1993

THE COMPLETE HANDBOOK OF

PRO
FOOTBALL

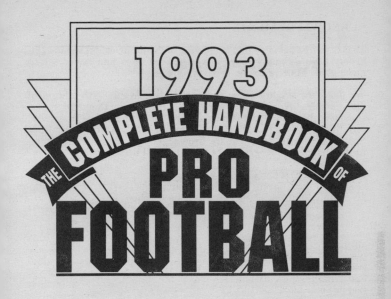

1993

THE COMPLETE HANDBOOK OF PRO FOOTBALL

EDITED BY
ZANDER HOLLANDER

AN ASSOCIATED FEATURES BOOK

A SIGNET BOOK

ACKNOWLEDGMENTS

Thanks to free agency, this is the year of the turnover! Never in NFL history have so many players switched teams . . . and never for so much gold. Tune in to see if payoffs make playoffs.

We thank the mighty corps that made possible this 19th edition of *The Complete Handbook of Pro Football*: contributing editor Eric Compton, the writers and Dot Gordineer, Linda Spain, Sue Powderly, Jerry Todd, Westchester Book Composition/Rainsford Type, Elias Sports Bureau, Fred Cantey, Joe Browne, Greg Aiello, Pete Abitante, Leslie Hammond, Reggie Roberts and the NFL team publicists.

PHOTO CREDITS: Cover—Mitch Reibel. Inside photos—George Gojkovich, Pete Groh, Vic Milton, Mitch Reibel, Wide World, CBS-TV and the NFL and college team photographers.

Zander Hollander

SIGNET
Published by the Penguin Group
Penguin Books USA Inc., 375 Hudson Street,
New York, New York 10014, U.S.A.
Penguin Books Ltd, 27 Wrights Lane,
London W8 5TZ, England
Penguin Books Australia Ltd, Ringwood,
Victoria, Australia
Penguin Books Canada Ltd, 10 Alcorn Ave.,
Toronto, Ontario, Canada M4V 3B2
Penguin Books (N.Z.,) Ltd, 182-190 Wairau Road,
Auckland 10, New Zealand

Penguin Books Ltd, Registered Offices:
Harmondsworth, Middlesex, England

First Signet Printing, August, 1993
10 9 8 7 6 5 4 3 2 1

Copyright © 1993 Associated Features Inc.
All rights reserved

 REGISTERED TRADEMARK—MARCA REGISTRADA

Printed in the United States of America

CONTENTS

Editor's Note: The material herein includes trades and rosters up to the final printing deadline.

THE GREENING OF TROY AIKMAN

By MIKE FISHER

In one transcendent game, Troy Aikman blossomed from "promising young quarterback" to one of *People* magazine's "50 Most Beautiful People."

In one dazzling 52-17 Super Bowl XXVII victory over the Buffalo Bills on Jan. 26, the Dallas Cowboys' quarterback quit having to answer every criticism he has ever heard and started having to answer phone calls from Jay Leno and David Letterman and Regis and Kathie Lee and Levi's and McDonald's.

That day in the Rose Bowl, the site of so many of Aikman's college highlights at UCLA and now of his MVP performance, ignited a dizzying offseason for football's newest celebrity.

"It seems like getting to the Super Bowl should take longer than it took us, because there are so many players who were in this league 10 or 12 years who never made it," said Aikman, who entered the NFL as the top overall pick in 1989. "I've talked to retired players who spent their whole lives waiting to win a Super Bowl, and were hoping to be able to say they went out on top. Me, I feel like my career is just starting.

"And for sure, what happened to me after the Super Bowl, as far as all the attention is concerned, is supposed to be the reward for years and years of production. In some ways, I got lucky."

It is true that Aikman is the beneficiary of some good fortune. He was blessed with a 6-4, 225-pound frame that allowed him to endure the pounding a quarterback naturally takes when his team

Mike Fisher, the Cowboys' beat man for the Fort Worth Star-Telegram, *has eyewitnessed the Troy Aikman adventure from its Dallas beginnings.*

MVP Troy Aikman rose to the occasion at Super Bowl.

was as bad as the Cowboys were in his early years. In 1989, when Dallas finished 1-15, Aikman missed five starts due to injury. He was not on the field when Dallas won that lone game. Even when he played well—against the Cardinals, when he threw for 379 yards—his Cowboys lost.

Aikman missed one start in 1990. A Week 15 shoulder injury sustained against the Eagles forced his exit from that game, prevented him from playing in a Week 16 loss to the Falcons, and probably cost the 7-9 Cowboys a playoff berth. He missed six more games in 1991, including two playoff outings. That time, it was a knee injury that ended his season prematurely.

"If he wasn't as durable as he is, he never would have survived some of those early times," offensive coordinator Norv Turner said.

But last year, with his supporting cast upgraded, Aikman stayed upright. And moved upstage.

Aikman's passing skills earned him a second straight Pro Bowl berth after a 1992 regular season in which he completed 64 percent

Aikman's 23 TD passes were second to Steve Young in NFC.

of his throws for 3,445 yards and 23 touchdowns, with 14 interceptions. Then he got better in the playoffs. Aikman's career postseason quarterback rating of 116.7 surpassed Bart Starr's record of 104.8 as Dallas scored 34, 30 and 52 points in the three postseason games, with Aikman throwing eight touchdown passes and no interceptions.

His Super Bowl statistics included 22 completions in 30 attempts for 273 yards and four touchdowns. In completing 73.3 percent of his throws, he outdid the more experienced Jim Kelly, the Buffalo quarterback. In running for 28 yards, he even outdid the Bills' All-Pro back, Thurman Thomas. And he won praise from everyone.

"He's as good as anyone in the league right now," said Dan Fouts, the San Diego Chargers' Hall-of-Famer, who compared Aikman to another famous Oklahoman, Mickey Mantle. "It must be an Oklahoma thing. But they've got the same eyes, the same hair, the same sideways grin. That same air of confidence comes through in everything they do."

From Sonny Jurgensen, the former Washington QB: "He's the next superstar in this league. He looks like a finished product to me. If you went to all 28 teams and let them take any quarterback they wanted . . . he'd probably be first."

From Archie Manning, the ex-New Orleans QB, whose son,

Peyton, was the Louisiana High School Player of the Year as a junior quarterback: "I pointed to Troy and said, 'Son, that's the way to want to handle yourself out there.' A young quarterback can learn a lot watching a guy like Troy. He does everything so well."

From Joe Theismann, the former Washington QB: "To me, he's like [Johnny] Unitas. He stands tall and takes it in the face almost to a degree that it hurts him . . . He's so good, people can't help but focus on him."

The experts now are moved to issue the usual round of comparisons. Aikman is like Unitas. Aikman is like Joe Montana. Or Dan Marino. Or John Elway. Or, of course, Roger Staubach, the Cowboys' monument whose legend Aikman finds himself chasing.

"Troy is a different sort of player than I was, and really, he's coming up with his own definition of what a quarterback can do," Staubach said. "He has a certain charisma that is important in a quarterback, and I think most of the great quarterbacks have to have that. And he is very gifted physically. But I don't like to make comparisons. I'm a great, great fan of Troy Aikman. I think Troy is just Troy."

"It takes a Super Bowl, I guess, for people to really appreciate the caliber of a player," Aikman said. "It was after the Super Bowl that people started coming out and saying, 'Now there was the game where he really became somebody.' But I honestly don't think I did much different in that game than I'd done most of the season. But things get magnified. I was the same as our whole team, which didn't raise its game. We tried to stay at the same high level all season."

That high level was achieved because Aikman is surrounded by gifted athletes young enough to still be striving to improve. Two of his offensive linemen, center Mark Stepnoski and guard Nate Newton, made the Pro Bowl. Behind him is Emmitt Smith, the league rushing champion for two straight years. His passing targets include wide receiver Michael Irvin and tight end Jay Novacek, both among the premier players at their positions. Dallas' defense in 1992 was the league's top-ranked.

Additionally, Aikman plays for an owner, Jerry Jones, and a head coach, Jimmy Johnson, whose commitment to success is exceeded by no one.

Even the city he lives in is a perfect fit for Aikman, who moved from the Los Angeles suburb of Cerritos, Cal., to tiny Henryetta, Okla., when he was 12, and definitely leans toward the southern-fried lifestyle.

"It's mostly my upbringing, though part of it is a conscious decision," said Aikman of a low-profile personal style that is now tested by a relentless public that wants a piece of him. "I was brought up not to brag. I've always disliked people who do. I kept quiet my first few years in Dallas for those reasons. Now, I can be myself."

Aikman loves Dallas. And Los Angeles. Both cities have plenty to offer a rich, single, young man. But Henryetta, a town of 6,000 that Rand-McNally almost skipped, is home. Of course, even in Henryetta, there is no escaping his celebrity.

Henryetta has an "Aikman Avenue" and "Home of Troy Aikman" signs at the city limits and now has an athletic center, thanks in part to funds donated by Aikman.

That town fostered an attachment that most NFL quarterbacks shed by the time they're making a million a year. (Aikman is scheduled to earn $1.170 million this year, though he and the club have talked about renegotiating.) He feels like he owes Henryetta a little something, because after all, it gave him football. Henryetta is one of the reasons Aikman feels lucky.

Had Kenneth and Charlyn Aikman not moved the family from California, Troy would not have played high school football. He would have stuck with baseball, as his California pals did. He would have relied on his 92 miles-per-hour fastball as an athletic claim to fame.

But eighth-grade boys in Henryetta went out for football. Concerned that not joining them would hurt his father, Troy Aikman tried out, too. Even in the 10th grade, he still considered quitting football to concentrate on baseball. But he thought it would let his father down.

The Henryetta Fighting Hens football teams were traditionally awful, and not even the tall, skinny quarterback could make them much better. His junior season, they finished 2-8, but somehow qualified for the state playoffs for the first time in 30 years. As a senior, Troy led them to a 6-4 mark, only their fourth winning record in 25 years.

"Those are still some of the greatest times in my life," Aikman said. "They are good people."

He won a scholarship to the University of Oklahoma, but after two years in the wishbone offense, transferred away from coach Barry Switzer to UCLA. After a redshirt season, Aikman led the Bruins to a 20-4 record in his final two years. Included were victories in the 1988 Aloha Bowl and 1989 Cotton Bowl. He was named an All-American after a career highlighted by a 64.8-percent completion ratio, 5.298 yards, 41 touchdowns and the third-best ranking in NCAA history.

Aikman shows sumo king Asahifuji how to pass in Tokyo.

But leaving Oklahoma didn't separate him from his roots there. Aikman was reunited with the people of Henryetta last March, when the city named him Henryettan of the Year and threw a parade in his honor. It was just one of the offseason events that were triggered by Aikman's new-found level of popularity.

There was one span in March when Aikman traveled to Germany as part of a promotional tour for Logo Athletics, then flew to San Francisco for a collectables show, then to Oklahoma City for an appearance, then to Washington, D.C., where he joined the Cowboys in their tour of the White House. In between have come a flood of requests. People want to meet him, want to hear him speak, want to touch him, want to hire him to peddle their products.

"Companies have come to me with so many endorsement opportunities, and there is a part of me that would like to have success in that area," Aikman said. "I mean, who wouldn't be flattered by all of it? But I also have seen what can happen to players who kind of get fat and sassy because of the celebrity part of it, and they forget what got them there in the first place. It can be fun to be noticed by people, to sign autographs, to be on 'Tonight' or whatever. But it can also be a distraction that I won't let affect my football.''

It will affect his pocketbook, however. Aikman's agent, Leigh Steinberg, is plotting to capitalize on the quarterback's success by signing him to endorsement deals that will earn him an additional seven-figure income.

''We always believed that Troy would be recognized as a premier quarterback, and that it would be in unison with the Cowboys having success as a team,'' Steinberg said. ''You have the combined mystique of the Cowboys and Troy—what a football name!—and you have a quarterback who is basically playing the leading man in a movie.''

But, Aikman said warily, ''I've made it clear to Leigh that I don't want to go berserk on that stuff. What I want to do is get back to another Super Bowl.''

At 26, that seems like a reasonable goal. But Aikman knows nothing is automatic. He knows what happened to Mark Rypien, the Redskins' quarterback who won the Super Bowl MVP award the year before him, then signed a new $3-million-a-year contract, then struggled through 1992, finishing as the league's lowest-ranked full-time quarterback.

''I take nothing for granted,'' Aikman said. ''There is a fine line between being comfortable and being too comfortable.''

Johnson's relationship with Aikman is better now that it's ever been. Winning a Super Bowl can do that to guys, even guys who in their early years together rarely saw eye-to-eye. Even their conflicts were created more by circumstances than personality.

The Aikman/Johnson mix can be volatile. Their strong wills and their inexperience at the professional level may have caused some uneasiness. The presence of Steve Walsh certainly contributed.

''The problems all began, really, when they brought Steve in,'' Aikman said. ''There probably would have been tension no matter what with any two young quarterbacks. But here was a situation where one of the young quarterbacks had won a national championship for Jimmy at the University of Miami. Jimmy didn't want to show favoritism—even though he had to have feelings for Steve—so he kept his distance from us. That caused problems for me.''

The Cowboys spent a No. 1 pick in the 1989 supplemental draft for Walsh. It wasn't until 1991, when Walsh was finally dealt to New Orleans, when Aikman and Johnson allowed themselves to get along. Slowly but surely, Aikman has developed some trust in his coach. At the same pace, Johnson has developed trust in his quarterback.

"Troy is an outstanding person and an outstanding quarterback," Johnson said. "He's not the kind of person who needs to go out and throw for 350 yards to be effective, or to feel like he's successful. He just wants to win. And the caliber of person he is, combined with the caliber of athlete he is, both those things make for a pretty good bottom line."

The bottom line on Aikman is that he seems to have a pretty good feel for controlling his environment. Will he get "fat and sassy?" He doesn't seem the type.

Aikman's buddy, Tom Whiteknight, tells the story of the day before a game at Texas Stadium when Aikman pulled his pickup truck into a filling station, paid for his gas, then pulled out five tickets to the game and handed them to the attendants.

"He'll kill me for telling that," Whiteknight said of Aikman, whose involvement in charity work, such as the Troy Aikman Foundation for children, is as extensive as any player's in football. "But this guy does things for people that he'll never talk about. He loves people, and people love him."

Now, of course, it makes sense for people to befriend Aikman. While he has been credited with wielding too much power—he labels as "unfair and ridiculous" suggestions that he helped fire former offensive coordinator Dave Shula after the 1990 season— he is one of the hubs of this team. He and Emmitt Smith are to the on-field product what Jones and Johnson are from the sidelines.

"Everyone knows that," said fullback Daryl Johnston. "But it takes a special person like Troy to put up with this 'Aikman Mystique' crap. He doesn't carry himself like he's a high-paid guy. It's just not in his makeup."

Aikman's makeup has led to a strong union with Turner, who came to Dallas before the 1991 season and became Aikman's mentor and friend. Both men are earthy, country-western music fans who shun the limelight and don't seem to know what all the fuss is about.

"Norv," Aikman said, "is one of the best things that has ever happened to me."

Turner installed a quick-drop, quick-pass scheme that fit Aikman perfectly. By 1992, he seemed to have it mastered. He helped beat the Atlanta Falcons, 41-17, by completing 13 straight throws. He helped beat the Denver Broncos, 31-27, in the game that clinched Dallas' playoff berth, by completing 25 of 35 passes for 231 yards and three touchdowns. Included was a late-game, 77-yard drive that was engineered by Aikman's arm and guile.

Troy's rush to the airport in Honolulu cost him $10,000.

"Those of us who watched him in practice every day didn't need any proof that Troy was a great quarterback," receiver Michael Irvin said. "But that might have been that one game that had all the football people around the country finally starting to sit up and take notice of him. And then in the playoffs and the Super Bowl, he was so incredible that even all the people out there who don't like football had to sit up and take notice."

The Cowboys defeated the Eagles, 34-10, in their Jan. 10 divisional playoff game. Aikman completed 15 of 25 passes for 200 yards, with two touchdowns and no interceptions. In the NFC game in San Francisco, Aikman completed 24 of 34 throws for 322 yards, two touchdowns and no interceptions. Dallas won, 30-20.

"The most impressive thing to me in the playoffs was how easy Troy made it for his wide receivers," Fouts said. "They never had to make diving, one-handed catches. Especially in the second half against San Francisco, every ball was right between the numbers. The guys had no choice but to catch it."

Maybe it is Aikman's naivete that caused his only major gaffe of last season. On Feb. 7, he bid a premature "Aloha" to the Pro Bowl. It created headlines all across the country when Aikman decided to depart Honolulu in the third quarter. His logic was simple: His stint in the game was over; the game was running long, and he had a plane to catch. Aikman told a few people of his plan, including 49er quarterback Steve Young, a friend. But Aikman failed to inform 49er coach George Seifert, who was in charge of the NFC squad. Seifert was befuddled. Hawaii was outraged. NFL commissioner Paul Tagliabue was quick to bring Aikman to his office in New York, where he penalized Aikman by handing out a $10,000 fine.

"I had a meeting back in Dallas that I wanted to get to, and my flight was all set up to get me to that meeting on time," Aikman said. "It wasn't the right thing to do. I think things kind of got blown out of proportion, though. I really didn't have any idea of what a big issue it would become."

That's because Aikman really didn't have a good grasp on what a big deal he had become. Steinberg, for one, cringed when he heard the news of Aikman's "quarterback sneak."

"I would have rather not had the Pro Bowl thing happen," Steinberg said. "It was not exactly part of the plan you lay out when you're trying to create a plan to market the Super Bowl MVP. But the way things happened is a part of who Troy is. He tolerates b.s. for about two seconds. That's part of Troy Aikman's charm."

Stockton-Visser: The First Couple Of Sports TV

By STAN ISAACS

It is a few hours before a Philadelphia Eagles game at Giants Stadium. Down on the field, Eagle backup quarterback Jim McMahon is playing catch and bantering with a woman.

She is Lesley Visser, the CBS roving reporter, who will work the game from the sidelines. She suddenly turns, points to the press box where Dick Stockton, the announcer who will call the play-by-play for the CBS telecast, is looking at his notes and setting up for the game. "Hey, Jim," she calls to McMahon, "it's my husband's birthday today."

McMahon turns and yells up to the press box, his voice carrying around the unfilled stadium, "Hey, Dick, happy birthday!" Stockton shakes his head wryly and looks down at his notes.

This is one of the few times the Stockton-Visser marital connection would be exposed to the public on a day when they are assigned to work the same telecast. When they are seen together on NFL games this season, it would be difficult for even the most knowing insider to detect anything that would give away that they are husband-and-wife when they are on the air.

Mark Wolff, a CBS producer who has worked with the pair on football, said, "They are very professional, very serious about what they do and would not intrude their personal life onto a telecast."

Bob Dekas, the producer for the Toronto-Oakland American

A savant of sports television, Stan Isaacs earned his letter as a columnist and critic on Newsday.

"Forever kids"—Lesley Visser and Dick Stockton.

League baseball championship series to which both were assigned last season, said, "You would never know during our production meetings before the games that they were married. I smile that they didn't even sit next to each other. Dick would sit next to Jim Kaat, his analyst on the games, Lesley elsewhere with people involved with the pre-game show."

It is essentially the same at a pro football production meeting. Visser says, "When they get around to the subject of the pre-game show ["NFL Today"] I'll be sitting with my producer and I might say we need a camera when [Troy] Aikman gets off the bus. I might also need an extra credential for whatever reason. The pre-game show is minor at these meetings. I might be off editing a piece I did earlier in the week while they are going into the details of the game telecast." Stockton adds, "I'll be involved with the story line for the game, what the coaches have told us. We'll put graphics in or out."

Not seen is the preparation they put into their work. Visser, who interviews players and coaches during the week, will invariably come up with more information than she will use on the air, and will pass on to Stockton and his analyst material that they might find useful. Stockton might come up with tidbits that are better presented by a reporter and pass it on to Visser.

Stockton says, "She is there during the week and gets to know the players better. Her personality warms them up and she winds up getting great stuff. With us, the players' attitude is that they do it because they are required to do so. With her, they like to do it."

Visser say "Sometimes it's the other way. I'll start talking to a guy and 'll say, 'I told your husband everything, I have nothing to say.'"

Stockton says, "Not only do I like to have her working the same game, so do all the others in our crew because her presence as a reporter means it is an important telecast." The joke is that CBS saves the expense of an extra hotel room by having them on the same assignment. "But when you consider the cost of room service and an extra phone," she says, "it's no great saving."

If they were once a novelty, now they could be regarded as pacesetters, the advance party of a movement that is flowering in the White House, where President Bill Clinton unabashedly praises his wife, Hillary, as a significant partner in his administration. A forerunner of sorts to Stockton-Visser in sports were Johnny Morris, the former Bear, and his wife, Jeannie, when he was an anchor and she a roving reporter on a local TV newscast in Chicago.

Visser, 39, came to television after a solid career as a reporter for the *Boston Globe*. She was the first woman to be a beat reporter covering an NFL team. At first when she arrived with the New England Patriots, television stations in every city would send a crew to cover her. She distinguished herself on the beat because she was a solid, knowledgeable reporter who had paid her dues.

Early on at the *Globe*, just out of Boston College, her first beat was high school football. "You'd take the ferry to Martha's Vineyard. You'd hold the umbrella in one hand and keep stats with the other," she says.

She has become one of the most visible of female sports journalists, particularly in Chicago, where she looms 32 feet tall on a mural on a building off an expressway, put up by Chicago clothing retailer Bigsby & Kruthers.

She speaks frquently about the role of woman sports journalists. "I tell women that success is as much about stamina as it is about talent." She acknowledges that there are relatively few women in

Lesley interviews Redskins' owner Jack Kent Cooke after Super Bowl XXVI as coach Joe Gibbs looks on.

sports television. "Because there are not so many jobs open, many go to ex-athletes and women can get tired of the fight. They have to fight on two fronts, internally for acceptance and externally for access."

When she was asked how long she was a woman journalist, she would answer, "That's like asking Randall Cunningham how long he has been a black quarterback." When she is asked, too frequently for her taste, by aspiring women journalists about the problem of women in the locker room, she answers, "That is only three percent of the job, so I will devote only three percent of my time to that subject." She said, "The best advice my mother ever gave me came from Dorothy Parker. She said, 'Never put all your eggs in one bastard.' "

Stockton, 50, says, "People who ask how I feel about Lesley doing what she is doing are in the dark ages. I say it's great. She has made a mark. She has tremendous talent, she gets more out of players than anybody I've seen."

They first met in 1975 when she was 21, he 32, when she was an intern at the *Globe*, and he was broadcasting Red Sox games. "We went out," she said, "but it seemed as if he was a million years old. I was into Springsteen, and he had attended only one concert, to see the Lettermen. He later told me he went into the back of his closet to look for college-boy clothes."

They met again on a plane after both worked an NBA game in 1982. "When we saw each other that time," Stockton said, "I knew I wouldn't let her get away. I would be an unhappy camper now if I didn't have her."

They were married Jan. 22, 1983. Stockton's family name had been shortened from the original, Stockvisser, so there are those who would suggest they should have taken Stockvisser as their married name. They roll their eyes at the suggestion.

They are an engaging pair, the First Couple of Sports Media, respected and well-liked. Visser is more exuberant, a vivacious, blue-eyed brunette with an infectious smile. Stockton, hazel-eyed with thinning hair that he often tends to smooth with his palm, is more reserved on the air, yet an engaging, witty fellow privately.

If they are strictly professional about each other on the air, they are social and fun-loving winding down with co-workers after a game. "We'll tell some of the things that we couldn't say on the air," Visser says. Producer Mark Wolff said, "I call them 'America's oldest teenagers' because they always seem to have fun."

Visser says, "I married him because he's the only guy I met who could name every starter of every Final Four team and play Gershwin on the piano." He demurs. "Only since 1957 with the Final Fours."

Stockton grew up in Queens, New York, an avid New York Giants baseball fan. He came out of Syracuse University in 1965 to a career in broadcasting that included stops in Philadelphia, Pittsburgh, Boston and New York before he settled in at CBS. He has worked basketball (NBA), football (NFL), baseball and the NCAA basketball tournament as well as calling, among others, pre-season Washington Redskin football. He did play-by-play on Oakland baseball games on radio this past season.

On one of their first dates, Stockton recited the details of the New York Giants' miracle run for the pennant in the 1951 season. Visser didn't think he was crazy. And shortly after they were

Stockton and Jim Kaat teamed up in baseball.

married and Stockton was into one of his reminiscences about growing up in the 1950s and going to the Polo Grounds, Visser said, "Why don't we go up there?"

"You mean it?" he said. "You don't think it's crazy?"

No, she didn't. And that is why every year on Oct. 3, the anniversary of Bobby Thomson's home run that won the 1951 pennant for the Giants, Stockton and Visser make a pilgrimage to Manhattan to stand at the site of the old Polo Grounds. Looking out over the housing project that is there now, Stockton reminisces about aspects of his childhood visits.

He has talked about the Chesterfield signs that hung from the stands, about the old popular songs played during batting practice. "Now, whenever I hear 'Because of You' and 'Perfidia' I think of batting practice."

Visser says, "Don't you think most people you like are a little bit eccentric? Most women, I believe, love the childhood of the men they like."

Visser grew up in Maryland, Ohio and Massachusetts, a tomboy. When she was in fourth grade, her brother gave her a subscription to *Sports Illustrated*. She idolized Tucker Frederickson and Sam Jones, wore their No. 24, and used to imitate Jones' jump shot at the playground.

For her bachelerette party before her wedding, her friends sprung a surprise as the guest of honor. He was Ike DeLock, the Red Sox journeyman pitcher of the 1950s whose baseball card Visser had carried in her wallet for almost 10 years. She adored DeLock for his name and his somewhat lumpy physique. "I was stunned," she says. "There we were drinking champagne and in walked my baseball card. He was older than I remembered him to be, but just as chunky; he was definitely still my baseball card."

After 13 years at the *Globe*, Visser joined CBS in 1988. "I didn't help her get the job," Stockton says. "It gets our goat to hear people even suggest that. CBS felt that the time was ripe for a woman in their sports operation. They knew of her abilities as a writer, knew she was smart, and knew people in the industry. I would never go in and say, 'Hire my wife.'"

"The first year at CBS," she says, "I was inadequate. I was so stiff on the air I looked as if I had rigor mortis. I knew I was way behind my level as a newspaperwoman. Dick was supportive. He said, 'You'll get better, you can't compress the experience. You'll get better just by doing it.' He didn't offer technical criticisms, but was emotionally supportive."

As she has come along, her natural ebullience putting interview subjects at ease, she jokes that her greatest problem on TV has been trying to make her hair look good on camera. "I have total hair-anoia," she has said, claiming membership in The Worst Hair in America Club.

Stockton's thinning hair has drawn the barbs of Don Imus, the carbuncle on New York's morning radio scene. Dick laughed off Imus' suggestion that Visser set Stockton's bed on fire. "If you take Imus seriously he'll kill you. We have gone down to the studio and let him have at us."

Stockton regards his TV call on NBC of Carlton Fisk's epic home run in the sixth game of the 1975 World Series as his No. 1 highlight as a broadcaster. "This was a fantastic game with so many subplots and it had the great replay of Fisk body-englishing the ball to stay fair. I recall that I said, 'If it stays fair . . . pause . . . it's a home run.' When he crossed the plate, I said, 'There will be a seventh game.' "

That was the day Stockton and Visser met for the first time in the Fenway Park press box before the game. She jokes, "Meeting me wasn't the best thing that happened to Dick that day. The Fisk home run was."

Lesley is a regular on "The NFL Today" with, from left, Greg Gumbel, Terry Bradshaw and Pat O'Brien.

He recalls as well "broadcasting all the Larry Bird-Magic Johnson duels and hosting the Villanova upset of Georgetown in the 1985 NCAA final. That was such a great upset. And when Brent Musburger threw the mike back to me after calling the game, I said, 'And that's why they play the game,' in relation to all the talk about Georgetown being a sure thing."

And then there was the time Stockton was just breaking in at CBS hosting a taped magazine show. Watching the show at home some weeks later, he was chagrinned to hear an out-take make it on air. He was heard saying, "Ah, let's do it again."

Visser's biggest moment on television came when she was reporting a story on how the unification of the two Germanys would change sports in Germany. "I felt that this was the story of the century, beyond sports. I stood up in front of the Berlin wall when it came down and said the next Wimbledon champions might come from the other side of the wall. I was proud to be there."

In Ali's healthier days, he was interviewed by Stockton.

She also cites her role presenting the Super Bowl trophy to the winning Washington Redskins after the 1992 Super Bowl in Minneapolis. "That's the biggest venue in sports. I felt I was representing women, CBS, myself. You want to demonstrate you are in control. Only Brent Musburger and Bob Costas have been in such a scene, and I have such respect for them because it is such a difficult assignment. You don't know after presenting the trophy which players you will get. So you have to know what each player has done should they come over to you."

Stockton said, "I gave her an 'A'. [CBS sports head] Neal Pilson said it was the best post-Super Bowl interviewing he had seen."

Then there was the time after a Los Angeles Laker-Seattle SuperSonic playoff game in which the Lakers came back from a 29-point deficit to win. "I had to interview Kareem Abdul Jabbar," she says. "He was very difficult. We were on the court and I gave him a pretty simple question. I asked what he attributed the comeback to. He paused for what seemed like an eternity. Then he said, 'What?' Just that. He stripped me on national TV."

Her toughest assignment? "Working behind the bench during the NBA playoffs. It is the most adversarial situation you can be in. The coach doesn't want anyone near him, but the producer wants you as close as you can get. Phil Jackson is a great guy off the court, but I have images of him glaring at me when I tried to get close to hear what he was saying in a timeout. We have been out socially with Pat Riley in Paris, yet Pat gave me that cold stare when I was behind him at the bench. It's difficult because you need them before or after the game for comments and yet you want to get something during the game despite their dirty looks. It's a push-pull dance.''

For Stockton, the toughest assignment is the opening round of the NCAA tournament, when he does four games in one day, a doubleheader in the afternoon and, another in the evening at the same site. ''The day before, you watch eight teams' practices, meet eight coaches, many from small schools you don't know much about. Then when you do the games, you may have only an hour and half between games; you never leave the arena. That's really a test.''

The Stockvissers have an apartment on New York's East Side and a condo in Boca Raton, Fla. They spend a third of the time in New York, a third in Florida and, a third, or possibly more, on the road. They claim they have never lit the stove in their apartments. Stockton says, ''We just pick up the phone and order out. And we eat out a lot. We leave it to the professionals.''

They used to play tennis wherever they went but Dick, Lesley says, ''has now been afflicted with the disease called golf.'' Stockton taught himself to play the piano, can read music and has more than 2,500 pieces of sheet music. ''When we are going out and Lesley is finishing up getting dressed,'' Stockton says, ''she will ask me to play a favorite song of hers. I'll play 'A Nightingale Sang in Barclay Square' or 'More I Cannot Wish You' from 'Guys and Dolls.' ''

He says their life is ''the best of all possible worlds. We love the work we do, but our relationship and life together takes precedence over work.''

They have no children. ''Our lifestyle doesn't lend itself to that,'' Stockton says. ''We are into a different kind of thing; we are kids ourselves. She's 11 and I'm 12.''

They take things as they come. They have thought about hosting a talk show together. Andrea Joyce, a CBS colleague whose husband Harry Smith was part of CBS' 1992 Winter Olympics coverage along with Joyce, thinks they would be terrific working together on an event if Dick did play-by-play and Lesley did color. ''She knows sports as well as anybody and they are a terrific pair together—witty, knowledgeable and they play off each other so well.''

Not, however, during a pro football telecast. They are, first of all, professionals.

Love Him or Not, Barry Foster Joins Steeler Legends

By MIKE PRISUTA

The lights dimmed, the video monitors strategically placed around Three Rivers Stadium's plush Allegheny Club blinked on and the capacity crowd at a Pittsburgh Chamber of Commerce luncheon crept to the edge of seats to witness a rerun most of those in attendance wouldn't soon forget. Especially the guest of honor.

It was Feb. 23, 1993. But once the highlight film started to roll, it was the fall of 1992 all over again. And Barry Foster was once again juking New York Jets, deking Detroit Lions and blasting his way through Cleveland Browns.

Everyone knew the outcome of this improbable epic, a record-topping, breakthrough season for Foster and a long-awaited return to the NFL playoffs for his Pittsburgh Steelers. Still, no one could take his eyes away from the action for an instant. Especially the guest of honor.

"That was something else," the Steelers' 1992 MVP said when the show finally drew to a close. "I was even moving around in my seat . . . reliving it, remembering it."

Foster couldn't forget it. He set Pittsburgh single-season records for carries (390), rushing yards (1,690), total yards from scrimmage (2,034), most 100-yard games (12) and fewest games needed to reach the 1,000-yard plateau (10), records that had previously belonged to Steelers' legend and Hall-of-Famer Franco Harris. Foster also etched his name in the NFL record book along-

---

Mike Prisuta of the Beaver County (Pa.) Times *has rarely missed a down since tackling the Steeler assignment in 1986.*

Barry Foster waved farewell to Franco Harris' records.

side Eric Dickerson's with the 12 100-yard efforts, finished second in the NFL in rushing and second among Steelers in receiving (with 36 catches, for 344 yards) and scoring (11 touchdowns for 66 points).

He came out of nowhere, carried the Steelers to the AFC Central Division championship and ended up in the Pro Bowl.

The Chamber of Commerce luncheon, an annual February event in Pittsburgh to celebrate the Steelers' MVP, was perhaps Foster's finest hour since the honor was bestowed upon him in a vote of his teammates.

"No one was more deserving," Steeler coach Bill Cowher declared. And yet, when lunch was done, when the politicians and prominent members of the community were done posing for pictures, collecting autographs, shaking hands and patting Foster on the back, there was Foster . . . apologizing for the actions and aspects of his dream season he'd just as soon forget.

"I don't like being a bad guy," insisted Foster, who was often perceived as such throughout 1992 despite his magnificant numbers. "I just want to do my job and be recognized for what I've done on the field, not a bunch of negative things. I really don't enjoy that."

As a 23-year-old third-year pro entering last season, Foster began making headlines long before the Steelers started winning games. Dissatisfied with the contract that called for him to receive a base salary of $124,800, the option year of his initial three-year deal with the Steelers, Foster decided brief holdouts at the outset of minicamp and training camp were in order. On both occasions, he was the only signed Steeler who declined to show.

Foster was fined and he responded, once he finally made it to training camp and on the sporadic occasions when he decided to grant reporters an audience, by complaining about being underpaid often enough to create a rift between himself and his team.

Foster accused management of "screwing the players." He insisted all problems would be solved if the Steelers would just give him "a couple of extra hundred thousand dollars." When he wasn't bitching, he was brooding.

The poisoned pens in the press poured it on. The Pittsburgh talk shows bristled with backlash. There were angry letters to the editor in local publications. Even Foster's agent, Jordan Woy, wondered why his client would opt for a holdout (negotiations for a new pact had been taking place) when he already had a signed contract.

The Steelers, meanwhile, were in the most uncomfortable position of being almost completely at odds with the man who, in the absence of the suspended Tim Worley, was supposed to become the feature back in a power offense installed by new coordinator Ron Erhardt that wouldn't function without one.

How strained were relations? During training camp at St. Vincent College in steamy Latrobe, Pa., a Steelers' official walked past a TV in a lounge that was tuned into a Pirates' game. Barry Bonds, the former resident problem child and malcontent of the Pittsburgh baseball clubhouse, was on the screen. The Steelers' official stopped for a moment, then shook his head. "What is it with this town and guys named Barry?" he wondered.

Finally, an uneasy peace was reached. Foster's base salary, including a signing bonus for a new three-year deal, was upgraded to $413,000. A generous incentive package with the potential to more than double the deal was included.

"I'm pretty sure they put a lot of money in the incentive

Foster carried most times (390) in NFL last season.

package not really believing I'd get it,'' Foster said.

Not so, says Steelers director of football operations Tom Donahoe. ''We put those incentives in there because you would hope, if the guy had a phenomenal year, you could reward him for it,'' he said. The Steelers at least had an inkling, Donahoe insisted, that Foster was capable of becoming something special. The problem was, while the two sides were negotiating, Foster was merely average at best. If that.

He picked up just 691 rushing yards in 1990 and 1991 combined, his first two professional seasons. He was best known for blanking out and failing to field a kickoff in San Francisco as a rookie in 1990. Perhaps more significantly, 392 of Foster's 488 yards in 1991 came in the Steelers' first six games. In Week Seven, an Oct. 20 home game against Seattle, Foster suffered a sprained ankle. He wound up missing six of the final nine contests. Questions about Foster's commitment were raised, even within the organization.

"Some people, unfairly probably, questioned what he was doing," Donahoe said. "I personally don't think you should ever do that with players. No one can tell someone how they feel. He said he was hurt and he couldn't play. I think you have to believe him and go with that. Maybe the thing wasn't diagnosed properly. Maybe we didn't treat it properly; I don't know. We just couldn't get him healthy."

Whatever the problem was, Foster's new contract, and the new opportunities supplied by Cowher and Erhardt solved it. And once the '92 season started, opponents had a hard enough time getting Foster down, let alone off the field. "Bad News Barry" even bounced back from a back injury suffered in a Monday night victory over Cincinnati on Oct. 19 in time to star in an upset win in Kansas City the following Sunday.

He did the same prior to the regular-season finale against Cleveland, then went out and tied Dickerson's record in the game's final seconds. The Three Rivers Stadium faithful went crazy that day, as Foster swept around the corner for the nine yards he needed to duplicate history. Steeler fans, who were in the habit of complaining about or cursing Foster's attitude Monday through Saturday and wildly cheering his every move on Sundays, responded with a standing ovation and by chanting his name.

Most still can't figure him out, and likely never will. Foster, who admits he has very few close, trusted friends on the team or anywhere else, likes it that way.

The product of a modest background and the prime supporter of an ailing mother back home in Grand Prairie, Tex., Foster has financial needs that go beyond merely wanting to live the good life while cruising the fast lane. That's one of the main reasons why Foster, a wishbone fullback who gained just 1,977 yards in three collegiate seasons, left Arkansas a year ahead of schedule in the first place.

As a pro, he prefers to go about his business, then go home and be left alone. He's into playing football, being well paid for doing so and fishing, probably not in that order.

Steeler fans had a problem with that. The Steelers did not. "We're all motivated by different things," Cowher said. "I don't get involved with what does it, as long as we all understand what we're after and by what means we go after it. That has not been a problem with this guy."

It wasn't from September to December, anyway. Before the "Cowher Power" era in Pittsburgh got started, all that was really widely known about Foster was, as former coach Chuck Noll liked to say, "Nobody likes to tackle him in practice." It became painfully obvious why starting Sept. 6 in Houston.

Foster worked his way through Luv Ya Blue for a hard-earned 107 yards and the Steelers pulled off a stunning 29-24 upset. The next week, Foster fumbled three times against the Jets, but Cowher kept calling his number. Foster responded with 190 yards. He was just getting started.

There were three 100-yard games in the season's first four, and six in the first eight. He became the first NFL back to crack the 1,000-yard plateau in '92 and ended up leading the league in rushing in 11 of the season's 17 weeks. Most games, the Steelers couldn't pass with much effectiveness, yet Foster still proved almost impossible to stop. He thrived by generating deceptive speed from his 5-10, 214-pound frame. Or by relying on a quick burst just prior to contact. Foster's low-to-the-ground, churning style offered defenders nothing to attack but thighs and shoulder pads. Rarely was he dropped on initial contact.

And when all of the above wasn't enough, toughness usually allowed him to at least move the sticks. Day or night, warm or cold, home or dome, Foster just kept rolling. "I definitely thought I could put up 1,000 yards," Foster said. "But I didn't think I'd be able to do it in 10 games, or have the season I had."

Foster was compared to the likes of Dickerson, Harris, Barry Sanders and Earl Campbell. No one snickered. The comparisons were legitimate. Foster was in the company of another great runner, Emmitt Smith of the eventual Super Bowl champion Cowboys, as well. The two went wire-to-wire for the NFL rushing title before Smith finally prevailed on the regular-season's final Sunday.

All the while, Foster's concentration on compensation kept hogging the spotlight. When asked what meant more to him, all the bonus money he was piling up or all the attention he was getting, he wondered, "What can you do with so much fame? You're in this game to get successful at your position, get as much money as you can and get a ring."

Finally, a week before the Steelers were to play the Bills in the AFC playoffs, the spit really hit the fan. At a press conference to announce Foster had been selected as the team's MVP, he once again went about the business of coldly and candidly alienating all of Pittsburgh. The new contract, less than a season old, was already out of date, Foster said. He deserved more up front, and less in incentives, he insisted. And if the Steelers didn't come through, he'd hold out again, all of next season if necessary.

Foster said he didn't care about the fans' reactions, and was unconcerned about honoring the final two years of his existing contract. "Teams don't honor contracts; why should I?" Foster said.

Management bit its lip in declining to respond. The fans fumed. Teammates just shook their heads. And Foster, as he had done all season, went out and played his heart out, gaining 104 yards in the Steelers' season-ending 24-3 loss to the Bills.

He went home to Texas, presumably to fish and count money. But when he returned for the February luncheon, a gathering the Steelers couldn't be sure Foster would even attend until he walked through the door, he came back a changed man.

"Even people in my hometown said, 'You had a great year, but you shouldn't have said those things,'" Foster admitted. "I really regret the things I said at that press conference. I just feel like after the season I had, I should have been more well-received by the fans and not left the city on a negative tone."

He doesn't intend to let it happen again. Woy, who has represented Foster for three years and understands him more than most, doesn't believe it will. "He's different than some. He's a little more of a loner and he's not a guy that hangs out with everybody on the team or knows everybody on the team's business," Woy said. "He kind of stays to himself. But deep down he's a great guy."

So why all the acrimony? "I think Barry, deep down in his own mind, knew from the moment he got drafted he had a chance to be a superstar in the league," Woy said. "But he was a fifth-round draft choice, then he wasn't used much as a rookie, and then he got hurt. There was a lot of frustration there. He wasn't being considered as a top-notch guy from a playing standpoint or from a pay standpoint."

Now that he's both, Foster has a new outlook, too. Although he made $530,000 in incentives last season and is scheduled to

He actually showed up to receive Steeler MVP award.

make $460,000 in base pay this year, Foster still wants more money. But he's no longer holding a holdout over the Steelers' heads to get it. "Money will always be an issue, with me or with any other player," Foster said. "But I'm anticipating that I'll be in [camp] on time. And I know I have to be more in control, and really be responsible for what I say. I worked so hard to win the fans over in the city of Pittsburgh. I'm willing to change. I'm trying."

As he does, Foster will attempt to elevate himself to the level of Sanders and Thurman Thomas, backs who have produced the type of remarkable stats Foster posted in 1992 over the course of several seasons, not just one. Until he does, Foster refuses to put himself in their class.

"At a card show, I think more people want to see Thurman Thomas and Barry Sanders than they do me," Foster said.

In Buffalo and Detroit, maybe. But in Pittsburgh, where they've been waiting for a new Franco Harris to emerge ever since the four Super Bowl trophies the Steelers won in the 1970s started gathering dust, the new Barry Foster is more than enough.

INSIDE THE NFC

By PHIL ANASTASIA

PREDICTED ORDER OF FINISH

EAST	CENTRAL	WEST
Dallas	Green Bay	San Francisco
Washington	Minnesota	Atlanta
Philadelphia	Detroit	New Orleans
Phoenix	Chicago	L.A. Rams
N.Y. Giants	Tampa Bay	

NFC Champion: Dallas

For 13 unlucky NFC teams, the most tumultuous of offseasons in league history had a title: "Chasing the Cowboys."

"They are the new standard of excellence," Eagles' owner Norman Braman said.

"Everybody is trying to catch up with them," 49ers president Carmen Policy said.

Free agency brought massive changes to the NFL during the spring of 1993. As a result of the long-awaited labor settlement, players with five years of service whose contracts had expired were free to sign with other teams for the first time in modern NFL history.

The results were staggering. Reggie White left Philadelphia for Green Bay. Tim McDonald left Phoenix for San Francisco. Tim Harris left San Francisco for Philadelphia. Players jumped from

---

Phil Anastasia follows the Eagles and the NFL for the Camden (N.J.) Courier-Post.

Sterling Sharpe's 108 catches set NFL record.

team to team and clubs scrambled to rebuild their rosters and remake their images.

Incredibly, the Cowboys, the most active of franchises over the previous several seasons, were quiet. The defending Super Bowl champions sustained only a couple of free-agent losses and made no major signings. The Cowboys even were sedate on draft day, trading out of the first round to acquire a pair of role players in the second round.

"They don't have to make a lot of moves," Phoenix coach Joe Bugel said. "They are the team to beat and they know it. Everybody else is chasing them."

The Cowboys are clearly the class of the NFC. Given the fact that free agency will be available for players after four years of service starting in 1994, the days of dynasties are probably history. But for one more year, the Cowboys should remain on their high horse.

"We understand the challenge," Dallas coach Jimmy Johnson said. "We can't be complacent and we don't intend to be. It's a challenge to try to defend the title and that's the way we're going to approach it."

In the very least, they should repeat in the NFC East, with big-play offensive stars Troy Aikman, Emmitt Smith and Michael Irvin, and a deep, relentless defense led by Charles Haley and Robert Jones.

The Redskins are in transition, with the big change at the top: Richie Petitbon replaces legendary coach Joe Gibbs. Age is becoming a problem for Washington, and the Redskins lost wide receiver Gary Clark and three defensive regulars as free agents.

Philadelphia is in a state of uncertainty. The Eagles lost superstar defensive end White, but they still have a big-play quarterback in Randall Cunningham and defensive stars Seth Joyner and Clyde Simmons.

Phoenix might be coming on strong. The Cardinals signed Clark and quarterback Steve Beuerlein, the backup in Dallas. With help from an impressive draft, led by running back Garrison Hearst, the Cardinals could be ready to challenge for a playoff berth.

The Giants have a new coach in Dan Reeves but many of the same old problems: an aging defense and a lack of big-play people on offense. Lawrence Taylor and Phil Simms are back for one more year.

Green Bay is a rising power in the Central. The Packers were 9-7 last year and have an emerging superstar in quarterback Brett Favre. In addition to White, they've made several other moves designed to vault them to the top of the division.

Minnesota won 11 games despite quarterback problems. The Vikings took some big hits to their offensive line, losing starters Brian Habib and Kirk Lowdermilk, but they added veteran quarterback Jim McMahon, who brings experience and a winning attitude. If McMahon stays healthy, the Vikings will be in the hunt.

Detroit will look to bounce back from a disastrous season. They still have superstar running back Barry Sanders and an offensive line rebuilt through free agency. The defense got a big boost when they traded for Pat Swilling, the Saints' pass-rush specialist.

Chicago will attempt to rebuild under new coach Dave Wannstedt, who led Dallas' defense to the top of the rankings last season. Tampa Bay needs to solve its quarterback problems, and several others, before it can challenge for the playoffs.

San Francisco was the best team in the NFL during the 1992 regular season. The Cowboys knocked the 49ers out of the playoffs, but the team from the Bay Area figures to challenge again. Reigning NFL Player of the Year Steve Young is the trigger man. The defense was hurt by the loss of free agents Pierce Holt and Harris, but the 49ers offset that somewhat by signing McDonald, a perennial Pro Bowl strong safety.

Atlanta signed Holt, a Pro Bowl defensive tackle, and several others to add muscle to their defense. The Falcons have plenty of offensive weapons, led by quarterback Chris Miller and wide receivers Andre Rison and Mike Pritchard, and should figure in the playoff mix.

The Saints are another NFC power in transition. They traded Swilling to Detroit and let quarterback Bobby Hebert walk as a free agent. They will regroup behind star defensive end Wayne Martin and emerging running back Vaughn Dunbar.

The Rams added some experience to their young defense by signing free agents Shane Conlan and Fred Stokes. They could jump out of the basement if the Saints stagger.

But it's all about catching Dallas, which was 13-3 and cruised through the playoffs, averaging 35 points. They appear to be too deep, too fast, too much.

ATLANTA FALCONS

TEAM DIRECTORY: Chairman: Rankin Smith Sr.; Pres.: Taylor Smith; VP-Player Personnel: Ken Herock; Dir. Pub. Rel.: Charlie Taylor; Head Coach: Jerry Glanville. Home field: Georgia Dome (71,594). Colors: Black, red, silver and white.

SCOUTING REPORT

OFFENSE: The Red Gun still can stun some people, but the Falcons need a ground game to become a complete offensive team.

Quarterback Chris Miller is a talented trigger man. He's expected back from injury in 1993 and could make another run at a Pro Bowl berth. Miller has good touch on his passes. For backup, the Falcons signed Bobby Hebert, New Orleans veteran.

The wide-receiving corps is second to none. Andre Rison is coming off another monster season and Mike Pritchard is an emerging star. Drew Hill can work the sidelines like a master and Michael Haynes is a secondary-scaring deep threat.

The line was rocked during free agency as the Falcons lost starting guards Houston Hoover and Bill Fralic. Tackles Mike Kenn and Chris Hinton are solid, and promising second-year man Bob Whitfield could move inside. Top pick Lincoln Kennedy of Washington will vie for playing time. Jamie Dukes is an underrated center.

The ground game lacks muscle. Second-year man Tony Smith has potential but he needs the football and some running room. Steve Broussard is a decent all-purpose back.

DEFENSE: Big news here. The Falcons signed defensive tackles Pierce Holt and Jumpy Geathers as free agents and finally have some muscle up front.

Holt cost $7.5 million in guaranteed money, so he'd better be good. He's a Pro Bowler who can rush the passer and play the run. Geathers is a powerful inside pass-rusher. Moe Gardner and Chuck Smith are undersized ends but should benefit from Holt's presence. Smith, in particular, could emerge as a big-time pass-rusher.

Jessie Tuggle is a highly productive inside linebacker and the Falcons still have high hopes for outside linebacker Darion Conner, who has the talent to become a big-play man. After two learning seasons, Conner might be ready to burst into prominence.

The Falcons have revamped their secondary. Cornerback Mel-

Andre Rison was a 1,000-yard receiver on way to Pro Bowl.

vin Jenkins, a good coverage man, was signed as a free agent. The Falcons also traded for cornerback Vinnie Clark and safety Alton Montgomery, a hard hitter. Cornerback Deion Sanders is a tremendous athlete, but the Falcons have to wait until he fulfills his baseball commitment.

SPECIAL TEAMS: A Jerry Glanville specialty. The Falcons attack in this area.

Norm Johnson is a good kicker. He made 18 of 22 field-goal attempts and all 39 of his extra points last year. Punter Scott Fulhage is dependable.

Sanders is perhaps the game's best kickoff-return man and is also a dangerous punt-returner. Tony Smith handles most of the return duties before Sanders' arrival.

The coverage teams are tenacious and the Falcons love to try to block placekicks and punts.

FALCONS VETERAN ROSTER

HEAD COACH—Jerry Glanville. Assistant Coaches—Bobby April, Jimmy Carr, June Jones, Tim Jorgensen, Bill Kollar, Keith Rowen, Jimmy Robinson, Doug Shively, Ollie Wilson.

No.	Name	Pos.	Ht.	Wt.	NFL Exp.	College
68	Agee, Mel	DL	6-5	298	2	Illinois
62	Alex, Keith	G	6-4	315	1	Texas A&M
—	Archambeau, Lester	DE	6-5	275	4	Stanford
44	Broussard, Steve	RB	5-7	201	4	Washington State
77	Bryan, Rick	DE	6-4	265	10	Oklahoma
72	Buddenberg, John	G	6-6	275	1	Akron
25	Case, Scott	S	6-1	188	10	Oklahoma
27	Clark, Vinnie	CB	6-0	194	3	Ohio State
56	Conner, Darion	LB	6-2	245	4	Jackson State
51	Dinkins, Howard	LB	6-1	223	2	Florida State
42	Donaldson, Jeff	S	6-1	190	10	Colorado
64	Dukes, Jamie	C	6-1	285	8	Florida State
32	Eaton, Tracey	S	6-1	195	6	Portland State
74	Epps, Tory	NT	6-1	280	4	Memphis State
29	Fishback, Joe	S	6-0	212	4	Carson-Newman
53	Forde, Brian	LB	6-3	235	6	Washington State
65	Fortin, Roman	G	6-5	290	4	San Diego State
17	Fulhage, Scott	P	6-1	193	7	Kansas State
76	Gann, Mike	DE	6-5	270	9	Notre Dame
67	Gardner, Moe	NT	6-2	258	3	Illinois
97	Geathers, Jumpy	DT	6-7	290	10	Wichita State
59	Giles, Oscar	LB	6-2	248	1	Texas
71	Goldberg, Bill	NT	6-2	266	1	Georgia
89	Grant, Marcus	WR	5-9	172	1	Houston
99	Green, Tim	DE	6-2	245	8	Syracuse
50	Hardy, Darryl	LB	6-2	220	1	Tennessee
81	Haynes, Michael	WR	6-0	180	8	Northern Arizona
3	Hebert, Bobby	QB	6-4	215	8	NW Louisiana
85	Hill, Drew	WR	5-9	172	14	Georgia Tech
75	Hinton, Chris	T	6-4	300	11	Northwestern
95	Holt, Pierce	DE	6-4	280	6	Angelo State
20	Jenkins, Melvin	CB	5-10	173	7	Cincinnati
9	Johnson, Norm	K	6-2	203	12	UCLA
38	Jones, Keith	RB	6-1	210	5	Illinois
83	Jones, Tony	WR	5-7	145	4	Texas
19	Kalal, Tim	P	6-3	205	1	Miami
78	Kenn, Mike	T	6-7	280	16	Michigan
88	Le Bel, Harper	TE	6-4	245	5	Colorado State
22	McKyer, Tim	CB	6-1	174	8	Texas-Arlington
12	Miller, Chris	QB	6-2	205	7	Oregon
87	Milling, James	WR	5-9	160	5	Maryland
24	Mitchell, Brian	CB	5-9	164	3	BYU
22	Montgomery, Alton	S	6-0	195	4	Houston
36	Moore, Derrick	RB	6-1	227	2	NE Oklahoma
98	Ostroski, Jerry	G	6-3	316	1	Tulsa
33	Pegram, Erric	RB	5-9	188	3	North Texas State
82	Phillips, Jason	WR	5-7	166	5	Houston
39	Pickens, Bruce	CB	5-11	190	3	Nebraska
35	Pritchard, Mike	WR	5-11	180	3	Colorado
30	Ray, Terry	S	6-1	187	2	Oklahoma
26	Riddick, Louis	S	6-2	216	2	Pittsburgh
80	Rison, Andre	WR	6-0	188	5	Michigan State
41	Rouse, James	RB	6-0	220	4	Arkansas
55	Ruether, Mike	C	6-4	286	8	Texas
21	Sanders, Deion	DB	6-0	185	5	Florida State
37	Shelley, Elbert	CB	5-11	185	7	Arkansas State
43	Sims, Kelly	CB	5-10	200	1	Cincinnati
90	Smith, Chuck	DE	6-2	242	2	Tennessee
28	Smith, Tony	RB	6-1	214	2	Southern Mississippi
54	Solomon, Jesse	LB	6-0	235	8	Florida State
52	Tippins, Ken	LB	6-1	230	5	Middle Tenn. State
11	Tolliver, Billy Joe	QB	6-1	218	5	Texas Tech
58	Tuggle, Jessie	LB	5-11	230	7	Valdosta State
40	Wallace, Anthony	RB	6-0	191	1	California
70	Whitfield, Bob	OT	6-5	308	2	Stanford

	TOP DRAFT CHOICES					
Rd.	Name	Sel. No.	Pos.	Ht.	Wt.	College
1	Kennedy, Lincoln	9	OT	6-6	358	Washington
2	Harper, Roger	38	S	6-2	223	Ohio State
3	Alexander, Harold	67	P	6-2	225	Appalachian State
5	George, Ron	121	LB	6-0	225	Stanford
6	Lyons, Mitch	151	TE	6-4	255	Michigan State

THE ROOKIES: The Falcons got the biggest man on the board when they took Kennedy in the first round. The 340-pound Kennedy projects as a perennial Pro Bowler if he can keep his weight under control. Atlanta got a Glanville-style hitter in the second round in Ohio State's mean safety, Roger Harper.

OUTLOOK: Improved. The Falcons were a rising power in 1991 but injuries took their toll last season, when they were 6-10. They should be strong again this season, challenging the 49ers for the division title.

FALCON PROFILES

CHRIS MILLER 28 6-2 205   Quarterback

Leader of the Falcons' offense hopes to bounce back from injury-marred season . . . Sat out final eight games with knee injury . . . Expected back in full health . . . Passed for 1,739 yards and 15 TDs in only eight games . . . Passed for 351 yards and four TDs in loss to Chicago . . . Had three TD passes in victory over Green Bay . . . Enters 1993 having thrown a TD pass in club-record 14 consecutive games . . . Best season was 1991, when he threw 26 TD passes and made the Pro Bowl . . . Led Falcons to playoff berth by throwing 20 TD passes as team went 8-1 down the stretch . . . Erratic at times, he threw four interceptions three different times in 1991 . . . Passed for career-high 3,459 yards in 1989 . . . Starter since 1988 . . . As a baseball shortstop, he was drafted by Toronto and Seattle . . . Falcons' No. 1 pick in 1987 out of Oregon . . . Born Aug. 9, 1965, in Pomona, Cal. . . . 1992 base salary: $1.2 million.

PIERCE HOLT 31 6-4 280   Defensive Lineman

Jumped to the Falcons from the 49ers as a free agent . . . Signed three-year, $7.5-million deal that was fully guaranteed . . . 49ers had a chance to keep his rights but declined . . . Falcons believe he will add muscle to their weak defense . . . Bruising inside player who excels against the run . . . Also an active, relentless pass-rusher . . . Finished 1992 season with 55 tackles and 5½ sacks . . . Led 49ers in playoffs with three sacks . . . Made the Pro Bowl for the first time . . . Played five seasons for the 49ers . . . The oldest player (26) selected in the 1988 draft . . . 49ers took him in the second round out of Angelo (Tex.) State . . . Lone Star Conference Defensive Player of the Decade in the 1980s . . . Born Jan. 1, 1962, in Marlin, Tex. . . . 1993 base salary: $2 million.

DEION SANDERS 26 6-0 185   Defensive Back

Versatile athlete makes the most of his part-time status . . . Made the Pro Bowl for the second consecutive year . . . As usual, missed time early in season because of his commitment to Atlanta Braves baseball team . . . Led Falcons in interceptions with three and made 66 tackles . . . Averaged 35 yards on interception returns . . . Led NFC in kickoff-return average with 26.7 . . . Returned two kickoffs for TDs . . . Only player in the NFL to catch a pass and run from scrimmage on offense, intercept a pass on defense and return kickoffs and punts . . . Caught 37-yard TD pass against Bucs . . . Produced 11 plays of 30 or more yards . . . Led major-league baseball with 14 triples in 1992 . . . Falcons' No. 1 pick in 1989 out of Florida State . . . Born Aug. 9, 1967, in Fort Myers, Fla. . . . 1992 salary: $2 million.

ANDRE RISON 26 6-0 188   Wide Receiver

Speedy, stylish athlete is the go-to guy in the Falcons' passing game . . . Set team single-season record with 93 receptions in 1992 . . . Generated 1,121 yards and 11 TDs . . . Returned to the Pro Bowl for third consecutive year . . . Holds NFL record for most receptions in first four seasons with 308 . . . Has averaged 85 receptions in three seasons with the Falcons

. . . Named transition player to Falcons during free-agency period . . . Burst into prominence with 82 receptions for 1,208 yards in 1990, his first season in Atlanta . . . Acquired by Falcons from Indianapolis in 1990 deal that sent No. 1 pick (Jeff George) to the Colts . . . Caught 52 passes for 820 yards as a rookie . . . Colts' No. 1 pick in 1989 out of Michigan State . . . Born March 19, 1967, in Muncie, Ind. . . . 1993 base salary: $475,000.

CHRIS HINTON 32 6-4 300   Tackle

One of the top all-around blockers in the NFL . . . Strong run-blocker who also excels in pass-protection . . . Started all 16 games in 1992 . . . His protection helped the Falcons set a team record with 33 TD passes . . . Seven-time Pro Bowler . . . Named transition player by Falcons during free-agency period . . . Key man in 1990 draft-day blockbuster trade . . . He came to Atlanta from Indianapolis along with wide receiver Andre Rison for No. 1 overall pick, which the Colts used for Jeff George . . . In seven seasons with the Colts, he made the Pro Bowl six times . . . Fourth pick in the 1983 draft, he was traded to the Colts in deal that sent John Elway to the Broncos . . . All-American at Northwestern . . . Born July 31, 1961, in Chicago . . . 1993 salary: $1.1 million.

TONY SMITH 23 6-1 214   Running Back

Talented athlete who was slowed by injuries and inexperience as a rookie . . . Missed time with five different ailments and ended season on injured-reserve list . . . Started five games . . . Second on the team in rushing with 329 yards . . . Ran for two of the Falcons' three rushing TDs . . . Team's top punt-returner with 9.7 average, including a 45-yarder . . . Falcons' second No. 1 pick (Bob Whitfield was the first) in 1992 draft out of Southern Mississippi . . . Second running back selected . . . Ran for 998 yards and eight TDs as a senior . . . Dangerous return man . . . Averaged 32.5 yards on kickoff returns and brought two back for TDs as a sophomore . . . Averaged 12.5 yards on punt returns and scored twice as a junior . . . Born June 29, 1970, in Vicksburg, Miss. . . . 1993 base salary: $440,000.

MICHAEL HAYNES 27 6-0 180   Wide Receiver

One of the most dangerous deep threats in the NFL . . . Led Falcons in yards-per-catch for the second year in a row with 16.8 . . . Caught 48 passes for 808 yards and 10 TDs . . . Joins teammate Andre Rison and 49ers' Jerry Rice as only players with 20 or more TDs catches in last two seasons . . . Has averaged 18 yards per catch in his career . . . Burst on the scene in 1991 with team-high 1,122 receiving yards and 11 TDs . . . Led the NFL that season with a 22.4-yard average . . . Crushed the Saints in 1991, generating 187 yards in regular-season victory and 144 yards, including game-winning TD, in playoff win . . . Falcons' seventh-round pick out of Northern Arizona in 1988 . . . Big Sky Conference 100- and 200-meter sprint champion . . . Born Dec. 24, 1965, in New Orleans . . . 1993 base salary: $800,000.

JAMES GEATHERS 33 6-7 290   Defensive Lineman

Jumped to the Falcons from the Redskins as a free agent . . . Signed a three-year, $2.9-million deal . . . Called "best bull-rusher in the NFL" by Falcons' coach Jerry Glanville . . . Played three seasons for the Redskins, who signed him in Plan B from New Orleans in 1990 . . . Recorded five sacks last season . . . Also notched a sack in Redskins' playoff victory over Minnesota . . . Had 4½ sacks in helping Redskins to the Super Bowl in 1991 season . . . Played first six seasons with New Orleans . . . Best statistical season was 1986, with nine sacks . . . Nicknamed "Jumpy" by his grandfather . . . Saints' second-round draft pick out of Wichita State in 1984 . . . Born June 6, 1960, in Georgetown, S.C. . . . 1993 base salary: $1.1 million.

MIKE KENN 37 6-7 280   Tackle

Grizzled veteran of the NFL's brashest team . . . Old man of the offensive line just keeps rolling along . . . Started all 16 games . . . Tremendous pass-blocker . . . Has started a remarkable total of 220 games in his Falcons' career . . . Taught the ropes to highly-touted rookie Bob Whitfield last year . . . Five-time Pro Bowl selection . . . Started 90 consecutive games at the beginning of his career . . . All-Rookie selection in

1978 . . . His 15 seasons with the Falcons are the second-most in team history to Jeff Van Note's 18 . . . Outspoken, thoughtful, highly respected by his peers . . . Hard worker whose offseason regimen has contributed to his incredible durability . . . Falcons' No. 1 pick in 1978 out of Michigan . . . One of handful of players left in the NFL who were drafted in the 1970s . . . Born Feb. 9, 1956, in Evanston, Ill. . . . 1993 base salary: $1 million.

MIKE PRITCHARD 23 5-11 180   Wide Receiver

Smooth, swift receiver is poised on the verge of stardom . . . Second on the team in receptions with 77 . . . Generated 827 yards and five TDs . . . Caught seven or more passes in six different games . . . Excels on crossing routes . . . Dangerous runner after the catch . . . Has 132 receptions in just two NFL seasons . . . Impact player as a rookie in 1991 when he caught 50 passes for 624 yards . . . Falcons' second No. 1 pick (Bruce Pickens was the first) in 1991, out of Colorado . . . An all-purpose star in college . . . Averaged 18.8 yards every time he touched the football as a runner, receiver and return man . . . Generated 1,528 all-purpose yards as a senior for co-national champions . . . Born Oct. 25, 1969, in Charleston, S.C. . . . 1993 base salary: $475,000.

BOBBY HEBERT 33 6-4 215   Quarterback

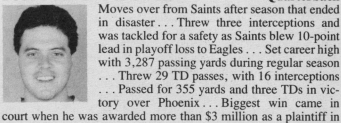

Moves over from Saints after season that ended in disaster . . . Threw three interceptions and was tackled for a safety as Saints blew 10-point lead in playoff loss to Eagles . . . Set career high with 3,287 passing yards during regular season . . . Threw 29 TD passes, with 16 interceptions . . . Passed for 355 yards and three TDs in victory over Phoenix . . . Biggest win came in court when he was awarded more than $3 million as a plaintiff in settlement with NFL . . . Sat out 1990 season in contract dispute . . . Set club record with 62.9 completion percentage in 1989 . . . Passed for 3,156 yards and 20 TDs in 1988 . . . Hometown hero who was born, raised and played college football in Louisiana . . . Played three seasons in USFL . . . Joined Saints as a free agent in 1985 . . . Played collegiately at Northwestern Louisiana . . . Born Aug. 19, 1960, in Galliano, La. . . . 1992 base salary: $1.43 million.

BRUCE PICKENS 25 5-11 190   Cornerback

Talented athlete has the potential to become one of the NFL's best defensive backs . . . Expected to step into starting lineup . . . Played in all 16 games, starting four, in 1992 . . . Registered 51 tackles . . . Ranked second on the team to Deion Sanders with two interceptions and 11 passes defended . . . Tremendous athlete with speed, quickness, leaping ability . . . Slowed by protracted contract holdout as a rookie in 1991 . . . Didn't sign until Oct. 4 and ended up playing in only seven games . . . Falcons' No. 1 pick, third overall, in 1991 draft out of Nebraska . . . Considered the best pure coverage cornerback in the draft that year . . . Consensus All-American at Nebraska . . . 1993 base salary: $450,000.

COACH JERRY GLANVILLE:

Battled through difficult third season in Atlanta . . . Injuries and a complete defensive meltdown doomed his team to a 6-10 record . . . Falcons surrendered 414 points, by far the highest total in the NFL . . . The collapse was especially frustrating because of the gains made in 1991 . . . That season, he led the Falcons to a 10-6 record and playoff berth . . . Falcons beat the Saints in the playoffs and looked like a rising NFL power . . . Before last season, his reconstruction job in Atlanta looked remarkably similar to the one he worked in Houston . . . Took Oilers to the playoffs in second season after five consecutive losing records . . . Controversial figure who energizes a franchise . . . Outspoken, colorful, quotable . . . His teams are known for their intensity and aggressive special teams . . . Career record as an NFL head coach is 54-59 . . . His teams have made the playoffs in four of the last six seasons . . . Falcons were 5-11 in his first season in 1990 . . . Led Oilers to three consecutive playoff berths but his controversial style led to his dismissal . . . Known for leaving tickets for Elvis Presley and other luminaries, real and fictional, dead and alive . . . Served as an assistant coach in Buffalo, Detroit and Atlanta before joining Oilers' staff as defensive coordinator in 1984 . . . Played linebacker at Northern Michigan . . . Drives race cars in offseason . . . Born Oct. 14, 1941, in Detroit.

A healthy Chris Miller hopes to pick up where he left off.

GREATEST INTERCEPTOR

The strong Falcon defenses of the 1970s featured a defensive back named Rolland Lawrence, who came out of little Tabor College in Hillsboro, Kan.

Playing for the Falcons from 1973-81, Lawrence was a smart, instinctive, consistent player. He led the team in interceptions five years in a row and finished his career with 39, tops on the Falcons' all-time list.

Lawrence's best season was 1975, when he was among the league leaders with nine interceptions and averaged 18.1 yards on returns, including an 87-yarder for a touchdown. Lawrence led the team in interceptions every year from 1975-79. He had a total of 34 interceptions in that period, never snatching fewer than six passes in a season. Lawrence holds the team record for career-return yardage with 658.

Deion Sanders rates a mention. Although he has played only four seasons for the Falcons, and spent parts of those seasons playing baseball, he already holds the team record for interception returns for touchdowns with three.

INDIVIDUAL FALCON RECORDS

Rushing

Most Yards Game:	202	Gerald Riggs, vs New Orleans, 1984
Season:	1,719	Gerald Riggs, 1985
Career:	6,631	Gerald Riggs, 1982-88

Passing

Most TD Passes Game:	5	Wade Wilson, 1992
Season:	31	Steve Bartkowski, 1980
Career:	149	Steve Bartkowski, 1975-85

Receiving

Most TD Passes Game:	3	8 times, most recently Andre Rison, vs Chicago, 1992
Season:	13	Alfred Jenkins, 1981
Career:	40	Alfred Jenkins, 1975-83

Scoring

Most Points Game:	18	8 times, most recently Andre Rison, vs Chicago, 1992
Season:	114	Mick Luckhurst, 1981
Career:	558	Mick Luckhurst, 1981-87
Most TDs Game:	3	8 times, most recently Andre Rison, vs Chicago, 1992
Season:	13	Alfred Jenkins, 1981
Career:	48	Gerald Riggs, 1982-88

CHICAGO BEARS

TEAM DIRECTORY: Chairman: Edward B. McCaskey; Pres.: Michael B. McCaskey; VP-Player Personnel: Bill Tobin; Dir. Adm.: Tim LeFevour; VP-Operations: Ted Phillips; Dir. Marketing and Communications: Ken Valdiserri; Pub. Rel. Dir.: Bryan Harlan; Head Coach: Dave Wannstedt. Home field: Soldier Field (66,960). Colors: Navy blue, orange and white.

SCOUTING REPORT

OFFENSE: The Bears committed themselves to quarterback Jim Harbaugh when they re-signed him in the spring. Harbaugh was a free agent, but the Bears spent the money to make him their highest-paid player. Harbaugh is an athletic, hard-nosed quarterback who lacks a great passing touch. He can run and make plays but is best when directing a balanced attack.

The Bears need to get the teeth back in their ground game.

Donnell Woolford had second-most interceptions (7) in NFL.

Their leading rusher in 1992, Neal Anderson, managed only 582 yards. Anderson still has some spring in his legs, and the Bears are hoping hard-running, hard-blocking fullback Craig ''Iron-head'' Heyward, signed as a free agent, will put some bite back in the ground attack.

The wide receivers are average. Wendell Davis is the best of the bunch but the Bears lack a big-play man. Perhaps top pick Curtis Conway of USC is that man. Tom Waddle is a solid possession receiver. The passing game would be helped tremendously by the addition of a receiving threat at tight end.

The line is solid. Jerry Fontenot is a good young center and the Bears have high hopes for young tackles Stan Thomas and Troy Auzenne. Mark Bortz and John Wojciechowski are decent guards.

DEFENSE: It's on this side of the football that new coach Dave Wannstedt is expected to make the most immediate impact. Wannstedt will try to restructure the Bears in the image of the Cowboys, stressing speed, depth and aggressiveness.

Age is a concern along the defensive line. Richard Dent and Steve McMichael remain productive players, but both are in their mid-30s. William Perry is an aging Refrigerator, but there is hope in young linemen Alonzo Spellman, Trace Armstrong and rookie Carl Simpson of Florida State.

A new era begins at linebacker with the retirement of future Hall of Famer Mike Singletary. Dante Jones will replace him. John Roper is a solid outside linebacker, but the Bears are still waiting on promising young player Ron Cox.

The secondary has a couple of big-play men in cornerback Donnell Woolford and safety Mark Carrier. Shaun Gayle and Lemuel Stinson are adequate but more speed and talent are needed.

SPECIAL TEAMS: The Bears have an excellent kicker in Kevin Butler, who made 19 of 26 field-goal attempts and has one of the strongest legs in the league.

Chris Gardocki is a solid punter. Woolford doubles as a decent punt-returner but the Bears are still looking to replace Johnny Bailey, the return specialist they lost to Phoenix in Plan B. He was a Pro Bowl pick last season.

The coverage teams are decent but nothing special. Wannstedt will restock the roster with speedy players, which should have an immediate effect on special teams.

BEARS VETERAN ROSTER

HEAD COACH—Dave Wannstedt. Assistant Coaches—Danny Abromowicz, Clarence Brooks, Ivan Fears, Carlos Mainford, David McGinnis, Joe Pendry, Mike Shula, Bob Slowik, Ron Turner, Tony Wise.

No.	Name	Pos.	Ht.	Wt.	NFL Exp.	College
79	Age, Louis	T	6-7	350	2	SW Louisiana
35	Anderson, Neal	RB	5-11	210	8	Florida
93	Armstrong, Trace	DE	6-4	260	5	Florida
70	Auzenne, Troy	T	6-7	290	2	California
89	Blackwell, Kelly	TE	6-1	255	2	TCU
47	Blaylock, Anthony	CB	5-10	185	6	Winston-Salem
62	Bortz, Mark	G	6-6	282	11	Iowa
6	Butler, Kevin	K	6-1	190	9	Georgia
92	Cain, Joe	LB	6-1	233	5	Oregon Tech
20	Carrier, Mark	S	6-1	180	4	USC
44	Christian, Bob	RB	5-10	225	1	Northwestern
96	Cooper, Reggie	LB	6-2	215	2	Nebraska
54	Cox, Ron	LB	6-2	235	4	Fresno State
82	Davis, Wendell	WR	5-11	188	6	LSU
95	Dent, Richard	DE	6-5	265	11	Tennessee State
37	Douglass, Maurice	CB	5-11	202	7	Kentucky
24	Fain, Richard	CB	5-10	180	3	Florida
67	Fontenot, Jerry	G-C	6-3	287	5	Texas A&M
2	Furrer, Will	QB	6-3	209	2	Virginia Tech
17	Gardocki, Chris	P-K	6-1	196	3	Clemson
23	Gayle, Shaun	S	5-11	202	10	Ohio State
29	Gentry, Dennis	WR	5-8	180	12	Baylor
31	Green, Mark	RB	5-11	190	5	Notre Dame
4	Harbaugh, Jim	QB	6-3	220	7	Michigan
45	Heyward, Craig	FB	5-11	260	6	Pittsburgh
85	Jennings, Keith	TE	6-4	260	4	Clemson
53	Jones, Dante	LB	6-2	238	6	Oklahoma
64	Jurkovic, Mirko	G	6-3	290	2	Notre Dame
94	Kmet, Frank	DL	6-3	289	1	Purdue
88	Kozlowski, Glen	WR	6-1	210	8	BYU
58	Leeuwenburg, Jay	C	6-2	290	2	Colorado
33	Lewis, Darren	RB	5-10	225	3	Texas A&M
39	Lincoln, Jeremy	CB	5-10	184	2	Tennessee
26	Mangum, John	CB	5-10	178	4	Alabama
76	McMichael, Steve	DT	6-2	270	14	Texas
81	Morgan, Anthony	WR	6-1	195	3	Tennessee
84	Morris, Ron	WR	6-1	198	7	SMU
51	Morrissey, Jim	LB	6-3	225	9	Michigan State
18	Obee, Terry	WR	5-10	188	1	Oregon
36	Paul, Markus	S	6-2	200	5	Syracuse
91	Paulk, Tim	LB	6-1	230	1	Florida
72	Perry, William	DT	6-2	335	9	Clemson
59	Rivera, Ron	LB	6-3	234	10	California
55	Roper, John	LB	6-1	228	5	Texas A&M
99	Ryan, Tim	DT	6-4	265	4	USC
52	Schwantz, Jim	LB	6-2	232	1	Purdue
69	Smith, Vernice	G	6-3	298	5	Florida A&M
90	Spellman, Alonzo	DE	6-4	280	2	Ohio State
32	Stinson, Lemuel	CB	5-9	180	6	Texas Tech
57	Thayer, Tom	G	6-4	284	9	Notre Dame
60	Thomas, Stan	T	6-5	295	3	Texas
78	Van Horne, Keith	T	6-6	290	13	USC
87	Waddle, Tom	WR	6-0	185	4	Boston College
86	Wagner, Barry	WR	6-3	220	1	Alabama A&M
71	Williams, James	DT	6-7	335	3	Cheyney State
10	Willis, Peter Tom	QB	6-2	204	4	Florida State
73	Wojciechowski, John	G	6-4	280	7	Michigan State
21	Woolford, Donnell	CB	5-9	187	5	Clemson
83	Wright, Eric	WR	6-0	203	2	Stephen F. Austin
97	Zorich, Chris	DT	6-1	284	3	Notre Dame

		TOP DRAFT CHOICES				
Rd.	Name	Sel. No.	Pos.	Ht.	Wt.	College
1	Conway, Curtis	7	WR	6-0	185	USC
2	Simpson, Carl	35	DE	6-2	280	Florida State
3	Gedney, Chris	61	TE	6-1	254	Syracuse
4	Perry, Todd	97	G-T	6-5	292	Kentucky
4	Baker, Myron	100	LB	6-0	224	Louisiana Tech

THE ROOKIES: The Bears added much-needed speed by taking Conway in the first round. One of the fastest players in the draft, he doubles as a dangerous return man. Simpson, a good pass-rusher, was added in the second round.

OUTLOOK: Wannstedt is under no pressure to win right away, and that's good. The Bears, 5-11 last year, needed a change from Mike Ditka but they need lots of good young players, too. They remain a year or two away from playoff contention.

BEAR PROFILES

NEAL ANDERSON 29 5-11 210   Running Back

Once-great player hopes to return to prominence . . . Coaching change could revitalize this talented athlete, who feuded at times with departed Mike Ditka . . . Ran for 582 yards in 1992, his lowest total since his rookie season in 1986 . . . Averaged only 3.7 yards per carry . . . Scored five TDs, breaking loose for a 49-yard scoring run against Falcons . . . Caught 42 passes for 399 yards and six TDs . . . Four-time Pro Bowl pick was regarded as one of the best all-around backs in the NFL in his prime . . . Slowed by injuries in 1991 . . . Rushed for 747 yards that season, his first time under 1,000 yards since 1987 . . . Ran for 1,106 yards and 12 TDs in 1988 . . . Had a career-high 1,275 yards in 1989 . . . Smooth receiver has 271 catches and 20 TD receptions in seven NFL seasons . . . Ranks second on the Bears' all-time list with 67 career TDs . . . Took the torch from Walton Payton, the NFL's leading all-time rusher . . . Born Aug. 14, 1964, in Graceville, Fla. . . . 1993 base salary: $1.6 million.

CRAIG HEYWARD 26 5-11 260   Running Back

Signed with Bears as free agent after five seasons with the Saints . . . Expected to add muscle to Bears' sagging running game . . . Bruising inside runner and powerful blocker . . . Ran for 416 yards on 104 carries (4.0 average) for the Saints in 1992 . . . Caught three passes for 57 yards and ran for TD in playoff loss to Eagles . . . Squabbled with management and coach Jim Mora at various times over his weight and off-the-field activities . . . When healthy and at his playing weight, he is one of the NFL's most powerful runners . . . Best statistical season was 1990, with 599 yards and 4.7 average . . . Has 67 receptions in five NFL seasons . . . Saints' No. 1 pick in 1988 out of Pittsburgh . . . Ran for 1,655 yards and 11 TDs as a junior . . . Entered draft after that season . . . Born Sept. 26, 1966, in Passaic, N.J. . . . 1992 base salary: $1.1 million.

ALONZO SPELLMAN 21 6-4 280   Defensive End

Imposing physical specimen who could flourish in Bears' new defensive system . . . Made strides as a rookie in 1992, when he had 37 tackles and four sacks . . . Strong, quick, intense . . . One of the youngest players in the NFL . . . He played his first three NFL games at the age of 20 . . . Bears saw a potential Pro Bowler when they selected him in the first round of the 1992 draft . . . Has 31½-inch vertical leap . . . Natural pass-rusher who needs to learn the pro game . . . Played three seasons at Ohio State . . . Named Buckeyes' MVP after junior season . . . Played outside linebacker as a freshman before switching to defensive end . . . Entered draft after junior season . . . Born Sept. 27, 1971, in Rancocas, N.J. . . . 1993 base salary: $405,000.

WENDELL DAVIS 27 5-11 188   Wide Receiver

Smooth receiver is the feature attraction in the Bears' passing game . . . Led the team in receptions for the second year in a row with 54 . . . Generated 734 yards and two TDs . . . His statistics have been limited by the Bears' offensive approach . . . Has spent much of his career as a blocker and decoy for run-oriented team . . . That could change as Bears enter new era under coach Dave Wannstedt . . . Best statistical season was 1991, with 61 receptions and 945 yards . . . Both totals were highest by a Bear since Dick Gordon in 1970 . . . Became starter in 1990 after serving as a backup during his first two NFL seasons . . . Bears' second No. 1 pick (Brad Muster was the first) in 1988 . . . Set career records at LSU for receptions (183) and yards (2,708) . . . Born Jan. 3, 1966, in Shreveport, La. . . . 1993 base salary: $750,000.

JOHN ROPER 27 6-1 228   **Linebacker**

Another talented athlete who could blossom in Bears' new defensive system . . . Has the speed and talent to become a big-play man . . . Great pass-rusher in college but has yet to consistently display that skill at the NFL level . . . Managed only 2½ sacks in injury-marred 1992 season . . . Started all 16 games in 1991 and finished third on the team with eight sacks . . . NFC Defensive Player of the Week after 11-tackle, two-sack game against Bucs . . . Starter as a rookie in 1989 but relegated to backup duty the following year . . . Bears' second-round pick in 1989 out of Texas A&M . . . Nicknamed "Ravage" by his college teammates for his intense play . . . SWC Defensive Player of the Year as a senior . . . Born Oct. 4, 1965, in Yates, Tex. . . . 1992 base salary: $250,000.

KEVIN BUTLER 31 6-1 190   **Placekicker**

Another Bear who feuded with former coach Mike Ditka . . . Has been one of the NFL's most consistent kickers since his rookie season in 1985 . . . Made 19 of 26 field-goal attempts in 1992 . . . Holds 16 club records . . . The Bears' all-time leading scorer with 813 points . . . Holds NFL record for consecutive field goals with 24, set in 1989 . . . Has made 72.5 percent of his career field-goal attempts (172 of 237) . . . Burst on the scene as a rookie, making 31 of 38 field-goal attempts and 51 of 51 extra points for Super Bowl-bound team . . . Set NFL rookie record with 144 points . . . Was 3-for-3 in field-goal attempts in Super Bowl XX . . . Bears' fourth-round pick in 1985 out of Georgia . . . Set NCAA record for most games with two or more field goals with 27 . . . Born July 24, 1962, in Atlanta . . . 1993 base salary: $475,000.

MARK CARRIER 25 6-1 180   Safety

Struggled through frustrating season... Finished without an interception as the Bears managed only 14 as a team... Missed the Pro Bowl for first time in his three-year career... Burst into prominence as a rookie in 1990... Was the big-play man in the Bears' deep secondary ... Led NFL in interceptions with 10 and also forced five fumbles... Consensus pick as NFL Defensive Rookie of the Year... His statistics dropped off in 1991 but he still made the Pro Bowl... Had two interceptions and finished second on the team in tackles with 93... The Bears' No. 1 pick in 1990, sixth overall, out of USC... Entered draft after junior season... Born April 28, 1968, in Lake Charles, La.... 1993 base salary: $500,000.

TRACE ARMSTRONG 27 6-4 260   Defensive End

Another talented young player around whom the Bears are attempting to rebuild their defense ... Put together solid season with 6½ sacks... Effective run-defender who is an active, persistent pass-rusher... Suffered through injury-marred season in 1991... Missed four full games and parts of others with a knee injury ... Managed only 1½ sacks... Burst on the scene in 1990 with 10 sacks... Regarded as solid defensive end who could flourish in the Bears' new system... Collected five sacks as a rookie reserve in 1989... That total led all NFC rookies ... Bears' second No. 1 pick (Donnell Woolford was the first) in 1989 out of Florida... Played only one season at Florida after transferring from Arizona State... Earned degree in psychology ... Born Oct. 5, 1965, in Birmingham, Ala.... 1992 base salary: $300,000.

DONNELL WOOLFORD 27 5-9 187   Cornerback

Emerged as one of the NFL's top cornerbacks ... Finished second in the NFC in interceptions with seven... Smooth coverage man who appears to be on the verge of Pro Bowl recognition ... Usually assigned the task of covering the opposition's best receiver... Development slowed by injuries and inexperience early in his career... Finally worked into starting lineup in

1991 . . . Had two interceptions and finished with 77 tackles that year . . . Spent much of 1989 and 1990 seasons in former coach Mike Ditka's doghouse . . . During his difficult rookie season, Ditka snarled, "This guy can't cover anybody." . . . Bears' first No. 1 pick (Trace Armstrong was the second) in 1989 out of Clemson . . . Born Jan. 6, 1966, in Fayetteville, N.C. . . . 1993 base salary: $400,000.

JIM HARBAUGH 29 6-3 220   Quarterback

Bears showed their commitment to this team leader by signing him to four-year, $13-million contract in the spring . . . Had been a free agent who was attracting interest from several teams . . . Passed for 2,486 yards and 13 TDs in 1992 . . . Hard-nosed, competitive player is regarded as one of the NFL's most underrated quarterbacks . . . Could blossom in new offensive system . . . Set club records for pass attempts (478) and completions (275) in 1991 when he became the first Bear to start all 16 games at quarterback since Vince Evans in 1981 . . . Good scrambler who has rushed for more than 1,200 yards in his career . . . Averaged 5.2 yards per carry last season . . . Became full-time starter in 1990 . . . Has 28-25 record as a starter . . . Bears' No. 1 pick in 1987 out of Michigan . . . Born Dec. 23, 1963, in Ann Arbor, Mich. . . . 1993 base salary: $3 million.

STEVE McMICHAEL 35 6-2 270   Defensive Tackle

Old man of the Bears' defense just keeps rolling along . . . Re-signed to two-year, $2.2-million deal after he attracted interest from several teams as a free agent in the spring . . . Led the Bears in sacks with 10½, the second-highest total of his 13-year career . . . Active, intense player . . . Regarded as team leader because of his experience and dedicated approach . . . Has 86½ career sacks . . . Best statistical season was 1988, with 88 tackles and 11½ sacks . . . Two-time Pro Bowl selection . . . Bears claimed him on waivers from New England in 1981 . . . Patriots' third-round pick in 1980 out of Texas . . . Born Oct. 17, 1957, in Freer, Tex. . . . 1993 base salary: $1.1 million.

COACH DAVE WANNSTEDT: Became the 11th head coach
in Bears' history after helping the Cowboys to
Super Bowl title as defensive coordinator . . .
Intense, emotional coach who was credited with
molding Cowboys into one of the NFL's most
aggressive defensive units . . . Dallas was
ranked No. 1 in the NFL in defense despite
absence of a single Pro Bowl player . . . Cowboys' defense overwhelmed Eagles in playoff
opener and Bills in Super Bowl . . . An expert at situational substitutions, using as many as 17 defensive players in regular rotation
in some games . . . Spent four seasons as Cowboys' defensive coordinator . . . Close friend with Dallas head coach Jimmy Johnson,
who advised him to take the Bears' job . . . Also spent three years
as Johnson's defensive coordinator at University of Miami . . .
During his time in Miami, the Hurricanes held opponents to 2.2
yards per rushing attempt and 10.9 points per game . . . An assistant coach at University of Pittsburgh, Oklahoma State and USC
. . . Played offensive tackle at Pitt . . . A captain of the 1973 team
that featured freshman Tony Dorsett . . . Drafted by Green Bay in
the 15th round and spent one NFL season on the injured-reserve
list . . . Born May 21, 1952, in Pittsburgh.

GREATEST INTERCEPTOR

The big, bad Bears' defense of the early and mid-1980s was
known for its pass-rushing and hard hitting. It was known for the
ferocity that helped the team to its only Super Bowl victory following the 1985 season.

Gary Fencik was the brains behind that brawn. The Yale grad-
uate played safety for those great defenses, and while he wasn't
adverse to hitting, he was better known for his smart, instinctive
play. And for his interceptions.

Fencik holds the club record for interceptions in a career with
38 (1976-87). He led the team in interceptions five times. A Pro
Bowl player in 1981 and 1982, he had his best season in 1981,
when he set personal bests with six interceptions and 121 return
yards.

New Washington coach Richie Petitbon deserves mention. Petitbon, who played in Chicago from 1959-68, ranks second in the
Bears' all-time list with 37 interceptions and holds the team record
with a 101-yard return for a touchdown.

INDIVIDUAL BEAR RECORDS

Rushing

Most Yards Game:	275	Walter Payton, vs Minnesota, 1977
Season:	1,852	Walter Payton, 1977
Career:	16,726	Walter Payton, 1975-87

Passing

Most TD Passes Game:	7	Sid Luckman, vs N.Y. Giants, 1943
Season:	28	Sid Luckman, 1943
Career:	137	Sid Luckman, 1939-50

Receiving

Most TD Passes Game:	4	2 times, most recently Mike Ditka, vs L.A. Rams, 1963
Season:	13	2 times, most recently Dick Gordon, 1970
Career:	50	Ken Kavanaugh, 1940-41, 1945-50

Scoring

Most Points Game:	36	Gale Sayers, vs San Francisco, 1965
Season:	144	Kevin Butler, 1985
Career:	813	Kevin Butler, 1985-92
Most TDs Game:	6	Gale Sayers, vs San Francisco, 1965
Season:	22	Gale Sayers, 1965
Career:	125	Walter Payton, 1975-87

DALLAS COWBOYS

TEAM DIRECTORY: Owner/Pres/GM: Jerry Jones; VP: Stephen Jones; Pub. Rel. Dir.: Rich Dalrymple; Head Coach: Jimmy Johnson. Home field: Texas Stadium (65,024). Colors: Royal blue, metallic blue and white.

SCOUTING REPORT

OFFENSE: Explosive young talent makes the Cowboys the most dangerous team in the league. They came of age in 1992 as the offensive line started performing at a level established by young stars such as quarterback Troy Aikman, running back Emmitt Smith and wide receiver Michael Irvin.

Aikman capped a breakthrough 13-3 season by winning the MVP award in the Cowboys' Super Bowl victory over Buffalo. He is a master at running Dallas' offensive system and appears to

Gatorade ritual gave Jimmy Johnson Super Bowl baptism.

have his best years ahead of him. Backup quarterback is a concern since Steve Beuerlein left as a free agent.

Smith, the two-time defending NFL rushing champion, is a workhorse back who sets up everything else the Cowboys do offensively. Daryl Johnston is a classic blocking fullback.

The passing game is excellent. Irvin is a two-time Pro Bowler and one of the best receivers in the game. Alvin Harper is an emerging star coming off a clutch performance in the playoffs. Jimmy Smith is expected to take Kelvin Martin's place as the third wide receiver. Tight end Jay Novacek, a Pro Bowler, is a superb third-down receiver.

The offensive line burst into prominence in 1992. Center Mark Stepnoski and guard Nate Newton are Pro Bowlers, but the real key is right tackle Erik Williams, a powerful force who is regarded by many as the best young offensive lineman in football.

DEFENSE: Speed and depth are the trademarks of the defense that ranked No. 1 in the NFL despite not having a single Pro Bowl player.

The line is young, deep and versatile. The Cowboys traded for big-play end Charles Haley, who responded with a strong season in 1992. Tackles Tony Casillas and Russell Maryland are productive, and end Tony Tolbert is an emerging star. There's also plenty of reserve talent in Jimmie Jones, Leon Lett, Jim Jeffcoat and Chad Henning, a former Air Force pilot who could emerge as a force.

Middle linebacker Robert Jones was solid as a rookie and is only going to get better. Outside linebackers Vinson Smith and Ken Norton put together strong seasons, and the Cowboys have high hopes for young Dixon Edwards.

The secondary got a lift last season when the Cowboys traded for safety Thomas Everett. He's a hard hitter who's still in the prime of his career. Second-year man Darren Woodson is expected to emerge as the free safety. The cornerbacks are young and talented. Kevin Smith was impressive as a rookie and Larry Brown is a former No. 12 pick who has made good.

SPECIAL TEAMS: Fast and aggressive. The Cowboys go for blocks and play with reckless abandon.

The Cowboys scored 20 points on special teams last season on two punt blocks (one for a TD, one for a safety) and two punt returns. They like to pressure their opponents.

The return game is a concern because of the loss of Martin, who signed with Seattle as a free agent. Jimmy Smith and Clayton

COWBOYS VETERAN ROSTER

HEAD COACH—Jimmy Johnson. Assistant Coaches—Hubbard Alexander, Joe Avezzano, John Blake, Joe Brodsky, Dave Campo, Butch Davis, Jim Eddy, Robert Ford, Steve Hoffman, Hudson Houck, Norv Turner, Mike Woicik.

No.	Name	Pos.	Ht.	Wt.	NFL Exp.	College
50	Abrams, Bobby	LB	6-3	230	4	Michigan
34	Agee, Tommie	FB	6-0	227	7	Auburn
8	Aikman, Troy	QB	6-4	222	5	UCLA
40	Bates, Bill	S	6-1	203	11	Tennessee
21	Beasley, Michael	RB	5-10	195	1	West Virginia
49	Biggins, Milton	TE	6-4	273	1	Western Kentucky
42	Briggs, Greg	S	6-3	212	2	Texas Southern
24	Brown, Larry	CB	5-11	185	3	TCU
75	Casillas, Tony	DT	6-3	277	8	Oklahoma
68	Cornish, Frank	C-G	6-4	285	4	UCLA
3	Daniel, Tim	WR	5-11	192	2	Florida A&M
6	Domingos, Steve	P	6-3	200	1	San Francisco State
58	Edwards, Dixon	LB	6-1	224	3	Michigan State
2	Elliott, Lin	K	6-0	182	2	Texas Tech
60	Evans, Melvin	T	6-2	303	2	Texas Southern
27	Everett, Thomas	S	5-9	183	7	Baylor
39	Gainer, Derrick	RB	5-11	240	3	Florida A&M
29	Gant, Kenneth	S	5-11	191	4	Albany State
17	Garrett, Jason	QB	6-2	195	1	Princeton
32	Garrett, Judd	RB	6-1	205	1	Princeton
63	Gesek, John	G	6-5	282	7	Cal-Sacramento
66	Gogan, Kevin	G-T	6-7	319	7	Washington
94	Haley, Charles	DE	6-5	230	8	James Madison
80	Harper, Alvin	WR	6-3	207	3	Tennessee
38	Hall, Chris	S	6-2	184	1	East Carolina
70	Hellestrae, Dale	G-C	6-5	283	9	SMU
95	Hennings, Chad	DL	6-6	267	2	Air Force
90	Hill, Tony	DE	6-6	255	3	Tenn.-Chattanooga
47	Holmes, Clayton	CB	5-10	181	2	Carson-Newman
20	Horton, Ray	S	5-11	188	11	Washington
88	Irvin, Michael	WR	6-2	200	6	Miami (Fla.)
77	Jeffcoat, Jim	DE	6-5	276	11	Arizona State
19	Jett, John	P	6-0	184	1	East Carolina
48	Johnston, Daryl	FB	6-2	236	5	Syracuse
97	Jones, Jimmie	DL	6-4	276	4	Miami (Fla.)
55	Jones, Robert	LB	6-2	238	2	East Carolina
69	Jones, Todd	G	6-3	295	2	Henderson State
78	Lett, Leon	DL	6-6	292	3	Emporia State
67	Maryland, Russell	DT	6-1	277	3	Miami (Fla.)
7	Millen, Hugh	QB	6-5	216	8	Washington
98	Myles, Godfrey	LB	6-1	242	3	Florida
61	Newton, Nate	G	6-3	303	8	Florida A&M
51	Norton, Ken	LB	6-2	238	6	UCLA
84	Novacek, Jay	TE	6-4	231	9	Wyoming
52	Pruitt, Mickey	LB	6-1	218	6	Colorado
64	Rankin, Alex	G	6-9	312	1	Angelo State
72	Richards, James	G	6-4	288	1	California
87	Roberts, Alfredo	TE	6-3	251	6	Miami (Fla.)
4	Saxon, Mike	P	6-3	200	9	San Diego State
22	Smith, Emmitt	RB	5-9	203	4	Florida
82	Smith, Jimmy	WR	6-1	205	2	Jackson State
26	Smith, Kevin	CB	5-11	177	2	Texas A&M
57	Smith, Vinson	LB	6-2	237	5	East Carolina
53	Stepnoski, Mark	C	6-2	271	5	Pittsburgh
92	Tolbert, Tony	DE	6-6	265	5	Texas-El Paso
71	Tuinei, Mark	T	6-5	298	11	Hawaii
76	Veingrad, Alan	G-T	6-5	280	8	East Texas State
89	Wacasey, Fallon	TE	6-7	263	1	Tulsa
37	Washington, James	S	6-1	203	6	UCLA
79	Williams, Erik	T	6-6	319	3	Central State (Ohio)
23	Williams, Robert	S	5-10	186	7	Baylor
86	Williams, Tyrone	WR	6-5	207	1	Western Ontario
28	Woodson, Darren	S	6-1	215	2	Arizona State

TOP DRAFT CHOICES

Rd.	Name	Sel. No.	Pos.	Ht.	Wt.	College
2	Williams, Kevin	46	WR	5-9	190	Miami
2	Smith, Darrin	54	LB	6-0	228	Miami
3	Middleton, Mike	84	DB	5-10	210	Indiana
4	Lassic, Derrick	94	RB	5-9	188	Alabama
4	Stone, Ron	96	OT	6-4	296	Boston College

Holmes are the top candidates to replace him as return specialist.

The coverage teams are strong and reflect the Cowboys' philosophy of drafting for speed.

Punter Mike Saxon is a solid veteran. Kicker Lin Elliott struggled a little as a rookie but came on strong late in the year. At one point, he made 13 consecutive field-goal attempts.

THE ROOKIES: The Cowboys traded out of the first round and ended up with two No. 2 picks, which they used on Miami's Kevin Williams, a wide receiver, and linebacker Darrin Smith. Williams is an explosive return man who will fill the role vacated by departed free agent Kelvin Martin. Smith fits the Cowboys' mold: he has blazing speed and probably will make an immediate impact on special teams.

OUTLOOK: The team to beat in the NFC East and in all of football. The salary cap and complacency might eventually get the best of this team, but not this year. There's too much young talent, too many good players dying to strut their stuff. Another Super Bowl title for Jimmy Johnson's gang looks within reach.

COWBOY PROFILES

TROY AIKMAN 26 6-4 222   Quarterback

Hottest property in the NFL . . . Led the Cowboys to the Super Bowl title with a sensational playoff performance . . . Threw eight touchdown passes without an interception in three playoff victories . . . MVP of the Super Bowl . . . Made Pro Bowl for second year in a row . . . Young, handsome athlete considered the next superstar in terms of endorsements and national visibility . . . Passed for 3,445 yards and 23 touchdowns in leading Dallas to NFC East title . . . Tied for NFC lead in completions with 302 . . . Threw for nine touchdowns without an interception in victories over Atlanta, Phoenix and Denver . . . Ranks fourth all-time in NFL passing completion percentage at 60.2 . . . Injuries cost him playing time and slowed his development in first three NFL seasons . . . Tough, competitive player regarded as a team leader . . . First pick in the 1989 draft out of UCLA . . . Began college career at Oklahoma but transferred to Bruins . . . Born Nov. 21, 1966, in Cerritos, Cal. . . . 1993 base salary: $1.17 million.

EMMITT SMITH 24 5-9 203   Running Back

An unquestioned NFL superstar before the age of 25 . . . Won NFL rushing title for the second season in a row . . . First player to win back-to-back rushing titles since Eric Dickerson in 1983-84 . . . Ran for team-record 1,713 yards . . . Set another team record with 18 rushing touchdowns . . . Ran for 174 yards against Atlanta . . . Established the Cowboys' superiority in NFC East with 163 yards against the Eagles' tough defense . . . Has 4,213 rushing yards and 41 rushing touchdowns in just three NFL seasons . . . Has 18 100-yard games . . . Cowboys are 26-1 when he carries 20 or more times . . . Also emerged as receiving threat in 1992 with 59 receptions, including 12 in a game against Phoenix . . . NFC Offensive Player of the Month in both November and December . . . Led NFL in rushing with 1,563 yards in 1991 . . . Consensus NFL Rookie of the Year with 937 rushing yards in 1990 . . . Cowboys' No. 1 pick in 1990 . . . Entered draft after junior season at Florida . . . Ran for 8,804 yards and 106 touchdowns in his career at Escambia (Fla.) High School . . . Born May 15, 1969, in Pensacola, Fla. . . . 1992 base salary: $335,000.

MICHAEL IRVIN 27 6-2 200   Wide Receiver

Flashy athlete is the Cowboys' go-to man . . . Caught 78 passes for 1,396 yards and seven TDs in 1992 . . . Made Pro Bowl for second year in a row . . . Monster game against Phoenix featured eight catches for 210 yards and three TDs . . . First Cowboy ever to surpass 75 catches and 1,300 receiving yards in consecutive seasons . . . Has averaged 97.5 yards in last 21 regular-season games . . . Breakthrough season in 1991 when he set team records for receptions (93) and receiving yards (1,523) ... Demonstrative, emotional athlete in tradition of many University of Miami players ... Was on pace for 1,000-yard season when he suffered knee injury in 1989 ... Cowboys' No. 1 pick out of Miami in 1988 ... Holds school career records for catches (143), receiving yards (2,423) and TD receptions (26) ... One of 17 children ... Born March 5, 1966, in Fort Lauderdale, Fla. ... 1993 base salary: $1.25 million.

JAY NOVACEK 30 6-4 231   Tight End

One of the great Plan B finds ... Made the Pro Bowl for the second consecutive year following 1992 season ... Set club record for receptions by a tight end with 68 ... Caught TD pass in playoff victory over Eagles and another in Super Bowl victory over Bills ... Has led all NFC tight ends in receptions since arriving in Dallas as Plan B free agent from Phoenix in 1990 ... Blossomed into a Pro Bowl player in 1991 when he caught 59 passes for 664 yards and four TDs ... Finesse player known more as a receiver than blocker ... Played five seasons for the Cardinals, catching 83 passes ... Cardinals' sixth-round pick in 1985 out of Wyoming ... Born Oct. 24, 1962, in Gothenburg, Neb. ... 1993 base salary: $900,000.

DARYL JOHNSTON 27 6-2 236   Fullback

Clears the way for rushing champion Emmitt Smith ... Regarded as one of the NFL's top blocking backs ... Carried the football only 17 times for 61 yards in 1992 ... Effective receiver who made 32 catches for 249 yards ... Caught 14-yard TD pass to seal important regular-season victory over Eagles ... Has been starter since 1990 season ... Special-teams ace who made his mark early in career by covering kicks ... Cowboys' second-round draft pick in 1989, the second selection made by coach Jimmy Johnson ... An All-American at Syracuse ... Has degree in economics ... Had 4.0 grade-point average at Lewiston-Porter High School (Youngstown, N.Y.) ... Born Feb. 10, 1966, in Youngstown, N.Y. ... 1992 base salary: $287,000.

ERIK WILLIAMS 24 6-6 319   Tackle

Emerging star of the NFL's most improved offensive line . . . Tremendous run-blocker who helped pave the way for NFL rushing champion Emmitt Smith . . . Started all 16 games in 1992 . . . Cornerstone of an offensive line that set a franchise record by allowing only 23 sacks . . . Aggressive, emotional player with fierce game-day demeanor . . . Named NFC Offensive Player of the Week, a rarity for a lineman, for his performance against Reggie White in victory over the Eagles . . . Played in 11 games, starting three, as a rookie in 1991 . . . Cowboys' third-round pick out of Central (Ohio) State . . . First Central State lineman ever drafted by NFL . . . His blocking helped Central State win NAIA title by scoring an average of 54.8 points per game . . . Philadelphia native who grew up as an Eagles' fan . . . Born Sept. 7, 1968, in Philadelphia . . . 1993 base salary: $250,000.

MARK STEPNOSKI 26 6-2 271   Center

Anchor of the Cowboys' strong offensive line . . . Voted to the Pro Bowl after 1992 season . . . Part of an offensive line that allowed just 23 sacks and led NFL with only 112 yards lost due to sacks . . . His run-blocking helped Emmitt Smith win the NFL rushing title for the second year in a row . . . Has started last 54 games, longest streak among Cowboys' offensive linemen . . . Became starter late in his rookie season . . . Dallas' third-round pick out of Pittsburgh in 1989 . . . Four-year starter and Outland Trophy finalist at Pitt . . . Two-time Academic All-American who has degree in communications . . . Born Jan. 20, 1967, in Erie, Pa. . . . 1993 base salary: $600,000.

CHARLES HALEY 29 6-5 230   Defensive End

Emotional leader of the NFL's top-ranked defense . . . Supplied experience and inspiration to young defense after he was acquired in a trade with San Francisco before the start of the 1992 season . . . Cowboys surrendered second-round pick in 1993 draft to acquire talented but temperamental star . . . Managed only six sacks but led team with total of 42 quarterback pressures, more than double any teammate . . . Forced a fumble by

Jim Kelly that teammate Jimmie Jones returned for a touchdown in Super Bowl win over Buffalo . . . Spent first six seasons with the 49ers, helping them win two Super Bowls . . . One of a handful of active NFL players with three Super Bowl rings . . . Led NFC with 16 sacks in 1990 . . . Three-time Pro Bowl selection . . . A steal in the 1986 draft, the 49ers got him in the fourth round out of James Madison . . . Born Jan. 6, 1964, in Gladys, Va. . . . 1993 base salary: $1.8 million.

RUSSELL MARYLAND 24 6-1 277   Defensive Tackle

Key man in the NFL's youngest, quickest defense . . . Started 14 games and led team in tackles behind line of scrimmage with five . . . Also tied for team lead in fumble recoveries with two . . . Made 47 tackles . . . Had two sacks in playoff victory over Eagles . . . Quick, active player fits perfectly into Cowboys' defensive scheme . . . Intelligent, personable athlete is regarded as a team leader . . . Emerged as a force late in rookie season in 1991 . . . Started seven games as a rookie and finished with 63 tackles and 4½ sacks . . . Registered another sack in playoff victory over Chicago . . . Top pick in 1991 draft . . . Known as "The Conscience" by his University of Miami teammates for his work ethic and ability to influence others . . . Born March 22, 1969, in Chicago . . . 1993 base salary: $825,000.

TONY CASILLAS 29 6-3 277   Defensive Tackle

Veteran leader of young Dallas defense . . . Second among club's defensive linemen in tackles with 55 . . . Strong run-defender . . . Found new life with Cowboys after several frustrating seasons with Falcons . . . Emerged as a team leader in his first season in Dallas in 1991 . . . Acquired by Dallas from Atlanta in exchange for second-round draft pick . . . His turbulent stay in Atlanta included contract problems and bitter dispute with Falcons' coach Jerry Glanville . . . Atlanta's No. 1 pick, the second overall, out of Oklahoma in 1986 . . . Pro Bowl alternate in 1986 and 1987 . . . Consensus All-American at Oklahoma . . . Voted Big Eight Conference's Defensive Player of the Decade in the 1980s . . . His wife, Lisa, is a doctor . . . Born Oct. 26, 1963, in Tulsa, Okla. . . . 1993 base salary: $725,000.

Emmitt Smith targets third straight rushing crown.

KEN NORTON 27 6-2 238   Linebacker

Put together his finest season in 1992 . . . Became the first player other than a middle linebacker to lead Cowboys in tackles since 1988 . . . Led team with 120 tackles from his outside linebacker spot . . . Tied for team lead with two fumble recoveries . . . Forced and recovered fumble in playoff victory over Eagles . . . Has been starter since 1989, his second season . . . Made 119 tackles in 1990 . . . Missed most of rookie season in 1988 with broken thumb . . . Cowboys' No. 2 pick in 1988 out of UCLA . . . Son of former heavyweight boxing champion Ken Norton . . . Didn't play football until his junior season at Westchester High School in Los Angeles . . . Born Sept. 29, 1966, in Los Angeles . . . 1993 base salary: $565,000.

COACH JIMMY JOHNSON: Completed resurrection of the

Cowboys with victory over Buffalo in Super Bowl . . . His personnel decisions and leadership have transformed Cowboys from a league laughingstock into the NFL's premier team in just four years . . . Has built young, speedy team that is expected to be Super Bowl contender for years to come . . . In 1992, led Dallas to 13-3 record and first NFC East title since 1985 . . . Cowboys powered through three playoff games, scoring 34, 30 and 52 points . . . Has 32-32 record in four regular seasons . . . Including playoff games, his teams have gone 32-11 since losing 22 of first 26 games . . . Led Cowboys to 11-5 record in 1991 . . . Named NFL Coach of the Year by AP after leading Cowboys to 7-9 mark in 1990 . . . His first team in 1989 went 1-15, beating only Washington . . . Has turned over the roster since replacing legendary Tom Landry on Feb. 25, 1989 . . . The second head coach in Cowboys' history . . . Unlike many NFL coaches, he has complete authority over personnel decisions . . . Close friend and former college roommate of Cowboys' owner Jerry Jones . . . Compiled 52-9 record in five seasons as head coach at University of Miami . . . His confident, talented Miami teams were regarded as the "bad boys" of college football . . . Had 29-25-3 record in five seasons as head coach at Oklahoma State . . . Played defensive tackle on Arkansas' 1964 national championship team . . . Born July 16, 1942, in Port Arthur, Tex.

GREATEST INTERCEPTOR

The Cowboys knew they had somebody special after Mel Renfro's first season in 1964. The defensive back from Oregon led the team in interceptions as a rookie with seven. By the end of his distinguished career, Renfro would hold the team record for interceptions with 52 and for interception-return yardage with 626.

Rangy and fast, Renfro was a big-play man for the Cowboys' emerging dynasty in the mid- and late 1960s. He would stick around through the 1977 season, playing in four Super Bowls for the Cowboys.

Renfro also holds the team record for kickoff-return yardage in a career with 2,246, a 26.4 average. He scored two touchdowns on kick returns and three touchdowns on interception returns, including a 90-yarder.

Special mention goes to Everson Walls, an undrafted free agent out of Grambling who joined the Cowboys in 1981 and played nine seasons in Dallas. Compensating for a lack of speed with remarkable instincts, Walls finished his Cowboy career with 44 interceptions, including a league-leading 11 in his rookie season.

INDIVIDUAL COWBOY RECORDS

Rushing

Most Yards Game:	206	Tony Dorsett, vs Philadelphia, 1978
Season:	1,713	Emmitt Smith, 1992
Career:	12,036	Tony Dorsett, 1977-87

Passing

Most TD Passes Game:	5	7 times, most recently Danny White, vs N.Y. Giants, 1983
Season:	29	Danny White, 1983
Career:	154	Danny White, 1976-87

Receiving

Most TD Passes Game:	4	Bob Hayes, vs Houston, 1970
Season:	14	Frank Clarke, 1962
Career:	71	Bob Hayes, 1965-74

Scoring

Most Points Game:	24	5 times, most recently Emmitt Smith, vs Phoenix, 1990
Season:	123	Rafael Septien, 1983
Career:	874	Rafael Septien, 1978-86
Most TDs Game:	4	5 times, most recently Emmitt Smith, vs Phoenix 1990
Season:	19	Emmitt Smith, 1992
Career:	86	Tony Dorsett, 1977-87

DETROIT LIONS

TEAM DIRECTORY: Pres.: William Clay Ford; Exec VP/CEO: Charles Schmidt; VP-Adm./Gen Counsel: Michael Huyghue; Dir. Player Personnel: Ron Hughes; Dir. Marketing, Broadcasting and Communication: Bill Keenist; Media Rel. Coordinator: Mike Murray; Head Coach: Wayne Fontes. Home field: Pontiac Silverdome (80,500). Colors: Honolulu blue and silver.

SCOUTING REPORT

OFFENSE: As long as they have Barry Sanders, the Lions will be dangerous. Sanders overcome a slow start last season to finish with 1,352 yards and nine TDs. He is a threat every time he touches the football.

To help Sanders, the Lions spent their free-agent dollars to rebuild their offensive line. They signed David Lutz, Bill Fralic and David Richards to serve as bodyguards for No. 20. Left tackle Lomas Brown is one of the best in the business.

The Lions have some talented wide receivers in Willie Green, Brett Perriman and Herman Moore, who is an emerging star. But more depth in this area is crucial. The Lions also need more consistent play from their tight ends.

Quarterback is a problem area. The Lions have rotated quarterbacks because of injuries or ineffectiveness for much of the last three seasons. They need to settle on someone and hope he stays healthy and at the top of his game.

This might be the season that Andre Ware finally begins to approach his potential. He played pretty well at the end of last season and will go to training camp with a great chance to win the job. Rodney Peete remains in the mix, as does Erik Kramer.

DEFENSE: The Lions continue to search for more pass-rushing. It's the missing ingredient from a solid but unspectacular defense.

The line has some promising young players in Marc Spindler, Kelvin Pritchett and Robert Porcher. The Lions will need a replacement for the traded Jerry Ball (Browns), one of the best nose tackles in the NFL. Dan Owens is a solid backup.

Chris Spielman and Dennis Gibson are productive inside linebackers who excel in run-defense and the Lions landed Pat Swilling in a draft-day deal with the Saints. George Jamison is a good all-around player at left linebacker, and the Lions think they might have a future star in right linebacker Tracy Scroggins, a relentless pass-rusher.

The secondary was hurt by cornerback Melvin Jenkins' flight to Atlanta as a free agent, but Ray Crockett is a solid cornerback. The safety tandem of William White and Bennie Blades is a good one. Blades, in particular, is a hard hitter and big-play man.

SPECIAL TEAMS: The Lions have the NFL's reigning return king in Mel Gray, who excels at bringing back both punts and

Barry Sanders rumbled without suing for lack of support.

LIONS VETERAN ROSTER

HEAD COACH—Wayne Fontes. Assistant Coaches—Hank Bullough, Don Clemons, Frank Gansz, Dan Henning, Bert Hill, Lamar Leachman, Dave Levy, Billie Matthews, Herb Paterra, Charlie Sanders, Jerry Wampfler.

No.	Name	Pos.	Ht.	Wt.	NFL Exp.	College
6	Arnold, Jim	P	6-3	211	11	Vanderbilt
40	Barrett, Reggie	WR	6-3	215	3	Texas-El Paso
33	Bennett, Antoine	CB	5-11	185	3	Florida A&M
36	Blades, Bennie	S	6-1	221	6	Miami (Fla.)
66	Bouwens, Shawn	OG	6-4	290	3	Nebraska-Wesleyan
75	Brown, Lomas	T	6-4	287	9	Florida
68	Burton, Leonard	C	6-3	275	8	South Carolina
87	Campbell, Jeff	WR	5-8	173	4	Colorado
50	Caston, Toby	ILB	6-1	243	7	Louisiana State
32	Clay, Willie	CB	5-9	184	2	Georgia Tech
55	Cofer, Michael	OLB	6-5	244	11	Tennessee
48	Coleman, Sidney	LB	6-2	250	5	Southern Mississippi
21	Colon, Harry	S	6-0	203	3	Missouri
76	Conover, Scott	T	6-4	285	3	Purdue
39	Crockett, Ray	CB	5-9	181	5	Baylor
67	Dallafior, Ken	G-C	6-4	283	9	Minnesota
52	Derby, John	LB	6-0	232	1	Iowa
95	Ford, Darryl	LB	6-1	225	2	New Mexico State
79	Fralic, Bill	G	6-5	280	9	Pittsburgh
98	Gibson, Dennis	ILB	6-2	243	7	Iowa State
53	Glover, Kevin	C	6-2	282	9	Maryland
23	Gray, Mel	WR-KR	5-9	162	8	Purdue
86	Green, Willie	WR	6-2	181	3	Mississippi
74	Griffin, Willie	DE	6-3	286	1	Nebraska
4	Hanson, Jason	K	5-11	183	2	Washington State
99	Hayworth, Tracy	LB	6-3	260	4	Tennessee
81	Holman, Rodney	TE	6-3	238	11	Tulane
44	Iaquaniello, Mike	S	6-3	208	2	Michigan State
58	Jamison, George	LB	6-1	235	7	Cincinnati
89	Johnson, Jimmie	TE	6-2	255	5	Howard
	Jones, James	RB	6-3	232	11	Florida
57	Jones, Victor	ILB	6-2	250	6	Virginia Tech
45	Kent, Phillip	LB	6-1	244	1	Mississippi
12	Kramer, Erik	QB	6-1	199	4	North Carolina State
72	Linn, Jack	G-T	6-5	285	2	West Virginia
16	Long, Chuck	QB	6-4	217	7	Iowa
73	Lutz, Dave	G-T	6-6	305	11	Georgia Tech
26	Lynch, Eric	RB	5-10	224	1	Grand Valley State
83	Matthews, Aubrey	WR	5-7	165	8	Delta State
92	McLemore, Thomas	TE	6-5	245	2	Southern
84	Moore, Herman	WR	6-3	205	3	Virginia
90	Owens, Dan	DE	6-3	280	4	USC
9	Peete, Rodney	QB	6-0	193	5	USC
80	Perriman, Brett	WR	5-9	180	6	Miami (Fla.)
96	Pete, Lawrence	NT	6-0	275	5	Nebraska
91	Porcher, Robert	DE	6-3	283	2	South Carolina State
94	Pritchett, Kelvin	DE	6-2	281	3	Mississippi
77	Reynolds, Don	DE	6-3	278	1	Virginia
28	Richards, Curvin	RB	5-9	195	2	Pittsburgh
63	Richards, Dave	G	6-4	310	6	UCLA
5	Riley, Mike	P	6-0	217	1	Mississippi State
27	Robinson, Junior	CB	5-9	161	3	East Carolina
64	Rodenhauser, Mark	C	6-5	280	6	Illinois State
20	Sanders, Barry	RB	5-8	203	5	Oklahoma State
38	Scott, Kevin	CB	5-9	175	3	Stanford
59	Scroggins, Tracy	LB	6-2	255	2	Tulsa
54	Spielman, Chris	ILB	6-1	247	6	Ohio State
92	Spindler, Marc	DE	6-5	290	4	Pittsburgh
56	Swilling, Pat	LB	6-3	242	8	Georgia Tech

continued on page 478

Rd.	Name	Sel. No.	Pos.	Ht.	Wt.	College
	TOP DRAFT CHOICES					
2	McNeil, Ryan	33	CB	6-3	175	Miami
3	London, Antonio	62	LB	6-2	234	Alabama
3	Compton, Mike	68	C-G	6-6	294	West Virginia
6	Jeffries, Greg	147	DB	5-9	183	Virginia
7	Hallock, Ty	174	LB	6-2	254	Michigan State

kickoffs. Gray went the distance with both a punt return and kickoff return in 1992.

Punter Jim Arnold is one of the NFL's best, averaging an impressive 43.9 yards last season. The Lions turned the place-kicking over to rookie Jason Hanson and he responded by making 21 of 26 field-goal attempts, including 18 of his final 19. He was perfect on extra points, too.

The coverage teams are strong but will miss Jenkins, their top tackler in 1992.

THE ROOKIES: The Lions traded their No. 1 pick to New Orleans for Swilling, who should make a big impact on their defense. The Lions stuck with defense with their own picks, taking Miami's smooth cornerback Ryan McNeil in the second round and speedy Alabama linebacker Antonio London in the third round.

OUTLOOK: From 12-4 to 5-11, Wayne Fontes' Lions fell hard in 1992. Injuries were a factor, but the Lions also lost the confidence that marked their play in 1991. This season, they will show they really aren't as bad as they looked last season—or as good as they looked in 1991.

LION PROFILES

BARRY SANDERS 25 5-8 203   Running Back

The best pure runner in football . . . Continues his assault on the NFL record book . . . Ran for 1,352 yards in 1992 . . . Recovered from slow start to generate 985 yards in final 10 games . . . Was hampered by decimation of the Lions' offensive line . . . One of just four NFL running backs to generate 1,000 yards each of his first four seasons . . . Has 5,674 career rushing yards

. . . Remarkable quickness and change of direction . . . Has 52 career rushing TDs . . . Understated athlete who hands the football to the referee after scoring TD . . . Four-time Pro Bowl selection . . . Led NFL with 17 TDs in 1991 . . . Ran for 1,437 yards and won NFL Rookie of the Year honors in 1989 . . . Lions' No. 1 pick, third overall, after winning Heisman Trophy at Oklahoma State . . . Entered draft after junior season . . . Scored 56 TDs in three college seasons . . . Born July 16, 1968, in Wichita, Kan. . . . 1993 base salary: $1 million.

LOMAS BROWN 30 6-4 287   Tackle

Cornerstone of the Lions' offensive line . . . His value was clear when the Lions named him their franchise player during the offseason free-agency period . . . Island of stability in storm-tossed offensive line . . . Started all 16 games . . . Smooth pass-blocker who protects quarterback's blind side . . . Has helped clear the way for Barry Sanders to run for more than 5,600 yards in four NFL seasons . . . Has made Pro Bowl three years in a row . . . Durable player who has started 91 of the last 92 games . . . Quietly developed into one of the NFL's best offensive linemen . . . Didn't make Pro Bowl until his sixth season . . . Lions' No. 1 pick in 1985 out of Florida . . . One of the Lions' most active players in community service . . . Born March 30, 1963, in Miami . . . 1992 base salary: $925,000.

PAT SWILLING 28 6-3 242   Linebacker

Joins Lions after draft-day trade from Saints . . . His production dropped a bit in 1992 when he managed only 10½ sacks, the third-highest total on the team . . . Ranked sixth on Saints in tackles with 49 . . . Forced three fumbles . . . Regarded by many as the best outside linebacker in the NFL . . . Put together monster season in 1991 with NFL-high 17 sacks . . . Named NFL Defensive Player of the Year by Associated Press . . . Signed offer sheet for three-year, $5.475-million contract from Lions in March, but Saints matched the offer under old free-agency system and kept his rights. Then they traded him to Detroit anyway . . . Explosive outside pass-rusher in the mold of Giants' Lawrence Taylor . . . Four-time Pro Bowler . . . Has 76½ sacks in seven NFL seasons . . . A steal in the 1986 draft, the Saints got him in the third round out of Georgia Tech . . . Played stand-up defensive end in college and some scouts wondered about his ability to convert to linebacker . . . Born Oct. 25, 1964, in Toccoa, Ga. . . . 1993 base salary: $1.2 million.

BENNIE BLADES 26 6-1 221   Safety

Hard hitter is the key man in the Lions' secondary . . . Third on the team in tackles in 1992 with 96 . . . Also had three interceptions . . . Special-teams standout who blocked two punts, returning one for a TD . . . Pro Bowl pick after the 1991 season . . . Gives excellent run support . . . His heavy hitting makes Lions' secondary a dangerous place for wide receivers . . . Switched from strong safety to free safety midway in the 1989 season . . . Productive player has 471 tackles in five NFL seasons . . . Forced four fumbles and recovered three as a rookie in 1988 . . . Named transition player during free-agency period . . . Lions' No. 1 pick, third overall, out of Miami in 1988 . . . His brother, Brian, plays wide receiver for Seattle . . . Born Sept. 3, 1966, in Ft. Lauderdale, Fla. . . . 1993 base salary: $950,000.

RODNEY PEETE 27 6-0 193   Quarterback

Make-or-break season for this talented but inconsistent player . . . Has been unable to hold starting position because of injuries and ineffectiveness . . . Expected to receive strong challenge from Andre Ware in 1993 . . . Started 10 games in 1992 and led Lions in passing yards (1,702) and TDs (nine) . . . Also threw nine interceptions and was sacked 28 times . . . Benched in midseason in favor of Erik Kramer and then again late in the season in favor of Ware . . . Smart, athletic player but lacks strong arm and durability . . . Career-best game featured 306 passing yards and four TD throws in 1990 victory over Chicago . . . Started eight games as a rookie in 1989 . . . Lions' No. 6 pick in 1989 out of USC . . . Second in the Heisman Trophy balloting in 1988 to future teammate Barry Sanders . . . Born March 16, 1966, in Tucson, Ariz. . . . 1993 base salary: $850,000.

MEL GRAY 32 5-9 162   Kick Returner

More happy returns for this ageless athlete in 1992 . . . Made the Pro Bowl for the third year in a row . . . Returned two kickoffs and one punt for touchdowns . . . Averaged 24 yards on kickoff returns, with a pair of 89-yarders for scores . . . Ranks second on the NFL's all-time list with 5,706 career yards on kickoff returns . . . Daring, sure-handed player who has a remarkable knack for finding running room . . . Former USFL player found new life in the NFL . . . Lions acquired him as a Plan B free agent from Saints in 1989 . . . Started his pro career as a running back for the Los Angeles Express of the USFL . . . Led Purdue in rushing his final two seasons . . . Born March 16, 1961, in Williamsburg, Va. . . . 1993 base salary: $575,000.

DAVE LUTZ 33 6-6 305   Offensive Lineman

Free-agent Chief signed two-year, $2.6-million contract with Lions . . . Should help team's blocking needs . . . Spent his first six seasons as offensive tackle, starting 60 games from 1983 to 1988 . . . Switched to guard in 1989 and had one of his best seasons . . . During three years at guard, the Chiefs had three 1,000-yard rushing seasons by a running back . . . Has played 123 of 139 games since being drafted in the second round of the 1983 draft by the Chiefs . . . Never played guard in college . . . Started at tackle for four years at Georgia Tech . . . Didn't miss a snap during final two collegiate seasons . . . Born Dec. 30, 1959, in Monroe, N.C. . . . 1993 base salary: $1,000,000, plus $500,000 in bonuses.

ANDRE WARE 25 6-2 205   Quarterback

Another disappointing Lions' quarterback under pressure to break through in 1993 . . . Lions still are waiting for this talented but unproven athlete to realize his potential . . . Showed flashes late last year . . . Started final three games and led Lions to two victories . . . Threw two TD passes without an interception in victory over Browns in his first start of the season . . . Came back the next week to pass for 290 yards in victory over Chicago . . . Will be given every opportunity to seize starting job this year . . . Played in just five games, starting one, in 1990 and 1991 . . . Slow to pick up Lions' offensive system after playing in unique offense at University of Houston . . . Lions' No. 1 pick in 1990 . . . Record-setter at Houston who passed for 46 TDs and won Heisman Trophy as a junior . . . Entered draft after that season . . . Born July 31, 1968, in Dickinson, Tex. . . . 1993 base salary: $1 million.

DAVID RICHARDS 27 6-4 310   Guard

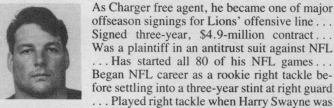

As Charger free agent, he became one of major offseason signings for Lions' offensive line . . . Signed three-year, $4.9-million contract . . . Was a plaintiff in an antitrust suit against NFL . . . Has started all 80 of his NFL games . . . Began NFL career as a rookie right tackle before settling into a three-year stint at right guard . . . Played right tackle when Harry Swayne was hurt during the second week last season . . . Returned to finish at right guard . . . Was fourth-round selection of Chargers in 1988 draft . . . One of only seven NFL rookies to start every game in 1988 as a rookie . . . Transferred to UCLA after sophomore season when SMU's football program folded . . . Born April 11, 1966, on Staten Island, N.Y. . . . 1993 base salary: $1,525,000, plus $800,000 in bonuses.

HERMAN MOORE 23 6-3 205   Wide Receiver

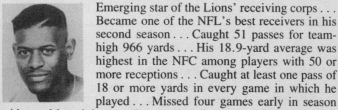

Emerging star of the Lions' receiving corps . . . Became one of the NFL's best receivers in his second season . . . Caught 51 passes for team-high 966 yards . . . His 18.9-yard average was highest in the NFC among players with 50 or more receptions . . . Caught at least one pass of 18 or more yards in every game in which he played . . . Missed four games early in season with quadricep injury . . . Returned to lineup in dramatic fashion by catching 45 passes for 884 yards in 11-game span . . . In that stretch, he caught seven passes covering more than 40 yards . . . Played sparingly as a rookie in 1991, catching only 11 passes . . . Lions' No. 1 pick out of Virginia in 1991 . . . Holds school records for career receiving yards (2,504) and TD catches (27) . . . Won ACC high-jump competition in 1990 with leap of 7-2¾ . . . Born Oct. 20, 1969, in Danville, Va. . . . 1993 base salary: $475,000.

KEVIN GLOVER 30 6-2 282   Center

His return to health could help revitalize Lions' offensive line . . . Missed final nine games in 1992 with leg injury . . . Expected back to full strength . . . Had been durable, consistent player before injury . . . Started every game from 1988 through middle of 1992 season . . . Underrated player whose run-blocking has cleared the way for Barry Sanders . . . Pro Bowl alternate in 1991 . . . Good athlete for his position, he once returned a kickoff 19 yards against the Rams . . . Injuries slowed development early in his career . . . Lions' second-round pick out of Maryland in 1985 . . . Born June 17, 1963, in Largo, Md. . . . 1993 base salary: $850,000.

TRACY SCROGGINS 24 6-2 255   Linebacker

Came on strong late in his rookie season and led the Lions in sacks with 7½ . . . Only the second rookie to lead Detroit in sacks (Al Baker was the other in 1978) . . . Recorded at least one sack in six of his seven starts . . . Had two sacks in Thanksgiving Day game against Houston . . . Strong blitzer . . . Outstanding athlete who still is learning the nuances of his position . . . Lions' second-round pick in 1992 out of Tulsa . . . Played two seasons at Tulsa . . . A standout running back at Coffeyville (Kan.) Junior College . . . Switched to outside linebacker at Tulsa . . . Born Sept. 11, 1969, in Checotah, Okla. . . . 1993 base salary: $325,000.

RODNEY HOLMAN 33 6-3 238   Tight End

Was informed by Bengals that he was no longer wanted because he couldn't get deep for pass receptions anymore. . . . So he signed with Lions . . . Caught 308 passes for 4,329 yards and 34 touchdowns in 11-year career with Bengals . . . Caught 26 passes for 326 yards and two touchdowns last season . . . A quiet player who does his job without much fanfare . . . Can be an effective blocker, but isn't as dominant as he was in early years . . . Best season was in 1989, when he caught 50 passes for 736 yards and nine touchdowns . . . Has been to Pro Bowl three times . . . Is Tulane's all-time leading receiver with 135 catches . . . Was third-round draft choice in 1982 and sat for two years until he cracked starting lineup . . . Born April 20, 1960, in Ypsilanti, Mich. . . . 1992 base salary: $750,000.

CHRIS SPIELMAN 27 6-1 247   Linebacker

Born linebacker with the instincts and demeanor for the position . . . Led the Lions in tackles for the fifth straight season . . . Finished with 146 tackles, the fourth-highest total by a Lion since 1973 . . . Made 13 tackles in games against Pittsburgh, Cincinnati and Green Bay . . . First player to lead the Lions in tackles five straight seasons . . . Hard-hitting, emotional player . . . Has 559 tackles in five NFL seasons . . . Two-time Pro Bowl selection . . . Set team record with 153 tackles as a rookie in 1988 . . . Lions' second-round pick out of Ohio State in 1988 . . . Lombardi Award winner as nation's outstanding linebacker as a senior . . . Remarkable total of 205 tackles as a junior . . . Born Oct. 11, 1965, in Canton, Ohio . . . 1993 base salary: $975,000.

BILL FRALIC 31 6-5 280   Guard

Signed with Lions as free agent after eight seasons in Atlanta . . . Became highest-paid guard in NFL history when he signed three-year, $5.4-million deal . . . Joins David Richards, formerly of San Diego, as free agents expected to upgrade the Lions' offensive line . . . Powerful run-blocker should have appreciative teammate in Barry Sanders . . . Starter since the first game of his rookie season in 1985 . . . Four-time Pro Bowl selection . . . Named to NFL's All-Decade Team for the 1980s . . . Outspoken critic of steroid use in the NFL . . . Participated in Wrestlemania II after rookie season . . . Falcons' No. 1 pick in 1985 . . . Three-time All-American tackle at University of Pittsburgh . . . Born Oct. 31, 1961, in Penn Hills, Pa. . . . 1993 base salary: $2.1 million.

COACH WAYNE FONTES: Vows to return the Lions to prom-

inence after difficult 1992 season . . . "I'll say this: 1991 wasn't the fluke, 1992 was the fluke," he said after Lions tumbled to 5-11 record . . . Tried to hold team together despite injuries and tragedy . . . Team was devastated in 1992 offseason by death in traffic accident of guard Eric Andolsek . . . Suffered another blow when his brother and assistant coach, Len Fontes, died of a heart attack . . . These tragedies came on heels of paralyzing injury to guard Mike Utley . . . Emotional coach who is popular with his players . . . Named NFL Coach of the Year after leading the Lions to 12-4 record and NFC Central title in 1991 . . . Lions reached NFC title game that season before losing to Washington . . . Has 33-37 career record . . . Became interim coach following firing of Darryl Rogers midway in 1988 season . . . Spent four seasons as Lions' defensive coordinator before becoming head coach . . . An assistant coach at Tampa Bay for nine seasons . . . A defensive back for the New York Jets of the AFL in 1962 . . . Once returned an interception 83 yards for a TD, a Jets' record until Erik McMillan went 93 yards in 1989 . . . College assistant coach at Dayton, Iowa and USC . . . Played football and baseball at Michigan State . . . Born Feb. 2, 1940, in Canton, Ohio.

GREATEST INTERCEPTOR

Great defensive backs have been part of the Lions' history. From Yale Lary to Jack Christiansen to Dick "Night Train" Lane to Lem Barney, the Lions have featured a series of future Hall of Famers in their secondary.

But the Detroit team record for interceptions doesn't belong to a Hall of Famer. It goes to Dick LeBeau, a smart, instinctive player who made only three Pro Bowls but finished his 14-year career with 62 interceptions.

LeBeau, who made the Pro Bowl in 1965, 1966 and 1967, finished his distinguished career in 1972. He was consistent but not spectacular, never once intercepting 10 passes in a season or managing 200 return yards.

Special mention goes to Barney, who was inducted in the Hall of Fame in 1992. Barney played for the Lions from 1967-77 and finished his career with 56 interceptions and a team-record 1,051 return yards.

The NFL's Defensive Rookie of the Year in 1967, Barney burst on the scene that season with 10 interceptions, three of which he returned for touchdowns.

INDIVIDUAL LION RECORDS

Rushing

Most Yards Game:	220	Barry Sanders, vs Minnesota, 1991
Season:	1,584	Barry Sanders, 1991
Career:	5,674	Barry Sanders, 1989-92

Passing

Most TD Passes Game:	5	Gary Danielson, vs Minnesota, 1978
Season:	26	Bobby Layne, 1951
Career:	118	Bobby Layne, 1950-58

Receiving

Most TD Passes Game:	4	Cloyce Box, vs Baltimore, 1950
Season:	15	Cloyce Box, 1952
Career:	35	Terry Barr, 1957-65

Scoring

Most Points Game:	24	2 times, most recently, Barry Sanders, vs Minnesota, 1991
Season:	128	Doak Walker, 1950
Career:	1,113	Eddie Murray, 1980-91
Most TDs Game:	4	2 times, most recently, Barry Sanders, vs Minnesota, 1991
Season:	17	Barry Sanders, 1991
Career:	56	Barry Sanders, 1989-92

GREEN BAY PACKERS

TEAM DIRECTORY: Pres./CEO: Bob Harlan; Exec. VP/GM: Ron Wolf; Chief Fin. Officer: Michael Reinfeldt; Dir. Pub. Rel.: Lee Remmel; Head Coach: Mike Holmgren. Home fields: Lambeau Field (59,543) and County Stadium, Milwaukee (56,051). Colors: Green and gold.

SCOUTING REPORT

OFFENSE: One of the reasons Reggie White cited for his decision to sign with Green Bay was the presence of young quarterback Brett Favre. In his first season as a starter, Favre made that much of an impression in 1992 in leading the Packers to a 9-7 season.

Favre adapted quickly to the controlled passing game that first-year coach Mike Holmgren brought from San Francisco. Making good decisions and throwing accurate passes, Favre went straight to the Pro Bowl. He is expected to get even better.

Wide receiver Sterling Sharpe was a record-setter with his 108 catches. He will remain the feature guy in the passing game, but the Packers want to take some of the load off him. Ron Lewis and Robert Brooks are promising young wideouts.

Jackie Harris looks like a future Pro Bowler at tight end. He caught 55 passes and should continue to flourish in the Packers' offense. And they signed 10-year Dolphin wide receiver Mark Clayton.

The running backs are solid but unspectacular. Vince Workman was on his way to a great season but got hurt. Darrell Thompson is talented but inconsistent. The Packers have high hopes for young players Edgar Bennett and Dexter McNabb.

The line is led by tackle Ken Ruettgers, a dependable player. James Campen is a solid center. The Packers also addressed this area in free agency, signing Harry Galbreath and Tunch Ilkin.

DEFENSE: The big news is the addition of White, a seven-time Pro Bowler with the Eagles. He moves into the left defensive end spot and gives the Packers instant pass-rush and credibility.

The Packers also added nose tackle Bill Maas as a free agent. Matt Brock will move to right end, but the Packers still lack depth and talent in this area.

The linebackers are strong. Johnny Holland and Brian Noble are solid inside and the Packers also like second-year man Mark

Reggie White's biggest sack netted $17 million.

D'Onofrio. George Koonce is a a good all-around player, and Tony Bennett looks like a future Pro Bowler as a pass-rushing right linebacker. White's presence on the other side should help Bennett, who had 13½ sacks last season. Rookie Wayne Simmons of Clemson adds depth.

The secondary has a pair of big-play men in cornerback Terrell Buckley and safety LeRoy Butler. Roland Mitchell is solid at the other corner. The Packers lost Pro Bowl safety Chuck Cecil, but filled the void with free agent Mike Prior and rookie George Teague of Alabama.

SPECIAL TEAMS: Chris Jacke is a solid placekicker. He made 22 of 29 field-goal attempts last season, including a 41-yarder as

PACKERS VETERAN ROSTER

HEAD COACH—Mike Holmgren. Assistant Coaches—Greg Blache, Nolan Cromwell, Jon Gruden, Gil Haskell, Dick Jauron, Kent Johnston, Sherman Lewis, Jim Lind, Tom Lovat, Steve Mariucci, Andy Reid, Ray Rhodes, Bob Valesente.

No.	Name	Pos.	Ht.	Wt.	NFL Exp.	College
43	Anderson, Jesse	TE	6-2	255	4	Mississippi State
74	Archambeau, Lester	DE	6-5	275	4	Stanford
78	Barrie, Sebastian	DE	6-2	270	2	Liberty
82	Beach, Sanjay	WR	6-1	194	3	Colorado State
—	Beauford, Terry	G	6-1	296	1	Florida A&M
34	Bennett, Edgar	RB	6-0	223	2	Florida State
90	Bennett, Tony	LB	6-2	243	4	Mississippi
35	Berry, Latin	RB	5-10	196	3	Oregon
97	Bethune, George	DE	6-4	255	3	Alabama
51	Brady, Jeff	LB	6-1	235	3	Kentucky
62	Brock, Matt	DE	6-5	290	5	Oregon
87	Brooks, Robert	WR	6-0	171	2	South Carolina
27	Buckley, Terrell	CB	5-9	174	2	Florida State
36	Butler, LeRoy	S	6-0	200	4	Florida State
63	Campen, James	C	6-2	280	7	Tulane
21	Carter, Carl	CB	5-11	190	8	Texas Tech
89	Chmura, Mark	TE	6-5	240	1	Boston College
—	Clayton, Mark	WR	5-9	181	11	Louisville
55	Collins, Brett	LB	6-1	226	2	Washington
49	Crews, Terry	LB	6-2	240	2	Western Michigan
99	Davey, Don	DE	6-4	280	3	Wisconsin
56	Dent, Burnell	LB	6-1	238	8	Tulane
11	Detmer, Ty	QB	6-0	183	1	Brigham Young
58	D'Onofrio, Mark	LB	6-2	235	1	Penn State
4	Favre, Brett	QB	6-2	220	3	Southern Mississippi
76	Galbreath, Harry	G	6-1	271	6	Tennessee
—	Grant, David	NT	6-4	275	5	West Virginia
71	Gray, Cecil	T	6-4	292	3	North Carolina
—	Hallstrom, Ron	G	6-6	310	12	Iowa
30	Harris, Corey	DB	5-11	195	2	Vanderbilt
80	Harris, Jackie	TE	6-3	243	4	NE Louisiana
24	Hauck, Tim	S	5-10	181	4	Montana
81	Holder, Chris	WR	6-0	182	1	Tuskegee
40	Holland, Jamie	WR-KR	6-1	195	7	Ohio State
50	Holland, Johnny	LB	6-2	235	7	Texas A&M
79	Ilkin, Tunch	T	6-3	272	14	Indiana State
48	Ingram, Darryl	TE	6-3	250	3	California
13	Jacke, Chris	K	6-0	197	5	Texas-El Paso
64	Jurkovic, John	NT	6-2	300	3	Eastern Illinois
53	Koonce, George	LB	6-1	238	2	East Carolina
28	Kyles, Troy	WR	6-1	190	2	Howard
85	Lewis, Ron	WR	5-11	180	3	Florida State
77	Maas, Bill	NT	6-5	275	10	Pittsburgh
77	Majkowski, Don	QB	6-2	203	7	Virginia
83	McKay, Orlando	WR	5-10	175	1	Washington
44	McNabb, Dexter	FB	6-1	245	2	Florida
—	Milling, James	WR	5-9	160	5	Maryland
47	Mitchell, Roland	CB	5-11	195	7	Texas Tech
57	Moran, Rich	G	6-3	280	9	San Diego State
61	Neville, Tom	G	6-5	288	5	Fresno State
91	Noble, Brian	LB	6-4	250	9	Arizona State
8	O'Brien, Ken	QB	6-4	212	11	Cal-Davis
98	Oglesby, Alfred	NT	6-3	285	4	Houston
96	Patterson, Shawn	DE	6-5	273	5	Arizona State
95	Paup, Bryce	LB	6-5	247	4	Northern Iowa
45	Prior, Mike	S	6-0	210	8	Illinois State
54	Randle, Ervin	LB	6-1	251	9	Baylor
75	Ruettgers, Ken	T	6-6	286	9	Southern California
22	Sanders, Tracey	CB	6-0	180	1	Florida State
84	Sharpe, Sterling	WR	6-1	205	6	South Carolina

continued on page 478

			TOP DRAFT CHOICES			
Rd.	Name	Sel. No.	Pos.	Ht.	Wt.	College
1	Simmons, Wayne	15	LB	6-2	236	Clemson
1	Teague, George	29	S	6-0	185	Alabama
3	Dotson, Earl	81	OT	6-3	315	Texas A&I
5	Brunell, Mark	118	QB	6-1	208	Washington
5	Willis, James	119	LB	6-2	235	Auburn

time expired to upset the Eagles.

The Packers have high hopes for Buckley, who was an electrifying return man in college. He struggled with fumbles as a rookie but showed flashes of his ability, including a punt return for a TD.

Veteran punter Bryan Wagner was added midway in the season. He was an improvement over Paul McJulien, but the Packers still want to upgrade this area. The coverage teams are excellent, allowing just 15.8 yards on kickoff returns and 8.8 yards on punt returns.

THE ROOKIES: The Pack went for defense, drafting Simmons with their own No. 1 pick, then trading with Dallas to get the Cowboys' No. 1 pick and grabbing Teague. Both players add speed and big-play ability to the Packers' suddenly-formidable defense. Texas A&I tackle Earl Dotson might be a sleeper in the third round.

OUTLOOK: The Pack looks back. There's an air of confidence and anticipation around this team, which made big moves in free agency. If they can stay healthy, they are the team to beat in the division.

PACKER PROFILES

REGGIE WHITE 31 6-5 290   Defensive End

The most coveted free agent of the Class of 1993 . . . Signed with Green Bay after long process that included visits to Cleveland, Atlanta, Detroit, Washington, San Francisco and the New York Jets . . . Signed four-year, $17-million deal that included $4.5-million signing bonus . . . Left the Eagles in part because of his hard feelings toward team owner Norman Braman . . . Future Hall of Famer has been regarded as the best defensive lineman in NFL for the last six seasons . . . Only player in NFL history with more sacks than games played . . . Has 124 sacks in 121 games since entering the NFL in 1985 . . . A Pro Bowl starter seven seasons in a row . . . A licensed Baptist minister, his nickname is "The Minister of Defense" . . . Along with his wife, Sara, has built a second home called "Hope Palace" for unwed mothers on their property in Knoxville, Tenn. . . . Remarkably durable player who has never missed a game in professional career because of injury . . . Best NFL season was 1987, when he had 21 sacks in 12 games . . . Played two seasons for Memphis Showboats of USFL . . . All-American at University of Tennessee . . . Selected by Eagles in 1984 NFL supplemental draft . . . Born Dec. 19, 1961, in Chattanooga, Tenn. . . . 1993 base salary: $4.5 million.

BRETT FAVRE 23 6-2 220   Quarterback

The NFL's hottest young quarterback . . . Made the Pro Bowl in his first season as a starter . . . Led the Packers to six consecutive victories in remarkable late-season surge . . . Passed for 3,227 yards and 18 TDs despite not starting until fourth game . . . Tied Dallas' Troy Aikman for most completions (302) in the NFC . . . Set Packers' record by passing for 200 yards in 11 consecutive games . . . Went 11-for-11 in the first half of upset of Philadelphia . . . Ran for winning TD in dramatic victory in Houston . . . His potential was cited by Reggie White as one of the reasons White joined the Packers as a free agent . . . Acquired by the Packers from Falcons on Feb. 10, 1992 in exchange for No. 1 pick . . . Was Falcons' second-round pick out of Southern Mississippi in 1991 . . . Born Oct. 10, 1969, in Gulfport, Miss. . . . 1993 base salary: $360,000.

STERLING SHARPE 28 6-1 205   Wide Receiver

Smooth, speedy wide receiver put his name at the top of the NFL record book in 1992 . . . Set NFL record with 108 catches, breaking the mark of 106 by Washington's Art Monk . . . Also led NFL with 1,461 receiving yards and 13 TD catches . . . First player to lead the NFL in receptions, receiving yards and receiving TDs since Green Bay's Don Hutson in 1944

. . . Caught six or more passes in 12 games . . . Caught 11 passes for 160 yards against Giants . . . Has 389 receptions in first five NFL seasons, another league record . . . Three-time Pro Bowl selection . . . Has caught a pass in 71 consecutive games . . . Packers' No. 1 pick in 1988, out of South Carolina . . . Born April 6, 1965, in Glenville, Ga. . . . 1993 base salary: $1.3 million.

HARRY GALBREATH 28 6-1 271   Guard

Signed whopping three-year, $4.45-million contract with Packers . . . Considered one of prime free-agent guards available during offseason . . . One of the headiest offensive linemen in league with Dolphins . . . Started 52 consecutive games and has been at or near Pro Bowl level for past couple of years . . . *Sports Illustrated* named him to its All-Pro team in 1991 . . . Known as ''Dirty Harry,'' he gets occasionally flagged for holding penalties . . . Knows every trick to stop defensive linemen . . . Don Shula says he's the type of player who battles to the very last ounce . . . Taken in eighth round of 1988, out of Tennessee, and moved into starting lineup for final 13 weeks . . . Born Jan. 1, 1965, in Clarksville, Tenn. . . . 1993 base salary: $1,260,000, plus $1,500,000 signing bonus.

KEN RUETTGERS 31 6-6 286   Tackle

Regained his standing as one of the NFL's best left tackles in 1992 . . . Put together strong, injury-free season . . . His pass-blocking helped quarterback Brett Favre make the Pro Bowl . . . His value was reflected in the Packers' decision to name him a transition player in free-agency period . . . Injuries cost him large chunks of 1991 and 1990 seasons . . . Missed 17 games those two years with variety of ailments . . . A starter since first game of 1986 . . . Hard worker who is renowned for his offseason conditioning regimen . . . Started 59 of 60 non-strike games between 1986 and 1990 . . . Packers' No. 1 pick out of USC in 1985 . . . They traded with Buffalo to move up in draft order and get him . . . Born Aug. 20, 1962, in Bakersfield, Cal. . . . 1992 base salary: $825,000.

VINCE WORKMAN 25 5-10 205   Running Back

Was headed to breakthrough season in 1992 . . . Led team in rushing with 631 yards despite missing final 6½ games with shoulder injury . . . Also caught 47 passes . . . Projected over full season, he was on his way to 1,100 yards on the ground and 60-plus catches . . . Versatile back fits nicely into Packers' offensive scheme . . . Caught 12 passes in season-opener against Vikings . . . Broke off 44-yard run and scored first rushing TD of the season against Eagles in mid-November . . . Hurt his shoulder later that game and never returned . . . Led Packers with seven rushing TDs in 1991 . . . Packers' fifth-round pick out of Ohio State in 1989 . . . Senior season was cut short after two games when he was ruled ineligible for dealings with an agent . . . Gained 1,030 yards as a running back in 1986 and caught 26 passes as a flanker in 1987 . . . Born May 9, 1968, in Buffalo . . . 1993 base salary: $300,000.

JOHNNY HOLLAND 28 6-3 235   Linebacker

Has developed into one of the NFL's most productive linebackers . . . Led the Packers in tackles with 122 despite missing last two games with neck injury . . . Expected back at full strength in 1993 . . . Hard hitter with good instincts . . . Flows easily to the ball from his inside linebacker spot . . . Has made 100 or more tackles in each of the last five seasons . . . Also had three interceptions in 1992, as well as recovering two fumbles and forcing two fumbles . . . Has been a starter since the first game of his rookie season in 1987 . . . Packers' second-round pick in 1989 out of Texas A&M . . . Born March 11, 1965, in Belleville, Tex. . . . 1992 base salary: $600,000.

LeROY BUTLER 25 6-0 195   Safety

Poised on brink of stardom . . . Solid, dependable player who needs to make more big plays to be considered among NFL elite . . . Finished fourth on team in tackles with 73 . . . Defended 13 passes . . . His fumble recovery and 27-yard return fueled comeback victory over Philadelphia . . . Registered three interceptions in both 1990 and 1991 . . . Broke into starting lineup in

1991 . . . Used in passing situations and on special teams as rookie in 1990 . . . Can line up at either safety and cornerback . . . Packers' No. 2 pick out of Florida State in 1990 . . . Played cornerback as a senior at Florida State after spending most of his career at free safety . . . Born July 19, 1968, in Jacksonville, Fla. . . . 1993 base salary: $500,000.

TERRELL BUCKLEY 22 5-9 175 Cornerback

The Packers expect big things from this supremely talented but unproven player . . . Struggled as a rookie after missing most of training camp in contract dispute . . . Started final 12 games . . . Finished with three interceptions and led team with 16 passes defended . . . Had troubles with fumbles as a punt-returner . . . Averaged 10 yards on punt returns and brought back 58-yarder for touchdown in victory over Bengals . . . One of the youngest players in the NFL in 1992 at the age of 21 . . . Entered draft after junior season at Florida State . . . Holds school record with 21 career interceptions . . . Holds NCAA record with 501 yards on interception returns . . . Scored seven TDs on returns in three college seasons . . . Has signed minor-league baseball contract with Atlanta Braves . . . Born June 7, 1971, in Pascagoula, Miss. . . . 1993 base salary: $725,000.

TONY BENNETT 26 6-2 242 Linebacker

Explosive pass-rusher . . . Should benefit from addition of Reggie White on other side of the defense . . . Led Packers in sacks for the second year in a row with 13½ . . . Third on the team in tackles with 82 . . . Burst into prominence in 1991 when he registered 13 sacks, third-highest total in the NFL . . . Speed, agility and tenacity make him prototype pass-rushing outside linebacker . . . Slowed by injuries and inexperience as a rookie in 1990 . . . Played in 14 games but did not start . . . Packers' first No. 1 pick (Darrell Thompson was the second) in 1990 out of Mississippi . . . Packers got the pick in trade with Cleveland . . . Was reserve defensive tackle his first two seasons at Mississippi . . . Set state record in discus throw (158-10) in high school . . . Born July 1, 1967, in Clarksdale, Miss. . . . 1992 base salary: $350,000.

MIKE PRIOR 29 6-0 210 Safety

Free agent from Colts is sixth on Indy's all-time interception list with 27 . . . Intercepted three passes in Dec. 20 victory over Cardinals . . . Was second on team with 91 tackles . . . Drafted in seventh round in 1985 by Tampa Bay . . . Went from injured reserve to being released Sept. 30, 1986 . . . Colts signed him in 1987 . . . Took over a starting job in 1988 and never surrendered it . . . Missed seven games in 1991 with an abdominal injury . . . Born Nov. 14, 1963, in Chicago Heights, Ill. . . . 1992 base salary: $425,000.

COACH MIKE HOLMGREN: Has the Packers on the verge

of prominence . . . Instilled winning attitude in his first season . . . Led the team to six consecutive late-season victories and 9-7 overall record . . . Loss in season-finale to Minnesota cost the Packers the NFC Central title . . . Became Packers' 11th head coach after six seasons as an assistant with San Francisco . . . Brought in former 49er assistants Ray Rhodes and Sherman Lewis as defensive and offensive coordinators, respectively . . . Helped the 49ers to five NFC East titles and back-to-back Super Bowl crowns . . . Named 49ers' offensive coordinator in 1989 after three seasons as quarterback coach . . . Pursued by five other teams but reached agreement with Packers . . . Attracted by challenge of returning Packers to previous glory . . . An assistant coach for four years at BYU before joining Bill Walsh's staff with the 49ers . . . Played quarterback at USC in the late 1960s . . . Drafted by Cardinals but never played in the NFL . . . Spent 10 years as a high-school coach in northern California . . . His Sacred Heart High team in San Francisco once lost 21 consecutive games . . . At 6-5, he is the tallest coach in Packers' history . . . Born June 15, 1948, in San Francisco.

GREATEST INTERCEPTOR

The two most famous defensive backs in Green Bay's illustrious history are Willie Wood and Herb Adderley. They are Super Bowl heroes and Hall of Famers. But the greatest interceptor in Packer history is Bobby Dillon, who finished his eight-year career in 1959 with 52 interceptions.

Dillon was remarkably consistent. He had nine interceptions in three different seasons—1953, 1955 and 1957. He had seven interceptions in 1954 and 1956. Those were 12-game seasons, too.

Wood and Adderley made a dynamic duo for the Packers' great teams in the 1960s. Wood finished his 12-year career in 1971 with 48 interceptions. He was a Pro Bowl pick eight times and played in six NFL championship games.

Adderley finished his nine-year career with the Packers in 1969 with 39 interceptions. Including three seasons with Dallas, Adderley returned seven interceptions for touchdowns in his career, the second-highest total in NFL history.

INDIVIDUAL PACKER RECORDS

Rushing

Most Yards Game:	186	Jim Taylor, vs N.Y. Giants, 1961
Season:	1,474	Jim Taylor, 1962
Career:	8,207	Jim Taylor, 1958-66

Passing

Most TD Passes Game:	5	4 times, most recently Lynn Dickey, vs Houston, 1983
Season:	32	Lynn Dickey, 1983
Career:	152	Bart Starr, 1956-71

Receiving

Most TD Passes Game:	4	Don Hutson, vs Detroit, 1945
Season:	17	Don Hutson, 1943
Career:	99	Don Hutson, 1935-45

Scoring

Most Points Game:	33	Paul Hornung, vs Baltimore, 1961
Season:	176	Paul Hornung, 1960
Career:	823	Don Hutson, 1935-45
Most TDs Game:	5	Paul Hornung, vs Baltimore, 1961
Season:	19	Jim Taylor, 1962
Career:	105	Don Hutson, 1935-45

LOS ANGELES RAMS

TEAM DIRECTORY: Pres.: Georgia Frontiere; Exec. VP: John Shaw; VP-Football Operations/Head Coach: Chuck Knox; VP-Media and Community Rel.: Marshall Klein; Adm. Football Operations: Jack Faulkner; Dir. Player Personnel: John Becker; Dir. Marketing: Pete Donovan; Dir. Pub. Rel.: Rick Smith. Home field: Anaheim Stadium (69,008). Colors: Royal blue, gold and white.

SCOUTING REPORT

OFFENSE: The Rams know they can't rely too much on quarterback Jim Everett, who lacks the athletic ability to excel in difficult situations. The running game is the key.

Everett has a great passing touch and knowledge of the game. He can get the football upfield and pick apart a defense with precision passes. He just needs time.

Cleveland Gary put together a strong season at running back. If he can avoid fumbles, he could be the Rams' feature back for many seasons. David Lang averaged 6.2 yards per carry in limited action last season and could emerge as the starter at fullback, but top pick Jerome Bettis of Notre Dame will battle him for the job.

The receiving corps is strong. The Rams lost Aaron Cox in free agency, but Henry Ellard and Willie Anderson form an imposing tandem. Jeff Chadwick is a good possession receiver.

The line is the key. The Rams want to run the football, control the clock and rest their defense. That's the philosophy that Chuck Knox has followed through his coaching career.

Left tackle Gerald Perry was lost as a free agent, but the Rams signed Irv Eatman to replace him. Ageless Jackie Slater plans to return for another season at right tackle. Tom Newberry is a good guard but the Rams need Bern Brostek to emerge as a powerful force in the interior of their line.

DEFENSE: The Rams have added some muscle on this side of the football, but they aren't intimidating. Not yet, anyway. But they get after people.

The key man is young defensive tackle Sean Gilbert, an emerging star. He could be a Pro Bowler for years and years. Another young defensive lineman with potential is Marc Boutte. Bill Hawkins and Gerald Robinson are journeymen, but the Rams beefed up their pass rush by signing Fred Stokes as a free agent.

Shane Conlan, signed as a free agent, will run the defense from

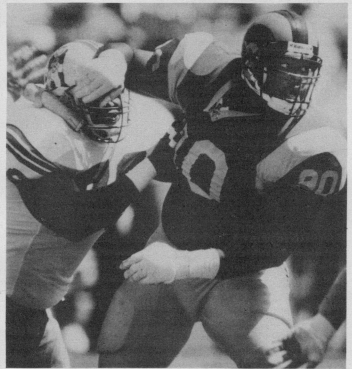

Mammoth Sean Gilbert proved he has the right stuff.

his middle-linebacker spot. He's an instinctive player who comes from a winning team in Buffalo and will add a lot. Kevin Greene was lost as a free agent but the Rams might have an emerging star in Roman Phifer, an active, athletic outside linebacker.

The secondary has a terrific coverage man in cornerback Todd Lyght. Darryl Henley is the other cornerback. Pat Terrell is a good young safety but the Rams need more speed, depth and big-play ability in this department.

SPECIAL TEAMS: A bright spot for the Rams.

Todd Kinchen, who returned two punts for TDs, has speed, moves and courage. Vernon Turner is a dependable kickoff-returner.

Kicker Tony Zendejas is deadly accurate. He was 15-for-20

RAMS VETERAN ROSTER

HEAD COACH—Chuck Knox. Assistant Coaches—Chris Clausen, George Dyer, Jim Erkenbeck, Chick Harris, Milt Jackson, Rod Perry, Dick Seicer, Howard Tippett, Ted Tollner, Joe Vitt, Ernie Zampese.

No.	Name	Pos.	Ht.	Wt.	NFL Exp.	College
83	Anderson, Willie	WR	6-0	175	6	UCLA
75	Ashmore, Darryl	T	6-7	300	1	Northwestern
28	Bailey, Robert	CB	5-9	176	3	Miami (Fla.)
96	Boutte, Marc	DT	6-4	298	2	Louisiana State
17	Bracken, Don	P	6-1	211	8	Michigan
61	Brostek, Bern	C	6-3	300	4	Washington
9	Buchanan, Richard	WR	5-10	178	1	Northwestern
35	Buckley, Eric	S	5-11	212	1	Central Florida
51	Bush, Blair	C	6-3	275	16	Washington
88	Carter, Pat	TE	6-4	250	6	Florida State
89	Chadwick, Jeff	WR	6-3	185	11	Grand Valley State
56	Conlan, Shane	LB	6-3	230	7	Penn State
25	Crooms, Chris	S	6-2	211	2	Texas A&M
77	Eatman, Irv	T	6-7	300	8	UCLA
80	Ellard, Henry	WR	5-11	180	11	Fresno State
11	Everett, Jim	QB	6-5	212	8	Purdue
6	Foster, Sean	WR	6-1	190	1	Long Beach State
63	Garten, Joe	G	6-2	290	1	Colorado
43	Gary, Cleveland	RB	6-0	226	5	Miami (Fla.)
16	Gaspard, Curtis	WR	6-0	180	1	Washington
90	Gilbert, Sean	DT	6-4	315	2	Pittsburgh
79	Goeas, Leo	G-T	6-4	292	4	Hawaii
42	Griffin, Courtney	CB	5-10	180	1	Fresno State
67	Harper, Shawn	T	6-4	292	1	Indiana
62	Harris, Kelvin	C	6-2	272	1	Miami (Fla.)
70	Hawkins, Bill	DE	6-6	269	5	Miami (Fla.)
20	Henley, Darryl	CB	5-9	172	5	UCLA
57	Homco, Thomas	LB	6-0	245	1	Northwestern
31	Israel, Steve	CB	5-11	186	2	Pittsburgh
72	Jenkins, Robert	T	6-5	285	8	UCLA
86	Johnson, Damone	TE	6-4	250	9	Cal Poly SLO
52	Kelm, Larry	LB	6-4	240	7	Texas A&M
81	Kinchen, Todd	WR	6-0	187	2	Louisiana State
22	Kors, R.J.	S	6-0	195	3	Long Beach State
38	Lang, David	RB	5-11	213	3	Northern Arizona
34	Lester, Tim	RB	5-9	215	2	Eastern Kentucky
27	Lilly, Sammy	CB	5-11	175	6	Georgia Tech
41	Lyght, Todd	CB	6-0	186	3	Notre Dame
53	Martin, Chris	LB	6-2	241	11	Auburn
82	McNeal, Travis	TE	6-3	244	5	Tenn.-Chattanooga
30	Moore, Reggie	WR	5-9	181	1	UCLA
66	Newberry, Tom	G	6-2	285	8	Wisconsin-LaCrosse
26	Newman, Anthony	S	6-0	199	6	Oregon
14	Pagel, Mike	QB	6-2	220	12	Arizona State
69	Pahukoa, Jeff	G-T	6-2	298	3	Washington
58	Phifer, Roman	LB	6-2	230	3	UCLA
95	Piel, Mike	DT	6-4	270	5	Illinois
98	Powers, Warren	DE	6-6	287	5	Maryland
87	Price, Jim	TE	6-4	247	3	Stanford
97	Robinson, Gerald	DE	6-3	262	6	Auburn
92	Rocker, David	DT	6-4	267	3	Auburn
59	Rolling, Henry	LB	6-2	225	6	Nevada-Reno
12	Rubley, T.J.	QB	6-3	205	2	Tulsa
78	Slater, Jackie	T	6-4	285	18	Jackson State
50	Stephen, Scott	LB	6-3	243	7	Arizona State
23	Stewart, Michael	S	6-0	195	7	Fresno State
60	Stokes, Fred	DE	6-3	274	7	Georgia Southern
65	Subis, Nick	T	6-4	278	2	San Diego State
37	Terrell, Pat	S	6-0	195	4	Notre Dame
32	Thompson, Anthony	RB	6-0	210	4	Indiana
54	Townsend, Brian	LB	6-3	242	2	Michigan
55	White, Leon	LB	6-3	242	8	Brigham Young
68	Williams, Anthony	LB	6-2	245	1	Alabama A&M
76	Young, Robert	DE	6-6	273	3	Mississippi State
10	Zendejas, Tony	K	5-8	165	9	Nevada-Reno

TOP DRAFT CHOICES

Rd.	Name	Sel. No.	Pos.	Ht.	Wt.	College
1	Bettis, Jerome	10	RB	5-11	248	Notre Dame
2	Drayton, Troy	39	TE	6-2	253	Penn State
3	White, Russell	73	RB	5-10	216	California
5	La Chapelle, Sean	122	WR	6-3	207	UCLA
5	Belin, Chuck	127	G	6-2	312	Wisconsin

last season in field-goal attempts and made all 38 of his extra points. He is regarded a clutch, late-game kicker.

Don Bracken is a solid punter and the coverage teams are strong.

THE ROOKIES: Ground Chuck, the Rams' ball-control offensive system, got a featured running back in Bettis. He projects as an immediate starter. The Rams stayed on that side of the football when they took Penn State's speedy tight end Troy Drayton in the second round and California's talented but underachieving running back Russell White in the third round.

OUTLOOK: Knox has the Rams moving in the right direction. They play hard, especially on defense. But this team, 6-10 a year ago, still is feeling the effect of several bad drafts and isn't ready to challenge for a playoff spot yet.

RAM PROFILES

JIM EVERETT 30 6-5 212   Quarterback

Bounced back with solid season . . . Fresh approach under new coaching staff seemed to rejuvenate his sagging career . . . Passed for 3,323 yards and 22 TDs . . . His 80.2 passing rating was his best since his breakthrough season of 1989 . . . Slumped badly in 1990 and 1991, throwing 37 interceptions . . . Threw NFC-high 20 interceptions as Rams tumbled to 3-13 record in 1991 . . . Looked like the NFL's best young quarterback in 1989 when he passed for team-record 4,310 yards and also threw 29 TD passes . . . Led Rams to playoff victories over Eagles and Giants that season before they lost to 49ers in NFC title game . . . The third pick in the 1986 draft, the Rams got him in a trade with Houston for defensive end William Fuller, guard Kent Hull, two No. 1 draft picks and a fifth-rounder . . . Three-year starter at Purdue . . . Born Jan. 3, 1963, in Emporia, Kan. . . . 1993 base salary: $2 million.

SEAN GILBERT 23 6-4 315   Defensive Lineman

The foundation of the Rams' future . . . Imposing physical specimen who could develop into a dominating defensive force . . . Struggled early in his rookie season in 1992 but came on strong in final six weeks . . . Started all 16 games . . . Finished with 54 tackles and five sacks . . . Has size and strength to excel against the run and quickness to rush the passer . . . The Rams made him their No. 1 pick in the 1992 draft, the third overall selection . . . Rams' coach Chuck Knox said drafting him was "the first step in rebuilding this football team" . . . Entered the draft after his junior season at University of Pittsburgh . . . Consensus All-American as a junior . . . Played in only six games as a sophomore in 1991 because of knee injury and sat out freshman year in 1990 because of academics . . . Born April 10, 1970, in Aliquippa, Pa. . . . 1993 base salary: $650,000.

WILLIE ANDERSON 28 6-0 175   Wide Receiver

Dangerous deep threat . . . Combines great speed with explosive burst to beat defenders for long balls . . . Caught 38 passes for 657 yards in 1992 . . . Led the Rams with seven TD receptions . . . Has averaged a remarkable 21.3 yards per catch during his five-year NFL career . . . Slowed by injuries in 1991 when he missed four full games and parts of two others after fracturing a small bone in his back . . . Led NFL in yards-per-catch average in both 1989 and 1990 . . . Caught 51 passes for 1,097 yards (21.5) average in 1990 . . . Burst into prominence in 1989 with 44 receptions for 1,146 yards (26.0) average . . . Set NFL record in 1989 game against Saints with 336 yards on 15 receptions . . . Nicknamed "Flipper" by his grandmother, who said his cry as a baby sounded like the TV dolphin . . . Rams' second-round pick in 1988 out of UCLA . . . Born March 7, 1965, in Paulsboro, N.J. . . . 1993 base salary: $800,000.

TODD LYGHT 24 6-0 186   Cornerback

Smooth coverage man . . . Started 12 games, missing four with leg injury . . . Made 65 tackles and defended 14 passes . . . Registered three interceptions . . . Averaged 26.7 yards on interception returns . . . Has the speed, leaping ability and instincts to develop into Pro Bowl cornerback . . . Slowed by contract holdout and injuries early in his rookie season in 1991 . . . Played in 12 games as a rookie, starting final eight . . . Rams' No. 1 pick in 1991, fifth overall, out of Notre Dame . . . Consensus All-American . . . Had eight interceptions as a junior . . . Intercepted 19 passes in senior season at Luke Powers Catholic High School in Flint, Mich. . . . Born Feb. 9, 1969, in Kwajalein, Marshall Islands . . . 1993 base salary: $600,000.

MARC BOUTTE 24 6-4 298   Defensive Lineman

Teams with Sean Gilbert to form foundation of the Rams' young defensive line . . . Started final 15 games as a rookie in 1992 . . . Made 32 tackles and knocked down six passes . . . Powerful inside player who specializes in run defense . . . Needs to improve pass-rush to become top-caliber player . . . Managed only one sack in 1992 . . . Saw increased playing time late in the season . . . Rams got him in the third round in 1992 out of LSU . . . Versatile athlete who played all defensive line positions in college . . . Made 236 career tackles . . . Four-year starter . . . Nicknamed ''Big Boo'' . . . Born July 25, 1969, in Lake Charles, La. . . . 1993 base salary: $280,000.

SHANE CONLAN 29 6-3 230   Linebacker

Signed three-year, $5.1-million contract with Rams after six years as Bills' dominant inside linebacker . . . Will play middle linebacker in Chuck Knox's 4-3 . . . Specialty is stopping the run . . . Ankle injury last season limited him to 12 regular-season games . . . Finished fourth on team with 82 tackles . . . Averages 91 tackles a season . . . Went to Pro Bowl in 1988, '89 and '90 . . . Was 1987 Rookie of the Year . . . Came to Bills in draft-day exchange of first-round choices with Oilers . . . Started his first five games as a rookie at outside linebacker before moving to inside linebacker after the Cornelius Bennett trade . . . Led Penn State to 12-0 national-championship season as an All-American linebacker . . . Attracted pro interest in high school as a catcher on the baseball team . . . Born March 4, 1964, in Frewsburg, N.Y.

FRED STOKES 29 6-3 274   **Defensive End**

Signed with Rams as a free agent after four seasons with the Redskins . . . His return was a homecoming of sorts since he played his first two NFL seasons for the Rams . . . Projected to provide experience, leadership and outside pass-rush to young defensive line . . . Natural pass-rusher with speed, outside burst and knack for finding the quarterback . . . Signed by the Redskins in Plan B in 1989 . . . Expected to serve as a situational player, he emerged as the Redskins' starting right end in 1991 . . . Registered 36 tackles and 6½ sacks in helping Redskins to Super Bowl . . . Had six tackles, sack, forced fumble and fumble recovery in Super Bowl victory over Buffalo . . . Rams' seventh-round draft choice in 1987 out of Georgia Southern . . . Born March 14, 1964, in Vadalia, Ga. . . . 1993 base salary: $1.1 million.

CLEVELAND GARY 27 6-0 226   **Running Back**

Good-news, bad-news season in 1992 . . . Finished sixth in the NFC with 1,125 rushing yards, by far the highest total of his disappointing career . . . Also led the team in receptions with 52 and touchdowns with 10 . . . But continued to be plagued by fumbles . . . Lost the handle nine times . . . Has size, speed and moves to be Pro Bowl running back but has lacked consistency . . . Struggled through injury-marred season in 1991 when he started only two games because of hamstring and knee injuries and finished with just 245 rushing yards . . . Showed flashes of his potential in 1990 with 808 rushing yards and 15 TDs, second-highest total in the NFL . . . Fumbled 12 times that season, losing seven . . . Baseball prospect who has played in the Montreal Expos' minor-league system . . . Rams' No. 1 pick in 1989 out of Miami . . . Born May 4, 1966, in Indiantown, Fla. . . . 1992 base salary: $350,000.

HENRY ELLARD 32 5-11 180   Wide Receiver

This elegant pass-catcher continues to carve his place in the Rams' record book . . . Caught 47 passes for 727 yards and three TDs . . . Finished second on the team in receptions after leading the Rams in that category eight years in a row . . . Rams' record holder for most career receptions (533), most career receiving yards (8,716) and most receptions in a season (86 in 1988) . . . Has generated four 1,000-yard seasons . . . Smart, crafty receiver who runs precise patterns . . . Shifty runner after the catch . . . Led the NFL in receiving yards with 1,414 in 1988 . . . Three-time Pro Bowl selection, twice as a receiver, once as a punt-returner . . . Rams' second-round pick in 1983 out of Fresno State . . . Born July 21, 1961, in Fresno, Cal. . . . 1993 base salary: $850,000.

PAT TERRELL 25 6-0 195   Safety

Hard-hitting defensive back is another key man in Rams' rebuilding project . . . Started 11 games in 1992, missing five with injuries . . . Finished with 55 tackles . . . Good range and instincts . . . Moved into starting lineup in 1991 . . . Finished third on the team in tackles with 74 . . . Played in 15 games as a rookie, starting once . . . Rams' second-round pick in 1990 out of Notre Dame . . . Played wide receiver and cornerback early in college career . . . Key member of the 1989 national championship team . . . Earned degree in business administration . . . Working on acquiring pilot's license . . . Born March 18, 1968, in Memphis, Tenn. . . . 1993 base salary: $250,000.

TOM NEWBERRY 30 6-2 285   Offensive Lineman

Anchor of the Rams' offensive line . . . Started all 16 games at left guard . . . Strong, athletic player is regarded as one of the top interior offensive linemen in the NFL . . . Powerful run-blocker . . . Pro Bowl pick after the 1988 and 1989 seasons . . . Has been timed in 4.7 seconds in 40-yard dash and has 34-inch vertical leap . . . In 1986, he became the first pure rookie since Eric Dickerson to start for the Rams . . . Started 73 consecutive non-strike games before missing 1990 finale with a sprained ankle . . . Rams' second-round pick out of Wisconsin-LaCrosse in 1986 . . . Won NCAA Division III shot-put and discus titles in 1984 and 1985 . . . Earned degree in geography . . . Born Oct. 20, 1962, in Onalaska, Wis. . . . 1993 base salary: $750,000.

COACH CHUCK KNOX: Revamped the Rams' roster and playing style in his first season back with his old team . . . Led Rams to 6-10 record, doubling their win total from 1991 . . . Returned to the Rams after nine seasons with Seahawks . . . Rehired by the Rams 14 years after he was dismissed as their head coach . . . Given title of club vice-president, with authority over college draft and player personnel decisions . . . Roster shakeup continued in 1993 offseason as he signed free agents Irv Eatman, Shane Conlan and Fred Stokes and traded for Leo Goeas . . . Ranks second to Miami's Don Shula among active coaches with 176 career victories . . . Only coach in NFL history to win division titles with three different teams (Rams, Bills, Seahawks) . . . Compiled 54-15 record and won five NFC West titles during great stretch with the Rams in the mid-1970s . . . Dismissed in part because of his conservative style . . . Favors strong running game, so his offensive system usually is called ''Ground Chuck'' . . . Spent five seasons as head coach of the Bills, winning AFC East title in 1980 . . . His teams made the playoffs four times in his nine seasons with Seattle . . . Has 176-124-1 overall record . . . Played tackle at Juniata (Pa.) College . . . Wrote a book entitled ''Hard Knox'' that chronicled his rise from a tough neighborhood outside Pittsburgh . . . An NFL assistant with the Jets and Lions for 10 seasons . . . College assistant at Kentucky and Wake Forest . . . Born April 27, 1932, in Sewickley, Pa.

GREATEST INTERCEPTOR

The Rams' defenses of the 1960s had the Fearsome Foursome. They also had Ed Meador.

Meador, a Ram from 1959-70, finished his career with 46 interceptions, tops on the team's all-time list. He never had as many as nine interceptions in a season, but he was a solid, consistent player who served as a great complement to those ferocious defensive fronts.

Meador was a five-time Pro Bowl selection and led the Rams in interceptions five times. His best season was 1967, when he collected a career-best eight interceptions and returned two for touchdowns. He also returned two interceptions for touchdowns in 1969.

Meador is tied with LeRoy Irvin for the Rams' career record for interception returns for touchdowns in a career with five. Irvin ranks third on the all-time list with 34 interceptions.

Special mention goes to Hall of Famer Dick "Night Train" Lane, who set an NFL record with 14 interceptions as a Rams' rookie in 1952.

INDIVIDUAL RAM RECORDS

Rushing

Most Yards Game:	248	Eric Dickerson, vs Dallas, 1985
Season:	2,105	Eric Dickerson, 1984
Career:	7,245	Eric Dickerson, 1983-87

Passing

Most TD Passes Game:	5	7 times, most recently Jim Everett, vs N.Y. Giants, 1988
Season:	31	Jim Everett, 1988
Career:	154	Roman Gabriel, 1962-72

Receiving

Most TD Passes Game:	4	3 times, most recently Harold Jackson, vs Dallas, 1973
Season:	17	Elroy Hirsch, 1951
Career:	53	Elroy Hirsch, 1949-57

Scoring

Most Points Game:	24	3 times, most recently Harold Jackson, vs Dallas, 1973
Season:	130	David Ray, 1973
Career:	789	Mike Lansford, 1982-90
Most TDs Game:	4	3 times, most recently Harold Jackson, vs Dallas, 1973
Season:	20	Eric Dickerson, 1983
Career:	58	Eric Dickerson, 1983-87

MINNESOTA VIKINGS

TEAM DIRECTORY: Chairman: John Skoglund; Pres. and CEO: Roger Headrick; VP-Finance: Jim Miller; VP-Adm./Team Oper.: Jeff Diamond; Dir. Football Oper.: Jerry Reichow; Pub. Rel. Dir.: David Pelletier; Dir. Communications: Dan Endy; Head Coach: Dennis Green; Home field: Hubert H. Humphrey Metrodome (63,000). Colors: Purple, white and gold.

SCOUTING REPORT

OFFENSE: The Vikings' big move in free agency was signing quarterback Jim McMahon, who had been Randall Cunningham's backup in Philadelphia. McMahon will start. But will he finish?

Smart, instinctive and loaded with leadership qualities, McMahon is good enough to turn the Vikings into an offensive power. But his durability is a real concern. Sean Salisbury and Rich Gannon are backups with starting experience.

The running game is potent. Terry Allen emerged as a star with 1,201 yards and is also a good receiver. Roger Craig and Keith Henderson are decent backups and top pick Robert Smith of Ohio State should see some action.

McMahon could use another receiving threat. Cris Carter is a talented wide receiver with the ability to get in the end zone, but Anthony Carter is well past his prime and Hassan Jones is a journeyman. Jake Reed might emerge as a starter, but rookie Qadry Ismail of Syracuse is in the mix, too.

The line was devastated in free agency by the defections of Brian Habib and Kirk Lowdermilk. The left side remains intact with tackle Gary Zimmerman and guard Randall McDaniel, but Tim Irwin is near the end of his career at right tackle. The interior of the line is a big concern.

DEFENSE: This remarkably aggressive, opportunistic unit scored an incredible eight touchdowns in 1992.

The line lost Al Noga in free agency but remains strong with end Chris Doleman and tackles Henry Thomas and John Randle. Doleman re-emerged as a force in 1992 with 14½ sacks.

Middle linebacker Jack Del Rio is solid against the run, while left linebacker Carlos Jenkins is a speedy young athlete with big-play ability. He scored two TDs in 1992. Veteran Mike Merriweather is the right linebacker.

The secondary is solid. Cornerback Audray McMillian and

Terry Allen ran and caught for 1,679-yard season.

safety Todd Scott are Pro Bowlers. Carl Lee is a smooth coverage man at the other cornerback spot.

SPECIAL TEAMS: Kicker Fuad Reveiz had a good year, making 19 of 25 field-goal attempts and all 45 of his extra points.

Harry Newsome is an excellent punter who led the NFC with a 45-yard average. The coverage teams are decent.

The Vikings lack a big-play return man.

THE ROOKIES: With a No. 1 pick for the first time since 1988, the Vikings grabbed Smith, a speedy, productive player. More speed arrived in the second round in the person of Ismail, the

VIKINGS VETERAN ROSTER

HEAD COACH—Dennis Green. Assistant Coaches—Tom Batta, Brian Billick, Jack Burns, Tony Dungy, Chris Foerster, Monte Kiffin, John Michels, Tom Moore, Willie Shaw, Richard Solomon, John Teerlinck, Steve Wetzel, Tyrone Willingham.

No.	Name	Pos.	Ht.	Wt.	NFL Exp.	College
72	Adams, Scott	OL	6-5	281	2	Georgia
21	Allen, Terry	RB	5-10	197	3	Clemson
92	Barker, Roy	DT	6-4	292	1	North Carolina
52	Bavaro, David	LB	6-0	228	3	Syracuse
50	Berry, Ray	LB	6-2	230	7	Baylor
67	Boyd, Tracy	T	6-4	296	1	Elizabeth City State
81	Carter, Anthony	WR	5-11	176	9	Michigan
80	Carter, Cris	WR	6-3	198	7	Ohio State
62	Christy, Jeff	C	6-3	289	1	Pittsburgh
94	Conover, Frank	DT	6-5	325	3	Syracuse
33	Craig, Roger	RB	6-0	219	11	Nebraska
77	Culpepper, Brad	DT	6-1	267	1	Florida
75	Dafney, Bernard	G	6-5	317	1	Tennessee
55	Del Rio, Jack	LB	6-4	250	9	USC
79	Dixon, David	G	6-5	350	1	Arizona State
56	Doleman, Chris	DE	6-5	270	9	Pittsburgh
29	Evans, Chuck	RB	6-1	217	1	Clark
49	Evans, Patt	TE	6-6	261	1	Minnesota
43	Fisher, Luke	TE	6-2	235	1	East Carolina
40	Gaddis, Mike	RB	6-0	217	1	Oklahoma
16	Gannon, Rich	QB	6-3	208	7	Delaware
25	Glenn, Vencie	S	6-0	189	8	Indiana State
37	Graham, Lorenzo	RB	5-11	200	1	Livingston
99	Harris, James	DE	6-4	275	1	Tempe
90	Harris, Robert	DE	6-4	285	1	Southern
30	Henderson, Keith	RB	6-1	230	4	Georgia
98	Hinkle, George	DT	6-5	288	6	Arizona
53	Holmes, Bruce	LB	6-2	237	1	Minnesota
76	Irwin, Tim	T	6-7	297	13	Tennessee
51	Jenkins, Carlos	LB	6-3	219	3	Michigan State
28	Jenkins, Izel	CB	5-10	190	6	North Carolina State
14	Johnson, Brad	QB	6-4	218	1	Florida State
89	Johnson, Joe	WR	5-8	170	5	Notre Dame
83	Jordan, Steve	TE	6-3	240	12	Brown
69	Kalis, Todd	G	6-5	291	6	Arizona State
39	Lee, Carl	CB	5-11	182	11	Marshall
45	Lenseigne, Tony	TE	6-4	235	1	East Washington
91	Manusky, Greg	LB	6-1	237	6	Colgate
58	McDaniel, Ed	LB	5-11	232	1	Clemson
64	McDaniel, Randall	G	6-4	275	6	Arizona State
9	McMahon, Jim	QB	6-1	195	12	Brigham Young
26	McMillian, Audray	CB	6-0	190	8	Houston
68	Morris, Mike	C	6-5	273	6	NE Missouri State
18	Newsome, Harry	P	6-0	185	9	Wake Forest
85	Novoselsky, Brent	TE	6-2	237	6	Pennsylvania
82	Paige, Stephone	WR	6-2	188	10	Fresno State
27	Parker, Anthony	CB	5-10	179	3	Arizona State
23	Pearson, Jayice	CB	5-11	186	7	Washington
93	Randle, John	DT	6-1	270	4	Texas A&I
19	Randolph, Joe	WR	5-7	155	1	Elon
86	Reed, Jake	WR	6-3	220	2	Grambling
7	Reveiz, Fuad	K	5-11	226	9	Tennessee
12	Salisbury, Sean	QB	6-5	217	5	USC
60	Schreiber, Adam	C-G	6-4	290	10	Texas
38	Scott, Todd	CB	5-10	191	3	SW Louisiana
63	Smith, Daryle	T	6-5	276	6	Tennessee
73	Strickland, Fred	LB	6-2	250	6	Purdue
46	Tennell, Derek	TE	6-2	258	6	UCLA

continued on page 478

TOP DRAFT CHOICES

Rd.	Name	Sel. No.	Pos.	Ht.	Wt.	College
1	Smith, Robert	21	RB	6-1	193	Ohio State
2	Ismail, Qadry	52	WR	6-0	192	Syracuse
3	Gerak, John	58	G	6-4	276	Penn State
3	Brown, Gilbert	79	DT	6-2	337	Kansas
4	Sheppard, Ashley	106	LB	6-3	258	Clemson

brother of former Heisman Trophy winner "Rocket" Ismail. The Vikings also got a jump on rebuilding their offensive line with Penn State's tough guard John Gerak.

OUTLOOK: If McMahon can stay healthy, Dennis Green's Vikings will be a tough team. But the heart of the offensive line was lost in free agency, and that doesn't bode well for the health of any quarterback. Still, this team, 11-5 last year, has the talent and the confidence to withstand Green Bay's challenge for the division title the Vikings won in '92.

VIKING PROFILES

CHRIS DOLEMAN 31 6-5 270   **Defensive End**

Bounced back in a big way in 1992 . . . Re-established himself as one of the NFL's best pass-rushers . . . Finished third in the NFC in sacks with 14½ . . . Big-play man forced six fumbles and recovered three, returning one for a TD . . . Also snared the fourth interception of his career . . . Returned to the Pro Bowl . . . Difficult season in 1991 . . . Managed only seven sacks and missed the Pro Bowl for the first time in five years . . . Led NFL in sacks with 21 in 1989 . . . Also forced five fumbles and recovered five more during that monster season . . . Durable player who has started every game (90) since the end of the 1987 strike . . . Has 75½ sacks in eight NFL seasons . . . Only an average player at linebacker in his first two seasons . . . Burst into prominence after switch to defensive end in 1987 . . . Vikings' No. 1 pick, fourth overall, out of Pittsburgh in 1985 . . . Born Oct. 16, 1961, in Indianapolis . . . 1993 base salary: $1.1 million.

JIM McMAHON 34 6-1 195   Quarterback

Signed by Vikings as free agent after spending three seasons with Eagles . . . Projected by the Vikings as the answer to their long-standing quarterback problems . . . Signed two-year deal for $3.2 million . . . Intelligent, instinctive player with great feel for the position . . . Natural leader . . . Downside is lack of durability . . . Has missed time because of injuries in nearly every season . . . Played in only two games in 1992 as backup to Randall Cunningham . . . Started 11 games in 1991 after Cunningham went down with knee injury . . . Led Eagles to 10-6 record, including six straight wins . . . Best game was a 341-yard passing performance in rallying the Eagles from 23-0 deficit to 32-30 win over Browns . . . Played seven seasons in Chicago, one in San Diego . . . Set 71 NCAA records at BYU . . . Born Aug. 21, 1959, in Jersey City, N.J. . . . 1993 base salary: $1.6 million.

TERRY ALLEN 25 5-10 197   Running Back

Emerging star . . . Set Vikings' record with 1,201 rushing yards in 1992 . . . Tied team record with 13 rushing TDs . . . Second on the team in receptions with 49 for 478 yards and two TDs . . . Generated 191 all-purpose yards and three TDs in victory over Rams . . . Ran for two TDs against Eagles . . . Burst into prominence in his first full season as a starter . . . Had started seven games in 1991 but split time with Herschel Walker . . . Ran for 563 yards (4.7 average) in 1991 . . . NFC Offensive Player of the Week after rushing for 127 yards against Bucs . . . Sat out 1990 season after suffering knee injury in training camp . . . Vikings' ninth-round pick in 1990 out of Clemson . . . Born Feb. 21, 1968, in Commerce, Ga. . . . 1993 base salary: $425,000.

RANDALL McDANIEL 28 6-4 275   Guard

Perhaps the best guard in the NFL . . . Strong, quick, smart . . . Explosive run-blocker . . . Great footwork makes him one of the NFL's most athletic interior linemen . . . Made the Pro Bowl for the fourth year in a row after 1992 season . . . Started all 16 games for the third year in a row . . . His blocking cleared the way for Terry Allen to set team record for rushing yards . . . Crunching block led Allen into end zone against Eagles' renowned goal-line defense . . . A starter since the second game of his rookie season . . . Vikings named him a transition player during the free-agency period . . . Can dunk a basketball wearing full football uniform . . . Vikings' top pick out of Arizona State in 1988 . . . Holds NCAA record with 620-pound deadlift . . . Born Dec. 19, 1964, in Phoenix . . . 1993 base salary: $925,000.

GARY ZIMMERMAN 31 6-6 286   Tackle

Solid player at important position along offensive line . . . His value as left tackle was evident by Vikings' decision to name him transition player during free-agency period . . . Combines with Randall McDaniel to form powerful left side of offensive line . . . Four-time Pro Bowl selection . . . Durable player has started 108 consecutive games, longest streak on the team . . . Named to second team on NFL's All-Decade Team of the 1980s . . . Played two seasons for Los Angeles Express of the USFL . . . Giants made him the third overall pick in the 1984 supplemental draft (just before Eagles took Reggie White) . . . Traded to Vikings in exchange for two No. 2 picks in 1986 draft . . . Three-year starter at Oregon . . . Born Dec. 13, 1961, in Fullerton, Cal. . . . 1992 base salary: $650,000.

CRIS CARTER 27 6-3 198   Wide Receiver

Feature receiver in Vikings' passing attack . . . Led team in receptions with 53 despite missing final four games with separated shoulder . . . Also caught six TD passes . . . Strong, physical receiver with great leaping ability . . . Excels at catching alley-oop passes in the end zone . . . Led Vikings with 72 catches for 962 yards in 1991 . . . Good runner after the catch . . . Selected by the Eagles in the fourth round of the 1987 supplemental draft . . . Entered draft after he was ruled ineligible for his senior season . . . Burst into prominence with 761 receiving yards in 1988 . . . Caught 11 TD passes in 1989 . . . Released by the Eagles in part because of off-the-field problems . . . Claimed on waivers by Vikings . . . All-American at Ohio State . . . Born Nov. 25, 1965, in Middletown, Ohio . . . 1993 base salary: $800,000.

HENRY THOMAS 28 6-2 268   Defensive Tackle

Recognition finally came his way in 1992 when he was named to the Pro Bowl for the first time . . . Finished with 50 tackles and six sacks . . . Powerful run-defender and has improved his pass rush . . . Long regarded as one of the best-kept secrets in the NFL . . . Has 40 sacks in six NFL seasons . . . Best statistical season was 1989, with nine sacks, three forced fumbles, three fumble recoveries . . . Overshadowed by linemates Keith Millard (since traded) and Chris Doleman . . . Has scored two TDs on returns in his career . . . A starter since the first game of his rookie season . . . Vikings' third-round pick in 1987 out of LSU . . . MVP of the 1987 Sugar Bowl . . . Fond of fishing . . . Born Jan. 12, 1965, in Houston . . . 1993 base salary: $900,000.

JOHN RANDLE 25 6-1 270   Defensive Lineman

Little-known player has developed into one of the NFL's top pass-rushers . . . Registered 11½ sacks in 1992 . . . Made 44 tackles and recovered two fumbles . . . Started 15 games at defensive tackle . . . Decent run-defender . . . Specializes in active pass rush . . . Speedy, athletic, relentless . . . Has 21 sacks over past two seasons . . . Burst on scene in 1991 with 9½ sacks . . . Played in all 16 games as a rookie in 1990 . . . One of the Vikings' best free-agent finds . . . Signed as rookie free agent before training camp in 1990 . . . Played two seasons at Texas A&I after transferring from Trinity Valley Community College . . . Born Dec. 2, 1967, in Hearne, Tex. . . . 1993 base salary: $350,000.

AUDRAY McMILLIAN 31 6-0 190   Cornerback

Stardom came late to this journeyman defensive back . . . Burst into prominence in 1992 . . . Led the NFC with eight interceptions and 157 return yards . . . Returned two interceptions for TDs . . . Also ranked fourth on the team in tackles with 69 . . . Made the Pro Bowl for the first time in his career . . . Big-play man for a defense that scored a remarkable eight TDs . . . Became a full-time starter for the first time in his career in 1992 . . . Reserve defensive back for Vikings from 1989-91 . . . Signed by Vikings as Plan B free agent from Houston . . . Was a backup during his four seasons in Houston . . . Originally third-round draft pick by New England in 1985 . . . Cut by Patriots at end of training camp and signed by Oilers . . . Standout at University of Houston . . . Returned interception for TD in 1984 Cotton Bowl . . . Born Aug. 13, 1962, in Carthage, Tex. . . . 1992 base salary: $355,000.

ANTHONY CARTER 32 5-11 176   Wide Receiver

This acrobatic athlete has entered the twilight of his career . . . Age and injuries slowed him down in 1992 . . . Finished with 41 receptions for 580 yards . . . The reception total was his lowest since 1987, the yardage total the lowest of his career . . . One of the best wide receivers in Vikings' history . . . Holds team record with 6,759 career receiving yards . . . Fourth on the team's all-time list with 48 TDs . . . Deceptive speed, great leaping ability and instincts . . . Despite slight frame, he specializes in slants and crossing patterns . . . Best season was 1988, with 72 receptions for 1,225 yards . . . Broke NFL playoff records in 1987 for most receiving yards in a game (227 against 49ers) and most punt-return yards in a game (143 against Saints) . . . Spent three seasons with Michigan Panthers and Oakland Invaders of the USFL . . . Vikings acquired his NFL rights in a trade with Dolphins . . . Three-time All-American at the University of Michigan . . . Born Sept. 17, 1960, in Riviera Beach, Fla. . . . 1993 base salary: $1 million.

TODD SCOTT 25 5-10 191   Safety

Burst into prominence in 1992 . . . Switched to safety to replace Joey Browner and made Pro Bowl in his first season as a starter . . . Finished third on the team in tackles with 73 . . . Emerged as big-play man for NFL's most opportunistic defense . . . Had five interceptions . . . Returned an interception for TD and fumble recovery for another score as Vikings' defense produced remarkable eight TDs . . . Won job in training camp and started all 16 games . . . Played in all 16 games as a rookie in 1991, starting once . . . Used mostly as extra cornerback in passing situations . . . Vikings' sixth-round pick in 1991 draft out of Southwest Louisiana . . . Four-year starter in college . . . Earned degree in business management . . . Born Jan. 23, 1968, in Galveston, Tex. . . . 1992 base salary: $66,000.

COACH DENNIS GREEN: Revitalized the Vikings in his first season . . . Led team to 11-5 record and just its second NFC Central Division title since 1980 . . . Brought toughness and enthusiasm to a team that was lacking both . . . Made hard decisions to release or trade veterans such as Herschel Walker, Joey Browner and Keith Millard . . . Injected roster with youth . . . Became the Vikings' fifth head coach on Jan. 10, 1992 . . . Just the second black head coach in NFL history, following the Raiders' Art Shell . . . "There's a new sheriff in town," he said in promising to instill discipline in a team regarded as talented underachievers . . . Compiled 16-18 record in three seasons as head coach at Stanford . . . An NFL assistant coach under Bill Walsh with the 49ers . . . Popular with his players for his honest but tough-minded approach . . . Was 10-45 in five seasons as head coach at Northwestern in mid-1980s . . . Was the Big Ten's first black head coach . . . Two-year starter as a tailback at Iowa and also played for British Columbia Lions of the CFL . . . Assistant coach at Dayton and Iowa . . . Born Feb. 17, 1949, in Harrisburg, Pa.

GREATEST INTERCEPTOR

The big names on the great Minnesota defenses of the late 1960s and early 1970s were linemen such as Carl Eller, Jim Marshall and Alan Page. They were the Purple People Eaters. But there was a big-play man in the back of that defense, too. Safety Paul Krause was a six-time Pro Bowl player and one of the toughest, smartest defensive backs of his era.

Krause finished his career with 53 interceptions, a Vikings' record. He also holds the team record for interception-return yardage with 852.

Krause was an opportunistic player who took advantage of the problems created for offenses by the Vikings' overpowering defensive front. His heady play helped the Vikings dominate the NFC in those years and advance to four Super Bowls.

Krause's best season probably was 1975, when he set team records for interceptions with 10 and for return yardage with 201.

INDIVIDUAL VIKING RECORDS

Rushing

Most Yards Game:	200	Chuck Foreman, vs Philadelphia, 1976
Season:	1,201	Terry Allen, 1992
Career:	5,879	Chuck Foreman, 1973-79

Passing

Most TD Passes Game:	7	Joe Kapp, vs Baltimore, 1969
Season:	26	Tommy Kramer, 1981
Career:	239	Francis Tarkenton, 1961-66, 1972-78

Receiving

Most TD Passes Game:	4	Ahmad Rashad, vs San Francisco, 1979
Season:	11	Jerry Reichow, 1961
Career:	50	Sammy White, 1976-85

Scoring

Most Points Game:	24	2 times, most recently Ahmad Rashad, vs San Francisco, 1979
Season:	132	Chuck Foreman, 1975
Career:	1,365	Fred Cox, 1963-77
Most TDs Game:	4	2 times, most recently Ahmad Rashad, vs San Francisco, 1979
Season:	22	Chuck Foreman, 1975
Career:	76	Bill Brown, 1962-74

NEW ORLEANS SAINTS

TEAM DIRECTORY: Owner: Tom Benson; Pres/GM: Jim Finks; VP-Administration: Jim Miller; Bus. Mgr/Controller: Bruce Broussard; Dir. Media Rel.: Rusty Kasmiersky; Head Coach: Jim Mora. Home field: Superdome (69,056). Colors: Old gold, black and white.

SCOUTING REPORT

OFFENSE: Big changes. The Saints cut their ties with long-time quarterback Bobby Hebert, who broke their hearts with a disastrous second-half meltdown in a playoff loss to the Eagles.

To replace Hebert, the Saints signed veteran Wade Wilson as a free agent. Wilson is talented and experienced but a little erratic. He could emerge as a starter but will have to beat out Steve Walsh and strong-armed youngster Mike Buck. In any event, the Saints will look and act differently without Hebert, now a Falcon.

The ground game depends on second-year man Vaughn Dunbar, and Brad Muster. Dunbar led the team in rushing as a rookie. He could emerge as a franchise back. Ex-Bear fullback Muster replaces Craig "Ironhead" Heyward, now a Bear.

The Saints need more big plays from their wide receivers. Eric Martin is a terrific possession receiver but lacks deep speed. Quinn Early is decent but nothing special. Floyd Turner could be a dangerous deep threat if he can stay healthy.

The line is solid. Left tackle Richard Cooper is underrated, while guard Jim Dombrowski and center Joel Hilgenberg are tough inside. Louisiana Tech tackle Willie Roaf will be there if needed. John Tice is a good blocking tight end but the Saints need more production in the passing game from that position. That's why they took Notre Dame tight end Irv Smith with their second pick.

DEFENSE: The Saints have plenty of muscle on this side of the football, but they are getting a little old.

The linebacking corps is second to none. Sam Mills and Vaughan Johnson hit like demolition balls in run-defense and Rickey Jackson is a ferocious pass-rusher.

The strong line is led by end Wayne Martin, who burst into prominence with 15½ sacks. The Redskins tried to sign him as a free agent but the Saints matched the offer. Renaldo Turnbull is a talented young end who lacks consistency.

The secondary is solid. Gene Atkins and Brett Maxie are de-

Rickey Jackson keeps adding to his Saints' sack mark.

pendable safeties and Keith Taylor provides good depth. Vince Buck is a good coverage cornerback and Reggie Jones has the talent to develop into one of the NFL's best.

SPECIAL TEAMS: The key here is kicker Morten Andersen, one of the best in NFL history. He put together another sensational season in 1992.

Tommy Barnhardt is a good punter who averaged 44 yards in 1992, second-best in the NFC. The coverage teams are strong.

The Saints lack sizzle in the return game. Pat Newman averaged just 6.9 yards on punt returns and Fred McAfee was mediocre on kickoff returns. This team continues to rue the day they let Mel Gray get away as a Plan B free agent.

SAINTS VETERAN ROSTER

HEAD COACH—Jim Mora. Assistant Coaches—Paul Boudreau, Vic Fangio, Joe Marciano, Jim Mora Jr., Russell Paternostro, John Pease, Steve Sidwell, Jim Skipper, Carl Smith, Steve Walters.

No.	Name	Pos.	Ht.	Wt.	NFL Exp.	College
7	Andersen, Morten	K	6-2	221	12	Michigan State
28	Atkins, Gene	FS	6-1	200	7	Florida A&M
78	Backes, Tom	T	6-4	273	1	Oklahoma
6	Barnhardt, Tommy	P	6-2	207	7	North Carolina
74	Bowles, Scott	G-T	6-5	280	3	North Texas State
64	Brennan, Mike	G-T	6-5	285	3	Notre Dame
85	Brenner, Hoby	TE	6-5	245	13	USC
67	Brock, Stan	T	6-6	290	14	Colorado
16	Buck, Mike	QB	6-3	227	4	Maine
26	Buck, Vince	CB	6-0	198	4	Central State (Ohio)
80	Carroll, Wesley	WR	6-0	183	3	Miami (Fla.)
41	Cook, Toi	CB	5-11	188	7	Stanford
71	Cooper, Richard	T	6-5	290	4	Tennessee
72	Dombrowski, Jim	G-T	6-5	298	8	Virginia
19	Dowdell, Marcus	WR	5-10	179	1	Tennessee State
63	Dunbar, Karl	DE	6-4	275	2	LSU
32	Dunbar, Vaughn	RB	5-10	204	2	Indiana
89	Early, Quinn	WR	6-0	190	6	Iowa
91	Goff, Robert	DE-NT	6-3	270	6	Auburn
61	Hilgenberg, Joel	C-G	6-2	252	10	Iowa
21	Hilliard, Dalton	RB	5-8	204	8	LSU
57	Jackson, Rickey	LB	6-2	243	13	Pittsburgh
68	Jetton, Paul	C-G	6-4	288	6	Texas
53	Johnson, Vaughan	LB	6-3	245	8	North Carolina State
27	Jones, Reginald	CB	6-1	202	3	Memphis State
60	Kennard, Derek	G	6-3	300	8	Nevada-Reno
43	Legette, Tyrone	CB	5-9	177	2	Nebraska
62	Leggett, Brad	C	6-4	270	2	USC
46	Lumpkin, Sean	S	6-0	206	2	Minnesota
47	Mack, Cedric	CB	5-11	190	11	Baylor
84	Martin, Eric	WR	6-1	195	9	LSU
42	Martin, Sammy	WR	5-11	182	5	LSU
93	Martin, Wayne	DE	6-5	275	5	Arkansas
39	Maxie, Brett	S	6-2	194	9	Texas Southern
25	McAfee, Fred	RB	5-10	195	3	Mississippi College
76	McGuire, Gene	C	6-2	284	2	Notre Dame
69	Miller, Les	DE-NT	6-7	285	7	Ft. Hays State
51	Mills, Sam	LB	5-9	225	8	Montclair State
22	Muster, Brad	FB	6-3	231	6	Stanford
36	Ned, Derrick	RB	6-1	210	1	Grambling
86	Newman, Patrick	WR	5-11	189	4	Utah State
70	Port, Chris	G-T	6-5	290	3	Duke
—	Robbins, Tootie	T	6-5	310	11	East Carolina
83	Small, Torrance	WR	6-3	201	2	Alcorn State
99	Smeenge, Joel	LB	6-5	250	4	Western Michigan
37	Spencer, Jimmy	CB	5-9	180	2	Florida
49	Stowers, Tommie	TE	6-3	240	2	Missouri
20	Taylor, Craig	FB	6-0	228	4	West Virginia
29	Taylor, Keith	S	5-11	206	6	Illinois
97	Turnbull, Renaldo	LB	6-4	250	4	West Virginia
88	Turner, Floyd	WR	5-11	188	5	NW Louisiana
12	Verdugo, Kevin	QB	6-3	211	1	Colorado State
87	Wainright, Frank	TE	6-3	245	3	Northern Colorado
4	Walsh, Steve	QB	6-3	204	5	Miami (Fla.)
73	Warren, Frank	DE	6-4	290	12	Auburn
94	Wilks, Jim	DE-NT	6-5	275	13	San Diego State
90	Williams, James	LB	6-0	230	4	Mississippi State
48	Williams, Ronnie	TE	6-4	260	2	Oklahoma State
18	Wilson, Wade	QB	6-3	206	13	East Texas State
92	Winston, DeMond	LB	6-2	239	4	Vanderbilt

TOP DRAFT CHOICES

Rd.	Name	Sel. No.	Pos.	Ht.	Wt.	College
1	Roaf, Willie	8	OT	6-4	303	Louisiana Tech
1	Smith, Irv	20	TE	6-3	255	Notre Dame
2	Freeman, Reggie	53	LB	6-1	235	Florida State
4	Neal, Lorenzo	89	FB	5-10	236	Fresno State
4	Brown, Derek	109	RB	5-9	183	Nebraska

THE ROOKIES: The Swilling trade enabled the Saints to use the Lions' No. 1 pick to select Roaf, the highest-rated blocker on the board. More muscle for the front line arrived later in the first round when the Saints used their own pick for tight end Smith, a powerful blocker. Florida State stand-up defensive end Reggie Freeman projects as an outside linebacker for the Saints.

OUTLOOK: Jim Mora's Saints (12-4) were devastated to lose in the first round of the playoffs for the fourth time in a row last season. They still have talent but their confidence could be shaky. They appear to be heading in the wrong direction.

SAINT PROFILES

WADE WILSON 34 6-3 206   **Quarterback**

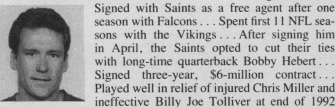

Signed with Saints as a free agent after one season with Falcons . . . Spent first 11 NFL seasons with the Vikings . . . After signing him in April, the Saints opted to cut their ties with long-time quarterback Bobby Hebert . . . Signed three-year, $6-million contract . . . Played well in relief of injured Chris Miller and ineffective Billy Joe Tolliver at end of 1992 season . . . Started Falcons' last three games and passed for 1,040 yards and 10 TDs with just two interceptions . . . Remarkable performance in victory over Bucs included 324 passing yards and 5 TDs without an interception . . . In and out of the starting lineup during his long stay with the Vikings . . . Pro Bowl selection after passing for career-best 2,746 yards in 1988 . . . Passed for 12,135 yards and 66 TDs in 11 seasons with the Vikings . . . Minnesota's eighth-round pick out of East Texas State in 1981 . . . Born Feb. 1, 1959, in Greenville, Tex. . . . 1993 base salary: $2 million.

RICKEY JACKSON 35 6-2 243   Linebacker

Old man keeps rolling along . . . Grizzled veteran of the NFL's top linebacking corps . . . Put together another strong season with 13½ sacks, six forced fumbles, three fumble recoveries . . . The 13½ sacks marked his career high, set at the age of 34 . . . Made 66 tackles . . . Forced fumble with a sack in playoff loss to Eagles . . . Team record-holder for career sacks (110½) and fumble recoveries (23) . . . A remarkably durable player, he has started every non-strike game (179) of his 12-year NFL career . . . Four-time Pro Bowl selection . . . Saints' second-round pick out of Pittsburgh in 1981 . . . Born March 20, 1958, in Pahokee, Fla. . . . 1993 base salary: $1.3 million.

VAUGHN DUNBAR 24 5-10 204   Running Back

Led Saints in rushing as a rookie with 565 yards . . . Broke off 24-yard run and caught 32-yard pass in playoff loss to Eagles . . . Had Saints' biggest single-game rushing effort of the season with 91 yards against Rams . . . Scored three TDs . . . Has speed, moves and instincts to become 1,000-yard rusher . . . Saints' No. 1 pick out of Indiana in 1992 . . . Consensus All-American as a senior when he ran for 1,802 yards and 12 TDs . . . Had 265-yard game against Missouri . . . Ran for 2,568 yards and scored 40 TDs as a senior at Fort Wayne (Ind.) High School . . . Product of the same high school as Steelers' star Rod Woodson . . . Born Sept. 4, 1968, in Fort Wayne . . . 1993 base salary: $365,000.

JIM DOMBROWSKI 29 6-5 298   Guard

Cornerstone of the Saints' powerful offensive line . . . Started all 16 games in 1992 . . . Part of an offensive line that allowed league-low 15 quarterback sacks . . . Potent run-blocker . . . Durable player who has started 90 consecutive games . . . Named transition player during free-agency period . . . Started his career at left tackle but made smooth transition to left guard midway in 1989 season . . . Missed most of his rookie season in 1986 with a broken foot . . . The first player drafted (sixth overall) by new Saints' braintrust of coach Jim Mora and general manager Jim Finks in 1986 . . . Consensus All-American at Virginia . . . Has degree in biology, and hopes for career as orthopedic surgeon . . . Born Oct. 19, 1963, in Williamsville, N.Y. . . . 1992 base salary: $775,000.

BRAD MUSTER 28 6-3 231   Fullback

Signed with Saints as free agent after five seasons with Bears . . . Switched places with fullback Craig "Ironhead" Heyward, who signed with Bears after five seasons with Saints . . . Projected as Saints' starting fullback . . . Smooth receiver with good moves as a runner . . . Hampered by injuries for much of career . . . Started all 16 games for Bears in 1992 . . . Second on team with 414 rushing yards (4.2 average) . . . Caught 34 passes for 389 yards . . . Has scored 27 TDs in five NFL seasons . . . Best statistical season was 1990, with 664 rushing yards and 47 receptions . . . Scored eight TDs in 1989 . . . Bears' No. 1 pick out of Stanford in 1988 . . . Pac-10 Offensive Player of the Year as a junior . . . Born April 11, 1965, in San Marin, Cal. . . . 1992 base salary: $1.3 million.

ERIC MARTIN 31 6-1 195   Wide Receiver

Smart, steady receiver has been the go-to guy in the Saints' passing attack for several seasons . . . Led the team in receptions for the sixth year in a row with 68 . . . Generated 1,041 yards and scored five TDs . . . Caught eight passes for 151 yards against Cardinals and six passes for 103 yards against Rams . . . Has caught a pass in a club-record 89 consecutive games . . . Has played in a club-record 127 consecutive games . . . The Saints' all-time leader in receptions (466), receiving yardage (6,904) and TD catches (45) . . . Solid, unspectacular player has never been to the Pro Bowl . . . Set SEC receiving record for career yardage at LSU . . . Saints drafted him in the seventh round in 1985 . . . Born Nov. 8, 1961, in Van Vleck, Tex. . . . 1992 base salary: $800,000.

SAM MILLS 34 5-9 225 — Linebacker

Little man isn't short on respect from his peers ... Made Pro Bowl for the third time ... Led Saints with career-high 130 tackles ... Forced four fumbles and recovered four ... His sack and fumble return for TD sealed victory over Jets ... Instinctive, hard-hitting player ... Reads and reacts quickly ... Opposing blockers sometimes complain they can't find him ... Shortest linebacker in the NFL ... NFC Defensive Player of the Month in September, 1991 ... Began his pro career in USFL, where he played under Saints' coach Jim Mora ... Played at tiny Montclair (N.J.) State and wasn't drafted ... Signed with Browns as free agent but was cut in training camp ... Taught school before joining USFL Philadelphia Stars ... Born June 3, 1959, in Neptune, N.J. ... 1992 base salary: $940,000.

VAUGHAN JOHNSON 31 6-3 245 — Linebacker

Another USFL refugee who has flourished with the Saints ... Made the Pro Bowl for the fourth consecutive time ... Hard hitter who is regarded as one of the NFL's best inside linebackers ... Solid as a cement truck against the run ... Second on the team in tackles with 84 ... Forced three fumbles ... Led Saints in tackles in 1987 and 1988 ... Played two seasons for Jacksonville Bulls of the USFL ... Saints made him their No. 1 pick in NFL's supplemental draft in 1984 ... Attended North Carolina State ... Born March 4, 1962, in Morehead City, N.C. ... 1993 base salary: $950,000.

QUINN EARLY 28 6-0 190 — Wide Receiver

Free-agent find who has developed into solid starter for the Saints ... Caught 30 passes for 566 yards (18.9 average) and five TDs ... Had big game in playoff loss to Eagles, catching TD pass ... Smooth, steady receiver with decent speed and hands ... Runs good patterns ... Saints got him in Plan B from San Diego in 1991 ... Moved right into starting lineup and responded with career-best 32 receptions for 541 yards ... Can double as kick-returner . . . Chargers' third-round pick out of Iowa in 1988 . . . Started 17 games for the Chargers from 1988-90 and caught 55 passes . . . Led Big Ten as a junior with 22.3-yard average per reception . . . Earned degree in commercial art . . . Talented artist who produced illustrations for Iowa media guide . . . Born April 13, 1965, in West Hempstead, N.Y. . . . 1992 base salary: $375,000.

MORTEN ANDERSEN 33 6-2 221   Placekicker

One of the greatest kickers in NFL history produced another sensational season . . . Tied for first in NFC with 120 points . . . His 85.3 success rate on field-goal attempts (29 of 34) was tops in the NFC . . . Made his final 20 attempts of the season . . . Returned to the Pro Bowl for the sixth time . . . Has made 21 field goals from 50 yards or longer, an all-time NFL record . . . His 60-yard field goal in 1991 was the longest in the NFL since 1984 . . . Enters 1993 having made 127 of his last 128 extra-point attempts . . . Ranks second to Chiefs' Nick Lowery in career field-goal accuracy with a 78.1 percentage (246 of 315) . . . Saints' all-time leader in points (1,085) and field goals (246) . . . Named transition player during free-agency period . . . Saints' fourth-round pick out of Michigan State in 1982 . . . Came to America from Denmark as an exchange student in 1977 . . . Born Aug. 19, 1960, in Struer, Denmark . . . 1992 base salary: $500,000.

WAYNE MARTIN 27 6-5 275   Defensive End

Burst into prominence in 1992 . . . Led the team and finished third in the NFC with 15½ sacks . . . Tied team record with four sacks against Falcons . . . Named NFC Defensive Player of the Week for that performance . . . Redskins signed him to a four-year, $10.1-million offer sheet as a restricted free agent in April but Saints matched the offer, making him the team's highest-paid defensive player . . . Natural pass-rusher with good size, speed, moves . . . Recovered fumble in playoff loss to Eagles . . . Saints' No. 1 pick out of Arkansas in 1989 . . . Recorded 25½ sacks in his college career . . . Born Oct. 26, 1965, in Forrest City, Ark. . . . 1993 base salary: $2.4 million.

COACH JIM MORA: Frustrated by Saints' failure to advance
in playoffs . . . Called playoff loss to Eagles last
season the most devastating of his career . . .
Has 0-4 mark in NFL playoff games . . . Led
Saints to 12-4 record in regular season . . . Has
69-47 record in seven seasons with Saints, by
far the best mark in team history . . . Led 1991
Saints to 11-5 record and NFC West title . . .
Named NFL Coach of the Year after Saints
went 12-3 and made the playoffs for the first time in franchise
history in 1987 . . . His leadership and attention to detail have
helped turn one of the NFL's worst franchises into a perennial
playoff contender . . . Had remarkable success as coach in the
USFL . . . Led Philadelphia/Baltimore to three consecutive berths
in USFL title game . . . His team won the USFL title in 1984 and
1985 . . . NFL assistant coach with Seattle and New England . . .
College assistant at Colorado, Stanford, Washington and UCLA
. . . Spent three years as head coach of his alma mater, Occidental
(Cal.) College . . . Played tight end at Occidental and roomed with
future NFL quarterback and U.S. Senator Jack Kemp . . . Born
May 24, 1935, in Glendale, Cal.

GREATEST INTERCEPTOR

Dave Waymer was a solid player whose durability and consistency propelled him to the top of Saints' all-time list for interceptions. A Notre Dame product who played much of his career
for losing teams in New Orleans, Waymer managed 37 interceptions in 10 seasons. His total bettered by one the previous team
mark set by Tommy Myers. Waymer's high was nine in 1986.

Special mention goes to Jim Merlo, the Stanford product who
in 1976 averaged 35.5 yards on four interception returns and
brought back two for touchdowns, a New Orleans record.

INDIVIDUAL SAINT RECORDS

Rushing

Most Yards Game:	206	George Rogers, vs St. Louis, 1983
Season:	1,674	George Rogers, 1981
Career:	4,267	George Rogers, 1981-84

Passing

Most TD Passes Game:	6	Billy Kilmer, vs St. Louis, 1969
Season:	23	Archie Manning, 1980
Career:	155	Archie Manning, 1971-81

Receiving

Most TD Passes Game:	3	Dan Abramowicz, vs San Francisco, 1971
Season:	9	Henry Childs, 1977
Career:	45	Eric Martin, 1985-92

Scoring

Most Points Game:	18	8 times, most recently Reuben Mayes, vs Phoenix, 1990
Season:	121	Morten Andersen, 1987
Career:	1,085	Morten Andersen, 1982-92
Most TDs Game:	3	8 times, most recently Reuben Mayes, vs Phoenix, 1990
Season:	18	Dalton Hilliard, 1989
Career:	50	Dalton Hilliard, 1986-92

NEW YORK GIANTS

TEAM DIRECTORY: Pres.: Wellington Mara; Chairman: Bob Tisch; VP/GM: George Young; Dir. Pro Personnel: Tom Boisture; Dir. Pub. Rel.: Pat Hanlon; Head Coach: Dan Reeves. Home field: Giants Stadium (77,311). Colors: Blue, red and white.

SCOUTING REPORT

OFFENSE: It's back to the future as the Giants, under new coach Dan Reeves, have turned the reins over to 37-year-old quarterback Phil Simms. He'll be asked to run the offense and tutor young quarterback Dave Brown, the Giants' big hope for the years ahead.

Simms still can play, provided the Giants can protect him with good line play and a strong running game. The ground game has muscle in tailback Rodney Hampton, a Pro Bowler with speed and moves. Fullback Jarrod Bunch is a promising young player.

The line is key, especially given Simms' age. Left tackle Jumbo Elliott is a top-caliber player and Williams Roberts is a solid guard. The Giants still are waiting for Brian Williams to beat out veteran Bart Oates at center. Bob Kratch is a promising guard but Doug Riesenberg is only a journeyman right tackle.

The passing game lacks punch. The Giants signed wide receivers Mark Jackson and Mike Sherrard to compensate for the loss of Mark Ingram. Ed McCaffrey is a good possession receiver but the Giants lack a deep threat. The Giants need tight end Derek Brown, their top pick in 1992, to step up and become a productive player.

DEFENSE: Like Simms, Lawrence Taylor is back for another shot at glory. The greatest outside linebacker in NFL history won't find it at age 34, but he could smooth the Giants' transition to the Reeves era.

Taylor's return means the Giants will stay in a 3-4 defense. The strength of the defense remains the linebackers, with Taylor outside and ex-Bronco Michael Brooks and big-play man Pepper Johnson inside. (Nine-year veteran Carl Banks signed with the Redskins.) The Giants also have high hopes for young linebackers Corey Miller and Kanavis McGhee.

The line is young but promising. Gone is Leonard Marshall, who signed with the Jets as a free agent. Erik Howard and Eric Dorsey are still around, but the Giants' hope for improvement in this area rests with the likes of Keith Hamilton, Corey Widmer and top pick Michael Strahan of Texas Southern.

Can Lawrence Taylor supply his old magic and might?

The secondary has a solid coverage man in cornerback Mark Collins. Phillippi Sparks played well as a rookie and probably will emerge as the other cornerback. Myron Guyton and Greg Jackson are decent safeties, but the Giants would like more impact. Jesse Campbell, a former high draft pick cut loose by Philadelphia, could step in here.

SPECIAL TEAMS: The Giants used to excel in this area. Now, they are average at best.

Dave Meggett remains a great kick-returner. He averaged 23 yards on kickoff returns in 1992 and brought a 92-yarder back for a TD.

GIANTS VETERAN ROSTER

HEAD COACH—Dan Reeves. Assistant Coaches—Don Blackmon, James Daniel, Joe DeCamillis, George Hershaw, Earl Leggett, Pete Mangurian, Al Miller, Mike Nolan, Dick Rehbein, George Sefcik, Zaven Yaralian.

No.	Name	Pos.	Ht.	Wt.	NFL Exp.	College
41	Allred, Brian	DB	5-10	175	2	Cal-Sacramento
24	Anderson, Ottis	RB	6-2	225	15	Miami (Fla.)
9	Bahr, Matt	K	5-10	175	15	Penn State
54	Bailey, Carlton	LB	6-3	235	6	North Carolina
85	Baker, Stephen	WR	5-8	160	7	Fresno State
—	Bradley, Shazzon	DL	6-1	270	1	Tennesee
82	Brandes, John	TE	6-2	249	6	Cameron
—	Brooks, Michael	LB	6-1	235	7	Louisiana State
17	Brown, Dave	QB	6-5	215	2	Duke
86	Brown, Derek	TE	6-6	252	2	Notre Dame
2	Bruun, Eric	P	6-2	215	1	Purdue
33	Bunch, Jarrod	FB	6-2	248	3	Michigan
80	Calloway, Chris	WR	5-10	185	4	Michigan
37	Campbell, Jesse	S	6-1	215	2	North Carolina State
25	Collins, Mark	CB	5-10	190	8	Cal-Fullerton
87	Cross, Howard	TE	6-5	245	5	Alabama
99	DeOssie, Steve	LB	6-2	248	10	Boston College
71	Dillard, Stacey	DE	6-5	288	2	Oklahoma
77	Dorsey, Eric	DE	6-5	280	8	Notre Dame
76	Elliott, John	T	6-7	305	6	Michigan
73	Flythe, Mark	DE	6-7	290	1	Penn State
93	Fox, Mike	DE	6-6	275	4	West Virginia
10	Graham, Kent	QB	6-5	220	2	Ohio State
29	Guyton, Myron	S	6-1	205	5	Eastern Kentucky
75	Hamilton, Keith	DE	6-6	280	2	Pittsburgh
27	Hampton, Rodney	RB	5-11	215	4	Georgia
74	Howard, Erik	NT	6-4	268	8	Washington State
47	Jackson, Greg	S	6-1	200	5	LSU
—	Jackson, Mark	WR	5-9	180	8	Purdue
69	Johnson, Jim	T	6-5	305	1	Michigan State
52	Johnson, Pepper	LB	6-3	248	8	Ohio State
68	Jones, Clarence	T	6-6	280	3	Maryland
26	Kaumeyer, Thom	S	5-11	190	4	Oregon
61	Kratch, Bob	G	6-3	288	5	Iowa
5	Landeta, Sean	P	6-0	210	9	Towson State
81	McCaffrey, Ed	WR	6-5	215	3	Stanford
96	McGhee, Kanavis	LB	6-4	257	3	Colorado
38	McGriggs, Lamar	DB	6-3	210	3	Western Illinois
30	Meggett, David	RB	5-7	180	5	Towson State
57	Miller, Corey	LB	6-2	255	3	South Carolina
60	Moore, Eric	T	6-5	290	6	Indiana
83	Myles, Lee	WR	5-6	156	1	Baylor
67	Novak, Jeff	OT	6-6	300	1	SW Texas State
65	Oates, Bart	C	6-3	265	9	Brigham Young
84	Pierce, Aaron	TE	6-5	246	2	Washington
51	Powell, Andre	LB	6-1	226	1	Penn State
39	Raymond, Corey	S	5-11	180	2	LSU
95	Reynolds, Ed	LB	6-5	242	11	Virginia
72	Riesenberg, Doug	T	6-5	275	7	California
66	Roberts, William	T	6-5	280	9	Ohio State
91	Rooks, George	DE	6-4	275	2	Syracuse
—	Sherrard, Mike	WR	6-2	187	6	UCLA
11	Simms, Phil	QB	6-3	214	15	Morehead State
88	Smith, Joey	WR	5-10	177	3	Louisville
22	Sparks, Philippi	CB	5-11	186	2	Arizona State
56	Taylor, Lawrence	LB	6-3	243	13	North Carolina
34	Tillman, Lewis	RB	6-0	195	5	Jackson State
90	Widmer, Corey	DE	6-3	276	2	Montana State
59	Williams, Brian	C-G	6-5	300	5	Minnesota
23	Williams, Perry	CB	6-2	203	10	North Carolina State
3	Willis, Ken	K	5-11	190	4	Kentucky
36	Wright, Mike	CB	6-0	182	2	Washington State

TOP DRAFT CHOICES

Rd.	Name	Sel. No.	Pos.	Ht.	Wt.	College
2	Strahan, Michael	40	DE	6-4	262	Texas Southern
3	Buckley, Marcus	66	LB	6-3	235	Texas A&M
4	Bishop, Greg	93	OT	6-6	291	Pacific
5	Thigpen, Tommy	123	LB	6-1	234	North Carolina
6	Davis, Scott	150	G	6-3	279	Iowa

The coverage teams are mediocre and the Giants continue to search for a placekicker. Matt Bahr was consistent but missed the end of 1992 with a knee injury and his future is uncertain. Ken Willis filled in for the final four games.

THE ROOKIES: The Giants had used their No. 1 pick in the 1992 supplemental draft to get Dave Brown, their quarterback of the future. With their top picks in the 1993 draft, they continued to rebuild their aging defense by taking Strahan in the second round and Texas A&M linebacker Marcus Buckley in the third round.

OUTLOOK: The Giants, 6-10 last year, should improve under Reeves, who is a much better coach than the dismissed Ray Handley. But this team has a long road back to Super Bowl contention. They might take the first step back to respectability in 1993, but they won't close the gap on the Cowboys until they add a lot more young, talented players.

GIANT PROFILES

LAWRENCE TAYLOR 34 6-3 243   Linebacker

Bolstered by new two-year contract worth $5.05 million, he hopes to bounce back from Achilles injury that cost him the final seven games of 1992 season . . . At the time, his illustrious career appeared over, but he is hoping to return for two more seasons . . . Registered 47 tackles and five sacks before his injury . . . Considered the best outside linebacker in NFL history . . . Holds NFL record with 126½ quarterback sacks . . . Ten-time Pro Bowl selection . . . Unanimous selection to NFL's All-Decade Team of the 1980s . . . Revolutionized the sport by serving as the prototype for the pass-rushing outside linebacker . . . Second overall pick (behind George Rogers) out of North Carolina in 1981 draft . . . Golf enthusiast . . . Born Feb. 4, 1959, in Williamsburg, Va. . . . 1992 base salary: $1.45 million.

PHIL SIMMS 37 6-3 214   Quarterback

The Giants made commitment to this old-timer when they signed him to two-year, $5-million deal after the 1992 season . . . Expected to return to starting lineup and help tutor young quarterback Dave Brown . . . Frustrated by injuries and lack of playing time in previous two seasons . . . Played only four games in 1992 before sitting out rest of season with elbow ailment . . . Backup to Jeff Hostetler in 1991 . . . Started final four games that season when Hostetler went down with back injury . . . Has backing of new coach Dan Reeves . . . In 1990, led Giants to 10-0 start but suffered foot injury late in season . . . Set NFL record by completing 22 of 25 passes in Giants' victory over Denver in Super Bowl XXI . . . Giants' top pick out of Morehead (Ky.) State in 1979 . . . Born Nov. 3, 1955, in Springfield, Ky. . . . 1993 base salary: $2.5 million.

JUMBO ELLIOTT 28 6-7 305   Tackle

One of the NFL's best left tackles . . . Giants thought so much of him they made him their franchise player during free-agency period following 1992 season . . . Tremendous run-blocker who has improved his pass-blocking . . . His blocking has helped Rodney Hampton put together consecutive 1,000-yard seasons . . . Consistent, durable player who has avoided injuries in recent seasons . . . Burst into prominence with dominating performance against Bears' Pro Bowl end Richard Dent in 1990 playoffs . . . His powerful blocking helped the Giants rush for 194 yards in 31-3 victory that day . . . Injuries slowed his development early in career . . . Started five games as a rookie in 1988 . . . Giants' No. 2 pick out of Michigan in 1988 . . . Born April 1, 1965, in Lake Ronkonkoma, N.Y. . . . 1992 base salary: $600,000.

RODNEY HAMPTON 24 5-11 215   Running Back

Bright spot in dismal 1992 season . . . Feature runner around whom the Giants are attempting to rebuild . . . Ran for 1,141 yards and 14 TDs . . . Made Pro Bowl for the first time . . . Tied team record with three rushing TDs against Kansas City . . . Became only the second rusher in franchise history to produce consecutive 1,000-yard seasons . . . Ran for 1,059 yards in 1991 despite missing first two games with shoulder injury . . . Strong, fast runner with good cutback moves . . . Saw limited time as a rookie in 1990 . . . Finished with 455 yards . . . Missed NFC title game and Super Bowl with fractured fibula . . . Giants' No. 1 pick in 1990 out of Georgia . . . Entered draft after junior season . . . Born April 3, 1969, in Houston . . . 1993 base salary: $425,000.

DEREK BROWN 23 6-6 252   Tight End

The Giants are counting on this talented but unproven player . . . Saw little action as a rookie in 1992 . . . Reported late to training camp and never made smooth adjustment to NFL game . . . Caught only four passes for 31 yards . . . His development as a receiver was slowed by problems at the quarterback position . . . Tall, fast athlete has the tools to become an excellent NFL tight end . . . Consensus All-America selection at Notre Dame . . . Three-year starter for the Irish . . . Considered one of the best high-school players in the country in 1988 . . . Giants' No. 1 pick in 1992 draft . . . Born March 31, 1970, in Fairfax, Va. . . . 1993 base salary: $500,000.

KEITH HAMILTON 22 6-6 280   Defensive End

Emerging star as a pass-rusher . . . Came on strong during second half of rookie season . . . Finished with only 3½ sacks but put consistent pressure on quarterbacks . . . Led team with three forced fumbles . . . One of the youngest players in the NFL in 1992 at the age of 21 . . . Natural pass-rusher with smooth upfield moves . . . Expected to move into starting lineup in place of departed Leonard Marshall . . . Star freshman at University of Pittsburgh in 1989 . . . Slowed by injuries as a sophomore and junior . . . Decided to enter draft after junior season . . . Giants' fourth-round pick in 1992 . . . Born May 25, 1971, in Lynchburg, Va. . . . 1993 base salary: $175,000.

MARK COLLINS 29 5-10 190   Cornerback

Injuries slowed this smooth coverage man in 1992 . . . Should combine with impressive youngster Phillippi Sparks to form solid cornerback combination for several seasons . . . Led Giants in passes defended with 11 . . . Also credited with 71 tackles . . . Managed just one interception, a career-low . . . Has been a starter since the middle of his rookie season . . . Injuries have been a problem through much of his career . . . Tied for team lead in interceptions with four in 1991 . . . Giants' second-round pick out of Cal-Fullerton in 1986 . . . Born Jan. 16, 1964, in San Bernardino, Cal. . . . 1993 base salary: $900,000.

CARLTON BAILEY 28 6-3 235   Linebacker

Recovered from disappointment of being Super Bowl backup by signing three-year, $5.25-million contract with Giants . . . Will work with Pepper Johnson to form formidable pursuing inside-linebacking tandem . . . Started 10 games with Bills before coaching decision made Cornelius Bennett inside-linebacking starter . . . Hasn't really had a chance to show all of his skills . . . Won Lawrence Taylor Award in 1987 for being best defensive player at North Carolina, Taylor's alma mater . . . Had 132 tackles and 10 sacks as senior. . . . Was ninth-round Bills' draft choice in 1988. . . . Spent two seasons as Bills' best special-teams player. . . . Started six games in 1990 . . . Born Dec. 15, 1964, in Baltimore. . . . 1993 base salary: $1,700,000, with $1,250,000 in bonuses.

MICHAEL BROOKS 29 6-1 235   Linebacker

Bronco free agent has signed three-year, $5.4-million Giant contract . . . Was one of the AFC's best inside linebackers because of his ability to disrupt running offenses . . . Led team in tackles (167) and earned spot in Pro Bowl for first time . . . Led Broncos in tackles for past three years, averaging 165 a season . . . His 175-tackle season in 1990 was his best . . . As junior at Louisiana State, he was third in voting for Butkus Award ... Knee injury, which required major surgery, dropped him to third round of 1987 draft ... Played special teams during rookie year while he rehabilitated the knee ... Started at outside linebacker during the final four games of 1988 season and averaged 10 tackles ... Youngest of 13 children ... Born March 2, 1964, in Ruston, La. ... 1993 base salary: $400,000.

PEPPER JOHNSON 29 6-3 248   Linebacker

Emotional player has emerged as the leader of the Giants' defense ... Led team in tackles for the fourth time with 116 stops in 1992 ... Outspoken athlete was critical of former defensive coordinator Rod Rust ... Named transition player during free-agency period ... Three-time Pro Bowl selection ... Has replaced Lawrence Taylor as Giants' big-play linebacker ... His interception return sparked late-season upset of Kansas City ... Broke Taylor's team record with 4½ sacks in a 1991 game against Tampa Bay ... His best friend is Eagles' running back Keith Byars, his roommate at Ohio State ... Earned nickname from aunt who saw him sprinkle pepper on cereal ... Giants' second-round pick in 1986 ... Born June 29, 1964, in Detroit ... 1993 base salary: $1.2 million.

DAVE MEGGETT 27 5-7 180   Running Back

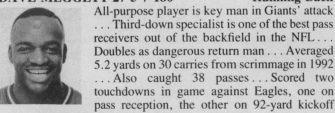

All-purpose player is key man in Giants' attack ... Third-down specialist is one of the best pass receivers out of the backfield in the NFL ... Doubles as dangerous return man ... Averaged 5.2 yards on 30 carries from scrimmage in 1992 ... Also caught 38 passes ... Scored two touchdowns in game against Eagles, one on pass reception, the other on 92-yard kickoff return ... Caught career-high 50 passes in 1991 ... Regarded as the steal of the 1989 draft ... Made the Pro Bowl as a rookie ... Accounted for 1,806 all-purpose yards that season and scored the Giants' three longest touchdowns ... Giants' fifth-round pick in 1989, out of Towson (Md.) State ... Born April 30, 1966, in Charleston, S.C. ... 1992 base salary: $625,000.

COACH DAN REEVES: Joined the Giants after 12 successful

seasons as head coach of the Broncos . . . Was dismissed by Denver because of differences with owner Pat Bowlen . . . Replaced Ray Handley, who was dismissed after two difficult seasons with the Giants . . . Returns to the NFC East, where he spent years as player and assistant coach with Cowboys . . . Tough-minded, hard-working coach . . . Led Denver to five first-place and three second-place finishes in AFC West . . . Took Broncos to three AFC titles . . . Flip side of that is three lopsided losses in the Super Bowl . . . Has 117 career victories as a head coach, including playoffs . . . Winning percentage of .605 . . . Recovered from heart problems in 1991 . . . Rejuvenated by challenge of rebuilding Giants into Super Bowl contenders . . . Ran for 1,990 yards and scored 42 TDs during eight-year career as all-purpose back for Cowboys . . . Was player-coach in Dallas in 1970-71 . . . Has been to eight Super Bowls as a player, assistant coach and head coach . . . Hired by Broncos in 1981 . . . Born Jan. 19, 1944, in Americus, Ga.

GREATEST INTERCEPTOR

Emlen Tunnell was a defensive back who made a habit of finding the football during his career with the Giants.

Tunnell played 11 seasons for the Giants and made 74 interceptions on his way to the Pro Football Hall of Fame. Playing from 1948-58, Tunnell set standards for a defensive back that still dominate the Giants' record book. He made the Pro Bowl seven years in a row and set his interception records during an era of 12-game seasons.

Tunnell twice intercepted passes in five consecutive games. He made three interceptions in a game on four occasions between 1949 and 1957. He returned two interceptions for touchdowns in 1949 and over his career returned two other interceptions for scores.

Tunnell didn't make the Pro Bowl until 1951, his fourth NFL season, but he was elected to the NFL's all-star game every year from then until 1957.

INDIVIDUAL GIANT RECORDS

Rushing

Most Yards Game:	218	Gene Roberts, vs Chicago Cardinals, 1950
Season:	1,516	Joe Morris, 1986
Career:	5,296	Joe Morris, 1982-89

Passing

Most TD Passes Game:	7	Y.A. Tittle, vs Washington, 1962
Season:	36	Y. A. Tittle, 1963
Career:	184	Phil Simms, 1979-92

Receiving

Most TD Passes Game:	4	Earnest Gray, vs St. Louis, 1980
Season:	13	Homer Jones, 1967
Career:	48	Kyle Rote, 1951-61

Scoring

Most Points Game:	24	2 times, most recently Earnest Gray, vs St. Louis, 1980
Season:	127	Ali Haji-Sheikh, 1983
Career:	646	Pete Gogolak, 1966-74
Most TDs Game:	4	2 times, most recently Earnest Gray, vs St. Louis, 1980
Season:	21	Joe Morris, 1985
Career:	78	Frank Gifford, 1952-60, 1962-64

PHILADELPHIA EAGLES

TEAM DIRECTORY: Owner: Norman Braman; Pres./CEO: Harry Gamble; VP-Finance: Mimi Box; VP: Suzi Braman; VP-Marketing: Decker Uhlhorn; Dir. Pro Scouting: Tom Gamble; Dir. Player Personnel: Joe Woolley; Dir. Pub. Rel.: Ron Howard; Head Coach: Rich Kotite. Home field: Veterans Stadium (65,356). Colors: Kelly green, white and silver.

SCOUTING REPORT

OFFENSE: The Eagles continue to count on talented but inconsistent quarterback Randall Cunningham, who struggled through a difficult season in 1992. In his first season back from a severe knee injury, Cunningham looked like his old self: brilliant one moment, baffling the next.

The Eagles hope Cunningham, like many athletes, will be better in his second season after a knee injury. He remains one of the most talented players in the NFL, a tremendous scrambler and big-play man.

The running game improved dramatically last season as Herschel Walker ran for 1,070 yards and Heath Sherman came on strong late in the year. The Eagles have depth here with James Joseph and two high 1992 draft picks, Siran Stacy and Tony Brooks. And there is always versatile Keith Byars.

The passing game hit the skids despite the presence of wide receiver Fred Barnett, a dangerous deep threat. The other wide receiver, Calvin Williams, is a decent complement to Barnett but the team lacks depth and talent at this position. Tight end Mark Bavaro was signed as a free agent from Cleveland, but his best years are behind him.

The offensive line remains a concern. Right tackle Antone Davis improved in 1992 but still isn't close to a dominant player. There are age and health concerns at left tackle, left guard and center. Right guard Eric Floyd played well. Top pick Lester Holmes of Jackson State may get some time.

DEFENSE: Two years ago, they were the best in the business. Now, they are in transition.

Pro bowl defensive tackle Jerome Brown was killed in a car accident in June 1992 and Pro Bowl defensive end Reggie White signed with Green Bay as a free agent in April. End Clyde Simmons, who led the NFL in sacks last season with 19, is the last remaining top player from one of the best defensive lines in recent history. Leonard Renfro of Colorado could step in.

Left linebacker Seth Joyner is a big-play man who returned two interceptions for TDs in 1992. Middle linebacker Byron Evans is underrated and right linebacker William Thomas is a promising young player. Tim Harris comes over from the 49ers to add explosiveness.

The secondary has a Pro Bowler in left cornerback Eric Allen and a lot of question marks. The Eagles are counting on a return to health of cornerback Ben Smith, who sat out 1992 with a knee injury. Age is a concern in the deep secondary, where veteran Wes Hopkins and Andre Waters both are past 31 and coming off leg injuries. Depth is another problem.

SPECIAL TEAMS:: The Eagles improved in this area as return specialist Vai Sikahema provided a spark and first-year coach Larry Pasquale had his units playing with aggressiveness.

Eagles need consistency from Randall Cunningham.

EAGLES VETERAN ROSTER

HEAD COACH—Rich Kotite. Assistant Coaches—Dave Atkins, Zeke Brat-
kowski, Lew Carpenter, Bud Carson, Peter Giunta, Dale Haupt, Bobby
Hammonds, Bill Muir, Larry Pasquale, Jim Vechiarella, Jim Williams,
Richard Wood.

No.	Name	Pos.	Ht.	Wt.	NFL Exp.	College
72	Alexander, David	C	6-3	275	7	Tulsa
21	Allen, Eric	CB	5-10	180	6	Arizona State
62	Baldinger, Brian	G-T	6-4	278	12	Duke
86	Barnett, Fred	WR	6-0	203	4	Arkansas State
50	Bartley, Ephesians	LB	6-2	213	2	Florida
24	Barlow, Corey	CB	5-9	182	1	Auburn
84	Bavaro, Mark	TE	6-4	245	9	Notre Dame
83	Beach, Pat	TE	6-4	250	11	Washington State
39	Brooks, Tony	RB	6-0	230	2	Notre Dame
47	Bruton, Tim	TE	6-3	260	1	Missouri
41	Byars, Keith	TE-RB	6-1	240	8	Ohio State
12	Cunningham, Randall	QB	6-4	205	9	Nevada-Las Vegas
78	Davis, Antone	T	6-4	325	3	Tennessee
56	Evans, Byron	LB	6-2	235	7	Arizona
6	Feagles, Jeff	P	6-1	205	6	Miami
95	Flores, Mike	DE	6-3	256	3	Louisville
61	Floyd, Eric	T-G	6-5	310	4	Auburn
33	Frizzell, William	S	6-3	206	10	North Carolina Central
93	Gardner, Donnie	DL	6-4	270	1	Kentucky
25	Gerhart, Tom	S	6-1	195	1	Ohio U.
81	Green, Roy	WR	6-1	195	15	Henderson State
54	Hager, Britt	LB	6-1	225	5	Texas
91	Harmon, Andy	DT	6-4	265	3	Kent State
97	Harris, Tim	LB	6-6	258	8	Memphis State
80	Hess, Bill	WR	5-8	171	1	West Chester
48	Hopkins, Wes	FS	6-1	215	11	SMU
68	Houston, Brandon	T	6-4	284	1	Oklahoma
76	Hudson, John	G-C	6-2	275	3	Auburn
98	Jeter, Tommy	DT	6-5	282	2	Texas
87	Johnson, Maurice	TE	6-2	243	3	Temple
32	Joseph, James	RB	6-2	222	3	Auburn
59	Joyner, Seth	LB	6-2	240	8	Texas-El Paso
57	Kowalkowski, Scott	LB	6-2	228	3	Notre Dame
42	McMillan, Erik	S	6-2	200	6	Missouri
29	McMillian, Mark	CB	5-7	162	2	Alabama
38	Miano, Rich	S	6-1	200	8	Hawaii
77	Millard, Keith	DT	6-5	263	9	Washington State
3	Petetti, Carl	K	5-7	195	1	Miami
74	Pitts, Mike	DT	6-5	280	11	Alabama
55	Rose, Ken	LB	6-1	215	7	Nevada-Las Vegas
9	Ruzek, Roger	K	6-1	200	7	Weber State
79	Schad, Mike	G	6-5	290	6	Queens (Canada)
75	Selby, Rob	G	6-3	286	3	Auburn
23	Sherman, Heath	RB	6-0	205	5	Texas A&I
22	Sikahema, Vai	WR-KR	5-9	196	8	Brigham Young
96	Simmons, Clyde	DE	6-6	280	8	Western Carolina
26	Smith, Ben	CB	5-11	185	4	Georgia
30	Smith, Otis	CB	5-11	184	3	Missouri
27	Stacy, Siran	RB	5-11	203	2	Alabama
85	Sydner, Jeff	WR-KR	5-6	170	2	Hawaii
51	Thomas, William	LB	6-2	218	3	Texas A&M
71	Thompson, Broderick	T-G	6-5	295	9	Kansas
34	Walker, Herschel	RB	6-1	225	9	Georgia
20	Waters, Andre	SS	5-11	200	10	Cheyney State
11	Weldon, Casey	QB	6-1	200	2	Florida State
89	Williams, Calvin	WR	5-11	190	4	Purdue

TOP DRAFT CHOICES

Rd.	Name	Sel. No.	Pos.	Ht.	Wt.	College
1	Holmes, Lester	19	OT	6-3	284	Jackson State
1	Renfro, Leonard	24	DT	6-2	292	Colorado
2	Bailey, Victor	50	WR	6-2	196	Missouri
3	Frazier, Derrick	75	CB	5-10	178	Texas A&M
3	Reid, Mike	77	S	6-1	218	North Carolina State

Sikahema averaged 12.6 yards on punt returns and broke off a team-record 87-yarder. He's tough and dependable. Rookie Jeff Sydner showed some flashes of return ability.

Punter Jeff Feagles was inconsistent early in the year but came on strong. He had a monster playoff game against the Saints. Kicker Roger Ruzek is solid and dependable, although the Eagles would like to see him improve his kickoffs.

THE ROOKIES: With two No. 1 picks, the Eagles addressed both lines by taking offensive guard Holmes and defensive tackle Renfro. Holmes is a powerful but unpolished 303-pounder who should add some toughness to the Eagles' front line. Renfro will see immediate action as the Eagles attempt to rebuild a defensive front that has been devastated by the death of Brown and the flight of Reggie White.

OUTLOOK: A team in decline. Rick Kotite's Eagles, 11-5 last year, took their shot from 1988-92 and they never made the top. In fact, they never even made the conference title game. Now, they are rebuilding with youth. Cunningham will make plays and there are still some great athletes on defense, but this team is headed in the wrong direction in a hurry.

EAGLE PROFILES

RANDALL CUNNINGHAM 30 6-4 205   Quarterback

Talented but inconsistent . . . Needs to become more of a team leader . . . Struggled through difficult season in 1992 . . . Started quickly, winning NFC Offensive Player of the Month award for September . . . Was benched for one game in midseason because of ineffectiveness . . . Never regained his rhythm or confidence after returning to the lineup . . . Completed 233 of 384 passes for 2,775 yards and 19 touchdowns, with 11 interceptions . . . Subpar play in playoff loss to Dallas raised anew questions about his ability to lead Eagles to Super Bowl . . . Has 1-4 record as a playoff starter . . . Sat out most of 1991 season after suffering severe knee injury in season opener . . . Put together his best season in 1990 with 30 touchdown passes and 942 rushing yards . . . Three-time Pro Bowl selection . . . MVP of 1988 Pro Bowl . . . Second-round pick out of UNLV in 1985 . . . Born March 27, 1963, in Santa Barbara, Cal. . . . 1993 base salary: $2.5 million.

SETH JOYNER 28 6-2 240   **Linebacker**

Intense player is the emotional leader of the Eagles' defense . . . Finished third on the team in tackles with 121 . . . Tied for team lead in interceptions with four, returning two for touchdowns . . . His interception was big play in rally for playoff victory over New Orleans . . . Devastated in June of 1992 by the death of defensive tackle Jerome Brown, one of his closest friends on Eagles . . . Big-play man has scored four touchdowns on returns in last two seasons . . . Made Pro Bowl after breakthrough 1991 season when he led the team with six forced fumbles and four fumble recoveries . . . *Sports Illustrated's* NFL Player of the Year in 1991 . . . Intense competitor who doesn't hesitate to criticize teammates or coaches . . . Plaintiff in lawsuit against NFL, he will be unrestricted free agent after 1993 season . . . Eighth-round draft pick out of UTEP . . . Born Nov. 18, 1964, in Spring Valley, N.Y. . . . 1993 base salary: $1.1 million.

CLYDE SIMMONS 29 6-6 280   **Defensive End**

Led NFL in sacks with 19 . . . Acknowledged as one of the NFL's best defensive linemen after spending years in former teammate Reggie White's shadow . . . Has made last two Pro Bowls . . . Put together big games against Phoenix (three sacks) and the Giants (3½ sacks) . . . Made 96 tackles in '92 . . . Quiet, unassuming manner stands in contrast to his ferocious play on the field . . . Has 71½ sacks in seven NFL seasons . . . Burst into prominence in 1991 when he made 115 tackles and had 13 sacks . . . Durable player has started every Eagles' game since 1987 . . . Ninth-round draft pick out of Western Carolina in 1986 . . . Born Aug. 4, 1964, in Lane, S.C. . . . 1993 base salary: $1.1 million.

ERIC ALLEN 27 5-10 180   **Cornerback**

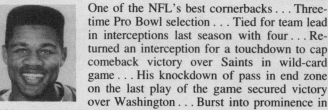

One of the NFL's best cornerbacks . . . Three-time Pro Bowl selection . . . Tied for team lead in interceptions last season with four . . . Returned an interception for a touchdown to cap comeback victory over Saints in wild-card game . . . His knockdown of pass in end zone on the last play of the game secured victory over Washington . . . Burst into prominence in 1989 when he led the NFC in interceptions with eight . . . Has been starter at right cornerback since first game of his rookie season in 1988 . . . Eagles' second-round pick in 1988 out of Arizona State . . . Born Nov. 11, 1965, in San Diego . . . 1993 base salary: $1.15 million.

HERSCHEL WALKER 31 6-1 225   **Running Back**

Found new life with his fourth professional team . . . Became the first Eagle to rush for 1,000 yards since 1985 . . . Finished with 1,070 yards, the second-highest total of his NFL career . . . Had five 100-yard games . . . Made good first impression on his new teammates with back-to-back, 100-yard games in the first two weeks of the season . . . Joined the Eagles as a free agent June 22, 1992, after the Vikings released him . . . Played two-plus seasons for the Vikings, who had traded five players and eight draft picks to acquire him from Dallas . . . Best NFL seasons in Dallas were 1987 and 1988, when he made the Pro Bowl . . . A legend in the old USFL, running for 2,411 yards for the New Jersey Generals in 1985 . . . Off-the-field pursuits include track, ballet and Olympic bobsledding . . . Heisman Trophy winner as a junior at Georgia . . . Born March 3, 1962, in Wrightsville, Ga. . . . 1993 base salary: $1.5 million.

KEITH BYARS 29 6-1 240   Running Back

One of the NFL's most versatile offensive players . . . Made switch to tight end midway through 1992 season after playing running back since high school . . . Caught 56 passes for 502 yards . . . His 38-yard touchdown catch fueled comeback victory over the Giants . . . Ranks fourth on the Eagles' all-time list with 371 career receptions . . . Versatile player who can line up as halfback, fullback, H-back, tight end or wide receiver . . . Threw four touchdown passes in 1990 . . . Second-leading rusher in Ohio State history . . . Sings backup on gospel album recorded by his wife, Margaret Bell Byars . . . Eagles' No. 1 draft pick in 1986, the first selection made by then-coach Buddy Ryan . . . Born Oct. 14, 1963, in Dayton, Ohio . . . Runs free football camp every summer for Dayton-area youngsters . . . 1992 base salary: $825,000.

HEATH SHERMAN 26 6-0 205   Running Back

Became the Eagles' feature runner in the second half of the 1992 season . . . Gained 497 of his 583 yards in final eight games . . . Had the Eagles' four longest touchdown runs of the season, covering 30 (twice), 21 and 17 yards . . . Ran for 109 yards against the Giants . . . Ran for 96 yards and scored touchdown in crucial late-season victory over Washington . . . Produced 105 rushing yards in wild-card victory over the Saints . . . Led Eagles in rushing in 1990 with 685 yards, including back-to-back 100-yard games . . . Struggled in 1991 after reporting overweight and out of shape to training camp . . . Eagles' sixth-round draft choice in 1989 out of Texas A&I . . . Born March 27, 1967, in Wharton, Tex. . . . 1992 base salary: $365,000.

FRED BARNETT 27 6-0 203   Wide Receiver

Burst into prominence in 1992 . . . Led Eagles in receptions (67) and receiving yards (1,083) . . . Named to the Pro Bowl for the first time . . . Caught two touchdown passes in wild-card victory over New Orleans . . . Set career high in receiving yards with 193 on eight catches in regular-season victory over Phoenix . . . Caught nine passes for 161 yards against Seattle . . .

Has nine 100-yard games in three NFL seasons . . . Tremendous athlete with speed, strength and leaping ability . . . Caught eight touchdown passes as a rookie in 1990 . . . Caught a 95-yard TD pass from Randall Cunningham that season that ranks as the second-longest play in Eagles' history . . . A third-round draft pick out of Arkansas State in 1990 . . . Did not play football until his senior year at Rosedale (Miss.) High School because his mother, Earlean, thought it was too dangerous . . . Mississippi state high-jump champion as a senior with a leap of 6-11 . . . Born June 17, 1966, in Shelby, Miss. . . . 1992 base salary: $190,000.

TIM HARRIS 28 6-6 258   Linebacker

Comes to Eagles after two seasons with the 49ers . . . Finished tied for second in the NFL in sacks with 17 . . . Put together six multiple-sack games . . . Added three sacks in the play-offs . . . Relentless pass-rusher with great up-field speed . . . Finished third on the 49ers with 64 tackles . . . Acquired by 49ers from Packers in 1991 in exchange for two No. 2 draft picks . . . Has 75 sacks in seven NFL seasons . . . Packers' fourth-round pick out of Memphis State in 1986 . . . Burst into prominence in 1988 with 13½ sacks . . . Recorded two safeties that season . . . Set career-high with 19½ sacks in 1989 . . . Managed just three sacks in difficult 1991 season . . . Sat out first four games with Packers, then was traded to 49ers . . . Three-year starter at Memphis State, where he played defensive end . . . Born Sept. 10, 1964, in Birmingham, Ala. . . . 1992 base salary: $825,000.

BYRON EVANS 29 6-2 235   Linebacker

Underrated player is one of the NFL's best middle linebackers . . . Led Eagles in tackles in 1992 with 152 . . . Hard hitter who excels against the run . . . Had career-high four interceptions in '92 . . . Credited with 20 tackles in game against Phoenix . . . Made memorable play that game when his jarring hit kept Johnny Bailey out of the end zone as part of remarkable seven-play, goal-line stand . . . Made 16 tackles against 49ers . . . Had big game in victory over Dallas with interception and forced fumble . . . Played major role in defense that ranked No. 1 in most categories in 1991 . . . Overshadowed at times by Pro Bowl teammates Reggie White, Clyde Simmons, Seth Joyner and Eric Allen . . . Leads Eagles in tackles over last five seasons with 559 . . . Became starter for good in 1989 . . . Undersized but productive linebacker at Arizona . . . Eagles' fourth-round draft choice in 1987 . . . Born Feb. 23, 1964, in Phoenix . . . 1993 base salary: $925,000.

CALVIN WILLIAMS 26 5-11 190   Wide Receiver

Smart, productive player is good complement to big-play wide receiver Fred Barnett . . . Led the Eagles in touchdown catches for the second time in his three seasons with seven . . . Caught 42 passes for 598 yards . . . Caught five passes for 108 yards and two TDs against Broncos . . . Lacks deep speed but runs good patterns and has dependable hands . . . Has knack for scoring touchdowns . . . Set Eagles' rookie record with nine TD catches in 1990 . . . Has 19 TD catches in three seasons despite missing much of 1991 with injured shoulder . . . Caught TD pass in waning moments of playoff loss to Dallas last season . . . Has been starter since training camp of rookie season . . . Made smooth transition to NFL after playing in pro-style offense at Purdue . . . Was Eagles' fifth-round draft pick in 1990 . . . Born March 3, 1967, in Baltimore . . . 1993 base salary: $850,000.

ANTONE DAVIS 26 6-4 325   Tackle

Put together decent sophomore season after struggling as a rookie . . . Drastically reduced penalties and sacks allowed . . . Started 15 games . . . Has great size and strength, but foot speed is a liability . . . Expectations were high after the Eagles traded two No. 1 picks to move into position to draft him in 1991 . . . Troubled rookie season included nine penalties, 10 sacks allowed and a one-game benching . . . Was overweight for much of his rookie season, according to Eagles coach Rich Kotite . . . Good run-blocker but susceptible to speedy pass-rushers . . . Consensus All-American at the University of Tennessee . . . His five-year, $4.7-million contract made him the highest-paid offensive lineman in Eagles' history . . . Born Feb. 28, 1967, in Sweetwater, Tenn. . . . 1993 base salary: $450,000.

COACH RICH KOTITE: Led the Eagles to an 11-5 record  and their first playoff victory since 1980 . . . Rewarded with one-year contract extension after the season by owner Norman Braman . . . Now signed to coach the Eagles through 1994 . . . Made difficult decision to bench quarterback Randall Cunningham for one game midway last season . . . Criticized at times by outspoken players such as linebacker Seth Joyner . . . Unlike his predecessor, Buddy Ryan, he is careful not to alienate management, a stance that bothers some players left over from Ryan era . . . Has 21-11 record in his first two seasons, the best two-year record of any coach in Eagles' history . . . Led Eagles to 10-6 record in 1991 when he kept the team together despite injury problems at quarterback position . . . Lost Cunningham for the season in the first game and ended up starting four different quarterbacks . . . His personnel decisions such as trading two No. 1 picks for Antone Davis and signing Pat Ryan as a free agent have been criticized by some . . . Promoted to head coach from offensive coordinator Jan. 8, 1991, the same day Ryan was dismissed . . . Outraged some media members by closing practices . . . In 1990, his only season as offensive coordinator, the Eagles set a team record with 396 points and led the NFL in rushing . . . Spent previous seven seasons as assistant coach with the Jets . . . Began NFL coaching career as assistant to Hank Stram in New Orleans in 1977 . . . Spent next four years on Sam Rutigliano's staff in Cleveland . . . Little All-American tight end at Wagner College in Staten Island, N.Y. . . . Born Oct. 13, 1942, in Brooklyn, N.Y.

GREATEST INTERCEPTOR

He was a bright spot in a dark era in Eagles' history. Bill Bradley played eight seasons for the Eagles. Not once in those eight years did the Eagles manage a winning record, much less contend for a playoff berth.

A free safety from Texas, Bradley joined the Eagles in 1969. The team went 4-9-1 in his first season, which should have been an omen. Philadelphia would go 35-72-4 during Bradley's time with the team.

He was a rangy, instinctive player who had a knack for finding the football. He set a team record with 11 interceptions in 1971. He intercepted nine more passes in 1972. He finished his career with 34 interceptions and 536 return yards, both team records.

INDIVIDUAL EAGLE RECORDS

Rushing

Most Yards Game:	205	Steve Van Buren, vs Pittsburgh, 1949
Season:	1,512	Wilbert Montgomery, 1979
Career:	6,538	Wilbert Montgomery, 1977-84

Passing

Most TD Passes Game:	7	Adrian Burk, vs Washington, 1954
Season:	32	Sonny Jurgensen, 1961
Career:	167	Ron Jaworski, 1977-85

Receiving

Most TD Passes Game:	4	2 times, most recently Ben Hawkins, vs Pittsburgh, 1969
Season:	13	3 times, most recently Mike Quick, 1983
Career:	79	Harold Carmichael, 1971-83

Scoring

Most Points Game:	25	Bobby Walston, vs Washington, 1954
Season:	116	Paul McFadden, 1984
Career:	881	Bobby Walston, 1951-62
Most TDs Game:	4	6 times, most recently Wilbert Montgomery, vs Washington, 1979
Season:	18	Steve Van Buren, 1945
Career:	79	Harold Carmichael, 1971-83

PHOENIX CARDINALS

TEAM DIRECTORY: Pres.: William V. Bidwill; VP/GM: Larry Wilson; Exec. VP: Joe Rhein; Dir. Pro Personnel: Erik Widmark; Dir. College Scouting: Bob Ackles; Dir. Pub. Rel.: Paul Jensen; Media Coordinator: Greg Gladysiewski; Head Coach: Joe Bugel. Home field: Sun Devil Stadium (73,521). Colors: Cardinal red, white and black.

SCOUTING REPORT

OFFENSE: The Cardinals have the talent to score points. If they can get more consistent play from the quarterback spot, they will be a dangerous team.

Cardinals chose Georgia's Garrison Hearst with No. 4.

Wide receiver Gary Clark was imported from Washington as a free agent to spruce up the passing game. Clark combines with speedy Randal Hill and dependable Ricky Proehl to form an imposing trio of wide receivers.

The running game was the problem in 1992 as the Cardinals ranked 26th in the NFL in rushing offense. The Cardinals hope they solved the problem with the addition of Georgia running back Garrison Hearst.

The offensive line is another trouble spot. The Cardinals have a solid left tackle in Luis Sharpe but age, injuries and inexperience conspired to turn the rest of the line into a area of weakness. Second-year man Ed Cunningham looks promising and the Cardinals will try to squeeze another season out of Mark May.

The key, of course, is the quarterback. Chris Chandler played well at times last season but lacked consistency. The Cardinals went hard after Joe Montana but failed. Timm Rosenbach's once-promising career has lost its luster and Tony Sacca, their top pick in 1992, isn't ready to contribute. But they hope to have a solution in Steve Beuerlein, the Cowboy backup signed as a free agent.

DEFENSE: Hope springs in the desert. The Cardinals have rebuilt their line with young players such as Eric Swann, Michael Bankston, Mike Jones and Reuben Davis. Swann looks like an emerging star and the rest of the "Young Guns," as they are called, can make life miserable for opposing offenses.

The linebacking corps is solid when healthy. But both outside linebackers, Ken Harvey and Freddie Joe Nunn, were out with knee injuries at the end of 1992. Harvey, the team's best pass-rusher, might not be back until after the start of this season. Eric Hill is a strong middle linebacker.

The secondary took a shot when Pro Bowl safety Tim McDonald signed with San Francisco as a free agent. The Cardinals replaced him with Chuck Cecil, a Pro Bowl pick from Green Bay.

The cornerbacks are solid. Aeneas Williams and Robert Massey are solid coverage men. Massey emerged as a big-play man with three interception returns for TDs last year. The Cardinals need depth in this area.

SPECIAL TEAMS: The Cardinals have one of the NFL's best punters in Rich Camarillo, who made the Pro Bowl for the fourth time in his career.

Another Pro Bowler was return specialist Johnny Bailey, who averaged 24.6 yards on kickoff returns and an NFL-high 13.2 yards bringing back punts.

Kicker Greg Davis suffered through a difficult season, making

CARDINALS VETERAN ROSTER

HEAD COACH—Joe Bugel. Assistant Coaches—Ted Cottrell, Bobby Jackson, Jim Johnson, Steve Loney, John Matsko, LeCharles McDaniel, Mike Murphy, Ted Plumb, Joe Pascale, Jerry Rhome, Pete Rodriguez, Bob Rogucki, Fritz Shurmur.

No.	Name	Pos.	Ht.	Wt.	NFL Exp.	College
20	Bailey, Johnny	RB-KR	5-8	187	4	Texas A&I
63	Bankston, Michael	DL	6-1	285	2	Sam Houston State
70	Baxley, Rob	T	6-5	287	2	Iowa
7	Beuerlein, Steve	QB	6-2	209	6	Notre Dame
25	Blount, Eric	RB-KR	5-9	190	2	North Carolina
42	Booty, John	S	6-0	180	6	Texas Christian
54	Braxton, David	OLB	6-2	240	5	Wake Forest
33	Brown, Ivory Lee	RB	6-2	245	2	Arkansas-Pine Bluff
16	Camarillo, Rich	P	5-11	195	13	Washington
26	Cecil, Chuck	S	6-0	190	6	Arizona
37	Centers, Larry	RB	6-0	212	4	Steven F. Austin
17	Chandler, Chris	QB	6-4	220	6	Washington
84	Clark, Gary	WR	5-9	173	9	James Madison
59	Cunningham, Ed	C	6-3	290	2	Washington
64	Cunningham, Rick	T	6-6	307	3	Texas A&M
21	Davis, Dexter	CB	5-10	180	3	Clemson
5	Davis, Greg	K	6-0	195	7	Citadel
93	Davis, Reuben	DL	6-4	292	6	North Carolina
22	Duerson, Dave	S	6-1	215	11	Notre Dame
83	Edwards, Anthony	WR	5-9	188	5	N. Mexico Highlands
94	Faulkner, Jeff	DE	6-4	290	4	Southern
31	Harris, Odie	S	6-0	190	6	Sam Houston State
56	Harvey, Ken	OLB	6-2	225	6	California
91	Henson, David	DL	6-2	280	1	Arkansas Central
58	Hill, Eric	ILB	6-2	250	5	Louisiana State
81	Hill, Randal	WR	5-10	180	3	Miami (Fla.)
97	Hyche, Steve	ILB	6-2	245	4	Livingston
41	Jackson, Robert	WR	6-1	190	1	Central State (Ohio)
53	Jax, Garth	ILB	6-3	250	8	Florida State
86	Jones, Ernie	WR	6-0	200	6	Indiana
55	Jones, Jock	OLB	6-2	245	4	Virginia Tech
75	Jones, Mike	DE	6-4	287	3	North Carolina State
57	Kauahi, Kani	C	6-3	275	11	Hawaii
44	LaDuke, Nathan	S	5-11	200	1	Arizona State
28	Lofton, Steve	CB	5-9	195	3	Texas A&M
29	Lynch, Lorenzo	CB	5-10	200	7	Cal-Sacramento
40	Massey, Robert	CB	5-10	185	5	North Carolina Central
73	May, Mark	G	6-6	300	3	Pittsburgh
50	Nunn, Freddie Joe	OLB	6-4	255	9	Mississippi
27	Oldham, Chris	CB	5-9	183	4	Oregon
87	Proehl, Ricky	WR	6-0	190	4	Wake Forest
89	Reeves, Walter	TE	6-3	265	5	Auburn
82	Rolle, Butch	HB-TE	6-4	250	8	Michigan State
3	Rosenbach, Timm	QB	6-1	215	4	Washington State
79	Rucker, Keith	DL	6-3	325	2	Ohio Wesleyan
19	Sacca, Tony	QB	6-5	230	2	Penn State
32	Searcy, George	RB	5-11	225	1	East Tennessee State
67	Sharpe, Luis	T	6-4	295	12	UCLA
52	Small, Jessie	OLB	6-3	240	5	Eastern Kentucky
61	Smith, Lance	G	6-3	286	9	Louisiana State
90	Stowe, Tyronne	ILB	6-1	247	7	Rutgers
98	Swann, Eric	DL	6-4	310	3	None
95	Taylor, Alophonso	DL	6-1	325	1	Temple
85	Ware, Derek	HB-TE	6-2	255	2	Central State (Okla.)
35	Williams, Aeneas	CB	5-10	187	3	Southern
60	Williams, Willie	T	6-6	295	3	Louisiana State
80	Wolf, Joe	OL	6-6	296	5	Boston College
92	Wright, Willie	TE-HB	6-4	240	2	Wyoming
38	Zordich, Michael	S	6-1	201	7	Penn State

			TOP DRAFT CHOICES			
Rd.	Name	Sel. No.	Pos.	Ht.	Wt.	College
1	Hearst, Garrison	3	RB	5-9	205	Georgia
1	Dye, Ernest	18	OT	6-6	330	South Carolina
2	Coleman, Ben	32	OT	6-5	314	Wake Forest
4	Moore, Ronald	87	RB	5-10	228	Pittsburgh State
6	Wallerstedt, Brett	143	LB	6-0	237	Arizona State

only 13 of 26 field-goal attempts and misfiring four times from inside the 30.

The Cardinals' coverage teams are strong. They were second in the NFL in punt coverage (6.4 yards allowed) and fourth in kickoff coverage (18.3 yards allowed).

THE ROOKIES: The Cardinals might have landed the best player in the draft when they traded up one spot to take Hearst. He has been favorably compared to Dallas' Emmitt Smith. The Cardinals also restocked their offensive line by taking tackles Earnest Dye of South Carolina and Ben Coleman of Wake Forest.

OUTLOOK: Joe Bugel, his coaching staff and some members of the front office are under pressure to win this season, and the Cardinals, 4-12 last year, just might be able to do it. With the Giants, Eagles and Redskins in apparent decline, the Cardinals could finally become a playoff contender in the NFC East.

CARDINAL PROFILES

STEVE BEUERLEIN 28 6-2 209 Quarterback

Signed with Cardinals as free agent after two years with Cowboys . . . Agreed to three-year, $7.5-million contract . . . Projected as Cardinals' starting quarterback . . . Spent all of 1992 as backup to Troy Aikman for Super Bowl champion Cowboys . . . Made his mark in 1991 when he replaced the injured Aikman and led Cowboys to five consecutive victories and their first playoff berth since 1985 . . . Threw a TD pass in each of those five victories . . . Threw 111 consecutive passes without an interception during 1991 season . . . Spent four seasons with Raiders, although he saw action in just two of them . . . Sat out rookie season in 1987 on injured-reserve list and did not play in 1990 after bitter contract dispute . . . Started seven games for Raiders in 1989 and threw for 375 yards in victory over Rams . . . Raiders traded him to Cowboys for fifth-round draft pick . . . Raiders' fourth-round pick out of Notre Dame in 1987 . . . A four-year starter for Fighting Irish . . . Born March 7, 1965, in Hollywood, Cal. . . . 1992 base salary: $2 million.

MICHAEL BANKSTON 23 6-1 285   Defensive Lineman

Key part of Cardinals' rebuilding program . . . Started final six games as a rookie and helped the team's defensive resurgence . . . Finished with 24 tackles and two sacks . . . Joins with Eric Swann and Mike Jones to form "Young Guns" trio on defensive line . . . Strong inside player who ties up blocker and frees teammates to make tackles . . . Squat, powerful player is a natural nose tackle . . . Cardinals' fourth-round draft choice in 1992 out of Sam Houston State . . . Ranks third on his school's all-time list with 41 tackles for losses . . . Three-time All-Southland Conference selection . . . Born March 12, 1970, in East Bernard, Tex. . . . 1993 base salary: $200,000.

ERIC SWANN 23 6-4 310   Defensive Lineman

Intriguing player appears on the verge of stardom . . . Became a defensive force after joining the starting lineup for the final 11 games in 1992 . . . Made 70 tackles, including 11 for losses . . . Has remarkable blend of size, speed and strength, but still is learning NFL game . . . Never played a down of college football . . . Slowed in his rookie season of 1991 and again early in 1992 by injuries and inexperience . . . Sat out first four games of rookie season after knee surgery . . . Part-time player as a rookie who finished with 22 tackles and four sacks . . . Signed with North Carolina State but failed to qualify academically . . . Worked odd jobs and played for Bay State (Lynn, Mass.) Titans, a minor-league football team . . . Cardinals were fascinated and took him with the sixth overall pick in the 1991 draft . . . First non-college player drafted by the NFL since Emil "Six-Yard" Sitko by the Rams in 1946 . . . Born Aug. 16, 1970, in Swann Station, N.C. . . . 1993 base salary: $475,000.

FREDDIE JOE NUNN 31 6-4 255   Linebacker

Veteran influence on young defense . . . Hoping to bounce back from injury-marred 1992 season . . . Sat out last five games with knee injury . . . Finished with only 28 tackles and four sacks . . . Sack total was his lowest since his rookie season in 1985 . . . Forced two fumbles, recovered one . . . Returned to outside linebacker in 1991 after spending four seasons at defensive end . . . Led Cardinals in forced fumbles with six and was second in sacks with six . . . Has 59½ sacks in eight NFL seasons . . . One of the NFL's best pass-rushers in 1988, with 14 sacks . . . Cardinals' No. 1 pick in 1985 out of Mississippi . . . Cousin of boxer Michael Nunn . . . Born April 9, 1962, in Noxubee, Miss. . . . 1993 base salary: $1.2 million.

ERIC HILL 26 6-2 250   Linebacker

Run-stuffer in middle of Cardinals' defense . . . Key man in defensive surge over last 11 weeks in 1992 . . . Helped Cardinals hold eight of their final 11 opponents to under 100 rushing yards . . . Finished with 104 tackles, second on team . . . Combined with fellow inside linebacker Tyrone Stowe for 80 tackles over last six weeks . . . Led Cardinals in tackles in 1991 with 107 . . . Returned a fumble 85 yards for a touchdown against the Rams . . . Has made 330 tackles in first four NFL seasons . . . Starter since first game of rookie season in 1989 . . . Emotional player who once was ejected from a game against Dallas in 1990 following consecutive personal-foul penalties . . . Cardinals' No. 1 pick in 1989 out of LSU . . . Three-year starter at LSU . . . Born Nov. 14, 1966, in Galveston, Tex. . . . 1992 base salary: $425,000.

AENEAS WILLIAMS 25 5-10 187   Cornerback

Smooth coverage man is regarded as one of the NFL's best young cornerbacks . . . Struggled a bit in 1992 after sensational rookie season . . . Started all 16 games and had 48 tackles and three interceptions . . . Surrendered some big plays with ill-advised gambles . . . Led team with 13 passes defensed . . . One of the best rookies in the NFL in 1991 when he tied for the NFC lead with six interceptions . . . First rookie to hold or share NFC lead in that category since Everson Walls in 1981 . . . Confident player who made an interception in his first NFL exhibition game and first NFL regular-season game . . . Starred at Southern University . . . Former walk-on who finished college career with 20 interceptions . . . Cardinals' third-round pick in 1991 . . . Born Jan. 29, 1968, in New Orleans . . . 1993 base salary: $250,000.

ROBERT MASSEY 26 5-10 185   Cornerback

Emerged as standout in second season with Cardinals . . . Led team in interceptions with five, and returned three of them for touchdowns to become just the 11th player in NFL history to manage that feat . . . Returned two interceptions for touchdowns in upset of Redskins . . . Also returned interception for score against Falcons . . . Acquired by Cardinals before 1991 season from Saints in trade for guard Derek Kennard . . . Started five games for Cardinals that season . . . Had five interceptions for the Saints in 1990 . . . Named to *Pro Football Weekly's* All-Rookie team after starting all 16 games in 1989 . . . Saints' second-round draft pick in 1989 . . . Made 19 interceptions during standout career at North Carolina Central . . . Born Feb. 17, 1967, in Rock Hill, S.C. . . . 1992 base salary: $450,000.

LUIS SHARPE 33 6-4 295   Tackle

The anchor of the Cardinals' offensive line . . . His value was evident when the Cardinals named him a transition player during the free-agency period following last season . . . Started 15 games and put together one of his best seasons . . . Accomplished pass-blocker excels against the NFL's best speed-rushers . . . Cardinals would like to see him improve his run-blocking . . . Pro Bowl pick after 1987, 1988 and 1989 seasons . . . Has been a starter for the Cardinals since his rookie season of 1982 . . . Fluent in two languages, he sometimes does interviews with Spanish radio stations . . . Cardinals' No. 1 pick in 1982 out of UCLA . . . Born June 16, 1960, in Havana, Cuba . . . Family moved to Detroit when he was six . . . 1992 base salary: $975,000.

KEN HARVEY 28 6-2 225   Linebacker

Hoping to bounce back from injury-shortened 1992 season . . . Sat out last six games after suffering severe knee injury against Atlanta Nov. 15 . . . Projected to return to action early in 1993 season . . . Big-play man was missed by Cardinals . . . The team's best pure pass-rusher with outside burst . . . Still tied for team lead in sacks with six . . . Has 38 sacks in five NFL seasons . . . Recognition has been slow to arrive for this underrated player because of the Cardinals' low profile . . . Led Cardinals in sacks with 10 in 1990 and nine in 1991 . . . Weightlifting legend at University of California . . . Cardinals' No. 1 pick in 1988 . . . MVP of both Senior Bowl and East-West Shrine Game after senior season . . . Born May 6, 1965, in Austin, Tex. . . . 1993 base salary: $1.5 million.

CHRIS CHANDLER 27 6-4 220   Quarterback

Emerged as the Cardinals' offensive leader in 1992 . . . Seized opportunity when starter Timm Rosenbach was injured in second game . . . Started 13 of final 14 games and set career bests in pass attempts (413), completions (245), yards (2,832), completion percentage (59.3) and touchdown passes (15) . . . Led Cardinals to upset of Redskins with game-winning, 85-yard touchdown drive in final 41 seconds . . . Threw three touchdown passes in upset of 49ers . . . Completed 21 of 30 passes for 224 yards in victory over Rams . . . Claimed by Cardinals on waivers Nov. 5, 1991, following release by Bucs . . . Acquired by Bucs from Indianapolis in exchange for No. 1 draft pick . . . Colts' third-round draft pick in 1988 after starring at Washington . . . Tied NCAA record with four TD passes in one quarter . . . Born Oct. 12, 1965, in Everett, Wash. . . . 1993 base salary: $900,000.

RICKY PROEHL 25 6-0 190   Wide Receiver

One of the NFL's best possession receivers . . . Led Cardinals in receptions for the second time in his three-year career . . . Caught 60 passes for 744 yards and three TDs . . . His streak of 33 consecutive games with a reception was snapped by Cowboys but he bounced back with 100-yard games the next two weeks . . . Has 171 catches in three NFL seasons . . . Remarkably consistent player has collected 56, 55 and 60 receptions in his three NFL seasons . . . Set Cardinals' rookie record with 56 catches in 1990, leading all NFL first-year receivers . . . Caught seven passes for 132 yards against Eagles in final game of rookie season . . . Caught 25 touchdown passes in career at Wake Forest . . . Cardinals' third-round draft pick in 1990 . . . Born March 7, 1968, in Belle Mead, N.J. . . . 1992 base salary: $220,000.

GARY CLARK 31 5-9 173   Wide Receiver

Jumped to Cardinals as a free agent after eight outstanding seasons with Redskins . . . Signed three-year deal for $6 million that made him the second-highest paid wide receiver in the NFL . . . Adds instant credibility to Cardinals' receiving corps . . . Caught 64 passes for 912 yards and five TDs in final season with Redskins . . . Generated more than 1,000 receiving yards in each of previous three seasons . . . Never has caught fewer than 56 passes in an NFL season . . . Best season was 1991, with 70 catches for 1,340 yards and 10 TDs . . . Played two years for Jacksonville Bulls of USFL . . . Signed by Redskins as a free agent in 1985 . . . All-time leading receiver at James Madison University . . . Born May 1, 1962, in Dublin, Va. . . . 1993 base salary: $2 million.

CHUCK CECIL 28 6-0 190   Safety

Signed by the Cardinals as a free agent after five seasons with Green Bay . . . Hard-hitting sentry in the back of the secondary . . . Second on the team in tackles with 105 . . . Led team in interceptions with four . . . Unleashed two jarring hits on David Meggett of the Giants . . . Sarcastically called "Rhodes Scholar" by Eagles' coach Rich Kotite after he made derogatory comments about Herschel Walker . . . Has started every game the last two seasons . . . Made 110 tackles in 1991 . . . Missed 13 games in 1989 and 1990 with hamstring ailment . . . Had four interceptions playing part-time as a rookie in 1988 . . . Packers' fourth-round pick out of Arizona in 1988 . . . Set Pac-10 record with 21 career interceptions . . . Born Nov. 8, 1964, in Red Bluff, Cal. . . . 1992 base salary: $390,000.

COACH JOE BUGEL: Under pressure to produce a winner in his fourth season . . . Upbeat, positive coach hasn't been able to turn the Cardinals around . . . Suffered through back-to-back 4-12 seasons in 1991 and 1992 . . . Has 13-35 record in three seasons in Phoenix . . . Saw signs of hope in 1992 when defensive resurgence kept Cardinals competitive in most games in second half of season . . . With victories over Washington and San Francisco, the Cardinals beat the winners of three of the previous four Super Bowls . . . Cardinals' schedule in 1992 featured opponents with combined .570 winning percentage, highest in the NFL . . . Needs to post winning season in 1993 to avoid become the eighth ex-Cardinals coach since 1977 . . . Enthusiastic coach is popular with his players . . . Spent nine seasons as assistant coach in Washington . . . Developed the "Hogs" of the offensive line and helped the Redskins win two Super Bowl titles . . . An assistant in Detroit (1975-76) and Houston (1977-80) before joining Joe Gibbs' staff in Washington . . . Assistant coach at Ohio State, Iowa State, Navy and Western Kentucky . . . Roomed with Falcons' coach Jerry Glanville when both were assistants at Western Kentucky . . . Played in Little League World Series . . . Born March 10, 1940, in Pittsburgh.

GREATEST INTERCEPTOR

These days, Larry Wilson is a decision-maker with the Cardinals as their general manager. In his playing days, Wilson was a big-play-maker for the Cardinals. Playing from 1960 through 1972, Wilson was regarded as one of the best defensive backs in the NFL. He made the Pro Bowl eight times between 1962 and 1970.

Wilson was the prototype ballhawk. He finished his career with 52 interceptions and once went seven consecutive games with at least one interception. Wilson also holds Cardinals' team records for interception-return yardage with an even 800 and for interceptions returned for touchdowns with five. He returned two interceptions more than 90 yards for touchdowns, a 96-yarder against Cleveland and a 91-yarder against Philadelphia.

Wilson's best season probably was 1966, when he tied for the NFL lead in interceptions with 10 and went seven games in a row with an interception. And he returned two interceptions for TDs.

Wilson's best game was in 1965 against Cleveland. He picked off three passes, returning one 96 yards for a touchdown, and set a team record for total return yardage with 155.

INDIVIDUAL CARDINAL RECORDS

Rushing

Most Yards Game:	203	John David Crow, vs Pittsburgh, 1960	
Season:	1,605	Ottis Anderson, 1979	
Career:	7,999	Ottis Anderson, 1979-86	

Passing

Most TD Passes Game:	6	3 times, most recently Charley Johnson, vs New Orleans, 1969
Season:	28	2 times, most recently Neil Lomax, 1984
Career:	205	Jim Hart, 1966-82

Receiving

Most TD Passes Game:	5	Bob Shaw, vs Baltimore, 1950
Season:	15	Sonny Randle, 1960
Career:	66	Roy Green, 1979-1990

Scoring

Most Points Game:	40	Ernie Nevers, vs Chicago, 1929
Season:	117	2 times, most recently Neil O'Donoghue, 1984
Career:	1,380	Jim Bakken, 1962-78
Most TDs Game:	6	Ernie Nevers, vs Chicago, 1929
Season:	17	John David Crow, 1962
Career:	69	Roy Green, 1979-1990

SAN FRANCISCO 49ERS

TEAM DIRECTORY: Owner: Edward J. DeBartolo Jr.; Pres: Carmen Policy; VP-Football Adm.: John McVay; Dir. Pub. Rel.: Rodney Knox; Head Coach: George Seifert. Home field: Candlestick Park (66,445). Colors: 49er gold and scarlet.

SCOUTING REPORT

OFFENSE: Year after year after year, the 49ers are among the most explosive teams in the NFL. This year should be no different.

Quarterback Steve Young is the reigning NFL Player of the Year. He led the NFL in passing, scrambled his way to 537 yards, and is at the top of his multi-faceted game.

The running game was rejuvenated by Ricky Watters, who collected 1,013 yards in his first season as a starter. He's also a fine receiver. Tom Rathman remains a top fullback, a solid blocker, hard inside runner and decent receiver. Amp Lee is a talented backup running back.

The receivers are excellent. Jerry Rice continues his assault on the NFL record books. John Taylor missed much of 1992 with an injury but is expected back. Depth is a bit of concern after Mike Sherrard fled to the Giants as a free agent. Tight end Brent Jones is a Pro Bowler because of his receiving skills but he's a decent blocker, too. Veteran wide receiver Mervyn Fernandez was acquired from the Raiders.

The line is the unheralded key to this offensive show. Steve Wallace and Harris Barton are top-shelf tackles. Guy McIntyre is a powerful run-blocker at left guard and center Jesse Sapulo remains at the top of his game.

DEFENSE: Big changes here. The 49ers lost a stud when defensive end Pierce Holt fled to Atlanta as a free agent.

Michael Carter is still solid against the run, but the 49ers need Ted Washington and Dennis Brown to step up and play more consistently. Kevin Fagan is a solid end and Garin Veris, signed as a free agent last September, could emerge as a pass-rush threat after a year in the defensive system. Rookies Dana Stubblefield of Kansas and Todd Kelly of Tennessee add depth.

Bill Romanowski is an excellent outside linebacker. Tim Harris is the team's designated pass-rusher and Keith DeLeon and Mike Walter are solid against the run. But the 49ers lack speed in this area.

Stats and leadership made Steve Young Player of the Year.

The secondary got a big boost with the addition of Pro Bowl safety Tim McDonald, who was signed as a free agent. He will team with second-year man Dana Hall to form an imposing tandem of deep backs. McDonald, who made the Pro Bowl three years in a row for Phoenix, is a hard hitter with good instincts for the position.

Don Griffin is a top coverage man at cornerback. Eric Davis is solid at the other corner and Merton Hanks is a dependable nickel back.

SPECIAL TEAMS: A problem area. Every year, the 49ers vow to improve in this area.

Kicker Mike Cofer is inconsistent. He made some big kicks in 1992 after nearly losing his job, but he remains a concern.

Punter Klaus Wilmsmeyer was nothing special, averaging fewer than 40 yards per kick. The coverage teams are decent but not spectacular.

Dexter Carter is a dangerous return man but is prone to injuries.

49ERS VETERAN ROSTER

HEAD COACH—George Seifert. Assistant Coaches—Jerry Attaway, Dwaine Board, Jeff Fisher, Carl Jackson, Alan Lowry, John Marshall, Bobb McKittrick, Bill McPherson, Mike Shanahan, Ray Sherman, Mike Solari, Eric Wright, Bob Zeman.

No.	Name	Pos.	Ht.	Wt.	NFL Exp.	College
21	Alexander, Mike	WR	6-3	190	3	Penn State
79	Barton, Harris	T-T	6-4	286	7	North Carolina
67	Birch, Swift	DE	6-4	270	1	Temple
65	Boatswain, Harry	T	6-4	295	3	New Haven
71	Bollinger, Brian	G	6-5	285	2	North Carolina
13	Bono, Steve	QB	6-4	211	9	UCLA
15	Bridewell, Jeff	QB	6-5	220	1	Cal-Davis
96	Brown, Dennis	DE	6-4	290	4	Washington
27	Brown, Hurlie	S	6-0	195	1	Miami (Fla.)
35	Carter, Dexter	RB	5-9	174	4	Florida State
95	Carter, Michael	NT	6-2	285	10	SMU
76	Childs, Jason	T	6-4	285	1	North Dakota
6	Cofer, Mike	K	6-1	190	6	North Carolina State
85	Covington, Tom	TE	6-3	241	2	Georgia Tech
25	Davis, Eric	CB	5-11	178	4	Jacksonville State
63	Deese, Derrick	G	6-3	270	2	USC
59	DeLong, Keith	LB	6-2	250	5	Tennessee
54	Donahue, Mitch	LB	6-2	254	3	Wyoming
71	Downing, Tim	DE	6-5	284	1	Washington State
51	Dressel, Robert	C	6-4	290	1	Purdue
31	Evans, Kevin	WR	6-4	190	1	San Jose State
75	Fagan, Kevin	DE	6-3	265	7	Miami (Fla.)
17	Faison, Derrick	WR	6-4	210	2	Howard
57	Faryniarz, Brett	LB	6-3	230	5	San Diego State
88	Fernandez, Mervyn	WR	6-3	200	7	San Jose State
67	Foster, Roy	G	6-4	290	12	USC
31	Gash, Thane	S	5-11	198	5	East Tennessee State
98	Goss, Antonio	LB	6-4	228	4	North Carolina
24	Grant, Alan	CB	5-10	187	4	Stanford
29	Griffin, Don	CB	6-0	176	8	Middle Tenn. State
77	Haggins, Odell	NT	6-2	275	2	Florida State
28	Hall, Dana	S	6-2	206	2	Washington
36	Hanks, Merton	CB	6-2	185	3	Iowa
56	Harrison, Martin	LB	6-5	240	2	Washington
38	Hillman, Jay	FB	6-0	230	1	Boston
20	Holland, John Robert	CB	5-10	186	1	Sacramento State
23	Johnson, Barry	WR	6-2	197	2	Maryland
55	Johnson, John	LB	6-3	230	3	Clemson
84	Jones, Brent	TE	6-4	230	8	Santa Clara
90	Jordan, Darin	LB	6-2	245	4	Northeastern
68	LaBounty, Matt	DE	6-4	254	1	Oregon
22	Lee, Amp	RB	5-11	200	2	Florida State
43	Logan, Marc	RB	6-0	212	7	Kentucky
20	Loville, Derek	RB	5-10	205	3	Oregon
46	McDonald, Tim	S	6-2	207	7	USC
26	McGruder, Michael	CB	5-10	190	5	Kent State
62	McIntyre, Guy	G	6-3	265	10	Georgia
52	Moss, Anthony	LB	6-4	238	1	Florida State
51	Mott, Joe	LB	6-4	255	3	Iowa
14	Musgrave, Bill	QB	6-2	205	3	Oregon
77	Parrish, James	T	6-6	315	1	Temple
69	Peery, Ryan	DE	6-5	265	1	California
49	Popson, Ted	TE	6-4	250	1	Portland State
44	Rathman, Tom	FB	6-1	232	8	Nebraska
80	Rice, Jerry	WR	6-2	200	9	Miss. Valley State
91	Roberts, Larry	DE	6-3	275	8	Alabama
53	Romanowski, Bill	LB	6-4	240	7	Boston College
38	Russell, Damien	S	6-1	204	2	Virginia Tech

continued on page 479

TOP DRAFT CHOICES

Rd.	Name	Sel. No.	Pos.	Ht.	Wt.	College
1	Stubblefield, Dana	26	DT	6-2	288	Kansas
1	Kelly, Todd	27	DE	6-3	260	Tennessee
2	Hardy, Adrian	48	CB	6-0	194	NW Louisiana
5	Smith, Artie	116	DT	6-4	291	Louisiana Tech
6	Dalman, Chris	166	G	6-4	293	Stanford

Alan Grant handles most of the punt returns but averaged just 8.6 yards last season.

THE ROOKIES: With two No. 1 picks, the 49ers went right after their problems on the defensive line. They selected Stubblefield, a powerful inside player, and Kelly, a productive pass-rusher. Another impact player might have arrived in the second round in the person of Northwest Louisiana defensive back Adrian Hardy.

OUTLOOK: George Seifert's 49ers are still the team to beat in the division. They might not go 14-2 again, but they have too much talent and confidence to finish anywhere but at the top. This team just knows how to win.

49ER PROFILES

STEVE YOUNG 31 6-2 200   **Quarterback**

Escaped from Joe Montana's imposing shadow with a breakthrough season in 1992 . . . Named NFL Player of the Year after leading the 49ers to a 14-2 record . . . Won NFL passing title for second year in a row with a 107 rating . . . Passed for 3,465 yards and 25 TDs, with only seven interceptions . . . One of the NFL's best scramblers, he also ran for 537 yards and four TDs . . . Named NFC Offensive Player of the Week after running for one TD and passing for two in rallying 49ers over Saints . . . Long-time backup to the legendary Montana . . . Moved into starting lineup in 1991 . . . Won NFL passing title with 101.8 rating but missed final six games with knee injury . . . Despite his impressive statistics, 49ers were just 5-5 in his 10 starts . . . Acquired

by 49ers from Bucs in exchange for No. 2 and No. 4 picks in 1987 draft-day deal . . . Played two seasons in Tampa and two seasons with Los Angeles Express of the USFL . . . Second in Heisman Trophy balloting (to Mike Rozier) as a senior at BYU in 1983 . . . Born Oct. 11, 1961, in Salt Lake City . . . 1992 base salary: $2.5 million.

TIM McDONALD 28 6-2 207   Safety

Signed with the 49ers as a free agent . . . Made joining a winning team his top priority . . . Agreed to four-year, $10-million deal . . . Returns to native northern California . . . One of the NFL's best defensive backs . . . Made the Pro Bowl for the third time after the 1992 season . . . Led Cardinals in tackles for the fourth time in five seasons with 107 . . . Hard hitter with good range and instincts . . . Has averaged 121 tackles in five seasons as a starter . . . Named franchise player by the Cardinals but was allowed to become unrestricted free agent because he had been named a plaintiff in a lawsuit against the NFL . . . Another in long line of star defensive backs at USC . . . Cardinals' second-round draft pick in 1987 . . . Born Jan. 6, 1965, in Fresno, Cal. . . . 1993 base salary: $1.8 million.

RICKY WATTERS 24 6-1 212   Running Back

Burst on the scene in 1992 . . . Generated 1,013 rushing yards and ran for nine TDs in his first NFL season . . . Made the Pro Bowl despite missing much of December with a shoulder injury . . . Caught 43 passes for 405 yards and two TDs . . . Named NFC Offensive Player of the Week after 163-yard rushing game against Falcons . . . Quick, instinctive runner . . . Good receiver who fits nicely in 49ers' offensive scheme . . . Emotional player is regarded as inspiration to older, more sedate teammates . . . Sat out entire 1991 season with foot injury . . . 49ers' second-round pick in 1991 out of Notre Dame . . . Standout all-purpose player in college . . . Set school record by returning three punts for TDs . . . Averaged 5.5 yards per rush and scored 22 TDs . . . Born April 7, 1969, in Harrisburg, Pa. . . . 1992 base salary: $250,000.

JERRY RICE 30 6-2 200   Wide Receiver

The greatest wide receiver in NFL history... Continues his relentless assault on the record book... Became the NFL's all-time TD reception leader with 103, breaking Steve Largent's old mark of 100... Holds team records for career receiving yardage (10,273) and total TDs (108)... Caught 84 passes for 1,201 yards in 1992; it was his seventh straight season over 1,000 yards... Seven-time Pro Bowl selection... Remarkable durability... Has not missed a non-strike game in his career, 124 and counting... Tremendous hands, concentration, speed, moves after the catch... NFL's MVP in 1987 after catching 22 TD passes in strike-shortened 12-game season... 49ers' No. 1 pick in 1985 out of Mississippi Valley State... Born Oct. 13, 1962, in Starkville, Miss.... 1993 base salary: $2 million.

STEVE WALLACE 28 6-5 278   Tackle

Recognition finally came his way in 1992... Named to the Pro Bowl for the first time... Started all 16 games at left tackle... His consistent blocking helped the 49ers lead the NFL in yards (387.2) and points (26.9) per game... Named transition player during free-agency period... Versatile player has started at both tackle positions... Improved footwork and technique has made him a better pass-blocker at left tackle spot... Starter at left tackle in 1992 and 1991, at right tackle in 1990, at left tackle in 1988... Sat out much of 1989 with ankle problems... A backup in 1987 and 1986... 49ers' fourth-round pick in 1986 out of Auburn... His blocking in college helped Bo Jackson win the Heisman... All-SEC selection as a senior... Born Dec. 27, 1964, in Atlanta... 1993 base salary: $975,000.

JOHN TAYLOR 31 6-1 185   Wide Receiver

Has spent his career in the shadow of teammate Jerry Rice... Accomplished player in his own right... One of the most dangerous open-field runners in the NFL... Missed eight games in 1992 with fractured fibula but finished with 25 receptions, 428 yards, three TDs... Has fashioned two 1,000-yard receiving seasons... Caught 64 passes for 1,011 yards and nine TDs in 1991 . . . Caught 60 for 1,077 and 10 TDs in 1989 . . . Also a dangerous punt-returner . . . Two-time Pro Bowl selection, once as receiver, once as returner . . . Career-best game featured 11 receptions for 286 yards against the Rams in 1989 . . . Returned from four-game suspension for substance abuse in 1988 to catch game-winning TD pass against Bengals in Super Bowl XXIII . . . 49ers' third-round pick out of Delaware State in 1986 . . . Born March 31, 1962, in Camden, N.J. . . . 1993 base salary: $825,000.

TOM RATHMAN 30 6-1 232   Fullback

Tough, hard-nosed player is one of the unsung heroes of the 49ers' celebrated offense . . . Excellent blocker, receiver and short-yardage runner . . . Classic fullback who does dirty work for big-play performers . . . Started 15 games, missing one with injury . . . Caught 44 passes for 343 yards and four TDs . . . Also ran for five scores . . . Moved into starting lineup in 1988 and helped the 49ers to back-to-back Super Bowl titles . . . Had best rushing season in 1988, with 427 yards and 4.2 average . . . Led all NFL running backs with 73 receptions in 1989 . . . Scored two TDs against Denver in Super Bowl XXIV . . . 49ers' third-round pick out of Nebraska in 1986 . . . Has 284 receptions in NFL after catching only five passes in four seasons at Nebraska . . . Born Oct. 7, 1962, in Grand Island, Neb. . . . 1993 base salary: $950,000.

BRENT JONES 30 6-4 230   Tight End

Another late bloomer who has emerged a Pro Bowl player late in his career . . . Made Pro Bowl for the first time at age 29 . . . Caught 45 passes for 628 yards and four TDs . . . Caught two TD passes in fourth quarter as 49ers rallied for victory over Saints . . . Second among NFL tight ends in receiving yardage . . . A free agent who made good . . . Signed by the 49ers in 1987 after Pittsburgh released him . . . Reserve for two seasons, he emerged as a starter in 1989 . . . Smooth receiver fits in well with 49ers' passing scheme . . . Burst into prominence in 1989 with 500 receiving yards in regular season and three TDs in playoffs . . . Drafted in the fifth round by Steelers in 1986 out of Santa Clara . . . Born Feb. 12, 1963, in San Jose, Cal. . . . 1993 base salary: $800,000.

GUY McINTYRE 32 6-3 265   Guard

Classic late bloomer . . . Has been to four consecutive Pro Bowls after spending early part of his career in anonymity . . . Put together another strong season in 1992 as his blocking helped 49ers' offense lead the NFL in points and yards . . . Strong run-blocker . . . Good athlete for his position, he excels on pulls and traps . . . Served as backup for four years . . . Finally became a starter in 1988 and helped the 49ers to two consecutive Super Bowls . . . Created a stir in 1984 playoffs when he was used as a blocking back . . . That moved inspired the Bears to use William "The Refrigerator" Perry in that role in 1985 . . . 49ers' third-round pick out of Georgia in 1984 . . . Born Feb. 17, 1961, in Thomasville, Ga. . . . 1993 base salary: $900,000.

DON GRIFFIN 29 6-0 176   Cornerback

Smooth, dependable coverage man has been rock of stability in unsettled 49ers' secondary . . . Started all 16 games for the fourth season in a row . . . Led team with five interceptions . . . Also made 60 tackles and defended team-high 19 passes . . . Quiet, confident player has been steady through seven NFL seasons . . . Has been starter since the first game of his rookie season . . . Doubles as a punt-returner on occasion . . . Returned a punt 76 yards for a TD as a rookie in 1986 . . . Had five interceptions in 1987 . . . Has 19 career interceptions . . . 49ers' sixth pick, out of Middle Tennessee State, in 1986 . . . Born March 17, 1964, in Pelham, Ga. . . . 1993 base salary: $985,000.

COACH GEORGE SEIFERT: By far the top active NFL coach in terms of winning percentage . . . Has won a remarkable 81 percent of his games in four seasons . . . Has 57-14 overall record, including 5-2 mark in the playoffs . . . Led the 49ers to a 14-2 record and NFC West title in 1992 . . . His first 49ers team in 1989 went 14-2 in the regular season and drove to the Super Bowl title . . . His 1990 and 1992 teams reached the NFC title game . . . His 1991 team overcame injuries to win its last six games

Nobody has caught more TD passes (103) than Jerry Rice.

to finish 10-6, but missed the playoffs . . . Named NFL Coach of the Year in 1990 by *Football News* and *Boston Globe* . . . Praised by some players for creating looser, warmer atmosphere around team following retirement of former coach Bill Walsh . . . Paid his dues, spending nine years as a 49ers assistant before getting his chance . . . An assistant on three 49ers Super Bowl champion teams . . . Helped mold the 49ers' disciplined defensive approach since become coordinator in 1983 . . . Head coach at Westminster (Utah) College and Cornell . . . Won only three games in two seasons a Cornell in the mid-1970s . . . An assistant coach at Iowa, Oregon and Stanford . . . As a schoolboy, served as an usher at 49ers games at Kezar Stadium . . . Played end and guard at Utah . . Born Jan. 22, 1940, in San Francisco.

GREATEST INTERCEPTOR

He started his career as a cornerback and wound up as a safety In between, Ronnie Lott played in nine Pro Bowls and four Supe Bowls as the heart of the 49ers' defense in the 1980s.

Lott finished a 10-year career with the 49ers with 51 interceptions, tops on the team's all-time list. He also ranks first in career interception-return yardage with 643 and in returns for touchdowns with five.

Lott, who starred at USC, began his professional career as a cornerback and started in the Super Bowl as a rookie following the 1981 season. He made the Pro Bowl four times as a cornerback.

He switched to safety in 1986, became one of the game's hardest-hitting defensive backs and was an unquestioned leader of a team that dominated the 1980s. Lott was voted to the Pro Bowl five times as a safety. He became a Raider in 1991 and is a Jet in 1993.

Jimmy Johnson deserves mention, as well. Johnson played 16 seasons for the 49ers in a career that ended in 1976. He ranks second to Lott on the team's all-time list in interceptions with 47 and return yardage with 615.

INDIVIDUAL 49ER RECORDS

Rushing

Most Yards Game:	194	Delvin Williams, vs St. Louis, 1976
Season:	1,502	Roger Craig, 1988
Career:	7,344	Joe Perry, 1948-60, 1963

Passing

Most TD Passes Game:	6	Joe Montana, vs Atlanta, 1990
Season:	31	Joe Montana, 1987
Career:	244	Joe Montana, 1979-92

Receiving

Most TD Passes Game:	5	Jerry Rice, vs Atlanta, 1990
Season:	22	Jerry Rice, 1987
Career:	103	Jerry Rice, 1985-92

Scoring

Most Points Game:	30	Jerry Rice, vs Atlanta, 1990
Season:	138	Jerry Rice, 1987
Career:	896	Ray Wersching, 1977-86
Most TDs Game:	5	Jerry Rice, vs Atlanta, 1990
Season:	23	Jerry Rice, 1987
Career:	108	Jerry Rice, 1985-92

TAMPA BAY BUCCANEERS

TEAM DIRECTORY: Owner: Hugh Culverhouse; Pres.: Gay Culverhouse; Head Coach/Dir. Football Operations: Sam Wyche; VP-Football Administration: Rich McKay; Dir. Player Personnel: Jerry Angelo; Dir. Pub. Rel.: Rick Odioso. Home field: Tampa Stadium (74,321). Colors: Florida orange, white and red.

SCOUTING REPORT

OFFENSE: The Bucs finally tired of trying to convince themselves that Vinny Testaverde was a quality NFL quarterback, so they let him fly to Cleveland as a free agent. And while coach Sam Wyche is regarded as a brilliant offensive strategist, his Xs and Os mean little unless he can get quality play from his quarterback. And who will it be? Mark Vlasic, acquired as a free agent, joins 15-year veteran Steve DeBerg in the scramble along with inexperienced Craig Erickson and Mike Pawlawski.

The Bucs have an improved running game. Reggie Cobb is a strong young runner and Gary Anderson remains a dangerous all-purpose back. And free-agent signee Vince Workman had a 4.0-yard average as the Packers' top runner last year.

The receiving corps was hurt by the loss of Mark Carrier as a free agent. But Lawrence Dawsey is a good young player and the Bucs have high hopes for Courtney Hawkins, their top pick in 1992. Tight end Ron Hall was slowed by injuries last season but he's a nifty receiver.

The line is led by left tackle Paul Gruber, the NFL's ironman. He's played every offensive snap of every game for five seasons. Bruce Reimers is a solid guard and Tony Mayberry is an emerging force at center. The Bucs still are waiting for greatness from right tackle Charles McCrae. Meanwhile, they signed Anthony Munoz, 13-year Bengal tackle who had announced his retirement.

DEFENSE: The Bucs made some moves in free agency to put bite into their defense, signing linebacker Hardy Nickerson and cornerback Martin Mayhew.

The line has an emerging star in left end Santana Dotson. Mark Wheeler and Mark Duckens are decent inside, but the Bucs are still hoping that either Keith McCants or Alabama rookie Eric Curry will develop into a big-play man. Depth is a concern.

Nickerson will play middle linebacker. Broderick Thomas is a force at right linebacker and veteran Jimmy Williams can still

Reggie Cobb's 1,000-yard season bodes well for Bucs.

make plays on the left side. Darrick Brownlow provides good depth.

Mayhew and Rick Reynolds form a solid pair of cornerbacks, but safety is a problem area. The Bucs' starters at the end of last season were journeymen Marty Carter and Joe King.

SPECIAL TEAMS: Nothing special here. The Bucs' return teams are average. Anderson is a decent kickoff-returner but the Bucs are looking for a punt-returner.

Kicker Eddie Murray, imported last season, is past his prime and punter Dave Stryzinski is average. The coverage teams are

BUCCANEERS VETERAN ROSTER

HEAD COACH—Sam Wyche. Assistant Coaches—Maxie Baughan, Jeff Fitzgerald, Harold Jackson, Eddie Khayat, Willie Peete, Floyd Peters, Turk Schonert, Steve Shafer, George Stewart, Richard Wood, Bob Wylie.

No.	Name	Pos.	Ht.	Wt.	NFL Exp.	College
59	Alexander, Elijah	LB	6-2	230	2	Kansas State
44	Anderson, Darren	CB	5-10	180	1	Toledo
40	Anderson, Gary	RB	6-1	190	8	Arkansas
86	Armstrong, Tyji	TE	6-4	255	2	Mississippi
36	Barber, Chris	CB	6-0	190	3	North Carolina A&T
62	Beckles, Ian	OG	6-1	295	4	Indiana
1	Bennett, Tracy	K	6-0	180	1	Mesa State
53	Brady, Ed	LB	6-2	235	10	Illinois
55	Brownlow, Darrick	LB	6-0	235	3	Illinois
50	Burnette, Reggie	LB	6-2	240	2	Houston
27	Bussey, Barney	S	6-0	210	8	South Carolina State
23	Carter, Marty	S	6-1	200	3	Middle Tenn. State
57	Chamblee, Al	DE	6-1	240	3	Virginia Tech
15	Claiborne, Robert	WR	5-10	175	2	San Diego State
34	Cobb, Reggie	RB	6-0	215	4	Tennessee
25	Covington, Tony	S	5-11	190	3	Virginia
80	Dawsey, Lawrence	WR	6-0	195	3	Florida State
17	DeBerg, Steve	QB	6-3	215	17	San Jose State
76	Dill, Scott	OT	6-5	285	6	Memphis State
71	Dotson, Santana	DL	6-5	270	2	Baylor
7	Erickson, Craig	QB	6-2	200	2	Miami (Fla.)
20	Gray, Jerry	DB	6-0	185	9	Texas
26	Green, Rogerick	DB	5-10	180	2	Kansas State
74	Gruber, Paul	T	6-5	290	6	Wisconsin
91	Hall, Rhett	DL	6-2	260	3	California
82	Hall, Ron	TE	6-4	245	7	Hawaii
89	Harrison, Todd	TE	6-4	260	1	North Carolina State
85	Hawkins, Courtney	WR	5-9	180	2	Michigan State
95	Hayes, Eric	DL	6-3	290	3	Florida State
8	Howfield, Ian	K	6-2	195	2	Tennessee
30	Humphries, Leonard	CB	5-9	175	1	Penn State
24	Jones, Roger	CB	5-9	175	3	Tennessee State
41	King, Joe	S	6-2	200	3	Oklahoma State
22	Lewis, Garry	CB	5-11	185	4	Alcorn State
21	Mack, Milton	CB	5-11	185	7	Alcorn State
61	Mayberry, Tony	C	6-4	290	4	Wake Forest
78	Mayfield, Corey	DL	6-3	280	2	Oklahoma
16	Mayfield, Curtis	WR	6-0	180	1	Oklahoma State
35	Mayhew, Martin	CB	5-8	175	6	Florida State
6	McAlister, Scot	P	6-2	210	1	North Carolina
52	McCants, Keith	DE	6-3	260	4	Alabama
45	McClendon, Willie	RB	6-0	225	1	Florida
37	McDowell, Anthony	FB	5-11	230	2	Texas Tech
73	McHale, Tom	G	6-4	290	7	Cornell
70	McRae, Charles	T	6-7	300	3	Tennessee
83	Moore, Dave	TE	6-2	245	1	Pittsburgh
78	Munoz, Anthony	OL	6-6	285	14	USC
3	Murray, Eddie	K	5-11	185	14	Tulane
56	Nickerson, Hardy	LB	6-2	226	7	California
9	Pawlawski, Mike	QB	6-1	205	2	California
31	Pollard, Darryl	CB	5-11	185	6	Weber State
66	Reimers, Bruce	G	6-7	300	10	Iowa State
29	Reynolds, Ricky	CB	5-11	190	7	Washington State
33	Royster, Mazio	RB	6-1	205	2	USC
64	Ryan, Tim	G	6-2	280	3	Notre Dame
98	Seals, Ray	DE	6-3	270	4	None
4	Stryzinski, Dan	P	6-1	195	4	Indiana
67	Sullivan, Mike	OL	6-3	290	2	Miami (Fla.)
72	Taylor, Rob	T	6-6	290	8	Northwestern
51	Thomas, Broderick	LB	6-4	245	5	Nebraska
58	Tiggle, Calvin	LB	6-1	235	3	Georgia Tech
68	Tomberlin, Pat	OL	6-2	300	4	Florida State

continued on page 478

TOP DRAFT CHOICES

Rd.	Name	Sel. No.	Pos.	Ht.	Wt.	College
1	Curry, Eric	6	DE	6-6	265	Alabama
2	DuBose, Demetrius	34	LB	6-1	232	Notre Dame
3	Thomas, Lamar	60	WR	6-1	163	Miami
3	Lynch, John	82	S	6-1	219	Stanford
4	Harris, Rudy	91	FB	6-1	250	Clemson

so-so. For a below-average team, below-average special teams are deadly, and that's part of the Bucs' problem.

THE ROOKIES: The Bucs snatched Curry, the best pass-rusher in the draft, in the first round. Curry is a natural right end, and his development should allow McCants to move back to line-backer. The Bucs got a productive, hard-hitting inside linebacker in Notre Dame's Demetrius DeBose in the second round.

OUTLOOK: The Bucs, 5-11 last year, have some talent but lack consistency. They don't have a personality, either. If everything falls right, they could be a .500 team, but the playoffs are out of their reach.

BUCCANEER PROFILES

REGGIE COBB 25 6-0 215   **Running Back**

One of the NFL's best young running backs . . . Became feature back for Bucs in 1992 and responded with 1,171 yards, fourth-highest total in the NFC . . . Ran for nine TDs . . . Decent receiver, he caught 21 passes in 1992 . . . Put together four 100-yard games . . . Named transition player during free-agency period . . . Instinctive runner with good speed and strength
. . . Ran for 752 yards in 1991 . . . Played fullback as a rookie in 1990 . . . Caught 39 passes that season for 299 yards . . . Bucs' second-round pick out of Tennessee in 1990 . . . College highlight was a 225-yard game against Auburn . . . Entered draft after junior season . . . Nephew of former baseball great Lou Brock . . . Born July 7, 1968, in Knoxville, Tenn. . . . 1993 base salary: $600,000.

PAUL GRUBER 28 6-5 290   Tackle

Durable athlete enters 1993 on one of the most remarkable streaks in NFL history . . . Has never missed a snap in five-year NFL career . . . Has participated in all 4,850 of the Bucs' offensive plays since entering the NFL in 1988 . . . His value was evident when the Bucs named him their franchise player during free-agency period . . . Smooth pass-blocker with good footwork . . . Protects quarterback's blind side . . . Combines with Charles McCrae to form tackle combination of high No. 1 picks . . . Was not penalized for holding during 1989 season (1,025 plays) . . . All-Rookie selection in 1988 . . . First offensive lineman selected in 1988 draft (fourth overall pick) . . . Consensus All-American at Wisconsin . . . Born Feb. 24, 1965, in Madison, Wis. . . . 1992 base salary: $650,000.

LAWRENCE DAWSEY 25 6-0 195   Wide Receiver

Smooth athlete is the feature man in the Bucs' passing game . . . Led team in receptions in 1992 with 60 . . . Generated 776 yards, averaging 12.9 yards per catch . . . Could put up huge numbers if Bucs ever settle their quarterback problems . . . Impact player as a rookie in 1991 . . . Caught 55 passes, more than any other NFL rookie . . . Produced 818 yards and scored three TDs . . . Moved into starting lineup midway in rookie season . . . Bucs' third-round pick out of Florida State in 1991 . . . Caught 143 passes for 2,329 yards in his college career . . . 10th of 11 children . . . All-state running back in high school in Alabama . . . Born Nov. 16, 1967, in Dothan, Ala. . . . 1992 base salary: $183,000.

BRODERICK THOMAS 26 6-4 245   Linebacker

Talented but inconsistent, he's a symbol of the Bucs' defense . . . Put together monster season in 1991 but tailed off last year . . . Finished with 113 tackles and five sacks . . . Big plays were few and far between after he regularly made them in 1991 . . . That was his breakthrough season, with team-record 174 tackles and 11 sacks . . . Remarkable game in upset of Eagles that season featured 12 tackles, a sack, a forced fumble and downing of the punter . . . Started to emerge as big-play man in 1990 with 7½ sacks and team-high 33 quarterback pressures . . . Struggled as rookie in 1989 after missing all of training camp in contract dispute . . . Bucs' No. 1 pick, sixth overall, out of Nebraska in 1989 . . . Consensus All-American at Nebraska . . . Big Eight Player of the Year as a senior . . . Nephew of former Chicago Bears' great Mike Singletary . . . Born Feb. 20, 1967, in Houston . . . 1993 base salary: $1 million.

RON HALL 29 6-4 245   Tight End

Looking to bounce back from injury-marred season . . . Has receiving skills to become feature target in Bucs' offensive system . . . Caught 39 passes for 351 yards and four TDs in 1992 . . . Missed four full games and parts of others with injuries . . . Good all-around athlete needs only to stay healthy to emerge as one of the NFL's top tight ends . . . Caught 31 passes in 1991, another season shortened by injuries . . . Named first-team All-Pro by *Sports Illustrated* after 1990 season . . . Averaged 15 yards per catch that season . . . Nicknamed "Ironman" by his teammates for his mental and physical toughness . . . Bucs' fourth-round draft pick out of Hawaii in 1987 . . . Walked on hot coals as a college player to improve his concentration . . . Born March 15, 1964, in Ft. Huachuca, Ariz. . . . 1993 base salary: $750,000.

HARDY NICKERSON 28 6-2 226   Linebacker

Signed three-year, $5.1-million contract with the Bucs . . . Couldn't have been protected by Steelers because he was a named plaintiff in antitrust suit against NFL . . . Reluctantly accepted 10-percent raise in 1992 to give him a one-year contract that set up his freedom . . . Led Steelers with 114 tackles, including 68 solos . . . Topped Steelers with 94 tackles the previous year . . . A mobile inside linebacker who covers the field sideline-to-sideline . . . Started at inside linebacker for the Steelers for five seasons, but figures as middle linebacker in Floyd Peters' 4-3 defense . . . Was fifth-round draft choice in 1987 who moved into starting lineup in 1988 . . . Registered 501 tackles in three-year career at California . . . Born Sept. 1, 1965, in Los Angeles. . . . 1993 base salary: $1,400,000, plus $950,000 in bonuses.

SANTANA DOTSON 23 6-5 270   Defensive Lineman

Impact player as a rookie... One of the surprises of the Class of 1992... Led Bucs with 10 sacks, twice as many as any teammate... Also led team with 11 tackles for losses and 25 quarterback pressures... Started all 16 games... Finished with 71 tackles... Bucs' fifth-round pick... Overlooked by some scouts despite sensational senior season at Baylor... Consensus All-American... Led Jack Yates High School in Houston to 36-4 record and a state title in his three-year career... His father, Alphonse, was a defensive lineman for Kansas City, Miami and Oakland... Born Dec. 19, 1969, in New Orleans... 1993 base salary: $130,000.

RICKY REYNOLDS 28 5-11 190   Cornerback

Has gradually become one of the NFL's top cornerbacks... Set team record in 1992 with 24 passes defensed... Also made 65 tackles and came up with two interceptions... Named transition player by Bucs during free-agency period... Has been starter since first game of rookie season... Best statistical season was 1989, with five interceptions... Special-teams standout blocked two field-goal attempts as a rookie in 1987... Made two interceptions in 1989 game against 49ers... Bucs' second-round pick out of Washington State in 1987... Three-year starter in college... Once blocked two field-goal attempts in a game against San Jose State... Sprint champion in high school... Born Jan. 19, 1965, in Sacramento... 1993 base salary: $800,000.

BRUCE REIMERS 33 6-7 300   Guard

Durable, consistent offensive lineman... Signed by the Bucs as a Plan B free agent before 1992 season... Started all 16 games... "A big, ol' lumberjack kind of guy," according to Bucs' line coach Jim McNally... Reunited with Bucs' coach Sam Wyche, his coach during his career in Cincinnati... Played eight seasons for the Bengals, starting the last five...

Started every game as Bengals drove to the Super Bowl in 1988 . . . Regarded as a dominant run-blocker . . . Helped Bucs' back Reggie Cobb crack 1,000-yard barrier in 1992 . . . Bengals' eighth-round pick out of Iowa State in 1984 . . . Defensive lineman early in college career . . . Likes to ride motorcycles . . . Born Sept. 28, 1960, in Algoona, Iowa . . . 1993 base salary: $625,000.

KEITH McCANTS 24 6-3 260   Defensive End

Bucs are still waiting for this talented but inconsistent player to realize his potential . . . Put together another so-so season in 1992, with 58 tackles and five sacks . . . That's not what the Bucs had in mind when they made him the fourth overall pick in the 1990 draft . . . Made transition to defensive end in 1991 after spending his rookie season at linebacker . . . Shows flashes of greatness but disappears from the action for large stretches . . . Has the skills to be a terrific pass-rusher . . . Big disappointment as a rookie linebacker, starting just four games and making only 44 tackles . . . Entered NFL after junior season at Alabama . . . Consensus All-American who was regarded as the top defensive player in the nation that season . . . Born Nov. 19, 1968, in Mobile, Ala. . . . 1993 base salary: $750,000.

COURTNEY HAWKINS 23 5-9 180   Wide Receiver

Expected to emerge as key man in Bucs' offense in 1993 . . . Impact player as a rookie last year . . . Caught 20 passes for 336 yards (16.8 average) and three TDs . . . Speedy, shifty player who doubles as dangerous kick-returner . . . Lacking a No. 1 pick, the Bucs made him their first selection in the 1992 draft . . . Picked in the second round out of Michigan State . . . Caught 47 passes for 656 yards as a senior . . . Also averaged 26 yards on kick returns . . . Broke Andre Rison's single-season school record with 60 catches as a sophomore . . . Named Michigan high school Player of the Year as a senior . . . Scored 63 TDs in career at Beacher High School in Flint, Mich. . . . All-State in football, basketball and track . . . Born Dec. 12, 1969, in Flint, Mich. . . . 1993 base salary: $340,000.

COACH SAM WYCHE: Struggled through difficult first season  with the Bucs . . . A 3-1 start raised hopes, but Bucs lost 10 of their next 12 games and finished 5-11 . . . "We hoped for a Cinderella season but we didn't produce one on the scoreboard," Wyche said . . . Brought respectability to the Bucs' offense, which averaged 298 yards per game . . . Disappointed by his inability to get the best from quarterback Vinny Testaverde, who fled to Cleveland as a free agent after the season . . . Hired by the Bucs after nine seasons as head coach of the Bengals . . . Resigned after frustrating 3-13 season in 1991 . . . Regarded as brilliant, innovative offensive coach who perfected the no-huddle offense . . . Emotional, outspoken . . . Passionate about social issues . . . Worked with the homeless in Cincinnati . . . Fined $28,000 by the NFL for banning *USA Today* female reporter from the locker room . . . Compiled 61-63 record in Cincinnati . . . Led team to AFC title in 1988 . . . Bengals lost that Super Bowl to 49ers on a last-minute pass from Joe Montana to John Taylor . . . Played collegiately at Furman . . . Also played semipro football and finished his career as a backup quarterback with the Bills . . . An assistant under Bill Walsh in San Francisco . . . Head coach at Indiana University . . . Born Jan. 5, 1945, in Atlanta.

GREATEST INTERCEPTOR

He joined the Bucs in 1976, their first season in the NFL. He was an undrafted free agent from Kent State, a longshot to make the roster, much less set any team records. But Cedric Brown retired after the 1984 season with the Tampa Bay record for interceptions. His total of 29 still ranks atop the team's list.

Brown and Mike Washington, who ranks second with 28, are the only players in the Bucs' relatively short history to have more than 20 career interceptions. Brown was a versatile player who manned both the cornerback and safety positions and started 95 games in his career.

In 1978, he led the Bucs with six interceptions and 110 return yards; in 1981, he was among the league leaders with 10 interceptions and 215 return yards, a team record that still stands.

INDIVIDUAL BUC RECORDS

Rushing

Most Yards Game:	219	James Wilder, vs Minnesota, 1983	
Season:	1,544	James Wilder, 1984	
Career:	5,957	James Wilder, 1981-89	

Passing

Most TD Passes Game:	5	Steve DeBerg, vs Atlanta, 1987	
Season:	20	2 times, most recently Vinny Testaverde, 1989	
Career:	77	Vinny Testaverde, 1987-92	

Receiving

Most TD Passes Game:	4	Jimmie Giles, vs Miami, 1985	
Season:	9	3 times, most recently Mark Carrier, 1989	
Career:	34	Jimmie Giles, 1978-86	

Scoring

Most Points Game:	24	Jimmie Giles, vs Miami, 1985	
Season:	99	Donald Igwebuike, 1989	
Career:	416	Donald Igwebuike, 1985-89	
Most TDs Game:	4	Jimmie Giles, vs Miami, 1985	
Season:	13	James Wilder, 1984	
Career:	43	James Wilder, 1981-89	

WASHINGTON REDSKINS

TEAM DIRECTORY: Chairman/CEO: Jack Kent Cooke; Exec. VP: John Kent Cooke; GM: Charley Casserly; Asst. GM: Bobby Mitchell; Dir. Pro Scouting: Joe Mack; Dir. Pro Player Personnel: Kirk Mee; Dir. College Scouting: George Saimes; VP-Communications: Charlie Dayton; Dir. Information: John Autry; Dir. Media Rel.: Mike McCall; Head Coach: Richie Petitbon. Home field: Robert F. Kennedy Stadium (55,454). Colors: Burgundy and gold.

SCOUTING REPORT

OFFENSE: The Redskins' problems in 1992 can be traced to the play of quarterback Mark Rypien, the NFC's lowest-rated passer. After winning the MVP award in the Super Bowl following the 1991 season, Rypien never regained his rhythm. He is the key. If he displays touch on his passes and makes good decisions, the Redskins will be a formidable offensive team. They still have a strong line, explosive wide receivers and a muscular ground game.

The Redskins' line is led by left tackle Jim Lachey, one of the best in the business, and right guard Mark Schlereth, a powerful run-blocker. Center Raleigh McKenzie is solid, as is right tackle Ed Simmons. The Redskins have high hopes for young Mo Elewonibi.

The receiving corps took a shot when Gary Clark fled to Phoenix as a free agent, but the Redskins signed Tim McGee from Cincinnati to replace him. The big key, however, is second-year man Desmond Howard, the Heisman Trophy winner who was no factor as a rookie. Art Monk and Ricky Sanders have slowed down but remain crafty veterans.

Running back Earnest Byner's days as a workhorse might be over. But the Redskins got a big boost in the playoffs from Brian Mitchell, and Ricky Ervins remains an excellent change-of-pace runner.

DEFENSE: Free agency took some of the teeth from this unit as the Redskins lost linemen Jumpy Geathers and Fred Stokes and cornerback Martin Mayhew.

They added Al Noga, an active pass-rushing lineman, and he'll join Charles Mann, Tim Johnson, Eric Williams, Bobby Wilson,

Mark looks for return of Super Bowl Rypien.

Jason Buck and Shane Collins to form a deep, talented defensive line.

With Wilber Marshall presumably gone to the Oilers, the Redskins signed veteran Giant outside linebacker Carl Banks. He joins another big-play outside linebacker in Andre Collins. Kurt Gouveia is a solid middle linebacker.

The secondary could be a weak spot, even with the addition of Notre Dame rookie Tom Carter. Darrell Green is 33 and coming off an injury-marred season. A.J. Johnson is average at the other cornerback spot. The safeties, Brad Edwards and Danny Copeland, are journeymen who lack speed and big-play ability.

SPECIAL TEAMS: The Redskins' strength in this area is kicker Chip Lohmiller, whom they made a transition player during the free-agency period. Lohmiller made 30 of 40 field-goal attempts last season and is regarded as one of the NFL's best from long distance.

Mitchell and Howard are dangerous return men; each returned

REDSKINS VETERAN ROSTER

HEAD COACH—Richie Petitbon. Assistant Coaches—Don Breaux, Bobby DePaul, Rod Dowhower, Russ Grimm, Jim Hanifan, Larry Peccatiello, Dan Riley, Wayne Sevier, Rennie Simmons, Charlie Taylor, Emmitt Thomas, Torgy Torgeson.

No.	Name	Pos.	Ht.	Wt.	NFL Exp.	College
58	Banks, Carl	LB	6-4	235	10	Michigan State
98	Barker, Tony	LB	6-2	230	2	Rice
57	Bingham, Guy	C	6-3	260	14	Montana
53	Bostic, Jeff	C	6-2	278	14	Clemson
22	Bowles, Todd	S	6-2	205	8	Temple
59	Brantley, John	LB	6-3	240	2	Georgia
67	Brown, Ray	T	6-5	280	8	Arkansas State
99	Buck, Jason	DE	6-4	265	7	BYU
21	Byner, Earnest	RB	5-10	218	10	East Carolina
50	Caldwell, Ravin	LB	6-3	240	8	Arkansas
16	Cochrane, Chris	QB	6-3	220	1	Cornell
51	Coleman, Monte	LB	6-2	245	15	Central Arkansas
55	Collins, Andre	LB	6-1	233	4	Penn State
91	Collins, Shane	DE	6-3	267	2	Arizona State
12	Conklin, Cary	QB	6-4	215	2	Washington
26	Copeland, Danny	S	6-2	213	5	Eastern Kentucky
27	Edwards, Brad	S	6-2	207	6	South Carolina
25	Eilers, Pat	S	5-11	195	3	Notre Dame
64	Elewonibi, Mo	T	6-4	282	4	BYU
52	Elliott, Matt	C	6-1	265	2	Michigan
32	Ervins, Ricky	RB	5-7	200	3	USC
73	Fuhler, Tom	DL	6-4	290	1	Tennessee
2	Goodburn, Kelly	P	6-2	199	7	Emporia State
54	Gouveia, Kurt	LB	6-1	228	7	BYU
90	Graf, Rick	LB	6-5	244	7	Wisconsin
28	Green, Darrell	CB	5-8	170	11	Texas A&I
39	Green, Robert	RB	5-8	207	2	William & Mary
36	Gulledge, David	S	6-1	203	2	Jacksonville State
6	Hakel, Chris	QB	6-2	230	2	William & Mary
24	Harry, Carl	WR	5-9	170	1	Utah
34	Hoage, Terry	S	6-2	201	10	Georgia
86	Hobbs, Stephen	WR	5-11	200	6	North Alabama
80	Howard, Desmond	WR	5-9	183	2	Michigan
66	Jacoby, Joe	G-T	6-6	314	13	Louisville
88	Jenkins, James	TE	6-2	234	3	Rutgers
47	Johnson, Anthony	CB	5-8	170	5	SW Texas State
45	Johnson, Sidney	CB	5-9	175	6	California
78	Johnson, Tim	DT	6-3	283	7	Penn State
79	Lachey, Jim	T	6-6	294	9	Ohio State
8	Lohmiller, Chip	K	6-3	210	6	Minnesota
71	Mann, Charles	DE	6-6	272	11	Nevada-Reno
20	Mays, Alvoid	CB	5-9	180	4	West Virginia
85	McGee, Tim	WR	5-10	183	8	Tennessee
63	McKenzie, Raleigh	C-G	6-2	279	9	Tennessee
87	Middleton, Ron	TE	6-2	270	8	Auburn
30	Mitchell, Brian	RB	5-10	209	4	SW Louisiana
81	Monk, Art	WR	6-3	210	14	Syracuse
62	Moore, Darryl	G	6-2	292	2	Texas-El Paso
97	Noga, Al	DE	6-1	269	6	Hawaii
89	Orr, Terry	TE	6-2	235	9	Texas
56	Powell, Boone	LB	6-3	237	2	Texas
95	Rogers, Ted	LB	6-2	240	2	Williams
82	Rowe, Ray	TE	6-2	256	2	San Diego State
11	Rypien, Mark	QB	6-4	234	7	Washington State
83	Sanders, Ricky	WR	5-11	180	8	SW Texas State
69	Schlereth, Mark	G	6-3	287	5	Idaho
74	Siever, Paul	G	6-5	293	2	Penn State
76	Simmons, Ed	T	6-5	300	7	Eastern Washington
61	Steele, Derek	DE	6-3	265	1	Maryland
20	Stock, Mark	WR	6-0	185	3	VMI
41	Thomas, Johnny	CB	5-9	191	5	Baylor
77	Wahler, Jim	DT	6-4	275	5	UCLA
75	Williams, Eric	DT	6-4	290	10	Washington State
94	Wilson, Bobby	DT	6-2	283	3	Michigan State

TOP DRAFT CHOICES

Rd.	Name	Sel. No.	Pos.	Ht.	Wt.	College
1	Carter, Tom	17	DB	5-11	187	Notre Dame
2	Brooks, Reggie	45	RB	5-7	209	Notre Dame
3	Hamilton, Rick	71	LB	6-1	243	Central Florida
3	Bunn, Ed	80	P	6-2	185	Texas-El Paso
4	Palmer, Sterling	101	DE	6-6	258	Florida State

a punt for a TD in 1992. The coverage teams are solid.

Punting has been a problem. The Redskins will look for more consistency from Kelly Goodburn, who averaged fewer than 40 yards per punt.

THE ROOKIES: The Redskins address an area of concern by taking Carter in the first round. Carter was projected by many analysts as the best coverage man in the draft pool. Running back Reggie Brooks, a short, quick, powerful player who could flourish behind the Redskins' big offensive line, was the team's second pick.

OUTLOOK: The Redskins, 9-7 last year, are an aging team and the change in coaches from Joe Gibbs to Richie Petitbon could make for a rough season. There's still plenty of talent on the roster, and the organization is second to none. But, like the Eagles and Giants, they are an NFC East power in decline.

REDSKIN PROFILES

CARL BANKS 31 6-4 235   Linebacker

After nine seasons and two Super Bowls with Giants, he signed three-year Redskin contract estimated at $5.5 million . . . Became expendable when Giants signed Bronco free agent Michael Brooks and rescinded Banks' status as transition player . . . Had figured prominently in new Giant coach Dan Reeves' plans . . . Solid, unspectacular player who would love to reclaim his place among NFL's top linebackers . . . Made 55 tackles in 1992 . . . Also registered four sacks . . . Had spent entire career in long shadow cast by Giants' other outside linebacker, Lawrence

Taylor . . . Has been starter since rookie season . . . Made Pro Bowl after 1987 season . . . Led Giants in tackles in 1986 and 1987 . . . Giants' top pick in 1984, out of Michigan State . . . Born Aug. 29, 1962, in Flint, Mich. . . . 1992 base salary: $1.1 million.

DARRELL GREEN 33 5-8 170   Cornerback

This highly respected athlete is nearing the end of a great career . . . Hoping to bounce back from injury-marred 1992 season . . . Sat out eight regular-season games with broken forearm . . . Missed playoff opener against Vikings with sore heel . . . Finished with just 25 tackles and one interception, tying his career-low . . . Five-time Pro Bowl selection . . . Regarded as one of the NFL's best coverage cornerbacks . . . Helped Redskins to Super Bowl in 1991 with team-high five interceptions and 21 passes defensed . . . Ranks fourth on the team's all-time list with 30 career interceptions . . . Has twice won "Fastest Man" competition . . . Clinched 1987 playoff victory over Bears with 52-yard punt return for TD . . . Redskins' No. 1 pick out of Texas A&I in 1983 . . . Born Feb. 15, 1960, in Houston . . . 1993 salary: $1.55 million.

JIM LACHEY 30 6-6 294   Tackle

Perhaps the NFL's best offensive lineman . . . Hoping to bounce back from subpar 1992 season . . . Missed six games with knee injury and played tentatively in a few others . . . Named transition player by Redskins during free-agency period . . . As left tackle, he usually matches up with opponent's top pass-rusher . . . Was sensational in Redskins' drive to the Super Bowl in 1991 . . . Did not allow a sack all season . . . Three-time Pro Bowl pick . . . Named NFC Offensive Lineman of the Year in 1990 . . . Acquired by Redskins from Raiders in lopsided trade for Jay Schroeder on Sept. 3, 1988 . . . San Diego's No. 1 pick out of Ohio State in 1985 . . . Born June 4, 1963, in St. Henry, Ohio . . . 1993 base salary: $1.25 million.

MARK RYPIEN 30 6-4 234   Quarterback

Still another Redskins star hoping to bounce back from disappointing season . . . Struggled all season after missing much of training camp in contract dispute . . . Some attributed his problems to a letdown after his breakthrough 1991 season . . . The NFC's lowest-rated starting quarterback in 1992 with a 71.7 mark . . . Threw 17 interceptions and had only 13 touchdown passes . . . Threw two interceptions that were returned for touchdowns in shocking loss in Phoenix . . . Capped big season in 1991 by earning MVP award in Super Bowl victory over Buffalo . . . Named Pro Bowl starter that season after passing for 3,564 yards and 28 TDs . . . Monster game against Atlanta that season (442 yards, six TDs) . . . Has 46-21 record as a starting quarterback . . . Injuries slowed development early in his career . . . Redskins' sixth-round draft pick out of Washington State in 1986 . . . Born Oct. 2, 1962, in Calgary . . . 1993 base salary: $3 million.

EARNEST BYNER 30 5-10 218   Running Back

Fell just two yards short of his third consecutive 1,000-yard season . . . Led Redskins with 998 yards on 262 carries . . . Workhorse back has carried the football 967 times in his four seasons with the Redskins . . . Split time in one-back formation with Ricky Ervins . . . Scored TD in dominating playoff victory over Minnesota . . . Best season was 1990, with 1,219 yards . . . Made Pro Bowl after 1990 and 1991 seasons . . . Acquired by Redskins from Browns in trade for Mike Oliphant on April 22, 1989 . . . Ran for 1,002 yards for Browns in 1985 . . . Cleveland's 10th-round pick out of East Carolina in 1984 . . . Born Sept. 15, 1962, in Milledgeville, Ga. . . . 1993 base salary: $1 million.

DESMOND HOWARD 23 5-9 183   Wide Receiver

The Redskins expect big things from this talented but unproven player . . . Spent most of his rookie season on the bench . . . Missed all of training camp in contract dispute . . . Caught only three passes for paltry 20 yards . . . Saw some action on special teams . . . Returned six punts for 84 yards, including a 55-yarder for a touchdown . . . Returned 22 kickoffs for 462 yards (21.0 average) . . . Expected to move into starting lineup this season . . . Heisman Trophy winner after sensational junior season at Michigan . . . Caught 61 passes for 950 yards and 19 touchdowns . . . Set NCAA record with at least one touchdown catch in 10 consecutive games . . . Averaged 30 yards on kickoff returns, 12 yards on punt returns and caught nine TD passes as a sophomore . . . Entered draft after junior season . . . The Redskins traded up two spots to draft him with the fourth overall pick in 1992 . . . Born May 15, 1970, in Cleveland . . . 1993 base salary: $700,000.

MARK SCHLERETH 27 6-3 287   Guard

One of the best guards in the NFL . . . Two-time Pro Bowl selection who burst into prominence during Redskins' Super Bowl season in 1991 . . . Potent drive-blocker is one of the keys to the Redskins' formidable ground game . . . Started all 16 games in 1992 . . . Consistent, durable player during team's difficult, injury-marred season . . . First and only native-born Alaskan to play in the NFL . . . Thrust into lineup as unheralded rookie late in 1989, he was standout in upset victory over Philadelphia . . . Moved into starting lineup for good midway in 1990 season . . . Redskins' 10th-round draft pick out of Idaho in 1989 . . . Born Jan. 25, 1966, in Anchorage . . . 1993 base salary: $650,000.

ART MONK 35 6-3 210   Wide Receiver

The most prolific receiver in NFL history . . . Ranks first on the league's all-time list with 847 receptions . . . Broke Steve Largent's record of 819 receptions during a memorable Monday night game against Denver . . . Finished 1992 season with 46 catches for 644 yards and three TDs . . . Slowed down a bit in second half of season to raise concerns that his illustrious career is almost over . . . Put together a sensational season during Redskins' Super Bowl drive in 1991 . . . Caught 71 passes for 1,048 yards and eight TDs . . . Smart, physical receiver who specializes in sideline routes . . . Has 11,028 career receiving yards and 63 career TDs . . . Shy, understated athlete who tends to avoid interviews . . . Set NFL single-season record (since broken) with 106 receptions in 1984 . . . Redskins' No. 1 pick out of Syracuse in 1980 . . . Born Dec. 5, 1957, in White Plains, N.Y. . . . 1992 base salary: $1.1 million.

CHARLES MANN 32 6-6 272   Defensive End

Nagging injuries slowed down this potent pass-rusher in 1992 . . . Like so many of his teammates, he's hoping to bounce back with big season . . . Finished 1992 with 91 tackles but only 4½ sacks, his lowest total in that category since rookie season of 1983 . . . Put together marvelous season in 1991 when he led the Redskins with 11½ sacks and was named to the Pro Bowl for the fourth time in five years . . . Solid run-defender who plays within confines of disciplined defensive scheme . . . Has 81½ sacks in 10 NFL seasons . . . Redskins' third-round pick out of Nevada-Reno in 1983 . . . Born April 12, 1961, in Sacramento, Cal. . . . 1992 base salary: $900,000.

TIM McGEE 29 5-10 183   Wide Receiver

Signed by Redskins to be a replacement for departed Gary Clark, who signed with Phoenix . . . Has three-year, $4.4-million contract . . . Finished second last season on Bengals with 35 catches for 408 yards and three touchdowns . . . Received double coverage because injured Eddie Brown missed the season with neck injury . . . Averaged 53 catches for 917 yards from 1989 to 1991 . . . Will need to be more physical in the tough NFC East in order to make catches over the middle . . . Best season was 1989, when he caught 65 passes for 1,211 yards . . . Caught 123 passes for 2,042 yards and 15 touchdown at Tennessee . . . Was first-round choice of Bengals in 1986 and broke into the starting lineup before end of season . . . Born Aug. 7, 1964, in Cleveland . . . 1993 base salary: $1,200,000, plus $1,900,000 in bonuses.

RICKY ERVINS 24 5-7 200   Running Back

Sophomore jinx hit this talented runner in 1992 . . . Carried 151 times for 495 yards, a paltry 3.3 average . . . Sat out playoff victory over Vikings with ankle injury . . . Will be given opportunity to emerge as feature runner in 1993 . . . Speedy, shifty runner with low center of gravity . . . Burst on scene as a rookie in 1991 when he gained 680 yards on just 145 carries (4.7 average) and broke off the team's longest three runs of the season, covering 65, 37 and 34 yards . . . Ran for 133 yards against

Browns . . . Ran for 104 yards in playoff victory over Atlanta and 72 yards in Super Bowl victory over Buffalo . . . Good receiver who made 32 catches in 1992 . . . Redskins' third-round pick in 1991 out of USC . . . Led Pac-10 in rushing as junior with 1,395 yards but missed most of senior season with ankle injury . . . Born Dec. 7, 1968, in Fort Wayne, Ind. . . . 1993 base salary: $180,000.

COACH RICHIE PETITBON: Takes over for long-time friend Joe Gibbs, who shocked sports world with his retirement in February . . . Spent 15 seasons as a Redskins' assistant coach, the last 12 under Gibbs . . . Long regarded as one of the NFL's top defensive coordinators . . . Has tough task in trying to maintain standard set by Gibbs, who led Redskins to three Super Bowl titles . . . Has always said he only wanted to be a head coach with either the Redskins or Bears . . . Turned down numerous chances to explore head-coaching opportunities because of his loyalty to the Redskins . . . Has been a member of all five Redskins' Super Bowl teams either as a player or a coach . . . Master at situation substitutions and utilizing all the defensive players on his roster . . . Popular with players, most of whom applauded his promotion to head coach . . . His defense in 1991 allowed only 224 points and forced 41 turnovers in helping Redskins take Super Bowl title . . . Before joining Redskins as defensive assistant in 1978, he spent four seasons as secondary coach for the Oilers . . . A standout NFL player for Bears, Rams and Redskins from 1959-72 . . . Made four Pro Bowls as a defensive back and registered 48 career interceptions . . . Has spent last 33 years in the NFL as a player and coach . . . An all-SEC quarterback at Tulane . . . Born April 18, 1938, in New Orleans.

GREATEST INTERCEPTOR

He was a solid, unspectacular player who spent 12 seasons with the Redskins. Brig Owens never made the Pro Bowl. He led the team in interceptions in a season just twice. But Owens, a product of the University of Cincinnati, finished his career in 1977 with 36 interceptions, a Redskins' record.

Owens' best seasons were his early ones. He intercepted seven passes as a rookie in 1966 and set his personal best with eight interceptions two years later.

Over the next eight seasons, the Redskins' seasonal interception leaders ranged from Rickie Harris to Pat Fischer to Ken Stone to Joe Lavender. Owens tied Mike Bass for the Redskins' top spot with four interceptions in 1970.

But Owens still finished his career as the Redskins' all-time leader. He finished with five more interceptions than Sammy Baugh—yes, quarterback Sammy Baugh. Baugh finished his illustrious 16-year career in 1952 with 31 interceptions. Eleven of them came in 1943, when he led the NFL in that category.

INDIVIDUAL REDSKIN RECORDS

Rushing

Most Yards Game:	221	Gerald Riggs, vs Philadelphia, 1989
Season:	1,347	John Riggins, 1983
Career:	7,472	John Riggins, 1976-79, 1981-85

Passing

Most TD Passes Game:	6	3 times, most recently Mark Rypien, vs Atlanta, 1991
Season:	31	Sonny Jurgensen, 1967
Career:	187	Sammy Baugh, 1937-52

Receiving

Most TD Passes Game:	3	15 times, most recently Gary Clark, vs Atlanta, 1991
Season:	12	4 times, most recently Ricky Sanders, 1988
Career:	79	Charley Taylor, 1964-77

Scoring

Most Points Game:	24	2 times, most recently Larry Brown, vs Philadelphia, 1973
Season:	161	Mark Moseley, 1983
Career:	1,207	Mark Moseley, 1974-86
Most TDs Game:	4	2 times, most recently Larry Brown, vs Philadelphia, 1973
Season:	24	John Riggins, 1983
Career:	90	Charley Taylor, 1964-77

INSIDE THE AFC

By JOHN CLAYTON

PREDICTED ORDER OF FINISH

EAST	CENTRAL	WEST
Miami	Houston	Kansas City
Buffalo	Pittsburgh	Denver
N.Y. Jets	Cleveland	San Diego
Indianapolis	Cincinnati	L.A. Raiders
New England		Seattle

AFC Champion: Miami

"Break up the Buffalo Bills." That was the battle cry of 13 frustrated AFC teams after three unfulfilled trips to the Super Bowl by the Bills.

Since their 52-17 loss to Dallas in the Super Bowl, the Bills lost two of their main front-office architects—GM Bill Polian and top assistant Bob Ferguson. Free agency cost them Pro Bowl left tackle (Will Wolford), two mobile inside linebackers (Shane Conlan and Carlton Bailey) and a top backup lineman (Mitch Frerotte).

Marv Levy's Bills are no longer the class of the AFC. In fact, they aren't the class of the AFC East. Miami is the defending champ, and coach Don Shula revamped his receiving corps in order to pass his way to the Super Bowl. AFC teams watched the Bills lose championships to three different NFC teams, so the AFC imported some of the brightest minds and philosophies from, well, the NFC. New England brought back two-time Giant Super Bowl

---

John Clayton covers the Seahawks and the NFL for the Tacoma Morning News Tribune.

Stan Humphries' mission is to take Chargers all the way.

winner Bill Parcells after his TV sojourn. And Houston signed defensive guru Buddy Ryan as a key assistant.

Not only did teams such as Denver and Kansas City change to the 49ers' offensive scheme, but the Chiefs' Marty Schottenheimer traded a first-round choice to secure the quarterback who engineered it, Joe Montana. At 37, Montana makes a comeback after two years of elbow problems. No. 19 (16 is in the Bay) hopes to turn a string of four consecutive second-place finishes by the Chiefs into a championship.

Montana's goal won't be easy because San Diego's Bobby Ross taught a hungry group of talented Chargers how to win. The Chargers, led by quarterback Stan Humphries, will battle the Chiefs, Denver and the Raiders, quarterbacked by ex-Giant Jeff Hostetler, in what could be the league's tightest race.

Wade Phillips, a longtime defensive coordinator, replaces Dan Reeves (gone to the Giants) as the Broncos' coach, and he switched to a power offense by adding backs Rod Bernstine (Chargers) and Robert Delpino (Rams), plus 290-pound offensive linemen Don Maggs (Oilers) and Brian Habib (Vikings).

Tired of waiting for Jay Schroeder or Todd Marinovich, the Raiders' Art Shell signed Hostetler to handle his offense. In Seattle, Tom Flores, coming off a 2-14 season, will let Dan McGwire and Notre Dame's Rick Mirer (No. 2 in the draft) fight it out at quarterback.

The Dolphins' Dan Marino can throw to tight end Keith Jackson and proven receivers Mark Duper, Irving Fryar (Pats) and Mark Ingram (Giants). After a 9-7 season, Indianapolis invested in the Bills' Wolford and center Kirk Lowdermilk (Vikings).

The Jets went on a $10-million spending spree to acquire Bengal quarterback Boomer Esiason, Giant defensive lineman Leonard Marshall and Raider safety Ronnie Lott.

Parcells needs time and talent to turn around the 2-14 Pats, and he's banking on Drew Bledsoe, the Washington State quarterback who was No. 1 in the draft.

Seeking no more 35-point comeback losses in the playoffs, Houston hired Ryan to further motivate the conference's most talented defense. Jack Pardee's Oilers will have to hold off Bill Cowher's Steelers, featuring Barry Foster, and Bill Belichick's Browns, whose Bernie Kosar came back with a bang.

No small task confronts the Bengals' David Shula, who needs, among other things, all he can get from young David Klingler at quarterback.

And the winners are: Miami in the East, Houston in the Central and Kansas City in the West. Overall? Make it Miami.

Steelers' Rod Woodson looks for elusive Super Bowl ring.

BUFFALO BILLS

TEAM DIRECTORY: Pres.: Ralph Wilson; Exec. VP-Adm.: Jerry Foran; VP/Head Coach: Marv Levy; GM: John Butler; Corp. VP: Linda Bogdan; Dir. Pro Personnel: A.J. Smith; Dir. Media Rel.: Scott Berchtold; Dir. Pub. and Community Rel.: Denny Lynch. Home field: Rich Stadium (80,290). Colors: Scarlet red, royal blue and white.

SCOUTING REPORT

OFFENSE: Break up the Bills. After three failed trips to the Super Bowl, the Bills were struck a second major blow by the Colts in the harpooning of Jim Kelly's no-huddle offense. Last year the Colts hired former Bills' offensive coordinator Ted Marchibroda—Kelly's sideline brain—as head coach. During the off-season, the Colts stole Kelly's blindside protection, left tackle Will Wolford.

Losing such brain and brawn continues the drain of the frustrated AFC champs. Hardest hit is the offensive line, which also lost versatile backup Mitch Frerotte. John Fina, a 1992 first-round choice, moves into Wolford's vital left-tackle job. Another concern is left guard Jim Ritcher, who is 35. But coach Marv Levy is still blessed with a line that includes Kent Hull, Glenn Parker and Howard Ballard.

If anything, though, the Bills' offense got better by signing consistent Colt receiver Billy Brooks, who takes over for 37-year-old James Lofton. Brooks should surpass Lofton's 51-catch totals. Andre Reed and Brooks are ideal possession receivers, and Don Beebe will beat you deep. Halfback Thurman Thomas can kill defenses as a runner or receiver.

DEFENSE: Levy could accept the loss of inside linebackers Carlton Bailey, who signed with the Giants, and Shane Conlan, who bolted for the Rams. He wanted to keep Cornelius Bennett in the middle of the field to chase down plays and get 10 to 15 tackles a game. That might be tough.

He couldn't afford losing nose tackle Jeff Wright, who signed a four-year, $6-million offer sheet with the 49ers. As painful as it was to the Bills' budget, management matched Wright's offer. That's good news for ends Bruce Smith, who returned to dominating form, and Phil Hansen, a North Dakota State find who became a force last season.

Bruce Smith sacked his way to fifth Pro Bowl.

Except for free safety, where Mark Kelso is showing some age, the Bills have no worries. They have three cornerbacks—Nate Odomes, Kirby Jackson and James Williams—who can cover and let strong safety Henry Jones (eight interceptions) make the big plays. Top pick Thomas Smith of North Carolina adds depth.

BILLS VETERAN ROSTER

HEAD COACH—Marv Levy. Assistant Coaches—Tom Bresnahan, Walt Corey, Bruce DeHaven, Charlie Joyner, Rusty Jones, Don Lawrence, Chuck Lester, Elijah Pitts, Dick Roach, Dan Sekanovich, Jim Shofner.

No.	Name	Pos.	Ht.	Wt.	NFL Exp.	College
86	Awalt, Rob	TE	6-5	242	7	San Diego State
75	Ballard, Howard	T	6-6	330	6	Alabama A&M
77	Barnett, Oliver	DE	6-3	292	4	Kentucky
82	Beebe, Don	WR	5-11	180	5	Chadron State
97	Bennett, Cornelius	LB	6-2	238	7	Alabama
80	Brooks, Bill	WR	6-0	195	8	Boston University
2	Christie, Steve	K	6-0	185	4	William & Mary
66	Crafts, Jerry	OT	6-6	351	2	Louisville
43	Darby, Matt	S	6-1	200	2	UCLA
65	Davis, John	G	6-4	310	6	Georgia Tech
23	Davis, Kenneth	RB	5-10	208	8	Texas Christian
85	Edwards, Al	WR	5-8	173	4	NW Louisiana State
70	Fina, John	OL	6-4	285	2	Arizona
33	Fuller, Eddie	RB	5-9	198	4	LSU
35	Gardner, Carwell	FB	6-2	244	4	Louisville
7	Gilbert, Gale	QB	6-3	210	8	California
50	Goganious, Keith	LB	6-2	239	2	Penn State
17	Gordon, Bob	WR	5-10	185	1	Nebraska
98	Gray, Jim	DT	6-2	277	1	West Virginia
26	Hale, Chris	CB	5-7	179	5	USC
90	Hansen, Phil	DE	6-5	278	3	North Dakota State
15	Harris, Willie	WR	6-1	198	R	Mississippi State
67	Hull, Kent	C	6-4	275	8	Mississippi State
47	Jackson, Kirby	CB	5-10	180	7	Mississippi State
20	Jones, Henry	S	5-11	197	3	Illinois
12	Kelly, Jim	QB	6-3	218	8	Miami (Fla.)
38	Kelso, Mark	FS	5-11	180	8	William & Mary
81	Lamb, Brad	WR	5-10	177	3	Anderson
63	Lingner, Adam	C	6-4	268	11	Illinois
73	Lodish, Mike	NT	6-3	280	4	UCLA
79	Love, Sean	OL	6-3	290	1	Penn State
55	Maddox, Mark	LB	6-1	233	3	Northern Michigan
84	McKeller, Keith	TE	6-4	242	7	Jacksonville State
88	Metzelaars, Pete	TE	6-7	254	12	Wabash
9	Mohr, Chris	P	6-5	215	4	Alabama
60	Myslinski, Tom	G	6-2	295	2	Tennessee
37	Odomes, Nate	CB	5-10	199	7	Wisconsin
74	Parker, Glenn	G-T	6-5	305	4	Arizona
44	Paterra, Greg	FB	5-11	224	3	Slippery Rock
99	Patton, James	DL	6-3	287	2	Texas
53	Patton, Marvcus	LB	6-2	243	4	UCLA
94	Pike, Mark	DE	6-4	272	8	Georgia Tech
83	Reed, Andre	WR	6-2	190	9	Kutztown State
14	Reich, Frank	QB	6-4	205	9	Maryland
51	Ritcher, Jim	G	6-3	273	13	North Carolina State
8	Rodgers, Matt	QB	6-4	205	1	Iowa
19	Rose, Barry	WR	6-0	185	1	Wis.-Stevens Pt.
58	Sanders, Glenell	LB	6-0	235	2	Louisiana Tech
24	Schulz, Kurt	S	6-1	208	2	Eastern Washington
78	Smith, Bruce	DE	6-4	275	9	Virginia State
56	Talley, Darryl	LB	6-4	236	11	West Virginia
89	Tasker, Steve	WR	5-9	181	9	Northwestern
87	Thomas, Ed	TE	6-3	251	4	Houston
34	Thomas, Thurman	RB	5-10	198	6	Oklahoma State
21	Turner, Nate	RB	6-1	255	2	Nebraska
18	Walsh, Chris	WR	6-1	185	1	Stanford
25	Washington, Mickey	CB	5-9	191	3	Texas A&M
29	Williams, James	CB	5-10	186	4	Fresno State
93	Willis, Keith	DE	6-1	263	12	Northeastern
22	Wren, Darryl	CB	6-0	188	4	Pittsburg State
91	Wright, Jeff	NT	6-3	270	6	Central Missouri State

Rd.	Name	Sel. No.	Pos.	Ht.	Wt.	College
		TOP DRAFT CHOICES				
1	Smith, Thomas	28	CB	5-11	190	North Carolina
2	Parrella, John	55	DT	6-3	289	Nebraska
4	Copeland, Russell	111	WR	6-2	194	Memphis State
5	Devlin, Mike	136	C	6-1	281	Iowa
5	Savage, Sebastian	139	DB	5-11	192	North Carolina State

SPECIAL TEAMS: Former GM Bill Polian filled a one-time problem with solid players. Kicker Steve Christie made 24 of 30 field goals and scored 115 points. Chris Mohr, the former World Leaguer, punted for a 34.8 yards net. Few teams gained anything on returns (8.4 yards on punts and 20.3 on kickoffs). Cliff Hicks was dependable on punt returns with a 10-yard average.

THE ROOKIES: From walk-on to first-round choice, the Tar Heels' Thomas Smith has come a long way. His tenaciousness compensates for his seeming lack of speed. Second-rounder John Parrella, a 289-pound converted tight end from Nebraska, will vie for a spot on defensive line. The Bills took Memphis State wide receiver Russell Copeland in the fourth round.

OUTLOOK: The Dolphins nosed them out for the division title, but they have added talent while the Bills (11-5) have lost some. Though the Bills might still be good enough to be a playoff team, they should miss the Super Bowl for the first time in four years.

BILL PROFILES

CORNELIUS BENNETT 27 6-2 238　　　　　**Linebacker**

Earned fourth trip to the Pro Bowl despite missing training camp because of a contract dispute . . . Switched to inside linebacker Nov. 8 to take advantage of his ability to chase down ball-carriers . . . Former pass-rushing weak-side linebacker has become a model of 1990s linebackers by moving inside so that opponents can't run away from him . . . Had streak of 91 consecutive starts broken when he missed season-finale against Houston with bad ankle . . . Led Bills with three fumble reeoveries to increase his career total to 12 . . . Finished fifth on team with 81 tackles and had four sacks . . . Ranked second on team with 15 quarterback pressures and can destroy offenses with inside-linebacker blitzes . . . Has 4.5 speed in the 40 . . . Selected by Colts, out of Alabama, in first round of 1987 draft and came to Bills after a holdout and a complicated trade with Rams . . . Nicknamed "Biscuit" because of his love for mother's biscuits . . . Was a three-time All-American . . . Born Aug. 25, 1966, in Birmingham, Ala. . . . 1993 base salary: $1,300,000.

HENRY JONES 25 5-11 197   Safety

Selected to start in the Pro Bowl after season in which he intercepted eight passes . . . Opened year as first-time starter by picking off two Jim Everett passes, returning the first 68 yards . . . His 263 yards of interception returns was best in franchise history . . . Followed Ram game with 12 tackles against 49ers . . . Became the first Bill to return two interceptions for touchdowns in a season when he had 23- and 82-yarders against Colts . . . Was Bills' first-round choice in 1991 but rookie season was destroyed by contract holdout . . . Played 15 games, mostly on special teams, as a rookie . . . Promoted to starting strong safety role after release of injured Leonard Smith before last season . . . Played cornerback for Illinois and was All-Big 10 as junior and senior . . . Allowed only two touchdown receptions during college career . . . Born Dec. 29, 1967, in St. Louis . . . 1993 base salary: $415,000.

JIM KELLY 33 6-3 218   Quarterback

Earned fourth trip to Pro Bowl but missed the game because of a knee injury that plagued him through playoffs . . . Missed playoffs against Oilers and Steelers, but returned to complete 70.8 percent of his passes against the Dolphins in AFC title game . . . Completed 269 of 462 passes for 3,457 yards and 23 touchdowns last season . . . Was sacked only 20 times . . . Became only the second Bills' quarterback to pass for more than 20,000 yards during career . . . Had 403-yard game against 49ers, the first 400-yard game of his career . . . Showed no effects from departure of offensive coordinator Ted Marchibroda, who took his no-huddle offense to Indianapolis . . . Sprained right knee in season finale against Oilers . . . Was first-round draft choice of Bills in 1983 but opted to play two seasons with USFL Houston Gamblers . . . Threw 83 touchdown passes but was sacked 110 times in two seasons of Run-and-Shoot with the Gamblers . . . Signed with Bills in August 1986 . . . Born Feb. 14, 1960, in Pittsburgh . . . 1993 base salary: $2,400,000.

NATE ODOMES 28 5-10 199   Cornerback

Earned first trip to Pro Bowl . . . Rarely lets a defender get behind him . . . Since being drafted in 1987, he has started 104 consecutive games . . . Had two interceptions in season opener against Rams, including a one-hander against Jim Everett . . . Had five interceptions in 1991 and was named to the UPI All-AFC team, but was bypassed in Pro Bowl voting . . . Came to Bills in draft-day trade with Buccaneers at top of the second round . . . Was youngest defensive starter in NFL in 1987 at 22 . . . Ran a 4.37 40 at Wisconsin, where he was an All-American cornerback . . . Born Aug. 25, 1965, in Columbus, Ga. . . . 1993 base salary: $650,000.

ANDRE REED 29 6-2 190   Wide Receiver

Had seventh 50-plus catch season with 65 for 913 yards . . . Has been five-time participant in Pro Bowl . . . Had 10-catch, 144-yard game against 49ers Sept. 13, his fourth 10-catch game . . . Had eight catches for 136 yards and three touchdowns against Oilers in come-from-behind playoff win . . . His 534 career receptions leads next closest Bill, Elbert Dubenion, 296 . . . Has 21 regular-season and five playoff 100-yard games . . . His precise routes are almost impossible for defenders to cover . . . Was fourth-round choice from tiny Kutztown State in 1985

... Established himself quickly with a 48-catch rookie year ... Broke nine school records at Kutztown and had 142 catches for 2,020 yards and 14 touchdowns ... Born Jan. 29, 1964, in Allentown, Pa. ... 1993 base salary: $1,150,000.

BRUCE SMITH 30 6-4 275   Defensive End

Returned to being a dominant player by recording 14 sacks ... Selected to Pro Bowl for a fifth time ... His 89 tackles ranked third on team and was second-highest total of eight-year career ... Started 15 games, missing only the Nov. 20 game against New Orleans with three cracked ribs, but played finale and three playoff games ... Has 91½ career sacks ... Came back from major knee difficulties during 1991 season in which he needed three separate arthroscopes ... Appeared in only five regular-season games that year ... Was first selection in 1985 draft and earned NFL Defensive Rookie-of-the-Year honors ... Had 6½ sacks and started 13 games as rookie ... Used some at fullback during short-yardage blocking plays ... Won 1985 Outland Trophy to conclude 46-sack career at Virginia Tech ... Born June 18, 1963, in Norfolk, Va. ... 1993 base salary: $1,600,000.

DARRYL TALLEY 33 6-4 236   Linebacker

Had his third consecutive 100-tackle season and fourth of career ... Had 106 tackles, including 73 solos, and added four sacks ... Has averaged 108.6 tackles during past five seasons ... Considered one of the most underrated outside linebackers ... Is inspirational leader of Bills' defense ... Merited Pro Bowl honors in 1991 ... Moved into starting lineup in 1985 for the first five games before being benched by then-coach Hank Bullough ... Returned to starting lineup in 1986 and never gave up outside linebacker position ... Has played in 156 regular-season and 12 playoff games ... Started for four years at West Virginia, averaging 121 tackles ... Was second-round draft choice of Bills in 1983 . . . Born July 10, 1960, in Cleveland . . . 1993 base salary: $950,000.

JEFF WRIGHT 30 6-3 270   Nose Tackle

Stunned Bills by signing a four-year, $6-million offer sheet with 49ers . . . After considerable debate within organization, the Bills matched the offer, making him the team's highest-paid defensive player . . . Could have been signed for around $800,000 a season in late December . . . Has 25 career sacks . . . No player has sacked Miami's Dan Marino (four) more than Wright . . . His quickness and strength off the line of scrimmage is difficult for centers to handle . . . Best game was an eight-tackle, 1½-sack effort against Saints . . . Spent two years as a backup behind Fred Smerlas . . . Became starter in 1990 . . . Sacked Warren Moon twice during a playoff game . . . Was eighth-round choice of Bills in 1988 from Central Missouri State . . . Transferred from Tulsa and Coffeyville . . . Born June 13, 1963, in San Bernadeno, Cal. . . . 1993 base salary: $1,100,000, plus $1,600,000 bonus.

THURMAN THOMAS 27 5-10 198   Halfback

Became first player in NFL history to lead league in combined yardage from scrimmage for four consecutive seasons, breaking a Jim Brown record . . . Selected to fourth Pro Bowl but couldn't play because of ankle injury suffered in Super Bowl XXVII . . . His 1,487 yards on 312 carries was his best ever . . . Had 10 100-yard rushing games, including five consecutive 100-yard games . . . Caught 58 passes for 626 yards . . . In 78 career regular-season games, he has rushed for 6,316 yards on 1,376 carries and has caught 247 passes for 2,666 yards . . . Won 1991 MVP honors and rates as best all-purpose back of his era . . . Was a second-round steal in 1988 draft because of worries about knee troubles in college . . . Rushed for 4,595 yards and 43 touchdowns

at Oklahoma State . . . Suffered knee injury playing pickup basketball before junior season . . . Born May 16, 1966, in Houston . . . 1993 base salary: $1,000,000, plus $450,000 in bonuses.

BILL BROOKS 29 6-0 195   Wide Receiver

Signed three-year, $3.5-million contract with Bills after seven seasons for the rival AFC East Colts . . . Is expected to replace the departed James Lofton . . . Was second only to Raymond Berry as best receiver in Colts' history . . . Had 411 receptions for 5,818 yards and 28 touchdowns with Colts . . . Comes to the Bills with a 39-game reception string . . . Averaged 58.7 receptions as Colt . . . His six 50-plus receptions seasons is a Colts' record . . . Caught 44 passes for 468 yards last season . . . Has been durable enough to have had streak of 74 consecutive starts, but he missed last year's opener against Cleveland because of ankle injury . . . His only touchdown catch last season was a 19-yarder in season-finale against Bengals . . . Was fourth-round steal in 1986 and earned All-Rookie honors . . . Caught 228 passes during brilliant career at Boston University and had 32 touchdown receptions . . . Has gained more than 100 yards 13 times . . . Born April 6, 1964, in Boston . . . 1993 base salary: $1,100,000, plus $500,000 signing bonus.

KENT HULL 32 6-4 275   Center

One of the brainiest and best centers in football . . . Star status hasn't been appreciated as much because other teammates such as Howard Ballard and Will Wolford drew more national recognition . . . Co-captain for three consecutive seasons . . . Hasn't missed a game or a start in seven seasons . . . Best game last year was against Indianapolis, when he won game ball . . . After going to three consecutive Pro Bowls, he has been overlooked for the past two seasons . . . Played three seasons at center for New Jersey Generals of USFL . . . Was a four-year starter at Mississippi State . . . Signed as free agent by Bills at training camp in 1986 and moved right into starting lineup . . . Born Jan. 13, 1961, in Ponotoc, Miss. . . . 1993 base salary: $375,000.

HOWARD BALLARD 29 6-6 325   Tackle

Has become dominating right tackle . . . Named to Pro Bowl for first time and started . . . Has started 67 consecutive games . . . Understandable nickname is "House" . . . Selected in 11th round of 1987 draft but opted to stay at Alabama A&M for final season, signing with Bills in 1988 . . . Criticized early in his career by quarterback Jim Kelly for letting defensive players get around him . . . Became full-time starter in 1989 . . . Extremely effective on counter plays, as he slams his bulk into tacklers at line of scrimmage . . . Missed a season in college because of bad knee . . . Born Nov. 3, 1963, in Ashland, Ala. . . . 1993 base salary: $700,000.

COACH MARV LEVY: Has compiled a 75-40 record to become the Bills' winningest coach . . . His 8-5 career playoff record is best in franchise history and he has been to three consecutive Super Bowls . . . Only Don Shula and Levy have coached teams to three consecutive Super Bowls . . . Since 1988, he's made Rich Stadium the toughest place for visitors because of 41-5 home record, including playoffs . . . Hired

Nov. 3, 1986, from CFL's Montreal Alouettes . . . Using more than 30 years of coaching experience, Levy built Bills into AFC's most dominating franchise . . . Rebuilt Chiefs from a 2-12 loser to a winner from 1977 through 1982 but lost job after strike-ruined 1982 season . . . Then worked two years in broadcasting before heading to Montreal, where he led Alouettes to 50-34-4 record . . . Was an assistant for three pro franchises and was head coach at California and William & Mary . . . His all-time NFL head coaching record is 106-82, including playoffs . . . Born Aug. 3, 1928, in Chicago . . . Was running back at Coe College . . . NFL Coach of the Year in 1988.

GREATEST INTERCEPTOR

It was at a time when Jack Kemp was quarterback, with Daryle Lamonica as backup, and Lou Saban was the coach. It was 1964, an AFL championship season for the Bills, and it marked the rookie year for George "Butch" Byrd.

A fourth-round draft pick out of Boston University, he gained a starting cornerback berth and made an impact that he sustained for seven seasons.

Byrd set the club record for career interceptions with 40, returning five for touchdowns, and at 205 pounds he was a punishing hitter.

Current Bills' safety Henry Jones, who earned a trip to the Pro Bowl thanks to an eight-interception season, could challenge Byrd in the years ahead.

INDIVIDUAL BILL RECORDS

Rushing

Most Yards Game:	273	O.J. Simpson, vs Detroit, 1976
Season:	2,003	O.J. Simpson, 1973
Career:	10,183	O.J. Simpson, 1969-77

Passing

Most TD Passes Game:	5	2 times, most recently Jim Kelly, vs Houston, 1989
Season:	26	Joe Ferguson, 1983
Career:	181	Joe Ferguson, 1973-84

Receiving

Most TD Passes Game:	4	Jerry Butler, vs N.Y. Jets, 1979
Season:	10	Elbert Dubenion, 1964
Career:	49	Andre Reed, 1985-91

Scoring

Most Points Game:	30	Cookie Gilchrist, vs N.Y. Jets, 1963
Season:	138	O.J. Simpson, 1975
Career:	670	Scott Norwood, 1985-91
Most TDs Game:	5	Cookie Gilchrist, vs N.Y. Jets, 1963
Season:	23	O.J. Simpson, 1975
Career:	70	O.J. Simpson, 1969-77

CINCINNATI BENGALS

TEAM DIRECTORY: Chairman: Austin E. Knowlton; Pres.: John Sawyer; VP/GM: Michael Brown; Corp. Sec.-Legal Counsel: Katie Blackburn; Dir. Player Personnel: Pete Brown; Dir. Pub. Rel.: Allan Heim; Head Coach: David Shula. Home field: Riverfront Stadium (60,389). Colors: Orange, black and white.

Bengals couldn't ask for more from Harold Green.

SCOUTING REPORT

OFFENSE: Second-year coach David Shula isn't left with much. The Bengals lost wide receiver Tim McGee (35 catches) and tight end Rodney Holman (26 catches) to free agency. Left tackle Anthony Munoz finally retired (then signed with the Bucs). Wide receiver Eddie Brown's neck injury, which sidelined him last season, makes him a question mark.

To make matters worse, the Bengals traded away quarterback Boomer Esiason and have little choice than to rush David Klingler into the starting lineup. Klingler completed only 48 percent of his passes as a rookie and was sacked a scary 18 times in his limited duty. With so few tools to work with, Klingler, drafted to run more of a pass-oriented offense, could be in for a long season. Ex-Raider Jay Schroeder will be Klingler's backup.

Fortunately, Shula has Pro Bowler Harold Green in the backfield. Green rushed for 1,170 yards and led the team with 41 receptions. Derrick Fenner occasionally spelled him and helped by averaging 4.5 yards a carry. If Brown can't recover, though, the starting receiving assignments fall upon promising Carl Pickens and immature Reggie Rembert and Jeff Query.

Replacing Esiason, Munoz, McGee and Holman in one season, though, is too much to ask a unit.

DEFENSE: Defensive coordinator Ron Lynn brought the attack back into the defense, but he'll have to stop a major leakage of yards. The Bengals finished 26th, allowing 333 yards and 23 points a game. Perhaps John Copeland of Alabama, the Bengals' top pick, will help.

During this difficult changeover season for the defense, Lynn developed a few young stars. Cornerback Leonard Wheeler and free safety Darryl Williams improved as the season went along. Inside linebacker Ricardo McDonald emerged as a big-play man. Well-travelled outside linebacker Daniels Stubbs, with his fourth team in five seasons, came up with nine sacks.

Lynn's style is a gambling defense. It allowed the Bengals to record 45 sacks, but also allow 4.5 yards a rush. He'll also have to tighten up a secondary that allowed 7.4 yards per passing attempt.

Big seasons are expected from linebackers Alfred Williams and James Francis, but it comes as no surprise that the Bengals are trying to replace strong safety David Fulcher, who lacks the mobility to be a star in this defense.

BENGALS VETERAN ROSTER

HEAD COACH—Dave Shula. Assistant Coaches—Jim Anderson, Marv Braden, Mike Haluchak, Bob Karmelowicz, Ron Lynn, Jim McNally, Ron Meeks, Mike Pope, Richard Williamson, Kim Wood.

No.	Name	Pos.	Ht.	Wt.	NFL Exp.	College
65	Arthur, Mike	C	6-3	280	3	Texas A&M
42	Ball, Eric	RB	6-2	220	5	UCLA
57	Bentley, Ray	LB	6-2	235	8	Central Michigan
3	Breech, Jim	K	5-6	175	15	California
81	Brown, Eddie	WR	6-0	185	8	Miami (Fla.)
38	Dingle, Mike	RB	6-2	240	2	South Carolina
29	Dixon, Rickey	S	5-11	191	6	Oklahoma
44	Fenner, Derrick	RB	6-3	228	5	North Carolina
50	Francis, James	LB	6-5	252	4	Baylor
97	Frier, Mike	DE	6-5	299	2	Appalachian State
47	Frisch, David	TE	6-7	260	R	Colorado State
33	Fulcher, David	S	6-3	238	8	Arizona State
35	Garrett, Shane	WR	5-11	185	2	Texas A&M
58	Gordon, Alex	LB	6-5	245	7	Cincinnati
28	Green, Harold	RB	6-2	222	4	South Carolina
12	Hollas, Donald	QB	6-3	215	3	Rice
26	Isaiah, Richard	WR	6-0	175	1	Toledo
11	Johnson, Lee	P-K	6-2	200	9	Brigham Young
25	Jones, Rod	CB	6-0	185	8	SMU
55	Kirk, Randy	LB	6-2	231	5	San Diego State
7	Klingler, David	QB	6-2	205	2	Houston
64	Kozerski, Bruce	G	6-4	287	10	Holy Cross
69	Krumrie, Tim	NT	6-2	274	11	Wisconsin
56	McDonald, Ricardo	LB	6-2	235	2	Pittsburgh
62	Melander, Jon	G	6-7	280	3	Minnesota
36	Miles, Ostell	RB	6-0	236	2	Houston
73	Moyer, Ken	G-C	6-7	297	4	Toledo
95	Nix, Roosevelt	DE	6-6	292	2	Central State (Ohio)
23	Overton, Don	RB	6-1	225	4	Fairmont State
80	Pickens, Carl	WR	6-2	206	2	Tennessee
32	Price, Mitchell	CB	5-9	181	4	Tulane
89	Query, Jeff	WR	6-0	165	5	Millikin
61	Rayam, Tom	G	6-6	297	2	Alabama
52	Reasons, Gary	LB	6-4	234	10	NW Louisiana
88	Rembert, Reggie	WR	6-5	200	3	West Virginia
79	Rogers, Lamar	DE	6-4	292	3	Auburn
77	Sargent, Kevin	T	6-6	284	2	Eastern Washington
98	Savage, Tony	DT	6-3	285	2	Washington State
10	Schroeder, Jay	QB	6-4	215	10	UCLA
76	Scrafford, Kirk	G	6-6	255	4	Montana
90	Shaw, Eric	LB	6-3	248	2	Louisiana Tech
84	Stegall, Milt	WR	6-0	184	2	Miami (Ohio)
96	Stubbs, Daniel	DE	6-4	264	6	Miami (Fla.)
49	Thomason, Jeff	TE	6-4	233	2	Oregon
48	Thompson, Craig	TE	6-2	244	2	North Carolina A&T
86	Turner, Elbert	WR	5-11	165	1	Illinois
34	Vinson, Fernandus	S	5-10	197	3	North Carolina State
63	Walter, Joe	T	6-7	292	9	Texas Tech
37	Wheeler, Leonard	CB	5-11	189	2	Troy State
39	White, Sheldon	CB	5-11	190	6	Miami (Ohio)
4	Wilhelm, Erik	QB	6-3	217	4	Oregon State
94	Williams, Alfred	LB	6-6	240	3	Colorado
31	Williams, Darryl	S	6-0	191	2	Miami (Fla.)
60	Withycombe, Mike	C-G	6-5	297	6	Fresno State

		TOP DRAFT CHOICES				
Rd.	Name	Sel. No.	Pos.	Ht.	Wt.	College
1	Copeland, John	5	DT	6-4	280	Alabama
2	McGee, Tony	37	TE	6-4	246	Michigan
3	Tovar, Steve	59	LB	6-3	245	Ohio State
3	Parten, Ty	63	DT	6-5	264	Arizona
4	Simmons, Marcello	90	RB	5-11	185	SMU

SPECIAL TEAMS: They can't run off Jim Breech even though he's 37. This is his 15th season, but how do you replace a kicker who made 19 of 27 field goals and can still nail the 48-yarders? Lee Johnson settled into the punting job and averaged 42.1 yards. Breakdowns on special teams, though, left the Bengals exposed for three touchdowns on returns. Pickens averaged 12.7 yards on punt returns and is one of the best in the AFC.

THE ROOKIES: Defensive tackle Copeland and tight end Tony McGee from Michigan could immediately press for starting jobs. Copeland was the most complete defensive lineman available while McGee, the second-rounder, will work his way into Holman's old job. Steve Tovar from Ohio State will be tried at outside line.

OUTLOOK: The Bengals, 5-11 last year, will be pressed to come out of the cellar with an inexperienced second-year quarterback and a major talent drain on offense. The defense lacks powerful forces on the line, which allows them to be overrun.

BENGAL PROFILES

HAROLD GREEN 25 6-2 222 **Running Back**

Earned Pro Bowl selection by rushing for 1,170 yards, second-best in team history . . . Averaged 4.4 yards per carry . . . Led Bengals with 41 receptions for 214 yards . . . Team tried to protect him from free agency by putting on a restricted price tag of first- and third-round choices . . . Named transition player in 1994 to further protect him from free agency . . . Was recruited by the Redskins, who were almost willing to give up

first- and third-round choices to sign him as a restricted free agent
... Answered any questions about his durability ... Took the
flashes of excellence showed during his first two years and turned
himself into one of the league's elite backs ... An outstanding
receiving back in college, he left South Carolina as a junior to be
a second-round choice in 1990 ... Has steadily improved rushing
totals from 353 yards to 753 to 1,170 ... Has been to past two
Pro Bowls ... Ranks second on South Carolina's all-time rushing
list with 3,005 yards ... Born Jan. 29, 1968, in Ladson, S.C. ...
1992 base salary: $305,000.

DAVID KLINGLER 24 6-2 205   Quarterback

Showed he can throw deep passes accurately,
but needs to be more durable ... Left one game
with twisted knee and missed season finale with
hip pointer ... Given starting job over Boomer
Esiason in November and started four games
... Rookie completed 47 of 98 passes for 530
yards and had three touchdown passes ...
Threw only two interceptions but was sacked
18 times ... Was the Bengals' surprise first-round choice (No. 6
overall) when everyone thought they would select a defensive
player ... Broke tons of NCAA records at University of Houston,
where he operated out of the Run-and-Shoot ... Throws well out
of the pocket ... Has a congenital neck problem ... Passed for
9,430 yards and 91 touchdowns to break Southwest Conference
records ... Attributes strong arm to his genes. His father, Dick,
starred as a high-school quarterback ... Can dunk a basketball
flat-footed and high-jumps 6-foot-9 ... Born Feb. 17, 1969, in
Stratford, Tex. ... 1993 base salary: $1,000,000.

DARRYL WILLIAMS 23 6-0 191   Safety

Brought awesome speed to free safety ... Established himself as productive free safety during rookie season ... Led Bengals with four
interceptions and 13 passes defensed ... Finished third in tackles with 78, including 70 solos
... Had 4.34-second time in 40 during college
and can cover sideline-to-sideline ... A devastating hitter who loves to drill opponents ...
Considered best defensive back to come from University of Miami

since Bennie Blades . . . Left Miami after junior season and was first-round choice of the Bengals . . . Born Jan. 1, 1970, in Miami . . . 1993 base salary: $400,000.

ALFRED WILLIAMS 24 6-6 240   **Linebacker**

Should challenge and probably beat Daniel Stubbs as starting right outside linebacker . . . Became main pass-rush threat with 10-sack season . . . Started four games after disappointing rookie season . . . Had a heart problem—Wolfe Parkinson-White syndrome—that caused a rapid heartbeat . . . Had two surgeries last year, but made rapid recovery . . . Has 13 sacks during the past two seasons . . . Contract problems and a late arrival in training camp ruined rookie year . . . Was first-round choice in 1991 draft . . . Winner of the Butkus Award as top college linebacker . . . Holds Colorado sack record with 35 . . . His long reach enabled him to deflect three passes and force three fumbles . . . Had 263 career tackles at Colorado . . . Born Nov. 6, 1968, in Houston . . . 1993 base salary: $400,000.

JAMES FRANCIS 25 6-5 252   **Linebacker**

One of the biggest, strongest outside linebackers in league . . . Finished season on injured-reserve list because of knee injury that nagged him all season . . . Recorded only 39 tackles, five sacks and intercepted three passes during his short season . . . Began 1991 season as an inside linebacker to take advantage of his run pursuit, but is more comfortable on the outside . . . Still, the team's best all-around player on defense . . . Holds up tight ends with his strength, enabling him to make tackles . . . Was first-round choice in 1990, made All-Rookie teams and was *USA Today's* Defensive Rookie of the Year . . . Had eight sacks as rookie . . . Despite bulk, he has dropped into coverage to intercept six career passes . . . Tied for team lead with three forced fumbles . . . Was sixth man on Baylor basketball team . . . A rare athlete who played in the 1989 Liberty Bowl as a football player and in 1989 NCAA basketball tournament . . . Born Aug. 4, 1968, in Houston . . . 1993 base salary: $450,000.

BRUCE KOZERSKI 31 6-4 287 Guard

Because of need, he switched to left guard after spending five years as a standout center . . . Had his best season and has become the leader of offensive line . . . During past nine seasons, he has started at every spot on offensive line . . . As smart on the field as he was at Holy Cross, where he was an honor student with a 3.7 grade-point average, majoring in physics . . . Came to the Bengals as a ninth-round draft choice . . . He played against coach David Shula (Dartmouth) in college . . . Started at right guard in 1986, but was rushed into service at center . . . Played guard and tackle the next season before moving to center . . . Born April 3, 1962, in Plains, Pa. . . . 1993 base salary: $600,000.

LAMAR ROGERS 25 6-4 292 Defensive End

Continued to develop into the big defensive linemen that the Bengals need to battle 300-pound blockers . . . Is still developing pass-rushing skills and had four sacks last season . . . Might be the best Bengal defensive lineman against the run . . . Recorded 43 tackles last season and forced two fumbles . . . Was supposed to start during his rookie season, but struggled trying to live up to expectations . . . Drafted in the second round of 1991 draft . . . Originally went to Auburn as a tight end but shifted to linebacker and then to defensive end . . . Was highest-rated defensive lineman at 1991 scouting combine . . . Born Nov. 5, 1967, in Opp, Ala. . . . 1993 base salary: $355,000.

EDDIE BROWN 30 6-0 185 Wide Receiver

Missed the entire season with a neck injury aggravated in preseason . . . First injured the neck in 1991 on hit by Oiler safety Bubba McDowell in training camp . . . Prior to last year had been one of the league's consistent big-play receivers, averaging 52 catches and 16.9 yards per reception . . . Caught 50 passes in five of first seven seasons . . . His 59-catch season in 1991 was a personal high, but his best season was 1988, when he grabbed 53 receptions for 1,273 yards . . . Ranks third on the Bengals' all-time reception list with 363, trailing Isaac Curtis (420) and Cris Collinsworth (417) . . . Holds Bengal record for a 216-yard day against Pittsburgh in 1988 . . . Speciality is catching passes in the middle of the field and using open-field running ability . . . Used "Play-Doh" to strengthen his hands for receptions . . . Was first-round choice in 1985 from University of Miami . . . Began college career as a defensive back . . . Born Dec. 18, 1962, in Miami . . . 1993 base salary: $1,025,000.

TIM KRUMRIE 32 6-2 274   Defensive Tackle

Hasn't slowed down as much as the organization expected . . . Though he can't go sideline-to-sideline as he did in his early days, he led the Bengals in tackles for the first time since 1988 . . . One of the most productive nose tackles of the late 1980s, he recorded 97 tackles, four sacks, two forced fumbles and a fumble recovery . . . Led Bengals in tackles from 1985 through 1988, but broke his left leg in Super Bowl XXIII . . . It took him two years to regain full strength, but he didn't miss a season . . . Plays with a metal rod in the leg . . . "I'm a very good cheater," he says of his ability to slip past offensive linemen . . . Was a consensus All-American at Wisconsin in 1981 and 1982 . . . Was a heavyweight wrestling champ in high school . . . A 10th-round choice in 1983 draft . . . Born May 20, 1960, in Menomonie, Wisc. . . . 1993 base salary: $600,000.

CARL PICKENS 23 6-2 206   Wide Receiver

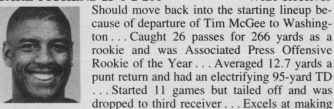

Should move back into the starting lineup because of departure of Tim McGee to Washington . . . Caught 26 passes for 266 yards as a rookie and was Associated Press Offensive Rookie of the Year . . . Averaged 12.7 yards a punt return and had an electrifying 95-yard TD . . . Started 11 games but tailed off and was dropped to third receiver . . . Excels at making the leaping catch and is tough enough to steal the ball from defensive backs . . . Best catch was game-winner against the Bears in overtime . . . Caught 109 passes at Tennessee to rank fourth on school's all-time list . . . Earned All-American honors for two seasons and was a high-jumper . . . Former Vols' coach Johnny Majors called him the most natural athlete he's seen in 23 years of coaching . . . Was second-round choice of Bengals in 1991 . . . Born March 23, 1970, in Murphy, N.C. . . . 1993 base salary: $365,000.

RICARDO McDONALD 23 6-2 235   **Linebacker**

Carries a big impact for what might be considered a tiny inside linebacker . . . Not only likes to hit people, but he loves to talk about it on the field . . . Was star of Bengals' offseason workouts . . . Started 14 games as left inside linebacker and was second on team with 95 tackles, two behind Tim Krumrie . . . Bench-presses 415 pounds and runs a 4.62 40 . . . Taken on fourth round last season . . . Returned to high-school position of inside linebacker after playing on outside at college . . . Started four seasons at Pitt and finished with 260 career tackles . . . Twin brother, Devon, was linebacking star at Notre Dame . . . Born Nov. 8, 1969, in Kingston, Jamaica, he might have become a cricket player . . . But the family moved to New Jersey when he was 12 . . . 1993 base salary: $220,000.

COACH DAVID SHULA: Son of Dolphin coach Don Shula

began the tough rebuilding process with a 5-11 record, a two-game improvement over the previous season . . . Opened first season with impressive victories over Seahawks, 21-3, and Raiders, 24-21 . . . Still the youngest coach in the NFL at 33 . . . He and dad are first father-son combination to be NFL head coaches at same time . . . Don was 33 when he first became head coach . . . The Eagles offered Dave a head-coaching job but he declined it to gain more experience . . . Is a meticulous student of the game whose specialty is organization . . . Began coaching career with Miami by coaching receivers and quarterbacks in 1982 . . . Was assistant head coach of Dolphins in 1988 . . . Cowboys hired him to be offensive coordinator and quarterback coach in 1989 . . . Left Dallas after two seasons to become receiver coach with the Bengals . . . Played wide receiver at Dartmouth and was a wide receiver/kick-returner for Colts in 1981 . . . Born May 28, 1959, in Lexington, Ky.

GREATEST INTERCEPTOR

He was one of the first players to use the stationary bike in the offseason to keep in shape. But there was nothing stationary about

Ken Riley, a 6-foot, 180-pound cornerback who stands as the Bengals' No. 1 all-time interceptor.

Riley was a product of Texas A&M who became a starter in the second year (1969) of what would be a 15-year career as a Bengal. He made 65 interceptions, returning five for touchdowns. In his final season he had eight interceptions and, on the heels of a Pro Bowl year, he joined former Bengal defensive coordinator Hank Bullough at Green Bay for a 16th season in 1984.

"Ken was a heady player," Bullough said. "There were those who were faster and stronger, but few cornerbacks who were better."

INDIVIDUAL BENGAL RECORDS

Rushing

Most Yards Game:	201	James Brooks, vs Houston, 1990	
Season:	1,087	James Brooks, 1986	
Career:	6,447	James Brooks, 1984-91	

Passing

Most TD Passes Game:	5	2 times, most recently Boomer Esiason, vs Tampa Bay, 1989
Season:	29	Ken Anderson, 1981
Career:	196	Ken Anderson, 1971-85

Receiving

Most TD Passes Game:	3	3 times, most recently Isaac Curtis, vs Baltimore, 1979
Season:	10	Isaac Curtis, 1974
Career:	53	Isaac Curtis, 1973-83

Scoring

Most Points Game:	24	Larry Kinnebrew, vs Houston, 1984
Season:	115	Jim Breech, 1981
Career:	963	Jim Breech, 1981-92
Most TDs Game:	4	Larry Kinnebrew, vs Houston, 1984
Season:	16	Pete Johnson, 1981
Career:	70	Pete Johnson, 1977-83

CLEVELAND BROWNS

TEAM DIRECTORY: Owner/Pres.: Art Modell; Exec. VP-Legal Administration: Jim Bailey; Asst. to Pres.: David Modell; VP-Pub. Rel.: Kevin Byrne; Dir. Personnel: Mike Lombardi; Head Coach: Bill Belichick. Home field: Cleveland Stadium (78,512). Colors: Seal brown, orange and white.

SCOUTING REPORT

OFFENSE: Bernie Kosar had his best season in years, and he also had his scariest. He completed 66.5 percent of his passes and had a hard-to-beat 87 quarterback rating, but he broke a bone in his right foot twice.

Browns need a healthy Bernie Kosar.

Kosar spent the offseason with two pins holding the foot together, but he is expected to lead the Browns' conservative offense this fall. And, bringing back some old memories, his former University of Miami backup, Vinny Testaverde, will be right behind him. Testaverde signed a two-year, $2.8-million contract to fill in for Kosar.

Testaverde isn't the only touch of Tampa Bay in the Browns' offense. Mark Carrier, the Bucs' all-time leading receiver, signed to give Kosar a wide-receiver target other than Michael Jackson from the backfield. Carrier and Jackson should start.

Big decisions need to be made at running back. Should coach Bill Belichick stay with veterans such as Kevin Mack and Leroy Hoard, or should he simply let Eric Metcalf and Tommy Vardell be the starters? The Browns added guard Houston Hoover to an improving offensive line whose best acquisition was center Jay Hilgenberg, who came to the Browns in a 1992 trade from the Bears. Top pick Steve Everitt of Michigan will back up Hilgenberg.

DEFENSE: Reggie White would have made the Browns' defensive line exceptional, but they already had a pretty good one. Anchored by Pro Bowl defensive tackle Michael Dean Perry, the Browns' front four gets better with the signing of ex-Lion Jerry Ball and the development of young players such as Anthony Pleasant, Rob Burnett, Pio Sagapolutele and promising young backup Bill Johnson.

The rest of the defense is strong up the middle. Middle linebacker Mike Johnson had his best season, but Belichick has to be concerned about age and uncertainty at his outside linebacker positions. Clay Matthews is 37. Former Plan B acquisition David Brandon continues to surprise the coaches with his ability to force fumbles, but he could be replaced.

Call the secondary the Comeback Capital of the NFL. Cornerback Terry Taylor overcame drug problems to consistently cover receivers for 16 starts. Long-time Brown Frank Minnifield overcame a strange urinary disorder. Strong safety Vince Newsome overcame rejection when the Rams released him two years ago. Next up is Najee Mustafaa, formerly Reggie Rutland of the Vikings, who is coming back from major knee surgery.

SPECIAL TEAMS: Matt Stover, once a raw prospect, settled into the Browns' job nicely by making 21 of 29 field goals and scoring 90 points. Punter Brian Hanson is an accurate punter who

BROWNS VETERAN ROSTER

HEAD COACH—Bill Belichick. Assistant Coaches—Ernie Adams, Jim Bates, Steve Crosby, Kirk Ferentz, Richard Mann, John Mitchell, Scott O'Brien, Nick Saban, Phil Savage, Mike Sheppard, Jerry Simmons, Kevin Spencer, Gary Tranquill, Woody Widenhofer.

No.	Name	Pos.	Ht.	Wt.	NFL Exp.	College
23	Baldwin, Randy	RB	5-10	216	3	Mississippi
93	Ball, Jerry	DT	6-1	300	7	Southern Methodist
37	Barnett, Harlon	S	5-11	200	4	Michigan State
58	Brandon, David	LB	6-4	230	7	Memphis State
52	Brown, Richard	LB	6-3	240	6	San Diego State
90	Burnett, Rob	DE	6-4	270	4	Syracuse
83	Carrier, Mark	WR	6-0	182	7	Nicholls State
80	Collins, Shawn	WR	6-2	207	5	Northern Arizona
72	Dahl, Bob	G-T	6-5	285	2	Notre Dame
79	Davis, Travis	DT	6-2	275	3	Michigan State
35	Douglas, Derrick	FB	5-10	222	3	Louisiana Tech
38	Ellison, Bernard	DB	6-0	192	3	Nevada
53	Figaro, Cedric	LB	6-3	255	6	Notre Dame
69	Fike, Dan	G-T	6-7	285	9	Florida
62	Fisher, John	C	6-3	280	1	Tennessee
81	Galbraith, Scott	TE	6-2	255	4	USC
8	Goebel, Brad	QB	6-3	198	3	Baylor
41	Haddix, Wayne	CB	6-1	204	5	Liberty
20	Haller, Alan	CB	5-11	185	2	Michigan State
11	Hansen, Brian	P	6-2	215	9	Sioux Falls
63	Hilgenberg, Jay	C	6-3	270	13	Iowa
39	Hilliard, Randy	CB	5-11	160	4	Northwestern State
33	Hoard, Leroy	RB	5-11	230	4	Michigan
89	Holohan, Pete	TE	6-4	244	13	Notre Dame
64	Hoover, Houston	G-T	6-2	300	6	Jackson State
1	Jackson, Michael	WR	6-4	195	3	Southern Mississippi
94	Johnson, Bill	DL	6-4	295	2	Michigan State
59	Johnson, Mike	LB	6-1	230	8	Virginia Tech
96	Jones, James	DT	6-2	290	3	Northern Iowa
16	Jones, Selwyn	CB	6-0	185	2	Colorado State
66	Jones, Tony	T	6-5	295	6	Western Carolina
10	Keen, Robbie	K	6-3	215	1	Cal-Berkeley
88	Kinchen, Brian	TE	6-2	232	6	LSU
68	King, Ed	G-T	6-4	303	3	Auburn
19	Kosar, Bernie	QB	6-5	215	9	Miami
97	Logan, Ernie	DL	6-3	285	3	East Carolina
34	Mack, Kevin	FB	6-0	220	9	Clemson
57	Matthews, Clay	LB	6-2	245	16	USC
87	McCardell, Keenan	WR	6-1	175	2	UNLV
21	Metcalf, Eric	RB	5-10	185	5	Texas
65	Milstead, Rod	G	6-2	290	2	Delaware State
31	Minnifield, Frank	CB	5-9	180	10	Louisville
27	Moore, Stevon	S	5-11	205	5	Mississippi
46	Mustafaa, Najee	CB	6-1	190	6	Georgia Tech
92	Perry, Michael Dean	DT	6-1	290	6	Clemson
17	Philcox, Todd	QB	6-4	225	4	Syracuse
98	Pleasant, Anthony	DE	6-5	258	4	Tennessee State
15	Pruitt, James	WR	6-2	198	6	Cal State-Fullerton
70	Rienstra, John	G	6-5	275	8	Temple
86	Rowe, Patrick	WR	6-1	195	2	San Diego State
75	Sagapolutele, Pio	DL	6-6	297	3	San Diego State
84	Smith, Rico	WR	6-0	185	2	Colorado
50	Stams, Frank	LB	6-2	240	5	Notre Dame
3	Stover, Matt	K	5-11	178	4	Louisiana Tech
49	Swilling, Ken	LB	6-2	245	1	Georgia Tech
24	Taylor, Terry	CB	5-10	185	10	Southern Illinois
12	Testaverde, Vinny	QB	6-5	215	7	Miami
91	Thornton, John	DT	6-3	303	2	Cincinnati
85	Tillman, Lawyer	WR	6-5	230	5	Auburn

continued on page 479

TOP DRAFT CHOICES

Rd.	Name	Sel. No.	Pos.	Ht.	Wt.	College
1	Everitt, Steve	14	C	6-5	284	Michigan
2	Footman, Dan	42	DE	6-5	281	Florida State
3	Caldwell, Mike	83	LB	6-1	226	Middle Tenn. State
5	Arvie, Herman	124	T	6-4	330	Grambling
6	McKenzie, Rich	153	LB	6-2	230	Penn State

placed 28 of his 74 attempts inside the 20. The Browns' return teams are as good as the coaches want it to be. Metcalf offers big plays on punt returns. Randy Baldwin is a no-nonsense kickoff returner.

THE ROOKIES: Bigger and better. That was the Browns motto' going into the draft. They traded down in the first round for Michigan's 280-pound center Everitt, who may be moved to guard. Dan Footman, the second-rounder, was a Florida State defensive end who outgrew the fullback position and overcame major knee troubles to become a 290-pound force.

OUTLOOK: A healthy Kosar, a solid running game and a couple hot receivers could take this team (7-9 in 1992) further than most preseason prognosticators project. The defense won't allow many points, but getting the touchdowns is a worry with this offense. They need Tommy Vardell to be a Touchdown Tommy.

BROWN PROFILES

BERNIE KOSAR 29 6-5 215   Quarterback

Browns have some concerns about right ankle that was broken twice last season...Two screws were surgically inserted after the season to help healing process...Fought off pain to have another impressive season...Would have been second in the AFC with an 87 quarterback rating but failed to meet the 224-pass qualifying minimum...Completed 103 of 155 passes for 1,160 yards, eight touchdowns and seven interceptions. ...Dolphin linebacker John Offerdahl broke the ankle in the second quarter of a Sept. 14 Monday night game...But he led 20-point fourth-quarter comeback and a 27-23 victory...Spent 10

weeks on the injured-reserve list. . . . Signed "lifetime" contract
extension through 1999 that pays him an average of $3.28 million
a season. . . . Kosar holds 19 team and five NFL passing records
. . . Has thrown only 78 interceptions in 3,012 attempts. . . . Played
only two seasons at Miami . . . Browns sent four draft choices to
Bills to make him 1985 supplemental pick . . . Born Nov. 25,
1963, in Boardman, Ohio. . . . 1993 base salary: $2,200,000.

MIKE JOHNSON 30 6-1 230   Linebacker

Grabbed back leadership role of defense with
best season . . . Led Browns with career-high
176 tackles and forced four fumbles . . . Tied
Len Ford's team record with five fumble recoveries . . . Had 10 or more tackles in 14
games . . . Has been to Pro Bowl twice . . . A
broken bone in right foot sidelined him for final
11 games of 1991, the only season since 1987
he hasn't been Browns' tackle leader . . . Was defensive star for
two years with Philadelphia Stars of USFL . . . Was 1984 USFL
supplemental choice of Browns, behind running back Kevin Mack
. . . Led Browns with special-teams tackles (33) in 1986 after leaving Stars . . . Beat out Anthony Griggs for inside linebacking job
in 1987. . . . Started four years at Virginia Tech with Bruce Smith
and Jesse Penn. . . . Born Nov. 26, 1962, in Southport, N.C.

KEVIN MACK 31 6-0 220   Fullback

Led the Browns with 543 rushing yards on 169
carries . . . Started season on four-week injury
list because of calf injury . . . Scored his 48th
career touchdown against Steelers Oct. 11 after
being activated . . . Rushed for six touchdowns,
fifth in the AFC . . . Moved past Greg Pruitt for
fourth place on team's all-time rushing list
(5,090 yards). . . . Went to Pro Bowl in 1985
and 1987 . . . Browns gave Bears four draft choices in order to
acquire him as 1984 USFL supplemental choice . . . Rushed for
330 yards in one season with USFL Los Angeles Express . . .
Joined Browns in 1985 and teamed with Earnest Byner to become
NFL's third pair of 1,000-yard backs . . . Is all-time Browns' postseason leader with 424 yards, but hasn't had a 100-yard game in
the playoffs . . . Rushed for 862 yards for Clemson in 1983. . . .
Born Aug. 9, 1962, in Kings Mountain, N.C. . . . 1992 base salary:
$850,000.

MARK CARRIER 27 6-0 182   Wide Receiver

Signed with Browns as a free agent after six seasons with Bucs... His three-year, $3.6-million deal made him the Browns' highest-paid wide receiver... Followed quarterback Vinny Testaverde, who also left the Bucs to sign with the Browns as a free agent last spring ... Caught 56 passes for 692 yards (12.4 average) and team-high 4 TDs for the Bucs... Caught 321 passes for 5,018 yards in six seasons with the Bucs ... Best season was 1989, when he made the Pro Bowl after catching 86 passes for 1,422 yards... Statistics dropped in subsequent seasons in part because of Testaverde's problems... Bucs' third-round pick in 1987 out of Nicholls (La.) State... Distant cousin of Bears' defensive back Mark Carrier... Born Oct. 28, 1965, in Lafayette, La.... 1993 base salary: $1.4 million.

TOMMY VARDELL 24 6-1 238   Fullback

"Touchdown Tommy" had impressive NFL beginning but is still looking for first pro touchdown... Finished second on team with 369 yards on 99 carries.... Started 10 games as rookie... Had 84-yard rushing day Sept. 14 against Dolphins... Finished season on injured reserve because of calf injury... Scored 34 touchdowns during final two years at Stanford ... Was the ninth overall choice in 1992 draft... Is prototype fullback who can run, block, catch and lead... Was high-school wrestling star at 195 pounds... Graduated from Stanford with a 3.2 grade-point average... Finished second to Darrin Nelson's 4,033 Stanford record with 2,940 yards.... Born Feb. 20, 1969, in El Cajon, Cal.... 1993 base salary: $400,000.

ERIC METCALF 25 5-10 185   Halfback

Battled 1992 offseason trade rumors to have one of his better seasons.... Though not an every-down player, the Browns let him do everything.... He's scored touchdowns via punt and kickoff returns, rushing and receiving, and he's even thrown a touchdown pass... Caught 47 passes for 614 yards and rushed for 301 yards on 73 carries.... In 56 career games,

Metcalf has 5,853 all-purpose yards, an average of 104 yards per game . . . Has 21 career touchdowns in four seasons . . . Had two 200-plus all-purpose-yard games last season . . . Recovered completely from 1991 shoulder injury that caused him to miss half the season. . . . Father, Terry, was former Cardinal and CFL star. . . . Was Heisman Trophy candidate and two-time NCAA long-jump champion at Texas. . . . Had 5,705 career all-purpose yards at Texas . . . Browns made him first-round choice in 1989 . . . Rushed for 633 yards as rookie. . . . Born Jan. 23, 1968, in Seattle. . . . 1993 base salary: $775,000.

MICHAEL DEAN PERRY 28 6-1 290   Defensive Tackle

Rebounded from early-season knee troubles to become Browns' only Pro Bowl player. . . . Missed most of training camp because of arthroscopic surgery . . . Made just one tackle on sore knee in season-opener against Indianapolis and sat out the next two games. . . . Finished strong with 8½ sacks in final 13 games . . . Selected to the Pro Bowl for fourth consecutive year . . . Ranks fifth on Browns' all-time sack list with 41½, averaging more than eight sacks per season . . . Complained often last season about Browns' "two-gap" scheme that prevented him from attacking on every down . . . He is the player Browns built their defense around . . . His quickness is virtually impossible for guards or centers to stop without help from other blockers . . . Tiny brother of Bear defensive tackle William (Refrigerator) Perry. . . . Holds Clemson's sack record with 28. . . . Was Browns' second-round choice in 1988. . . . Born Aug. 27, 1965, in Aiken, S.C. . . . 1993 base salary: $1,550,000.

ERIC TURNER 24 6-1 207   Safety

On the verge of being one of the AFC's top safeties. . . . Still adjusting to NFL pass coverage and had to be benched once . . . Strong finish hints that he is ready to explode as a defender . . . In 23 pro games, he's forced six fumbles and intercepted three passes . . . His 119 tackles ranked second on team . . . Ankle problems prevented him from starting three games last season . . . Missed first half of rookie season because of stress leg fracture, but still finished third on team with 84 tackles, including 52 solos . . . Was second choice in the 1991 draft, the highest chosen defensive back in NFL since Gary Glick by Steelers in 1956 . . . Ranks fourth in UCLA history with 369 career tackles . . . Was scholastic All-American . . . Born Sept. 20, 1968, in Ventura, Cal. . . . 1993 base salary: $700,000.

JAY HILGENBERG 33 6-3 270   Center

Became an instant anchor on Browns' offensive line . . . Started 16 games after being acquired from Bears a few days before season opener . . . Browns only gave up third-round choice to get him after he held out at training camp . . . Browns signed him to two-year, $2.1-million contract . . . Was seven-time Pro Bowler for Bears . . . Since 1984, he's missed only two starts . . . Handles snaps on field goals and extra points . . . His brother, Joel, is Saints' center . . . His uncle, Wally, was linebacker with Lions and Minnesota from 1964-79 . . . Signed by Bears in 1981 as an undrafted free agent out of Iowa . . . Replaced Dan Neal as Bears' starting center midway into his third season in 1983 . . . Born March 21, 1960, in Iowa City, Iowa. . . . 1993 base salary: $1,101,000.

CLAY MATTHEWS 37 6-2 245   Linebacker

The Browns' grand old man on defense is still a force . . . Spared from most pass-coverage situations, Matthews concentrated on stopping the run and rushing the passer . . . Tied Rob Burnett for team sack lead with nine. . . . Finished third with 111 tackles, his eighth 100-tackle season . . . Joins Ted Hendricks, Jack Reynolds, Jack Pardee, Ray Nitschke and Chuck Howley for surviving 15 seasons at linebacker . . . Passed Jerry Sherk on the all-time Browns' sack list with 71. . . . Tied with Lou ''The Toe'' Groza with 216 games played. . . . Since 1985, he has missed only one start. . . . Has been selected to five Pro Bowls . . . Brother, Bruce, is a perennial Pro Bowl offensive lineman with Oilers. . . .

One of five Browns in history to play in three decades . . . Was first-round choice of Browns in 1978 and has been mainstay at right outside linebacker. . . . Was middle linebacker at Southern Cal, where he was All-American . . . Born March 15, 1956, in Palo Alto, Cal. . . . 1992 base salary: $1,200,000.

ED KING 23 6-4 303   Guard

Struggled after sensational rookie season but started 14 games at right guard . . . Straightened out technique difficulties on final stretch in which Browns rushed for 100 yards in four of final five games . . . Might be moved to right tackle because of acquisition of guard Houston Hoover. . . . Earned consensus All-Rookie honors in 1991 after skipping senior year at Auburn . . . Started 14 games as a rookie at age 21 . . . One of finest linemen to ever play at Auburn. . . . Recruited as a *Parade* All-American . . . Browns drafted him in second round in 1991 . . . Born Dec. 3, 1969, in Fort Benning, Ga. . . . 1993 base salary: $350,000.

ROB BURNETT 26 6-4 270   Defensive End

Responded to the tough job of being the Browns' main pass-rusher from the defensive line. . . . Tied Clay Matthews for the team sack lead with nine. . . . After two years of grooming, Burnett has finally been turned loose . . . A foot injury limited him to eight starts in 1991 and left questions about his development. . . . Two sacks and a blocked field goal during the first month of last season erased doubts . . . Outperformed promising starting defensive end Anthony Pleasant in great debate as to who was best Browns' rookie in 1990. . . . Played defensive tackle at Syracuse but showed special ability to get to the quarterback (18 career sacks) . . . Was fifth-round choice in the 1990 draft . . . Started final six games of 1990 at left defensive end and ended up sixth on the team with 57 tackles. . . . Born Aug. 27, 1967, in Livingston, N.J. . . . 1992 base salary: $330,000.

COACH BILL BELICHICK: Continues to do miracles with  a defense that is in midst of transition . . . Stingy defense set five club records, including fewest touchdowns allowed (29), fewest rushing yards (1,605) and most sacks (48) . . . Two-year record as head coach is 13-19. . . . A tireless worker who learned the intracacies of NFL defenses from extensive film-room study . . . Began coaching career in 1975 as 23-year-old special assistant to Ted Marchibroda, current Colts' coach . . . In 1976, he became special-teams coach in Detroit and then moved to Denver as defensive coach . . . Ray Perkins hired him for Giants in 1979, and he became defensive coordinator in 1989 . . . His final defense with the Giants allowed a league-low 211 points and won a Super Bowl . . . The Browns hired him at the age of 38 to become the franchise's eighth head coach . . . Father, Steve, was a Lion fullback and a long-time assistant coach at the Naval Academy . . . Was a 170-pound center, defensive end, tight end and occasional linebacker at Wesleyan, where he majored in economics . . . Born April 16, 1952, in Nashville, Tenn.

GREATEST INTERCEPTOR

"Our franchise has been blessed with a lot of great interceptors," Browns' owner Art Modell said. "Clarence Scott was good. Warren Lahr intercepted a lot of passes (40). But the best might have been Thom Darden."

From 1972 through 1981, Darden established the standard of interceptions for this franchise. The Michigan grad picked off 45 passes, five more than Lahr and six more than Scott. His best season was 1978, when he set the club record with 10.

The Browns have a rich history for great play from their secondary. Back in 1950, Tommy James intercepted nine passes. Twice during his Browns' career, he had three-interception games. It was fitting when Hanford Dixon and Frank Minnifield combined to create the "Dawg Pound" during the late 1980s that the Browns would be known for its secondary.

INDIVIDUAL BROWN RECORDS

Rushing

Most Yards Game:	237	2 times, most recently Jim Brown, vs Philadelphia, 1961
Season:	1,863	Jim Brown, 1963
Career:	12,312	Jim Brown, 1957-65

Passing

Most TD Passes Game:	5	3 times, most recently Brian Sipe, vs Pittsburgh, 1979
Season:	30	Brian Sipe, 1980
Career:	154	Brian Sipe, 1974-83

Receiving

Most TD Passes Game:	3	7 times, most recently Calvin Hill, vs Baltimore, 1978
Season:	13	Gary Collins, 1963
Career:	70	Gary Collins, 1962-71

Scoring

Most Points Game:	36	Dub Jones, vs Chicago Bears, 1951
Season:	126	Jim Brown, 1965
Career:	1,349	Lou Groza, 1950-59, 1961-67
Most TDs Game:	6	Dub Jones, vs Chicago Bears, 1951
Season:	21	Jim Brown, 1965
Career:	126	Jim Brown, 1957-65

DENVER BRONCOS

TEAM DIRECTORY: Owner: Pat Bowlen; GM: John Beake; Dir. Football Oper./Player Personnel: Bob Ferguson; Dir. Media Rel.: Jim Saccomano; Head Coach: Wade Phillips. Home field: Mile High Stadium (76,273). Colors: Orange, blue and white.

SCOUTING REPORT

OFFENSE: Replacing Dan Reeves as head coach might have been too rash a change, but this offense was long overdue for an overhaul. Owner Pat Bowlen gave Wade Phillips, Reeves' defensive coordinator, the difficult assignment but supplied him some quality replacement parts.

How long can John Elway continue his comeback magic?

Imported were 290-pound left tackle Don Maggs and 6-7, 300-pound guard Brian Habib. Although Habib might be asked to move to right tackle if aging Ken Lanier falters, his job will be to handle the 300-pound defensive tackles such as Chester McGlockton and Cortez Kennedy in this division.

Maggs, a finesse type of blocker, will be quarterback John Elway's first well-paid bodyguard. Add these big bodies to dependable center Keith Kartz and powerful run-blocker Doug Widell and Elway can be satisfied with the front wall.

Former Charger Rod Bernstine will be the most powerful back at Elway's disposal. Bernstine has had Pro Bowl half-seasons for the past two years, but he can't stay healthy for 16 games. Just in case he can't, Robert Delpino was signed from the Rams.

What the Broncos lack is speed at the receiving position. Vance Johnson has been slowed by years of injuries. H-back Shannon Sharpe earned his Pro Bowl trip with 53 catches, but he isn't a speedster. Cedric Tillman and Arthur Marshall weren't good enough athletes to be drafted, and Derek Russell had injury problems last season.

DEFENSE: Promoting Phillips from defensive coordinator allowed the front office to keep the defense intact. Despite dropping from first to 13th in the AFC statistically, they are good enough to return to the top. Phillips sets up the defense so that a great group of linebackers makes tackles while safeties Steve Atwater and Dennis Smith come in for the kill. Atwater and Smith remain the best one-two punch at safety in the league.

The linebackers beat opponents every way possible. Simon Fletcher is the quarterback sacker. Karl Mecklenburg is the brains. Mike Croel can chase sprinting wide receivers. Although Mecklenburg's starting days might be numbered, his understudy, Keith Traylor, will have to prove a lot to take the starting job away from him. But tackling machine Michael Brooks has gone to the Giants.

More bulk is needed on the defensive line, but Greg Kragen shows what dedication can do. He's one of league's best nose tackles. Shane Dronett, a 280-pound rookie a year ago, was the first start in that process, and now he'll be joined by top pick Dan Williams, a defensive end from Toledo.

SPECIAL TEAMS: Brad Daluiso has the best kickoff leg in the game. David Treadwell can't make long field goals, but he's consistent on the short ones. A comeback from major knee surgery by Mike Horan will be critical to the punting game because the Broncos never found a replacement.

BRONCOS VETERAN ROSTER

HEAD COACH—Wade Phillips. Assistant Coaches—Vernon Banks, Barney Chavous, Jim Fassel, Mo Forte, Bishop Harris, John Levra, Al Reynolds, Harold Richardson, Richard Smith, Ernie Stautner, Les Steckel, Charlie Waters, John Paul Young.

No.	Name	Pos.	Ht.	Wt.	NFL Exp.	College
27	Atwater, Steve	S	6-3	217	5	Arkansas
33	Bernstine, Rod	RB	6-3	238	7	Texas A&M
34	Braxton, Tyrone	CB	5-11	185	7	North Dakota State
42	Brooks, Michael A.	S	6-0	189	3	North Carolina State
23	Coleman, Eric	CB	6-0	190	3	Wyoming
51	Croel, Mike	LB	6-3	231	3	Nebraska
5	Daluiso, Brad	K	6-2	207	3	UCLA
62	Davidson, Jeff	G	6-5	309	4	Ohio State
39	Delpino, Robert	RB	6-0	205	6	Missouri
29	Dimry, Charles	CB	6-0	175	7	Nevada-Las Vegas
99	Dronett, Shane	DE	6-6	275	2	Texas
7	Elway, John	QB	6-3	215	11	Stanford
73	Fletcher, Simon	LB	6-6	240	9	Houston
68	Freeman, Russell	T	6-7	290	2	Georgia Tech
92	Geater, Ron	NT	6-6	270	2	Iowa
75	Habib, Brian	T	6-7	292	5	Washington
93	Haliburton, Ronnie	LB	6-4	230	3	LSU
83	Harry, Emile	WR	5-11	186	7	Stanford
24	Henderson, Wymon	CB	5-10	186	7	Nevada-Las Vegas
2	Horan, Mike	P	5-11	190	10	Long Beach State
66	Johnson, Chuck	T	6-5	275	2	Texas
89	Johnson, Reggie	TE	6-2	256	3	Florida State
82	Johnson, Vance	WR	5-11	185	9	Arizona
55	Kacherski, John	LB	6-3	240	2	Ohio State
72	Kartz, Keith	C	6-4	270	7	California
71	Kragen, Greg	NT	6-3	265	9	Utah State
21	Lang, Le-Lo	CB	5-11	185	4	Washington
76	Lanier, Ken	T	6-3	290	13	Florida State
20	Lewis, Greg	RB	5-10	214	3	Washington
59	Lucas, Tim	LB	6-3	230	7	California
8	Maddox, Tommy	QB	6-4	195	2	UCLA
78	Maggs, Don	T	6-5	290	8	Tulane
86	Marshall, Arthur	WR	5-11	174	2	Georgia
77	Mecklenburg, Karl	LB	6-3	235	11	Minnesota
61	Meeks, Bob	C	6-2	279	2	Auburn
52	Mills, Jeff	LB	6-3	238	4	Nebraska
12	Moore, Shawn	QB	6-2	213	2	Virginia
74	Noonan, Danny	DT	6-4	275	7	Nebraska
26	Oliver, Muhammad	DB	5-11	170	2	Oregon
91	Oshodin, Willie	DE	6-4	260	3	Villanova
63	Pollack, Frank	G-T	6-5	285	4	Northern Arizona
38	Rivers, Reggie	RB	6-1	215	3	SW Texas State
36	Robinson, Frank	CB	5-11	174	2	Boise State
85	Russell, Derek	WR	6-0	179	3	Arkansas
30	Sewell, Steve	RB	6-3	210	9	Oklahoma
84	Sharpe, Shannon	TE	6-2	230	4	Savannah State
49	Smith, Dennis	S	6-3	200	13	USC
50	Sullins, John	LB	6-1	225	2	Alabama
81	Taylor, Kitrick	WR	5-11	189	6	Washington State
87	Tillman, Cedric	WR	6-2	204	2	Alcorn State
54	Traylor, Keith	LB	6-2	260	3	Central Oklahoma
9	Treadwell, David	K	6-1	180	5	Clemson
96	Walker, Kenny	DE	6-3	260	3	Nebraska
79	Widell, Dave	C-T	6-6	292	6	Boston College
67	Widell, Doug	G	6-4	287	5	Boston College

TOP DRAFT CHOICES

Rd.	Name	Sel. No.	Pos.	Ht.	Wt.	College
1	Williams, Dan	11	DE	6-3	281	Toledo
2	Milburn, Glyn	43	RB	5-8	177	Stanford
3	Jones, Rondell	69	S	6-2	220	North Carolina
3	Elam, Jason	70	P-K	5-11	192	Hawaii
4	Robinson, Jeff	98	DE	6-4	252	Idaho

THE ROOKIES: They drafted the best Williams available. Three of their 10 picks had the surname Williams. First-round Dan Williams could be the starting defensive end. Kevin Williams, a fifth-round UCLA halfback, and second-round running back Glyn Milburn from Stanford add speed to the backfield and special teams. Seventh-rounder Clarence Williams from Washington State could be a sleeper at tight end or H-back.

OUTLOOK: The Elway-Bernstine combo is a formidable one. With a defense that usually holds opponents to 17 or fewer points a game, the Broncos, 8-8 last year, should again challenge for the AFC title.

BRONCO PROFILES

ROD BERNSTINE 28 6-3 238   Running Back

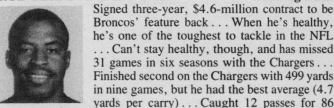

Signed three-year, $4.6-million contract to be Broncos' feature back . . . When he's healthy, he's one of the toughest to tackle in the NFL . . . Can't stay healthy, though, and has missed 31 games in six seasons with the Chargers . . . Finished second on the Chargers with 499 yards in nine games, but he had the best average (4.7 yards per carry) . . . Caught 12 passes for 86 yards . . . Rushed for 150 yards on 23 carries against Indianapolis Oct. 18, but suffered a shoulder injury that required surgery . . . Didn't return until Week 14 . . . Sprained an ankle on his first carry of wild-card playoff game and didn't return . . . Gained 2,007 yards as a Charger . . . Was first-round selection in 1987 following a controversial trade with Browns . . . Went from fullback to tight end at Texas A&M and had 65 career receptions . . . Played two

NFL seasons as a backup tight end before switching to running back and H-back in 1989 . . . His best season was 1991, when he rushed for 766 yards . . . Born Feb. 8, 1965, in Fairfield, Cal. . . . 1993 base salary: $1,000,000, plus $750,000 signing bonus.

JOHN ELWAY 33 6-3 215   Quarterback

Missed four games because of badly bruised right shoulder, and the Broncos lost all four games . . . It was first time in nine seasons he missed more than a game . . . Returned to start final two games . . . Became 15th player to pass for more than 30,000 yards . . . The true Comeback Kid, he has engineered an amazing 31 game-saving, fourth-quarter drives (30 wins and one tie) . . . Seventeen times, he's brought the Broncos from behind to win in the final three minutes, including eight times with less than a minute . . . Moved into eighth place in rushing among all-time quarterbacks (2,282 yards) . . . From 1984 through 1992, his 92-51-1 record, including postseason games, is best in the NFL . . . Has had seven 3,000-yard seasons during 10-year career . . . Last season he completed 174 of 316 passes for 2,242 yards and 10 touchdowns, with 17 interceptions . . . Set five NCAA passing records and nine Pac-10 marks during brilliant career at Stanford . . . Was first player selected in 1983 draft and was thrust into the starting lineup as a rookie . . . Led Broncos to 12-2 record in second season and has been to three Super Bowls . . . Signed four-year, $19.1-million contract extension . . . Born June 28, 1960, in Port Angeles, Wash. . . . 1993 base salary: $3 million, plus $600,000 signing bonus.

BRIAN HABIB 28 6-7 295   Tackle

Created a stir when he signed with Broncos as a free agent after five seasons in Minnesota . . . Relatively unknown player who started only one season for the Vikings . . . Got a three-year, $4.2-million deal from the Broncos . . . Briefly became the highest-paid offensive linemen in the NFL, but his contract was soon topped by those of other free agents . . . Deal included a

$700,000 signing bonus . . . Big, strong, athletic player who lacks experience . . . Broncos believe he will emerge as cornerstone of their rebuilt offensive line . . . Started all 16 games at right guard for the Vikings . . . Backup from 1989-91 . . . Spent rookie season in 1988 on injured-reserve . . . Vikings' 11th-round pick in 1988 out of Washington . . . Played tight end and defensive end in high school . . . State record-holder as an amateur swimmer . . . Born Dec. 2, 1964, in Ellensburg, Wash. . . . 1993 base salary: $1 million.

DON MAGGS 31 6-5 290   Tackle

Signed three-year, $3.7-million contract as an unrestricted free agent . . . Was three-year starter with Oilers . . . Had no problems after having arthroscopic elbow surgery to remove bone spurs prior to last season . . . Started pro career in USFL in 1984 with Pittsburgh Maulers, and moved to New Jersey Generals the following season . . . Signed with Oilers in 1986 and, after four seasons as backup, moved into starting lineup in 1990 . . . Was penalized only once in 1990 . . . Played left tackle for three seasons at Tulane . . . Maulers made him second-round choice in 1984 . . . Born Nov. 1, 1961, in Youngstown, Ohio . . . 1993 base salary: $1,000,000, plus $700,000 signing bonus.

STEVE ATWATER 26 6-3 217   Safety

Considered NFL's premier free safety because of his ability to deck ball-carriers . . . Selected to Pro Bowl three of his four seasons . . . Finished second on Broncos with 152 tackles, including 76 solo . . . Forced three fumbles, a career high . . . Has averaged 121 tackles a season since coming into the NFL . . . Has a tendency to overreact to quarterback pump fakes and was beaten deep for a few touchdowns . . . Was a three-time All-Southwest Conference safety and two-time All-American at Arkansas, where he was known as the Smiling Assassin . . . Intercepted 14 passes during college career . . . Broncos made him first-round choice in 1989 and he responded by earning All-Rookie honors . . . Best hit was a Monday night collision with Christian Okoye in which he knocked the 250-pound back off his feet . . . Came to Arkansas as a wishbone quarterback . . . Born Oct. 28, 1966, in Chicago . . . 1993 base salary: $850,000.

SIMON FLETCHER 31 6-6 240   Linebacker

When will the league recognize he's been playing Pro Bowl ball for past five years? . . . Finished second in the AFC with 16 sacks . . . Teammates named him their defensive player of year . . . Needs two sacks to break Rulon Jones' career sack record (73½) and has led team in sacks five times . . . Has averaged 12½ sacks past five seasons . . . Never missed a game in eight seasons with the Broncos and has 95 consecutive starts and 124 consecutive games . . . Forced team-high five fumbles . . . Was a standup defensive end for three seasons at University of Houston . . . Was second-round draft choice of Broncos in 1985 . . . Waited until his second season to be a starter . . . Bounced between defensive end and linebacker during early pro career . . . Born Feb. 18, 1962, in Bay City, Tex. . . . 1993 base salary: $1,000,000.

SHANNON SHARPE 25 6-2 230   Tight End

Went to Pro Bowl after emerging as one of the top H-backs in the NFL . . . Led team with 53 catches and had 640 receiving yards . . . He and his brother, Sterling of the Packers, became first brother combination to lead two different teams in receiving . . . Was only seventh-round choice in the 1990 draft because he lacked speed and came from tiny Savannah State . . . Made Broncos as wide receiver and special-teams performer . . . Switched from wide receiver to H-back in 1991 and caught 22 passes for 322 yards . . . Caught 192 passes during three seasons in college . . . Also starred in triple jump in high school . . . Born June 26, 1968, in Chicago.

MIKE CROEL 24 6-3 231   Linebacker

One of fastest linebackers in the NFL, with 4.45 speed in 40 . . . Still learning outside linebacker position but is tough to block in pass-rushing situations . . . Had five sacks to give him 15 for first two seasons . . . Earned Rookie of the Year honors in 1991 with 10 sacks . . . Tied Greg Kragen for fifth place in tackles with 101 . . . Was first-round choice in 1991, fourth player selected . . . Earned All-American honors at Nebraska . . . A track standout at 100 meters in high school . . . Is an accomplished artist and loves to paint abstracts . . . Has started at outside linebacker since third game of rookie year . . . Born June 6, 1969, in Sudbury, Mass. . . . 1993 base salary: $650,000.

GREG KRAGEN 31 6-3 265   Nose Tackle

Ranks among best nose tackles even though he concedes as many as 35 pounds to blockers . . . Signed two-year, $2.2-million contract prior to free-agent period . . . Set career high in sacks with 5½ . . . Earned first trip to the Pro Bowl in 1989 . . . Finished in a fifth-place tie on the Broncos with 101 tackles . . . Played at Utah State from 1980 through 1983 as defensive lineman . . . Signed as free agent, he was among the final cuts in 1984 training camp . . . Tried out the next year and earned backup job behind Rubin Carter . . . Moved into starting nose tackle three weeks into 1986 season . . . Born March 4, 1962, in Danville, Cal. . . . 1993 base salary: $1,000,000, plus $300,000 in bonuses.

DENNIS SMITH 34 6-3 200   Safety

Decided to play another season after considering retirement . . . Finished third on team with 127 tackles . . . Ignored in Pro Bowl voting despite the great year, but has been to five . . . Has had back-to-back seasons in which he didn't miss a start . . . One of the most honored athletes in Southern Cal history, he earned All-American honors in football and was seven-foot high-jumper in track . . . Was a first-round choice of Broncos in

1981... Played cornerback as rookie and was occasionally used as wide receiver... Had four interceptions last season to increase his career total to 27, nine during the past two years... Born Feb. 3, 1959, in Santa Monica, Cal.... 1993 base salary: $1,000,000.

VANCE JOHNSON 30 5-11 185   Wide Receiver

Is only remaining Amigo since the departures of Mark Jackson and Ricky Nattiel... Can't shake injuries that have nagged him throughout his career... Can still make the big play and have 100-yard game when healthy... Caught 24 passes for 294 yards and two touchdowns... Played in 11 games but started only six... Has only six starts during the past two years
... Has 367 career receptions for 5,008 yards as Bronco... Was second-round choice in 1985 because of his 4.36 speed in the 40 ... Played tailback at Arizona and finished fourth in school history with 3,442 all-purpose yards... Won 1982 long-jump championship and was an alternate on 1984 Olympic team... Is an acrylic fine-arts creator... Born March 13, 1963, in Trenton, N.J.... 1993 base salary: $750,000.

COACH WADE PHILLIPS:

Hired over former Broncos' assistant Mike Shanahan to replace Dan Reeves after 12 years... Was defensive coordinator for past four years... Twice during tenure with Broncos his defenses allowed fewest points in the AFC... His 1991 defense led the AFC in 12 categories, including fewest touchdowns (20), most sacks (52) and most interceptions (23)... A players' coach, Phillips stresses a zone defensive approach that allows safeties to hit and players to use their athletic skills... Is son of former Houston Oiler and New Orleans Saint head coach Bum Phillips... Was linebacker for three years at University of Houston... Began coaching career at Houston in 1969 and then coached high-school ball in Orange, Tex.... Spent five seasons with the Oilers, coaching linebackers and later defensive linemen... Served as his father's defensive coordinator at New Orleans from 1981 through 1985; Saints led league in defense in 1983... Was interim coach for four games in 1985 and had a 1-3 record... Was defensive coordinator and linebacker coach for Eagles from 1986 through 1988... Born June 21, 1947, in Orange, Tex.

Steve's safety slogan: "Don't go near the Atwater."

GREATEST INTERCEPTOR

Austin "Goose" Gonsoulin was the quiet member of the first Denver Bronco teams. The only time you heard from "Goose" was when quarterbacks threw passes downfield. The Baylor product answered with his body and his hands.

From 1960 through 1966, he intercepted 43 passes. Steve Foley, the consummate pro safety, intercepted one more pass during his career than Gonsoulin, but he spread his picks over 11 seasons (1976 through 1986).

"Goose never said much," said former Broncos' head coach Jack Faulkner, now a front-office exec with the Los Angeles Rams. "There wasn't anything flashy about him. He studied in meetings and did a great job of calling audibles on the field."

Bigger than most safeties, the 6-3 Gonsoulin wasn't reluctant to hit, either. "Very little excited him," Faulkner said. "But he was one good football player."

INDIVIDUAL BRONCO RECORDS

Rushing

Most Yards Game:	183	Otis Armstrong, vs Houston, 1974
Season:	1,407	Otis Armstrong, 1974
Career:	6,323	Floyd Little, 1967-75

Passing

Most TD Passes Game:	5	2 times, most recently John Elway, vs Minnesota, 1984
Season:	24	Frank Tripucka, 1960
Career:	158	John Elway, 1983-92

Receiving

Most TD Passes Game:	3	4 times, most recently Steve Watson, vs Baltimore, 1981
Season:	13	Steve Watson, 1981
Career:	44	Lionel Taylor, 1960-66
	44	Haven Moses, 1972-81

Scoring

Most Points Game:	21	Gene Mingo, vs Los Angeles, 1960
Season:	137	Gene Mingo, 1962
Career:	736	Jim Turner, 1971-79
Most TDs Game:	3	12 times, most recently Gaston Green, vs San Diego, 1991
Season:	13	3 times, most recently Steve Watson, 1981
Career:	54	Floyd Little, 1967-75

HOUSTON OILERS

TEAM DIRECTORY: Pres./Owner: K.S. (Bud) Adams; Exec. VP/GM: Mike Holovak; Exec. VP-Adm.: Mike McClure; Exec. VP-Finance: Scott Thompson; VP-Marketing and Broadcasting: Don MacLachlan; Dir. Business Oper.: Lewis Mangum; Dir. Media Services: Chip Namias; Head Coach: Jack Pardee. Home field: Astrodome (62,439). Colors: Scarlet, Columbia blue and white.

The Moon is still bursting out all over.

SCOUTING REPORT

OFFENSE: The clock is ticking. The pressure is on. It's probably Super Bowl or bust for quarterback Warren Moon, who turns 37 in November. Management kept the Run-and-Shoot offense together for one more season, and if it doesn't gun down a trip to the Super Bowl, expect major, major changes.

Moon knows that backup Cody Carlson received a $2.95-million contract during the offseason. He also knows that he has more offensive weapons than any quarterback in pro football. The renewed Fab Four of Haywood Jeffires, Curtis Duncan, Ernest Givins and Webster Slaughter should each catch between 70 and 100 passes. Slaughter was added more than a month into the season, and he still caught 39 passes.

The best news for Moon was that Lorenzo White is coming off his best season (1,226 rushing yards and 57 receptions). White is durable and has become dependable.

The bad news for Moon is that he lost his left tackle, Don Maggs, to the Broncos. Bruce Matthews moves from center to left tackle while John Flannery should take over at center. Mike Munchak continues as one of the best at guard. Top pick Brad Hopkins, a tackle from Illinois, adds bulk.

DEFENSE: Blowing a 35-point lead in the playoffs against the Bills cost coach Jack Pardee his defensive responsibilities. GM Mike Holovak handed them over to Buddy Ryan. If the Oilers don't go to the Super Bowl, Ryan could wind up as head coach.

Ryan will have plenty to work with because the Oilers are loaded with talent. Ray Childress is one of the game's best defensive tackles. William Fuller, Sean Jones and Lee Williams are Pro Bowl-caliber pass-rushers. Of course the biggest plus will be Redskin outside linebacker Wilber Marshall, assuming the deal is finalized.

Ryan's most important task is to make outside linebacker Lamar Lathon live up to his athletic potential. Lathon enters his fourth season and should be a dominating player. Middle linebacker Al Smith already is.

All is well in the secondary. Ryan has good safeties—Bubba McDowell, Bo Orlando and Marcus Robinson—and Pro Bowl cornerback Cris Dishman.

SPECIAL TEAMS: Al Del Greco was an upgrade from Ian Howfield the year before, but he still missed critical kicks. Overall, though, his numbers were good—21 of 27 field goals and 104 points. Greg Montgomery had an incredible year, averaging 46.9

OILERS VETERAN ROSTER

HEAD COACH—Jack Pardee. Assistant Coaches—Charlie Baggett, Tom Bettis, Frank Bush, Kevin Gilbride, Ronnie Jones, Frank Novak, Buddy Ryan, Jim Stanley, Steve Watterson, Gregg Williams, Bob Young.

No.	Name	Pos.	Ht.	Wt.	NFL Exp.	College
76	Alm, Jeff	DT	6-6	272	4	Notre Dame
58	Bowden, Joe	LB	5-11	230	2	Oklahoma
33	Brown, Gary	RB	5-11	229	3	Penn State
22	Brown, Tony	CB	5-9	183	2	Fresno State
98	Burns, Chris	DE	6-4	282	1	Middle Tenn. State
14	Carlson, Cody	QB	6-3	202	7	Baylor
79	Childress, Ray	DT-DE	6-6	272	9	Texas A&M
87	Coleman, Pat	WR	5-7	173	3	Mississippi
—	Cuba, Monte	DT	6-4	305	1	New Mexico
66	Dawson, Doug	G	6-3	288	6	Texas
3	Del Greco, Al	PK	5-10	200	10	Auburn
28	Dishman, Cris	CB	6-0	178	6	Purdue
77	Donnalley, Kevin	T	6-5	305	3	North Carolina
85	Drewrey, Willie	WR	5-7	164	7	West Virginia
38	Dumas, Mike	S	5-11	181	3	Indiana
80	Duncan, Curtis	WR	5-11	184	7	Northwestern
55	Flannery, John	G-C	6-3	304	3	Syracuse
95	Fuller, William	DE	6-3	274	8	North Carolina
81	Givins, Ernest	WR	5-9	172	8	Louisville
83	Harris, Leonard	WR	5-8	166	8	Texas Tech
—	Huerta, Carlos	PK	5-7	172	1	Miami (Fla.)
24	Jackson, Steve	CB	5-8	182	3	Purdue
84	Jeffires, Haywood	WR	6-2	201	7	North Carolina State
37	Joseph, Dale	CB	6-0	180	1	Howard Payne
96	Jones, Sean	DE	6-7	268	10	Northeastern
56	Kozak, Scott	LB	6-3	222	5	Oregon
57	Lathon, Lamar	LB	6-3	252	4	Houston
29	Lewis, Darryll	CB	5-9	188	3	Arizona
—	Little, Joseph	WR	5-10	157	1	Cal-Sacramento
—	Marshall, Wilber	LB	6-1	231	10	Florida
74	Matthews, Bruce	C-G-T	6-5	291	11	USC
86	Mays, Damon	WR	5-9	170	2	Missouri
25	McDowell, Bubba	S	6-1	198	5	Miami (Fla.)
94	Montgomery, Glenn	DT	6-0	278	5	Houston
9	Montgomery, Greg	P	6-4	215	6	Michigan State
1	Moon, Warren	QB	6-3	212	10	Washington
63	Munchak, Mike	G	6-3	284	12	Penn State
—	Nee, John	OL	6-5	295	1	Elon
64	Norgard, Erik	C-G	6-1	282	3	Colorado
45	Obradovich, Ed	LB	6-0	247	1	Michigan State
28	Orlando, Bo	S	5-10	180	4	West Virginia
21	Petry, Stan	CB	6-0	181	3	Texas Christian
7	Richardson, Bucky	QB	6-1	228	2	Texas A&M
68	Roberts, Tim	DT	6-6	318	2	Southern Mississippi
31	Robertson, Marcus	S-CB	5-11	197	3	Iowa State
50	Robinson, Eddie	LB	6-1	245	2	Alabama State
53	Seale, Eugene	LB	5-10	260	7	Lamar
89	Slaughter, Webster	WR	6-1	170	8	San Diego State
54	Smith, Al	LB	6-1	251	7	Utah State
71	Teeter, Mike	DT	6-2	260	1	Michigan
32	Tillman, Spencer	RB	5-11	206	7	Oklahoma
88	Wellman, Gary	WR	5-9	173	2	USC
44	White, Lorenzo	RB	5-11	222	6	Michigan State
73	Williams, David	T	6-5	297	5	Florida
39	Williams, James	CB	5-11	190	1	Texas Southern
97	Williams, Lee	DE-DT	6-6	271	10	Bethune-Cookman

TOP DRAFT CHOICES

Rd.	Name	Sel. No.	Pos.	Ht.	Wt.	College
1	Hopkins, Brad	13	OT	6-3	300	Illinois
2	Barrow, Michael	47	LB	6-1	236	Miami
4	Hannah, Travis	102	WR	5-7	161	USC
5	Mills, John Henry	131	TE	6-0	221	Wake Forest
6	Bradley, Chuck	158	T	6-5	310	Kentucky

yards a punt. In Slaughter and Pat Coleman, the Oilers have fine returners.

THE ROOKIES: Hopkins was taken in the first round as a candidate for Maggs' vacated tackle spot. Hopkins' specialty was run-blocking, but he needs work on the pass. Ryan pushed to make University of Miami middle linebacker Michael Barrows the second-round pick.

OUTLOOK: Nice guys might finish last, but Pardee probably has to finish first and win two playoff games to keep his job. Pardee is a nice guy, but the Oilers, 10-6 in 1992, have too many big salaries to keep together longer than this season.

OILER PROFILES

WARREN MOON 36 6-3 212   Quarterback

Missed five of final six regular-season games with a fractured upper left arm on a hit from Viking safety Vencie Glenn ... Despite missed time, he went to fifth Pro Bowl ... Ranked No. 1 in NFL with 89.3 quarterback rating and had career-best 64.7 completion percentage.... Has passed for 51,428 yards in 14 pro seasons, including 30,200 in the NFL and 21,228 in CFL ... In wild AFC playoff against Bills, he completed 36 of 50 passes for 371 yards and four first-half TDs ... But Bills came back from 28-3 halftime deficit to take it, 41-38 ... Rarely makes mistakes and has just thrown 38 interceptions in past 1,412 passes ... Completed 224 of 346 passes for 2,521 yards and 18 touchdowns ... Was sacked only 16 times last year ... Took University of Washington to Rose Bowl in 1977 ... Played six seasons for Edmonton Eskimos and won five consecutive Grey Cups ... Signed with Oilers in 1984 ... Born Nov. 18, 1956, in Los Angeles ... 1993 base salary: $4,000,000.

RAY CHILDRESS 30 6-6 272   Defensive Tackle

Has amazing big-play skills at restricting defensive tackle position . . . Was second on team with 90 tackles, including 60 solos . . . Led team and was ranked eighth in the AFC with career-high 13 sacks . . . His three multi-sack games increased his career total to 11 . . . An eight-tackle, two-sack game against Buffalo in season-finale earned him AFC Defensive Player of the Week honors . . . Selected to Pro Bowl for fourth time and has gone as an end and a tackle . . . Was defensive terror at Texas A&M, where he recorded 360 tackles, 26 sacks and nine fumble recoveries in four seasons . . . Was third overall choice in 1985 draft by the Oilers . . . Had 135 tackles as a rookie and was named to All-Rookie teams . . . Born Oct. 20, 1962, in Memphis . . . 1993 base salary: $825,000.

BRUCE MATTHEWS 32 6-5 291   Tackle

An amazing athlete . . . Has earned trips to the Pro Bowl at center and guard and now wants to do it at left tackle . . . The departure of left tackle Don Maggs forces Matthews to give up his Pro Bowl spot at center . . . Has gone to Pro Bowl five consecutive seasons . . . Serves as deep snapper on special teams . . . Considered one of the greatest offensive linemen to come out of Southern Cal . . . Was the ninth overall selection in 1983 draft. . . . Started 15 games at right guard as a rookie . . . Played center, right guard and right tackle in 1984 . . . Endured back problems all season, but was a steady influence at left tackle in 1986 . . . Went to his first Pro Bowl in 1988 . . . Born Aug. 8, 1961, in Raleigh, N.C. . . . 1993 base salary: $1,100,000.

ERNEST GIVINS 28 5-9 172   Wide Receiver

Caught 67 passes for 787 yards to earn his second trip to Pro Bowl . . . Protected from free agency by being named a transition player, which will make him one of 10 top-paid wide receivers . . . His 10 touchdown receptions were the most by any receiver in the AFC . . . Has missed only two games during seven-year career . . . Set club record with his seventh 50-plus-catch season . . . Has caught passes in 52 consecutive games

... His 438 career catches ranks second in club history behind Drew Hill, who is retiring with 480 ... Has 16 100-yard games ... Transferred from Northeast Oklahoma Junior College to Louisville, where he averaged 18.9 yards a catch in two seasons.... Was second-round choice of Oilers in 1986 and caught 61 passes as rookie ... Born Sept. 3, 1964, in St. Petersburg, Fla.... 1992 base salary: $800,000.

LORENZO WHITE 27 5-11 222   Halfback

Finally emerged as star NFL running back ... Started 16 games and earned his first trip to the Pro Bowl ... Rushed 265 times for 1,226 yards and scored seven touchdowns ... Finished fourth on the team with 57 catches for 641 yards and a touchdown.... Became first Oiler since Mike Rozier in 1988 to break the 1,000-yard barrier ... Had 10 games in which his running and receiving totals topped 100 yards ... Ranks second on team's all-time playoff rushing list with 264 yards ... Moved into fifth place on Oilers' all-time rushing list with 2,857 yards ... Rushed for 4,513 yards and scored 41 touchdowns during four-year career at Michigan State ... Was first-round choice of Oilers in 1988 ... Didn't get a start until his third pro season, when he rushed for 702 yards ... Was a backup in 1991 but started to explode in the final weeks of that season ... Born April 12, 1966, in Hollywood, Fla.

AL SMITH 28 6-1 251   Linebacker

Almost escaped through free agency, but he was saved when the Oilers made him a transition player at the last minute ... Earned second consecutive trip to the Pro Bowl as a starter ... Led team with 120 tackles.... Has had more than 100 tackles four times in six seasons, including three in a row ... He has been among team's top three tacklers his entire career ... Was dominant linebacker in the PCAA during three seasons at Utah State after transferring from Cal-Poly Pomona ... Was sixth-round draft choice of the Oilers in 1987 and had 11 starts as a rookie ... Born Nov. 26, 1964, in Los Angeles ... 1993 base salary: $500,000.

MIKE MUNCHAK 33 6-3 284   Guard

Tied club record by going to eighth Pro Bowl . . . Might be losing his ability to dominate defenders but his experience makes him difficult to get around . . . Missed two games, but has only missed five games since 1986 . . . Named to the NFL Team of the Decade for the 1980s at right guard . . . Played guard and tackle at Penn State and was considered one of the top college blockers in the country . . . Was eighth overall choice in 1982 . . . Started 16 games at left guard as rookie . . . Became league's top lineman by his second year . . . Born March 5, 1960, in Scranton, Pa. . . . 1993 base salary: $1,100,000.

CURTIS DUNCAN 28 5-11 184   Wide Receiver

Finally cracked the Pro Bowl roster after six tries . . . Oilers' most durable receiver, he has not missed a game since rookie season in 1987 and has made 64 consecutive starts . . . His 82 catches last year was a career high and he had a team-best 954 yards . . . He waited until the next-to-last game of the season to make his only touchdown catch . . . Has averaged 61 catches a season during past four years . . . Played four seasons at Northwestern and caught 67 passes for 1,159 yards . . . Averaged 26.2 yards a kickoff return in college . . . Drafted in 10th round by Oilers and spent two seasons as backup . . . Born Jan. 26, 1965, in Detroit . . . 1993 base salary: $525,000.

CRIS DISHMAN 28 6-0 178   Cornerback

Has emerged as one the toughest and best coverage cornerbacks in the conference . . . Held out until Sept. 10 but still started 15 games . . . Ranked second on the team with 21 passes defensed . . . Singlehandedly won the Sept. 23 game against Kansas City by stripping a fumble from hands of receiver J.J. Birden . . . Went to Pro Bowl in 1991 . . . Didn't become a full-time starter until Jack Pardee's first season as head coach in 1990 . . . Started 44 games at cornerback over past three seasons . . . One of two fifth-round choices in the 1988 draft and was used as a rookie in the nickel pass defense . . . Started 33 of 34 games at Purdue . . . One of the stars of the Purdue track team . . . Born Aug. 13, 1965, in Louisville . . . 1993 base salary: $825,000.

HAYWOOD JEFFIRES 28 6-2 201   Wide Receiver

Won Pro Bowl starting job for the second consecutive year . . . Led AFC with 90 catches and was fourth in conference with 913 yards . . . Became only the second player since 1970 to lead a conference in receiving three consecutive years . . . Has caught at least one pass in 48 consecutive games . . . The only knock against him is that he has a tendency to drop passes . . . A starter for only three years, he is averaging almost 85 receptions a season . . . Was Oilers' first-round choice in 1987 but played only 11 games and caught only nine passes during first two seasons . . . At North Carolina State, though, he had 111 receptions . . . Has great speed and leaping ability . . . Born Dec. 12, 1964, in Greensboro, N.C. . . . 1993 base salary: $1,000,000, plus $400,000 bonus.

WEBSTER SLAUGHTER 28 6-1 170   Wide Receiver

Signed as an unconditional free agent Sept. 29 after being Brown holdout . . . Was declared a free agent and he went to the highest bidder, the Oilers signing him to two-year, $2.3-million contract . . . Played in 12 games and started nine, ending up fifth on the team with 39 catches for 486 yards and four touchdowns . . . Passed the 5,000-yard career plateau against, appropriately, the Browns, Nov. 8 . . . Hasn't missed a game because of injury since 1988 . . . Played with fractured hand against Bills in playoffs and caught eight passes for 73 yards and a touchdown . . . Born Oct. 19, 1964, in Stockton, Cal. . . . 1993 base salary: $1,050,000 plus $100,000 bonus.

WILBER MARSHALL 31 6-1 231   Linebacker

Assuming deal is finally resolved, big-play man of Redskins' defense becomes an Oiler . . . Had been tabbed Redskins' franchise player . . . Led team last year in sacks with six, forced fumbles with three and passes defensed with 12 . . . Finished third with 138 tackles . . . Made Pro Bowl for third time in his career . . . Fiery player whose best season was 1991, when Redskins drove to Super Bowl title . . . Signed by the Redskins as a free agent in March 1988 after spending four seasons with Bears . . . One of only two players to change teams under the old free-agency system . . . Bears' No. 1 pick out of Florida in 1984 . . . Made Pro Bowl twice with Bears and helped team to Super Bowl title in 1985 . . . One of 12 children . . . Born April 18, 1962, in Titusville, Fla. . . . 1992 base salary: $1.3 million.

COACH JACK PARDEE:  After three trips to playoffs in three years, the pressure is on Pardee to go to the Super Bowl . . . GM Mike Holovak forced him to fire three assistants, including defensive coordinator Jim Eddy, and hire Buddy Ryan as Eddy's replacement . . . Three-year record with the Oilers is an impressive 30-18, but management is concerned about 1-3 playoff mark . . . He's defensive-minded coach who has updated offense with the revolutionary Run-and-Shoot attack . . . Oilers' defense ranked third in NFL, highest ranking for the franchise since 1970 AFL-NFL merger . . . Signed a five-year contract in 1990 . . . Moved from University of Houston, where he compiled a 22-10-1 record . . . After 15-year career as one of the NFL's top linebackers, he accepted assistant's job with Redskins and eventually ended up as head coach of the World Football League's Florida Blazers . . . Compiled 14-6 record but lost, 22-21, in championship game to Birmingham . . . Was three-year head coach of Bears with 20-22 record, three-year coach of Redskins with 24-24 and two-year head coach of USFL's Houston Gamblers with 23-13 . . . Known for his toughness, Pardee battled back from cancer during playing days . . . Born April 19, 1936, in Exira, Iowa.

GREATEST INTERCEPTOR

Jim Norton's nickname was "The Blade." Traditional NFL scouts thought Norton was too skinny for their league. He was perfect for the Oilers and the AFL.

Norton might not have been the best defensive back who put on an Oiler uniform during the franchise's formative years. That honor goes to Kenny Houston, whom the Oilers made the mistake of trading.

From 1960 through 1968, Norton set the Oilers' standard with 29 interceptions. He came to the pros with a feisty toughness. His scouting report was simple: tall, smart and intimidating.

Sometimes, he was too intimidating. His signature play was when he decked a Kansas City Chief in front of the team bench.

"He was the first Oiler to have his jersey retired," Oiler GM Mike Holovak said. "That's how good he was."

INDIVIDUAL OILER RECORDS

Rushing

Most Yards Game:	216	Billy Cannon, vs N.Y. Jets, 1961
Season:	1,934	Earl Campbell, 1980
Career:	8,574	Earl Campbell, 1978-84

Passing

Most TD Passes Game:	7	George Blanda, vs N.Y. Titans, 1961
Season:	36	George Blanda, 1961
Career:	175	Warren Moon, 1984-92

Receiving

Most TD Passes Game:	3	9 times, most recently Haywood Jeffires, vs Cincinnati, 1992
Season:	17	Bill Gorman, 1961
Career:	51	Charlie Hennigan, 1960-66

Scoring

Most Points Game:	30	Billy Cannon, vs N.Y. Titans, 1961
Season:	115	2 times, most recently Tony Zendejas, 1989
Career:	596	George Blanda, 1960-66
Most TDs Game:	5	Billy Cannon, vs N.Y. Titans, 1961
Season:	19	Earl Campbell, 1979
Career:	73	Earl Campbell, 1978-84

INDIANAPOLIS COLTS

TEAM DIRECTORY: Pres./Tres.: Robert Irsay; VP/GM: Jim Irsay; VP/Gen. Counsel: Michael Chernoff; Dir. Player Personnel: Jack Bushofsky; Dir. Pub. Rel.: Craig Kelly; Head Coach: Ted Marchibroda. Home field: Hoosier Dome (60,129). Colors: Royal blue and white.

SCOUTING REPORT

OFFENSE: Tired of watching one of the league's most porous offensive lines, GM Jimmy Irsay went on a spending spree. He signed Bills' left tackle Will Wolford to a three-year, $7.65-million contract and Viking center Kirk Lowdermilk to a three-year,

A low for Steve Emtman was his knee; a high was 90-yard TD.

$6.15-million deal. The two high-paid offensive linemen had better protect Jeff George from his usual three-and-four sack games.

Suddenly, George, the beleaguered franchise quarterback, finds two blockers making more money than he does, and a sense of urgency exists for his development. George, an inconsistent 54.6-percent passer, must step into the pocket this year and take the Colts to the playoffs. In many ways, backup Jack Trudeau outperformed him last year, making the best out of a talent-starved offense.

George's gains on the line came at the expense of losing his top receiver for three years, Bill Brooks, who signed with the Bills. Veterans Reggie Langhorne (65 catches) and Jessie Hester (52 catches) are decent fill-ins until a younger receiver develops. Tight end Kerry Cash and running back Anthony Johnson each topped the 40-catch plateau to offer alternatives, and top pick Sean Dawkins of California is a deep threat.

What George doesn't have is a running game. The Colts averaged a ridiculous 2.9 yards a carry and ranked last in the league on the ground.

DEFENSE: Defensive end Steve Emtman and linebacker Quentin Coryatt were impact players—for half a season. Then Emtman blew out a knee and Coryatt broke his wrist.

Still, the defense, rebuilt around the first two choices in the 1992 draft, should mature this year. Emtman and Coryatt make big plays. If the Colts make the playoffs, Emtman, Coryatt, inside linebacker Jeff Herrod and outside linebacker Duane Bickett could all earn trips to the Pro Bowl.

The Colts are solid at linebacker with pass-rushers on the outside—Bickett and Chip Banks—and run-pursuers on the inside—Herrod and Coryatt. The defensive line is led by Emtman and aided by the development of nose tackle Tony Siragusa, but aging defensive end Jon Hand is being phased out.

Improvements on the defensive line and a full season by Emtman should tighten up a pass defense that allowed 181 yards a game. The secondary will miss free safety Mike Prior, who signed with the Packers.

SPECIAL TEAMS: Dean Biasucci's decline as a field-goal specialist is becoming a concern. He missed 13 of 29 last year, not good for someone making his living in a domed stadium. Rohn Stark continues to be the game's best punter, booming a 44.8-yard average and planting 22 inside the 20. Clarence Verdin makes every return exciting.

COLTS VETERAN ROSTER

HEAD COACH—Ted Marchibroda. Assistant Coaches—Ron Blackledge, Fred Bruney, George Catavolos, Gene Huey, Nick Nicolau, Dwain Painter, Francis Peay, Jay Robertson, Brad Seely, Rick Venturi, Tom Zupancic.

No.	Name	Pos.	Ht.	Wt.	NFL Exp.	College
33	Ambrose, Ashley	DB	5-10	177	2	Miss. Valley State
81	Arbuckle, Charles	TE	6-3	248	2	UCLA
31	Ball, Michael	DB	6-0	220	6	Southern
51	Banks, Chip	LB	6-4	254	11	USC
36	Baylor, John	DB	6-0	208	5	Southern Mississippi
29	Belser, Jason	DB	5-9	187	2	Oklahoma
4	Biasucci, Dean	K	6-0	190	9	Western Carolina
50	Bickett, Duane	LB	6-5	251	9	USC
5	Borgognone, Dirk	K	6-2	220	1	Pacific
60	Brandon, Michael	DE	6-4	290	1	Florida
53	Butcher, Paul	LB	6-0	230	7	Wayne State
71	Call, Kevin	OT	6-7	308	10	Colorado State
88	Cash, Kerry	TE	6-4	252	3	Texas
76	Clancy, Sam	DE	6-7	300	10	Pittsburgh
32	Clark, Ken	RB	5-9	204	4	Nebraska
55	Coryatt, Quentin	LB	6-3	250	2	Texas A&M
80	Cox, Aaron	WR	5-10	178	6	Arizona State
35	Culver, Rodney	RB	5-9	224	2	Notre Dame
38	Daniel, Eugene	DB	5-11	188	10	Louisiana State
69	Dixon, Randy	OG	6-3	305	7	Pittsburgh
90	Emtman, Steve	DE	6-4	290	2	Washington
93	Garrett, Murray	DE	6-4	285	1	Eastern New Mexico
11	George, Jeff	QB	6-4	227	4	Illinois
37	Goode, Chris	DB	6-0	199	7	Alabama
59	Grant, Stephen	LB	6-0	231	2	West Virginia
47	Hall, Victor	TE	6-3	288	1	Auburn
94	Hamlet, Anthony	DE	6-3	260	1	Miami (Fla.)
78	Hand, Jon	DE	6-7	301	8	Alabama
56	Heldt, Michael	C	6-2	285	1	Notre Dame
54	Herrod, Jeff	LB	6-0	249	6	Mississippi
84	Hester, Jessie	WR	5-11	175	8	Florida State
25	Humphrey, Ronald	RB	5-10	201	1	Miss. Valley State
75	James, Clint	DL	6-6	288	1	Louisiana State
23	Johnson, Anthony	RB	6-0	222	4	Notre Dame
87	Johnson, Hendricks	WR	6-2	185	1	Northern Arizona
49	Jones, Mike	TE	6-3	255	4	Texas A&M
85	Langhorne, Reggie	WR	6-2	207	9	Elizabeth City State
63	Lowdermilk, Kirk	C	6-3	263	9	Ohio State
64	Matich, Trevor	OL	6-4	297	9	Brigham Young
95	McClendon, Skip	DL	6-7	302	7	Arizona State
61	McCoy, Tony	NT	6-0	279	2	Florida
86	Miller, Eddie	WR	6-0	185	2	South Carolina
73	Moss, Zefross	OT	6-6	338	5	Alabama State
96	Peguese, Willis	DE	6-4	273	4	Miami (Fla.)
97	Radecic, Scott	LB	6-3	240	10	Penn State
68	Ray, John	OT	6-8	350	1	West Virginia
74	Schultz, William	OT	6-5	305	4	USC
98	Siragusa, Tony	NT	6-3	303	4	Pittsburgh
66	Solt, Ron	OG	6-3	280	9	Maryland
45	Stargell, Tony	DB	5-11	189	4	Tennessee State
3	Stark, Rohn	P	6-3	203	12	Florida State
79	Staysniak, Joe	OT	6-4	296	2	Ohio State
28	Toner, Ed	RB	6-0	240	2	Boston College
27	Toy, Maury	RB	6-0	235	1	UCLA
10	Trudeau, Jack	QB	6-3	227	8	Illinois
7	Tupa, Tom	QB	6-4	230	6	Ohio State
72	Vander Poel, Mark	OT	6-7	303	3	Colorado
58	Vanderbeek, Matt	LB	6-3	258	4	Michigan State
83	Verdin, Clarence	WR	5-8	162	8	SE Louisiana
92	Walker, Tony	LB	6-3	246	4	SE Missouri State
67	Wolford, Will	OT	6-5	300	8	Vanderbilt

		TOP DRAFT CHOICES				
Rd.	Name	Sel. No.	Pos.	Ht.	Wt.	College
1	Dawkins, Sean	16	WR	6-4	213	California
2	Potts, Roosevelt	49	RB	6-0	258	NE Louisiana
3	Buchanan, Ray	65	DB	5-9	193	Louisville
4	Gray, Derwin	92	DB	5-10	190	Brigham Young
4	McDonald, Devon	107	LB	6-3	240	Notre Dame

THE ROOKIES: Efforts to trade up for Georgia halfback Garrison Hearst failed, but coach Ted Marchibroda was pleased with his top two choices—wide receiver Dawkins (No. 16) and Northeast Louisiana fullback Roosevelt Potts (No. 49). Dawkins is a 6-3 big-play maker in the mold of Jerry Rice. Potts is a 288-pound one-back with running and blocking skills.

OUTLOOK: Management has spent enough money to win. Their 9-7 season might been partially a result of an easy schedule, but the Colts will take a lot to beat. They could be the second-best team in the AFC East.

COLT PROFILES

STEVE EMTMAN 23 6-4 290   Defensive End

Might have been NFL Rookie of the Year were it not for a torn knee ligament suffered against Miami Nov. 8 . . . Reconstructive surgery was successful and he should be ready to be one of the dominating defenders in football . . . In nine games, he had 49 tackles, three sacks, six quarterback pressures and one forced fumble. . . . His 90-yard interception return for a touchdown against the Dolphins made him AFC Defensive Player of the Week . . . His overpowering strength, quickness and desire convinced the Colts to make him first choice in last year's draft . . . Signed four-year, $9.165-million contract . . . Out of the University of Washington, he was first Pac-10 player to win Lombardi Award and Outland Trophy . . . Dominated the Pac-10 for three seasons . . . Born April 16, 1970, in Cheyney, Wash. . . . 1993 base salary: $1,000,000.

KIRK LOWDERMILK 30 6-3 263   Center

Signed with Colts as a free agent after eight seasons with the Vikings . . . Signed three-year, $6-million contract that made him the highest-paid center in NFL history . . . Smart, physical player . . . Colts want him to anchor their rebuilt offensive line . . . Started all 16 games for the Vikings in 1992 . . . Run-blocking helped Terry Allen rush for more than 1,100 yards . . . Became a starter in 1987 . . . Also can long snap . . . Best season might have been 1989, when he was named honorable mention All-Pro by AP . . . Vikings got him in the third round of the 1985 draft out of Ohio State . . . His blocking as a senior helped Keith Byars run for more than 1,700 yards . . . Wrestled for two years at Ohio State . . . State high-school wrestling heavyweight champion in Ohio . . . Born April 10, 1963, in Canton, Ohio (home of the Pro Football Hall of Fame) . . . 1993 base salary: $2 million.

JEFF GEORGE 25 6-4 227   Quarterback

Injuries ruined his third season and limited him to 10 games. . . . Threw 15 interceptions compared to seven touchdown passes and twice had to be replaced by backup Jack Trudeau . . . Suffered stretched ligament in right thumb that sidelined him for first three regular-season games. . . . Cracked a metacarpal bone in his right hand against New England Nov. 15 and missed three more games . . . Had a string of 25 consecutive games broken by the injuries . . . Was 6-4 as a starter, compared to 5-7 and 1-15 during his first two years . . . Possesses one of football's strongest arms and drops back with the authority of a John Elway . . . Completed better than 50 percent of his passes in 31 of 39 career games . . . His three-year statistics rank among best of any top-choice quarterback who entered the league since 1970 . . . Has been sacked 120 times in three seasons, eight more than retired Jim Plunkett during his early years with Patriots . . . Completed 167 of 306 passes for 1,963 yards last season . . . Was No. 1 in 1990 draft via a trade with Falcons that involved tackle Chris Hinton, wide receiver Andre Rison and a No. 1 choice . . . Began college career at Purdue and wound up at Illinois, where he was 20-4 as starter . . . Born Dec. 8, 1967, in Indianapolis . . . 1993 base salary: $2,000,000.

QUENTIN CORYATT 23 6-3 250   Linebacker

Had a slow start in training camp because of injuries and had his season end Oct. 25 because of a displaced bone in left wrist . . . Was team's second-leading tackler with 54 at the time . . . Had the quickness to chase down Bills' halfback Thurman Thomas for a 14-yard loss Sept. 20 . . . His 11-tackle game against the Bills was his best . . . Has amazing straight-ahead speed, but is working on his tendency to overpursue and get caught out of position . . . On the morning of the draft, Colts almost made him first choice ahead of Steve Emtman . . . Signed four-year, $9.165-million contract . . . Earned All-American honors at Texas A&M, where he played inside linebacker in 3-4 . . . Has 4.5 speed in the 40 . . . Once sacked BYU's Ty Detmer for a 32-yard loss . . . Born Aug. 1, 1970, in St. Croix, Virgin Islands . . . 1993 base salary: $1,150,000.

JEFF HERROD 27 6-0 249   Linebacker

Rewarded with three-year, $5.2-million contract last spring . . . Led Colts over past four seasons with 154, 155, 160 and 138 tackles . . . Had 99 solo tackles last season . . . Had his first injury-free season and started all 16 games . . . Pelvic, groin and ankle injuries nagged him during his early days with franchise . . . Was 243rd choice in 1988 draft, as the Colts took him in the ninth round . . . Spent rookie season as a reserve linebacker and special-teamer . . . Started 14 of 15 games in 1989 . . . Was tackling machine at Arkansas State . . . Was Defensive Player of the Game in the Blue-Gray All-Star engagement . . . Had 17 tackles in that game. . . . Born July 29, 1966, in Birmingham, Ala. . . . 1993 base salary: $1.25 million, plus $400,000 signing bonus.

DUANE BICKETT 30 6-5 251   Linebacker

Named the franchise player to protect the Colts from losing him because of free agency . . . A classic big-play linebacker who consistently attacks offenses . . . Has 32 double-digit tackle games and 46½ sacks during eight seasons with the Colts . . . Has missed only two starts because of injuries . . . A hamstring injury against New England forced him to miss a game for first time since 1990 . . . Finished fourth on team with 89 tackles . . . Had 10 solo tackles against New England Dec. 6 . . . His 3½-sack performance that day was his best since 1987, when he had four sacks against Jets . . . Has 955 career tackles . . . Was fifth selection in the 1985 draft by the Colts and became immediate starter. . . . Played linebacker and defensive end at Southern Cal after entering school as tight end . . . Born Dec. 1, 1962, in Los Angeles . . . 1992 base salary: $1,100,000.

WILL WOLFORD 29 6-5 296   Tackle

Wrestled away from Bills via three-year, $7.65-million offer sheet. . . . The Bills thought he was protected against free agency by naming him a transition player . . . An arbitrator had to decide Wolford's fate because of tricky clauses written in the contract that made it tough for the Bills to match . . . Considered one of best blocking left tackles in the NFL . . . Earned second trip to the Pro Bowl but didn't play because of shoulder injury . . . His specialty is blocking pass-rushers without much help from other linemen . . . Bench-presses more than 500 pounds, but is flexible enough to have a 32-inch vertical jump . . . A first-round choice in 1986 by virtue of a trade with 49ers . . . Held out until early August 1986 but moved into the starting lineup by third preseason game. . . . Earned All-Rookie honors . . . Switched from right guard to left tackle in 1987 and has been there since. . . . Was one of the Southeastern Conference's top blockers at Vanderbilt . . . Born May 18, 1964, in Louisville . . . 1993 base salary: $1,800,000, plus $2,050,000 bonus.

JACK TRUDEAU 30 6-3 227   Quarterback

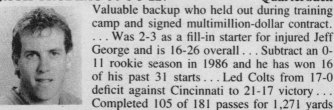

Valuable backup who held out during training camp and signed multimillion-dollar contract. . . . Was 2-3 as a fill-in starter for injured Jeff George and is 16-26 overall . . . Subtract an 0-11 rookie season in 1986 and he has won 16 of his past 31 starts . . . Led Colts from 17-0 deficit against Cincinnati to 21-17 victory . . . Completed 105 of 181 passes for 1,271 yards and had a team-best 68.6 quarterback rating . . . Enters eighth pro

season with the Colts after being second-round choice in 1986 . . .
Had major knee problems in 1990 . . . Threw 417 passes for 2,225
yards during rookie season in 1986 . . . Threw NCAA-record 215
passes without an interception at Illinois . . . Born Sept. 9, 1962,
in Forest Lake, Minn. . . . 1993 base salary: $1,000,000.

CHIP BANKS 33 6-4 254   Linebacker

Remarkable comeback continues . . . Following
drug problems, he came to the Colts for a third-
round choice in 1990 trade with Chargers, and
has started 51 of 53 games since then . . . A
fierce pass-rusher, Banks had nine sacks last
season to increase career total to 45½ . . . Had
51 tackles, including 37 solos and five quarterback pressures . . . Entered the NFL as first-
round choice of Browns in 1982 when he was third player selected
. . . Earned Rookie of the Year and Pro Bowl honors and followed
with another Pro Bowl season . . . Browns traded him to Buffalo
in 1985 in complicated three-draft-choice deal. When he failed to
report, he was eventually traded to San Diego for first- and second-
round choices . . . Was a first alternate to the Pro Bowl in 1987
for Chargers . . . Held out and didn't play in 1988 . . . Born Sept.
18, 1959, in Fort Lawton, Okla. . . . 1993 base salary: $750,000.

REGGIE LANGHORNE 30 6-2 207   Wide Receiver

Started only 12 games but led the Colts with
65 catches for 811 yards . . . Caught eight
passes in games against Pittsburgh and Cincinnati . . . Had seven catches in at least four
games and 14 multiple-reception games . . .
Came to the Colts as Plan B acquisition, March
25, 1992, when he signed two-year, $1.526-
million contract . . . Was left unprotected by
Browns because of numerous disagreements with coach Bill Belichick . . . Doesn't have the deep speed of his earlier days, but
can still get behind defenders . . . Had 60- and 57-catch seasons
with Browns in 1988-89 . . . Selected in seventh round of the 1985
draft, out of Elizabeth State . . . Started three games as a rookie,
but became a full-time starter in second season with Browns . . .
Has had only one season in past seven years in which he caught
less than 39 passes . . . Born April 7, 1963, in Suffolk, Va. . . .
1993 base salary: $763,000.

ROHN STARK 34 6-3 203   **Punter**

Won fourth trip to the Pro Bowl with another great season . . . Boomed 83 punts for 44.8-yard average, third-best in NFL . . . Averaged 50 yards in four games to increase his career total to 16 . . . Ranks behind only Sammy Baugh (45.1), Tommy Davis (44.7) and Yale Lary (44.3) on NFL all-time career punting list . . . Missed only two games during his career and had a 40-yard average in 129 of them . . . Set all standards for punters who operate in domed stadiums . . . Finished sixth in the NCAA decathlon competition after All-American track career at Florida State. . . . Averaged 46 yards a kick in college . . . Owns amateur pilot's license. . . . Enters 12th season with the Colts, who drafted in second round in 1982 . . . As rookie, he had second-best average (44.4) in NFL . . . Born May 4, 1959, in Minneapolis . . . 1993 base salary: $415,000.

COACH TED MARCHIBRODA: Brought back memories of

past glories by leading team to 9-7 record after a 1-15 season . . . Despite the absences of top defenders Quentin Coryett and Steve Emtman, the Colts finished with a five-game winning streak and allowed only 49 points . . . Took over 2-12 Baltimore Colts in 1974 and led them to a 10-4 record . . . Followed the 10-4 season with three division titles and had a stretch from Oct. 26, 1975, to Nov. 20, 1977, in which the Colts won 29 of 33 regular-season games . . . His lifetime head-coaching record with the Colts is 50-43 . . . Considered one of the offensive masterminds in football, he's known for developing young quarterbacks. . . . His no-huddle offense took Jim Kelly and the Bills to three Super Bowl appearances . . . The tireless Marchibroda began his NFL coaching career as a backfield coach for the Redskins in 1961 . . . He was an assistant with the Rams, Bears, Lions, Eagles and Bills . . . As a player, he was a first-round Steelers' draft choice as a quarterback out of U. of Detroit in 1953 . . . Played a year, served in the Army and rejoined Steelers in 1955-56, winding up playing career in 1957 with the Chicago Cardinals . . . Born March 15, 1931, in Franklin, Pa.

With new support, Jeff George expects less sack time.

GREATEST INTERCEPTOR

Bob Boyd couldn't run faster than a 4.8 40-yard dash. To think that a cornerback that slow could survive in the NFL is amazing. Of course, the Baltimore Colt secondary of the 1960s was amazing. Boyd, the cornerback out of Oklahoma, was a speedster compared to safeties Rick Volk and Jerry Logan

Boyd didn't earn his paycheck with his feet. He earned it with his ability to anticipate and his knowledge of the game. Tempted by his lack of speed, quarterbacks kept throwing to his side enough to allow Boyd to intercept 57 passes in nine seasons.

"He had great recognition and great instincts," said New York Giants' GM George Young, once the Colts' player personnel director. "Back in those days, you didn't have to have great speed. Defensive backs could chuck the receiver. They were playing a tougher brand of football, so it wasn't necessarily a speed thing."

Boyd led the Colts seven seasons with interceptions.

INDIVIDUAL COLT RECORDS

Rushing

Most Yards Game:	198	Norm Bulaich, vs N.Y. Jets, 1971
Season:	1,659	Eric Dickerson, 1988
Career:	5,487	Lydell Mitchell, 1972-77

Passing

Most TD Passes Game:	5	2 times, most recently Gary Hogeboom, vs Buffalo, 1987
Season:	32	John Unitas, 1959
Career:	287	John Unitas, 1956-72

Receiving

Most TD Passes Game:	3	6 times, most recently Roger Carr, vs Cincinnati, 1976
Season:	14	Raymond Berry, 1959
Career:	68	Raymond Berry, 1955-67

Scoring

Most Points Game:	24	5 times, most recently Eric Dickerson, vs Denver, 1988
Season:	120	Lenny Moore, 1964
Career:	678	Lenny Moore, 1956-67
Most TDs Game:	4	5 times, most recently Eric Dickerson, vs Denver, 1988
Season:	20	Lenny Moore, 1964
Career:	113	Lenny Moore, 1956-67

KANSAS CITY CHIEFS

TEAM DIRECTORY: Founder: Lamar Hunt; Pres./COO/GM: Carl Peterson; Exec. VP-Adm.: Tim Connolly; Dir. Pub. Rel.: Robert Moore; Head Coach: Marty Schottenheimer. Home field: Arrowhead Stadium (77,622). Colors: Red and gold.

SCOUTING REPORT

OFFENSE: Coach Marty Schottenheimer junked his big-back, ball-control offense in favor of the 49er passing attack. And he and Chiefs' president Carl Peterson landed the 49er legend, 37-year-old Joe Montana, to operate it.

The Chiefs expect that Montana's elbow woes of the past two seasons are behind him and that he will bring his Super Bowl magic. Montana, who threw only 21 times last season (15 completions), takes over the starting job from 34-year-old Dave Krieg, who completed 55.7 percent of his passes and threw for 15 TDs for the 10-6 Chiefs.

With halfback Harvey Williams coming off a disappointing season and Barry Word and Christian Okoye perhaps headed elsewhere, the Chiefs signed Raider veteran Marcus Allen, who jumped at the opportunity to play with Montana. The versatile Allen—running, receiving, blocking—will have opportunities he hasn't had in recent seasons. J.J. Birden leads the wide receivers with Willie Davis and Tim Barnett.

Center Tim Grunhard and left tackle John Alt are the sure things on an offensive line that must become more mobile for the moving pockets. Guard Dave Szott will be a factor, and so will ex-Raider right tackle Reggie McElroy.

DEFENSE: The major changes on this unit occurred last season. Concerned about poor play against the run, the Chiefs went to the 4-3. The strategy worked, but it almost cost them linebacker Derrick Thomas. Thomas, the game's most feared blitzing linebacker, almost accepted an offer sheet from the Lions. Money tempted him, and so did the Lions' 3-4 scheme. Thomas works better in a 3-4 because he's a pass-rushing threat on every down. The 4-3 works because end Neil Smith emerged into a franchise player, Dan Saleaumua and Joe Phillips are able tackles and Chris Martin and Tracy Simien are solid but not flashy linebackers.

The Chiefs offered cornerback Kevin Ross in trade discussions because they wanted to get Dale Carter into the starting lineup.

Joe Montana is a Chief after 14 years of 49er glory.

Carter thrilled fans with his gambling style at cornerback. Cornerback Albert Lewis can't shake injuries but receivers still can't shake him. The safety jobs were held by Martin Bayless, a run-stopper, and Charles Mincy, an underrated hitter at free safety.

SPECIAL TEAMS: Having kicker Nick Lowery make 22 of 24 field goals isn't a surprise. He's one of the best. Having Bryan Barker average 43.3 yards a punt is a surprise. Dale Carter is a game-breaker on kickoff and punt returns. Bennie Thompson leads an aggressive group on the coverage teams.

CHIEFS VETERAN ROSTER

HEAD COACH—Marty Schottenheimer. Assistant Coaches—Dave Adolph, Russ Ball, John Buntin, Herman Edwards, Alex Gibbs, Paul Hackett, Mike McCarthy, Tom Pratt, Jimmy Raye, Dave Redding, Al Saunders, Kurt Schottenheimer, Darvin Wallis.

No.	Name	Pos.	Ht.	Wt.	NFL Exp.	College
32	Allen, Marcus	RB	6-2	210	12	USC
76	Alt, John	T	6-8	295	10	Iowa
38	Anders, Kimble	RB	5-11	221	3	Houston
50	Anderson, Erick	MLB	6-1	241	2	Michigan
77	Baldinger, Rich	T-G	6-4	293	12	Wake Forest
4	Barker, Bryan	P	6-1	187	4	Santa Clara
82	Barnett, Tim	WR	6-1	201	3	Jackson State
30	Bayless, Martin	S	6-2	213	10	Bowling Green
88	Birden, J.J.	WR	5-9	170	5	Oregon
14	Blundin, Matt	QB	6-6	230	2	Virginia
11	Brown, John	WR	6-2	195	1	Houston
34	Carter, Dale	CB-KR	6-1	181	2	Tennessee
89	Cash, Keith	TE	6-4	245	2	Texas
24	Dandridge, Gary	S	6-0	213	2	Appalachian State
84	Davis, Willie	WR	6-0	170	2	Central Arkansas
71	Dohring, Tom	T	6-6	290	3	Michigan
87	Dyal, Mike	TE	6-2	240	6	Texas A&I
67	Earle, John	G-C	6-5	284	1	Western Illinois
22	Ervin, Corris	CB	6-1	183	1	Central Florida
94	Evans, Mike	DT-DE	6-3	269	2	Michigan
26	Flagler, Terrence	RB	6-0	200	6	Clemson
74	Graham, Derrick	T	6-4	306	4	Appalachian State
98	Griffin, Leonard	DE	6-4	278	8	Grambling
61	Grunhard, Tim	C	6-2	299	4	Notre Dame
56	Hackett, Dino	MLB	6-3	230	8	Appalachian State
81	Hargain, Tony	WR	6-0	194	3	Oregon
85	Hayes, Jonathan	TE	6-5	248	9	Iowa
40	Highsmith, Alonzo	RB	6-1	235	6	Miami (Fla.)
9	Jackson, Byron	WR	5-7	160	1	San Jose State
62	Jennings, Jim	G-C	6-4	295	1	San Diego State
80	Jones, Fred	WR	5-9	183	4	Grambling
91	Kirksey, William	OLB	6-2	237	3	Southern Mississippi
17	Krieg, Dave	QB	6-1	202	14	Milton
29	Lewis, Albert	CB	6-2	195	11	Grambling
21	Lewis, Tauhan	CB	5-10	175	2	Nebraska
8	Lowery, Nick	K	6-4	205	14	Dartmouth
49	Marrow, Vince	TE	6-3	251	1	Toledo
51	Marts, Lonnie	OLB	6-1	243	4	Tulane
99	McDaniels, Pellom	DE	6-3	278	1	Oregon State
—	McElroy, Reggie	T	6-6	290	11	West Texas State
48	McNair, Todd	RB	6-1	202	5	Temple
39	McWright, Robert	CB	5-8	170	1	Texas Christian
92	Mickell, Darren	DE	6-4	268	2	Florida
42	Mincy, Charles	S	5-11	197	3	Washington
19	Montana, Joe	QB	6-1	195	15	Notre Dame
96	Newton, Tim	DT	6-0	275	8	Florida
35	Okoye, Christian	RB	6-1	260	7	Azusa Pacific
40	Pharms, Charles	S	5-11	185	1	Miami (Fla.)
75	Phillips, Joe	DT	6-5	300	8	Southern Methodist
64	Ricketts, Tom	G	6-5	305	5	Pittsburgh
52	Rogers, Tracy	MLB	6-2	241	4	Fresno State
31	Ross, Kevin	CB	5-9	182	10	Temple
97	Saleaumua, Dan	DT	6-0	295	7	Arizona State
66	Siglar, Ricky	T-G	6-7	296	2	San Jose State
54	Simien, Tracy	MLB	6-1	250	3	Texas Christian
95	Sims, Tom	DT	6-2	291	4	Pittsburgh
93	Smith, Leroy	OLB	6-2	225	1	Iowa
83	Smith, Michael	WR	5-8	160	1	Kansas State
90	Smith, Neil	DE	6-4	275	6	Nebraska
6	Smith, Tony	WR	6-2	185	1	Notre Dame
55	Snow, Percy	MLB	6-2	250	3	Michigan State
53	Stephens, Santo	OLB	6-4	232	1	Temple

continued on page 479

TOP DRAFT CHOICES

Rd.	Name	Sel. No.	Pos.	Ht.	Wt.	College
3	Shields, Will	74	G	6-2	299	Nebraska
4	Fields, Jamie	103	LB	5-11	236	Washington
5	Knapp, Lindsay	130	G	6-5	276	Notre Dame
6	Turner, Darius	159	RB	5-11	232	Washington
7	Hughes, Danan	186	WR	6-1	203	Iowa

THE ROOKIES: The Montana trade and the Darren Mickell supplemental choice forced Schottenheimer to wait until the third and fifth rounds to draft for needs at guard. Will Shields, Outland Trophy winner from Nebraska, and Lindsay Knapp from Notre Dame will need time to develop, but one of the two could slip into the right guard slot. A sleeper? Sixth-round fullback Darius Turner from Washington.

OUTLOOK: Can Montana recapture the wizardry that brought four championship rings? The answer to that will determine in large part whether the Chiefs move into Super Bowl contention.

CHIEF PROFILES

JOE MONTANA 37 6-1 195　　　　　Quarterback

Future Hall of Famer plans to finish career with Chiefs . . . Traded to KC in April after 14 remarkable seasons with San Francisco . . . Chiefs sent 49ers first-round pick in trade and signed Montana to three-year, $12-million deal . . . Missed most of 1991 and 1992 seasons with elbow injury . . . His only playing time in 1992 came in second half of regular-season finale against Detroit . . . Completed 15 of 21 passes for 126 yards and two TDs . . . He and Terry Bradshaw are the only quarterbacks in NFL history to win four Super Bowls . . . The only three-time Super Bowl MVP . . . Seven-time Pro Bowl selection . . . Put together one of his best seasons in 1990 with 3,944 passing yards . . . 49ers' third-round pick out of Notre Dame in 1979 . . . Born June 11, 1956, in New Eagle, Pa. . . . 1993 base salary: $4 million.

DERRICK THOMAS 26 6-3 242   Linebacker

Sack master has been to Pro Bowl four consecutive years . . . Downed quarterbacks 14½ times last season, making his career total 57½ in 63 games . . . Stripping ball from runners is his specialty. He's caused 13 fumbles, recovering seven, in four years . . . With switch to the 4-3 at midseason, Thomas lost his chance to rush quarterbacks on first and second downs . . . Finished season with three-sack classic against Broncos' John Elway . . . Pressured quarterbacks 53 times last season. . . . Fans still can't forget his seven-sack game against Seahawks in 1990 . . . Was a first-round choice from Alabama in 1989 . . . Born Jan. 1, 1967, in Miami . . . 1992 base salary: $600,000.

NEIL SMITH 27 6-4 275   Defensive End

Rewarded after his best season by being designated Chiefs' franchise player . . . Tied Derrick Thomas with team-high 14½ sacks, which ranked third in the league . . . Terrorized Redskins' Mark Rypien with four pressures and three sacks Nov. 15 . . . But received only a backup spot in Pro Bowl . . . Returned an interception for 22-yard touchdown against Seattle Nov. 22 . . . Now Chief fans know why former GM Jim Schaaf surrendered second-round choice in 1988 draft to move up one spot to make him second pick . . . Was a 208-pounder when he entered Nebraska . . . Born April 10, 1966, in New Orleans. . . . 1992 base salary: $575,000.

TIM GRUNHARD 25 6-2 299   Center

Former Chiefs' offensive line coach Howard Mudd thinks he might be the best center in the league . . . Missed the final three games with foot injury. . . . Three different players filled in for him during that absence . . . Learned the center position in the pros after never playing it at Notre Dame or in high school. . . . Future Hall-of-Famer Mike Webster taught Grunhard the fine art of being a center during his rookie year. . . . At his best, Grunhard opens holes that enable Chief backs to gain 1,000 yards a season. . . . Started final two seasons at guard for Notre

Dame and the Irish went 24-1 . . . Was second-round draft choice in 1990 . . . Born May 17, 1968, in Chicago . . . 1993 base salary: $750,000, plus $165,000 in bonuses.

DAN SALEAUMUA 28 6-0 295   Defensive Tackle

Despite registering the most tackles among Chief defensive linemen, Saleaumua considered giving up football at the end of the season . . . Coach Marty Schottenheimer won't let him and dangled a financial carrot by naming him a 1994 transition player. Next year, he will be among 10 top-paid defensive tackles . . . Adjusted well from the midseason switch from nose tackle to defensive tackle, pressuring quarterbacks 26 times . . . Never had a chance to play much when he was Jerry Ball's backup for the Lions in 1987-88 . . . Considered the prize of four years of Plan B free agency . . . Has 14½ sacks during the past three seasons . . . Was seventh-round draft choice out of Arizona State, where he also threw shot-put and discus . . . A practical joker . . . Born Nov. 25, 1964, in San Diego . . . 1992 base salary: $600,000.

HARVEY WILLIAMS 26 6-2 222   Halfback

Hopes to rebound after disappointing second season . . . Finished third on the team with 262 rushing yards, 185 yards less than his rookie season . . . Only start was in playoff loss to Chargers, and he gained just 35 yards. Saw extensive regular-season duty in only three games . . . Strained a knee on his second carry of the second game against the Seahawks and missed the next start . . . Still led the team in the final eight games with 216 yards . . . Chiefs expect him to be feature back in their new 49er-style offense, following the lead blocks of fullback Christian Okoye . . . Had 1,118 all-purpose yards as a rookie . . . Led the Chiefs last season with 19.3 kickoff-return average . . . Has the potential to be a 50-catch receiver out of the backfield . . . Was first-round choice in 1991 out of Louisiana Tech, where he rushed for 2,860 yards . . . Born April 22, 1967, in Hempstead, Tex. . . . 1993 base salary: $400,000.

MARCUS ALLEN 33 6-2 210   Halfback

Resolved long-running feud with Raider boss Al Davis and launches new era after 11 seasons with Raiders . . . Unrestricted free agent signed three-year KC contract at estimated $1.5 million a year . . . Under-utilized, he'd started only two games since 1990 after being demoted to third-down role . . . Had just 67 carries (301 yards for a 4.5 average) and 28 receptions (277 for 9.9 average) last season . . . Is No. 12 on NFL career rushing list . . . Was MVP in 1985 when led league in rushing with Raider record of 1,759 yards . . . Was MVP of Super Bowl XVIII . . . Won 1981 Heisman Trophy and was 10th player selected in 1982 draft, out of USC . . . Born March 26, 1960, in San Diego . . . 1992 base salary: $1,100,000.

KEVIN ROSS 31 5-9 182   Cornerback

One of the hardest-hitting cornerbacks in the league . . . Has averaged 80.4 tackles a season, incredible for a cornerback . . . His only interception of the season was a 99-yarder in the season-opener against San Diego . . . Has returned five interceptions for touchdowns during his career . . . Teammates named his "Rock" as a rookie because of his toughness . . . Has missed only four starts during his nine-year career . . . Learned tackling technique as a high-school wrestler . . . Struggled and was beaten often as a rookie starter, but never lost confidence . . . Has been to Pro Bowl twice and was alternate once . . . Was seventh-round choice (172 players selected ahead of him) in 1984 . . . Born Jan. 16, 1962, in Camden, N.J. . . . 1993 base salary: $775,000.

DALE CARTER 23 6-1 181   Cornerback

Became an instant star as a rookie . . . Intercepted seven passes, including a 55-yard touchdown . . . Started nine games in place of Albert Lewis at left cornerback . . . Has a gambling style that occasionally gets him beat, but he has great makeup speed . . . Averaged 10.5 yards on punt returns, and exploded for an 86-yard touchdown against the Seahawks and 46 yards against the Chargers . . . Brother is Jake Reed, the Viking wide receiver . . . Was All-American at Tennessee, where he collected nine interceptions in two years and averaged 27.7 yards per kickoff return . . . Was 20th draft pick . . . Born Nov. 28, 1969, in Covington, Ga. . . . 1993 base salary: $375,000.

JOHN ALT 31 6-8 296   Left Tackle

Fought off preseason back problems to finally earn a trip to the Pro Bowl . . . Considered one of the best pass-blocking left tackles in NFL . . . Has started 69 consecutive games . . . His long arms enable him to control pass-rushers . . . Came to Chiefs in first round in 1985 draft as third offensive linemen taken . . . Played basketball and football in high school but was recruited by Iowa as tight end . . . Grew from 230 to 278 pounds as a sophomore and became offensive lineman . . . Injuries plagued him early in his career . . . Born May 30, 1962, in Stuttgart, Germany . . . 1993 base salary: $900,000.

DAVE KRIEG 34 6-1 192   Quarterback

It wasn't his fault the Chiefs didn't go farther in the playoffs . . . Completed 230 of 413 passes for 3,115 yards and 15 touchdowns after being signed as a Plan B free agent from the Seahawks . . . Struggled learning an offense that coach Marty Schottenheimer decided to change after the season . . . Is accurate, short-range passer who has the ability to improvise on the run . . . Should fit well into 49er-type offense because of his ability to throw from a moving pocket . . . Ranks ninth on all-time NFL quarterback list with an 82.2 rating . . . Completed 21 passes longer than 30 yards, including six more than 50 yards . . . His 7.54 yards per attempt last year topped the AFC . . . Since becoming an NFL starter, he's played 129 games and missed only 10 . . . Is 80-55 as a starter . . . Has completed 58.3 percent of his passes and thrown for 210 touchdowns . . . Undrafted free agent in 1980 by the Seahawks, out of Milton College . . . Got starting job midway through 1983 season and became the franchise quarterback in Seattle . . . Born Oct. 20, 1958, in Iola, Wis. . . . 1993 base salary: $1,950,000.

J.J. BIRDEN 28 5-9 170   Wide Receiver

The Chiefs wouldn't let him slip away to the Eagles through free agency . . . They matched a two-year, $1.6-million offer sheet from the Eagles . . . Developed into the most dependable of the Chief receivers last season with 42 catches for 644 yards . . . A big-play receiver with the ability to get deep . . . Averaged 15.4 yards per catch but has a 17.4 career average . . . Had his first 11 starts after being a backup for two seasons . . . Was eighth-round choice of Browns in 1988 but missed the training camp because of a knee injury . . . Cut by the Browns, he was signed by Dallas as a developmental player . . . Chiefs signed him in 1990 and he caught 15 passes for a 23.5-yard average . . . Went to Oregon on a track scholarship as high-jumper and high-hurdler . . . Played quarterback at Oregon behind Chris Miller before moving to wide receiver . . . Weighed only 139 pounds coming out of high school . . . Born June 16, 1965, in Portland, Ore. . . . 1993 base salary: $700,000, plus $200,000 signing bonus.

COACH MARTY SCHOTTENHEIMER:

His .615 winning percentage makes him winningest coach in Chiefs' history, .001 better than Hank Stram. . . . Has a 39-24-1 record and is three-for-four in playoff berths for Chiefs . . . Lifetime record as an NFL head coach is 83-51-1, a .618 winning percentage . . . Plans to revamp the offense by installing 49ers-style system . . . Changed his standard 3-4 defense at midseason last year to improve the run defense with a 4-3 . . . Brought winning attitude to Chiefs after 4½ successful years as head coach of Browns, where he went to two AFC title games . . . Has never had a losing season as a head coach. . . . Took over midway through 1984 season for Sam Rutigliano as Browns' coach . . . Was an All-American linebacker at Pitt and was named to the school's all-time team . . . Was a backup with Bills, Patriots and Steelers . . . Retired from football to work in real estate . . . Accepted a coaching job with the Portland Storm of WFL in 1974 and went on to assistant jobs with Giants, Lions and Browns . . . Born Sept. 23, 1943, in Canonsburg, Pa.

GREATEST INTERCEPTOR

From the late-60s through the mid-70s, the Chiefs' practice sessions featured fierce competition between wide receiver Otis Taylor and cornerback Emmitt Thomas. It made each among the best every Sunday and it played a role in Thomas emerging as the all-time interceptor (58) on a team that has been blessed with great cornerbacks, including Albert Lewis and Kevin Ross.

"Emmitt was 6-2, which is big for a cornerback," said former Chief GM Jim Schaaf. "He was durable and wouldn't miss games. And he's one of those guys who could lay a lick on you. But he was also smart enough to figure out the scheme, react to the ball and break on the ball well."

Thomas came from tiny Bishop College, a school so small that he played for the football team and in the band. On the same day.

INDIVIDUAL CHIEF RECORDS

Rushing

Most Yards Game:	200	Barry Word, vs Detroit, 1990
Season:	1,480	Christian Okoye, 1989
Career:	4,897	Christian Okoye, 1987-92

Passing

Most TD Passes Game:	6	Len Dawson, vs Denver, 1964
Season:	30	Len Dawson, 1964
Career:	237	Len Dawson, 1962-75

Receiving

Most TD Passes Game:	4	Frank Jackson, vs San Diego, 1964
Season:	12	Chris Burford, 1962
Career:	57	Otis Taylor, 1965-75

Scoring

Most Points Game:	30	Abner Haynes, vs Oakland, 1961
Season:	139	Nick Lowery, 1990
Career:	1,360	Nick Lowery, 1980-92
Most TDs Game:	5	Abner Haynes, vs Oakland, 1961
Season:	19	Abner Haynes, 1962
Career:	60	Otis Taylor, 1965-75

LOS ANGELES RAIDERS

TEAM DIRECTORY: President: Al Davis; Exec. Asst.: Ai LoCasale; Sr. Exec.: John Herrera; Sr. Administrator: Morris Bradshaw; Dir. Football Oper.: Steve Ortmayer; Pro Football Scouting Dir.: George Karras; Publications: Mike Taylor; Head Coach: Art Shell. Home field: Los Angeles Memorial Coliseum (92,487). Colors: Silver and black.

SCOUTING REPORT

OFFENSE: With patience wearing thin after years of inconsistency at quarterback, Raider boss Al Davis brought in Jay Hostetler, the seven-year Giant. Known for his toughness, the mobile quarterback won a Super Bowl ring but most recently lost to Phil Simms in New York's QB derby.

Todd Marinovich, last year's early starter, simply wasn't ready for the full-time job.

Two long-time Raiders are gone: halfback Marcus Allen to the Chiefs and wide receiver Mervyn Fernandez to the 49ers. And wide receiver Willie Gault may be phased out as he enters his 11th year in the NFL.

Davis and coach Art Shell wanted younger, faster legs. They found a few world-class speedsters. Gaston Green, acquired from the Broncos for a third-round choice, is the fastest halfback in football. Wide receiver Tim Brown comes off a big year and Alexander Wright provides another deep threat to go with all-time wide receiver James Lofton, returning to the Raiders after four years with the Bills.

The combination of youth (Nick Bell) and experience (Eric Dickerson) makes the backfield departure of Allen easier to take. Fullback Steve Smith resisted free-agent offers to be the main blocking back.

The addition of Rams' left tackle Gerald Perry makes the left side of the offensive line rock-solid. Perry, a talented pass-blocker, will benefit working next to Steve Wisniewski, a perennial Pro Bowl left guard. Bruce Wilkerson shifts from left to right tackle. Center Don Mosebar and right guard Max Montoya provide leadership on the line.

DEFENSE: Shell's toughest job is figuring out who to use and when on the defensive line. Nolan Harrison developed into a Howie Long clone at defensive tackle. Despite an off-season, Greg Townsend is a Pro Bowl-caliber end. Willie Broughton helped as

Ex-Giant Jeff Hostetler gets his shot as QB savior.

a run-stopper. Shell must find ways to find more time for end Anthony Smith, who had 13 sacks as a part-timer, and tackle Chester McGlockton, a 320-pound run-stopper. Long won't be the one to move aside. He's still one of the best.

The linebacking corps remains in a constant state of change. Aaron Wallace and Winston Moss should be the outside linebackers, while Joe Kelly, Anthony Bell and Riki Ellison compete for the inside positions.

Derrick Hoskins, a second-year safety, or rookie Patrick Bates draws the impossible assignment of replacing Ronnie Lott, now a Jet. Other than strong safety, the secondary is set. Cornerbacks Lionel Washington and Terry McDaniels are superb at coverage. Free safety Eddie Anderson is an impact player.

SPECIAL TEAMS: The Raiders have the strong field-goal leg of Jeff Jaeger and the ideal directional punter in Jeff Gossett. The return teams have Tim Brown and Alexander Wright. Coverage teams are loaded with top tacklers.

RAIDERS VETERAN ROSTER

HEAD COACH—Art Shell. Assistant Coaches—Fred Biletnikoff, Gunther Cunningham, Ray Hamilton, Jim Hasslett, Odis McKinney, Bill Meyers, Steve Ortmayer, Terry Robiskie, Joe Scannella, Todd Sperber, Jack Stanton, Tom Walsh, Mike White, Doug Wilkerson.

No.	Name	Pos.	Ht.	Wt.	NFL Exp.	College
33	Anderson, Eddie	S	6-1	210	7	Fort Valley State
59	Bell, Anthony	LB	6-3	245	8	Michigan State
38	Bell, Nick	RB	6-2	250	3	Iowa
97	Broughton, Willie	DT	6-5	280	6	Miami (Fla.)
81	Brown, Tim	WR	6-0	195	5	Notre Dame
56	Bruce, Aundray	DE	6-5	260	6	Auburn
92	Collons, Ferric	DE	6-6	305	1	California
29	Dickerson, Eric	RB	6-3	220	11	Southern Methodist
46	Dorn, Torin	CB	6-0	190	4	North Carolina
50	Ellison, Riki	LB	6-2	225	10	USC
11	Evans, Vince	QB	6-2	210	14	USC
73	FitzPatrick, James	G	6-8	325	7	USC
49	Freeman, Kyle	LB	6-1	225	1	Angelo State
83	Gault, Willie	WR	6-1	175	11	Tennessee
87	Glover, Andrew	TE	6-6	250	3	Grambling
79	Golic, Bob	DT	6-3	280	14	Notre Dame
7	Gossett, Jeff	P	6-2	195	12	Eastern Illinois
85	Graddy, Sam	WR	5-10	180	6	Tennessee
22	Green, Gaston	RB	5-11	190	6	UCLA
74	Harrison, Nolan	DT	6-5	285	3	Indiana
80	Hobbs, Daryl	WR	6-2	175	1	Pacific
88	Horton, Ethan	TE	6-4	240	7	North Carolina
20	Hoskins, Derrick	S	6-2	200	2	Southern Mississippi
15	Hostetler, Jeff	QB	6-3	212	9	West Virginia
18	Jaeger, Jeff	K	5-11	195	6	Washington
58	Jimerson, A.J.	LB	6-3	235	3	Norfolk State
26	Johnson, Dennis	CB	6-1	200	1	Winston-Salem
82	Jones, David	TE	6-3	225	2	Delaware State
52	Jones, Mike	LB	6-1	230	3	Missouri
57	Kelly, Joe	LB	6-2	235	8	Washington
25	Land, Dan	CB	6-0	195	6	Albany State
—	Lofton, James	WR	6-3	190	16	Stanford
75	Long, Howie	DE	6-5	270	13	Villanova
12	Marinovich, Todd	QB	6-4	215	3	USC
41	McCallum, Napoleon	RB	6-2	230	5	Naval Academy
36	McDaniel, Terry	CB	5-10	180	5	Tennessee
91	McGlockton, Chester	DT	6-4	320	2	Clemson
17	Montgomery, Tyrone	RB	6-0	185	1	Mississippi
65	Montoya, Max	G	6-5	295	15	UCLA
72	Mosebar, Don	C	6-6	305	11	Southern California
99	Moss, Winston	LB	6-3	240	7	Miami (Fla.)
43	Patterson, Elvis	S	5-11	195	10	Kansas
64	Peat, Todd	G	6-2	305	5	Northern Illinois
71	Perry, Gerald	T	6-6	305	6	Southern
62	Roth, Tom	G	6-5	285	1	Southern Illinois
78	Skrepenak, Greg	T	6-6	315	2	Michigan
94	Smith, Anthony	DE	6-3	270	3	Arizona
39	Smith, Kevin	TE	6-4	255	1	UCLA
35	Smith, Steve	RB	6-1	240	7	Penn State
55	Stephens, Rich	G	6-7	310	1	Tulsa
93	Townsend, Greg	DE	6-3	270	11	Texas Christian
67	Turk, Dan	C	6-4	300	8	Wisconsin
51	Wallace, Aaron	LB	6-3	235	4	Texas A&M
48	Washington, Lionel	CB	6-0	185	11	Tulane
98	Watts, Walter	DT	6-6	320	1	Utah
68	Wilkerson, Bruce	T	6-5	295	7	Tennessee
76	Wisniewski, Steve	G	6-4	285	5	Penn State
89	Wright, Alexander	WR	6-0	195	4	Auburn
66	Wright, Steve	T	6-6	285	11	Northern Iowa

		TOP DRAFT CHOICES				
Rd.	Name	Sel. No.	Pos.	Ht.	Wt.	College
1	Bates, Patrick	12	DB	6-3	224	Texas A&M
3	Hobert, Billy Joe	58	QB	6-2	234	Washington
3	Trapp, James	72	DB	6-0	178	Clemson
5	Truitt, Olanda	125	WR	6-0	188	Mississippi State
7	Biekert, Greg	181	LB	6-2	230	Colorado

THE ROOKIES: Who better to replace Lott than his biggest fan—the 6-3, 224-pound Bates? No. 12 overall, Bates is a big hitter from Texas A&M who could beat out Hoskins at strong safety. Washington quarterback Billy Joe Hobert was the Raiders' surprise third-round choice. Speedy cornerback James Trapp from Clemson also went in the third round.

OUTLOOK: As always, the Raiders, 7-9 last year, will go as far as their offense takes them. Big seasons are needed by Bell and Hostetler if the Raiders are to return to the top of the division.

RAIDER PROFILES

JEFF HOSTETLER 32 6-3 212   **Quarterback**

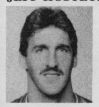

Comes to Raiders as a free agent after 10 seasons with the Giants . . . Signed three-year, $7.5-million deal . . . Raiders believe he can solve their long-time quarterback problems . . . Athletic player with good scrambling ability and decent throwing arm . . . Giants' starting quarterback in 1991 and 1992 . . . Missed four games last season with injuries . . . Passed for 1,225 yards and eight TDs with just three interceptions in run-oriented offense . . . Passed for career-high 2,032 yards in 1991 . . . Long-time backup got his chance to start when Phil Simms was injured late in 1990 season . . . Led the Giants on magical run that included Super Bowl victory over Buffalo . . . Did not attempt a pass until 1988, his fifth NFL season . . . Used mostly as a holder on placekicks early in his career . . . Giants' third-round pick out of West Virginia in 1984 . . . Born April 22, 1961, in Johnstown, Pa. . . . 1993 base salary: $2.5 million.

GERALD PERRY 28 6-6 305   Tackle

Signed with the Raiders as a free agent after two seasons with the Rams . . . Got three-year, $3.54-million contract that included $250,000 signing bonus and $250,000 bonus upon reporting to training camp . . . Big man with great agility . . . Superb pass-blocker at important left-tackle position . . . Started all 16 games for the Rams at left tackle in 1992 . . . Acquired by the Rams from Broncos in a 1991 draft-day trade for running back Gaston Green and fourth-round pick . . . Broncos' starter at left tackle in 1989 and 1990 . . . Started six games as a rookie in 1988 . . . Broncos' second-round pick out of Southern University in 1988 . . . Played basketball as well as football in college . . . Born Nov. 12, 1964, in Columbia, S.C. . . . 1993 base salary: $940,000.

TIM BROWN 27 6-0 195   Wide Receiver

Took control as the featured receiver after three seasons as the main threat off the bench . . . Led Raiders with 49 catches for 693 yards and seven touchdowns . . . Voted team MVP and was their best offensive player . . . Goes over the middle on third downs for tough catches . . . Continued to return punts and had 10.4-yard average . . . A two-time Pro Bowler because of his return ability . . . Dangerous runner after making catches downfield . . . Broke Gale Sayers' NFL record for most combined yardage as a rookie (2,316 yards) . . . Named a transition player once his contract expires after this season . . . Missed 15 games in 1989 after suffering major knee injury . . . Recovered to be important third-down receiver in 1990 and finished with 18 catches . . . Had 36 catches in 1991 . . . Won 1987 Heisman Trophy at Notre Dame . . . Born July 22, 1966, in Dallas . . . 1993 base salary: $650,000.

NICK BELL 25 6-2 250   Halfback

Tailed off after good rookie year, but had a couple of long runs that bulked up his average. Faces most critical season as Raiders' main back . . . Was named a transition player once his contract expired after the season . . . Finished second on team with 366 yards on 81 carries, 4.6 a carry . . . Has 4.4 speed, swift for a 250-pound back . . . Started only one game

. . . Scored three touchdowns, equal to his rookie season . . . Selected in the second round in 1991 following a draft-day trade with the Seahawks . . . Has had some of his best games against the Seahawks . . . Hamstring problems bothered him through his rookie season . . . Rushed for 945 yards and 10 touchdowns during his senior year at Iowa . . . Was a Nevada heavyweight wrestling champ in high school as a junior . . . Born Aug. 19, 1968, in Las Vegas . . . 1993 base salary: $350,000.

ERIC DICKERSON 33 6-3 220   Halfback

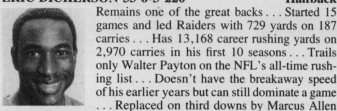

Remains one of the great backs . . . Started 15 games and led Raiders with 729 yards on 187 carries . . . Has 13,168 career rushing yards on 2,970 carries in his first 10 seasons . . . Trails only Walter Payton on the NFL's all-time rushing list . . . Doesn't have the breakaway speed of his earlier years but can still dominate a game . . . Replaced on third downs by Marcus Allen last year and often in the second half by Nick Bell . . . Has had six trips to Pro Bowl . . . Reached the 10,000-yard plateau faster than any player in league history, but he hasn't had a 1,000-yard season since 1989 . . . Was second player taken in 1983 draft and won Rookie of the Year honors with 1,808-yard season for Rams . . . Gained 2,105 yards in 1984 . . . Traded to Indianapolis in middle of 1987 season . . . Had two 1,000-yard seasons for Colts . . . Traded to Raiders for fourth- and eighth-round choices in 1992 . . . Rushed for 1,617 yards at Southern Methodist and finished third in Heisman Trophy voting in 1982 . . . Born Sept. 2, 1960, in Sealy, Tex. . . . 1993 base salary: $1,100,000.

STEVE WISNIEWSKI 26 6-4 285   Guard

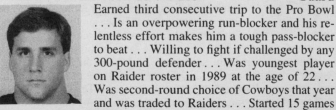

Earned third consecutive trip to the Pro Bowl . . . Is an overpowering run-blocker and his relentless effort makes him a tough pass-blocker to beat . . . Willing to fight if challenged by any 300-pound defender . . . Was youngest player on Raider roster in 1989 at the age of 22 . . . Was second-round choice of Cowboys that year and was traded to Raiders . . . Started 15 games at right guard as rookie . . . Moved to left guard for the past three seasons . . . Only the third offensive lineman in Penn State history to be named first-team All-American twice . . . Brother, Leo, was a defensive tackle with Baltimore Colts . . . Born April 7, 1967, in Rutland, Vt. . . . 1992 base salary: $300,000.

TODD MARINOVICH 24 6-4 215   Quarterback

Wasn't ready to be the full-time Raider quarterback after being pushed into the starting job. . . . Started seven games, but had a disappointing 58.2 rating . . . Completed 81 of 165 passes for 1,102 yards and five touchdowns . . . Was sacked 20 times and threw only five touchdown passes . . . Played in only one regular-season game before last year, throwing for three touchdowns against Chiefs in 1991 . . . The Chiefs turned around to stop him the following week in the playoffs . . . Started seven games after replacing Jay Schroeder following 0-2 start . . . Reacted poorly to being benched and missed a meeting . . . Was demoted to third-string during the second half of the season . . . Lacks the deep throws, but came to the Raiders known for his precision passing skills . . . Entered pros as 24th draft pick after two seasons with Southern Cal . . . Despite not playing high-school baseball, the California Angels drafted him in 1988 . . . Born May 8, 1969, in San Leandro, Cal. . . . 1993 base salary: $570,000.

TERRY McDANIEL 28 5-10 180   Cornerback

One of best coverage cornerbacks in the league . . . Had a team-high 20 passes defensed, and intercepted a team-high four passes . . . Earned first trip to Pro Bowl . . . Quarterbacks stopped challenging him late in the season . . . Raiders named him a transition player for when his contract expires after this season . . . He tied for sixth on the team with 63 tackles . . . Was a first-round choice in 1988 and became the first Raider rookie since Jack Tatum to start in the secondary . . . Missed the final 14 games because of a broken leg . . . Missed only three starts since his rookie year . . . Earned All-American honors at Tennessee in 1987 . . . Moved from wide receiver to cornerback during his sophomore season . . . Member of SEC champion 1,600-meter track team and holds Tennessee record for the 300-yard dash . . . Born Feb. 8, 1965, in Mansfield, Ohio . . . 1993 base salary: $800,000.

STEVE SMITH 29 6-1 240   Fullback

One of the hottest names in unconditional free agency during the offseason . . . Re-signed with the Raiders but almost left for rival Chiefs . . . He's the perfect power fullback to block for the conventional Raider running attack . . . Few hit the hole on lead blocks better than Smith . . . Is an all-purpose fullback who loves to block . . . Had only 44 carries for 129 yards last year . . . Tied Marcus Allen for third place on the Raiders with 28 catches . . . Has never had more than 117 carries during a season . . . Came to the Raiders in the third round of the 1987 draft . . . Became a full-time starter in 1989 and had his best season with 471 yards . . . Was starting fullback for the 1986 national championship team at Penn State . . . Was the Lions' offensive co-captain and played in three bowl games . . . Born Aug. 30, 1964, in Washington, D.C. . . . 1993 base salary: $1,000,000, plus $350,000 bonus.

JAMES LOFTON 37 6-3 190   Wide Receiver

After four years with Bills, he returned to Raiders with reported two-year, $1.8-million contract . . . Broke Steve Largent's all-time reception yardage mark of 13,089 last season when he posted 786 yards for a total of 13,821 . . . Had 51 receptions and six TDs . . . Age has diminished output but not his bag of tricks, such as never running the same pattern twice, and decoying by running at three-quarter speed . . . Packers made him No. 6 pick, out of Stanford, in 1978 . . . Traded to Raiders in '86 . . . Has played in Pro Bowl eight times . . . Born July 5, 1956, in Ford Ord, Cal.

AARON WALLACE 26 6-3 235   Linebacker

Cracked the starting lineup at outside linebacker after a two-year apprenticeship . . . Tried the strongside outside linebacker spot because of his strength in battling tight ends . . . Inconsistent with his pass-drops and in stopping the run. . . . Was fourth on team with 73 tackles . . . Conceded his pass-rushing role to Anthony Smith, but still came up with four sacks . . .

Started 16 games . . . A second-round choice in 1990 who had baptism as a pass-rushing linebacker . . . Earned All-Rookie honors by leading all rookies with nine sacks . . . Waited until the 1991 playoffs to get his first pro start . . . Holds Texas A&M record with 42 career sacks . . . Played in four bowl games . . . Was considered a second-round steal in 1990 . . . Born April 17, 1967, in Paris, Tex. . . . 1992 base salary: $275,000.

LIONEL WASHINGTON 32 6-0 185   Cornerback

Hasn't lost his touch or his speed as a coverage cornerback . . . Second only to Pro Bowler Terry McDaniel among Raiders with 13 passes defensed . . . Obtained by the Raiders in 1987 for only a fourth-round draft choice . . . Started 37 games for the Cardinals from 1983 through 1986 . . . Scored two touchdowns for Raiders in 1989 on interceptions . . . Intercepted two passes last season and has 28 for his career . . . Still hasn't matched his eight-interception season as Cardinal rookie in 1983 . . . Was fourth-round choice of the Cardinals after starting three seasons at Tulane . . . Was also sprinter on track team . . . Born Oct. 21, 1960, in New Orleans . . . 1993 base salary: $700,000.

HOWIE LONG 33 6-5 270   Defensive End

Stayed healthy for 16 games to re-establish himself as one of the league's elite defensive linemen . . . Finished second on the team with nine sacks . . . Usually draws double-team blocking that enables teammates to get the sacks . . . Voted alternate to the Pro Bowl and went because of an injury to Bills' Bruce Smith . . . Increased career sack total to 78 . . . Is a seven-time Pro Bowl selection . . . Named first-team defensive end on the All-NFL Team of the 1980s . . . Was second-round selection out of Villanova in 1981 . . . Became a starter five games into the 1982 season . . . Was NFL Defensive Lineman for the Year in 1984 after an 11-sack season . . . Born Jan. 6, 1960, in Somerville, Mass. . . . 1993 base salary: $1,500,000.

ANTHONY SMITH 26 6-3 270   **Defensive End**

It's hard to believe he isn't starting . . . His 13 sacks makes him one of the league's most feared pass-rushers and his explosion at the line of scrimmage makes him a solid run-stopper . . . Yet Raider coaches only started him once last year . . . He came off the bench to terrorize quarterbacks . . . Started two games in 1991 and had 10½ sacks . . . Missed 1990 rookie season because of major knee surgery . . . Came to the team as first-round choice in 1990 . . . Started college career at Alabama but transferred to Arizona for final season . . . Born June 28, 1967, in Elizabeth City, N.C. . . . 1993 base salary: $500,000, plus $112,500 in bonuses.

COACH ART SHELL: Missed playoffs for the first time as a

full-time head coach of the Raiders . . . Reshuffled coaching staff during difficult year and had to demote close friend Terry Robiskie as play-caller on offense . . . Has 35-25 record in four seasons . . . Is a stern displinarian who is trying to restore the Raider tradition . . . Took over for Mike Shanahan four weeks into the 1989 season and finished with 7-3 record . . . Went 12-4 and won AFC West the following year, earning Coach-of-the-Year honors . . . Raiders were 9-7 in 1991 and a wild-card playoff team . . . He was one of the great offensive linemen . . . Selected to the Pro Football Hall of Fame in 1989 . . . Played 15 seasons for Raiders and went to Pro Bowl eight times . . . His teams were 150-56-7 during his playing career . . . Earned two Super Bowl rings as player and one as assistant coach . . . Raiders made him a third-round choice in 1968 . . . He retired as an active player in 1983 and joined the coaching staff . . . Born Nov. 26, 1946, in Charleston, S.C.

GREATEST INTERCEPTOR

The numbers suggest a tie. Willie Brown and Lester Hayes each intercepted 39 passes during their illustrious Raider careers. Yet longtime Raiders give the nod to Hayes as being the greatest interceptor in team history.

"When you talk about bump-and-run coverage, the name you mention is Willie Brown; he was the foremost teacher of the art," retired Raider safety Vann McElroy said. "But when you talk about interceptors, it's Lester. The Judge [Hayes] always had the anticipation intangible there. If he had better hands, who knows how many interceptions he would have had?"

The colorful Hayes was a master thief. His 39 interceptions came in 10 seasons, two less than Brown. He returned 10, including two during the playoffs, for touchdowns.

"Lester watched a lot of film and was able to tell when a person was going to make his cut and where he was going to go with it," said McElroy, who came up with 37 interceptions. "The year that he used Stick'um was the year that he had 13 interceptions."

INDIVIDUAL RAIDER RECORDS

Rushing

Most Yards Game:	221	Bo Jackson, vs Seattle, 1987
Season:	1,759	Marcus Allen, 1985
Career:	8,545	Marcus Allen, 1982-92

Passing

Most TD Passes Game:	6	2 times, most recently Daryle Lamonica, vs Buffalo, 1969
Season:	34	Daryle Lamonica, 1969
Career:	150	Ken Stabler, 1970-79

Receiving

Most TD Passes Game:	4	Art Powell, vs Houston, 1963
Season:	16	Art Powell, 1963
Career:	76	Fred Biletnikoff, 1965-78

Scoring

Most Points Game:	24	2 times, most recently Marcus Allen, vs San Diego, 1984
Season:	117	George Blanda, 1968
Career:	863	George Blanda, 1967-75
Most TDs Game:	4	2 times, most recently Marcus Allen, vs San Diego, 1984
Season:	18	Marcus Allen, 1984
Career:	97	Marcus Allen, 1982-92

MIAMI DOLPHINS

TEAM DIRECTORY: Pres.: Timothy J. Robbie; Dir. Player Personnel: Tom Heckert; Dir. Media Relations: Harvey Greene; Head Coach: Don Shula. Home field: Joe Robbie Stadium (73,000). Colors: Aqua and orange.

SCOUTING REPORT

OFFENSE: Maybe the organization was a year too late upgrading its aging receiver corps, but credit owner Tim Robbie with doing a magnificent job on credit. Despite heavy debts hanging over the

Durable Dan Marino will pass 40,000-yard mark this season.

franchise, Robbie revamped the skills positions for big money. Combine money, Don Shula's coaching and Dan Marino's passing and watch out.

The offense is ready to advance past the AFC title game. Tight end Keith Jackson ($1.5 million a year) is capable of catching 60 Marino passes. Shula chased away mouthy Mark Clayton and began fazing out Mark Duper by signing Mark Ingram ($1.3 million) and trading for long-time nemesis Irving Fryar ($1.4 million). With Ingram and Fryar, the Dolphins acquired proven, big-play receivers who are great downfield blockers. And, as if Marino needed another target, the Dolphins picked up Penn State's O.J. McDuffie in the draft.

The backfield's success will depend on how well Bobby Humphrey comes back from offseason problems and whether Mark Higgs can get four yards a carry on first down.

The departure of right guard Harry Galbreath to the Packers leaves a big hole on the right side of the offensive line. The left side is secure with Richmond Webb and Keith Sims.

DEFENSE: Of all the playoff teams, the Dolphins had the youngest defense (25.7 years old). Things can only get better. Defensive end Marco Coleman and cornerback Troy Vincent, each on the verge of stardom, aren't rookies anymore. They are potential Pro Bowlers. And they've added veteran tackle Mike Golic from the Eagles.

Coleman, free safety Louis Oliver and linebacker Bryan Cox sometimes say too much and play with a chip on their shoulders. Why not? They are good enough to do that. If the Dolphins can keep inside linebacker John Offerdahl (adominal strain) healthy all season, they could vault from 10th in the league into the top five.

The Dolphins are exceptional at linebacker, have two of the finest coverage cornerbacks in the league (Vincent and J.B. Brown) and get a decent pass-rush from Coleman and defensive end Jeff Cross.

SPECIAL TEAMS: The Dolphins have no problems with the kicking game. Kicker Pete Stoyanovich has put together 121- and 124-point seasons and made 61 field goals during that span. He's won or tied nine games since 1989 with fourth-quarter kicks. Reggie Roby recovered from a torn Achilles tendon and knee problems to average 41.2 yards a punt. Coverage teams gave up too many yards (21.2 on kickoffs and 11.6 on punts) and Shula needs to pick a solid return specialist.

DOLPHINS VETERAN ROSTER

HEAD COACH—Don Shula. Assistant Coaches—Joe Greene, George Hill, Tony Nathan, Tom Olivadotti, Mel Phillips, John Sandusky, Larry Seiple, Gary Stevens, Junior Wade, Mike Westhoff.

No.	Name	Pos.	Ht.	Wt.	NFL Exp.	College
32	Alexander, Bruce	CB	5-8	178	5	Stephen F. Austin
—	Austin, Elijah	DT	6-2	290	1	North Carolina State
86	Banks, Fred	WR	5-10	185	8	Liberty
84	Baty, Greg	TE	6-6	240	7	Stanford
33	Bell, Kameno	FB	5-11	230	1	Illinois
96	Benson, Mitchell	NT	6-4	300	4	Texas Christian
66	Blake, Eddie	G	6-3	315	2	Auburn
53	Bolcar, Ned	LB	6-2	240	4	Notre Dame
36	Braggs, Stephen	CB	5-9	177	7	Texas
57	Brothen, Kevin	C	6-1	285	1	Vanderbilt
37	Brown, J.B.	CB	6-0	189	5	Maryland
2	Brown, Reggie	WR	5-11	174	1	Mesa
54	Bullough, Chuck	LB	6-1	226	1	Michigan State
43	Carswell, Chuck	CB	5-9	192	1	Georgia
90	Coleman, Marco	DE	6-3	259	2	Georgia Tech
52	Collins, Roosevelt	LB-DE	6-4	235	2	Texas Christian
51	Cox, Bryan	LB	6-3	235	3	Western Illinois
34	Craver, Aaron	RB	6-0	216	3	Fresno State
91	Cross, Jeff	DE	6-4	272	6	Missouri
65	Dellenbach, Jeff	T-C	6-5	296	9	Wisconsin
74	Dennis, Mark	T	6-6	292	7	Illinois
85	Duper, Mark	WR	5-9	192	12	NW Louisiana
8	Ford, Bernard	WR	5-9	183	4	Central Florida
80	Fryar, Irving	WR	6-0	200	10	Nebraska
35	Glenn, Kerry	CB	5-9	177	9	Minnesota
—	Golic, Mike	DT	6-5	275	8	Notre Dame
42	Green, Chris	CB-S	5-11	189	3	Illinois
92	Griggs, David	DE-LB	6-3	250	5	Virginia
59	Grimsley, John	LB	6-2	236	10	Kentucky
45	Harden, Bobby	S	6-0	202	4	Miami (Fla.)
7	Hatcher, Dale	P	6-2	237	8	Clemson
73	Heller, Ron	T	6-6	290	10	Penn State
20	Hickerson, Eric	S	6-2	215	1	Indiana
21	Higgs, Mark	RB	5-7	198	6	Kentucky
29	Hobley, Liffort	S	6-0	207	8	Louisiana State
76	Hochertz, Martin	DE	6-5	260	1	Southern Illinois
50	Hollier, Dwight	LB	6-2	245	2	North Carolina
70	Hope, Charles	G	6-3	310	1	Central State
44	Humphrey, Bobby	RB	6-1	201	5	Alabama
97	Hunter, Jeff	DE	6-4	291	4	Albany State (Ga.)
1	Ingram, Mark	WR	5-10	188	7	Michigan State
88	Jackson, Keith	TE	6-4	250	6	Oklahoma
24	Jackson, Vestee	CB	6-0	186	8	Washington
9	Johnson, Alex	WR	5-9	173	2	Miami (Fla.)
99	Klingbeil, Chuck	NT	6-1	288	3	Northern Michigan
47	Malone, Darrell	CB	5-10	182	2	Jacksonville State
13	Marino, Dan	QB	6-4	224	11	Pittsburgh
89	Martin, Tony	WR	6-0	177	4	Mesa
82	Miller, Scott	WR-KR	5-11	179	3	UCLA
19	Mitchell, Scott	QB	6-6	230	4	Utah
93	Odom, Cliff	LB	6-2	236	14	Texas Arlington
56	Offerdahl, John	LB	6-3	238	8	Western Michigan
25	Oliver, Louis	S	6-2	224	5	Florida
30	Parmalee, Bernie	RB	5-11	201	2	Ball State
14	Pederson, Doug	QB	6-3	209	1	NE Louisiana
27	Rasul, Amir	RB	5-11	198	1	Florida A&M
98	Richardson, Huey	DE	6-4	263	3	Florida

continued on page 479

TOP DRAFT CHOICES

Rd.	Name	Sel. No.	Pos.	Ht.	Wt.	College
1	McDuffie, O.J.	25	WR	5-10	186	Penn State
3	Kirby, Terry	78	RB	6-1	222	Virginia
4	Bradford, Ronnie	105	CB	5-10	188	Colorado
5	Gray, Chris	132	G	6-4	276	Auburn
6	O'Neal, Robert	164	DB	6-1	195	Clemson

THE ROOKIES: Shula wanted an explosive returner who could play a position, and he found one in McDuffie, whose elusive style makes him a strong candidate to beat out ineffective punt-returner Eddie Miller, known for his fair catch. Third-rounder Terry Kirby from Virginia could end up as a starting halfback if Higgs and Humphrey falter.

OUTLOOK: The Dolphins, 11-5 in 1992, couldn't be more ready to take the AFC. The defense is one of the best and Marino has never had as many weapons as he has now.

DOLPHIN PROFILES

DAN MARINO 31 6-4 224   Quarterback

His bio is spread over two dozen pages of Dolphin media guide . . . One of greatest quarterbacks in history . . . Completed 330 of 554 passes last season for 4,116 yards and 24 touchdowns . . . Despite history of knee problems, his durability is amazing . . . Has started 140 consecutive regular-season games, 60 more than Jim Everett, next closest active quarterback . . . Last season, he led Dolphins to six fourth-quarter comebacks, increasing career total to 24 . . . His quarterback rating in those games was 101.3 . . . Ranks fourth on NFL all-time passing list with 39,502 yards, trailing Fran Tarkenton (47,003), Dan Fouts (43,040) and Johnny Unitas (40,239) . . . Has quickest release in the NFL, but line breakdowns allowed him to be sacked 28 times last season . . . Has had five arthroscopic procedures on left knee . . . Was first-round choice in quarterback-rich 1983 draft after great career at Pitt, where he holds most of school's passing records . . . Born Sept. 15, 1961, in Pittsburgh . . . 1993 base salary: $4,300,000.

IRVING FRYAR 30 6-0 200   Wide Receiver

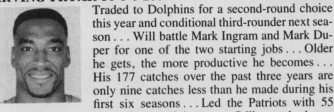

Traded to Dolphins for a second-round choice this year and conditional third-rounder next season . . . Will battle Mark Ingram and Mark Duper for one of the two starting jobs . . . Older he gets, the more productive he becomes . . . His 177 catches over the past three years are only nine catches less than he made during his first six seasons . . . Led the Patriots with 55 catches for 791 yards and four touchdowns . . . Still a tough, downfield blocker who loves to mix it up with defensive backs . . . Can be used in a pinch to return punts or kickoffs, a specialty of his during his first six seasons . . . Was first pick overall in 1984 draft by the Patriots and made instant impact on punt-return team with a 9.6-yard average, fourth-best in AFC . . . Became a full-time starter in 1985 and has had three 1,000-yard seasons . . . His 363 catches for 5,726 yards and 37 touchdowns are second-best on the Patriots' all-time list . . . Born Sept. 28, 1962, in Mount Holly, N.J. . . . 1993 base salary: $1,025,000.

MARK INGRAM 28 5-10 188   Wide Receiver

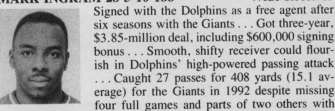

Signed with the Dolphins as a free agent after six seasons with the Giants . . . Got three-year, $3.85-million deal, including $600,000 signing bonus . . . Smooth, shifty receiver could flourish in Dolphins' high-powered passing attack . . . Caught 27 passes for 408 yards (15.1 average) for the Giants in 1992 despite missing four full games and parts of two others with injuries . . . Best season was 1991, with 51 receptions for 824 yards . . . Caught five TD passes in 1990 . . . Made big catch-and-run on a third down in the Giants' Super Bowl victory over Buffalo . . . Development slowed early in his career by injuries and inexperience . . . Caught only 32 passes in his first three seasons . . . Giants' top pick, out of Michigan State, in 1987 . . . Born Aug. 23, 1965, in Rockford, Ill. . . . 1993 base salary: $1.4 million.

TROY VINCENT 23 6-0 191   Cornerback

Enjoyed instant stardom as rookie left corner-back . . . Has the smooth coverage style of such greats as Albert Lewis and Mike Haynes . . . Didn't get to play a lot of man-to-man coverages until senior year at Wisconsin . . . Was known there as the "Stealth DB" for his quiet effectiveness . . . Started final 14 games at cornerback for the Dolphins . . . Reported to camp Aug. 8 after lengthy contract holdout . . . Was first of two first-round choices last season . . . Hamstring injury in final exhibition game forced him to miss first two games . . . Finished fifth on team with 77 tackles, but he led Dolphins with 13 passes defensed . . . Born June 8, 1970, in Yardley, Pa. . . . 1993 base salary: $600,000.

BRYAN COX 25 6-3 235   Linebacker

Feisty player has become the emotional leader of the defense . . . Tied for fifth in the AFC with 14 sacks, third-best in franchise history . . . Led Dolphins with 127 tackles . . . Signed contract extension through 1995 . . . Had sacks in nine of his 16 starts . . . Twice earned NFL Defensive Player of the Week honors and was Defensive Player of the Month in September . . . Grew up in violent East St. Louis neighborhood . . . Isn't afraid to intimidate opponents . . . Was fifth-round choice in 1991 draft and instantly established himself as a starter, earning All-Rookie honors . . . Was nickel back at Western Illinois . . . Had seven sacks during his first four games last season . . . Born Feb. 17, 1968, in East St. Louis, Ill. . . . 1993 base salary: $800,000.

MARK DUPER 34 5-9 192   Wide Receiver

Lone remaining member of the one of the greatest receiving tandems in NFL history . . . Plays his first season without Mark Clayton, his Marks Brothers teammate since 1983 . . . That duo combined for 17,512 yards on 1,061 catches and 50 100-yard games . . . Though he's lost some speed, he remains a dangerous deep threat . . . Caught 44 passes for 762 yards, a 17.3-yard average . . . Had seven touchdown catches . . . Has 511 career catches for 8,869 yards, a 17.4-yard average . . . Born Mark Dupas, he started calling himself Mark Duper as a youth because it sounded like Super Duper . . . Played two years at Northwestern (La.) State . . . Averaged 24.7 yards a catch in college . . . Ran anchor on 400-meter relay team . . . Ran 100 meters in 10.21 seconds . . . His high school didn't have a football team . . . Was a second-round choice in 1982 who spent most of season on bench . . . Born Jan. 25, 1959, in Pineville, La. . . . 1993 base salary: $1,250,000.

KEITH JACKSON 28 6-4 250   Tight End

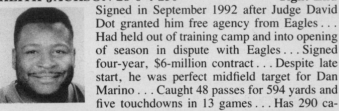

Signed in September 1992 after Judge David Dot granted him free agency from Eagles . . . Had held out of training camp and into opening of season in dispute with Eagles . . . Signed four-year, $6-million contract . . . Despite late start, he was perfect midfield target for Dan Marino . . . Caught 48 passes for 594 yards and five touchdowns in 13 games . . . Has 290 career catches for 3,507 yards and 25 touchdowns in five seasons . . . His 48 catches were second-most of any tight end in Dolphin history . . . Had seven-catch game against 49ers Dec. 6 . . . Has been to Pro Bowl four times in five years . . . Was Eagles' first-round choice in 1988 and had 81-catch season . . . Started four years at Oklahoma . . . Was *Parade* All-American in high school . . . Played cello in high school and college . . . Born April 19, 1965, in Little Rock, Ark. . . . 1993 base salary: $1,1250,000.

MARCO COLEMAN 23 6-3 259   Defensive End

Finished third on team with 84 tackles during brilliant rookie season . . . Tried at outside linebacker early in season, he made successful switch to defensive end for final 12 games . . . His quickness drives offensive tackles crazy . . . Recorded six sacks, the third-highest total of any rookie in club history . . . Held out until Aug. 1 and missed preseason opener . . . Sacked Bronco quarterback Tommy Maddox three times in Aug. 15 exhibition game in Berlin . . . Was a first-round choice after three years as Georgia Tech starter . . . Holds Georgia Tech's all-time sack lead with 28 . . . Averaged 70 tackles and nine sacks a season in college . . . Born Dec. 18, 1969, in Dayton, Ohio . . . 1993 base salary: $485,000.

LOUIS OLIVER 27 6-2 224   Safety

One of the most productive safeties in AFC . . . Has five interceptions in each of past five seasons . . . Had a three-interception game against Bills Oct. 4, returning one Jim Kelly pass 103 yards for a touchdown . . . Tends to infuriate opponents by taunting and talking to them on the field . . . Talks trash in print, too . . . Has 19 career interceptions . . . Finished second on team with 90 tackles . . . Averaged 78 tackles a season in first four years . . . Started three seasons at Florida after being walk-on . . . Was first-round pick in 1989 . . . Started 13 games as a rookie . . . Born March 9, 1966, in Belle Glade, Fla. . . . 1992 base salary: $350,000.

J.B. BROWN 26 6-0 189   Cornerback

An underrated cornerback who is one of the best in pro football covering wide receivers . . . Wasn't invited to NFL scouting combine and entered the league as a 12th-round choice in 1989 . . . Has started since his second season but played in the shadow of Tim McKyer . . . Had best season last year . . . Intercepted four passes . . . Played safety and cornerback at Maryland . . . Played backup cornerback as a rookie with Dolphins in 1990 . . . Helped to improve a secondary that ranked 18th in 1989 and fifth in 1990 . . . Held out entire 1991 training camp and began season on exempt list . . . Born Jan. 5, 1967, in Washington, D.C. . . . 1992 base salary: $450,000.

JEFF CROSS 27 6-4 272   Defensive End

Had to be moved to accommodate addition of rookie defensive end Marco Coleman . . . A fixture at right end for four seasons, he became left end . . . Played defensive tackle occasionally in 4-3 . . . Slowed slightly by various injuries . . . Has 33½ sacks in five seasons, five last year . . . Prior to last season, he led the Dolphins in sacks for three consecutive seasons . . .

Enters season with 64 consecutive starts. . . . Went to the Pro Bowl in 1990 after 11½-sack season . . . A surprising ninth-round choice in 1988 who began as backup defensive lineman . . . Played at Missouri after transferring from Riverside City College, where he was blocking tight end . . . Born March 25, 1966, in Riverside, Cal. . . . 1993 base salary: $1,000,000.

JOHN OFFERDAHL 29 6-3 232   Linebacker

Can't shake an injury bug that has forced him to miss 18 games over past two seasons . . . Abdominal strain sidelined him for eight games last year . . . Major knee problems wiped him out for 10 games in 1991 . . . Healthy, he's one of the dominating performers in the NFL . . . His ability to knock ball-carriers back with his powerful head-butts is legendary . . . Mobilized employees of his three Offerdahl's Bagel Gourmet Restaurants to distribute bagels to hurricane victims in Dade County last year . . . Was Pro Bowl selection for first five seasons before being hit with injuries . . . Was MVP for two of his four years as starting linebacker for Western Michigan . . . Dolphins made him second-round choice in 1986 . . . Born Aug. 17, 1964, in Wisconsin Rapids, Wis. . . . 1993 base salary: $1,250,000.

RICHMOND WEBB 26 6-6 298   Tackle

The best young pass-blocker in the game . . . Has been to the Pro Bowl in each of his first three seasons . . . No other Dolphin offensive lineman has been to as many Pro Bowls . . . Didn't miss any practice time as a rookie and was reasonably healthy through that season . . . Preseason knee-ligament problems in 1991 hampered him and forced him to miss the first two games . . . In 1990, the Dolphins allowed a league-low 16 sacks and Webb shut down Derrick Thomas once and Bruce Smith three times . . . Started three seasons at Texas A&M and was drafted in first round in 1990 . . . Born Jan. 11, 1967, in Dallas . . . 1993 base salary: $545,000.

MARK HIGGS 27 5-7 195   Halfback

Again led Dolphin rushers, with 915 yards, 10 more than in 1991 . . . Averaged 3.6 as the team's lead man on first and second downs . . . Had seven TDs . . . Will be coming back from offseason knee surgery . . . Was four-year starter at Kentucky, picked in eighth round (No. 205) by Cowboys in 1988 draft . . . Signed with Eagles in 1989 via Plan B, then went to Dolphins as free agent in 1990 . . . Had only 59 carries for 259 yards during first three NFL seasons . . . They've given him the ball since then . . . Born April 11, 1966, in Lexington, Ky. . . . 1992 base salary: $575,000

COACH DON SHULA: He's back at the top of his game, taking

Dolphins to AFC championship game . . . Fourteen of his 23 Dolphin teams have won or shared first place in AFC East . . . Over the past couple of years, he's developed a young defense that is the envy of the league . . . Starts 31st season in NFL . . . His regular-season record is 300-136-6; 318-151-6, including playoffs . . . Needs seven victories to pass George Halas on the NFL's all-time victory list . . . Since the 1970 merger, he is 60-17 against NFC teams . . . Has appeared in more Super Bowls (6) than any other coach . . . His teams are among fewest penalized and make fewest mental mistakes . . . Coached 1972 team to 17-0 record and Super Bowl VII crown . . . Had won Super Bowl V with Baltimore Colts in 1970 and then added third crown with Dolphins in 1973 . . . Played running back at John Carroll University . . . Intercepted 21 passes as cornerback with Browns, Baltimore Colts and Redskins . . . Assistant coach at Virginia in 1958 and Kentucky in 1959 before becoming offensive coordinator for Lions in 1960 . . . In 1963, he replaced Weeb Ewbank as coach of Colts . . . Compiled 71-23-4 record with the Colts . . . Took over as coach of Dolphins in 1970 . . . Born Jan. 4, 1930, in Grand River, Ohio.

GREATEST INTERCEPTOR

Jake Scott was smart. Defensive backs in the early 1970s had to have, in many cases, more brains and instincts than pure speed.

Rules allowed the defensive backs to be more physical. Corner-backs could chuck. Safeties could intimidate.

Scott and strong safety Dick Anderson were the safeties who won championships on the great Dolphin teams. Anderson was a heady strong safety. Scott was the interceptor who had 35 interceptions from 1970 through 1975.

"He was a tough, hard-nosed football player who was smart and could anticipate," said New York Giants' GM George Young. "He didn't have the great times in the 40; he made up for it by using his head."

INDIVIDUAL DOLPHIN RECORDS

Rushing

Most Yards Game:	197	Mercury Morris, vs New England, 1973
Season:	1,258	Delvin Williams, 1978
Career:	6,737	Larry Csonka, 1968-74, 1979

Passing

Most TD Passes Game:	6	2 times, most recently Dan Marino, vs N.Y. Jets, 1986
Season:	48	Dan Marino, 1984
Career:	290	Dan Marino, 1983-92

Receiving

Most TD Passes Game:	4	Paul Warfield, vs Detroit, 1973
Season:	18	Mark Clayton, 1984
Career:	81	Mark Clayton, 1983-92

Scoring

Most Points Game:	24	Paul Warfield, vs Detroit, 1973
Season:	124	Pete Stoyanovich, 1992
Career:	830	Garo Yepremian, 1970-78
Most TDs Game:	4	Paul Warfield, vs Detroit, 1973
Season:	18	Mark Clayton, 1984
Career:	82	Mark Clayton, 1983-92

NEW ENGLAND PATRIOTS

TEAM DIRECTORY: Chairman: James Orthwein; Vice Chairman: Mike O'Hallaron: Exec. VP-Business Oper.: Jim Hausmann; Exec. VP-Football Oper.: Patrick Forte; VP: Francis Kilroy; Dir. College Scouting: Charley Armey; Dir. Pro Scouting: Bobby Grier; Dir. Pub. Rel.: Mike Hanson; Head Coach: Bill Parcells. Home field: Foxboro Stadium (60,794). Colors: Red, white.

SCOUTING REPORT

OFFENSE: From Super Bowl to this? Former Giant coach Bill Parcells assumes the ultimate challenge in taking over the 2-14 Patriots in a setting that has a "For Sale" sign by owner James "I'd Rather Be In St. Louis" Orthwein hanging over the franchise.

Parcells must develop a rookie quarterback and some low-paid offensive players to resemble respectability, following the departure of the team's three highest-paid offensive players: quarterback Hugh Millen, wide receiver Irving Fryar and fullback John Stephens. If he can win six games with rookie Drew Bledsoe of Washington State or former Miami third-stringer Scott Secules as his starter, Parcells might be coach of the decade.

During camp, he had to determine whether Jon Vaughn (451 yards) or Leonard Russell (390) will be the featured back for his conservative offense. The Pats will need to run the ball because their only proven pass-catchers are Greg McMurtry and tight end Marv Cook.

Left tackle Bruce Armstrong may spend the season on the injured list because of knee problems, so Parcells will have to make do with two excellent, young tackles—Pat Harlow and Eugene Chung—and such interior lineman as Calvin Stephens, Gene Chilton and Steve Trapilo, who missed two seasons because of bad knees.

DEFENSE: Parcells' coaching should improve a defense that is rebuilding under the tightest budget in pro football. He acquired some defensive line depth: Former Steeler defensive end Aaron Jones adds speed to the pass-rush while former Bills' defensive end Leon Seals and ex-Falcon tackle John Washington should firm up the run defense along with Ray Agnew.

Little needs to be added to a respectable linebacking corps. Vincent Brown is about as good as there is and will continue to

Pats hope for fast progress by No. 1 draftee Drew Bledsoe.

emerge as a star at inside linebacker. Parcells is solid on the outside with Andre Tippett and Chris Singleton. Dwayne Sabb, a second-year player, could even challenge Singleton.

Problems still exist in the secondary. The Patriots lack coverage cornerbacks, surrendering 22 touchdown passes and letting quarterbacks complete 56 percent of their attempts for a relatively high seven-yard average. Maybe too much was asked of cornerbacks Jerome Henderson and the talented Maurice Hurst. After all, they don't get much help from the safeties. Starter Randy Robbins was released.

SPECIAL TEAMS: Punter Shawn McCarthy wishes he could shift some of the work over to kicker Charlie Baumann. McCarthy was the second-most active punter with 103 attempts and a respectable 35.4 net. Baumann attempted only 17 field goals, making 11, but made extra points an adventure by missing two of 24.

PATRIOTS VETERAN ROSTER

HEAD COACH—Bill Parcells. Assistant Coaches—David Atkins, Romeo Crennel, Al Groh, Fred Hoaglin, Chris Palmer, John Parker, Ray Perkins, Dante Scarnecchia, Mike Sweatman, Bob Trott, Charlie Weis.

No.	Name	Pos.	Ht.	Wt.	NFL Exp.	College
92	Agnew, Ray	DE	6-3	272	4	North Carolina State
78	Armstrong, Bruce	T	6-4	284	7	Louisville
4	Armstrong, Chris	WR	6-1	205	1	Fayetteville State (N.C.)
8	Baumann, Charlie	K	6-1	203	3	West Virginia
47	Brown, Roger	S	6-0	196	4	Virginia Tech
59	Brown, Vincent	LB	6-2	245	6	Miss. Valley State
64	Caliguire, Dean	OL	6-2	277	4	Pittsburgh
17	Carlson, Jeff	QB	6-3	215	4	Weber State
63	Chilton, Gene	C	6-3	286	7	Texas
69	Chung, Eugene	T	6-4	295	2	Virginia Tech
87	Coates, Ben	TE	6-4	245	3	Livingstone
54	Collins, Todd	LB	6-2	242	2	Carson-Newman
85	Cook, Marv	TE	6-4	234	5	Iowa
49	Dwight, Reggie	TE	6-3	285	1	Troy State
98	Edwards, Tim	DE	6-1	270	2	Delta State
81	Farr, Mike	WR	5-10	192	4	UCLA
91	Gannon, Chris	DE	6-6	260	5	SW Louisiana
33	Gash, Sam	RB	5-11	224	2	Penn State
61	Gibson, Don	DL	6-3	275	1	USC
67	Gisler, Mike	OL	6-4	300	1	Houston
72	Goad, Tim	NT	6-3	280	6	North Carolina
46	Golden, Al	TE	6-3	240	1	Penn State
41	Gordon, Tim	S	6-0	188	7	Tulsa
66	Gordon, Steve	C	6-3	279	1	California
25	Granby, John	S	6-1	200	1	Virginia Tech
77	Harlow, Pat	T	6-6	290	3	USC
19	Hawkins, Wayne	WR	5-10	182	1	SW Minnesota
36	Henderson, Jerome	CB	5-10	189	3	Clemson
60	Hobby, Marion	DE	6-4	277	4	Tennessee
13	Hodson, Tom	QB	6-3	195	4	Louisiana State
18	Hopkins, Wade	WR	6-2	195	1	SW Baptist
99	Howard, David	LB	6-4	230	9	Long Beach State
37	Hurst, Maurice	CB	5-10	185	5	Southern
93	Jones, Aaron	DL	6-5	267	6	Eastern Kentucky
28	Lambert, Dion	CB	6-0	185	2	UCLA
—	Lewis, Bill	C	6-6	290	8	Nebraska
51	Lockhart, Eugene	LB	6-2	233	10	Houston
40	Lockwood, Scott	RB	5-10	196	2	USC
5	McCarthy, Shawn	P	6-6	227	3	Purdue
58	McGovern, Rob	LB	6-2	234	4	Holy Cross
86	McMurtry, Greg	WR	6-2	207	4	Michigan
74	Olberding, Lance	OL	6-7	310	1	Iowa
62	Perez, Chris	OL	6-6	305	1	Kansas
27	Pool, David	CB	5-9	182	4	Carson-Newman
70	Redding, Reggie	G	6-4	305	4	Cal State-Fullerton
32	Russell, Leonard	RB	6-2	235	3	Arizona State
95	Sabb, Dwayne	LB	6-4	248	2	New Hampshire
97	Seals, Leon	DL	6-5	272	7	Jackson State
10	Secules, Scott	QB	6-3	223	6	Virginia
55	Singleton, Chris	LB	6-2	247	4	Arizona
22	Smith, Rod	CB	5-11	187	2	Notre Dame
68	Stephens, Calvin	G	6-2	285	3	South Carolina
50	Sutter, Eddie	LB	6-3	240	1	Northwestern
21	Thompson, Reyna	DB	6-0	193	8	Baylor
83	Timpson, Michael	WR	5-10	175	5	Penn State
56	Tippett, Andre	LB	6-3	241	12	Iowa
65	Trapilo, Steve	OL	6-5	289	7	Boston College
3	Tudors, Pumpy	P	5-7	203	1	Tenn.-Chattanooga
34	Turner, Kevin	RB	6-0	224	2	Alabama
94	Van Bellinger, Scott	LB	6-5	245	1	Tenn.-Chattanooga
24	Vaughn, Jon	RB	5-9	203	3	Michigan
76	Washington, John	DL	6-4	290	8	Oklahoma State
38	White, Adrian	DB	6-0	205	7	Florida
96	Williams, Brent	DE	6-4	275	8	Toledo
16	Zolak, Scott	QB	6-5	222	3	Maryland

TOP DRAFT CHOICES

Rd.	Name	Sel. No.	Pos.	Ht.	Wt.	College
1	Bledsoe, Drew	1	QB	6-5	223	Washington State
2	Slade, Chris	31	LB	6-4	234	Virginia
2	Rucci, Todd	51	T	6-5	296	Penn State
3	Brisby, Vincent	56	WR	6-1	185	NE Louisiana
4	Johnson, Kevin	86	DT	6-1	309	Texas Southern

THE ROOKIES: "Too many holes, not enough pegs," Parcells said after the draft. But he filled the quarterback spot for the rest of the decade by making the 6-5, 233-pound Bledsoe the first choice overall. Virginia linebacker Chris Slade could offer some pass-rush help, and Penn State tackle Todd Rucci, despite knee problems, is a solid young prospect.

OUTLOOK: Once Orthwein sells this club, Parcells might have a better chance. The owner is biding time until he's awarded the St. Louis expansion team this fall. Parcells is a good enough coach to steal a few victories and improve the record.

PATRIOT PROFILES

ANDRE TIPPETT 33 6-3 241　　　　　　　　Linebacker

He is the Lawrence Taylor of the Patriots, which makes him popular with new boss, Bill Parcells . . . Is all-time Patriots' sack leader with 91½ . . . Forced team-high three fumbles to increase his career total to 16 . . . Seems to have shaken stretch of bad luck with injuries . . . Led Patriots with seven sacks and finished with 40 tackles, including 33 solos . . . Teams still tend to run away from his side of the field . . . One of the nation's top martial-arts experts, with all sorts of black belts . . . Named to University of Iowa all-decade team for the 1980s . . . Played defensive end and outside linebacker after transferring from Ellsworth Junior College . . . Was Patriots' second-round draft choice in 1982 . . . Born Dec. 27, 1959, in Birmingham, Ala. . . . 1993 base salary: $750,000.

EUGENE CHUNG 24 6-4 295   Offensive Lineman

Started 14 of the 15 games in which he played . . . Worked at right guard before knee injury to left tackle Bruce Armstrong . . . The loss of his father during training camp had an effect . . . And then he couldn't practice for two weeks in camp because of poison ivy . . . Will stay at right tackle until Armstrong returns . . . Was first-round choice in 1992 because of athletic ability and pass-blocking techniques . . . Owns a brown belt in judo . . . Started three seasons at Virginia Tech and is one of best blockers to come out of the school . . . Bench-presses more than 400 pounds . . . Born June 14, 1969, in Prince George's County, Md. . . . 1993 base salary: $500,000.

BRUCE ARMSTRONG 27 6-4 284   Tackle

Blew out a knee Nov. 1 against Buffalo and missed final eight games . . . Went to Pro Bowl in 1990 and 1991, earning nod as one of best young left tackles in the NFL . . . His injury broke a string of 84 consecutive games in which he started . . . Was durable enough as a rookie to play the entire season wearing a shoulder harness . . . Came to Patriots as 23rd pick in 1987 and earned rookie honors . . . Is franchise's best blocker since John Hannah . . . Played tight end at Louisville until switched to tackle before junior year . . . Born Sept. 7, 1965, in Miami . . . 1993 base salary: $750,000.

VINCENT BROWN 28 6-2 245   Linebacker

A non-stop tackling machine . . . Led Patriots with 103 tackles, including 78 solos . . . Forced team-high two fumbles and had interception and fumble returns for touchdowns last season . . . Selected as transition player even though his contract doesn't run out until 1995 . . . Hates being called "The Undertaker," his college nickname . . . Has occasionally filled in when needed at outside linebacker, but remains one of the most active inside linebackers in NFL . . . Played four years at Mississippi Valley State, where he graduated with criminal justice degree . . . Plans to go to law school . . . Drafted in second round of 1988 draft and started 15 games as a rookie . . . Born Sept. 1, 1965, in Atlanta . . . 1993 base salary: $825,000.

MARV COOK 27 6-4 234   Tight End

Only the second Patriot to catch 50 passes in three consecutive seasons . . . Has averaged 62 catches during past three years . . . Is in 10th place on team's all-time list with 188 catches in four seasons . . . Earned second consecutive trip to the Pro Bowl . . . Ranked second on team with 52 catches last year and had 413 yards and two touchdowns . . . Set team record for tight-end receptions with 82 in 1991 . . . Is perfect target in middle of field against zone defenses . . . Starred at Iowa, where his 126 receptions is second to Ronnie Harmon in school history . . . After Patriots took him in third round in 1989, he was a backup but earned All-Rookie honors as a special-teamer . . . Born Feb. 24, 1966, in Iowa City, Iowa . . . 1993 base salary: $850,000.

SCOTT SECULES 28 6-3 223   Quarterback

An unknown from Dolphins who could end up as starting quarterback with Patriots . . . Signed two-year, $1.45-million contract . . . Has thrown only 69 passes during five-year pro career . . . Spent past four seasons on Miami bench behind Dan Marino and Scott Mitchell . . . Bill Parcells likes his leadership and his arm . . . Didn't throw a pass last year . . . Held on kick placements . . . Has 34 of 69 completions for 393 yards and two touchdowns during NFL career . . . Came to the Dolphins from Cowboys in 1989 in exchange for fifth-round choice . . . Played four seasons at Virginia behind Don Majkowski and started only one season . . . Completed 174 of 296 passes for 2,311 yards and 12 touchdowns as senior . . . Dallas took him in sixth round in 1988 and he was third quarterback most of season . . . Born Nov. 8, 1965, in Newport News, Va. . . . 1993 base salary: $600,000, plus $150,000 signing bonus.

PAT HARLOW 24 6-6 290   Tackle

One of the building blocks on Patriots' young offensive line . . . Started 16 games as rookie at right tackle in 1991 and replaced injured Pro Bowler Bruce Armstrong at left tackle during final eight games last season . . . A back operation forced him to play 25 pounds underweight last year because he couldn't lift weights . . . Battled all season and had an excellent year under the circumstances . . . The back is fine now . . . Has 32 career starts out of 32 possible games . . . If Armstrong recovers from knee injury, Harlow might be switched back to right tackle . . . Was 11th player selected in 1991 draft . . . Began Southern Cal career as defensive tackle but moved to offensive line as junior . . . Had an 88-percent grade for blocking consistency during senior year and didn't allow a sack . . . Born March 16, 1969, in Norco, Cal. . . . 1993 base salary: $330,000.

MAURICE HURST 25 5-10 185   Cornerback

Most active of Patriot cornerbacks, leading team with 18 passes defensed . . . Has averaged 15 starts a season since being drafted by Patriots in 1989 . . . Didn't have as good a season as he did in 1991, but the lack of a pass rush didn't help . . . Intercepted three passes to increase his career total to 12 and has averaged 54 tackles a season . . . His 63 tackles last season led all Patriots' defensive backs and ranked fifth on the team . . . Was a fourth-round pick who started 14 games as a rookie . . . Went to Southern University as a walk-on wide receiver, but switched to cornerback for his final two years . . . Born Sept. 17, 1967, in New Orleans . . . 1993 base salary: $500,000.

GREG McMURTRY 25 6-2 207   Wide Receiver

Begins third season as full-time starter . . . Caught 35 passes for 424 yards and one 65-yard touchdown . . . Is big receiver who breaks tackles after catching the ball . . . What he lacks in speed, he makes up with smarts . . . Considered more of a possession receiver, which should make him valuable in Bill Parcells' offense . . . Makes the tough downfield block . . .

Best season was in 1991, when he caught 41 passes for 614 yards . . . Took over for injured Hart Lee Dykes in October, 1990, with three-catch day . . . Came to the Patriots as a third-rounder in 1990 . . . Almost pursued a baseball career after Boston Red Sox made him a first-round choice in 1986, but opted for football . . . Was a *Parade* All-American in Brockton, Mass. . . . Started four seasons at Michigan . . . Born Oct. 15, 1967, in Jackson, Miss. . . . 1993 base salary: $450,000.

LEONARD RUSSELL 23 6-2 235   Halfback

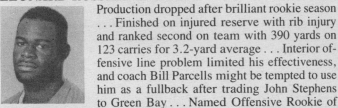

Production dropped after brilliant rookie season . . . Finished on injured reserve with rib injury and ranked second on team with 390 yards on 123 carries for 3.2-yard average . . . Interior offensive line problem limited his effectiveness, and coach Bill Parcells might be tempted to use him as a fullback after trading John Stephens to Green Bay . . . Named Offensive Rookie of the Year by Associated Press in 1991 . . . Started 15 games and rushed for 959 yards on 266 carries, with four touchdowns . . . An underclassman who was among the last to register for 1991 draft, Russell became a first-round choice, out of Arizona State . . . He previously starred at San Antonio JC in Walnut Creek, Cal. . . . Rushed for 810 yards in one season at Arizona State . . . Born Nov. 17, 1969, in Long Beach, Cal. . . . 1993 base salary: $450,000.

CHRIS SINGLETON 26 6-2 247   Linebacker

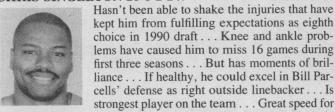

Hasn't been able to shake the injuries that have kept him from fulfilling expectations as eighth choice in 1990 draft . . . Knee and ankle problems have caused him to miss 16 games during first three seasons . . . But has moments of brilliance . . . If healthy, he could excel in Bill Parcells' defense as right outside linebacker . . . Is strongest player on the team . . . Great speed for a 247-pounder . . . A courageous individual who gave his twin brother, Kevin, a bone marrow transplant to help in battle against leukemia in 1989 . . . Started three seasons at Arizona and finished with 287 tackles . . . Holdout hampered rookie season and limited him to four starts . . . Born Feb. 20, 1967, in Omaha, Neb. . . . 1993 base salary: $580,000.

RAY AGNEW 25 6-3 272   Defensive End

Started 14 games and finished with 61 tackles, a career high . . . A solid-run stopper who is known for his consistency . . . Beginning to live up to the reputation that made him 10th choice in 1990 draft . . . Has had bad luck with minor injuries—broken hand, knee and shoulder . . . But plays hurt . . . Scouts say he should have solid 10-to-15 year NFL career, gaining Pro Bowl honors as he gains experience . . . Played at North Carolina State, where he was ACC Rookie of the Year in 1986 and proved a solid lineman for three more seasons . . . Was sports editor of high-school newspaper . . . Born Dec. 9, 1967, in Winston-Salem, N.C. . . . 1993 base salary: $510,000, plus $40,000 bonus.

COACH BILL PARCELLS:

Hired away from the world of TV at NBC, his job is to rebuild Patriots as he did Giants . . . Comes in wearing two Super Bowl rings . . . Professional coaching career as assistant began with Patriots in 1980 . . . Compiled 85-52-1 record with the Giants before resigning prior to the 1991 season . . . Overcame heart condition to return to the sidelines . . . Was courted by at least three franchises before last season but decided to stay at NBC . . . Has 8-3 record in the playoffs . . . Played linebacker at Wichita State and was seventh-round choice of the Lions, but opted not to play pro football, taking a coaching position at Hastings College . . . Coached at West Point, Wichita State, Florida State, Vanderbilt and Texas Tech before getting first head-coaching job at Air Force Academy . . . After year as linebackers' coach with Pats, he joined Giants in 1981 as defensive coordinator . . . Appointed head coach after Ray Perkins left in 1983 . . . Super Bowl triumphs came in 1986 and 1990 . . . Born Aug. 22, 1941, in Englewood, N.J.

GREATEST INTERCEPTOR

Raymond Clayborn was all athlete—a football and track star at Texas and the 16th player overall in the 1977 draft. He was an All-Pro kickoff-returner as a rookie and he fast became a superior cornerback, overpowering the smaller receivers and fighting for interceptions with the bigger ones.

He intercepted 36 passes from 1977 through 1989 and made the Pro Bowl in 1983, '85 and '86.

He had the good fortune to play with Mike Haynes, one of the smoothest cornerbacks of the past two decades. Haynes, a coverage specialist, rarely let any receiver he covered get open. That created opportunities for Clayborn.

"Some cornerbacks can run with the receivers, but they can't turn and find the ball," said former Patriots' GM Dick Steinberg, now with the Jets. "Ray always found it and was in front of the receiver to make the play."

INDIVIDUAL PATRIOT RECORDS

Rushing

Most Yards Game:	212	Tony Collins, vs N.Y. Jets, 1983
Season:	1,458	Jim Nance, 1966
Career:	5,453	Sam Cunningham, 1973-79, 1981-82

Passing

Most TD Passes Game:	5	3 times, most recently Steve Grogan, vs N.Y. Jets, 1979
Season:	31	Babe Parilli, 1964
Career:	182	Steve Grogan, 1975-90

Receiving

Most TD Passes Game:	3	6 times, most recently Stanley Morgan, vs Seattle, 1986
Season:	12	Stanley Morgan, 1979
Career:	67	Stanley Morgan, 1977-89

Scoring

Most Points Game:	28	Gino Cappelletti, vs Houston, 1965
Season:	155	Gino Cappelletti, 1964
Career:	1,130	Gino Cappelletti, 1960-70
Most TDs Game:	3	14 times, most recently Stanley Morgan, vs Seattle, 1986
Season:	13	2 times, most recently Stanley Morgan, 1979
Career:	67	Stanley Morgan, 1977-89

NEW YORK JETS

TEAM DIRECTORY: Chairman: Leon Hess; Pres.: Steve Gutman; VP/GM: Dick Steinberg; Dir. Player Personnel: Dick Haley; Asst. GM: James Harris; Dir. Pro Personnel: Jim Royer; Dir. Pub. Rel.: Frank Ramos; Head Coach: Bruce Coslet. Home field: Giants Stadium (77,311). Colors: Kelly green and white.

SCOUTING REPORT

OFFENSE: Bruce Coslet learned a valuable lesson: Don't rush youth. Quarterback Browning Nagle wasn't ready for the starting job, and Coslet's young pups paid a price for thinking they were better than they really were. They fell from 8-8 to 4-12, forcing owner Leon Hess to pay a bigger price in the offseason.

Hess opened his checkbook to give Coslet experienced leadership. Quarterback Boomer Esiason, a $3-million sure thing when Coslet coordinated the Bengal offense, returns to his native Long Island to re-direct the Jets. Fearing second-year tight end Johnny Mitchell might not be ready for full-time service, Hess spent $1 million a year for tight end James Thornton, a solid run-blocker from the Bears.

Esiason's job could be made easier if halfback Blair Thomas shakes three disappointing seasons and comes up with the 1,000 rushing yards GM Dick Steinberg expected when he selected him No. 2 in 1990. And former Pro Bowl back Johnny Johnson is a welcome addition from Phoenix. Mitchell should be more of a factor in view of the retirement of wide receiver Al Toon. Wide receivers Chris Burkett (57 catches) and Rob Moore (50) are dependable targets for Esiason, whose specialty is passing underneath zones.

The line is a question mark. Center Jim Sweeney might be the best returning starter but he has a bad neck. Dwayne White, a guard, wasn't as effective as in 1991.

DEFENSE: Defensive end Marvin Washington summed up the Jets' season: "horrible." Defensive end Dennis Byrd suffered a career-ending, temporarily paralyzing neck injury. Free safety Lonnie Young suffered a likely career-ending knee injury. Defensive end Jeff Lageman blew out his knee.

A great offseason followed the disaster. Byrd started walking. Lageman's knee healed ahead of schedule. Hess and Steinberg

Jets are counting on ex-Bengal Boomer Esiason.

bought a few hired guns—free safety Ronnie Lott ($1.8 million a year), defensive tackle Leonard Marshall ($1.58 million a year) and cornerback Eric Thomas ($1.158 million). And in the draft they added Florida State's Marvin Jones, a big-play linebacker.

Lott's leadership and crunching hits will inspire a talented secondary three-deep in cornerbacks (Thomas, James Hasty and Michael Brim) and underrated strong safety Brian Washington. Marshall's signing solidifies the weakside tackle of the defensive line and should trim from the 119.9 rushing yards allowed. With Lageman back and Washington developing, the pass rush will also be feared.

SPECIAL TEAMS: Kicker Cary Blanchard, acquired off waivers from New Orleans, replaced retired Pat Leahy and Jason Staurovsky and made 16 of 22 field goals, showing decent range of 47 yards. The rest of the units were average. Punter Louis Aguiar lacks powerful range. The Jets operated without a punt- or kick-return threat.

JETS VETERAN ROSTER

HEAD COACH—Bruce Coslet. Assistant Coaches—Paul Alexander, Larry Beightol, Pete Carroll, Ed Donatell, Foge Fazio, Walt Harris, Greg Mackrides, Chip Myers, Al Roberts, Greg Robinson, Johnny Roland.

No.	Name	Pos.	Ht.	Wt.	NFL Exp.	College
4	Aguiar, Louie	P	6-2	215	3	Utah State
16	Bailey, Mario	WR	5-9	168	1	Washington
98	Barber, Kurt	LB	6-4	241	2	USC
30	Baxter, Brad	RB	6-1	235	4	Alabama State
9	Blake, Jeff	QB	6-0	202	2	East Carolina
10	Blanchard, Cary	K	6-1	225	2	Oklahoma State
18	Boles, Eric	WR	6-3	211	2	Central Washington
76	Brown, James	T	6-6	321	1	Virginia State
87	Burkett, Chris	WR	6-4	200	9	Jackson State
66	Cadigan, Dave	G	6-4	285	6	USC
50	Cadrez, Glenn	LB	6-3	240	2	Houston
82	Carpenter, Rob	WR	6-2	190	3	Syracuse
28	Chaffey, Pat	RB	6-1	220	3	Oregon State
59	Clifton, Kyle	LB	6-4	236	10	Texas Christian
99	Coleman, Keo	LB	6-1	247	2	Mississippi State
69	Criswell, Jeff	T	6-7	291	6	Graceland
89	Dawkins, Dale	WR	6-1	190	4	Miami (Fla.)
52	Dixon, Cal	C	6-4	284	2	Florida
62	Duffy, Roger	C-G	6-3	285	4	Penn State
7	Esiason, Boomer	QB	6-5	220	10	Maryland
91	Frase, Paul	DT-DE	6-5	270	5	Syracuse
35	Graham, Scottie	RB	5-9	215	1	Ohio State
96	Gunn, Mark	DT-DE	6-5	279	3	Pittsburgh
40	Hasty, James	CB	6-0	201	6	Washington State
25	Hicks, Clifford	CB-KR	5-10	195	7	Oregon
55	Houston, Bobby	LB	6-2	239	3	North Carolina State
39	Johnson, Johnny	RB	6-2	216	4	San Jose State
78	Johnson, Mario	DT	6-3	288	2	Missouri
51	Jones, Don	LB	6-0	231	1	Washington
56	Lageman, Jeff	DE	6-5	266	5	Virginia
57	Lewis, Mo	LB	6-3	250	3	Georgia
42	Lott, Ronnie	FS	6-0	200	13	USC
75	Malamala, Siupeli	T	6-5	308	2	Washington
70	Marshall, Leonard	DE	6-3	285	11	Louisiana State
81	Mathis, Terance	WR-KR	5-10	177	4	New Mexico
74	McCullough, Russ	T	6-10	315	1	Missouri
94	Mersereau, Scott	DT	6-3	275	7	Southern Connecticut
83	Mitchell, Johnny	TE	6-3	237	2	Nebraska
85	Moore, Rob	WR	6-3	205	4	Syracuse
8	Nagle, Browning	QB	6-3	225	3	Louisville
3	Peters, Paul	WR	6-1	206	2	Cal State-Northridge
71	Pickel, Bill	DT	6-5	265	11	Rutgers
27	Porter, Kevin	S	5-10	214	6	Auburn
20	Price, Dennis	CB	6-1	182	6	UCLA
37	Prior, Anthony	CB-S	5-11	185	1	Washington State
19	Richardson, Paul	WR	6-3	204	1	UCLA
84	Sadowski, Troy	TE	6-5	250	4	Georgia
53	Sweeney, Jim	C-G	6-4	286	10	Pittsburgh
49	Tate, David	S-CB	6-1	200	6	Colorado
32	Thomas, Blair	RB	5-10	202	4	Penn State
22	Thomas, Eric	CB	5-11	181	7	Tulane
80	Thornton, James	TE	6-2	242	6	Cal State-Fullerton
23	Turner, Marcus	CB-S	6-0	190	5	UCLA
48	Washington, Brian	SS	6-1	218	5	Nebraska
97	Washington, Marvin	DE	6-6	272	5	Idaho
56	Whisenhunt, Ken	TE	6-3	235	8	Georgia Tech
67	White, Dwayne	G	6-2	315	4	Alcorn State
77	Willig, Matt	T	6-8	305	1	USC
72	Wilson, Karl	DT-DE	6-5	277	6	Louisiana State
38	Yancy, Kelly	RB	5-11	211	R	Morningside
31	Young, Lonnie	S-CB	6-1	196	9	Michigan State

TOP DRAFT CHOICES

Rd.	Name	Sel. No.	Pos.	Ht.	Wt.	College
1	Jones, Marvin	4	LB	6-1	237	Florida State
2	Rudolph, Coleman	36	DE	6-4	265	Georgia Tech
4	Ware, David	88	T	6-6	269	Virginia
5	Baxter, Fred	115	TE	6-4	245	Auburn
5	Murrell, Adrian	120	RB	5-10	202	West Virginia

THE ROOKIES: The Jets grabbed the best defensive player (Jones) in the draft. The fourth pick overall, he is a nasty, mean hitter who flies to the ball. Defensive end Coleman Rudolph, a second-round choice, has pass-rush skills.

OUTLOOK: If rumors that Boomer's left arm is dead are untrue, he could refuel the Jets and pilot them as a wild-card playoff contender. "I thought we were a middle-of-the-pack team that had a chance to crawl up a little bit if some of our young players developed," Coslet said of last season. This season, the inexperience excuse is gone.

JET PROFILES

BOOMER ESIASON 32 6-5 220   **Quarterback**

Reunited with former Bengal offensive coordinator Bruce Coslet, with whom he had some of his best seasons . . . Acquired for third-round choice this year and possibly a second-rounder next year, depending upon his playing time . . . Brought in because of experience and the hope he might lead Jets to Super Bowl . . . Bengals will get the second-round choice if he starts at least eight games and has a quarterback rating of 89, something he's done twice during his career . . . Bengal officials thought elbow problems and age might have taken away his ability to throw deep, but Esiason doesn't agree . . . He is a master of throwing under zone coverages . . . Completed 144 of 287 passes for 1,407 yards and 11 touchdowns, but had 15 interceptions . . . Replaced an aging Ken Anderson as Bengals' starting quarterback during rookie season in 1984 . . . Though he was born with the surname,

Norman, he became known as Boomer because he kicked as a baby all the time . . . Completed 56 percent of his passes and threw 174 touchdown passes as a Bengal . . . One of the best play-fakers in the game . . . Born April 17, 1961, in East Islip, N.Y. . . . 1993 base salary: $3,000,000.

RONNIE LOTT 34 6-0 200   Safety

Wants to cash his winning attitude in for a Super Bowl ring with the Jets, with whom he signed two-year, $3.6-million contract . . . Destined to be a Hall-of-Famer . . . Once had a portion of a finger surgically removed so he couldn't miss playing time during a season . . . Has survived 151 painful games but remains one of the most feared hitters . . . Led Raiders last year with 103 tackles . . . Leads active players with 60 interceptions . . . Played two seasons with Raiders after winning four Super Bowl rings with 49ers . . . Went to the Pro Bowl after 1991 season after intercepting eight passes . . . Has been to Pro Bowl 10 times in 12 years . . . Was first-round choice of 49ers in 1981 and finished runner-up to Lawrence Taylor for Rookie of the Year . . . Played cornerback during his first four seasons before moving to free safety . . . All-American at Southern Cal. . . . Born May 8, 1959, in Albuquerque, N.M. . . . 1993 base salary: $1,400,000, plus $500,000 signing bonus.

BRAD BAXTER 26 6-1 235   Fullback

Maybe the most underrated fullback in the NFL . . . Led Jets in rushing for first time in three-year career with 698 yards and 4.6-yard average . . . Has rushed for 23 touchdowns . . . His powerful blocks enabled Jets to finish sixth in the AFC with 109.5 rushing yards per game . . . Earned game balls from coach Bruce Coslet for 98-yard game against Buffalo and 103 yards against Miami . . . Originally selected in 11th round by Vikings, Baxter was cut and then signed with Jets' developmental squad in 1989 . . . Started 10 games at fullback in 1990 and finished second on team with 539 yards rushing . . . His 11 touchdowns in 1991 led the AFC . . . Started three seasons for Division I-AA Alabama State and had 19 career 100-yard games . . . Teammate Jim Sweeney compares his running style to that of Earl Campbell, the former Houston Oiler... Born May 5, 1967, in Dothan, Ala. ... 1992 base salary: $275,000.

BRIAN WASHINGTON 27 6-1 218   Safety

Voted the Jets' MVP... Close to being considered a Pro Bowler... Tied for fifth place in the AFC with six interceptions... Personally responsible for 10 of the Jets' 38 turnovers... Averaged 100 tackles a season for the past three years... Entered league as 10th-round pick of the Browns in 1988... Started 14 games at strong safety for the Browns, but was cut one week into the 1989 season... Signed with the Jets and quit after one practice to run his father-in-law's restaurant... Returned to the Jets in 1990 and started 13 games at strong safety... Was an All-Big Eight safety at Nebraska... Born Sept. 10, 1965, in Richmond, Va.... 1992 base salary: $290,000.

KYLE CLIFTON 31 6-4 236   Linebacker

Captain of the defense for the past three seasons ... In nine years, he's never finished lower than second on team in tackles... Had 138 tackles, including 88 solos, to rank second last year... Forte is the ability to drop into pass coverages ... Best effort last season was a 15-tackle game against Indianapolis... Has started 67 consecutive games... Increased career tackle total to 1,305... Not a flashy player, but he always finds ways to be in on the tackle... Played junior varsity quarterback for Texas Christian before switching to linebacker as sophomore... Set school record with 189 tackles as senior... Drafted by Jets in third round of 1984 draft... Born Aug. 23, 1962, in Onley, Tex.... 1993 base salary: $730,000.

JAMES HASTY 28 6-0 201   Cornerback

Best cornerback who hasn't been selected to Pro Bowl... To protect him from free agency, Jets named him their transition player... One of the bigger and more physical cornerbacks in NFL... His long arms and desire to hit enable him to jam receivers at line of scrimmage... Ranked fifth on the team with 65 tackles and led the squad with 17 passes defensed... In 79 career games, he has 31 takeaways (17 interceptions and 14 fumble recoveries) . . . Took over at right cornerback during his rookie season in 1988 . . . Earned All-Rookie honors and never seemed to be intimidated . . . Started at defensive back for two seasons at Washington State after transferring from Central Washington . . . Named to Pac-10 All-Academic team as senior . . . Drafted in third round in 1988 . . . Born May 23, 1965, in Seattle . . . Jets matched Bengals' offer last spring and he winds up with 1993 base salary of $1,500,000.

JOHNNY JOHNSON 25 6-2 216   Running Back

Traded to Jets on draft day after three seasons with Cardinals . . . Expected to emerge as feature back in Jets' offensive system . . . Smooth runner with deceptive quickness and change of direction . . . Came on strong late last season after contract holdout and injuries produced slow start . . . Gained 712 of his team-high 734 rushing yards in eight of final nine games . . . Put together three 100-yard games in second half of season . . . Ran for career-high 156 yards against Giants and 146 yards against Colts . . . Led Cardinals to upset of 49ers with 102 rushing yards . . . Burst into prominence as unheralded rookie in 1990 . . . Made Pro Bowl after leading all NFL rookies in yards from scrimmage with 1,167 . . . Cardinals' seventh-round pick in 1990 out of San Jose State . . . Left school after five games in senior season because of dispute with coach . . . As a junior, he became the first player in NCAA history to rush for more than 1,200 yards and catch 60 passes . . . Born June 11, 1968, in Santa Clara, Cal. . . . 1993 base salary: $850,000.

LEONARD MARSHALL 31 6-3 285   Defensive End

Comes to Jets as a free agent after 10 seasons with the Giants . . . Signed two-year, $3-million deal . . . Projected as the Jets' starting right defensive end . . . Played in 14 games, starting 13, in 1992 . . . Had 41 tackles and four quarterback sacks . . . Returned to prominence in 1991 when he put together big season with 58 tackles and team-high 11 sacks . . . Contract squabble slowed him down in 1990 . . . Active pass-rusher with decent upfield burst . . . Best season was 1985, with 15½ sacks . . . Named NFC's Defensive Lineman of the Year by the NFLPA after that season . . . Two-time Pro Bowl selection . . . Giants' second-round pick out of LSU in 1983 . . . Born Oct. 22, 1961, in Franklin, La. . . . 1993 base salary: $1.4 million.

JEFF LAGEMAN 26 6-5 266   Defensive End

Blew out his right knee during second week of season but is on schedule to resume role as one of defensive leaders . . . Signed two-year, $2.4-million contract after the season at a time when Jets officials were certain he could play this season . . . A streak of 49 consecutive starts ended because of the injury . . . Has grown from linebacker to defensive end in the pros and is a pass-rushing threat . . . Solid leverage and quickness off the ball make him a factor every play . . . Selected as a linebacker in first round of the 1989 draft and started 15 games as a rookie . . . Moved to defensive end the next season even though he weighed only 254 pounds . . . Increased weight in 1990 to 266 pounds, decreased his body fat 25 percent and increased leg strength from 575 to 675 pounds . . . Drives a Harley Davidson to practice . . . Had 10 sacks in 1991, a career high . . . Started at inside linebacker for three years at Virginia . . . Born July 18, 1967, in Great Falls, Va. . . . 1993 base salary: $925,000.

ERIC THOMAS 28 5-11 181   Cornerback

Expected to be the starting cornerback opposite James Hasty . . . Jets signed him to a three-year, $3.5-million contract . . . Might have lost a step but he is considered a top coverage cornerback . . . Six teams recruited him during free-agency period . . . Tore the anterior cruciate ligament in his right knee in 1990 in an offseason basketball game . . . Started 16 games last season for Bengals and had 40 tackles . . . Struggled early in the season adjusting to the Bengals' new defensive scheme, but played well toward the end of the season . . . One of the best punt-and kick-blockers in NFL . . . Didn't intercept a pass, but he had 15 during first five seasons with the Bengals . . . Was second-round draft choice out of Tulane in 1987 . . . Was also track star once clocked in 10.3 seconds at 100 meters . . . Wants to coach track after he retires from football . . . Born Sept. 11, 1964, in Sacramento, Cal. . . . 1993 base salary: $1,200,000, with $575,000 in bonuses.

MO LEWIS 23 6-3 250   Linebacker

Moved from left to right outside linebacker to take advantage of his pass-rushing skills . . . The switch became more important after the Jets lost pass-rushing defensive end Jeff Lageman because of a knee injury . . . Defensive coaches didn't turn him completely loose on the quarterback, so he had only two sacks . . . Forced three fumbles and recovered four . . . Led squad with 145 tackles . . . His 4.7 speed in 40 is exceptional for a 250-pound linebacker . . . Was third-round choice in 1991 . . . Started 16 games as a rookie and was named to every All-Rookie team . . . Started two seasons at Georgia . . . Is a distant cousin of former Pittsburgh Steeler Joe Greene . . . Has a first-degree black belt in karate . . . Born Oct. 21, 1969, in Atlanta . . . 1993 base salary: $285,000, plus $40,000 in bonuses.

ROB MOORE 24 6-3 205   Wide Receiver

Nagging injuries throughout the season didn't prevent him from starting 16 games and catching 50 passes . . . Led Jets with 726 receiving yards . . . Had a string of 35 games in which he caught passes broken against Indianapolis six weeks into the season . . . Runs a 4.4 40 and has an amazing 45-inch vertical jump . . . Is a long-striding receiver whose speed is deceiving for cornerbacks . . . Caught 22 touchdown passes, averaged 20 yards a catch and had 2,122 career yards during three-year career at Syracuse . . . Skipped senior year and became a first-round supplemental pick in 1990 . . . Caught 44 passes for 692 yards as rookie . . . Followed with spectacular 70-catch season that helped the Jets make playoffs . . . Born Sept. 27, 1968, in East Meadow, N.Y. . . . 1993 base salary: $700,000.

CHRIS BURKETT 31 6-4 200   Wide Receiver

Re-established career in New York after being released by Bills in 1989... Replaced retired wide receiver Al Toon 11 weeks into the season and led Jets with 57 catches for 724 yards... Rewarded after the season with two-year, $2-million contract... Is Jets' special-teams captain and one of best special-teamers in conference... Turns upfield quickly after a catch and specializes in snatching passes with his big hands... Averaged 34 catches a season during first four seasons with the Bills, who made him a second-round choice in 1985... Started six games for Jets in 1989 and caught 21 passes... Caught 94 passes to lead Jackson State during his junior and senior years... Born Aug. 21, 1962, in Laurel, Miss.... 1993 base salary: $775,000, plus $150,000 bonus.

MARVIN WASHINGTON 27 6-6 272   Defensive End

Almost stolen away by Seattle during free agency... After six days, the Jets matched three-year, $3-million offer sheet... Constant improvement led to best season... Topped Jets with 8½ sacks... Started final 14 games at right defensive end... Long arms enabled him to knock down eight passes... Had five quarterback pressures and eight tackles in late-season game against Bills... Finished sixth on Jets with 62 tackles... Played right defensive end and basketball at the University of Idaho... Set school record with 14½ sacks... Was key reserve on Texas-El Paso and Idaho basketball teams... Transferred from UTEP... Didn't play football in high school... Drafted in sixth round in 1989... Born Oct. 22, 1965, in Denver... 1993 base salary: $600,000, plus $400,000 signing bonus.

BLAIR THOMAS 25 5-10 202   Halfback

Knee, groin and hip injuries limited him to nine games... His 440 rushing yards were lowest in three-year career, but his 4.5-yard average was his second best... New running back coach Johnny Roland is expected to help him in what might be his most pivotal year... Might be asked to play at 195 pounds to accentuate his quickness... Was second choice overall in 1990 but is still looking to live up to his Penn State reputation . . . Worked on flexibility before last season to help hamstring and back problems . . . Penn State's Joe Paterno called him "the best all-around back I've ever coached." . . . Finished his college career 97 yards shy of Curt Warner's rushing record (3,398) . . . Came back from major knee surgery to rush for 1,341 yards as a senior . . . Compared to a Thurman Thomas-type of back who can beat you catching the ball or running it . . . Born Oct. 7, 1967, in Philadelphia . . . 1993 base salary: $700,000, plus $400,000 bonus.

JIM SWEENEY 31 6-4 286   Center

Has played every position on offensive line during eight-year Jets' career . . . Leads all active Jets with 126 consecutive starts since 1984 . . . Injuries, particularly some neck problems, might be catching up to him but he refuses to give up . . . His line calls were instrumental in enabling to Jets to rank sixth in AFC rushing . . . Drafted in second round in 1984 and was given the left guard job with two weeks left in the season . . . Switched to left tackle in 1986 and started for two seasons . . . Used at center from 1989 to the present . . . Idolized former Pittsburgh Steeler center Mike Webster while growing up in Pittsburgh . . . Played guard and center at the University of Pittsburgh for two seasons . . . Born Aug. 8, 1962, in Pittsburgh . . . 1993 base salary: $860,000.

BROWNING NAGLE 25 6-3 225   Quarterback

Needs more seasoning to be a solid NFL starter, so Jets got Boomer Esiason . . . Rushed into the starting lineup during his second pro season and struggled with a 55.7 quarterback rating . . . Earned starting job during 5-0 preseason in which he completed 34 of 64 passes for 544 yards . . . Completed 192 of 387 passes for 2,280 yards and only seven touchdowns . . . Was intercepted 17 times and sacked 27 times . . . Started 13 games . . . Benched for 12th game but was called into service in first quarter when Ken O'Brien injured thumb . . . His best game was a 366-yard effort against Falcons in the regular-season opener . . . Has the strong arm, toughness and running ability to be a big-time quarterback . . . Drafted in second round in 1991 and threw only two passes as a rookie . . . Coach Bruce Coslet worked feverishly with Nagle during the 1991 offseason to prepare him for the starting job . . . Played two seasons in Howard Schnellenberger's pro-style offense at Louisville . . . Threw for 5,104 yards in two seasons in college . . . Born April 29, 1968, in Largo, Fla. . . . 1992 base salary: $300,000.

COACH BRUCE COSLET: Owner Leon Hess gave him a partial vote of confidence with one-year extension through 1994 . . . Kept optimistic after a dropoff from 8-8 playoff season to 4-12 disappointment . . . Will team up with former pupil, quarterback Boomer Esiason, to rejuvenate an offense that produced only 20 touchdowns last season . . . Esiason credits Coslet for helping him with some of his best years with Bengals . . . As offensive coordinator, Coslet called plays for 1988 Bengal offense that led the NFL with 378.6 yards per game . . . "He knows more about how to dissect a defense than anyone I've ever seen," Esiason said. "He wasn't only my teacher, but my eyes." . . . Took over Jets in 1990 and struggled through 4-12 season . . . Jets earned a wild-card spot in the playoffs the following year . . . His three-year coaching record is 16-32 . . . An undrafted tight end, he played from 1969 through 1976 with Bengals and caught 64 passes for 877 yards . . . Had played in 1968 with Edmonton of the CFL . . . Operated a successful construction business in Stockton, Cal., for three years after retiring from football . . . Was an assistant coach for the San Francisco 49ers in 1980 and moved to Bengals, where he spent nine years as an assistant, final four as offensive coordinator . . . Born Aug. 5, 1946, in Oakdale, Cal. . . . Played tight end at College of the Pacific.

GREATEST INTERCEPTOR

Because the American Football League featured passers, defensive coordinators needed reactors. They needed free safeties who could roam the field and prevent quarterbacks from hitting the big plays.

Dainard Paulson was such a free safety. He roamed the field, preventing deep touchdowns, and he intercepted 29 attempts from 1961 through 1965.

"Back in those days, you weren't getting the nickel formations and things like that," said former Jets' assistant coach Chuck Knox. "Free safeties protected center field. They protected the deep hole and the post and they had to be able to read the quarterback."

Paulson did all of that. He studied film and watched receivers' moves. Back then, most teams played zone defenses. Paulson's job was to prevent the receivers from finding the seams.

"That's where he did the great job," Knox said. "He would get a jump on the ball and he'd fill the holes between the cornerbacks and the safeties."

INDIVIDUAL JET RECORDS

Rushing

Most Yards Game:	192	Freeman McNeil, vs Buffalo, 1985
Season:	1,331	Freeman McNeil, 1985
Career:	8,074	Freeman McNeil, 1981-92

Passing

Most TD Passes Game:	6	Joe Namath, vs Baltimore, 1972
Season:	26	2 times, most recently Joe Namath, 1967
Career:	170	Joe Namath, 1965-76

Receiving

Most TD Passes Game:	4	Wesley Walker, vs Miami, 1986
Season:	14	2 times, most recently Don Maynard, 1965
Career:	88	Don Maynard, 1960-72

Scoring

Most Points Game:	24	Wesley Walker, vs Miami, 1986
Season:	145	Jim Turner, 1968
Career:	1,470	Pat Leahy, 1974-91
Most TDs Game:	4	Wesley Walker, vs Miami, 1986
Season:	14	3 times, most recently Emerson Boozer, 1972
Career:	88	Don Maynard, 1960-72

PITTSBURGH STEELERS

TEAM DIRECTORY: Pres.: Daniel Rooney; VP: John McGinley; VP: Art Rooney Jr.; Dir. Football Operations: Tom Donahoe; Dir. Communications: Joe Gordon; Dir. Pub. Rel.: Dan Edwards; Head Coach: Bill Cowher. Home field: Three Rivers Stadium (59,600). Colors: Black and gold.

SCOUTING REPORT

OFFENSE: Last year, coach Bill Cowher needed to pick between Neal O'Donnell and Bubby Brister for his starting quarterback. He chose O'Donnell and won the AFC Central title. After O'Donnell signed a three-year, $8.2-million offer sheet from the Bucs, management had to determine if he should be their franchise quarterback.

And that is what O'Donnell has become, the Steelers deciding their future falls on the development of this third-year quarterback

Whatever it took, Steelers wouldn't let Neal O'Donnell get away.

who played in the Pro Bowl last year. He doesn't have the big-time arm, but he makes very few mistakes.

Of course, the conservative Cowher offense—coordinated by Ron Erhardt—doesn't allow for mistakes. It has Barry Foster getting the ball and running with it. He led the AFC with 1,690 yards and finished second on the team with 36 catches. Fullback Merril Hoge blocks for him.

Tight end Eric Green and halfback Tim Worley are both coming out of drug-ruined seasons, hoping to regain starting jobs. Green has the better chance, but Worley will help to spell Foster, who had 12 100-yard games. The Steelers count on another good year from an injury-recovered Jeff Graham, their leading receiver.

The hidden strength of the offense is a line that features Pro Bowl center Dermontti Dawson and right guard Carlton Haselrig, left tackle John Jackson, left guard Duval Love, and Leon Searcy, who takes over at right tackle for Tunch Ilkin.

DEFENSE: Cowher lost two starters who ranked first and fourth in tackles, so replacing inside linebacker Hardy Nickerson and outside linebacker Jerrol Williams won't be easy. They were two of the better young linebackers in the game.

The Steelers signed former Pro Bowl linebacker Kevin Greene from the Rams. Greene will be able to return to a more comfortable position at linebacker and become a factor in the pass rush. Cowher also hopes that veteran David Little stays around long enough to let second-year backup Levon Kirkland develop into a starter. Pro Bowler Greg Lloyd, the leader of the bunch, will keep everyone motivated.

This will be an important year for cornerback Rod Woodson. Concerned that the Steelers might be losing too many players, Woodson could be in his last season (his contract expires) with the Steelers. He covets a Super Bowl ring. In the secondary, the Steelers are loaded. D.J. Johnson is great at the other corner. Carnell Lake and Darren Perry excel at safety, and top pick Deon Figures of Colorado adds depth.

SPECIAL TEAMS: Kicker Gary Anderson hasn't lost much over his 12 seasons. He made 28 of 36 field-goal tries. Mark Royals, who averaged 42.7 yards per punt, made Steeler fans forget about the hard-to-spell Dan Strzyinski. As long as Woodson is around, the Steelers have one of the most dangerous return specialists in football.

THE ROOKIES: The Steelers went for a couple of Colorado teammates for their first two picks—cornerback Figures in the first

STEELERS VETERAN ROSTER

HEAD COACH—Bill Cowher. Assistant Coaches—Dom Capers, Ron Ehrhardt, Steve Furness, John Guy, Bob Harrison, Dick Hoak, Pat Hodgson, Dick LeBeau, Marvin Lewis, Kent Stephenson.

No.	Name	Pos.	Ht.	Wt.	NFL Exp.	College
1	Anderson, Gary	PK	5-11	181	12	Syracuse
43	Avery, Steve	RB	6-1	225	1	Northern Michigan
85	Campbell, Russ	TE	6-5	259	2	Kansas State
56	Clark, Greg	LB	6-0	225	6	Arizona State
87	Cooper, Adrian	TE	6-5	268	3	Oklahoma
51	Cooper, Louis	LB	6-1	235	8	Western California
80	Davenport, Charles	WR	6-3	210	2	North Carolina State
64	Davidson, Kenny	DE	6-5	277	4	Louisiana State
63	Dawson, Dermontti	C	6-2	288	6	Kentucky
88	Didio, Mark	WR	5-11	181	1	Connecticut
66	Evans, Donald	DE	6-2	275	6	Winston-Salem State
79	Finn, Mike	DL	6-4	296	1	Arkansas-Pine Bluff
29	Foster, Barry	RB	5-10	214	4	Arkansas
60	Gammon, Kendall	C	6-4	273	2	Pittsburg State
81	Graham, Jeff	WR	6-1	195	3	Ohio State
86	Green, Eric	TE	6-5	280	4	Liberty
91	Greene, Kevin	LB	6-3	247	9	Auburn
22	Griffin, Larry	S	6-0	199	7	North Carolina
49	Hargett, David	DB	6-1	200	1	Georgia
77	Haselrig, Carlton	G	6-1	290	4	Pitt-Johnstown
53	Hinkle, Bryan	LB	6-2	229	13	Oregon
33	Hoge, Merril	FB	6-2	226	7	Idaho State
36	Holloway, Cornell	CB	5-10	182	4	Pittsburgh
78	Howe, Garry	NT	6-1	298	2	Colorado
65	Jackson, John	OT	6-6	290	6	Eastern Kentucky
44	Johnson, D.J.	CB	6-0	189	5	Kentucky
25	Jones, Gary	S	6-2	215	4	Texas A&M
84	Jorden, Tim	TE	6-3	239	4	Indiana
99	Kirkland, Levon	LB	6-0	247	2	Clemson
37	Lake, Carnell	SS	6-1	210	5	UCLA
83	Lipps, Louis	WR	5-10	193	9	Southern Mississippi
50	Little, David	LB	6-1	239	13	Florida
95	Lloyd, Greg	LB	6-2	225	7	Fort Valley State
67	Love, Duval	G	6-3	291	9	UCLA
89	Mills, Ernie	WR	5-11	186	3	Florida
14	O'Donnell, Neil	QB	6-3	230	4	Maryland
55	Olsavsky, Jerry	LB	6-1	222	5	Pittsburgh
7	Owens, Darrick	WR	6-2	202	1	Mississippi
39	Perry, Darren	FS	5-10	194	2	Penn State
3	Royals, Mark	P	6-5	212	4	Appalachian State
72	Searcy, Leon	OT	6-3	305	2	Miami (Fla.)
74	Shaw, Rickie	OT	6-4	295	1	North Carolina
24	Shelton, Richard	CB	5-10	199	4	Liberty
2	Shepherd, Leslie	WR	5-11	180	1	Temple
61	Simpson, Tim	G-C	6-2	295	1	Illinois
40	Smagala, Stan	CB	5-10	177	4	Notre Dame
69	Solomon, Ariel	C-OT	6-5	286	3	Colorado
93	Steed, Joel	NT	6-2	290	2	Colorado
20	Stone, Dwight	WR-RB	6-0	187	7	Middle Tenn. State
11	Strom, Rick	QB	6-2	205	5	Georgia Tech
73	Strzelczyk, Justin	OT	6-6	305	4	Maine
94	Szymanski, Jim	DE	6-5	270	3	Michigan State
82	Thigpen, Yancey	WR	6-1	203	2	Winston-Salem State
34	Thompson, Leroy	RB	5-10	215	3	Penn State
18	Tomczak, Mike	QB	6-1	204	9	Ohio State
71	Viaene, David	OL	6-5	300	5	Minnesota-Duluth
23	Walker, Sammy	CB	5-11	200	3	Texas Tech
92	Webster, Elnardo	LB	6-2	243	2	Rutgers
41	Wilcots, Solomon	S	5-11	202	7	Colorado
98	Williams, Gerald	NT	6-3	289	8	Auburn
42	Williams, Warren	RB	6-0	214	6	Miami (Fla.)
26	Woodson, Rod	CB	6-0	202	7	Purdue

		TOP DRAFT CHOICES				
Rd.	Name	Sel. No.	Pos.	Ht.	Wt.	College
1	Figures, Deon	23	CB	6-0	192	Colorado
2	Brown, Chad	44	LB	6-2	236	Colorado
3	Hastings, Andre	76	WR	6-0	185	Georgia
4	Henry, Kevin	108	DE	6-3	266	Mississippi State
5	Palaiei, Lonnie	135	G	6-3	308	Nevada-Las vegas

round and outside linebacker Chad Brown in the second round. Figures is known for his powerful short-range coverage and Brown for his pass-rushing and open-field tackling. Third-round wide receiver Andre Hastings of Georgia brings great leaping credentials.

OUTLOOK: As a first-year coach, Cowher gave himself a tough act to follow with an 11-win start. The Oilers have more talent than the Steelers, but Cowher used good coaching and player hustle to win the division. This year, though, he won't catch the Oilers by surprise.

STEELER PROFILES

NEIL O'DONNELL 27 6-3 220　　　　　　　　Quarterback

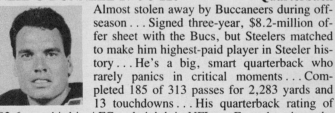

Almost stolen away by Buccaneers during off-season . . . Signed three-year, $8.2-million offer sheet with the Bucs, but Steelers matched to make him highest-paid player in Steeler history . . . He's a big, smart quarterback who rarely panics in critical moments . . . Completed 185 of 313 passes for 2,283 yards and 13 touchdowns . . . His quarterback rating of 83.6 was third in AFC and eighth in NFL . . . Earned a trip to the Pro Bowl after being selected as an alternate . . . Lacks deep arm strength, so his specialty is hitting the middle-range throws . . . Was 9-3 after as a starter after beating out Bubby Brister in training camp . . . Missed three games because of a cracked fibula but returned to play against Buffalo in playoffs . . . After being the third-string quarterback as a rookie in 1990, he had eight starts for an injured Brister the next year and had a 78.8 quarterback rating

. . . Statistically, finished behind only Boomer Esiason with 387 completions on 658 attempts and 4,989 yards at Maryland . . . Selected in third round in 1990 . . . Born July 3, 1966, in Morristown, N.J. . . . 1993 base salary: $2,150,000, plus $1,325,000 in bonuses.

ROD WOODSON 28 6-0 202   Cornerback

Had perhaps his best season with career-high 85 tackles . . . Destroyed quarterbacks' concentration, rushing from the corner for six sacks . . . Voted to Pro Bowl for fourth time . . . Averaged 11.4 yards per punt return and 18.8 yards on kickoffs . . . Owns virtually all Steeler return records . . . Is a plaintiff in antitrust suits against the NFL and can't be named a franchise or transition player after his contract expires this year . . . Continues to be one of fastest players in NFL . . . Occasionally a wide receiver . . . Was 10th player taken in 1987 draft, but he held out 94 days before signing a contract . . . Was nickel back during the final eight games of his rookie season . . . Earned co-MVP honors in his second year, leading team with 18 passes defensed . . . Broke 13 Purdue records . . . Was Big 10 hurdle champion . . . Born March 10, 1965, in Fort Wayne, Ind. . . . 1993 base salary: $1,200,000.

BARRY FOSTER 24 5-10 214   Halfback

Lost rushing title to Dallas' Emmitt Smith by 23 yards . . . Rushed for 1,690 yards on 390 carries and scored 11 touchdowns . . . Finished second on Steelers with 36 catches for 344 yards . . . Broke five Steeler offensive records with enormous season . . . His NFL-record-tying 12 100-yard games shattered Franco Harris' season club record of seven . . . Had 100-yard games in every home game, an NFL first . . . Has a career rushing average of 4.56 yards per carry . . . Has quick first steps and hits the hole with power and acceleration . . . Was on pace to 1,000-yard season in 1991 when he missed six of the final nine games with ankle problems . . . Came to Steelers in running-back-rich 1990 draft as fifth-round choice after three seasons at Arkansas . . . Skipped senior year . . . Averaged 5.6 yards a carry as a rookie but only had 36 attempts. . . . Born Dec. 8, 1968, in Hurst, Tex. . . . 1993 base salary: $460,000.

JEFF GRAHAM 24 6-1 195   Wide Receiver

Made Steeler fans forget about departure of Louis Lipps . . . Caught 49 passes for 711 yards after rather quiet rookie season . . . Had Pro Bowl-type of start, but was slowed down at the end of the season because of ankle injury . . . Saw limited action as a rookie, catching only two passes for 21 yards . . . Selected in second round in 1991 draft as tall, talented, big-play threat . . . Ranked sixth in Ohio State history with 98 receptions for 1,806 yards and 12 touchdowns . . . Was Buckeyes' MVP and All-Big 10 pick as a senior . . . Can be used as a punt- and kickoff-returner . . . Born Feb. 14, 1969, in Dayton, Ohio . . . 1993 base salary: $325,000.

DERMONTTI DAWSON 28 6-2 288   Center

Developing into one of game's best centers . . . Earned first trip to Pro Bowl . . . A durable blocker who has 68 consecutive starts and has only failed to start three games since middle of rookie season . . . Has played both guard positions during Steeler career . . . Missed eight games in 1988 when Bills' Art Still, an uncle by marriage, fell on his knee . . . Drafted in second round in 1988, out of Kentucky . . . Won SEC weightlifting competition . . . Born June 17, 1965, in Lexington, Ky. . . . 1993 base salary: $545,000.

ERIC GREEN 26 6-5 280   Tight End

Off-field problems aside, he might be the best tight end in the game . . . Missed six games because of drug suspension and finished as backup . . . Finished season behind Adrian Cooper but had 14 catches for 152 yards and two touchdowns . . . Played in seven games and started five . . . In 31 NFL games, Green has 89 catches and 15 touchdowns . . . Holds team record for touchdowns (7) by a tight end . . . Fast enough to outrun some strong safeties and is one of toughest receivers to tackle downfield . . . Selected in first round of 1990 draft . . . Caught 34 passes despite missing most of training camp because of contract troubles . . . Missed five games because of a broken ankle in 1991 but ended up with 41 catches for 582 yards and six touchdowns . . . Caught 99 passes for 1,442 yards and 16 touchdowns at Liberty University . . . Born June 22, 1967, in Savannah, Ga. . . . 1993 base salary: $475,000.

CARLTON HASELRIG 27 6-1 290   Guard

Not your typical developmental story . . . Attended tiny Johnstown campus at Pitt, where there was no football program . . . Was major star on wrestling team and won three NCAA titles each in Division I and Division II . . . His college wrestling record was 143-2-1 . . . Bloomed as Pro Bowl guard last season in second year as starter . . . Is exceptional pass-blocker, helped by great leverage he has from his wrestling background . . . Needs work on his run-blocking . . . Selected in 12th round of 1989 draft and spent season as a guard on the developmental squad . . . Started 16 games in 1991 as team's right guard . . . Born Jan. 22, 1966, in Johnstown, Pa . . . 1992 base salary: $99,000.

MERRIL HOGE 28 6-2 226   Fullback

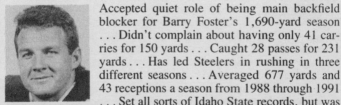

Accepted quiet role of being main backfield blocker for Barry Foster's 1,690-yard season . . . Didn't complain about having only 41 carries for 150 yards . . . Caught 28 passes for 231 yards . . . Has led Steelers in rushing in three different seasons . . . Averaged 677 yards and 43 receptions a season from 1988 through 1991 . . . Set all sorts of Idaho State records, but was only 10th-round draft pick in 1987 . . . Is hard-working and intense off and on field . . . Born Jan. 26, 1965, in Pocatello, Idaho . . . 1993 base salary: $500,000.

D.J. JOHNSON 27 6-0 189   Cornerback

Plays in the shadow of perennial Pro Bowl cornerback Rod Woodson . . . Led Steelers with 21 passes defensed . . . Has started 46 of the past 47 games . . . Had five interceptions to bring his career total to nine . . . Plays off the receiver a little more than Woodson, but doesn't let receivers get behind him . . . Has averaged 62 tackles a season in three years as a starter . . .

Started three years at left cornerback for Kentucky . . . Came to the Steelers in 1989 as seventh-round choice . . . Born July 14, 1966, in Louisville . . . 1993 base salary: $450,000.

GREG LLOYD 28 6-2 225   Linebacker

Selected to the Pro Bowl as a need player . . . Voted Pro Bowl alternate for two consecutive seasons . . . Atlanta's Jerry Glanville once called Lloyd the meanest man in the NFL . . . Though he excelled dropping into coverage, he led the Steelers with 6½ sacks . . . Doesn't leave the field when the Steelers bring in nickel or dime pass defenses . . . Finished third on the team with 96 tackles . . . Voted the Steelers' MVP in 1991, when he had eight sacks . . . Was sixth-round choice of the Steelers in 1987, out of Fort Valley State . . . Missed rookie season because of major knee surgery . . . Preseason knee injury sidelined him for first seven weeks in 1988 . . . Became full-time starter in 1989 . . . Born May 26, 1965, in Miami . . . 1992 base salary: $490,000.

BUBBY BRISTER 31 6-3 207   Quarterback

Despite losing the starting job to Neil O'Donnell, Bubby moved into second place on the all-time franchise list for passing attempts (1,452), moving ahead of Mark Malone and Jim Finks . . . Started four games and completed 63 of 116 passes for 719 yards and two touchdowns . . . Filled in for an injured O'Donnell during critical late-season stretch and kept playoff drive alive . . . Went 2-2 as a starter, making him 28-29 during his career . . . Has a strong arm and is known for fiery leadership . . . Underwent major knee surgery last February to repair damaged ligaments . . . Admitted after last season he reinjured knee during the last week of training camp but put off surgery . . . A multi-talented athlete who juggled football and baseball careers at Alabama, Tulane and Northeast Louisiana . . . Ranked seventh in the nation as college senior with a 134.8 quarterback rating at Northeast Louisiana . . . Taken in third round of 1986 draft . . . Beat out Todd Blackledge for starting job in third season and threw four touchdown passes longer than 65 yards in 1988 . . . Born Aug. 15, 1962, in Alexandria, La. . . . 1993 base salary: $1,200,000.

KEVIN GREENE 31 6-3 247   Linebacker

Signed with Steelers as a free agent after eight seasons with the Rams . . . Attracted by chance to play outside linebacker in 3-4 defensive scheme . . . Odd man out after the Rams switched to 4-3 alignment, but he still led Rams in tackles (75) and sacks (10) . . . Prototype pass-rushing outside linebacker has speed, moves, outside burst . . . Intense, emotional player . . . Struggled at defensive end in 1991 . . . Registered 46 sacks as an outside linebacker from 1988-90 . . . Pro Bowl choice in 1989 after second consecutive 16½-sack season . . . Also had three sacks in the playoffs after 1989 season . . . Spent three seasons as a backup before becoming starter in 1988 . . . Rams' fifth-round pick in 1987 out of Auburn . . . A college walk-on . . . Born July 31, 1962, in Granite City, Ill. . . . 1993 base salary: $1.8 million.

COACH BILL COWHER: Brought new energy and new ideas

that enabled the Steelers to return to the playoffs . . . Installed an approach that convinced players to create new traditions instead of reveling in the franchise's past successes . . . Not only opened his head-coaching career with an 11-5 record and the AFC Central title, but he earned the conference top seed in the playoffs. . . . One of only 12 coaches in NFL history to win 11 games in first season as head coach . . . Promoted an aggressive defense that led the NFL with 43 takeaways, including a league-leading 21 fumble recoveries . . . Served three seasons as defensive coordinator and linebacker coach for the Kansas City Chiefs . . . At the age of 32, his 1989 Chief defense led the AFC and was second in the NFL, allowing 268.3 yards a game . . . Coached under Marty Schottenheimer for four seasons at Cleveland, rising from special teams coach to secondary coach . . . Played five NFL seasons as a backup linebacker and special-teamer for the Browns and the Philadelphia Eagles. . . . His wife, Kaye, played professional basketball for the Women's Professional Basketball League . . . Started at linebacker for North Carolina State for three seasons . . . Born: May 8, 1957, in Grafton, Pa.

Center Greg Lloyd took his ball to the Pro Bowl.

GREATEST INTERCEPTOR

When Pro Football Hall of Fame selectors met to discuss candidates in 1990, Mel Blount's name offered no debate. Yes. Next candidate.

"Mel was as good a cornerback that has ever lived," said his former secondary coach, Bud Carson, now defensive coordinator of the Philadelphia Eagles. "He was just a great athlete."

Blount, out of Southern, was 6-3 and intimidating. Though he didn't lift weights, his natural strength enabled him to stuff receivers before they left the line of scrimmage. Bump-and-run was his specialty, and when the league limited contact in a 1978 rule change, it was mainly because of him.

From 1970 through 1983, he intercepted 57 passes. But he never seemed to slow down. In 1983, he ran a 4.5.

"He had everything you could possibly want in a cornerback," Carson said. "He caught every ball that went in his hands. He never dropped any."

INDIVIDUAL STEELER RECORDS

Rushing

Most Yards Game:	218	John Fuqua, vs Philadelphia, 1970
Season:	1,690	Barry Foster, 1992
Career:	11,950	Franco Harris, 1972-83

Passing

Most TD Passes Game:	5	2 times, most recently Mark Malone, vs Indianapolis, 1985
Season:	28	Terry Bradshaw, 1978
Career:	210	Terry Bradshaw, 1970-82

Receiving

Most TD Passes Game:	4	Roy Jefferson, vs Atlanta, 1968
Season:	12	2 times, most recently Louis Lipps, 1985
Career:	63	John Stallworth, 1974-87

Scoring

Most Points Game:	24	2 times, most recently Roy Jefferson, vs Atlanta, 1968
Season:	139	Gary Anderson, 1985
Career:	1,123	Gary Anderson, 1982-92
Most TDs Game:	4	2 times, most recently Roy Jefferson, vs Atlanta, 1968
Season:	14	Franco Harris, 1976
Career:	100	Franco Harris, 1972-83

SAN DIEGO CHARGERS

TEAM DIRECTORY: Chairman/Pres.: Alex G. Spanos; Vice Chairman: Dean Spanos; GM: Bobby Beathard; Dir. Player Personnel: Billy Davaney; Dir. Pro Personnel: Rudy Feldman; Dir. Pub. Rel.: Bill Johnston; Head Coach: Bobby Ross. Home field: San Diego Jack Murphy Stadium (61,863). Colors: Navy, white and gold.

SCOUTING REPORT

OFFENSE: Bobby Ross proved that the Chargers had the talent on offense to be a playoff force. After adjusting to Ross' system during an 0-4 start, the Charger offense overpowered teams on their way to an 11-5 mark and the Western Division crown— before they were eliminated by the Dolphins in the playoffs.

The most important acquisition was gutty quarterback Stan Humphries, acquired from the Redskins for a third-round choice. Humphries kept getting better as the season progressed and made management forget about promising young quarterback John Friesz, who blew out his knee during the preseason.

Humphries' arm was strong enough to get Anthony Miller, Shawn Jefferson and Nate Lewis completions 20 yards downfield. Getting receivers downfield cleared space for Ronnie Harmon to do his thing. Harmon is the best third-down back in the league. The departure of Rod Bernstine to Denver could allow Harmon to move up into a starting role. To do so, though, he'll have to beat Marion Butts, who fought off knee problems to lead the Chargers with 809 rushing yards.

Whoever the back is, he couldn't ask for a better line. Harry Swayne developed into a top left tackle and signed a $1.8-million-a-year contract in April. Guard Eric Moten and center Courtney Hall are budding stars. Former Ram Joe Milinichick replaces David Richards at right guard, leaving Broderick Thompson as the only aging player at right tackle.

DEFENSE: Bill Arnsparger proved great defensive minds don't grow old. They simply get better. His simple approach to the game won over the usually skeptical Chargers and turned them into AFC stalwarts.

This defense has the big names—Leslie O'Neal and Burt Grossman as defensive ends, Junior Seau as the do-everything inside linebacker and Gill Byrd at cornerback. Arnsparger puts them in

In the clutch, Chargers go to their MVP, Ronnie Harmon.

position to make plays, and this quartet does as as well as any in pro football.

GM Bobby Beathard finessed a few young defensive finds to grow with this defense this year. He stole outside linebacker Jerroll Williams from the Steelers. The 253-pounder was developing into a pass-rushing force in Pittsburgh and could be an impact player for the Chargers. Chris Mims, last year's first-round choice, should take over at a defensive-tackle spot.

Free safety Stanley Richard, a first-rounder two years ago, is ready to have a Pro Bowl season. Beathard signed cornerback Brian Davis to provide more depth and then added Darrien Gordon of Stanford in the draft.

SPECIAL TEAMS: The Chargers are set with some of the best special teams in the NFL. John Kidd is a solid punter and John Carney is a powerful, accurate kicker. Lewis can handle punt and kickoff returns skillfully.

CHARGERS VETERAN ROSTER

HEAD COACH—Bobby Ross. Assistant Coaches—Bill Arnsparger, Sylvester Croom, John Dunn, John Fox, Ralph Friedgen, Dale Lindsey, Carl Mauck, John Misciagna, George O'Leary, Chuck Priefer, Jack Reilly, Jerry Sullivan.

No.	Name	Pos.	Ht.	Wt.	NFL Exp.	College
52	Anno, Sam	LB	6-3	240	7	USC
85	Barnes, Johnnie	WR	6-1	180	2	Hampton
32	Bieniemy, Eric	RB	5-7	198	3	Colorado
13	Brennan, Brian	WR	5-10	185	10	Boston College
35	Butts, Marion	RB	6-1	248	5	Florida State
22	Byrd, Gill	CB-S	5-11	189	11	San Jose State
3	Carney, John	K	5-11	170	6	Notre Dame
29	Carrington, Darren	S	6-2	200	5	Northern Arizona
59	Clark, Reggie	LB	6-3	238	2	North Carolina
31	Davis, Brian	CB	6-2	190	7	Nebraska
28	Elder, Donnie	CB	5-9	178	9	Memphis State
6	Ethridge, Ray	WR	5-10	180	2	Pasadena City College
26	Fields, Floyd	SS	6-0	208	3	Arizona State
27	Frank, Donald	CB	6-0	192	4	Winston-Salem State
17	Friesz, John	QB	6-4	218	4	Idaho
40	Fuller, James	S	6-0	208	2	Portland State
56	Grayson, David	OLB	6-3	233	7	Fresno State
21	Griffith, Howard	RB	5-11	230	2	Illinois
92	Grossman, Burt	DE	6-4	270	5	Pittsburgh
84	Habersham, Shaun	WR	5-11	183	1	None
53	Hall, Courtney	C-G	6-1	281	5	Rice
36	Hall, Delton	SS	6-1	211	7	Clemson
33	Harmon, Ronnie	RB	5-11	200	8	Iowa
34	Hendrickson, Steve	HB-LB	6-0	250	5	California
12	Humphries, Stan	QB	6-2	224	5	NE Louisiana
80	Jefferson, Shawn	WR	5-11	172	3	Central Florida
74	Jonassen, Eric	T	6-5	303	2	Bloomsburg
10	Kidd, John	P	6-3	208	10	Northwestern
65	Lavin, Jim	T	6-4	275	1	Georgia Tech
98	Lee, Shawn	DT	6-2	300	6	North Alabama
81	Lewis, Nate	WR	5-11	197	4	Oregon Tech
95	Little, Kevin	DE	6-2	275	2	North Carolina A&T
13	Malone, Art	CB	5-10	190	1	Washington
88	May, Deems	TE	6-4	250	2	North Carolina
71	Milinichik, Joseph	G	6-5	290	8	North Carolina State
83	Miller, Anthony	WR	5-11	185	6	Tennessee
94	Mims, Chris	DT	6-5	270	2	Tennessee
73	Mooney, Mike	T	6-6	320	2	Georgia Tech
77	Moten, Eric	G	6-2	306	3	Michigan State
4	O'Hara, Pat	QB	6-3	205	3	USC
91	O'Neal, Leslie	DE	6-4	259	8	Oklahoma State
97	Paul, Arthur	DT	6-6	294	1	Arizona State
50	Plummer, Gary	ILB	6-2	244	8	California
30	Pope, Marquez	CB	5-10	188	2	Fresno State
86	Pupunu, Alfred	TE	6-2	252	2	Weber State
24	Richard, Stanley	FS	6-2	197	3	Texas
55	Seau, Junior	OLB	6-3	250	4	USC
23	Shelton, Anthony	S	6-1	195	4	Tennessee State
8	Stephens, Ralph	P	6-3	210	1	Georgia Southwestern
72	Swayne, Harry	T	6-5	290	7	Rutgers
93	Thornton, George	DT	6-3	300	3	Alabama
43	Tuipulotu, Peter	RB	5-11	210	2	Brigham Young
25	Vanhorse, Sean	CB	5-10	180	3	Howard
89	Walker, Derrick	TE	6-0	244	4	Michigan
90	White, Reggie	DT	6-4	291	2	North Carolina A&T
64	Whitley, Curtis	C	6-1	288	2	Clemson
57	Williams, Jerrol	OLB	6-5	263	5	Purdue
96	Winter, Blaise	DE	6-4	278	9	Syracuse
87	Young, Duane	TE	6-1	260	3	Michigan State
70	Zandofsky, Mike	C-G	6-2	305	5	Washington

Rd.	Name	Sel. No.	Pos.	Ht.	Wt.	College
	TOP DRAFT CHOICES					
1	Gordon, Darrien	22	CB	5-11	182	Stanford
2	Means, Natrone	41	RB	5-10	255	North Carolina
3	Cocozzo, Joe	64	G	6-3	295	Michigan
4	Johnson, Ray Lee	95	DE	6-3	245	Arkansas
4	Bush, Lewis	99	LB	6-2	238	Washington State

THE ROOKIES: Cornerback Gordon didn't go to postseason all-star games, but he shut out four first-round choices in his final four games. Beathard made him a first-round choice (No. 22) because he runs 4.4 40s and can cover. Natrone Means is a 255-pound back from North Carolina drafted in the second round (No. 41) to help fill the gap left by Bernstine.

OUTLOOK: The Chargers, aided partially by the fifth-place schedule, sneaked up on the rest of the AFC last year. This year's schedule is tougher, but so are the Chargers. With Ross in control and Beathard working behind the scenes, the Chargers are a force in the AFC West.

CHARGER PROFILES

STAN HUMPHRIES 28 6-2 224   Quarterback

 Gutty leader of Charger offense . . . Acquired in 1992 training-camp trade from Redskins for third-round choice . . . Selected first alternate to Pro Bowl behind Dan Marino, Warren Moon and Jim Kelly . . . Completed 263 of 454 passes for 3,356 yards and 16 touchdown passes . . . Didn't miss a playoff game despite dislocating his left shoulder in regular-season finale against Seattle . . . Completed 14 of 23 passes for 199 yards in Chargers' wild-card playoff victory over Kansas City . . . Is 15-6 as an NFL starting quarterback . . . Drafted in the sixth round in 1988 by Redskins . . . When Mark Rypien went down with a knee injury three weeks into 1988 season, he ended up with five starts before

spraining a knee against Philadelphia . . . Completed 58 percent of his passes that season, but had only three touchdown passes and 10 interceptions . . . Began college career at LSU before transferring to Northeast Louisiana, where he played behind Bubby Brister . . . Born April 14, 1965, in Shreveport, La., which produced Terry Bradshaw and Joe Ferguson . . . 1992 base salary: $400,000.

MARION BUTTS 27 6-1 248   Running Back

Slowed by knee problems but still led Chargers with 809 yards on 218 carries . . . Ranks behind Paul Lowe as franchise's second all-time rusher with 3,551 yards . . . Earned second alternate selection to Pro Bowl . . . Suffered knee sprain in season opener and aggravated it in the fifth week . . . A punishing runner who earned Pro Bowl honors in 1990 and 1991 by gaining 1,225 and 834 yards, respectively . . . Was Chargers' surprise leading runner as rookie with 683 yards . . . Carried the ball only 64 times at Florida State, where he was blocking fullback and special-teams star . . . Was seventh-round choice in 1987 . . . Born Aug. 1, 1966, in Worth County, Ga. . . . 1993 base salary: $405,000.

RONNIE HARMON 29 5-11 200   Halfback

Selected to the Pro Bowl even though he only started two games . . . Is simply the best third-down back in the game and might finally get a chance to start . . . Led NFL running backs with 79 receptions and led Chargers with 1,149 combined yards . . . Caught six passes or more in eight games . . . Rushed for 235 yards on 55 carries . . . Combines power and right moves . . . Voted Charger MVP in each of the past two seasons . . . Had 1,099 yards from scrimmage in 1991 . . . Has averaged 61 catches a season during three-year Charger career . . . Named a transition player by GM Bobby Beathard . . . Has 328 career receptions . . . Entered the league as first-round choice of Bills in 1986 . . . Best Bills' season was 1987, when he had 485 yards rushing and 56 receptions . . . Was left unprotected and signed through Plan B in 1990 by Chargers . . . One of the most productive backs in Big 10 history, gaining 2,442 yards at Iowa . . . Born May 7, 1964, in Queens, N.Y. . . . 1992 base salary: $550,000.

JUNIOR SEAU 24 6-3 250   **Linebacker**

Was only unanimous AFC Pro Bowl selection last season . . . Plays inside and outside linebacker and can attack from the defensive line . . . Despite missing a game with a groin injury, he led Chargers with 108 tackles . . . Topped team in 1991 with 129 tackles and was second as rookie with 85 . . . His 19-tackle playoff game against Miami might have been the best ever played by Charger defender . . . Was second alternate to Pro Bowl as a rookie and starter the following year . . . Didn't speak English until he was seven after growing up in American Samoa . . . Was a Prop 48 student who turned around his grades to be scholastic All-American . . . Skipped senior year at Southern Cal after All-American junior season . . . Was third player selected in the 1990 draft . . . Runs a 4.61 40 and bench-presses 440 pounds . . . Born Jan. 19, 1969, in San Diego . . . 1993 base salary: $600,000, plus $50,000 bonus.

JERROL WILLIAMS 26 6-5 263   **Linebacker**

Signed a remarkable $1.7 million, one-year contract with Chargers, a $1.58-million raise . . . The Steelers, who groomed him for four seasons, didn't match Charger offer and instead signed Ram linebacker Kevin Greene . . . Finished third on Steelers with six sacks, but has big-play capabilities . . . Had nine sacks in 1991 despite making only four starts . . . Combines speed and strength . . . Was a fourth-round choice in 1989 from Purdue . . . Had 276 tackles and 12½ sacks in two seasons at Purdue . . . Started only eight games during first three years as Steeler understudy . . . Didn't miss a start in 1992 and finished fourth on Steelers with 96 tackles . . . Born July 5, 1967, in Las Vegas . . . 1993 base salary: $1,100,000, plus $600,000 signing bonus.

HARRY SWAYNE 28 6-5 290   Tackle

Signed three-year, $5.4-million contract with Cardinals, but Chargers matched the offer, making him the highest-paid player on team . . . Voted the Chargers' Co-Lineman of the Year after starting 12 games at left tackle . . . Received same honors in 1991 . . . Selected as transition player but had five teams pursue him in free agency . . . Considered best athlete on the offensive line . . . Signed as Plan B find after four seasons with Buccaneers . . . Fractured lower left leg in 1991 season . . . Excels in pass blocking . . . Drafted as defensive lineman in 1987 in seventh round by Bucs . . . Spent two years as a backup defender . . . Backup offensive lineman for two seasons before leaving for Chargers . . . Played at Rutgers as a defensive lineman . . . Born Feb. 2, 1965, in Philadelphia . . . 1993 base salary: $1,500,000, plus $1,200,000 signing bonus.

ANTHONY MILLER 28 5-11 185   Wide Receiver

After disappointing, injury-plagued 1991 season, Miller regained his zest . . . With knee surgery behind him, he caught 72 passes for 1,060 yards and seven touchdowns . . . Despite double-team coverage most of his career, he has 290 career catches, sixth-best in team history . . . Selected to Pro Bowl for the third time . . . Has 13 career 100-yard games . . . Lost to Darrell Green in Fastest Man competition in 1989 . . . Played only one year of high-school football before signing track scholarship at San Diego State in 1984 . . . Transferred to Pasadena City College, then to Tennessee, where he starred as wide receiver . . . Was first-round choice in 1989 and caught 36 passes, fourth among rookies that season . . . Born April 5, 1965, in Pasadena, Cal. . . . 1993 base salary: $1,000,000.

BURT GROSSMAN 26 6-4 270   Defensive End

Added weight and returned as defensive line force . . . Placed third on the team with eight sacks and had 46 tackles . . . Had 2½ sacks in playoff game against Chiefs . . . Has 34 career sacks . . . Ankle problems have slowed him down . . . A durable defender who has missed only one start in four seasons . . . One of the most colorful and quotable characters in the league . . . His specialty is speed and his elusiveness makes him an effective outside pass-rusher . . . Tied Chiefs' Derrick Thomas with 10 sacks in 1989, when he was All-Rookie selection . . . Was eighth pick overall . . . Signed two-year, $3-million contract before this season . . . Has been juggled between right and left defensive end . . . His sister is Margo Adams of Wade Boggs fame . . . Had 26½ sacks in three seasons at Pitt . . . Born April 10, 1967, in Philadelphia . . . 1993 base salary: $1,500,000.

LESLIE O'NEAL 29 6-4 259   Defensive End

His 17 sacks was a half-sack shy of Gary Johnson's club record set in 1980 . . . Returned to right defensive end, a position he held before being switched to linebacker in 1989 . . . Had two sacks, forced a fumble and intercepted a pass in playoff victory over Kansas City . . . Named the Chargers' franchise player . . . Became team's all-time sack leader with 68½ . . .
Had arthroscopic knee surgery at midseason but returned after 10 days to have a two-sack game . . . Finished third on team with 68 tackles . . . Was first-round choice, out of Oklahoma State, in 1986 and led all rookies that year with 12½ sacks in 13 games . . . Missed 1987 season with what could have been career-ending knee injury . . . Regained full speed after two seasons and played linebacker for three years . . . Born May 7, 1964, in Little Rock, Ark. . . . 1992 base salary: $1,500,000.

STANLEY RICHARD 25 6-2 197   Safety

The Sheriff is back on patrol . . . After disappointing rookie season in which teammates wondered about his toughness, Richard lived up to reputation at Texas, where teammates called him "The Sheriff" because of his hits . . . Was given Wood County sheriff's badge . . . Appropriately, a criminal justice major . . .
Finished second on the team last year with 79 tackles, many of a violent nature . . . Missed two games toward end of the season because of hip flexor . . . Calls defensive signals and rarely makes wrong call . . . Started 14 games as rookie after Chargers made him ninth selection in 1991 draft . . . Led secondary with 59 tackles . . . Born Oct. 21, 1967, in Miniola, Tex. . . . 1993 base salary: $475,000.

GILL BYRD 32 5-11 189   Cornerback

Ranks fourth among active interceptors with 42 . . . Has intercepted more passes (31) over the past five seasons than any player in the NFL . . . Took second trip to Pro Bowl . . . Led Chargers with 20 passes defensed . . . Voted team's most inspirational player for fifth consecutive year . . . Was a plaintiff in antitrust suit but liked the Chargers so much he didn't solicit free-agency offers . . . Was first-round choice in 1983 and won a starting cornerback spot at minicamp . . . Has started 146 games in 10-year career as Charger . . . Lacks speed, but anticipation makes him one of league's premier cornerbacks . . . Was walk-on freshman at San Jose State who ended up starting at cornerback for four seasons . . . Born Feb. 20, 1961, in San Francisco . . . 1992 base salary: $775,000.

CHRIS MIMS 22 6-5 270   Defensive Tackle

Expected to win starting defensive tackle job after great rookie season . . . Recorded 10 sacks as rookie pass-rusher but gained most of his action as passing-down tackle . . . Eight of his sacks came from defensive left tackle . . . Finished fourth on team with 53 tackles . . . Started four games . . . Was first-round choice last year after winning All-SEC honors at Tennessee . . . Born Sept. 29, 1970, in Los Angeles . . . 1993 base salary: $375,000.

NATE LEWIS 26 5-11 197   Wide Receiver

Will be in dog-fight with Shawn Jefferson for starting job . . . Held off rapidly improving Jefferson by catching 34 passes for 580 yards, a team-high 17.1-yard average . . . Started eight games . . . Had 42-catch season in 1991 and established himself as big-play scoring threat . . . Scored seven touchdowns over past two seasons . . . Averaged 21.2 yards on 19 kickoff returns and 9.8 yards on 13 punt returns . . . Was third-round pick in 1990 and spent rookie season as a backup . . . Began college career at

Northeastern Oklahoma A&M, transferred to Georgia, then Oregon Tech . . . Born Oct. 19, 1966, in Moultrie, Ga. . . . 1993 base salary: $265,000, plus $45,000 in bonuses.

COACH BOBBY ROSS: Set tone that enabled Chargers to overcome early adversity and become a final-eight playoff team . . . Never panicked after 0-4 start . . . Won 11 of his last 12 regular-season games and captured AFC West . . . Turnaround parallels 5-20 start at Georgia Tech after which Tech won 18 of 20 and a share of national championship in 1990 . . . Operates a solid offensive gameplan that features power blocking and timing passes . . . Enters 28th season of pro or college coaching . . . Hired Jan. 2, 1992, by GM Bobby Beathard, who was looking for another Joe Gibbs . . . Although Ross made his name in the college ranks, he had four years of experience in the late 1970s as a Kansas City assistant . . . Was quarterback and defensive back at Virginia Military Institute before becoming a high-school coach . . . Served as assistant at William & Mary, Rice, VMI, Maryland and The Citadel . . . As head coach at The Citadel (1973-88), Maryland (1982-86) and Georgia Tech (1987-91), he compiled a 94-76-2 record . . . Born Dec. 23, 1936, in Richmond, Va.

GREATEST INTERCEPTOR

In 1961, Charlie McNeil, a cornerback out of Compton Jr. College, set the standard for Charger defensive backs. He intercepted nine passes that year, a figure that no Charger has ever topped.

Over the years, the Chargers weren't known for pass interceptors. But Gill Byrd, a walk-on at San Jose State who became a first-rounder for the Chargers in the 1983 draft, has become a worthy franchise holder in that department.

From his rookie year through 1992, Byrd has picked off 42 passes, including three seven-interception seasons (1988, '89, '90). And for the past two years he has gone to the Pro Bowl.

INDIVIDUAL CHARGER RECORDS

Rushing

Most Yards Game:	206	Keith Lincoln, vs Boston, 1964
Season:	1,225	Marion Butts, 1990
Career:	4,963	Paul Lowe, 1960-67

Passing

Most TD Passes Game:	6	Dan Fouts, vs Oakland, 1981
Season:	33	Dan Fouts, 1981
Career:	254	Dan Fouts, 1973-87

Receiving

Most TD Passes Game:	5	Kellen Winslow, vs Oakland, 1981
Season:	14	Lance Alworth, 1965
Career:	81	Lance Alworth, 1962-70

Scoring

Most Points Game:	30	Kellen Winslow, vs Oakland, 1981
Season:	118	Rolf Benirschke, 1980
Career:	766	Rolf Benirschke, 1977-86
Most TDs Game:	5	Kellen Winslow, vs Oakland, 1981
Season:	19	Chuck Muncie, 1981
Career:	83	Lance Alworth, 1962-70

SEATTLE SEAHAWKS

TEAM DIRECTORY: Pres.: David Behring; GM/Head Coach: Tom Flores; Exec. VP: Mickey Loomis; VP-Football Operations: Chuck Allen; Dir. Player Personnel: Mike Allman; VP-Adm./Pub. Rel.: Gary Wright. Home field: Kingdome (66,000). Colors: Blue, green and silver.

SCOUTING REPORT

OFFENSE: The Seahawk offense hit an all-time low last season. It scored a 16-game NFL-low 140 points, it averaged only 3.6 yards a play and it scored only 13 touchdowns. Major problems remain at quarterback.

Notre Dame's Rick Mirer, No. 2 overall, went to Seahawks.

Chased out of town was starter Kelly Stouffer, leaving Dan McGwire to contend now with Notre Dame quarterback Rick Mirer, the second overall pick in the draft. The other quarterback, Stan Gelbaugh, is a gutty leader, but he has yet to win an NFL start. Seahawk fans wondered why they didn't sign free agent Steve Beuerlein, but coach Tom Flores obviously decided to cast his lot with Mirer.

The only thing Flores could depend upon last season was his running attack. Chris Warren developed into a solid halfback who rushed for 1,017 yards while fullback John L. Williams blocked well and grabbed 74 receptions, mostly on third downs.

Injuries decimated the receiving corps, so Flores bought some depth by signing wide receiver Kelvin Martin from the Cowboys and tight end Ferrell Edmunds from the Dolphins. Martin figures to battle Tommy Kane for the job of taking double coverage away from Brian Blades, the team's franchise receiver.

Left tackle Ray Roberts and left guard Andy Heck will have a chance to work together for a second season and eliminate pass-blocking holes. The line, as a whole, allowed 67 sacks last season. That can't be repeated.

DEFENSE: The defense rallied around defensive tackle Cortez Kennedy for an incredible season. Despite an offense that punted after every five or six plays, the defense held together to rank among the league's top 10 while Kennedy was named Defensive Player of the Year, a first for a 2-14 team.

It won't be easy to repeat. Kennedy will draw more double- and triple-team blocking. Part of his success was the play of 32-year-old defensive linemen Jeff Bryant and Joe Nash.

The Seahawks can be upbeat because the corps of the defense are young players—Kennedy, 25, linebacker Terry Wooden, 26, and strong safety Robert Blackmon, 26.

At 28, linebacker Rufus Porter provides enthusiasm and pursuit from the left outside linebacker spot. Free safety Eugene Robinson, the brains of the outfit, calls the defensive adjustments. Cornerbacks Patrick Hunter and Dwayne Harper rarely get beat.

SPECIAL TEAMS: Kicker John Kasay had an off-season (14 of 22 field goals) but he should rebound. Punter Rick Tuten should have gone to the Pro Bowl after booming 108 punts for a 44.1-yard average. Martin will be the punt-returner. Coverage teams are good.

SEAHAWKS VETERAN ROSTER

HEAD COACH—Tom Flores. Assistant Coaches—Tommy Brasher, Bob Bratkowski, Dave Brown, Tom Catlin, Larry Kennan, Paul Moyer, Howard Mudd, Russ Purnell, Frank Raines, Clarence Shelman, Rusty Tillman.

No.	Name	Pos.	Ht.	Wt.	NFL Exp.	College
61	Adams, Theo	G	6-4	298	2	Hawaii
25	Blackmon, Robert	S	6-0	198	4	Baylor
89	Blades, Brian	WR	5-11	189	6	Miami
64	Brilz, Darrick	G	6-3	287	7	Oregon State
77	Bryant, Jeff	DE	6-5	281	12	Clemson
84	Clark, Louis	WR	6-0	195	7	Mississippi State
88	Daniels, David	WR	6-1	190	3	Penn State
50	Davis, Anthony	LB	6-0	231	1	Utah
74	Dees, Andrew	T	6-6	274	1	Syracuse
33	Dodge, Dedrick	S	6-2	184	3	Florida State
53	Donaldson, Ray	C	6-3	300	14	Georgia
9	Dugan, Chris	K	5-10	170	1	Arizona State
82	Edmunds, Ferrell	TE	6-6	254	6	Maryland
54	Feasel, Grant	C	6-7	283	9	Abilene Christian
31	Frank, Malcolm	CB	5-8	182	2	Baylor
51	Frerotte, Mitch	G	6-3	286	5	Penn State
18	Gelbaugh, Stan	QB	6-3	207	6	Maryland
7	Graham, Jeff	QB	6-5	220	1	Long Beach State
5	Green, Anthony	WR	5-11	190	1	Western Kentucky
87	Green, Paul	TE	6-3	230	2	Southern California
35	Hagy, John	S	6-0	190	4	Texas
23	Hairston, Stacey	CB	5-9	180	1	Northern Ohio
29	Harper, Dwayne	CB	5-11	174	6	South Carolina State
66	Heck, Andy	G	6-6	298	5	Notre Dame
76	Hitchcock, Bill	T	6-6	291	3	Purdue
27	Hunter, Patrick	CB	5-11	186	8	Nevada
20	Jefferson, James	CB	6-1	199	4	Texas A&I
43	Johnson, Tracy	FB	6-0	230	5	Clemson
30	Jones, James	FB	6-3	232	11	Florida
93	Junior, E.J.	LB	6-3	242	13	Alabama
83	Junkin, Trey	TE	6-2	237	11	Louisiana Tech
81	Kane, Tommy	WR	5-11	181	6	Syracuse
4	Kasay, John	K	5-10	189	3	Georgia
78	Keim, Mike	T	6-7	285	1	Brigham Young
96	Kennedy, Cortez	DT	6-3	293	4	Miami
63	Lee, Ronnie	T	6-3	296	15	Baylor
6	Martin, Kelvin	WR	5-9	162	7	Boston College
36	Mayes, Rueben	RB	5-11	201	6	Washington State
44	McCloughan, Dave	S	6-1	185	3	Colorado
10	McGwire, Dan	QB	6-8	243	3	San Diego State
47	McKinney, Darian	TE	6-6	240	1	Central Michigan
71	Millard, Bryan	G	6-5	277	9	Texas
98	Murphy, Kevin	LB	6-2	235	8	Oklahoma
72	Nash, Joe	DT	6-3	278	12	Boston College
97	Porter, Rufus	LB	6-1	227	6	Southern
73	Roberts, Ray	T	6-6	304	2	Virginia
41	Robinson, Eugene	S	6-0	191	9	Colgate
37	Robinson, Rafael	S	5-11	200	2	Wisconsin
91	Rodgers, Tyrone	DT	6-3	266	2	Washington
24	Shamsid-Deen, M.	RB	5-11	200	1	Tenn-Chattanooga
70	Sinclair, Michael	DE	6-4	255	2	Eastern New Mexico
59	Spitulski, Bob	LB	6-3	235	2	Central Florida
94	Stephens, Rod	LB	6-1	237	5	Georgia Tech
48	Stayner, Larry	TE	6-5	241	1	Boise State
85	Thomas, Doug	WR	5-10	178	3	Clemson
86	Thomas, Robb	WR	5-11	175	5	Oregon State
56	Tofflemire, Joe	C	6-3	273	4	Arizona
21	Treggs, Brian	WR	5-9	161	1	California
62	Tuatagaloa, Natu	DE	6-4	274	5	California
14	Tuten, Rick	P	6-2	218	5	Florida State
42	Warren, Chris	RB	6-2	225	4	Ferrum
90	Wooden, Terry	LB	6-3	236	4	Syracuse
32	Williams, John L.	FB	5-11	231	8	Florida
57	Woods, Tony	DE	6-4	269	7	Pittsburgh
92	Wyman, David	LB	6-2	248	7	Stanford

TOP DRAFT CHOICES

Rd.	Name	Sel. No.	Pos.	Ht.	Wt.	College
1	Mirer, Rick	2	QB	6-2	216	Notre Dame
2	Gray, Carlton	30	CB	6-0	182	UCLA
4	Wells, Dean	85	LB	6-2	238	Kentucky
5	Warren, Terrance	114	WR	6-0	193	Hampton
7	McCrary, Michael	170	DE	6-3	243	Wake Forest

THE ROOKIES: Mirer could win the starting job. His Joe Montana coolness will be put to a supreme test behind a line that allowed 67 sacks. UCLA cornerback Carlton Gray was a tempting second-round choice because he's a refined man-to-man technician. Fourth-rounder Dean Wells from Kentucky could help the special teams.

OUTLOOK: The easier schedule that goes with a fifth-place finish might help, but the Seahawks can't go anywhere until they've settled the quarterback position. Unless Mirer works miracles, it should be another long season.

SEAHAWK PROFILES

CORTEZ KENNEDY 25 6-3 293   **Defensive Tackle**

Named NFL Defensive Player of the Year, an amazing accomplishment for player on 2-14 team . . . Voted MVP by teammates . . . Dedicated season to best friend, Jerome Brown, who died in 1992 car accident . . . Led Seahawks with 14 sacks, powerful numbers for an interior tackle who is double- and triple-teamed . . . Has great quickness and power at line of scrimmage . . . Set team record for most tackles behind line of scrimmage (28) . . . Had career-best 92 tackles . . . Was third player selected in 1990 following a trade in which Seahawks surrendered two first-round choices to draft him . . . Held out of training camp as a rookie and had a disappointing first season . . . Rebounded in second year to have a Pro Bowl season, recording 73 tackles and 6½ sacks . . . Was 320-pound bench-warmer on Miami Hurricane

team as a junior but lost 27 pounds and became an All-American
. . . Born Aug. 23, 1968, in Wilson, Ark. . . . 1993 base salary:
$875,000, plus $100,000 in bonuses.

CHRIS WARREN 26 6-2 226   Halfback

Blossomed into top NFL running back in first
season as a starter. . . . Became second player
in team history to rush for 1,000 yards . . .
Rushed for 1,017 yards on 223 carries, a 4.6-
yard average . . . Only one of eight players in
league history to rush for 1,000 yards on a team
that won less than three games . . . Had 100-
yard games against New England, Washington
and Kansas City . . . A 30-yard touchdown against San Diego in
the season finale put him over the 1,000-yard mark . . . Backfield
coach Clarence Shelman gets credit for improving his fundamen-
tals as running back . . . Has been one of AFC's top return specialists but will probably be replaced by Kelvin Martin in that role
this season . . . Drafted in fourth round in 1990 from tiny Ferrum
College . . . Originally went to Virginia and played defensive back
and running back . . . Born Jan. 24, 1967, in Silver Springs, Md.
. . . 1992 base salary: $150,000.

FERRELL EDMUNDS 28 6-6 254   Tight End

Gets new start after signing three-year, $4.45
million contract with the Seahawks . . . Dolphin
free agent rated as best tight end available . . .
Could catch 60-to-70 passes in Tom Flores'
Vertical Stretch offense that allows the tight end
to be one of the prime receivers on almost any
down . . . Missed 14 games during past two seasons because of injuries . . . Caught only 10
passes for 91 yards in limited duty last year . . . Planned his Dolphin departure after they signed Keith Jackson to four-year, $6-
million contract last September . . . Had bone chips surgically
removed from his right knee twice last season . . . Third-most productive tight end in AFC from 1988 through 1991 with 107 catches
and two trips to Pro Bowl . . . Considered excellent blocker . . .
Had 117 career catches for 1,612 yards and 10 touchdowns in five
seasons with the Dolphins . . . Was four-year starter at Maryland,

where he made 101 catches . . . Has speed to get deep . . . Dolphins drafted him in third round in 1988 . . . Born April 16, 1965, in South Boston, Va. . . . 1993 base salary: $1,400,000, plus $750,000 signing bonus.

JOHN L. WILLIAMS 28 5-11 231   Fullback

Took over leadership role after being voted offensive captain . . . Had one of his best seasons as a blocker . . . Led team in receiving for a third time in five years . . . Caught 74 passes for 556 yards . . . Has five 50-plus catch seasons, including three with more than 70 . . . Ranks behind Steve Largent on Seahawks' list with 413 receptions . . . Only five running backs in NFL history have caught more passes than Williams . . . Caught 11 passes in Oct. 25 game against Giants . . . With Chris Warren getting most of the action, he rushed only 114 times for 339 yards . . . Missed the Pro Bowl for first time in three years . . . Was first-round choice in 1986 and started in backfield upon arrival . . . Has 4,208 career rushing yards . . . Ranks third on Florida's all-time rushing list with 2,409 yards . . . Teamed in college backfield with the Bears' Neal Anderson . . . Has body of a fullback but runs like a halfback . . . Born Nov. 23, 1964, in Palatka, Fla . . . 1992 base salary: $1,000,000, plus $200,000 in bonuses.

EUGENE ROBINSON 30 6-0 191   Safety

Hit high point of determined career by being selected to Pro Bowl for first time . . . Came into the league as undrafted free agent in 1985 and fought off numerous challenges to win starting job as Seahawk free safety . . . Led team with 94 tackles and had a career high seven interceptions . . . Had three-interception day against Steelers . . . Has started 106 games during his career . . . Calls all defensive adjustments in secondary . . . Is punishing tackler in middle of field . . . Plays saxophone in training camp and in locker room . . . Is unofficial team barber . . . Started two seasons at Colgate and graduated with a degree in computer science . . . Has not missed a game during his career because of an injury . . . Hasn't finished lower than third in tackles since becoming starter in 1986 . . . Born May 28, 1963, in Hartford, Conn. . . . 1993 base salary: $650,000.

DAN McGWIRE 25 6-8 243　　　　Quarterback

Will battle Notre Dame rookie Rick Mirer for starting quarterback job . . . Has had disappointing first two seasons in which he played only three games . . . Has only thrown 37 pro passes in two seasons . . . Completed 17 of 30 passes last year for 116 yards and had three interceptions . . . Broke his left hip being sacked in a loss to Cowboys and spent 10 weeks on injured reserve . . . Has trouble avoiding the rush while in the pocket . . . Took boxing lessons to improve his hand and foot speed . . . Is tallest quarterback ever to play in the NFL . . . Played two seasons at San Diego State after transferring from Iowa . . . Passed for 7,484 yards and had 528 completions at San Diego State . . . Brother, Mark, plays for Oakland A's . . . Born Dec. 18, 1967, in Pomona, Cal. . . . 1993 base salary: $1,000,000.

ROBERT BLACKMON 26 6-0 198　　　　Safety

One of the best two-way safeties in league . . . Can cover receivers as well as he can hit ball-carriers . . . Had career-high 65 tackles . . . Missed only two games in three-year career . . . Drafted in second round in 1990 and was given the starting job at strong safety . . . Tendinitis in a knee caught up to him and he ended up being a backup for 10 games of rookie season . . . Takes losing so personally, he considered giving up the game in rookie year . . . Despite making only five starts, he earned All-Rookie designation . . . Was All-American at Baylor. . . . Intercepted eight passes as a senior . . . Played quarterback in high school . . . Born May 12, 1967, in Bay City, Tex. . . . 1992 base salary: $275,000 . . . Seahawks matched offer from Eagles, giving him three-year, $3.25-million pact.

ANDY HECK 26 6-6 298　　　　Guard

Successfully switched late in 1992 training camp from left tackle to left guard . . . After struggling for a month, he developed consistency . . . Is student of the game who spends endless hours in preparation . . . Has become leader among young group of offensive linemen . . . Seahawks named him a transition player after his contract expires this year . . . Missed three games with bad ankle injury that forced him to miss his first plays in almost two years . . . Drafted in first round in 1989 and was immediately thrust into starting lineup . . . Benched for seven weeks but finished the season as a starter . . . Missed only nine plays over two-year span of 1990 to 1991 . . . Didn't play on offensive line until senior year at Notre Dame . . . Was a promising tight end who excelled as a blocker for the Irish . . . Born Jan. 1, 1967, in Fargo, N.D. . . . 1993 base salary: $500,000.

RUFUS PORTER 28 6-1 227   Linebacker

Has developed into a complete linebacker. . . . Aggressiveness allows him to pursue plays all over the field, but he worked on coverage skills . . . A quick outside rusher . . . Had 9½ sacks to increase his career total to 35, an average of seven a season . . . Had a career-high 90 tackles . . . His 2½-sack game against Eagles Dec. 13 was his best last season . . . Went to Pro Bowl his first two seasons as special-teamer . . . Moved into full-time job at right outside linebacker in 1990 . . . Missed last year's minicamp because he suffered burns while cooking catfish . . . Signed by Seahawks as undrafted 208-pound linebacker . . . Had 211 tackles in two seasons at Southern University . . . One of most popular players on the team . . . Born May 18, 1965, in Amite, La. . . . 1993 base salary: $725,000.

BRIAN BLADES 28 5-11 189   Wide Receiver

A training-camp-long holdout created nightmare season . . . Reported to camp the week before regular-season opener and broke collarbone on first play . . . Missed 10 games as a result . . . Caught only 19 passes for 256 yards and one touchdown . . . His only 100-yard game (103) of the season was against San Diego . . . Management put contract problems aside and named him transition player after this season . . . Has eight 100-yard games during career . . . Older brother, Bennie, plays safety for Lions . . . Went to Pro Bowl in 1989 and was voted MVP by his teammates for making 79 catches . . . Averaged 59 catches a season before last season . . . Considered one of the better downfield blockers among wide receivers . . . As a former defensive back, he likes to mix it up as he fights for receptions . . . Never shy about making catches over the middle . . . Was second-round draft choice from University of Miami . . . Learned his routes from retired Seahawk great Steve Largent . . . Born July 24, 1965, in Ft. Lauderdale, Fla. . . . 1993 base salary: $850,000.

TERRY WOODEN 26 6-3 236   Linebacker

Knee problems plagued him for second time in three years . . . Played first half of season on bad right knee . . . Underwent arthroscopic surgery and missed final eight games . . . Ranked second on team at time of injury with 55 tackles . . . Battled back from major knee reconstruction in 1990 to have a great season in 1991, when he led Seahawks with 100 tackles . . . Is a heady player who is always around the ball . . . Brother, Jo Jo, played linebacker at Syracuse last year . . . The 49ers almost signed him to an offer sheet in offseason . . . Despite some knee problems in college, he had 273 career tackles, 23 sacks and seven interceptions at Syracuse . . . Born Jan. 14, 1967, in Hartford, Conn. . . . 1992 base salary: $275,000.

RAY ROBERTS 24 6-6 304   Tackle

Had difficult transition into NFL . . . Was beaten for 17 sacks and was flagged 17 times for penalties . . . Held out during the early part of training camp and missed valuable practice time . . . Put into starting lineup upon his arrival and faced some of the league's top pass-rushers . . . Needs to work on his technique and to improve his quickness picking up rushers . . . Improved steadily as the season progressed in opening holes on the run . . . Was a first-round choice in 1992 draft and the second offensive lineman taken . . . Started 39 of 40 games at Virginia and was finalist in Lombardi and Outland Trophy competition . . . Began college career as defensive lineman . . . Born June 3, 1969, in Asheville, N.C. . . . 1993 base salary: $400,000.

COACH TOM FLORES: Kept a bad team competitive through

16 games . . . Maintained an atmosphere in which players stayed focused and played hard each week . . . Owner Ken Behring promoted his son, David, to take title as team president, but Flores remained GM in charge of all personnel and organization decisions . . . Hired by Behring as team president Feb. 22, 1989 . . . Replaced Chuck Knox as head coach Jan. 6, 1992, after Knox left for Rams . . . Served nine seasons as head coach of Raiders . . . Compiled a 83-53 record from 1979 through 1987 and won two Super Bowls . . . His 1983 Raiders were last AFC team to win the Super Bowl . . . Won three AFC West division titles during Raider tenure . . . Has an 85-67 record as NFL head coach . . . Prefers the Vertical Stretch offense that allows receivers to go deep to catch passes . . . Was quarterback who bounced around camps with Calgary of the CFL and Washington before signing with AFL Raiders in 1960 . . . Played six seasons with Raiders but missed 1962 because of a lung problem . . . Traded to Bills in 1967 . . . Finished his career with Chiefs . . . Was a Bills' assistant in 1971 before moving to Raiders the next season . . . Took over for John Madden in 1979 . . . Born March 21, 1937, in Fresno, Cal.

GREATEST INTERCEPTOR

Dave Brown met frustration early during his career. He was a first-round draft choice out of Michigan in 1975 on a Super Bowl powerhouse Pittsburgh Steeler team that eventually won four Super Bowls. As good as he was, Brown wasn't good enough to start. Mel Blount was a future Hall-of-Famer. J.T. Thomas was a former first-round draft choice.

When the NFL expanded, the Steelers left Brown unprotected. He was the first selection of the Seattle Seahawks in 1976 and became one of their first stars. During a brilliant 11-year career, Brown intercepted 50 passes and he was one of the first to be inducted to the Seahawks Wall of Fame that encircles the Kingdome.

Brown kept himself in supreme shape by hiring a track coach during the offseason to enable him to cover faster receivers. That dedication enabled him to stay in the NFL until he was 38 years old.

Seahawk coach Tom Flores, knowing Brown's attention to detail, hired him to be a cornerback coach in 1992. Someday, it could lead to an NFL head coaching job.

INDIVIDUAL SEAHAWK RECORDS

Rushing

Most Yards Game:	207	Curt Warner, vs Kansas City, 1983
Season:	1,481	Curt Warner, 1986
Career:	6,705	Curt Warner, 1983-89

Passing

Most TD Passes Game:	5	3 times, most recently Dave Krieg, vs L.A. Raiders, 1988
Season:	32	Dave Krieg, 1984
Career:	195	Dave Krieg, 1980-91

Receiving

Most TD Passes Game:	4	Daryl Turner, vs San Diego, 1985
Season:	13	Daryl Turner, 1985
Career:	100	Steve Largent, 1976-89

Scoring

Most Points Game:	24	2 times, most recently Curt Warner, vs Denver, 1988
Season:	110	Norm Johnson, 1984
Career:	810	Norm Johnson, 1982-90
Most TDs Game:	4	2 times, most recently Curt Warner, vs Denver, 1988
Season:	15	3 times, most recently Derrick Fenner, 1990
Career:	101	Steve Largent, 1976-89

OFFICIAL 1992 NFL STATISTICS

(Compiled by Elias Sports Bureau)

RUSHING

YARDS

NFC:	1713	Emmitt Smith, Dallas
AFC:	1690	Barry Foster, Pittsburgh

YARDS, GAME

AFC:	190	Barry Foster, Pittsburgh vs. Jets, September 13, (33 attempts, 2 TD)
		Harold Green, Cincinnati vs. New England, December 20, (31 attempts, TD)
NFC:	174	Emmitt Smith, Dallas at Atlanta, December 21, (24 attempts, 2 TD)

LONGEST

NFC:	71	David Lang, Rams at Green Bay, December 20
AFC:	69	Barry Foster, Pittsburgh at Green Bay, September 27

ATTEMPTS

AFC:	390	Barry Foster, Pittsburgh
NFC:	373	Emmitt Smith, Dallas

ATTEMPTS, GAME

AFC:	37	Thurman Thomas, Buffalo vs. Pittsburgh, November 8 (155 yards)
NFC:	36	Johnny Johnson, Phoenix vs. Giants, December 12 (156 yards)

YARDS PER ATTEMPT

NFC:	5.2	Heath Sherman, Philadelphia
AFC:	4.8	Thurman Thomas, Buffalo

TOUCHDOWNS

NFC:	18	Emmitt Smith, Dallas
AFC:	11	Barry Foster, Pittsburgh

TEAM LEADERS, YARDS

AFC:

BUFFALO	1487	Thurman Thomas
CINCINNATI	1170	Harold Green
CLEVELAND	543	Kevin Mack
DENVER	648	Gaston Green
HOUSTON	1226	Lorenzo White
INDIANAPOLIS	592	Anthony Johnson
KANSAS CITY	607	Barry Word
L.A. RAIDERS	729	Eric Dickerson
MIAMI	915	Mark Higgs
NEW ENGLAND	451	Jon Vaughn
N.Y. JETS	698	Brad Baxter
PITTSBURGH	1690	Barry Foster
SAN DIEGO	809	Marion Butts
SEATTLE	1017	Chris Warren

NFC:

ATLANTA	363	Steve Broussard
CHICAGO	582	Neal Anderson
DALLAS	1713	Emmitt Smith
DETROIT	1352	Barry Sanders
GREEN BAY	631	Vince Workman
L.A. RAMS	1125	Cleveland Gary
MINNESOTA	1201	Terry Allen
NEW ORLEANS	565	Vaughn Dunbar
N.Y. GIANTS	1141	Rodney Hampton
PHILADELPHIA	1070	Herschel Walker
PHOENIX	734	Johnny Johnson
SAN FRANCISCO	1013	Ricky Watters
TAMPA BAY	1171	Reggie Cobb
WASHINGTON	998	Earnest Byner

TEAM CHAMPION

AFC:	2436	Buffalo
NFC:	2388	Philadelphia

TOP TEN RUSHERS

	Att	Yards	Avg	Long	TD
Smith, Emmitt, Dal.	373	1713	4.6	68t	18
Foster, Barry, Pit.	390	1690	4.3	69	11
Thomas, Thurman, Buf.	312	1487	4.8	44	9
Sanders, Barry, Det.	312	1352	4.3	55t	9
White, Lorenzo, Hou.	265	1226	4.6	44	7
Allen, Terry, Min.	266	1201	4.5	51	13
Cobb, Reggie, T.B.	310	1171	3.8	25	9
Green, Harold, Cin.	265	1170	4.4	53	2
Hampton, Rodney, NY-G	257	1141	4.4	63t	14
Gary, Cleveland, Rams	279	1125	4.0	63	7

AFC - INDIVIDUAL RUSHERS

	Att	Yards	Avg	Long	TD
Foster, Barry, Pit.	390	1690	4.3	69	11
Thomas, Thurman, Buf.	312	1487	4.8	44	9
White, Lorenzo, Hou.	265	1226	4.6	44	7
Green, Harold, Cin.	265	1170	4.4	53	2
Warren, Chris, Sea.	223	1017	4.6	52	3
Higgs, Mark, Mia.	256	915	3.6	23	7
Butts, Marion, S.D.	218	809	3.7	22	4
Dickerson, Eric, Rai.	187	729	3.9	40t	2
Baxter, Brad, NY-J	152	698	4.6	30	6
Green, Gaston, Den.	161	648	4.0	67t	2
Davis, Kenneth, Buf.	139	613	4.4	64t	6
Word, Barry, K.C.	163	607	3.7	44t	4
Johnson, Anthony, Ind.	178	592	3.3	19	0
Mack, Kevin, Cle.	169	543	3.2	37	6
Fenner, Derrick, Cin.	112	500	4.5	35t	7
Bernstine, Rod, S.D.	106	499	4.7	25t	4
Humphrey, Bobby, Mia.	102	471	4.6	21	1
Vaughn, Jon, N.E.	113	451	4.0	36	1
Okoye, Christian, K.C.	144	448	3.1	22	6
Thomas, Blair, NY-J	97	440	4.5	19	0
Russell, Leonard, N.E.	123	390	3.2	23	2
Vardell, Tommy, Cle.	99	369	3.7	35	0
Bell, Nick, Rai.	81	366	4.5	66t	3
Williams, John L., Sea.	114	339	3.0	14	1
Culver, Rodney, Ind.	121	321	2.7	36t	7
Allen, Marcus, Rai.	67	301	4.5	21	2
Metcalf, Eric, Cle.	73	301	4.1	31	1
Rivers, Reggie, Den.	74	282	3.8	48	3
Stephens, John, N.E.	75	277	3.7	19	2
Lewis, Greg, Den.	73	268	3.7	22	4
Bieniemy, Eric, S.D.	74	264	3.6	21	3
Williams, Harvey, K.C.	78	262	3.4	11	1
Hoard, Leroy, Cle.	54	236	4.4	37	0
Harmon, Ronnie, S.D.	55	235	4.3	33	3
Chaffey, Pat, NY-J	27	186	6.9	32	1
McNeil, Freeman, NY-J	43	170	4.0	18	0
Gardner, Carwell, Buf.	40	166	4.2	19	2

t = Touchdown
Leader based on most yards gained

	Att.	Yards	Avg.	Long	TD
Lockwood, Scott, N.E.	35	162	4.6	23	0
Schroeder, Jay, Rai.	28	160	5.7	19	0
Thompson, Leroy, Pit.	35	157	4.5	25	1
Hoge, Merril, Pit.	41	150	3.7	15	0
Moon, Warren, Hou.	27	147	5.4	23	1
Clark, Ken, Ind.	40	134	3.4	13	0
Smith, Steve, Rai.	44	129	2.9	15	0
McNair, Todd, K.C.	21	124	5.9	30	1
Stone, Dwight, Pit.	12	118	9.8	30	0
Hollas, Donald, Cin.	20	109	5.5	24	0
Millen, Hugh, N.E.	17	108	6.4	26	0
Elway, John, Den.	34	94	2.8	9	2
Smith, Sammie, Den.	23	94	4.1	15	0
Brown, Gary, Hou.	19	87	4.6	26	1
Evans, Vince, Rai.	11	79	7.2	16	0
Gelbaugh, Stan, Sea.	16	79	4.9	22	0
Humphries, Stan, S.D.	28	79	2.8	25	4
Carlson, Cody, Hou.	27	77	2.9	13	1
Givins, Earnest, Hou.	7	75	10.7	44	0
Krieg, Dave, K.C.	37	74	2.0	17	2
Mayes, Rueben, Sea.	28	74	2.6	14	0
Zolak, Scott, N.E.	18	71	3.9	19	0
Hector, Johnny, NY-J	24	67	2.8	14	0
Esiason, Boomer, Cin.	21	66	3.1	15	0
Marino, Dan, Mia.	20	66	3.3	12	0
Reed, Andre, Buf.	8	65	8.1	24	0
Nagle, Browning, NY-J	24	57	2.4	20	0
Marshall, Arthur, Den.	11	56	5.1	16	0
Ball, Eric, Cin.	16	55	3.4	17	2
Kelly, Jim, Buf.	31	53	1.7	10	1
Klingler, David, Cin.	11	53	4.8	12	0
Brown, A.B., NY-J	24	42	1.8	9	0
Turner, Kevin, N.E.	10	40	4.0	11	0
Fuller, Eddie, Buf.	6	39	6.5	15	0
Moore, Shawn, Den.	8	39	4.9	11	0
Tomczak, Mike, Cle.	24	39	1.6	16	0
Parmalee, Bernie, Mia.	6	38	6.3	20	0
Stouffer, Kelly, Sea.	9	37	4.1	11	0
Carlson, Jeff, N.E.	11	32	2.9	7	0
Baldwin, Randy, Cle.	10	31	3.1	11	0
Marinovich, Todd, Rai.	9	30	3.3	11	0
Graham, Scottie, NY-J	14	29	2.1	6	0
Harry, Emile, K.C.	1	27	27.0	27	0
George, Jeff, Ind.	14	26	1.9	13	1
Johnson, Tracy, Sea.	3	26	8.7	19	0
Mathis, Terance, NY-J	3	25	8.3	10t	1
Miles, Ostell, Cin.	8	22	2.8	9	0
Jackson, Michael, Cle.	1	21	21.0	21	0
Moore, Rob, NY-J	1	21	21.0	21	0
Maddox, Tommy, Den.	9	20	2.2	11	0
Mills, Ernie, Pit.	1	20	20.0	20	0
Slaughter, Webster, Hou.	3	20	6.7	10	0
Brister, Bubby, Pit.	10	16	1.6	8	0
Tillman, Lawyer, Cle.	2	15	7.5	15	0
Brooks, Bill, Ind.	2	14	7.0	8	0
McGwire, Dan, Sea.	3	13	4.3	11	0
Kosar, Bernie, Cle.	5	12	2.4	8	0
Hodson, Tom, N.E.	5	11	2.2	5	0
Mohr, Chris, Buf.	1	11	11.0	11	0

	Att.	Yards	Avg.	Long	TD
Paige, Tony, Mia.	7	11	1.6	6	1
Gainer, Derrick, Rai.	2	10	5.0	6	0
Mitchell, Scott, Mia.	8	10	1.3	8	0
Canley, Sheldon, NY-J	4	9	2.3	4	0
Carthon, Maurice, Ind.	4	9	2.3	5	0
Craver, Aaron, Mia.	3	9	3.0	8	0
Tasker, Steve, Buf.	1	9	9.0	9	0
Tupa, Tom, Ind.	3	9	3.0	10	0
Edwards, Al, Buf.	1	8	8.0	8	0
Harris, Leonard, Hou.	1	8	8.0	8	0
O'Brien, Ken, NY-J	8	8	1.0	7	0
Gash, Sam, N.E.	5	7	1.4	4	1
Johnson, Reggie, Den.	2	7	3.5	8	0
Lewis, Nate, S.D.	2	7	3.5	4	0
Saxon, James, Mia.	4	7	1.8	4	0
Thomas, Doug, Sea.	3	7	2.3	8	0
Fryar, Irving, N.E.	1	6	6.0	8	0
Gault, Willie, Rai.	1	6	6.0	6	0
Trudeau, Jack, Ind.	13	6	0.5	5	0
Blades, Brian, Sea.	1	5	5.0	5	0
O'Donnell, Neil, Pit.	27	5	0.2	9	1
McMurtry, Greg, N.E.	2	3	1.5	2	0
Carpenter, Rob, NY-J	1	2	2.0	2	0
Coates, Ben, N.E.	1	2	2.0	2	0
Wolfley, Ron, Cle.	1	2	2.0	2	0
Anders, Kimble, K.C.	1	1	1.0	1	0
Query, Jeff, Cin.	1	1	1.0	1	0
Tillman, Spencer, Hou.	1	1	1.0	1	0
Tuten, Rick, Sea.	1	0	0.0	0	0
Williams, Warren, Pit.	2	0	0.0	2	0
Jackson, Mark, Den.	3	-1	-0.3	1	0
Miller, Anthony, S.D.	1	-1	-1.0	-1	0
Perryman, Bob, Den.	3	-1	-0.3	1	0
Richardson, Bucky, Hou.	1	-1	-1.0	-1	0
Thomas, Robb, Sea.	1	-1	-1.0	-1	0
Blake, Jeff, NY-J	2	-2	-1.0	1	0
Herrmann, Mark, Ind.	3	-2	-0.7	0	0
Martin, Tony, Mia.	1	-2	-2.0	-2	0
Brown, Tim, Rai.	3	-4	-1.3	3	0
Gagliano, Bob, S.D.	3	-4	-1.3	0	0
Beebe, Don, Buf.	1	-6	-6.0	-6	0
Sharpe, Shannon, Den.	2	-6	-3.0	-3	0
Langhorne, Reggie, Ind.	1	-7	-7.0	-7	0
Reich, Frank, Buf.	9	-9	-1.0	0	0
McCarthy, Shawn, N.E.	3	-10	-3.3	0	0
Davis, Willie, K.C.	1	-11	-11.0	-11	0
Gossett, Jeff, Rai.	1	-12	-12.0	-12	0
Kidd, John, S.D.	2	-13	-6.5	0	0
Montgomery, Greg, Hou.	2	-14	-7.0	0	0

NFC - INDIVIDUAL RUSHERS

	Att.	Yards	Avg.	Long	TD
Smith, Emmitt, Dal.	373	1713	4.6	68t	18
Sanders, Barry, Det.	312	1352	4.3	55t	9
Allen, Terry, Min.	266	1201	4.5	51	13
Cobb, Reggie, T.B.	310	1171	3.8	25	9

	Att.	Yards	Avg.	Long	TD
Hampton, Rodney, NY-G	257	1141	4.4	63t	14
Gary, Cleveland, Rams	279	1125	4.0	63	7
Walker, Herschel, Phi.	267	1070	4.0	38	8
Watters, Ricky, S.F.	206	1013	4.9	43	9
Byner, Earnest, Was.	262	998	3.8	23	6
Johnson, Johnny, Pho.	178	734	4.1	42t	6
Workman, Vince, G.B.	159	631	4.0	44	2
Sherman, Heath, Phi.	112	583	5.2	34	5
Anderson, Neal, Chi.	156	582	3.7	49t	5
Dunbar, Vaughn, N.O.	154	565	3.7	25	3
Cunningham, Randall, Phi.	87	549	6.3	30	5
Young, Steve, S.F.	76	537	7.1	39t	4
Bunch, Jarrod, NY-G	104	501	4.8	37	3
Ervins, Ricky, Was.	151	495	3.3	25	2
Hilliard, Dalton, N.O.	115	445	3.9	22	3
Craig, Roger, Min.	105	416	4.0	21	4
Heyward, Craig, N.O.	104	416	4.0	23	3
Muster, Brad, Chi.	98	414	4.2	35	3
Lewis, Darren, Chi.	90	382	4.2	33	4
Broussard, Steve, Atl.	84	363	4.3	27	1
Lee, Amp, S.F.	91	362	4.0	43	2
Smith, Tony, Atl.	87	329	3.8	32	2
Jones, Keith, Atl.	79	278	3.5	26	0
Harbaugh, Jim, Chi.	47	272	5.8	17	1
Thompson, Darrell, G.B.	76	254	3.3	33	2
Bailey, Johnny, Pho.	52	233	4.5	15	1
Bennett, Edgar, G.B.	61	214	3.5	18	0
Lang, David, Rams	33	203	6.2	71	5
Favre, Brett, G.B.	47	198	4.2	19	1
Testaverde, Vinny, T.B.	36	197	5.5	18	2
Anderson, Gary, T.B.	55	194	3.5	18	1
Brown, Ivory Lee, Pho.	68	194	2.9	13	2
Gannon, Rich, Min.	45	187	4.2	14	0
Byars, Keith, Phi.	41	176	4.3	23	1
Richards, Curvin, Dal.	49	176	3.6	15	1
Hostetler, Jeff, NY-G.	35	172	4.9	27	3
Meggett, Dave, NY-G	32	167	5.2	30	0
Sydney, Harry, G.B.	51	163	3.2	19	2
Henderson, Keith, S.F.-Min.	44	150	3.4	12	1
Chandler, Chris, Pho.	36	149	4.1	18	1
Centers, Larry, Pho.	37	139	3.8	28	0
Everett, Jim, Rams	32	133	4.2	22	0
Ware, Andre, Det.	20	124	6.2	32	0
Delpino, Robert, Rams	32	115	3.6	31	0
McAfee, Fred, N.O.	39	114	2.9	19	1
Green, Mark, Chi.	23	107	4.7	18	2
Aikman, Troy, Dal.	37	105	2.8	19	1
Hebert, Bobby, N.O.	32	95	3.0	18	0
Miller, Chris, Atl.	23	89	3.9	16	0
Pegram, Erric, Atl.	21	89	4.2	15	0
Peete, Rodney, Det.	21	83	4.0	12	0
McDowell, Anthony, T.B.	14	81	5.8	23	0
Mitchell, Brian, Was.	6	70	11.7	33	0
Morgan, Anthony, Chi.	3	68	22.7	35	0
Carter, Anthony, Min.	16	66	4.1	14	1
Thompson, Anthony, Pho.-Rams	19	65	3.4	12	1
Wilson, Wade, Atl.	15	62	4.1	12	0
Johnston, Daryl, Dal.	17	61	3.6	14	0
Rice, Jerry, S.F.	9	58	6.4	26t	1

	Att.	Yards	Avg.	Long	TD
Agee, Tommie, Dal.	16	54	3.4	10	0
Rypien, Mark, Was.	36	50	1.4	11	2
Green, Robert, Was.	8	46	5.8	23	0
Monk, Art, Was.	6	45	7.5	16	0
Brooks, James, Cle.-T.B.	18	44	2.4	13	0
Logan, Marc, S.F.	8	44	5.5	26	1
Davis, Wendell, Chi.	4	42	10.5	21	0
Stradford, Troy, Rams-Det.	12	41	3.4	11	0
Pritchard, Mike, Atl.	5	37	7.4	22	0
Graham, Kent, NY-G	6	36	6.0	15	0
Kramer, Erik, Det.	12	34	2.8	11	0
Majkowski, Don, G.B.	8	33	4.1	8	0
Anderson, Ottis, NY-G	10	31	3.1	6	0
Montana, Joe, S.F.	3	28	9.3	16	0
Johnson, Joe, Min.	4	26	6.5	9	0
Jennings, Stanford, T.B.	5	25	5.0	10	0
Bono, Steve, S.F.	15	23	1.5	19	0
Highsmith, Alonzo, T.B.	8	23	2.9	5	0
McMahon, Jim, Phi.	6	23	3.8	11	0
Proehl, Ricky, Pho.	3	23	7.7	10	0
Tillison, Ed, Det.	4	22	5.5	10	0
McGee, Buford, G.B.	8	19	2.4	4	0
Clark, Gary, Was.	2	18	9.0	12	0
Simms, Phil, NY-G	6	17	2.8	7	0
Carter, Cris, Min.	5	15	3.0	6	0
Harper, Alvin, Dal.	1	15	15.0	15	0
Tolliver, Billy Joe, Atl.	4	15	3.8	15	0
Brooks, Robert, G.B.	2	14	7.0	8	0
Howard, Desmond, Was.	3	14	4.7	7	0
Turner, Vernon, Rams	2	14	7.0	9	0
Martin, Kelvin, Dal.	2	13	6.5	8	0
Tillman, Lewis, NY-G	6	13	2.2	6	0
Solomon, Jesse, Atl.	2	12	6.0	12	0
McNabb, Dexter, G.B.	2	11	5.5	8	0
Rosenbach, Timm, Pho.	9	11	1.2	10	0
Harris, Corey, G.B.	2	10	5.0	7	0
Taylor, John, S.F.	1	10	10.0	10	0
Carter, Dexter, S.F.	4	9	2.3	6	0
Sharpe, Sterling, G.B.	4	8	2.0	14	0
Stryzinski, Dan, T.B.	1	7	7.0	7	0
Nelson, Darrin, Min.	10	5	0.5	9	0
Hill, Randal, Pho.	1	4	4.0	4	0
DeBerg, Steve, T.B.	3	3	1.0	4	0
Gentry, Dennis, Chi.	5	2	0.4	3	0
Sikahema, Vai, Phi.	2	2	1.0	1	0
Willis, Peter Tom, Chi.	1	2	2.0	2	0
Goodburn, Kelly, Was.	2	1	0.5	5	0
Jones, Hassan, Min.	1	1	1.0	1	0
Fulhage, Scott, Atl.	1	0	0.0	0	0
Pagel, Mike, Rams	1	0	0.0	0	0
Salisbury, Sean, Min.	11	0	0.0	4	0
Wilmsmeyer, Klaus, S.F.	2	0	0.0	10	0
Blount, Eric, Pho.	1	-1	-1.0	-1	0
Brown, Dave, NY-G	2	-1	-0.5	1	0
Early, Quinn, N.O.	3	-1	-0.3	7	0
Erickson, Craig, T.B.	1	-1	-1.0	-1	0
Barnhardt, Tommy, N.O.	4	-2	-0.5	12	0
Jones, Ernie, Pho.	2	-3	-1.5	1	0
Buck, Mike, N.O.	3	-4	-1.3	-1	0

	Att.	Yards	Avg.	Long	TD
Conklin, Cary, Was.	3	-4	-1.3	-1	0
Sanders, Deion, Atl.	1	-4	-4.0	-4	0
Sanders, Ricky, Was.	4	-6	-1.5	3	0
Beuerlein, Steve, Dal.	4	-7	-1.7	-1	0
Irvin, Michael, Dal.	1	-9	-9.0	-9	0
Barnett, Fred, Phi.	1	-15	-15.0	-15	0

AMERICAN FOOTBALL CONFERENCE - RUSHING

	Att.	Yards	Avg.	Long	TD
Buffalo	549	2436	4.4	64t	18
Pittsburgh	518	2156	4.2	69	13
Cincinnati	454	1976	4.4	53	11
San Diego	489	1875	3.8	33	18
L.A. Raiders	434	1794	4.1	66t	7
N.Y. Jets	424	1752	4.1	32	8
Houston	353	1626	4.6	44	10
Cleveland	451	1607	3.6	37	7
Seattle	402	1596	4.0	52	4
New England	419	1550	3.7	36	6
Kansas City	446	1532	3.4	44t	14
Miami	407	1525	3.7	23	9
Denver	403	1500	3.7	67t	11
Indianapolis	379	1102	2.9	36t	8
AFC Total	6128	24027	3.9	69	144
AFC Average	437.7	1716.2	3.9	—	10.3

NATIONAL FOOTBALL CONFERENCE - RUSHING

	Att.	Yards	Avg.	Long	TD
Philadelphia	516	2388	4.6	38	19
San Francisco	482	2315	4.8	43	22
Dallas	500	2121	4.2	68t	20
N.Y. Giants	458	2077	4.5	63t	20
Minnesota	497	2030	4.1	51	19
Chicago	427	1871	4.4	49t	15
Washington	483	1727	3.6	33	10
Tampa Bay	438	1706	3.9	25	12
L.A. Rams	393	1659	4.2	71	12
Detroit	378	1644	4.3	55t	9
New Orleans	454	1628	3.6	25	10
Green Bay	420	1555	3.7	44	7
Phoenix	395	1491	3.8	42t	11
Atlanta	322	1270	3.9	32	3
NFC Total	6163	25482	4.1	71	189
NFC Average	440.2	1820.1	4.1	—	13.5
League Total	12291	49509	—	71	333
League Average	439.0	1768.2	4.0	—	11.9

PASSING

HIGHEST RATING
NFC:	107.0	Steve Young, San Francisco
AFC:	89.3	Warren Moon, Houston

COMPLETION PERCENTAGE
NFC:	66.7	Steve Young, San Francisco
AFC:	65.6	Cody Carlson, Houston

ATTEMPTS
AFC:	554	Dan Marino, Miami
NFC:	479	Mark Rypien, Washington

COMPLETIONS
AFC:	330	Dan Marino, Miami
NFC:	302	Troy Aikman, Dallas
		Brett Favre, Green Bay

YARDS
AFC:	4116	Dan Marino, Miami
NFC:	3465	Steve Young, San Francisco

YARDS, GAME
NFC:	449	Steve Young, San Francisco vs. Buffalo, September 13, (26-37, 3 TD)
AFC:	403	Jim Kelly, Buffalo at San Francisco, September 13, (22-33, 3 TD)

LONGEST
NFC:	89	Chris Miller (to Michael Haynes), Atlanta at Washington, September 13 - TD
AFC:	83	David Klingler (to Jeff Query), Cincinnati at San Diego, December 13 - TD

YARDS PER ATTEMPT
NFC:	8.62	Steve Young, San Francisco
AFC:	7.54	Dave Krieg, Kansas City

TOUCHDOWN PASSES
NFC:	25	Steve Young, San Francisco
AFC:	24	Dan Marino, Miami

TOUCHDOWN PASSES, GAME
AFC:	5	Warren Moon, Houston at Cincinnati, October 11, (21-32, 216 yards)
NFC:	5	Wade Wilson, Atlanta at Tampa Bay, December 13, (19-26, 324 yards)

LOWEST INTERCEPTION PERCENTAGE
NFC:	1.7	Steve Young, San Francisco
AFC:	2.9	Neil O'Donnell, Pittsburgh

TEAM CHAMPION (MOST NET YARDS)
AFC:	4029	Houston
NFC:	3880	San Francisco

TOP TEN PASSERS

	Att	Comp	Pct Comp	Yds	Avg Gain
Young, Steve, S.F.	402	268	66.7	3465	8.62
Miller, Chris, Atl.	253	152	60.1	1739	6.87
Aikman, Troy, Dal.	473	302	63.8	3445	7.28
Moon, Warren, Hou.	346	224	64.7	2521	7.29
Cunningham, Randall, Phi.	384	233	60.7	2775	7.23
Favre, Brett, G.B.	471	302	64.1	3227	6.85
Marino, Dan, Mia.	554	330	59.6	4116	7.43
O'Donnell, Neil, Pit.	313	185	59.1	2283	7.29
Hebert, Bobby, N.O.	422	249	59.0	3287	7.79
Kelly, Jim, Buf.	462	269	58.2	3457	7.48

AMERICAN FOOTBALL CONFERENCE - PASSING

	Att	Comp	Pct Comp	Gross Yards	Yds/ Att	Yds/ Comp
Houston	573	373	65.1	4231	7.38	11.34
Miami	563	332	59.0	4148	7.37	12.49
Buffalo	509	293	57.6	3678	7.23	12.55
San Diego	496	282	56.9	3614	7.29	12.82
Indianapolis	546	305	55.9	3584	6.56	11.75
Denver	473	258	54.5	3312	7.00	12.84
Kansas City	413	230	55.7	3115	7.54	13.54
Cleveland	398	238	59.8	3102	7.79	13.03
Pittsburgh	431	249	57.8	3046	7.07	12.23
N.Y. Jets	495	251	50.7	2962	5.98	11.80
L.A. Raiders	471	233	49.5	2950	6.26	12.66
New England	444	244	55.0	2492	5.61	10.21
Seattle	476	230	48.3	2323	4.88	10.10
Cincinnati	435	227	52.2	2284	5.25	10.06
AFC Total	6723	3745	—	44841	—	—
AFC Average	480.2	267.5	55.7	3202.9	6.67	11.97

NATIONAL FOOTBALL CONFERENCE - PASSING

	Att	Comp	Pct Comp	Gross Yards	Yds/ Att	Yds/ Comp
San Francisco	480	319	66.5	4054	8.45	12.71
Atlanta	548	336	61.3	3892	7.10	11.58
Dallas	491	314	64.0	3597	7.33	11.46
Green Bay	527	340	64.5	3498	6.64	10.29
L.A. Rams	495	289	58.4	3422	6.91	11.84
Tampa Bay	511	299	58.5	3399	6.65	11.37
Phoenix	517	298	57.6	3344	6.47	11.22
Washington	485	272	56.1	3339	6.88	12.28
Chicago	479	266	55.5	3334	6.96	12.53
New Orleans	426	251	58.9	3297	7.74	13.14
Minnesota	458	258	56.3	3162	6.90	12.26
Detroit	406	231	56.9	3150	7.76	13.64
Philadelphia	429	255	59.4	3054	7.12	11.98
N.Y. Giants	433	232	53.6	2628	6.07	11.33
NFC Total	6685	3960	—	47170	—	—
NFC Average	477.5	282.9	59.2	3369.3	7.06	11.91
League Total	13408	7705	—	92011	—	—
League Average	478.9	275.2	57.5	3286.1	6.86	11.94

Leader based on net yards

TD	Pct TD	Long	Int	Pct Int	Sack	Yds Lost	Rating Points
25	6.2	80t	7	1.7	29	152	107.0
15	5.9	89t	6	2.4	16	103	90.7
23	4.9	87t	14	3.0	23	112	89.5
18	5.2	72	12	3.5	16	105	89.3
19	4.9	75t	11	2.9	60	437	87.3
18	3.8	76t	13	2.8	34	208	85.3
24	4.3	62t	16	2.9	28	173	85.1
13	4.2	51	9	2.9	27	208	83.6
19	4.5	72t	16	3.8	15	119	82.9
23	5.0	65t	19	4.1	20	145	81.2

Sacked	Yds Lost	Net Yards	TD	Pct TD	Long	Int	Pct Int
32	202	4029	27	4.71	72	23	4.0
28	173	3975	24	4.26	62t	17	3.0
29	221	3457	23	4.52	65t	21	4.1
33	268	3346	16	3.23	67t	21	4.2
44	318	3266	13	2.38	81·	26	4.8
52	382	2930	16	3.38	81t	29	6.1
48	323	2792	15	3.63	77t	12	2.9
34	217	2885	18	4.52	69t	16	4.0
40	296	2750	15	3.48	51	14	3.2
39	283	2679	12	2.42	55t	24	4.8
48	360	2590	20	4.25	68t	23	4.9
65	458	2034	13	2.93	65t	19	4.3
67	545	1778	9	1.89	57	23	4.8
45	341	1943	16	3.68	83t	17	3.9
604	4387	40454	237	—	83t	285	—
43.1	313.4	2889.6	16.9	3.5	—	20.4	4.2

Sacked	Yds Lost	Net Yards	TD	Pct TD	Long	Int	Pct Int
32	174	3880	29	6.04	80t	9	1.9
40	259	3633	33	6.02	89t	15	2.7
23	112	3485	23	4.68	87t	15	3.1
43	268	3230	20	3.80	76t	15	2.8
26	204	3218	23	4.65	67t	20	4.0
45	334	3065	17	3.33	81t	20	3.9
36	258	3086	15	2.90	72t	24	4.6
23	176	3163	15	3.09	62t	17	3.5
45	264	3070	17	3.55	83t	24	5.0
15	119	3178	19	4.46	72t	16	3.8
40	293	2869	18	3.93	60t	15	3.3
59	354	2796	16	3.94	78t	21	5.2
64	462	2592	20	4.66	75t	13	3.0
45	283	2345	14	3.23	46	10	2.3
536	3560	43610	279	—	89t	234	—
38.3	254.3	3115.0	19.9	4.2	—	16.7	3.5
1140	7947	84064	516	—	89t	519	—
40.7	283.8	3002.3	18.4	3.8	—	18.5	3.9

AFC - INDIVIDUAL PASSERS

	Att	Comp	Pct Comp	Yds	Avg Gain
Moon, Warren, Hou.	346	224	64.7	2521	7.29
Marino, Dan, Mia.	554	330	59.6	4116	7.43
O'Donnell, Neil, Pit.	313	185	59.1	2283	7.29
Kelly, Jim, Buf.	462	269	58.2	3457	7.48
Carlson, Cody, Hou.	227	149	65.6	1710	7.53
Krieg, Dave, K.C.	413	230	55.7	3115	7.54
Humphries, Stan, S.D.	454	263	57.9	3356	7.39
Elway, John, Den.	316	174	55.1	2242	7.09
Schroeder, Jay, Rai.	253	123	48.6	1476	5.83
George, Jeff, Ind.	306	167	54.6	1963	6.42
Esiason, Boomer, Cin.	278	144	51.8	1407	5.06
Nagle, Browning, NY-J	387	192	49.6	2280	5.89
Gelbaugh, Stan, Sea.	255	121	47.5	1307	5.13
(Nonqualifiers)					
Philcox, Todd, Cle.	27	13	48.1	217	8.04
Hollas, Donald, Cin.	58	35	60.3	335	5.78
Kosar, Bernie, Cle.	155	103	66.5	1160	7.48
Herrmann, Mark, Ind.	24	15	62.5	177	7.38
Tomczak, Mike, Cle.	211	120	56.9	1693	8.02
Evans, Vince, Rai.	53	29	54.7	372	7.02
Millen, Hugh, N.E.	203	124	61.1	1203	5.93
Hodson, Tom, N.E.	91	50	54.9	496	5.45
Trudeau, Jack, Ind.	181	105	58.0	1271	7.02
O'Brien, Ken, NY-J.	98	55	56.1	642	6.55
Klingler, David, Cin.	98	47	48.0	530	5.41
Brister, Bubby, Pit.	116	63	54.3	719	6.20
Zolak, Scott, N.E.	100	52	52.0	561	5.61
Marinovich, Todd, Rai.	165	81	49.1	1102	6.68
Maddox, Tommy, Den.	121	66	54.5	757	6.26
Tupa, Tom, Ind.	33	17	51.5	156	4.73
Stouffer, Kelly, Sea.	190	92	48.4	900	4.74
Reich, Frank, Buf.	47	24	51.1	221	4.70
Gagliano, Bob, S.D.	42	19	45.2	258	6.14
Moore, Shawn, Den.	34	17	50.0	232	6.82
Carlson, Jeff, N.E.	49	18	36.7	232	4.73
McGwire, Dan, Sea.	30	17	56.7	116	3.87
(Fewer than 10 attempts)					
Blake, Jeff, NY-J	9	4	44.4	40	4.44
Breech, Jim, Cin.	1	1	100.0	12	12.00
Carpenter, Rob, NY-J	1	0	0.0	0	0.00
Foster, Barry, Pit.	1	0	0.0	0	0.00
Goebel, Brad, Cle.	3	2	66.7	32	10.67
Johnson, Anthony, Ind.	1	0	0.0	0	0.00
Lewis, Greg, Den.	1	0	0.0	0	0.00
Marshall, Arthur, Den.	1	1	100.0	81	81.00
Martin, Tony, Mia.	1	0	0.0	0	0.00
McMurtry, Greg, N.E.	1	0	0.0	0	0.00
Metcalf, Eric, Cle.	1	0	0.0	0	0.00
Mitchell, Scott, Mia.	8	2	25.0	32	4.00
Richardson, Bucky, Hou.	0	0	—	0	—
Royals, Mark, Pit.	1	1	100.0	44	44.00
Stark, Rohn, Ind.	1	1	100.0	17	17.00
Stover, Matt, Cle.	1	0	0.0	0	0.00
Tuten, Rick, Sea.	1	0	0.0	0	0.00

t = Touchdown
Leader based on rating points, minimum 224 attempts

TD	Pct TD	Long	Int	Pct Int	Sack	Yds Lost	Rating Points
18	5.2	72	12	3.5	16	105	89.3
24	4.3	62t	16	2.9	28	173	85.1
13	4.2	51	9	2.9	27	208	83.6
23	5.0	65t	19	4.1	20	145	81.2
9	4.0	65	11	4.8	15	90	81.2
15	3.6	77t	12	2.9	48	323	79.9
16	3.5	67t	18	4.0	28	218	76.4
10	3.2	80t	17	5.4	36	272	65.7
11	4.3	53	11	4.3	25	180	63.3
7	2.3	57t	15	4.9	27	188	61.5
11	4.0	38	15	5.4	19	150	57.0
7	1.8	51	17	4.4	27	215	55.7
6	2.4	57	11	4.3	34	265	52.9
3	11.1	69t	1	3.7	1	6	97.3
2	3.4	24t	0	0.0	8	45	87.9
8	5.2	69t	7	4.5	21	126	87.0
1	4.2	27	1	4.2	1	5	81.4
7	3.3	52	7	3.3	12	85	80.1
4	7.5	50	3	5.7	3	26	78.5
8	3.9	39	10	4.9	33	204	70.3
2	2.2	54t	2	2.2	12	96	68.8
4	2.2	81	8	4.4	11	85	68.6
5	5.1	55t	6	6.1	10	61	67.6
3	3.1	83t	2	2.0	18	146	66.3
2	1.7	42	5	4.3	13	88	61.0
2	2.0	65t	4	4.0	17	137	58.8
5	3.0	68t	9	5.5	20	154	58.2
5	4.1	38	9	7.4	10	60	56.4
1	3.0	19	2	6.1	5	40	49.6
3	1.6	33	9	4.7	26	222	47.7
0	0.0	21	2	4.3	9	76	46.5
0	0.0	55	3	7.1	5	50	35.6
0	0.0	40	3	8.8	6	50	35.4
1	2.0	40	3	6.1	3	21	33.7
0	0.0	20	3	10.0	7	58	25.8
0	0.0	19	1	11.1	2	7	18.1
0	0.0	12	0	0.0	0	0	116.7
0	0.0	0	0	0.0	0	0	39.6
0	0.0	0	0	0.0	0	0	39.6
0	0.0	22	0	0.0	0	0	102.1
0	0.0	0	0	0.0	0	0	39.6
0	0.0	0	0	0.0	0	0	39.6
1	100.0	81t	0	0.0	0	0	158.3
0	0.0	0	0	0.0	0	0	39.6
0	0.0	0	0	0.0	0	0	39.6
0	0.0	0	0	0.0	0	0	39.6
0	0.0	18	1	12.5	0	0	4.2
0	—	—	0	—	1	7	—
0	0.0	44	0	0.0	0	0	118.8
0	0.0	17	0	0.0	0	0	118.8
0	0.0	0	1	100.0	0	0	0.0
0	0.0	0	0	0.0	0	0	39.6

NFC - INDIVIDUAL PASSERS

	Att	Comp	Pct Comp	Yds	Avg Gain
Young, Steve, S.F.	402	268	66.7	3465	8.62
Miller, Chris, Atl.	253	152	60.1	1739	6.87
Aikman, Troy, Dal.	473	302	63.8	3445	7.28
Cunningham, Randall, Phi.	384	233	60.7	2775	7.23
Favre, Brett, G.B.	471	302	64.1	3227	6.85
Hebert, Bobby, N.O.	422	249	59.0	3287	7.79
Everett, Jim, Rams	475	281	59.2	3323	7.00
Chandler, Chris, Pho.	413	245	59.3	2832	6.86
Harbaugh, Jim, Chi.	358	202	56.4	2486	6.94
Testaverde, Vinny, T.B.	358	206	57.5	2554	7.13
Gannon, Rich, Min.	279	159	57.0	1905	6.83
Rypien, Mark, Was.	479	269	56.2	3282	6.85
(Nonqualifiers)					
Montana, Joe, S.F.	21	15	71.4	126	6.00
Wilson, Wade, Atl.	163	111	68.1	1366	8.38
Bono, Steve, S.F.	56	36	64.3	463	8.27
Simms, Phil, NY-G	137	83	60.6	912	6.66
Salisbury, Sean, Min.	175	97	55.4	1203	6.87
Hostetler, Jeff, NY-G	192	103	53.6	1225	6.38
Peete, Rodney, Det.	213	123	57.7	1702	7.99
Majkowski, Don, G.B.	55	38	69.1	271	4.93
Ware, Andre, Det.	86	50	58.1	677	7.87
DeBerg, Steve, T.B.	125	76	60.8	710	5.68
Tolliver, Billy Joe, Atl.	131	73	55.7	787	6.01
Beuerlein, Steve, Dal.	18	12	66.7	152	8.44
Erickson, Craig, T.B.	26	15	57.7	121	4.65
Willis, Peter Tom, Chi.	92	54	58.7	716	7.78
McMahon, Jim, Phi.	43	22	51.2	279	6.49
Kramer, Erik, Det.	106	58	54.7	771	7.27
Graham, Kent, NY-G	97	42	43.3	470	4.85
Rosenbach, Timm, Pho.	92	49	53.3	483	5.25
Pagel, Mike, Rams	20	8	40.0	99	4.95
Furrer, Will, Chi.	25	9	36.0	89	3.56
Sacca, Tony, Pho.	11	4	36.4	29	2.64
(Fewer than 10 attempts)					
Brown, Dave, NY-G	7	4	57.1	21	3.00
Buck, Mike, N.O.	4	2	50.0	10	2.50
Byars, Keith, Phi.	1	0	0.0	0	0.00
Byner, Earnest, Was.	3	1	33.3	41	13.67
Carter, Anthony, Min.	1	0	0.0	0	0.00
Conklin, Cary, Was.	2	2	100.0	16	8.00
Gardocki, Chris, Chi.	3	1	33.3	43	14.33
Henderson, Keith, Min.	1	1	100.0	36	36.00
Jones, Hassan, Min.	1	1	100.0	18	18.00
Jones, Keith, Atl.	1	0	0.0	0	0.00
McJulien, Paul, G.B.	1	0	0.0	0	0.00
Mitchell, Brian, Was.	1	0	0.0	0	0.00
Muster, Brad, Chi.	1	0	0.0	0	0.00
Newsome, Harry, Min.	1	0	0.0	0	0.00
Proehl, Ricky, Pho.	1	0	0.0	0	0.00
Sanders, Barry, Det.	1	0	0.0	0	0.00
Stryzinski, Dan, T.B.	2	2	100.0	14	7.00
Walker, Herschel, Phi.	1	0	0.0	0	0.00
Watters, Ricky, S.F.	1	0	0.0	0	0.00

t = Touchdown
Leader based on rating points, minimum 224 attempts

TD	Pct TD	Long	Int	Pct Int	Sack	Yds Lost	Rating Points
25	6.2	80t	7	1.7	29	152	107.0
15	5.9	89t	6	2.4	16	103	90.7
23	4.9	87t	14	3.0	23	112	89.5
19	4.9	75t	11	2.9	60	437	87.3
18	3.8	76t	13	2.8	34	208	85.3
19	4.5	72t	16	3.8	15	119	82.9
22	4.6	67t	18	3.8	26	204	80.2
15	3.6	72t	15	3.6	29	226	77.1
13	3.6	83t	12	3.4	31	167	76.2
14	3.9	81t	16	4.5	35	259	74.2
12	4.3	60t	13	4.7	25	177	72.9
13	2.7	62t	17	3.5	23	176	71.7
2	9.5	17	0	0.0	1	8	118.4
13	8.0	60t	4	2.5	8	58	110.1
2	3.6	36	2	3.6	2	14	87.1
5	3.6	38	3	2.2	10	67	83.3
5	2.9	51	2	1.1	15	116	81.7
8	4.2	46	3	1.6	24	148	80.8
9	4.2	78t	9	4.2	28	170	80.0
2	3.6	32	2	3.6	9	60	77.2
3	3.5	59	4	4.7	16	104	75.6
3	2.4	28t	4	3.2	8	66	71.1
5	3.8	30t	5	3.8	16	98	70.4
0	0.0	27	1	5.6	0	0	69.7
0	0.0	24	0	0.0	2	9	69.6
4	4.3	68t	8	8.7	10	58	61.7
1	2.3	42t	2	4.7	4	25	60.1
4	3.8	77t	8	7.5	15	80	59.1
1	1.0	44	4	4.1	7	49	44.6
0	0.0	45	6	6.5	7	32	41.2
1	5.0	22	2	10.0	0	0	33.1
0	0.0	16	3	12.0	4	39	.7.3
0	0.0	16	2	18.2	0	0	5.3
0	0.0	8	0	0.0	4	19	62.2
0	0.0	10	0	0.0	0	0	56.3
0	0.0	0	0	0.0	0	0	39.6
1	33.3	41t	0	0.0	0	0	121.5
0	0.0	0	0	0.0	0	0	39.6
1	50.0	10t	0	0.0	0	0	139.6
0	0.0	43	0	0.0	0	0	81.9
1	100.0	36t	0	0.0	0	0	158.3
0	0.0	18	0	0.0	0	0	118.8
0	0.0	0	0	0.0	0	0	39.6
0	0.0	0	0	0.0	0	0	39.6
0	0.0	0	0	0.0	0	0	39.6
0	0.0	0	1	100.0	0	0	0.0
0	0.0	0	0	0.0	0	0	39.6
0	0.0	0	1	100.0	0	0	0.0
0	0.0	0	0	0.0	0	0	39.6
0	0.0	12	0	0.0	0	0	95.8
0	0.0	0	0	0.0	0	0	39.6
0	0.0	0	0	0.0	0	0	39.6

PASS RECEIVING

RECEPTIONS
NFC:	108	Sterling Sharpe, Green Bay
AFC:	90	Haywood Jeffires, Houston

RECEPTIONS, GAME
NFC:	12	Vince Workman, Green Bay vs. Minnesota, September 6, (50 yards) (OT)
		Emmitt Smith, Dallas at Phoenix, November 22, (67 yards)
AFC:	11	John L. Williams, Seattle at Giants, October 25, (45 yards)

YARDS
NFC:	1461	Sterling Sharpe, Green Bay
AFC:	1060	Anthony Miller, San Diego

YARDS, GAME
NFC:	210	Michael Irvin, Dallas vs. Phoenix, September 20, (8 receptions - 3 TD)
AFC:	177	Eric Metcalf, Cleveland at Raiders, Septmeber 20, (5 receptions - 3 TD)

LONGEST
NFC:	89	Michael Haynes (from Chris Miller), Atlanta at Washington, September 13 - TD
AFC:	83	Jeff Query (from David Klingler), Cincinnati at San Diego, December 13 - TD

YARDS PER RECEPTION
AFC:	21.0	Willie Davis, Kansas City
NFC:	18.9	Herman Moore, Detroit

TOUCHDOWNS
NFC:	13	Sterling Sharpe, Green Bay
AFC:	10	Ernest Givins, Houston

TEAM LEADERS, RECEPTIONS

AFC:			NFC:		
BUFFALO	65	Andre Reed	ATLANTA	93	Andre Rison
CINCINNATI	41	Harold Green	CHICAGO	54	Wendell Davis
CLEVELAND	47	Mark Jackson	DALLAS	78	Michael Irvin
		Eric Metcalf			
DENVER	53	Shannon Sharpe	DETROIT	69	Brett Perriman
HOUSTON	90	Haywood Jeffires	GREEN BAY	108	Sterling Sharpe
INDIANAPOLIS	65	Reggie Langhorne	L.A. RAMS	52	Cleveland Gary
KANSAS CITY	44	Todd McNair	MINNESOTA	53	Cris Carter
L.A. RAIDERS	49	Tim Brown	NEW ORLEANS	68	Eric Martin
MIAMI	54	Bobby Humphrey	N.Y. GIANTS	49	Ed McCaffrey
NEW ENGLAND	55	Irving Fryar	PHILADELPHIA	67	Fred Barnett
N.Y. JETS	57	Chris Burkett	PHOENIX	60	Ricky Proehl
PITTSBURGH	49	Jeff Graham	SAN FRANCISCO	84	Jerry Rice
SAN DIEGO	79	Ronnie Harmon	TAMPA BAY	60	Lawrence Dawsey
SEATTLE	74	John L. Williams	WASHINGTON	64	Gary Clark

TOP TEN PASS RECEIVERS

	Yards	No	Avg	Long	TD
Sharpe, Sterling, G.B.	108	1461	13.5	76t	13
Rison, Andre, Atl.	93	1119	12.0	71t	11
Jeffires, Haywood, Hou.	90	913	10.1	47	9
Rice, Jerry, S.F.	84	1201	14.3	80t	10
Duncan, Curtis, Hou.	82	954	11.6	72	1
Harmon, Ronnie, S.D.	79	914	11.6	55	1
Irvin, Michael, Dal.	78	1396	17.9	87t	7
Pritchard, Mike, Atl.	77	827	10.7	38t	5
Williams, John L., Sea.	74	556	7.5	27	2
Miller, Anthony, S.D.	72	1060	14.7	67t	7

TOP TEN RECEIVERS BY YARDS

	Yards	No	Avg	Long	TD
Sharpe, Sterling, G.B.	1461	108	13.5	76t	13
Irvin, Michael, Dal.	1396	78	17.9	87t	7
Rice, Jerry, S.F.	1201	84	14.3	80t	10
Rison, Andre, Atl.	1119	93	12.0	71t	11
Barnett, Fred, Phi.	1083	67	16.2	71t	6
Miller, Anthony, S.D.	1060	72	14.7	67t	7
Martin, Eric, N.O.	1041	68	15.3	52t	5
Moore, Herman, Det.	966	51	18.9	77t	4
Duncan, Curtis, Hou.	954	82	11.6	72	1
Harmon, Ronnie, S.D.	914	79	11.6	55	1

AFC - INDIVIDUAL RECEIVERS

	No	Yards	Avg	Long	TD
Jeffires, Haywood, Hou.	90	913	10.1	47	9
Duncan, Curtis, Hou.	82	954	11.6	72	1
Harmon, Ronnie, S.D.	79	914	11.6	55	1
Williams, John L., Sea.	74	556	7.5	27	2
Miller, Anthony, S.D.	72	1060	14.7	67t	7
Givins, Earnest, Hou.	67	787	11.7	41	10
Reed, Andre, Buf.	65	913	14.0	51	3
Langhorne, Reggie, Ind.	65	811	12.5	34	1
Thomas, Thurman, Buf.	58	626	10.8	43	3
Burkett, Chris, NY-J	57	724	12.7	37t	1
White, Lorenzo, Hou.	57	641	11.2	69t	1
Fryar, Irving, N.E.	55	791	14.4	54t	4
Humphrey, Bobby, Mia.	54	507	9.4	26	1
Sharpe, Shannon, Den.	53	640	12.1	55	2
Hester, Jessie, Ind.	52	792	15.2	81	1
Cook, Marv, N.E.	52	413	7.9	27	2
Lofton, James, Buf.	51	786	15.4	50	6
Moore, Rob, NY-J	50	726	14.5	48t	4
Graham, Jeff, Pit.	49	711	14.5	51	1
Brown, Tim, Rai.	49	693	14.1	68t	7
Johnson, Anthony, Ind.	49	517	10.6	57t	3
Jackson, Mark, Den.	48	745	15.5	51t	8
Jackson, Keith, Mia.	48	594	12.4	42	5
Paige, Tony, Mia.	48	399	8.3	30	1
Jackson, Michael, Cle.	47	755	16.1	69t	7
Metcalf, Eric, Cle.	47	614	13.1	69t	5
Rivers, Reggie, Den.	45	449	10.0	37	1
Duper, Mark, Mia.	44	762	17.3	62t	7
Brooks, Bill, Ind.	44	468	10.6	26	1
McNair, Todd, K.C.	44	380	8.6	36	1
Clayton, Mark, Mia.	43	619	14.4	44t	3
Cash, Kerry, Ind.	43	521	12.1	41	3
Birden, J.J., K.C.	42	644	15.3	72t	3
Green, Harold, Cin.	41	214	5.2	19	0
Slaughter, Webster, Hou.	39	486	12.5	36t	4
Davis, Willie, K.C.	36	756	21.0	74t	3
Foster, Barry, Pit.	36	344	9.6	42	0

t = Touchdown
Leader based on receptions

	No	Yards	Avg	Long	TD
Harris, Leonard, Hou.	35	435	12.4	47	2
McMurtry, Greg, N.E.	35	424	12.1	65t	1
McGee, Tim, Cin.	35	408	11.7	36	3
Lewis, Nate, S.D.	34	580	17.1	62	4
Stone, Dwight, Pit.	34	501	14.7	49	3
Walker, Derrick, S.D.	34	393	11.6	59	2
Beebe, Don, Buf.	33	554	16.8	65t	2
Martin, Tony, Mia.	33	553	16.8	55t	2
Horton, Ethan, Rai.	33	409	12.4	30	2
Toon, Al, NY-J.	31	311	10.0	32	2
Mills, Ernie, Pit.	30	383	12.8	22	3
Metzelaars, Pete, Buf.	30	298	9.9	53t	6
Jefferson, Shawn, S.D.	29	377	13.0	51	2
Allen, Marcus, Rai.	28	277	9.9	40	1
Hoge, Merril, Pit.	28	231	8.3	20	1
Smith, Steve, Rai.	28	217	7.8	19	1
Gault, Willie, Rai.	27	508	18.8	53	4
Kane, Tommy, Sea.	27	369	13.7	31	3
Marshall, Arthur, Den.	26	493	19.0	80t	1
Pickens, Carl, Cin.	26	326	12.5	38	1
Timpson, Michael, N.E.	26	315	12.1	25	1
Hoard, Leroy, Cle.	26	310	11.9	46t	1
Holman, Rodney, Cin.	26	266	10.2	26t	2
Culver, Rodney, Ind.	26	210	8.1	27	2
Tillman, Lawyer, Cle.	25	498	19.9	52	0
Bavaro, Mark, Cle.	25	315	12.6	39	2
Barnett, Tim, K.C.	24	442	18.4	77t	4
Johnson, Vance, Den.	24	294	12.3	40	2
Banks, Fred, Mia.	22	319	14.5	39t	3
Mathis, Terance, NY-J	22	316	14.4	55t	3
Thompson, Leroy, Pit.	22	278	12.6	29	0
Jones, James, Sea.	21	190	9.0	30	0
Stephens, John, N.E.	21	161	7.7	32	0
Clark, Louis, Sea.	20	290	14.5	33	1
Coates, Ben, N.E.	20	171	8.6	22t	3
Holohan, Pete, Cle.	20	170	8.5	24	0
Blades, Brian, Sea.	19	256	13.5	37	1
Rembert, Reggie, Cin.	19	219	11.5	27	0
Thompson, Craig, Cin.	19	194	10.2	32	2
Brennan, Brian, Cin.-S.D.	19	188	9.9	21	1
Boyer, Mark, NY-J	19	149	7.8	23	0
Jones, Fred, K.C.	18	265	14.7	56	0
Hargain, Tony, K.C.	17	205	12.1	25	0
Query, Jeff, Cin.	16	265	16.6	83t	3
Mitchell, Johnny, NY-J	16	210	13.1	37t	1
Cooper, Adrian, Pit.	16	197	12.3	27	3
McNeil, Freeman, NY-J	16	154	9.6	32	0
Higgs, Mark, Mia.	16	142	8.9	21	0
Warren, Chris, Sea.	16	134	8.4	33	0
Glover, Andrew, Rai.	15	178	11.9	30	1
Davis, Kenneth, Buf.	15	80	5.3	22	0
Green, Eric, Pit.	14	152	10.9	24	2
McKeller, Keith, Buf.	14	110	7.9	26	0
Dickerson, Eric, Rai.	14	85	6.1	15	1
Carpenter, Rob, NY-J	13	161	12.4	51	1
Arbuckle, Charles, Ind.	13	152	11.7	23t	1.
Vardell, Tommy, Cle.	13	128	9.8	23	0
Vaughn, Jon, N.E.	13	84	6.5	28	0
Mack, Kevin, Cle.	13	81	6.2	23	0

	No	Yards	Avg	Long	TD
Tillman, Cedric, Den.	12	211	17.6	81t	1
Wright, Alexander, Rai.	12	175	14.6	41t	2
Russell, Derek, Den.	12	140	11.7	22	0
Cash, Keith, K.C.	12	113	9.4	19	2
Bernstine, Rod, S.D.	12	86	7.2	16	0
Heller, Ron, Sea.	12	85	7.1	17	0
Thomas, Robb, Sea.	11	136	12.4	31	0
Riggs, Jim, Cin.	11	70	6.4	17	0
Russell, Leonard, N.E.	11	24	2.2	12	0
Graddy, Sam, Rai.	10	205	20.5	48	1
Johnson, Reggie, Den.	10	139	13.9	48	1
Edmunds, Ferrell, Mia.	10	91	9.1	15	1
Green, Gaston, Den.	10	79	7.9	33	0
Davenport, Charles, Pit.	9	136	15.1	31	0
Fernandez, Mervyn, Rai.	9	121	13.4	21	0
Word, Barry, K.C.	9	80	8.9	22	0
Hayes, Jonathan, K.C.	9	77	8.6	21	2
Butts, Marion, S.D.	9	73	8.1	22	0
Green, Paul, Sea.	9	67	7.4	15	1
Thomas, Doug, Sea.	8	85	10.6	19	0
Lamb, Brad, Buf.	7	139	19.9	53	0
Gardner, Carwell, Buf.	7	67	9.6	17	0
Chaffey, Pat, NY-J	7	56	8.0	14	0
Kay, Clarence, Den.	7	56	8.0	15	0
Turner, Kevin, N.E.	7	52	7.4	19t	2
Thomas, Blair, NY-J	7	49	7.0	10	0
Fenner, Derrick, Cin.	7	41	5.9	15	1
Ball, Eric, Cin.	6	66	11.0	35t	2
Jorden, Tim, Pit.	6	28	4.7	8	2
Daniels, David, Sea.	5	99	19.8	57	0
Anders, Kimble, K.C.	5	65	13.0	28	0
Smith, Rico, Cle.	5	64	12.8	21	0
Bieniemy, Eric, S.D.	5	49	9.8	25	0
Clark, Ken, Ind.	5	46	9.2	17	0
Saxon, James, Mia.	5	41	8.2	14	0
Williams, Harvey, K.C.	5	24	4.8	12	0
Galbraith, Scott, Cle.	4	63	15.8	28	1
Young, Duane, S.D.	4	45	11.3	14	0
Bell, Nick, Rai.	4	40	10.0	16	0
Awalt, Robert, Buf.	4	34	8.5	10	0
Baxter, Brad, NY-J	4	32	8.0	12	0
Brown, A.B., NY-J	4	30	7.5	20	0
Lewis, Greg, Den.	4	30	7.5	16	0
Stanley, Walter, N.E.	3	63	21.0	36	0
Clark, Robert, Mia.	3	59	19.7	45	0
Williams, Mike, Mia.	3	43	14.3	18	0
Didio, Mark, Pit.	3	39	13.0	18	0
Verdin, Clarence, Ind.	3	37	12.3	21	0
Stegall, Milt, Cin.	3	35	11.7	13	1
Collins, Shawn, Cle.	3	31	10.3	11	0
Junkin, Trey, Sea.	3	25	8.3	13	1
Baty, Greg, Mia.	3	19	6.3	12	1
Jones, Mike, Sea.	3	18	6.0	7	0
Jones, Victor, Den.	3	17	5.7	16	0
Carthon, Maurice, Ind.	3	10	3.3	6	0
Baldwin, Randy, Cle.	2	30	15.0	20	0
Jones, David, Rai.	2	29	14.5	25	0
Holland, Jamie, Cle.	2	27	13.5	16	0
Edwards, Al, Buf.	2	25	12.5	20	0

	No	Yards	Avg	Long	TD
Tasker, Steve, Buf.	2	24	12.0	17	0
Fuller, Eddie, Buf.	2	17	8.5	17	0
Perryman, Bob, Den.	2	15	7.5	9	0
Thomason, Jeff, Cin.	2	14	7.0	10	0
Hector, Johnny, NY-J	2	13	6.5	9	0
Mayes, Rueben, Sea.	2	13	6.5	7	0
McCallum, Napoleon, Rai.	2	13	6.5	7	0
Whisenhunt, Ken, NY-J	2	11	5.5	10	0
Coleman, Pat, Hou.	2	10	5.0	6	0
Wolfley, Ron, Cle.	2	8	4.0	6	1
Jones, Bill, K.C.	2	6	3.0	5	0
Frerotte, Mitch, Buf.	2	4	2.0	2t	2
Brooks, James, Cle.	2	-1	-0.5	4	0
Williams, Warren, Pit.	1	44	44.0	44	0
Sadowski, Troy, NY-J	1	20	20.0	20	0
Prior, Mike, Ind.	1	17	17.0	17	0
Claiborne, Robert, S.D.	1	15	15.0	15	0
Young, Mike, Den.	1	11	11.0	11	0
McCardell, Keenan, Cle.	1	8	8.0	8	0
Dyal, Mike, K.C.	1	7	7.0	7	0
Brown, Gary, Hou.	1	5	5.0	5	0
Okoye, Christian, K.C.	1	5	5.0	5	0
Schultz, William, Ind.	1	3	3.0	3t	1
Thigpen, Yancey, Pit.	1	2	2.0	2	0
Fina, John, Buf.	1	1	1.0	1t	1
Jones, James, Cle.	1	1	1.0	1t	1
Hodson, Tom, N.E.	1	-6	-6.0	-6	0
Widell, Doug, Den.	1	-7	-7.0	-7	0

NFC - INDIVIDUAL RECEIVERS

	No	Yards	Avg	Long	TD
Sharpe, Sterling, G.B.	108	1461	13.5	76t	13
Rison, Andre, Atl.	93	1119	12.0	71t	11
Rice, Jerry, S.F.	84	1201	14.3	80t	10
Irvin, Michael, Dal.	78	1396	17.9	87t	7
Pritchard, Mike, Atl.	77	827	10.7	38t	5
Perriman, Brett, Det.	69	810	11.7	40t	4
Martin, Eric, N.O.	68	1041	15.3	52t	5
Novacek, Jay, Dal.	68	630	9.3	34	6
Barnett, Fred, Phi.	67	1083	16.2	71t	6
Clark, Gary, Was.	64	912	14.3	47	5
Dawsey, Lawrence, T.B.	60	776	12.9	41	1
Proehl, Ricky, Pho.	60	744	12.4	63t	3
Hill, Drew, Atl.	60	623	10.4	43	3
Smith, Emmitt, Dal.	59	335	5.7	26t	1
Hill, Randal, Pho.	58	861	14.8	49	3
Carrier, Mark, T.B.	56	692	12.4	40	4
Byars, Keith, Phi.	56	502	9.0	46	2
Harris, Jackie, G.B.	55	595	10.8	40	2
Davis, Wendell, Chi.	54	734	13.6	40	2
Carter, Cris, Min.	53	681	12.8	44	6
Gary, Cleveland, Rams	52	293	5.6	22	3
Moore, Herman, Det.	51	966	18.9	77t	4
Sanders, Ricky, Was.	51	707	13.9	62t	3
Centers, Larry, Pho.	50	417	8.3	26	2
McCaffrey, Ed, NY-G	49	610	12.4	44	5

	No	Yards	Avg	Long	TD
Allen, Terry, Min.	49	478	9.8	36t	2
Sydney, Harry, G.B.	49	384	7.8	20	1
Haynes, Michael, Atl.	48	808	16.8	89t	10
Hilliard, Dalton, N.O.	48	465	9.7	41	4
Ellard, Henry, Rams	47	727	15.5	33t	3
Workman, Vince, G.B.	47	290	6.2	21	0
Waddle, Tom, Chi.	46	674	14.7	68t	4
Monk, Art, Was.	46	644	14.0	49t	3
Jones, Brent, S.F.	45	628	14.0	43	4
Rathman, Tom, S.F.	44	343	7.8	27t	4
Watters, Ricky, S.F.	43	405	9.4	35	2
Williams, Calvin, Phi.	42	598	14.2	49t	7
Anderson, Neal, Chi.	42	399	9.5	30t	6
Carter, Anthony, Min.	41	580	14.1	54	2
Hall, Ron, T.B.	39	351	9.0	32	4
Byner, Earnest, Was.	39	338	8.7	29	1
Anderson, Willie, Rams	38	657	17.3	51	7
Sherrard, Mike, S.F.	38	607	16.0	56	0
Jones, Ernie, Pho.	38	559	14.7	72t	4
Walker, Herschel, Phi.	38	278	7.3	41	2
Meggett, Dave, NY-G	38	229	6.0	24	2
Harper, Alvin, Dal.	35	562	16.1	52	4
Muster, Brad, Chi.	34	389	11.4	44t	2
Price, Jim, Rams	34	324	9.5	25	2
Anderson, Gary, T.B.	34	284	8.4	34	0
Green, Willie, Det.	33	586	17.8	73t	5
Bailey, Johnny, Pho.	33	331	10.0	34	1
Martin, Kelvin, Dal.	32	359	11.2	27	3
Ervins, Ricky, Was.	32	252	7.9	19	0
Johnston, Daryl, Dal.	32	249	7.8	18	2
Early, Quinn, N.O.	30	566	18.9	59t	5
Chadwick, Jeff, Rams	29	362	12.5	27t	3
Sanders, Barry, Det.	29	225	7.8	48	1
Jordan, Steve, Min.	28	394	14.1	60t	2
Hampton, Rodney, NY-G	28	215	7.7	31	0
Ingram, Mark, NY-G	27	408	15.1	34	1
Cross, Howard, NY-G	27	357	13.2	29	2
Calloway, Chris, NY-G	27	335	12.4	28	1
McDowell, Anthony, T.B.	27	258	9.6	51t	2
Taylor, John, S.F.	25	428	17.1	54t	3
Small, Torrance, N.O.	23	278	12.1	33	3
Jennings, Keith, Chi.	23	264	11.5	23	1
Orr, Terry, Was.	22	356	16.2	58	3
Jones, Hassan, Min.	22	308	14.0	43t	4
Craig, Roger, Min.	22	164	7.5	22	0
Johnson, Joe, Min.	21	211	10.0	37	1
Cobb, Reggie, T.B.	21	156	7.4	27	0
Hawkins, Courtney, T.B.	20	336	16.8	49	2
Carter, Pat, Rams	20	232	11.6	25	3
Lee, Amp, S.F.	20	102	5.1	17	2
Heyward, Craig, N.O.	19	159	8.4	21	0
Carroll, Wesley, N.O.	18	292	16.2	72t	2
Lang, David, Rams	18	283	15.7	67t	1
Cox, Aaron, Rams	18	261	14.5	26	0
Sherman, Heath, Phi.	18	219	12.2	75t	1
Lewis, Darren, Chi.	18	175	9.7	30	0
Delpino, Robert, Rams	18	139	7.7	12t	1
Baker, Stephen, NY-G	17	333	19.6	46	2
Beach, Sanjay, G.B.	17	122	7.2	20	1

	No	Yards	Avg	Long	TD
Drewrey, Willie, T.B.	16	237	14.8	32	2
Farr, Mike, Det.	15	115	7.7	14	0
Morgan, Anthony, Chi.	14	323	23.1	83t	2
Edwards, Anthony, Pho.	14	147	10.5	25t	1
Jones, Tony, Atl.	14	138	9.9	24	1
Johnson, Johnny, Pho.	14	103	7.4	26	0
Lewis, Ronald, G.B.	13	152	11.7	27	0
Sikahema, Vai, Phi.	13	142	10.9	22	0
Thompson, Darrell, G.B.	13	129	9.9	43	1
Bennett, Edgar, G.B.	13	93	7.2	22	0
Rolle, Butch, Pho.	13	64	4.9	12	0
Brenner, Hoby, N.O.	12	161	13.4	23	0
Brooks, Robert, G.B.	12	126	10.5	18	1
Gentry, Dennis, Chi.	12	114	9.5	18	0
Jones, Keith, Atl.	12	94	7.8	15	0
Broussard, Steve, Atl.	11	96	8.7	24	1
Bunch, Jarrod, NY-G	11	50	4.5	13	1
Turner, Odessa, S.F.	9	200	22.2	57	2
Wainright, Frank, N.O.	9	143	15.9	29	0
Matthews, Aubrey, Det.	9	137	15.2	24	0
Jennings, Stanford, T.B.	9	69	7.7	20t	1
Dunbar, Vaughn, N.O.	9	62	6.9	13	0
Campbell, Jeff, Det.	8	155	19.4	78t	1
Green, Roy, Phi.	8	105	13.1	21	0
Beach, Pat, Phi.	8	75	9.4	16	2
Armstrong, Tyji, T.B.	7	138	19.7	81t	1
Green, Mark, Chi.	7	85	12.1	43	0
Williams, Jamie, S.F.	7	76	10.9	21	1
Brown, Ivory Lee, Pho.	7	54	7.7	18	0
Middleton, Ron, Was.	7	50	7.1	16	0
Reed, Jake, Mln.	6	142	23.7	51	0
McGee, Buford, G.B.	6	60	10.0	15	0
Harry, Emile, K.C.-Rams	6	58	9.7	13	0
Thomas, George, Atl.	6	54	9.0	18	0
Johnson, Jimmy, Det.	6	34	5.7	9	0
Reeves, Walter, Pho.	6	28	4.7	12	0
Tice, Mike, Min.	5	65	13.0	34t	1
Henderson, Keith, S.F.-Min.	5	64	12.8	23	0
Wright, Eric, Chi.	5	56	11.2	24	0
Blackwell, Kelly, Chi.	5	54	10.8	18	0
Turner, Floyd, N.O.	5	43	8.6	18	0
Turner, Vernon, Rams	5	42	8.4	16	0
Highsmith, Alonzo, T.B.	5	28	5.6	11	0
Thompson, Anthony, Rams	5	11	2.2	7	0
McNeal, Travis, Rams	4	79	19.8	38	0
Barrett, Reggie, Det.	4	67	16.8	24	1
Novoselsky, Brent, Min.	4	63	15.8	34	0
Morris, Ron, Chi.	4	44	11.0	26	0
Brown, Derek, NY-G.	4	31	7.8	9	0
West, Ed, G.B.	4	30	7.5	10	0
Phillips, Jason, Atl.	4	26	6.5	8	1
Warren, Don, Was.	4	25	6.3	11	0
Stowers, Tommie, N.O.	4	23	5.8	8	0
Sanders, Deion, Atl.	3	45	15.0	37t	1
Smith, Joey, NY-G.	3	45	15.0	22	0
Dixon, Floyd, Phi.	3	36	12.0	19	0
Roberts, Alfredo, Dal.	3	36	12.0	18	0
Mitchell, Brian, Was.	3	30	10.0	17	0
Hinnant, Mike, Det.	3	28	9.3	13	0

	No	Yards	Avg	Long	TD
Milling, James, Atl.	3	25	8.3	15	0
Newman, Pat, N.O.	3	21	7.0	8	0
Howard, Desmond, Was.	3	20	6.7	8	0
Agee, Tommie, Dal.	3	18	6.0	8	0
Blount, Eric, Pho.	3	18	6.0	18	0
Richards, Curvin, Dal.	3	8	2.7	6	0
Taylor, Kitrick, G.B.	2	63	31.5	35t	1
Pegram, Erric, Atl.	2	25	12.5	19	0
Logan, Marc, S.F.	2	17	8.5	13	0
Johnson, Maurice, Phi.	2	16	8.0	13	0
Stradford, Troy, Det.	2	15	7.5	12	0
Smith, Tony, Atl.	2	14	7.0	8	0
McLemore, Thomas, Det.	2	12	6.0	6	0
Tennell, Derek, Min.	2	12	6.0	8	0
Carter, Dexter, S.F.	1	43	43.0	43t	1
Barber, Mike, T.B.	1	32	32.0	32	0
McAfee, Fred, N.O.	1	16	16.0	16	0
Wagner, Barry, Chi.	1	16	16.0	16	0
Tillman, Lewis, NY-G	1	15	15.0	15	0
Ware, Derek, Pho.	1	13	13.0	13	0
Fullington, Darrell, T.B.	1	12	12.0	12	0
Parker, Jeff, T.B.	1	12	12.0	12	0
Moore, Dave, T.B.	1	10	10.0	10	0
Royster, Mazio, T.B.	1	8	8.0	8	0
Kozlowski, Glen, Chi.	1	7	7.0	7	0
Dowdell, Marcus, N.O.	1	6	6.0	6	0
Green, Robert, Was.	1	5	5.0	5	0
Jackson, John, Pho.	1	5	5.0	5t	1
Gesek, John, Dal.	1	4	4.0	4	0
Whitaker, Danta, Min.	1	4	4.0	4	0
Lipps, Louis, N.O.	1	1	1.0	1	0
Hinton, Chris, Atl.	1	-2	-2.0	-2	0
Favre, Brett, G.B.	1	-7	-7.0	-7	0
Cooper, Richard, N.O.	0	20	—	20	0

INTERCEPTIONS

INTERCEPTIONS
AFC:	8	Henry Jones, Buffalo
NFC:	8	Audray McMillian, Minnesota

INTERCEPTIONS, GAME
AFC:	3	Louis Oliver, Miami at Buffalo, October 4 - TD
		Eugene Robinson, Seattle at Pittsburgh, December 6
		Mark Kelso, Buffalo vs. Denver, December 12
		Mike Prior, Indianapolis vs. Phoenix, December 20
NFC:	3	Todd Scott, Minnesota at Cincinnati, September 27
		Audray McMillian, Minnesota vs. Cleveland, November 22 - TD
		Brad Edwards, Washington vs. Phoenix, November 29 - TD
		Vencie Glenn, Minnesota vs. Green Bay, December 27

YARDS
AFC:	263	Henry Jones, Buffalo
NFC:	157	Brad Edwards, Washington
		Audray McMillian, Minnesota

LONGEST
AFC:	103	Louis Oliver, Miami at Buffalo, October 4 - TD
NFC:	84	Jack Del Rio, Minnesota at Chicago, November 2 - TD

TOUCHDOWNS
NFC:	3	Robert Massey, Phoenix
AFC:	2	Henry Jones, Buffalo
		Charles Mincy, Kansas City

TEAM LEADERS, INTERCEPTIONS

AFC:
BUFFALO	8	Henry Jones
CINCINNATI	4	Darryl Williams
CLEVELAND	3	Vince Newsome
DENVER	4	Wymon Henderson, Dennis Smith
HOUSTON	6	Jerry Gray
INDIANAPOLIS	6	Mike Prior
KANSAS CITY	7	Dale Carter
L.A. RAIDERS	4	Terry McDaniel
MIAMI	5	Louis Oliver
NEW ENGLAND	3	Jerome Henderson, Maurice Hurst
N.Y. JETS	6	Mike Brim, Brian Washington
PITTSBURGH	6	Darren Perry
SAN DIEGO	6	Darren Carrington
SEATTLE	7	Eugene Robinson

NFC:
ATLANTA	3	Deion Sanders
CHICAGO	7	Donnell Woolford
DALLAS	3	Kenneth Gant, James Washington
DETROIT	4	Ray Crockett, Mel Jenkins, Kevin Scott, William White
GREEN BAY	4	Chuck Cecil
L.A. RAMS	4	Darryl Henley, Anthony Newman
MINNESOTA	8	Audray McMillian
NEW ORLEANS	8	Toi Cook
N.Y. GIANTS	4	Greg Jackson
PHILADELPHIA	4	Eric Allen, Byron Evans, Seth Joyner
PHOENIX	5	Robert Massey
SAN FRANCISCO	5	Don Griffin
TAMPA BAY	3	Marty Carter, Darrell Fullington, Milton Mack
WASHINGTON	6	Brad Edwards

TEAM CHAMPION
NFC:	28	Minnesota
AFC:	25	San Diego

TOP TEN INTERCEPTORS

	No	Yards	Avg	Long	TD
Jones, Henry, Buf.	8	263	32.9	82t	2
McMillian, Audray, Min.	8	157	19.6	51t	2
Carter, Dale, K.C.	7	65	9.3	36t	1
Kelso, Mark, Buf.	7	21	3.0	13	0
Robinson, Eugene, Sea.	7	126	18.0	49	0
Woolford, Donnell, Chi.	7	67	9.6	32	0
Brim, Michael, NY-J	6	139	23.2	77t	1
Carrington, Darren, S.D.	6	152	25.3	69	1
Cook, Toi, N.O.	6	90	15.0	48t	1
Edwards, Brad, Was.	6	157	26.2	53t	1
Gray, Jerry, Hou.	6	24	4.0	22	0
Perry, Darren, Pit.	6	69	11.5	34	0
Prior, Mike, Ind.	6	44	7.3	19	0
Washington, Brian, NY-J	6	59	9.8	23t	1

AFC - INDIVIDUAL INTERCEPTORS

	No	Yards	Avg	Long	TD
Jones, Henry, Buf.	8	263	32.9	82t	2
Robinson, Eugene, Sea.	7	126	18.0	49	0
Carter, Dale, K.C.	7	65	9.3	36t	1
Kelso, Mark, Buf.	7	21	3.0	13	0
Carrington, Darren, S.D.	6	152	25.3	69	1
Brim, Michael, NY-J	6	139	23.2	77t	1
Perry, Darren, Pit.	6	69	11.5	34	0
Washington, Brian, NY-J	6	59	9.8	23t	1
Prior, Mike, Ind.	6	44	7.3	19	0
Gray, Jerry, Hou.	6	24	4.0	22	0
Oliver, Louis, Mia.	5	200	40.0	103t	1
Johnson, David, Pit.	5	67	13.4	35	0
Odomes, Nate, Buf.	5	19	3.8	10	0
McDaniel, Terry, Rai.	4	180	45.0	67	0
Mincy, Charles, K.C.	4	128	32.0	39	2
Brown, J.B., Mia.	4	119	29.8	48	1
Woodson, Rod, Pit.	4	90	22.5	57	0
Byrd, Gill, S.D.	4	88	22.0	44	0
Henderson, Wymon, Den.	4	79	19.8	46t	1
Williams, Darryl, Cin.	4	65	16.3	30	0
Frank, Donald, S.D.	4	37	9.3	33	0
Thompson, Bennie, K.C.	4	26	6.5	25	0
Smith, Dennis, Den.	4	10	2.5	8	0
Anderson, Eddie, Rai.	3	131	43.7	102t	1
Francis, James, Cin.	3	108	36.0	66t	1
Griffin, Larry, Pit.	3	98	32.7	65t	1
Harper, Dwayne, Sea.	3	74	24.7	41	0
Jackson, Vestee, Mia.	3	63	21.0	30t	1
Newsome, Vince, Cle.	3	55	18.3	29	0
McDowell, Bubba, Hou.	3	52	17.3	26t	1
Henderson, Jerome, N.E.	3	43	14.3	34	0
Dishman, Cris, Hou.	3	34	11.3	17	0
Hurst, Maurice, N.E.	3	29	9.7	27	0

t = Touchdown
Leader based on interceptions

	No	Yards	Avg	Long	TD
Belser, Jason, Ind.	3	27	9.0	21	0
Richard, Stanley, S.D.	3	26	8.7	20	0
Walls, Everson, NY-G-Cle.	3	26	8.7	24	0
Jackson, Steve, Hou.	3	18	6.0	18	0
Simien, Tracy, K.C.	3	18	6.0	10	0
Fulcher, David, Cin.	3	0	0.0	0	0
Brandon, David, Cle.	2	123	61.5	92t	1
Goode, Chris, Ind.	2	93	46.5	47	0
Braxton, Tyrone, Den.	2	54	27.0	40	0
Pool, David, N.E.	2	54	27.0	41t	1
Seau, Junior, S.D.	2	51	25.5	29	0
Vincent, Troy, Mia.	2	47	23.5	32	0
Plummer, Gary, S.D.	2	40	20.0	38	0
Davis, Brian, Sea.	2	36	18.0	36	0
Williams, Jarvis, Mia.	2	29	14.5	25	0
Robbins, Randy, N.E.	2	27	13.5	20	0
Stargell, Tony, Ind.	2	26	13.0	15	0
Atwater, Steve, Den.	2	22	11.0	22	0
Washington, Lionel, Rai.	2	21	10.5	18	0
Hasty, James, NY-J	2	18	9.0	18	0
Turner, Marcus, NY-J	2	15	7.5	14	0
Williams, James, Buf.	2	15	7.5	15	0
Jones, Rod, Cin.	2	14	7.0	14	0
Little, David, Pit.	2	6	3.0	6	0
Minnifield, Frank, Cle.	2	6	3.0	5	0
Cain, Joseph, Sea.	2	3	1.5	3	0
Blaylock, Anthony, S.D.	2	0	0.0	0	0
Hunter, Patrick, Sea.	2	0	0.0	0	0
Ross, Kevin, K.C.	1	99	99.0	99t	1
Emtman, Steve, Ind.	1	90	90.0	90t	1
Singleton, Chris, N.E.	1	82	82.0	82t	1
Blackmon, Robert, Sea.	1	69	69.0	69	0
Brown, Vincent, N.E.	1	49	49.0	49t	1
Marts, Lonnie, K.C.	1	36	36.0	36t	1
Lloyd, Greg, Pit.	1	35	35.0	35	0
Robertson, Marcus, Hou.	1	27	27.0	27	0
Lang, Le-Lo, Den.	1	26	26.0	26	0
Smith, Al, Hou.	1	26	26.0	26	0
Smith, Neil, K.C.	1	22	22.0	22t	1
Houston, Bobby, NY-J	1	20	20.0	20t	1
Brooks, Michael, Den.	1	17	17.0	17	0
Kors, R.J., NY-J	1	16	16.0	16	0
Bickett, Duane, Ind.	1	14	14.0	14	0
Dodge, Dedrick, Sea.	1	13	13.0	13	0
Wheeler, Leonard, Cin.	1	12	12.0	12	0
Vanhorse, Sean, S.D.	1	11	11.0	11	0
Terry, Doug, K.C.	1	9	9.0	9	0
Conlan, Shane, Buf.	1	7	7.0	7	0
Dorn, Torin, Rai.	1	7	7.0	7	0
Matthews, Clay, Cle.	1	6	6.0	6	0
Turner, Eric, Cle.	1	6	6.0	6	0
Herrod, Jeff, Ind.	1	4	4.0	4	0
Williams, Jerrol, Pit.	1	4	4.0	4	0
Banks, Chip, Ind.	1	3	3.0	3	0
Bussey, Barney, Cin.	1	3	3.0	3	0
Mitz, Alonzo, Cin.	1	3	3.0	3	0
Wooden, Terry, Sea.	1	3	3.0	3	0
Dimry, Charles, Den.	1	2	2.0	2	0
Baylor, John, Ind.	1	1	1.0	1	0

	No	Yards	Avg	Long	TD
Clifton, Kyle, NY-J	1	1	1.0	1	0
Howard, David, N.E.	1	1	1.0	1	0
Lewis, Mo, NY-J	1	1	1.0	1	0
Alexander, Bruce, Mia.	1	0	0.0	0	0
Bayless, Martin, K.C.	1	0	0.0	0	0
Cox, Bryan, Mia.	1	0	0.0	0	0
Daniel, Eugene, Ind.	1	0	0.0	0	0
Dumas, Mike, Hou.	1	0	0.0	0	0
Fields, Floyd, S.D.	1	0	0.0	0	0
Graf, Rick, Hou.	1	0	0.0	0	0
Johnson, Mike, Cle.	1	0	0.0	0	0
Jones, Sean, Hou.	1	0	0.0	0	0
Land, Dan, Rai.	1	0	0.0	0	0
Lewis, Albert, K.C.	1	0	0.0	0	0
Lott, Ronnie, Rai.	1	0	0.0	0	0
McDonald, Ricardo, Cin.	1	0	0.0	0	0
Price, Dennis, NY-J	1	0	0.0	0	0
Radecic, Scott, Ind.	1	0	0.0	0	0
Smith, Rod, N.E.	1	0	0.0	0	0
Taylor, Terry, Cle.	1	0	0.0	0	0
Tuatagaloa, Natu, Sea.	1	0	0.0	0	0
Shelton, Richard, Pit.	0	15	—	15	0

AMERICAN FOOTBALL CONFERENCE - INTERCEPTIONS

	No	Yards	Avg	Long	TD
San Diego	25	405	16.2	69	1
Kansas City	24	403	16.8	99t	6
Buffalo	23	325	14.1	82t	2
Pittsburgh	22	384	17.5	65t	1
N.Y. Jets	21	269	12.8	77t	3
Indianapolis	20	302	15.1	90t	1
Houston	20	181	9.1	27	1
Seattle	20	324	16.2	69	0
Miami	18	458	25.4	103t	3
Cincinnati	16	205	12.8	66t	1
Denver	15	210	14.0	46t	1
New England	14	285	20.4	82t	3
Cleveland	13	222	17.1	92t	1
L.A. Raiders	12	339	28.3	102t	1
AFC Total	263	4312	16.4	103t	25
AFC Average	18.8	308.0	16.4	—	1.8

NFC - INDIVIDUAL INTERCEPTORS

	No	Yards	Avg	Long	TD
McMillian, Audray, Min.	8	157	19.6	51t	2
Woolford, Donnell, Chi.	7	67	9.6	32	0
Edwards, Brad, Was.	6	157	26.2	53t	1
Cook, Toi, N.O.	6	90	15.0	48t	1
Massey, Robert, Pho.	5	147	29.4	46t	3
Scott, Todd, Min.	5	79	15.8	35t	1
Glenn, Vencie, Min.	5	65	13.0	39	0
Griffin, Don, S.F.	5	4	0.8	2	0
Joyner, Seth, Phi.	4	88	22.0	43t	2
Evans, Byron, Phi.	4	76	19.0	43	0
Jackson, Greg, NY-G	4	71	17.8	36	0
White, William, Det.	4	54	13.5	28	0
Cecil, Chuck, G.B.	4	52	13.0	29	0
Crockett, Ray, Det.	4	50	12.5	35	0
Allen, Eric, Phi.	4	49	12.3	36	0
Henley, Darryl, Rams	4	41	10.3	25	0
Scott, Kevin, Det.	4	35	8.8	26	0
Jenkins, Mel, Det.	4	34	8.5	14	0
Newman, Anthony, Rams	4	33	8.3	17	0
Sanders, Deion, Atl.	3	105	35.0	55	0
Lyght, Todd, Rams	3	80	26.7	39	0
Bailey, Robert, Rams	3	61	20.3	37	1
Mayhew, Martin, Was.	3	58	19.3	33	0
Blades, Bennie, Det.	3	56	18.7	34	0
Davis, Eric, S.F.	3	52	17.3	37	0
Gouveia, Kurt, Was.	3	43	14.3	28	0
Johnson, A.J., Was.	3	38	12.7	29	0
Zordich, Mike, Pho.	3	37	12.3	23	0
Buckley, Terrell, G.B.	3	33	11.0	33t	1
Washington, James, Dal.	3	31	10.3	16	0
Holland, Johnny, G.B.	3	27	9.0	22	0
Fullington, Darrell, T.B.	3	25	8.3	16	0
Williams, Aeneas, Pho.	3	25	8.3	23	0
Parker, Anthony, Min.	3	23	7.7	23	0
Booty, John, Phi.	3	22	7.3	22	0
Gant, Kenneth, Dal.	3	19	6.3	11	0
Hopkins, Wes, Phi.	3	6	2.0	4	0
Carter, Marty, T.B.	3	1	0.3	1	0
Atkins, Gene, N.O.	3	0	0.0	0	0
Mack, Milton, T.B.	3	0	0.0	0	0
Pollard, Darryl, T.B.	2	99	49.5	75	0
Del Rio, Jack, Min.	2	92	46.0	84t	1
Thomas, Broderick, T.B.	2	81	40.5	56t	1
Jones, Reggie, N.O.	2	71	35.5	71t	1
Clark, Vinnie, G.B.	2	70	35.0	43	0
Thompson, Reyna, NY-G	2	69	34.5	69t	1
Buck, Vince, N.O.	2	51	25.5	34t	1
White, Leon, Rams	2	49	24.5	40	0
Stinson, Lemuel, Chi.	2	46	23.0	46	0
Johnson, Pepper, NY-G	2	42	21.0	38	0
Mitchell, Roland, G.B.	2	40	20.0	35	0
Gayle, Shaun, Chi.	2	39	19.5	30	0
McDonald, Tim, Pho.	2	35	17.5	20	0
Hall, Dana, S.F.	2	34	17.0	34	0
Everett, Thomas, Dal.	2	28	14.0	17	0
Davis, Dexter, Pho.	2	27	13.5	27	0
White, Sheldon, Det.	2	26	13.0	20	0

	No	Yards	Avg	Long	TD
King, Joe, T.B.	2	24	12.0	24	0
Lee, Carl, Min.	2	20	10.0	20	0
Marshall, Wilber, Was.	2	20	10.0	20t	1
Taylor, Keith, N.O.	2	20	10.0	20	0
Mays, Alvoid, Was.	2	18	9.0	13	0
Pickens, Bruce, Atl.	2	16	8.0	16	0
Horton, Ray, Dal.	2	15	7.5	15t	1
Maxie, Brett, N.O.	2	12	6.0	8	0
Holt, Issiac, Dal.	2	11	5.5	8	0
Miller, Corey, NY-G	2	10	5.0	10	0
Smith, Kevin, Dal.	2	10	5.0	7	0
Hanks, Merton, S.F.	2	5	2.5	4	0
Thomas, William, Phi.	2	4	2.0	4	0
Williams, Jimmy, T.B.	2	4	2.0	3	0
Case, Scott, Atl.	2	0	0.0	0	0
Reynolds, Ricky, T.B.	2	0	0.0	0	0
Bowles, Todd, Was.	1	65	65.0	65	0
Collins, Andre, Was.	1	59	59.0	59	0
Johnson, John, S.F.	1	56	56.0	56t	1
Miano, Rich, Phi.	1	39	39.0	39	0
Brown, Larry, Dal.	1	30	30.0	30	0
Doleman, Chris, Min.	1	27	27.0	27t	1
Jones, Jock, Pho.	1	27	27.0	27	0
Waters, Andre, Phi.	1	23	23.0	23	0
Morrissey, Jim, Chi.	1	22	22.0	22	0
Wright, Felix, Min.	1	20	20.0	20	0
Jenkins, Carlos, Min.	1	19	19.0	19t	1
Roberts, Larry, S.F.	1	19	19.0	19	0
Kelm, Larry, Rams	1	16	16.0	16	0
Green, Darrell, Was.	1	15	15.0	15	0
Myles, Godfrey, Dal.	1	13	13.0	13	0
Solomon, Jesse, Atl.	1	13	13.0	13	0
Johnson, Sidney, Was.	1	12	12.0	12	0
Mills, Sam, N.O.	1	10	10.0	10	0
Paul, Markus, Chi.	1	10	10.0	10	0
Singletary, Mike, Chi.	1	4	4.0	4	0
Phifer, Roman, Rams	1	3	3.0	3	0
DeLong, Keith, S.F.	1	2	2.0	2	0
Harper, Alvin, Dal.	1	1	1.0	1	0
Tuggle, Jessie, Atl.	1	1	1.0	1	0
Brown, Dennis, S.F.	1	0	0.0	0	0
Butler, Leroy, G.B.	1	0	0.0	0	0
Collins, Mark, NY-G	1	0	0.0	0	0
Lewis, Garry, T.B.	1	0	0.0	0	0
McKyer, Tim, Atl.	1	0	0.0	0	0
McMillian, Mark, Phi.	1	0	0.0	0	0
Mitchell, Brian, Atl.	1	0	0.0	0	0
Smith, Otis, Phi.	1	0	0.0	0	0
Sparks, Phillipi, NY-G	1	0	0.0	0	0
Whitmore, David, S.F.	1	0	0.0	0	0
Williams, Perry, NY-G	1	0	0.0	0	0

NATIONAL FOOTBALL CONFERENCE - INTERCEPTIONS

	No	Yards	Avg	Long	TD
Minnesota	28	502	17.9	84t	6
Philadelphia	24	307	12.8	49	2
Washington	23	485	21.1	65	2
Detroit	21	255	12.1	35	0
Tampa Bay	20	234	11.7	75	1
New Orleans	18	254	14.1	71t	3
L.A. Rams	18	283	15.7	40	1
San Francisco	17	172	10.1	56t	1
Dallas	17	158	9.3	30	1
Phoenix	16	298	18.6	46t	3
Green Bay	15	222	14.8	43	1
N.Y. Giants	14	192	13.7	69t	1
Chicago	14	188	13.4	46	0
Atlanta	11	135	12.3	55	0
NFC Total	256	3685	14.4	84t	22
NFC Average	18.3	263.2	14 4	—	1.6
League Total	519	7997	—	103t	47
League Average	18.5	285.6	15.4	—	1.7

Vikings' Audray McMillian tied for most interceptions (8).

PUNT RETURNS

YARDS PER RETURN
NFC:	13.2	Johnny Bailey, Phoenix
AFC:	11.4	Rod Woodson, Pittsburgh

YARDS
NFC:	532	Kelvin Martin, Dallas
AFC:	429	Eric Metcalf, Cleveland

YARDS, GAME
NFC:	111	Vai Sikahema, Philadelphia at Giants, November 22 (4 returns - TD))
AFC:	100	Carl Pickens, Cincinnati at Green Bay, September 20 (2 returns - TD)
		Dale Carter, Kansas City at Seattle, November 22 (4 returns - TD)
		Eric Metcalf, Cleveland vs. Chicago, November 29 (5 returns - TD)

LONGEST
AFC:	95	Carl Pickens, Cincinnati at Green Bay, September 20 - TD
NFC:	87	Vai Sikahema, Philadelphia at Giants, November 22 -TD

RETURNS
AFC:	44	Eric Metcalf, Cleveland
NFC:	42	Kelvin Martin, Dallas

RETURNS, GAME
NFC:	8	Vai Sikahema, Philadelphia at Seattle, December 13 (57 yards) (OT)
AFC:	7	Chris Hale, Buffalo vs. Indianapolis, September 20 (83 yards)
		Eric Metcalf, Cleveland at Houston, November 8 (87 yards)

FAIR CATCHES
AFC:	25	Chris Warren, Seattle
NFC:	18	Kelvin Martin, Dallas

TOUCHDOWNS
AFC:	2	Dale Carter, Kansas City
		Clarence Verdin, Indianapolis
NFC:	2	Todd Kinchen, Rams
		Kelvin Martin, Dallas

TEAM CHAMPION
NFC:	12.5	Dallas
AFC:	11.9	Cincinnati

TOP TEN PUNT RETURNERS

	No	FC	Yards	Avg	Long	TD
Bailey, Johnny, Pho.	20	8	263	13.2	65	0
Martin, Kelvin, Dal.	42	18	532	12.7	79t	2
Sikahema, Vai, Phi.	40	10	503	12.6	87t	1
Woodson, Rod, Pit.	32	13	364	11.4	80t	1
Verdin, Clarence, Ind.	24	12	268	11.2	84t	2
Marshall, Arthur, Den.	33	16	349	10.6	47	0
Carter, Dale, K.C.	38	6	398	10.5	86t	2
Brown, Tim, Rai.	37	19	383	10.4	40	0
Parker, Anthony, Min.	33	17	336	10.2	42	0
Buckley, Terrell, G.B.	21	5	211	10.0	58t	1

AFC - INDIVIDUAL PUNT RETURNERS

	No	FC	Yards	Avg	Long	TD
Woodson, Rod, Pit.	32	13	364	11.4	80t	1
Verdin, Clarence, Ind.	24	12	268	11.2	84t	2
Marshall, Arthur, Den.	33	16	349	10.6	47	0
Carter, Dale, K.C.	38	6	398	10.5	86t	2
Brown, Tim, Rai.	37	19	383	10.4	40	0
Hicks, Cliff, Buf.	29	6	289	10.0	42	0
Metcalf, Eric, Cle.	44	10	429	9.8	75t	1
Stanley, Walter, N.E.	28	17	227	8.1	50	0
Bieniemy, Eric, S.D.	30	3	229	7.6	21	0
Carpenter, Rob, NY-J	28	9	208	7.4	21	0
Warren, Chris, Sea.	34	25	252	7.4	16	0
Miller, Scott, Mia.	24	18	175	7.3	19	0
Slaughter, Webster, Hou.	20	8	142	7.1	20	0
(Nonqualifiers)						
Pickens, Carl, Cin.	18	9	229	12.7	95t	1
Hale, Chris, Buf.	14	2	175	12.5	27	0
Lewis, Nate, S.D.	13	5	127	9.8	25	0
Timpson, Michael, N.E.	8	2	47	5.9	14	0
Coleman, Pat, Hou.	7	4	35	5.0	19	0
Price, Mitchell, Cin.	6	2	56	9.3	25	0
Harris, Corey, Hou.	6	0	17	2.8	13	0
Vincent, Troy, Mia.	5	0	16	3.2	6	0
Treggs, Brian, Sea.	4	2	31	7.8	13	0
McCallum, Napoleon, Rai.	4	1	19	4.8	13	0
Mathis, Terance, NY-J	2	0	24	12.0	12	0
Prior, Mike, Ind.	1	12	7	7.0	7	0
Dimry, Charles, Den.	1	0	4	4.0	4	0
Mincy, Charles, K.C.	1	1	4	4.0	4	0
Brennan, Brian, S.D.	1	1	3	3.0	3	0
Lambert, Dion, N.E.	1	0	0	0.0	0	0
Martin, Tony, Mia.	1	0	0	0.0	0	0
Williams, Jarvis, Mia.	1	1	0	0.0	0	0
Birden, J.J., K.C.	0	1	0	—	—	0
Byrd, Gill, S.D.	0	3	0	—	—	0
Fernandez, Mervyn, Rai.	0	1	0	—	—	0
Fryar, Irving, N.E.	0	1	0	—	—	0

t = Touchdown
Leader based on average return, minimum 20 returns

NFC - INDIVIDUAL PUNT RETURNERS

	No	FC	Yards	Avg	Long	TD
Bailey, Johnny, Pho.	20	8	263	13.2	65	0
Martin, Kelvin, Dal.	42	18	532	12.7	79t	2
Sikahema, Vai, Phi.	40	10	503	12.6	87t	1
Parker, Anthony, Min.	33	17	336	10.2	42	0
Buckley, Terrell, G.B.	21	5	211	10.0	58t	1
Mitchell, Brian, Was.	29	9	271	9.3	84t	1
Meggett, Dave, NY-G	27	11	240	8.9	39	0
Grant, Alan, S.F.	29	10	249	8.6	46	0
Turner, Vernon, Rams	28	6	207	7.4	23	0
Newman, Pat, N.O.	23	10	158	6.9	18	0
(Nonqualifiers)						
Gray, Mel, Det.	18	9	175	9.7	58t	1
Smith, Tony, Atl.	16	4	155	9.7	45	0
Blount, Eric, Pho.	13	4	101	7.8	16	0
Hawkins, Courtney, T.B.	13	8	53	4.1	17	0
Sanders, Deion, Atl.	13	9	41	3.2	14	0
Woolford, Donnell, Chi.	12	3	127	10.6	36	0
Dowdell, Marcus, N.O.	12	6	37	3.1	34	0
Brooks, Robert, G.B.	11	1	102	9.3	22	0
Waddle, Tom, Chi.	8	10	28	3.5	13	0
Drewrey, Willie, T.B.	7	6	62	8.9	17	0
Sydner, Jeff, Phi.	7	5	52	7.4	17	0
Howard, Desmond, Was.	6	3	84	14.0	55t	1
Griffin, Don, S.F.	6	2	69	11.5	29	0
Anderson, Gary, T.B.	6	1	45	7.5	13	0
Harry, Emile, Rams	6	4	34	5.7	11	0
Lipps, Louis, N.O.	5	1	22	4.4	16	0
Kinchen, Todd, Rams	4	1	103	25.8	61t	2
Lewis, Ronald, S.F.	4	0	23	5.8	9	0
Morgan, Anthony, Chi.	3	1	21	7.0	13	0
Campbell, Jeff, Det.	3	0	15	5.0	9	0
Turner, Floyd, N.O.	3	0	10	3.3	5	0
Buck, Vince, N.O.	2	4	4	2.0	3	0
Hanks, Merton, S.F.	1	0	48	48.0	48t	1
Smith, Kevin, Dal.	1	0	17	17.0	17	0
Hauck, Tim, G.B.	1	0	2	2.0	2	0
Horton, Ray, Dal.	1	0	1	1.0	1	0
Stradford, Troy, Rams	1	0	1	1.0	1	0
Cecil, Chuck, G.B.	1	0	0	0.0	0	0
Clark, Vinnie, G.B.	1	0	0	0.0	0	0
Johnson, Sidney, Was.	1	0	0	0.0	0	0
Thomas, Johnny, Was.	1	0	0	0.0	0	0
Johnson, Joe, Min.	0	1	0	—	—	0
Phillips, Jason, Atl.	0	1	0	—	—	0

AMERICAN FOOTBALL CONFERENCE - PUNT RETURNS

	No	FC	Yards	Avg	Long	TD
Cincinnati	24	11	285	11.9	95t	1
Pittsburgh	32	13	364	11.4	80t	1
Indianapolis	25	24	275	11.0	84t	2
Buffalo	43	8	464	10.8	42	0
Denver	34	16	353	10.4	47	0
Kansas City	39	8	402	10.3	86t	2
L.A. Raiders	41	21	402	9.8	40	0
Cleveland	44	10	429	9.8	75t	1
San Diego	44	12	359	8.2	25	0
N.Y. Jets	30	9	232	7.7	21	0
Seattle	38	27	283	7.4	16	0
New England	37	20	274	7.4	50	0
Miami	31	19	191	6.2	19	0
Houston	33	12	194	5.9	20	0
AFC Total	495	210	4507	9.1	95t	7
AFC Average	35.4	15.0	321.9	9.1	—	0.5

NATIONAL FOOTBALL CONFERENCE - PUNT RETURNS

	No	FC	Yards	Avg	Long	TD
Dallas	44	18	550	12.5	79t	2
Philadelphia	47	15	555	11.8	87t	1
Phoenix	33	12	364	11.0	65	0
Minnesota	33	18	336	10.2	42	0
San Francisco	40	12	389	9.7	48t	1
Washington	37	12	355	9.6	84t	2
Detroit	21	9	190	9.0	58t	1
Green Bay	35	6	315	9.0	58t	1
N.Y. Giants	27	11	240	8.9	39	0
L.A. Rams	39	11	345	8.8	61t	2
Chicago	23	14	176	7.7	36	0
Atlanta	29	14	196	6.8	45	0
Tampa Bay	26	15	160	6.2	17	0
New Orleans	45	21	231	5.1	34	0
NFC Total	479	188	4402	9.2	87t	10
NFC Average	34.2	13.4	314.4	9.2	—	0.7
League Total	974	398	8909	—	95t	17
League Average	34.8	14.2	318.2	9.1	—	0.6

KICKOFF RETURNS

YARDS PER RETURN
AFC:	28.2	Jon Vaughn, New England
NFC:	26.7	Deion Sanders, Atlanta

YARDS
NFC:	1067	Deion Sanders, Atlanta
AFC:	815	Clarence Verdin, Indianapolis

YARDS, GAME
NFC:	190	Deion Sanders, Atlanta at New Orleans, December 3 (6 returns)
AFC:	125	Scott Lockwood, New England at Kansas City, December 13 (6 returns)

LONGEST
AFC:	100	Jon Vaughn, New England at Cincinnati, December 20 - TD
NFC:	99	Deion Sanders, Atlanta at Washington, September 13 - TD

RETURNS
NFC:	42	Mel Gray, Detroit
AFC:	39	Clarence Verdin, Indianapolis

RETURNS, GAME
NFC:	8	Mel Gray, Detroit vs. Dallas, November 8 (178 yards)
AFC:	7	Walter Stanley, New England at Atlanta, November 29 (120 yards)

TOUCHDOWNS
NFC:	2	Deion Sanders, Atlanta
AFC:	1	Jon Vaughn, New England

TEAM CHAMPION
NFC:	23.9	Atlanta
AFC:	21.5	New England

TOP TEN KICKOFF RETURNERS

	No	Yards	Avg	Long	TD
Vaughn, Jon, N.E.	20	564	28.2	100t	1
Sanders, Deion, Atl.	40	1067	26.7	99t	2
Bailey, Johnny, Pho.	28	690	24.6	63	0
Gray, Mel, Det.	42	1006	24.0	89t	1
Meggett, Dave, NY-G	20	455	22.8	92t	1
Baldwin, Randy, Cle.	30	675	22.5	47	0
Lewis, Darren, Chi.	23	511	22.2	97t	1
Montgomery, Alton, Den.	21	466	22.2	64	0
Logan, Marc, S.F.	22	478	21.7	82	0
Nelson, Darrin, Min.	29	626	21.6	53	0

AFC - INDIVIDUAL KICKOFF RETURNERS

	No	Yards	Avg	Long	TD
Vaughn, Jon, N.E.	20	564	28.2	100t	1
Baldwin, Randy, Cle.	30	675	22.5	47	0
Montgomery, Alton, Den.	21	466	22.2	64	0
Verdin, Clarence, Ind.	39	815	20.9	42	0
Ball, Eric, Cin.	20	411	20.6	48	0

t = Touchdown
f = Fair Catch (Turner, Kevin, N.E.: 2 fair catches)
Leader based on average return, minimum 20 returns

	No	Yards	Avg	Long	TD
Williams, Harvey, K.C.	21	405	19.3	37	0
McMillan, Erik, NY-J	22	420	19.1	45	0
Woodson, Rod, Pit.	25	469	18.8	32	0
Warren, Chris, Sea.	28	524	18.7	34	0
Stanley, Walter, N.E.	29	529	18.2	40	0
Mathis, Terance, NY-J	28	492	17.6	32	0
Stegall, Milt, Cin.	25	430	17.2	39	0
Wright, Alexander, Dal.-Rai.	26	442	17.0	33	0
(Nonqualifiers)					
Lewis, Nate, S.D.	19	402	21.2	62	0
Williams, Mike, Mia.	19	328	17.3	28	0
Mayes, Rueben, Sea.	19	311	16.4	29	0
Bieniemy, Eric, S.D.	15	257	17.1	30	0
Coleman, Pat, Hou.	14	290	20.7	28	0
Parmalee, Bernie, Mia.	14	289	20.6	32	0
McCallum, Napoleon, Rai.	14	274	19.6	41	0
Davis, Kenneth, Buf.	14	251	17.9	35	0
Edwards, Al, Buf.	12	274	22.8	34	0
Stone, Dwight, Pit.	12	219	18.3	28	0
Lockwood, Scott, N.E.	11	233	21.2	36	0
Carter, Dale, K.C.	11	190	17.3	39	0
Tillman, Spencer, Hou.	10	157	15.7	33	0
Metcalf, Eric, Cle.	9	157	17.4	30	0
Craver, Aaron, Mia.	8	174	21.8	44	0
Lewis, Darryll, Hou.	8	171	21.4	26	0
Fuller, Eddie, Buf.	8	134	16.8	28	0
Marshall, Arthur, Den.	8	132	16.5	21	0
Miles, Ostell, Cin.	8	128	16.0	27	0
Ambrose, Ashley, Ind.	8	126	15.8	26	0
Russell, Derek, Den.	7	154	22.0	33	0
Harmon, Ronnie, S.D.	7	96	13.7	30	0
Lamb, Brad, Buf.	5	97	19.4	31	0
Graddy, Sam, Rai.	5	85	17.0	21	0
Green, Gaston, Den.	5	76	15.2	20	0
Robinson, Frank, Cin.-Den.	4	89	22.3	26	0
Clark, Ken, Ind.	3	54	18.0	20	0
Jones, Fred, K.C.	3	51	17.0	23	0
Thompson, Leroy, Pit.	2	51	25.5	33	0
Johnson, Reggie, Den.	2	47	23.5	34	0
Thigpen, Yancey, Pit.	2	44	22.0	29	0
Fenner, Derrick, Cin.	f2	38	19.0	19	0
Hoard, Leroy, Cle.	2	34	17.0	25	0
Smith, Sammie, Den.	2	31	15.5	21	0
Paige, Tony, Mia.	2	29	14.5	19	0
Hoge, Merril, Pit.	2	28	14.0	17	0
Timpson, Michael, N.E.	2	28	14.0	28	0
Land, Dan, Rai.	2	27	13.5	14	0
McNair, Todd, K.C.	2	20	10.0	14	0
Price, Mitchell, Cin.	2	20	10.0	13	0
Brown, Tim, Rai.	2	14	7.0	14	0
Hendrickson, Steve, S.D.	2	14	7.0	8	0
Vardell, Tommy, Cle.	2	14	7.0	13	0
Cash, Keith, K.C.	1	36	36.0	36	0
Miller, Anthony, S.D.	1	33	33.0	33	0
Slaughter, Webster, Hou.	1	21	21.0	21	0
Anders, Kimble, K.C.	1	20	20.0	20	0
Oliver, Muhammad, Den.	1	20	20.0	20	0
Thomas, Doug, Sea.	1	19	19.0	19	0
Bussey, Barney, Cin.	1	18	18.0	18	0

	No	Yards	Avg	Long	TD
Humphrey, Bobby, Mia.	1	18	18.0	18	0
Bentley, Albert, Pit.	1	17	17.0	17	0
Bell, Nick, Rai.	1	16	16.0	16	0
Jones, James, Sea.	1	16	16.0	16	0
Brown, Gary, Hou.	1	15	15.0	15	0
Hector, Johnny, NY-J	1	15	15.0	15	0
Johnson, Tracy, Sea.	1	15	15.0	15	0
Montgomery, Glenn, Hou.	1	13	13.0	13	0
Query, Jeff, Cin.	1	13	13.0	13	0
Traylor, Keith, Den.	1	13	13.0	13	0
Flannery, John, Hou.	1	12	12.0	12	0
Hobby, Marion, N.E.	1	11	11.0	11	0
Mills, Ernie, Pit.	1	11	11.0	11	0
Turner, Kevin, N.E.	f1	11	11.0	11	0
Brennan, Brian, S.D.	1	10	10.0	10	0
Dawkins, Dale, NY-J	1	10	10.0	10	0
Cooper, Adrian, Pit.	1	8	8.0	8	0
Duffy, Roger, NY-J	1	7	7.0	7	0
Dixon, Cal, NY-J	1	6	6.0	6	0
Vanderbeek, Matt, Ind.	1	6	6.0	6	0
Hicks, Cliff, Buf.	1	5	5.0	5	0
Turk, Daniel, Rai.	1	3	3.0	3	0
Campbell, Russ, Pit.	1	0	0.0	0	0
Frerotte, Mitch, Buf.	1	0	0.0	0	0
Williams, Warren, Pit.	1	0	0.0	0	0
Anderson, Jesse, Pit.	f0	0	—	—	0
Awalt, Robert, Buf.	f0	0	—	—	0
Whisenhunt, Ken, NY-J	f0	0	—	—	0

NFC - INDIVIDUAL KICKOFF RETURNERS

	No	Yards	Avg	Long	TD
Sanders, Deion, Atl.	40	1067	26.7	99t	2
Bailey, Johnny, Pho.	28	690	24.6	63	0
Gray, Mel, Det.	f42	1006	24.0	89t	1
Meggett, Dave, NY-G	20	455	22.8	92t	1
Lewis, Darren, Chi.	23	511	22.2	97t	1
Logan, Marc, S.F.	22	478	21.7	82	0
Nelson, Darrin, Min.	29	626	21.6	53	0
Mitchell, Brian, Was.	23	492	21.4	47	0
Howard, Desmond, Was.	22	462	21.0	42	0
Martin, Kelvin, Dal.	24	503	21.0	59	0
Harris, Corey, Hou.-G.B.	33	691	20.9	50	0
Sikahema, Vai, Phi.	26	528	20.3	41	0
Turner, Vernon, Rams	29	569	19.6	35	0
Anderson, Gary, T.B.	29	564	19.4	39	0
Smith, Joey, NY-G	30	564	18.8	35	0
(Nonqualifiers)					
McAfee, Fred, N.O.	19	393	20.7	38	0
Brooks, Robert, G.B.	18	338	18.8	30	0
Sydner, Jeff, Phi.	17	368	21.6	45	0
Gentry, Dennis, Chi.	16	330	20.6	66	0
Lee, Amp, S.F.	14	276	19.7	33	0
Lang, David, Rams	13	228	17.5	26	0
Blount, Eric, Pho.	11	251	22.8	52	0
Green, Mark, Chi.	11	224	20.4	29	0
Dunbar, Vaughn, N.O.	10	187	18.7	27	0

	No	Yards	Avg	Long	TD
Pegram, Erric, Atl.	9	161	17.9	42	0
Hawkins, Courtney, T.B.	9	118	13.1	18	0
Edwards, Anthony, Pho.	8	143	17.9	24	0
Smith, Tony, Atl.	7	172	24.6	60	0
Hilliard, Dalton, N.O.	7	130	18.6	48	0
Stradford, Troy, Rams-Det.	7	94	13.4	21	0
Jones, Keith, Atl.	6	114	19.0	29	0
Delpino, Robert, Rams.	6	83	13.8	18	0
Henderson, Keith, Min.	5	111	22.2	29	0
Bennett, Edgar, G.B.	5	104	20.8	33	0
Johnson, Joe, Min.	5	79	15.8	25	0
Morgan, Anthony, Chi.	4	71	17.8	30	0
Kinchen, Todd, Rams.	4	63	15.8	19	0
Campbell, Jeff, Det.	4	61	15.3	21	0
Perriman, Brett, Det.	4	59	14.8	22	0
Thompson, Anthony, Rams	4	34	8.5	14	0
Thomas, George, T.B.	3	72	24.0	37	0
Grant, Alan, S.F.	3	70	23.3	47	0
Holmes, Clayton, Dal.	3	70	23.3	28	0
Walker, Herschel, Phi.	3	69	23.0	34	0
Newman, Pat, N.O.	3	62	20.7	29	0
Brooks, James, T.B.	3	49	16.3	24	0
Jurkovic, John, G.B.	3	39	13.0	14	0
Scott, Kevin, Det.	3	5	1.7	3	0
Carter, Dexter, S.F.	2	55	27.5	32	0
Parker, Anthony, Min.	2	30	15.0	15	0
Calloway, Chris, NY-G	2	29	14.5	17	0
Bunch, Jarrod, NY-G	2	27	13.5	17	0
West, Ronnie, Min.	2	27	13.5	27	0
Ryan, Tim, T.B.	2	24	12.0	13	0
Sparks, Phillipi, NY-G	2	23	11.5	14	0
Mayfield, Corey, T.B.	2	22	11.0	15	0
Smith, Lance, Pho.	2	16	8.0	13	0
Stephen, Scott, Rams	2	12	6.0	7	0
Tillison, Ed, Det.	1	27	27.0	27	0
Wilson, Charles, T.B.	1	23	23.0	23	0
Jordan, Buford, N.O.	1	18	18.0	18	0
Jackson, John, Pho.	1	17	17.0	17	0
Workman, Vince, G.B.	1	17	17.0	17	0
McNabb, Dexter, G.B.	1	15	15.0	15	0
Heyward, Craig, N.O.	1	14	14.0	14	0
Barnett, Oliver, Atl.	1	13	13.0	13	0
Booty, John, Phi.	1	11	11.0	11	0
Brooks, Tony, Phi.	1	11	11.0	11	0
Kennard, Derek, N.O.	1	11	11.0	11	0
Sims, Joe, G.B.	1	11	11.0	11	0
Rolle, Butch, Pho.	1	10	10.0	10	0
Anderson, Willie, Rams	1	9	9.0	9	0
Chamblee, Al, T.B.	1	9	9.0	9	0
Green, Robert, Was.	1	9	9.0	9	0
Smith, Kevin, Dal.	1	9	9.0	9	0
Davey, Don, G.B.	1	8	8.0	8	0
Gouveia, Kurt, Was.	1	7	7.0	7	0
Leeuwenburg, Jay, Chi.	1	7	7.0	7	0
Fortin, Roman, Atl.	1	5	5.0	5	0
Orr, Terry, Was.	1	3	3.0	3	0
Reed, Jake, Min.	1	1	1.0	1	0
Adams, Scott, Min.	1	0	0.0	0	0
Edwards, Dixon, Dal.	1	0	0.0	0	0

	No	Yards	Avg	Long	TD
Johnson, Jimmy, Det.	1	0	0.0	0	0
Rivera, Ron, Chi.	1	0	0.0	0	0
Turner, Odessa, S.F.	f1	0	0.0	0	0
West, Ed, G.B.	1	0	0.0	0	0
Israel, Steve, Rams	1	-3	-3.0	-3	0
Epps, Tory, Atl.	f0	0	—	—	0
Gash, Thane, S.F.	f0	0	—	—	0

AMERICAN FOOTBALL CONFERENCE - KICKOFF RETURNS

	No	Yards	Avg	Long	TD
New England	64	1376	21.5	100t	1
Cleveland	43	880	20.5	47	0
Denver	51	1028	20.2	64	0
Indianapolis	51	1001	19.6	42	0
Houston	46	885	19.2	42	0
Miami	44	838	19.0	44	0
Buffalo	41	761	18.6	35	0
Kansas City	39	722	18.5	39	0
San Diego	45	812	18.0	62	0
Cincinnati	59	1058	17.9	48	0
Seattle	50	885	17.7	34	0
Pittsburgh	48	847	17.6	33	0
N.Y. Jets	54	950	17.6	45.	0
L.A. Raiders	43	744	17.3	41	0
AFC Total	678	12787	18.9	100t	1
AFC Average	48.4	913.4	18.9	—	0.1

NATIONAL FOOTBALL CONFERENCE - KICKOFF RETURNS

	No	Yards	Avg	Long	TD
Atlanta	64	1532	23.9	99t	2
Phoenix	51	1127	22.1	63	0
San Francisco	42	879	20.9	82	0
Philadelphia	48	987	20.6	45	0
Chicago	56	1143	20.4	97t	1
Washington	48	973	20.3	47	0
Detroit	59	1193	20.2	89t	1
N.Y. Giants	56	1098	19.6	92t	1
Minnesota	45	874	19.4	53	0
New Orleans	42	815	19.4	48	0
Dallas	37	699	18.9	59	0
Green Bay	54	1017	18.8	50	0
Tampa Bay	50	881	17.6	39	0
L.A. Rams	63	1054	16.7	35	0
NFC Total	715	14272	20.0	99t	5
NFC Average	51.1	1019.4	20.0	—	0.4
League Total	1393	27059	—	100t	6
League Average	49.8	966.4	19.4	—	0.2

PUNTING

AVERAGE YARDS PER PUNT

AFC:	46.9	Greg Montgomery, Houston
NFC:	45.0	Harry Newsome, Minnesota

NET AVERAGE YARDS PER PUNT

NFC:	39.6	Rich Camarillo, Phoenix
AFC:	39.3	Rohn Stark, Indianapolis

LONGEST

NFC:	84	Harry Newsome, Minnesota at Pittsburgh, December 20
AFC:	73	Brian Hansen, Cleveland vs. Denver, September 27

PUNTS

AFC:	108	Rick Tuten, Seattle
NFC:	82	Jeff Feagles, Philadelphia

PUNTS, GAME

AFC:	11	Shawn McCarthy, New England vs. New Orleans, November 8 (395 yards)
		Rich Rodriguez, Denver at Seattle, November 30 (445 yards) (OT)
		Rick Tuten, Seattle vs. Philadelphia, December 13 (506 yards) (OT)
NFC:	10	Jeff Feagles, Philadelphia at Seattle, December 13 (425 yards) (OT)

TEAM CHAMPION

AFC:	45.2	Houston
NFC:	44.4	Minnesota

TOP TEN PUNTERS

	No	Yards	Long	Avg	Total Punts
Montgomery, Greg, Hou.	53	2487	66	46.9	55
Newsome, Harry, Min.	72	3243	84	45.0	73
Stark, Rohn, Ind.	83	3716	64	44.8	83
Tuten, Rick, Sea.	108	4760	65	44.1	108
Barnhardt, Tommy, N.O.	67	2947	62	44.0	67
Arnold, Jim, Det.	65	2846	71	43.8	66
Landeta, Sean, NY-G	53	2317	71	43.7	55
Barker, Bryan, K.C.	75	3245	65	43.3	76
Saxon, Mike, Dal.	61	2620	58	43.0	61
Gardocki, Chris, Chi.	79	3393	61	42.9	79

Oilers' Greg Montgomery led the NFC in punting average.

TB	Blk	Opp Ret	Ret Yds	In 20	Net Avg
9	2	31	255	14	37.3
15	1	34	339	19	35.7
7	0	45	313	22	39.3
8	0	56	416	29	38.7
10	0	31	218	19	37.7
10	1	30	356	12	34.7
9	2	30	406	13	31.5
13	1	35	300	16	35.3
9	0	34	397	19	33.5
9	0	38	351	19	36.2

AFC - INDIVIDUAL PUNTERS

	No	Yards	Long	Avg
Montgomery, Greg, Hou.	53	2487	66	46.9
Stark, Rohn, Ind.	83	3716	64	44.8
Tuten, Rick, Sea.	108	4760	65	44.1
Barker, Bryan, K.C.	75	3245	65	43.3
Royals, Mark, Pit.	73	3119	58	42.7
Kidd, John, S.D.	68	2899	65	42.6
Gossett, Jeff, Rai.	77	3255	56	42.3
Mohr, Chris, Buf.	60	2531	61	42.2
Johnson, Lee, Cin.	76	3196	64	42.1
Hansen, Brian, Cle.	74	3083	73	41.7
McCarthy, Shawn, N.E.	103	4227	61	41.0
Aguiar, Louie, NY-J	73	2993	65	41.0
(Nonqualifiers)				
Horan, Mike, Den.	37	1681	62	45.4
Roby, Reggie, Mia.	35	1443	60	41.2
Parker, Daren, Den.	12	491	61	40.9
Daluiso, Brad, Den.	10	467	67	46.7
Sullivan, Kent, K.C.	6	247	59	41.2
Lowery, Nick, K.C.	4	141	39	35.3
Stoyanovich, Pete, Mia.	2	90	48	45.0

Leader based on average, minimum 40 punts

NFC - INDIVIDUAL PUNTERS

	No	Yards	Long	Avg
Newsome, Harry, Min.	72	3243	84	45.0
Barnhardt, Tommy, N.O.	67	2947	62	44.0
Arnold, Jim, Det.	65	2846	71	43.8
Landeta, Sean, NY-G	53	2317	71	43.7
Saxon, Mike, Dal.	61	2620	58	43.0
Gardocki, Chris, Chi.	79	3393	61	42.9
Camarillo, Rich, Pho.	54	2317	73	42.9
Feagles, Jeff, Phi.	82	3459	68	42.2
Rodriguez, Ruben, Den.-NY-G	46	1907	55	41.5
Fulhage, Scott, Atl.	68	2818	56	41.4
Bracken, Don, Rams	76	3122	59	41.1
Stryzinski, Dan, T.B.	74	3015	57	40.7
Goodburn, Kelly, Was.	64	2555	66	39.9
Wilmsmeyer, Klaus, S.F.	49	1918	58	39.1
(Nonqualifiers)				
McJulien, Paul, G.B.	36	1386	67	38.5
Prokop, Joe, Mia.-NY-G	32	1184	56	37.0
Wagner, Bryan, G.B.	30	1222	52	40.7
Davis, Greg, Pho.	4	167	52	41.8
Johnson, Norm, Atl.	1	37	37	37.0

Leader based on average, minimum 40 punts

Total Punts	TB	Blk	Opp Ret	Ret Yds	In 20	Net Avg
55	9	2	31	255	14	37.3
83	7	0	45	313	22	39.3
108	8	0	56	416	29	38.7
76	13	1	35	300	16	35.3
74	9	1	39	308	22	35.6
68	9	0	24	244	22	36.4
77	3	0	40	385	17	36.5
60	7	0	22	185	12	36.8
76	9	0	32	284	15	35.9
75	7	1	27	234	28	36.1
103	4	0	59	499	19	35.4
73	3	0	26	189	21	37.6
38	1	1	14	132	7	40.2
35	3	0	16	183	11	34.3
12	1	0	7	88	1	31.9
10	1	0	6	40	3	40.7
6	0	0	4	18	2	38.2
4	0	0	1	10	0	32.8
2	0	0	0	0	0	45.0

Total Punts	TB	Blk	Opp Ret	Ret Yds	In 20	Net Avg
73	15	1	34	339	19	35.7
67	10	0	31	218	19	37.7
66	10	1	30	356	12	34.7
55	9	2	30	406	13	31.5
61	9	0	34	397	19	33.5
79	9	0	38	351	19	36.2
54	2	0	22	141	23	39.6
82	7	0	36	295	26	36.9
47	4	1	23	205	9	34.5
69	3	1	44	482	11	33.0
76	4	0	48	522	20	33.2
74	11	0	22	117	15	36.2
65	5	1	27	332	17	32.7
49	2	0	23	177	19	34.7
38	4	2	10	157	8	30.2
32	0	0	22	258	2	28.9
30	5	0	16	73	10	35.0
4	1	0	0	0	0	36.8
1	0	0	0	0	1	37.0

AMERICAN FOOTBALL CONFERENCE - PUNTING

	Total Punts	Yards	Long
Houston	55	2487	66
Indianapolis	83	3716	64
Seattle	108	4760	65
Denver	85	3705	67
San Diego	68	2899	65
L.A. Raiders	77	3255	56
Kansas City	86	3633	65
Buffalo	60	2531	61
Pittsburgh	74	3119	58
Cincinnati	76	3196	64
Cleveland	75	3083	73
New England	103	4227	61
N.Y. Jets	73	2993	65
Miami	61	2424	60
AFC Total	1084	46028	73
AFC Average	77.4	3287.7	—

NATIONAL FOOTBALL CONFERENCE - PUNTING

	Total Punts	Yards	Long
Minnesota	73	3243	84
New Orleans	67	2947	62
Detroit	66	2846	71
Dallas	61	2620	58
Chicago	79	3393	61
Phoenix	58	2484	73
Philadelphia	82	3459	68
L.A. Rams	76	3122	59
Atlanta	70	2855	56
Tampa Bay	74	3015	57
N.Y. Giants	85	3451	71
Washington	65	2555	66
San Francisco	49	1918	58
Green Bay	68	2608	67
NFC Total	973	40516	84
NFC Average	69.5	2894.0	—
NFL Total	2057	86544	84
NFL Average	73.5	3090.9	—

Avg	TB	Blk	Opp Ret	Return Yards	Inside the 20	Net Avg
45.2	9	2	31	255	14	37.3
44.8	7	0	45	313	22	39.3
44.1	8	0	56	416	29	38.7
43.6	6	1	39	382	15	37.7
42.6	9	0	24	244	22	36.4
42.3	3	0	40	385	17	36.5
42.2	13	1	40	328	18	35.4
42.2	7	0	22	185	12	36.8
42.1	9	1	39	308	22	35.6
42.1	9	0	32	284	15	35.9
41.1	7	1	27	234	28	36.1
41.0	4	0	59	499	19	35.4
41.0	3	0	26	189	21	37.6
39.7	3	0	33	382	13	32.5
—	97	6	513	4404	267	—
42.5	6.9	0.4	36.6	314.6	19.1	36.6

Avg	TB	Blk	Opp Ret	Return Yards	Inside the 20	Net Avg
44.4	15	1	34	339	19	35.7
44.0	10	0	31	218	19	37.7
43.1	10	1	30	356	12	34.7
43.0	9	0	34	397	19	33.5
42.9	9	0	38	351	19	36.2
42.8	3	0	22	141	23	39.4
42.2	7	0	36	295	26	36.9
41.1	4	0	48	522	20	33.2
40.8	3	1	44	482	12	33.0
40.7	11	0	22	117	15	36.2
40.6	10	3	46	548	18	31.8
39.3	5	1	27	332	17	32.7
39.1	2	0	23	177	19	34.7
38.4	9	2	26	230	18	32.3
—	107	9	461	4505	256	—
41.6	7.6	0.6	32.9	321.8	18.3	34.8
—	204	15	974	8909	523	—
42.1	7.3	0.5	34.8	318.2	18.7	35.8

FIELD GOALS

FIELD GOAL PERCENTAGE

AFC:	.917	Nick Lowery, Kansas City
NFC:	.853	Morten Andersen, New Orleans

FIELD GOALS

AFC:	30	Pete Stoyanovich, Miami
NFC:	30	Chip Lohmiller, Washington

FIELD GOAL ATTEMPTS

NFC:	40	Chip Lohmiller, Washington
AFC:	37	Pete Stoyanovich, Miami

LONGEST FIELD GOAL

AFC:	54	Al Del Greco, Houston vs. Kansas City, September 20
		Jeff Jaeger, Raiders vs. Giants, October 4
		Steve Christie, Buffalo at Miami, November 16
NFC:	54	Norm Johnson, Atlanta vs. Jets, September 6
		Norm Johnson, Atlanta vs. New England, November 29

AVERAGE YARDS MADE

AFC:	39.2	Jeff Jaeger, Raiders
NFC:	38.7	Norm Johnson, Atlanta

Reliable Saint Morten Andersen had best FG pct. in NFC.

AMERICAN FOOTBALL CONFERENCE - FIELD GOALS

	FG	FGA	Pct	Long
Kansas City	23	25	.920	52
San Diego	26	32	.813	50
Miami	30	37	.811	53
Buffalo	24	30	.800	54
Denver	20	25	.800	46
Pittsburgh	28	36	.778	49
Houston	21	27	.778	54
Cleveland	21	29	.724	51
Cincinnati	19	28	.679	48
New England	11	17	.647	44
Seattle	14	22	.636	43
N.Y. Jets	19	30	.633	47
L.A. Raiders	15	26	.577	54
Indianapolis	16	29	.552	52
AFC Total	287	393	——	54
AFC Average	20.5	28.1	.730	—

NATIONAL FOOTBALL CONFERENCE - FIELD GOALS

	FG	FGA	Pct	Long
New Orleans	29	34	.853	52
Atlanta	18	22	.818	54
Detroit	21	26	.808	52
N.Y. Giants	18	23	.783	47
Minnesota	19	25	.760	52
Green Bay	22	29	.759	53
L.A. Rams	15	20	.750	49
Washington	30	40	.750	53
Chicago	19	26	.731	50
Dallas	24	35	.686	53
San Francisco	18	27	.667	46
Philadelphia	16	25	.640	50
Tampa Bay	12	22	.545	47
Phoenix	13	26	.500	49
NFC Total	274	380	——	54
NFC Average	19.6	27.1	.721	—
League Total	561	773	——	54
League Average	20.0	27.6	.726	—

AFC - INDIVIDUAL FIELD GOALS

	1-19 Yards	20-29 Yards	30-39 Yards	40-49 Yards
Lowery, Nick, K.C.	0-0 —	9-10 .900	9-9 1.000	3-4 .750
Treadwell, David, Den.	1-1 1.000	9-10 .900	6-8 .750	4-5 .800
Carney, John, S.D.	0-0 —	13-14 .929	5-7 .714	7-8 .875
Stoyanovich, Pete, Mia.	0-0 —	9-9 1.000	14-16 .875	4-4 1.000
Christie, Steve, Buf.	2-2 1.000	9-9 1.000	3-6 .500	7-8 .875
Anderson, Gary, Pit.	0-0 —	12-13 .923	12-15 .800	4-6 .667
Del Greco, Al, Hou.	3-3 1.000	8-9 .889	5-6 .833	4-8 .500
Blanchard, Cary, NY-J	2-2 1.000	2-3 .667	5-7 .714	7-9 .778
Stover, Matt, Cle.	1-1 1.000	11-11 1.000	6-8 .750	2-6 .333
Breech, Jim, Cin.	0-0 —	8-8 1.000	7-7 1.000	4-11 .364
Baumann, Charlie, N.E.	2-2 1.000	4-4 1.000	3-7 .429	2-4 .500
Kasay, John, Sea.	0-0 —	4-5 .800	8-11 .727	2-6 .333
Jaeger, Jeff, Rai.	0-0 —	3-5 .600	4-6 .667	5-9 .556
Biasucci, Dean, Ind.	0-0 —	3-3 1.000	6-11 .545	6-12 .500
Nonqualifiers:				
Staurovsky, Jason, NY-J	1-1 1.000	0-0 —	1-2 .500	1-5 .200
Daluiso, Brad, Den.	0-0 —	0-0 —	0-0 —	0-0 —
Johnson, Lee, Cin.	0-0 —	0-0 —	0-0 —	0-0 —
AFC Total	12-12 1.000	104-113 .920	94-126 .746	62-105 .590
League Total	21-21 1.000	181-201 .900	192-253 .759	131-226 .580

Leader based on percentage, minimum 16 field goal attempts

50 or Longer	Totals	Avg. Yds. Att.	Avg Yds Made	Avg. Yds. Miss	Long
1-1 1.000	22-24 .917	31.6	31.6	34.5	52
0-0 —	20-24 .833	31.9	31.5	34.0	46
1-3 .333	26-32 .813	34.4	32.8	41.2	50
3-8 .375	30-37 .811	36.8	34.3	47.1	53
3-5 .600	24-30 .800	36.5	34.8	43.3	54
0-2 .000	28-36 .778	33.8	32.3	38.9	49
1-1 1.000	21-27 .778	33.7	31.7	40.8	54
0-1 .000	16-22 .727	36.4	35.6	38.7	47
1-3 .333	21-29 .724	33.9	30.3	43.5	51
0-1 .000	19-27 .704	36.0	31.7	46.0	48
0-0 —	11-17 .647	33.6	29.8	40.7	44
0-0 —	14-22 .636	34.2	32.7	36.9	43
3-6 .500	15-26 577	41.0	39.2	43.5	54
1-3 .333	16-29 .552	39.6	37.1	42.6	52
0-0 —	3-8 .375	38.5	31.3	42.8	43
0-1 .000	0-1 .000	54.0	0.0	54.0	—
0-1 .000	0-1 .000	59.0	0.0	59.0	—
15-37 .405	287-393 *.730	35.6	33.2	41.9	54
36-72 .500	561-773 .726	36.1	34.0	41.6	54

NFC - INDIVIDUAL FIELD GOALS

	1-19 Yards	20-29 Yards	30-39 Yards	40-49 Yards
Andersen, Morten, N.O.	0-0 —	10-10 1.000	8-10 .800	8-11 .727
Johnson, Norm, Atl.	0-0 —	6-6 1.000	4-5 .800	4-7 .571
Hanson, Jason, Det.	0-0 —	5-5 1.000	10-10 1.000	4-6 .667
Bahr, Matt, NY-G	2-2 1.000	1-1 1.000	10-11 .909	3-5 .600
Reveiz, Fuad, Min.	0-0 —	4-6 .667	7-7 1.000	5-8 .625
Jacke, Chris, G.B.	0-0 —	5-7 .714	9-10 .900	6-9 .667
Lohmiller, Chip, Was.	2-2 1.000	9-9 1.000	9-15 .600	8-12 .667
Zendejas, Tony, Rams	2-2 1.000	3-4 .750	7-9 .778	3-5 .600
Butler, Kevin, Chi.	1-1 1.000	8-8 1.000	9-10 .900	0-4 .000
Elliott, Lin, Dal.	0-0 —	6-7 .857	10-14 .714	5-10 .500
Cofer, Mike, S.F.	0-0 —	7-8 .875	5-8 .625	6-10 .600
Ruzek, Roger, Phi.	2-2 1.000	3-3 1.000	4-6 .667	6-13 .462
Willis, Ken, T.B.-NY-G	0-0 —	4-4 1.000	1-4 .250	5-8 .625
Davis, Greg, Pho.	0-0 —	6-10 .600	3-4 .750	4-9 .444
Nonqualifiers:				
Murray, Eddie, K.C.-T.B.	0-0 —	0-0 —	2-4 .500	2-4 .500
NFC Total	9-9 1.000	77-88 .875	98-127 .772	69-121 .570
League Total	21-21 1.000	181-201 .900	192-253 .759	131-226 .580

Leader based on percentage, minimum 16 field goal attempts

50 or Longer	Totals	Avg. Yds. Att.	Avg Yds Made	Avg. Yds. Miss	Long
3-3 1.000	29-34 .853	36.1	35.2	41.2	52
4-4 1.000	18-22 .818	39.0	38.7	40.5	54
2-5 .400	21-26 .808	38.8	35.8	51.4	52
0-2 .000	16-21 .762	36.0	32.9	45.8	47
3-4 .750	19-25 .760	37.8	37.6	38.3	52
2-3 .667	22-29 .759	37.6	37.0	39.4	53
2-2 1.000	30-40 .750	35.9	34.4	40.3	53
0-0 —	15-20 .750	33.3	31.5	38.6	49
1-3 .333	19-26 .731	34.7	30.5	45.9	50
3-4 .750	24-35 .686	37.7	36.6	40.0	53
0-1 .000	18-27 .667	35.6	33.4	39.9	46
1-1 1.000	16-25 .640	37.7	35.4	41.8	50
0-0 —	10-16 .625	36.5	33.5	41.5	45
0-3 .000	13-26 .500	36.5	32.1	40.9	49
1-1 1.000	5-9 .556	39.4	40.8	37.8	52
21-35 .600	274-380 .721	36.7	34.9	41.4	54
36-72 .500	561-773 .726	36.1	34.0	41.6	54

SCORING

POINTS

AFC:	124	Pete Stoyanovich, Miami
NFC:	120	Morten Andersen, New Orleans
		Chip Lohmiller, Washington

TOUCHDOWNS

NFC:	19	Emmitt Smith, Dallas
AFC:	12	Thurman Thomas, Buffalo

EXTRA POINTS

NFC:	53	Mike Cofer, San Francisco
AFC:	43	Steve Christie, Buffalo

FIELD GOALS

AFC:	30	Pete Stoyanovich, Miami
NFC:	30	Chip Lohmiller, Washington

FIELD GOAL ATTEMPTS

NFC:	40	Chip Lohmiller, Washington
AFC:	37	Pete Stoyanovich, Miami

LONGEST FIELD GOAL

AFC:	54	Al Del Greco, Houston vs. Kansas City, September 20
		Jeff Jaeger, Raiders vs. Giants, October 4
		Steve Christie, Buffalo at Miami, November 16
NFC:	54	Norm Johnson, Atlanta vs. Jets, September 6
		Norm Johnson, Atlanta vs. New England, November 29

MOST POINTS, GAME

AFC:	24	Thurman Thomas, Buffalo vs. Rams, September 6 (4 TD)
		Eric Metcalf, Cleveland at Raiders, September 20 (4 TD)
NFC:	18	Tom Rathman, San Francisco at Giants, September 6 (3 TD)
		Michael Irvin, Dallas vs. Phoenix, September 20 (3 TD)
		Andre Rison, Atlanta at Chicago, September 27 (3 TD)
		Terry Allen, Minnesota at Cincinnati, September 27 (3 TD)
		Jerry Rice, San Francisco vs. Atlanta, October 18 (3 TD)
		Ricky Watters, San Francisco vs. Atlanta, October 18 (3 TD)
		Emmitt Smith, Dallas at Raiders, October 25 (3 TD)
		Emmitt Smith, Dallas at Detroit, November 8 (3 TD)
		Terry Allen, Minnesota at Rams, November 29 (3 TD)
		Rodney Hampton, Giants vs. Kansas City, December 19 (3 TD)

TEAM LEADERS, POINTS

AFC:			NFC:		
BUFFALO	115	Steve Christie	ATLANTA	93	Norm Johnson
CINCINNATI	88	Jim Breech	CHICAGO	91	Kevin Butler
CLEVELAND	92	Matt Stover	DALLAS	119	Lin Elliott
DENVER	88	David Treadwell	DETROIT	93	Jason Hanson
HOUSTON	104	Al Del Greco	GREEN BAY	96	Chris Jacke
INDIANAPOLIS	72	Dean Biasucci	L.A. RAMS	83	Tony Zendejas
KANSAS CITY	105	Nick Lowery	MINNESOTA	102	Fuad Reveiz
L.A. RAIDERS	73	Jeff Jaeger	NEW ORLEANS	120	Morten Andersen
MIAMI	124	Pete Stoyanovich	N.Y. GIANTS	84	Rodney Hampton
NEW ENGLAND	55	Charlie Baumann	PHILADELPHIA	88	Roger Ruzek
N.Y. JETS	65	Cary Blanchard	PHOENIX	67	Greg Davis
PITTSBURGH	113	Gary Anderson	SAN FRANCISCO	107	Mike Cofer
SAN DIEGO	113	John Carney	TAMPA BAY	54	Reggie Cobb
SEATTLE	56	John Kasay	WASHINGTON	120	Chip Lohmiller

TEAM CHAMPION

NFC:	431	San Francisco
AFC:	381	Buffalo

TOP TEN SCORERS - KICKERS

	XP	XPA	FG	FGA	PTS
Stoyanovich, Pete, Mia.	34	36	30	37	124
Lohmiller, Chip, Was.	30	30	30	40	120
Andersen, Morten, N.O.	33	34	29	34	120
Elliott, Lin, Dal.	47	48	24	35	119
Christie, Steve, Buf.	43	44	24	30	115
Carney, John, S.D.	35	35	26	32	113
Anderson, Gary, Pit.	29	31	28	36	113
Cofer, Mike, S.F.	53	54	18	27	107
Lowery, Nick, K.C.	39	39	22	24	105
Del Greco, Al, Hou.	41	41	21	27	104

TOP TEN SCORERS - NONKICKERS

	TD	TDR	TDP	TDM	PTS
Smith, Emmitt, Dal.	19	18	1	0	114
Allen, Terry, Min.	15	13	2	0	90
Hampton, Rodney, NY-G.	14	14	0	0	84
Sharpe, Sterling, G.B.	13	0	13	0	78
Thomas, Thurman, Buf.	12	9	3	0	72
Foster, Barry, Pit.	11	11	0	0	66
Rice, Jerry, S.F.	11	1	10	0	66
Rison, Andre, Atl.	11	0	11	0	66
Anderson, Neal, Chi.	11	5	6	0	66
Watters, Ricky, S.F.	11	9	2	0	66

AFC - INDIVIDUAL SCORERS

KICKERS

	XP	XPA	FG	FGA	PTS
Stoyanovich, Pete, Mia.	34	36	30	37	124
Christie, Steve, Buf.	43	44	24	30	115
Anderson, Gary, Pit.	29	31	28	36	113
Carney, John, S.D.	35	35	26	32	113
Lowery, Nick, K.C.	39	39	22	24	105
Del Greco, Al, Hou.	41	41	21	27	104
Stover, Matt, Cle.	29	30	21	29	92
Breech, Jim, Cin.	31	31	19	27	88
Treadwell, David, Den.	28	28	20	24	88
Jaeger, Jeff, Rai.	28	28	15	26	73
Biasucci, Dean, Ind.	24	24	16	29	72
Blanchard, Cary, NY-J	17	17	16	22	65
Kasay, John, Sea.	14	14	14	22	56
Baumann, Charlie, N.E.	22	24	11	17	55
Staurovsky, Jason, NY-J	6	6	3	8	15
Daluiso, Brad, Den.	0	0	0	1	0
Johnson, Lee, Cin.	0	0	0	1	0

NONKICKERS

	TD	TDR	TDP	TDM	PTS
Thomas, Thurman, Buf.	12	9	3	0	72
Foster, Barry, Pit.	11	11	0	0	66
Givins, Earnest, Hou.	10	0	10	0	60
Culver, Rodney, Ind.	9	7	2	0	54

	TD	TDR	TDP	TDM	PTS
Jeffires, Haywood, Hou.	9	0	9	0	54
Fenner, Derrick, Cin.	8	7	1	0	48
Jackson, Mark, Den.	8	0	8	0	48
Miller, Anthony, S.D.	8	0	7	1	48
White, Lorenzo, Hou.	8	7	1	0	48
Brown, Tim, Rai.	7	0	7	0	42
Duper, Mark, Mia.	7	0	7	0	42
Higgs, Mark, Mia.	7	7	0	0	42
Jackson, Michael, Cle.	7	0	7	0	42
Metcalf, Eric, Cle.	7	1	5	1	42
Baxter, Brad, NY-J	6	6	0	0	36
Davis, Kenneth, Buf.	6	6	0	0	36
Lofton, James, Buf.	6	0	6	0	36
Mack, Kevin, Cle.	6	6	0	0	36
Metzelaars, Pete, Buf.	6	0	6	0	36
Okoye, Christian, K.C.	6	6	0	0	36
Jackson, Keith, Mia.	5	0	5	0	30
Ball, Eric, Cin.	4	2	2	0	24
Barnett, Tim, K.C.	4	0	4	0	24
Bernstine, Rod, S.D.	4	4	0	0	24
Butts, Marion, S.D.	4	4	0	0	24
Fryar, Irving, N.E.	4	0	4	0	24
Gault, Willie, Rai.	4	0	4	0	24
Harmon, Ronnie, S.D.	4	3	1	0	24
Humphries, Stan, S.D.	4	4	0	0	24
Lewis, Greg, Den.	4	4	0	0	24
Lewis, Nate, S.D.	4	0	4	0	24
Mathis, Terance, NY-J	4	1	3	0	24
Moore, Rob, NY-J	4	0	4	0	24
Rivers, Reggie, Den.	4	3	1	0	24
Slaughter, Webster, Hou.	4	0	4	0	24
Word, Barry, K.C.	4	4	0	0	24
Allen, Marcus, Rai.	3	2	1	0	18
Banks, Fred, Mia.	3	0	3	0	18
Bell, Nick, Rai.	3	3	0	0	18
Bieniemy, Eric, S.D.	3	3	0	0	18
Birden, J.J., K.C.	3	0	3	0	18
Carter, Dale, K.C.	3	0	3	0	18
Cash, Kerry, Ind.	3	0	3	0	18
Clayton, Mark, Mia.	3	0	3	0	18
Coates, Ben, N.E.	3	0	3	0	18
Cooper, Adrian, Pit.	3	0	3	0	18
Davis, Willie, K.C.	3	0	3	0	18
Dickerson, Eric, Rai.	3	2	1	0	18
Johnson, Anthony, Ind.	3	0	3	0	18
Kane, Tommy, Sea.	3	0	3	0	18
McGee, Tim, Cin.	3	0	3	0	18
Mills, Ernie, Pit.	3	0	3	0	18
Mincy, Charles, K.C.	3	0	0	3	18
Query, Jeff, Cin.	3	0	3	0	18
Reed, Andre, Buf.	3	0	3	0	18
Stone, Dwight, Pit.	3	0	3	0	18
Warren, Chris, Sea.	3	3	0	0	18
Williams, John L., Sea.	3	1	2	0	18
Bavaro, Mark, Cle.	2	0	2	0	12
Beebe, Don, Buf.	2	0	2	0	12
Brandon, David, Cle.	2	0	0	2	12
Brown, Vincent, N.E.	2	0	0	2	12
Cash, Keith, K.C.	2	0	2	0	12

	TD	TDR	TDP	TDM	PTS
Cook, Marv, N.E.	2	0	2	0	12
Elway, John, Den.	2	2	0	0	12
Frerotte, Mitch, Buf.	2	0	2	0	12
Gardner, Carwell, Buf.	2	2	0	0	12
Green, Eric, Pit.	2	0	2	0	12
Green, Gaston, Den.	2	2	0	0	12
Green, Harold, Cin.	2	2	0	0	12
Harris, Leonard, Hou.	2	0	2	0	12
Hayes, Jonathan, K.C.	2	0	2	0	12
Holman, Rodney, Cin.	2	0	2	0	12
Horton, Ethan, Rai.	2	0	2	0	12
Humphrey, Bobby, Mia.	2	1	1	0	12
Jefferson, Shawn, S.D.	2	0	2	0	12
Johnson, Vance, Den.	2	0	2	0	12
Jones, Henry, Buf.	2	0	0	2	12
Jorden, Tim, Pit.	2	0	2	0	12
Krieg, Dave, K.C.	2	2	0	0	12
Martin, Tony, Mia.	2	0	2	0	12
McNair, Todd, K.C.	2	1	1	0	12
Paige, Tony, Mia.	2	1	1	0	12
Pickens, Carl, Cin.	2	0	1	1	12
Russell, Leonard, N.E.	2	2	0	0	12
Sharpe, Shannon, Den.	2	0	2	0	12
Stephens, John, N.E.	2	2	0	0	12
Thompson, Craig, Cin.	2	0	2	0	12
Toon, Al, NY-J	2	0	2	0	12
Turner, Kevin, N.E.	2	0	2	0	12
Vaughn, Jon, N.E.	2	1	0	1	12
Verdin, Clarence, Ind.	2	0	0	2	12
Walker, Derrick, S.D.	2	0	2	0	12
Wright, Alexander, Rai.	2	0	2	0	12
Anderson, Eddie, Rai.	1	0	0	1	6
Arbuckle, Charles, Ind.	1	0	1	0	6
Baty, Greg, Mia.	1	0	1	0	6
Bentley, Ray, Cin.	1	0	0	1	6
Blades, Brian, Sea.	1	0	1	0	6
Brennan, Brian, Cin.	1	0	1	0	6
Brim, Michael, NY-J	1	0	0	1	6
Brooks, Michael, Den.	1	0	0	1	6
Brooks, Bill, Ind.	1	0	1	0	6
Brown, Gary, Hou.	1	1	0	0	6
Brown, J.B., Mia.	1	0	0	1	6
Burkett, Chris, NY-J	1	0	1	0	6
Carlson, Cody, Hou.	1	1	0	0	6
Carpenter, Rob, NY-J	1	0	1	0	6
Carrington, Darren, S.D.	1	0	0	1	6
Chaffey, Pat, NY-J	1	1	0	0	6
Childress, Ray, Hou.	1	0	0	1	6
Clark, Louis, Sea.	1	0	1	0	6
Davenport, Charles, Pit.	1	0	0	1	6
Duncan, Curtis, Hou.	1	0	1	0	6
Edmunds, Ferrell, Mia.	1	0	1	0	6
Emtman, Steve, Ind.	1	0	0	1	6
Fina, John, Buf.	1	0	1	0	6
Francis, James, Cin.	1	0	0	1	6
Fuller, William, Hou.	1	0	0	1	6
Galbraith, Scott, Cle.	1	0	1	0	6
Gash, Sam, N.E.	1	1	0	0	6
George, Jeff, Ind.	1	1	0	0	6

	TD	TDR	TDP	TDM	PTS
Glover, Andrew, Rai.	1	0	1	0	6
Goad, Tim, N.E.	1	0	0	1	6
Graddy, Sam, Rai.	1	0	1	0	6
Graham, Jeff, Pit.	1	0	1	0	6
Green, Paul, Sea.	1	0	1	0	6
Griffin, Larry, Pit.	1	0	0	1	6
Harper, Dwayne, Sea.	1	0	0	1	6
Henderson, Wymon, Den.	1	0	0	1	6
Hester, Jessie, Ind.	1	0	1	0	6
Hoard, Leroy, Cle.	1	0	1	0	6
Hoge, Merril, Pit.	1	0	1	0	6
Houston, Bobby, NY-J	1	0	0	1	6
Jackson, Vestee, Mia.	1	0	0	1	6
Johnson, Mike, Cle.	1	0	0	1	6
Johnson, Reggie, Den.	1	0	1	0	6
Jones, James, Cle.	1	0	1	0	6
Junkin, Trey, Sea.	1	0	1	0	6
Kelly, Jim, Buf.	1	1	0	0	6
Langhorne, Reggie, Ind.	1	0	1	0	6
Lodish, Mike, Buf.	1	0	0	1	6
Marshall, Arthur, Den.	1	0	1	0	6
Marts, Lonnie, K.C.	1	0	0	1	6
McDowell, Bubba, Hou.	1	0	0	1	6
McMurtry, Greg, N.E.	1	0	1	0	6
Meads, Johnny, Hou.	1	0	0	1	6
Mitchell, Johnny, NY-J	1	0	1	0	6
Moon, Warren, Hou.	1	1	0	0	6
Moore, Stevon, Cle.	1	0	0	1	6
O'Donnell, Neil, Pit.	1	1	0	0	6
Oliver, Louis, Mia.	1	0	0	1	6
Patterson, Elvis, Rai.	1	0	0	1	6
Pool, David, N.E.	1	0	0	1	6
Rogers, Tracy, K.C.	1	0	0	1	6
Ross, Kevin, K.C.	1	0	0	1	6
Schultz, William, Ind.	1	0	1	0	6
Singleton, Chris, N.E.	1	0	0	1	6
Smith, Neil, K.C.	1	0	0	1	6
Smith, Steve, Rai.	1	0	1	0	6
Stegall, Milt, Cin.	1	0	1	0	6
Thomas, Derrick, K.C.	1	0	0	1	6
Thompson, Leroy, Pit.	1	1	0	0	6
Tillman, Cedric, Den.	1	0	1	0	6
Timpson, Michael, N.E.	1	0	1	0	6
Vinson, Fernandus, Cin.	1	0	0	1	6
Washington, Brian, NY-J	1	0	0	1	6
Williams, Harvey, K.C.	1	1	0	0	6
Wolfley, Ron, Cle.	1	0	1	0	6
Woodson, Rod, Pit.	1	0	0	1	6
Grossman, Burt, S.D.	0	0	0	0	*4
Hale, Chris, Buf.	0	0	0	0	*2
Harrison, Nolan, Rai.	0	0	0	0	*2
Mims, Chris, S.D.	0	0	0	0	*2
Washington, Marvin, NY-J	0	0	0	0	*2

---

* Safety
Team safety credited to Houston.

NFC - INDIVIDUAL SCORERS

KICKERS

	XP	XPA	FG	FGA	PTS
Andersen, Morten, N.O.	33	34	29	34	120
Lohmiller, Chip, Was.	30	30	30	40	120
Elliott, Lin, Dal.	47	48	24	35	119
Cofer, Mike, S.F.	53	54	18	27	107
Reveiz, Fuad, Min.	45	45	19	25	102
Jacke, Chris, G.B.	30	30	22	29	96
Hanson, Jason, Det.	30	30	21	26	93
Johnson, Norm, Atl.	39	39	18	22	93
Butler, Kevin, Chi.	34	34	19	26	91
Ruzek, Roger, Phi.	40	44	16	25	88
Zendejas, Tony, Rams	38	38	15	20	83
Bahr, Matt, NY-G	29	29	16	21	77
Davis, Greg, Pho.	28	28	13	26	67
Willis, Ken, T.B.-NY-G	27	27	10	16	57
Murray, Eddie, K.C.-T.B.	13	13	5	9	28
Camarillo, Rich, Pho.	0	1	0	0	0

NONKICKERS

	TD	TDR	TDP	TDM	PTS
Smith, Emmitt, Dal.	19	18	1	0	114
Allen, Terry, Min.	15	13	2	0	90
Hampton, Rodney, NY-G	14	14	0	0	84
Sharpe, Sterling, G.B.	13	0	13	0	78
Anderson, Neal, Chi.	11	5	6	0	66
Rice, Jerry, S.F.	11	1	10	0	66
Rison, Andre, Atl.	11	0	11	0	66
Watters, Ricky, S.F.	11	9	2	0	66
Gary, Cleveland, Rams	10	7	3	0	60
Haynes, Michael, Atl.	10	0	10	0	60
Sanders, Barry, Det.	10	9	1	0	60
Walker, Herschel, Phi.	10	8	2	0	60
Cobb, Reggie, T.B.	9	9	0	0	54
Rathman, Tom, S.F.	9	5	4	0	54
Anderson, Willie, Rams	7	0	7	0	42
Byner, Earnest, Was.	7	6	1	0	42
Hilliard, Dalton, N.O.	7	3	4	0	42
Irvin, Michael, Dal.	7	0	7	0	42
Williams, Calvin, Phi.	7	0	7	0	42
Barnett, Fred, Phi.	6	0	6	0	36
Carter, Cris, Min.	6	0	6	0	36
Johnson, Johnny, Pho.	6	6	0	0	36
Lang, David, Rams	6	5	1	0	36
Novacek, Jay, Dal.	6	0	6	0	36
Sherman, Heath, Phi.	6	5	1	0	36
Clark, Gary, Was.	5	0	5	0	30
Cunningham, Randall, Phi.	5	5	0	0	30
Early, Quinn, N.O.	5	0	5	0	30
Green, Willie, Det.	5	0	5	0	30
Lewis, Darren, Chi.	5	4	0	1	30
Martin, Eric, N.O.	5	0	5	0	30
Martin, Kelvin, Dal.	5	0	3	2	30
McCaffrey, Ed, NY-G	5	0	5	0	30
Muster, Brad, Chi.	5	3	2	0	30
Pritchard, Mike, Atl.	5	0	5	0	30
Bunch, Jarrod, NY-G	4	3	1	0	24
Carrier, Mark, T.B.	4	0	4	0	24

	TD	TDR	TDP	TDM	PTS
Craig, Roger, Min.	4	4	0	0	24
Hall, Ron, T.B.	4	0	4	0	24
Harper, Alvin, Dal.	4	0	4	0	24
Jones, Brent, S.F.	4	0	4	0	24
Jones, Ernie, Pho.	4	0	4	0	24
Jones, Hassan, Min.	4	0	4	0	24
Lee, Amp, S.F.	4	2	2	0	24
Moore, Herman, Det.	4	0	4	0	24
Perriman, Brett, Det.	4	0	4	0	24
Waddle, Tom, Chi.	4	0	4	0	24
Young, Steve, S.F.	4	4	0	0	24
Byars, Keith, Phi.	3	1	2	0	18
Carter, Anthony, Min.	3	1	2	0	18
Carter, Pat, Rams	3	0	3	0	18
Chadwick, Jeff, Rams	3	0	3	0	18
Dunbar, Vaughn, N.O.	3	3	0	0	18
Ellard, Henry, Rams	3	0	3	0	18
Heyward, Craig, N.O.	3	3	0	0	18
Hill, Drew, Atl.	3	0	3	0	18
Hill, Randal, Pho.	3	0	3	0	18
Hostetler, Jeff, NY-G	3	3	0	0	18
Massey, Robert, Pho.	3	0	0	3	18
Meggett, Dave, NY-G	3	0	2	1	18
Monk, Art, Was.	3	0	3	0	18
Orr, Terry, Was.	3	0	3	0	18
Proehl, Ricky, Pho.	3	0	3	0	18
Sanders, Deion, Atl.	3	0	1	2	18
Sanders, Ricky, Was.	3	0	3	0	18
Small, Torrance, N.O.	3	0	3	0	18
Sydney, Harry, G.B.	3	2	1	0	18
Taylor, John, S.F.	3	0	3	0	18
Thompson, Darrell, G.B.	3	2	1	0	18
Bailey, Johnny, Pho.	2	1	1	0	12
Baker, Stephen, NY-G	2	0	2	0	12
Beach, Pat, Phi.	2	0	2	0	12
Broussard, Steve, Atl.	2	1	1	0	12
Brown, Ivory Lee, Pho.	2	2	0	0	12
Buckley, Terrell, G.B.	2	0	0	2	12
Carroll, Wesley, N.O.	2	0	2	0	12
Centers, Larry, Pho.	2	0	2	0	12
Cross, Howard, NY-G	2	0	2	0	12
Davis, Wendell, Chi.	2	0	2	0	12
Drewrey, Willie, T.B.	2	0	2	0	12
Ervins, Ricky, Was.	2	2	0	0	12
Goff, Robert, N.O.	2	0	0	2	12
Gray, Mel, Det.	2	0	0	2	12
Green, Mark, Chi.	2	2	0	0	12
Harris, Jackie, G.B.	2	0	2	0	12
Hawkins, Courtney, T.B.	2	0	2	0	12
Jenkins, Carlos, Min.	2	0	0	2	12
Johnston, Daryl, Dal.	2	0	2	0	12
Jordan, Steve, Min.	2	0	2	0	12
Joyner, Seth, Phi.	2	0	0	2	12
Kinchen, Todd, Rams	2	0	0	2	12
McDowell, Anthony, T.B.	2	0	2	0	12
McMillian, Audray, Min.	2	0	0	2	12
Morgan, Anthony, Chi.	2	0	2	0	12
Price, Jim, Rams	2	0	2	0	12
Rypien, Mark, Was.	2	2	0	0	12

	TD	TDR	TDP	TDM	PTS
Smith, Tony, Atl.	2	2	0	0	12
Testaverde, Vinny, T.B.	2	2	0	0	12
Turner, Odessa, S.F.	2	0	2	0	12
Workman, Vince, G.B.	2	2	0	0	12
Doleman, Chris, Min.	1	0	0	1	8
Aikman, Troy, Dal.	1	1	0	0	6
Anderson, Gary, T.B.	1	1	0	0	6
Armstrong, Tyji, T.B.	1	0	1	0	6
Bailey, Robert, Rams	1	0	0	1	6
Ball, Jerry, Det.	1	0	0	1	6
Barrett, Reggie, Det.	1	0	1	0	6
Beach, Sanjay, G.B.	1	0	1	0	6
Bennett, Tony, G.B.	1	0	0	1	6
Blades, Bennie, Det.	1	0	0	1	6
Brooks, Robert, G.B.	1	0	1	0	6
Buck, Vince, N.O.	1	0	0	1	6
Calloway, Chris, NY-G	1	0	1	0	6
Campbell, Jeff, Det.	1	0	1	0	6
Carter, Dexter, S.F.	1	0	1	0	6
Chandler, Chris, Pho.	1	1	0	0	6
Cook, Toi, N.O.	1	0	0	1	6
Copeland, Danny, Was.	1	0	0	1	6
Dawsey, Lawrence, T.B.	1	0	1	0	6
Delpino, Robert, Rams	1	0	1	0	6
Del Rio, Jack, Min.	1	0	0	1	6
Dotson, Santana, T.B.	1	0	0	1	6
Edwards, Anthony, Pho.	1	0	1	0	6
Edwards, Brad, Was.	1	0	0	1	6
Favre, Brett, G.B.	1	1	0	0	6
Hanks, Merton, S.F.	1	0	0	1	6
Harbaugh, Jim, Chi.	1	1	0	0	6
Henderson, Keith, Min.	1	1	0	0	6
Horton, Ray, Dal.	1	0	0	1	6
Howard, Desmond, Was.	1	0	0	1	6
Ingram, Mark, NY-G	1	0	1	0	6
Jackson, John, Pho.	1	0	1	0	6
Jenkins, Mel, Det.	1	0	0	1	6
Jennings, Keith, Chi.	1	0	1	0	6
Jennings, Stanford, T.B.	1	0	1	0	6
Johnson, John, S.F.	1	0	0	1	6
Johnson, Joe, Min.	1	0	1	0	6
Jones, Tony, Atl.	1	0	1	0	6
Jones, Reggie, N.O.	1	0	0	1	6
Jones, Roger, T.B.	1	0	0	1	6
Logan, Marc, S.F.	1	1	0	0	6
Marshall, Wilber, Was.	1	0	0	1	6
Maryland, Russell, Dal.	1	0	0	1	6
McAfee, Fred, N.O.	1	1	0	0	6
Mills, Sam, N.O.	1	0	0	1	6
Mitchell, Brian, Was.	1	0	0	1	6
Parker, Anthony, Min.	1	0	0	1	6
Phillips, Jason, Atl.	1	0	1	0	6
Reynolds, Ricky, T.B.	1	0	0	1	6
Richards, Curvin, Dal.	1	1	0	0	6
Rose, Ken, Phi.	1	0	0	1	6
Scott, Todd, Min.	1	0	0	1	6
Sherrard, Mike, S.F.	1	0	0	1	6
Sikahema, Vai, Phi.	1	0	0	1	6
Taylor, Kitrick, G.B.	1	0	1	0	6

	TD	TDR	TDP	TDM	PTS
Thomas, Broderick, T.B.	1	0	0	1	6
Thompson, Anthony, Pho.	1	1	0	0	6
Thompson, Reyna, NY-G	1	0	0	1	6
Tice, Mike, Min.	1	0	1	0	6
Tuggle, Jessie, Atl.	1	0	0	1	6
White, Reggie, Phi.	1	0	0	1	6
Williams, Jamie, S.F.	1	0	1	0	6
Williams, Robert, Dal.	1	0	0	1	6

AMERICAN FOOTBALL CONFERENCE - SCORING

	TD	TDR	TDP	TDM
Buffalo	44	18	23	3
Houston	41	10	27	4
Kansas City	40	14	15	11
Miami	36	9	24	3
San Diego	36	18	16	2
Pittsburgh	31	13	15	3
Cincinnati	31	11	16	4
Cleveland	30	7	18	5
Denver	29	11	16	2
L.A. Raiders	29	7	20	2
N.Y. Jets	23	8	12	3
Indianapolis	24	8	13	3
New England	25	6	13	6
Seattle	14	4	9	1
AFC Total	433	144	237	52
AFC Average	30.9	10.3	16.9	3.7

NATIONAL FOOTBALL CONFERENCE - SCORING

	TD	TDR	TDP	TDM
San Francisco	54	22	29	3
Dallas	48	20	23	5
Minnesota	45	19	18	8
Philadelphia	44	19	20	5
New Orleans	35	10	19	6
Atlanta	39	3	33	3
L.A. Rams	38	12	23	3
N.Y. Giants	36	20	14	2
Washington	30	10	15	5
Chicago	34	15	17	2
Green Bay	30	7	20	3
Detroit	30	9	16	5
Tampa Bay	33	12	17	4
Phoenix	29	11	15	3
NFC Total	525	189	279	57
NFC Average	37.5	13.5	19.9	4.1
NFL Total	958	333	516	109
NFL Average	34.2	11.9	18.4	3.9

	TD	TDR	TDP	TDM	PTS
Zorich, Chris, Chi.	1	0	0	1	6
Greene, Kevin, Rams	0	0	0	0	*2
Holt, Issiac, Dal.	0	0	0	0	*2
Swann, Eric, Pho.	0	0	0	0	*2

* Safety
Team safety credited to Philadelphia.

XP	XPA	FG	FGA	SAF	POINTS
43	44	24	30	1	381
41	41	21	27	1	352
39	40	23	25	0	348
34	36	30	37	0	340
35	36	26	32	3	335
29	31	28	36	0	299
31	31	19	28	0	274
29	30	21	29	0	272
28	29	20	25	0	262
28	29	15	26	1	249
23	23	19	30	1	220
24	24	16	29	0	216
22	25	11	17	0	205
14	14	14	22	0	140
420	433	287	393	7	3893
30.0	30.9	20.5	28.1	0.5	278.1

XP	XPA	FG	FGA	SAF	POINTS
53	54	18	27	0	431
47	48	24	35	1	409
45	45	19	25	1	374
40	44	16	25	1	354
33	35	29	34	0	330
39	39	18	22	0	327
38	38	15	20	1	313
36	36	18	23	0	306
30	30	30	40	0	300
34	34	19	26	0	295
30	30	22	29	0	276
30	30	21	26	0	273
33	33	12	22	0	267
28	29	13	26	1	243
516	525	274	380	5	4498
36.9	37.5	19.6	27.1	0.4	321.3
936	958	561	773	12	8391
33.4	34.2	20.0	27.6	0.4	299.7

SACKS

MOST SACKS
NFC:	19.0	Clyde Simmons, Philadelphia
AFC:	17.0	Leslie O'Neal, San Diego

MOST SACKS, GAME
AFC:	4.0	Chip Banks, Indianapolis vs. Cleveland, September 6
		Anthony Smith, Raiders at Seattle, October 18
		Derrick Thomas, Kansas City vs. San Diego, November 8
		Leslie O'Neal, San Diego at Phoenix, December 6
NFC:	4.0	Wayne Martin, New Orleans vs. Atlanta, December 3

TEAM CHAMPION
NFC:	57	New Orleans
AFC:	51	San Diego

TOP TEN LEADERS - SACKS

Simmons, Clyde, Phi.	19.0
Harris, Tim, S.F.	17.0
O'Neal, Leslie, S.D.	17.0
Fletcher, Simon, Den.	16.0
Martin, Wayne, N.O.	15.5
Doleman, Chris, Min.	14.5
Smith, Neil, K.C.	14.5
Thomas, Derrick, K.C.	14.5
Cox, Bryan, Mia.	14.0
Kennedy, Cortez, Sea.	14.0
Smith, Bruce, Buf.	14.0
White, Reggie, Phi.	14.0

AMERICAN FOOTBALL CONFERENCE - SACKS

	Sacks	Yards
San Diego	51	356
Kansas City	50	391
Houston	50	321
Denver	50	317
Cleveland	48	315
Seattle	46	317
L.A. Raiders	46	320
Cincinnati	45	294
Buffalo	44	351
Indianapolis	39	336
Pittsburgh	36	248
N.Y. Jets	36	240
Miami	36	283
New England	20	114
AFC Total	597	4203
AFC Average	42.6	300.2

NATIONAL FOOTBALL CONFERENCE - SACKS

	Sacks	Yards
New Orleans	57	376
Philadelphia	55	385
Minnesota	51	342
Dallas	44	347
Chicago	43	286
San Francisco	41	273
Washington	39	279
Tampa Bay	36	230
Green Bay	34	219
Atlanta	31	241
L.A. Rams	31	188
Detroit	29	185
Phoenix	27	196
N.Y. Giants	25	197
NFC Total	543	3744
NFC Average	38.8	267.4
League Total	1140	7947
League Average	40.7	283.8

AFC - INDIVIDUAL SACKS

O'Neal, Leslie, S.D.	17.0
Fletcher, Simon, Den.	16.0
Smith, Neil, K.C.	14.5
Thomas, Derrick, K.C.	14.5
Cox, Bryan, Mia.	14.0
Kennedy, Cortez, Sea.	14.0
Smith, Bruce, Buf.	14.0
Childress, Ray, Hou.	13.0
Smith, Anthony, Rai.	13.0
Williams, Lee, Hou.	11.0
Mims, Chris, S.D.	10.0
Williams, Alfred, Cin.	10.0
Porter, Rufus, Sea.	9.5
Banks, Chip, Ind.	9.0
Burnett, Rob, Cle.	9.0
Long, Howie, Rai.	9.0
Matthews, Clay, Cle.	9.0
Stubbs, Danny, Cin.	9.0
Jones, Sean, Hou.	8.5
Perry, Michael Dean, Cle.	8.5
Washington, Marvin, NY-J	8.5
Fuller, William, Hou.	8.0
Grossman, Burt, S.D.	8.0
Hansen, Phil, Buf.	8.0
Mecklenburg, Karl, Den.	7.5
Tippett, Andre, N.E.	7.0
Bickett, Duane, Ind.	6.5
Dronett, Shane, Den.	6.5
Lloyd, Greg, Pit.	6.5
Coleman, Marco, Mia.	6.0
Francis, James, Cin.	6.0
Saleaumua, Dan, K.C.	6.0
Winter, Blaise, S.D.	6.0
Woodson, Rod, Pit.	6.0
Wright, Jeff, Buf.	6.0
Kragen, Greg, Den.	5.5
Croel, Mike, Den.	5.0
Cross, Jeff, Mia.	5.0
Frase, Paul, NY-J	5.0
Mersereau, Scott, NY-J	5.0
Townsend, Greg, Rai.	5.0
Bryant, Jeff, Sea.	4.5
Clancy, Sam, Ind.	4.5
Nash, Joe, Sea.	4.5
Seau, Junior, S.D.	4.5
Williams, Jerrol, Pit.	4.5
Bennett, Cornelius, Buf.	4.0
Houston, Bobby, NY-J	4.0
Jones, James, Cle.	4.0
Krumrie, Tim, Cin.	4.0
Pleasant, Anthony, Cle.	4.0
Rogers, Lamar, Cin.	4.0
Talley, Darryl, Buf.	4.0
Wallace, Aaron, Rai.	4.0
Williams, Brent, N.E.	4.0
Blackmon, Robert, Sea.	3.5
Bruce, Aundray, Rai.	3.5
Baylor, John, Ind.	3.0
Emtman, Steve, Ind.	3.0
Evans, Donald, Pit.	3.0
Griggs, David, Mia.	3.0
Little, David, Pit.	3.0
McGlockton, Chester, Rai.	3.0
Mitz, Alonzo, Cin.	3.0
Ridgle, Elston, Cin.	3.0
Sims, Tom, K.C.	3.0
Siragusa, Tony, Ind.	3.0
Tuatagaloa, Natu, Sea.	3.0
Williams, Gerald, Pit.	3.0
Woods, Tony, Sea.	3.0
Goad, Tim, N.E.	2.5
Griffin, Leonard, K.C.	2.5
Harrison, Nolan, Rai.	2.5
Phillips, Joe, K.C.	2.5
Conlan, Shane, Buf.	2.0
Coryatt, Quentin, Ind.	2.0
Daniel, Eugene, Ind.	2.0
Davidson, Kenny, Pit.	2.0
Gunn, Mark, NY-J	2.0
Herrod, Jeff, Ind.	2.0
Hobley, Liffort, Mia.	2.0
Howe, Garry, Pit.	2.0
Johnson, Mario, NY-J	2.0
Johnson, Mike, Cle.	2.0
Johnson, Bill, Cle.	2.0
Jones, Aaron, Pit.	2.0
Lake, Carnell, Pit.	2.0
Lewis, Mo, NY-J	2.0
McMillan, Erik, NY-J	2.0
Mills, Jeff, Den.	2.0
Moore, Stevon, Cle.	2.0
Moss, Winston, Rai.	2.0
Newsome, Vince, Cle.	2.0
Nickerson, Hardy, Pit.	2.0
Patton, Marvcus, Buf.	2.0
Thornton, George, S.D.	2.0
Williams, Darryl, Cin.	2.0
Lathon, Lamar, Hou.	1.5
Maas, Bill, K.C.	1.5
McDowell, Bubba, Hou.	1.5
Offerdahl, John, Mia.	1.5
Sochia, Brian, Den.	1.5
Thompson, Bennie, K.C.	1.5
Walker, Kenny, Den.	1.5
Webster, Larry, Mia.	1.5
Agnew, Ray, N.E.	1.0
Alm, Jeff, Hou.	1.0
Anderson, Eddie, Rai.	1.0
Atwater, Steve, Den.	1.0
Bailey, Carlton, Buf.	1.0
Braggs, Stephen, Mia.	1.0
Brandon, David, Cle.	1.0
Broughton, Willie, Rai.	1.0
Brown, Richard, Cle.	1.0
Byrd, Dennis, NY-J	1.0
Clifton, Kyle, NY-J	1.0
Dodge, Dedrick, Sea.	1.0
Edwards, Tim, N.E.	1.0
Ellison, Riki, Rai.	1.0
Fulcher, David, Cin.	1.0

Glasgow, Nesby, Sea.	1.0	Pike, Mark, Buf.	1.0
Gordon, Alex, Cin.	1.0	Rembert, Johnny, N.E.	1.0
Graf, Rick, Hou.	1.0	Robinson, Eddie, Hou.	1.0
Hall, Delton, S.D.	1.0	Rolling, Henry, S.D.	1.0
Hand, Jon, Ind.	1.0	Sabb, Dwayne, N.E.	1.0
Hicks, Cliff, Buf.	1.0	Simien, Tracy, K.C.	1.0
Hilliard, Randy, Cle.	1.0	Sinclair, Mike, Sea.	1.0
Hollier, Dwight, Mia.	1.0	Smith, Al, Hou.	1.0
Howard, David, N.E.	1.0	Traylor, Keith, Den.	1.0
Jackson, Steve, Hou.	1.0	Turner, Eric, Cle.	1.0
Klingbeil, Chuck, Mia.	1.0	Vinson, Fernandus, Cin.	1.0
Lageman, Jeff, NY-J.	1.0	Walker, Tony, Ind.	1.0
Lambert, Dion, N.E.	1.0	Washington, Brian, NY-J	1.0
Lang, Le-Lo, Den.	1.0	White, Reggie, S.D.	1.0
Lewis, Darryll, Hou.	1.0	Barber, Kurt, NY-J.	0.5
Logan, Ernie, Cle.	1.0	Brown, Vincent, N.E.	0.5
McClendon, Skip, Ind.	1.0	Holmes, Ron, Den.	0.5
McCoy, Tony, Ind.	1.0	Lee, Shawn, S.D.	0.5
Millard, Keith, Sea.	1.0	Martin, Chris, K.C.	0.5
Nix, Roosevelt, Cin.	1.0	Montgomery, Glenn, Hou.	0.5
Odomes, Nate, Buf.	1.0	Ross, Kevin, K.C.	0.5
Pearson, J.C., K.C.	1.0	Walls, Everson, Cle.	0.5
Pickel, Bill, NY-J	1.0		

Team sacks credited to Denver, Kansas City, and L.A. Raiders.

NFC - INDIVIDUAL SACKS

Simmons, Clyde, Phi.	19.0	Gilbert, Sean, Rams	5.0
Harris, Tim, S.F.	17.0	McCants, Keith, T.B.	5.0
Martin, Wayne, N.O.	15.5	Robinson, Gerald, Rams	5.0
Doleman, Chris, Min.	14.5	Seals, Ray, T.B.	5.0
White, Reggie, Phi.	14.0	Taylor, Lawrence, NY-G	5.0
Bennett, Tony, G.B.	13.5	Thomas, Broderick, T.B.	5.0
Jackson, Rickey, N.O.	13.5	Wheeler, Mark, T.B.	5.0
Randle, John, Min.	11.5	Gardner, Moe, Atl.	4.5
Jeffcoat, Jim, Dal.	10.5	Mann, Charles, Was.	4.5
McMichael, Steve, Chi.	10.5	Solomon, Jesse, Atl.	4.5
Swilling, Pat, N.O.	10.5	Banks, Carl, NY-G	4.0
Dotson, Santana, T.B.	10.0	Brock, Matt, G.B.	4.0
Greene, Kevin, Rams	10.0	Jenkins, Carlos, Min.	4.0
Noga, Al, Min.	9.0	Jones, Jimmie, Dal.	4.0
Dent, Richard, Chi.	8.5	Marshall, Leonard, NY-G	4.0
Tolbert, Tony, Dal.	8.5	Nunn, Freddie Joe, Pho.	4.0
Scroggins, Tracy, Det.	7.5	Pitts, Mike, Phi.	4.0
Conner, Darion, Atl.	7.0	Spellman, Alonzo, Chi.	4.0
Harmon, Andy, Phi.	7.0	Warren, Frank, N.O.	4.0
Armstrong, Trace, Chi.	6.5	Wilks, Jimmy, N.O.	4.0
Joyner, Seth, Phi.	6.5	Brown, Dennis, S.F.	3.5
Paup, Bryce, G.B.	6.5	Hamilton, Keith, NY-G	3.5
Pritchett, Kelvin, Det.	6.5	Harrison, Martin, S.F.	3.5
Haley, Charles, Dal.	6.0	Lett, Leon, Dal.	3.5
Harvey, Ken, Pho.	6.0	Stokes, Fred, Was.	3.5
Johnson, Tim, Was.	6.0	Buck, Jason, Was.	3.0
Jones, Mike, Pho.	6.0	Casillas, Tony, Dal.	3.0
Marshall, Wilber, Was.	6.0	Coleman, Monte, Was.	3.0
Thomas, Henry, Min.	6.0	Gant, Kenneth, Dal.	3.0
Holt, Pierce, S.F.	5.5	Green, Tim, Atl.	3.0
Geathers, James, Was.	5.0	Merriweather, Mike, Min.	3.0

Mills, Sam, N.O.	3.0
Piel, Mike, Rams	3.0
Ryan, Tim, Chi.	3.0
Tippins, Kenny, Atl.	3.0
Ball, Jerry, Det.	2.5
Fox, Mike, NY-G	2.5
Maryland, Russell, Dal.	2.5
Roper, John, Chi.	2.5
Spindler, Marc, Det.	2.5
Bankston, Michael, Pho.	2.0
Carter, Marty, T.B.	2.0
Cofer, Mike, Det.	2.0
Collins, Andre, Was.	2.0
Davis, Reuben, Pho.	2.0
Del Rio, Jack, Min.	2.0
Dorsey, Eric, NY-G	2.0
Gann, Mike, Atl.	2.0
Golic, Mike, Phi.	2.0
Hawkins, Bill, Rams	2.0
Jamison, George, Det.	2.0
Jurkovic, John, G.B.	2.0
Miller, Corey, NY-G	2.0
Noble, Brian, G.B.	2.0
Owens, Dan, Det.	2.0
Perry, William, Chi.	2.0
Rucker, Keith, Pho.	2.0
Smith, Chuck, Atl.	2.0
Stewart, Michael, Rams	2.0
Swann, Eric, Pho.	2.0
Washington, Ted, S.F.	2.0
Williams, Jimmy, T.B.	2.0
Wilson, Bobby, Was.	2.0
Young, Robert, Rams	2.0
Zorich, Chris, Chi.	2.0
Koonce, George, G.B.	1.5
Thomas, William, Phi.	1.5
Turnbull, Renaldo, N.O.	1.5
Wilkins, David, S.F.	1.5
Archambeau, Lester, G.B.	1.0
Boutte, Marc, Rams	1.0
Brown, Robert, G.B.	1.0
Carter, Michael, S.F.	1.0
Chamblee, Al, T.B.	1.0
Collins, Shane, Was.	1.0
Cook, Toi, N.O.	1.0
Copeland, Danny, Was.	1.0
Cox, Ron, Chi.	1.0
Crockett, Ray, Det.	1.0
Dent, Burnell, G.B.	1.0
Donaldson, Jeff, Atl.	1.0
Fagan, Kevin, S.F.	1.0
Gouveia, Kurt, Was.	1.0
Hall, Dana, S.F.	1.0
Hyche, Steve, Pho.	1.0
Jackson, Johnny, S.F.-G.B.	1.0
Johnson, John, S.F.	1.0
Johnson, Pepper, NY-G	1.0
Johnson, Vaughan, N.O.	1.0
Jones, Jock, Pho.	1.0
Jones, Robert, Dal.	1.0
Maxie, Brett, N.O.	1.0
Mays, Alvoid, Was.	1.0
McKyer, Tim, Atl.	1.0
Miller, Les, N.O.	1.0
Morrissey, Jim, Chi.	1.0
Pete, Lawrence, Det.	1.0
Pickens, Bruce, Atl.	1.0
Porcher, Robert, Det.	1.0
Raymond, Corey, NY-G	1.0
Reynolds, Ricky, T.B.	1.0
Riddick, Louis, Atl.	1.0
Rivera, Ron, Chi.	1.0
Roberts, Larry, S.F.	1.0
Romanowski, Bill, S.F.	1.0
Scott, Todd, Min.	1.0
Singletary, Mike, Chi.	1.0
Smith, Vinson, Dal.	1.0
Spielman, Chris, Det.	1.0
Tuaolo, Esera, G.B.	1.0
Tuggle, Jessie, Atl.	1.0
Walter, Michael, S.F.	1.0
Woodson, Darren, Dal.	1.0
Buck, Vince, N.O.	0.5
Faulkner, Jeff, Pho.	0.5
Holland, Johnny, G.B.	0.5
McDonald, Tim, Pho.	0.5
Smeenge, Joel, N.O.	0.5

Team sacks credited to L.A. Rams and Philadelphia.

FUMBLES

MOST FUMBLES
NFC:	13	Randall Cunningham, Philadelphia
AFC:	12	John Elway, Denver
		Boomer Esiason, Cincinnati
		Browning Nagle, Jets
		Kelly Stouffer, Seattle

MOST FUMBLES, GAME
NFC:	5	Andre Ware, Detroit at Green Bay, December 6
AFC:	3	John Elway, Denver vs. Raiders, September 6
		Barry Foster, Pittsburgh vs. Jets, September 13
		Browning Nagle, Jets at Rams, September 27
		John Elway, Denver vs. Kansas City, October 4
		Stan Gelbaugh, Seattle vs. Raiders, October 18
		Stan Humphries, San Diego vs. Denver, October 25
		Mike Tomczak, Cleveland at Cincinnati, November 1
		Stan Humphries, San Diego at Kansas City, November 8
		Warren Moon, Houston at Minnesota, November 15
		Boomer Esiason, Cincinnati vs. Detroit, November 22
		Tommy Maddox, Denver at Raiders, November 22
		Kelly Stouffer, Seattle vs. Denver, November 30 (OT)
		Dave Krieg, Kansas City at Raiders, December 6
		Browning Nagle, Jets at Buffalo, December 6
		Cody Carlson, Houston vs. Chicago, December 7
		John Elway, Denver at Kansas City, December 27
		Donald Hollas, Cincinnati vs. Indianapolis, December 27

OWN FUMBLES RECOVERED
AFC:	6	Boomer Esiason, Cincinnati
		Dave Krieg, Kansas City
NFC:	4	Vinny Testaverde, Tampa Bay

MOST OWN FUMBLES RECOVERED, GAME
NFC:	3	Don Majkowski, Green Bay vs. Minnesota, September 6 (OT)
		Marcus Dowdell, New Orleans at Phoenix, October 18
AFC:	2	Victor Jones, Denver at Philadelphia, September 20
		Kelly Stouffer, Seattle at New England, September 20
		John Flannery, Houston at Denver, October 18
		Boomer Esiason, Cincinnati at Chicago, November 8 (OT)
		Tommy Maddox, Denver at Raiders, November 22
		Dave Krieg, Kansas City at Raiders, December 6
		Cody Carlson, Houston vs. Chicago, December 7
		Bubby Brister, Pittsburgh vs. Minnesota, December 20
		Donald Hollas, Cincinnati vs. Indianapolis, December 27

OPPONENTS' FUMBLES RECOVERED
AFC:	5	Mike Johnson, Cleveland
NFC:	4	Kevin Greene, Rams

MOST OPPONENTS' FUMBLES RECOVERED, GAME
AFC:	2	Brian Washington, Jets vs. Miami, November 1
NFC:	2	Danny Copeland, Washington vs. Dallas, December 13
		Thomas Everett, Dallas at Atlanta, December 21

YARDS
AFC:	115	Stevon Moore, Cleveland
NFC:	76	Sam Mills, New Orleans

LONGEST
NFC:	76	Sam Mills, New Orleans at Jets, December 26 - TD
AFC:	75	Ray Bentley, Cincinnati at Seattle, September 6 - TD

AFC - TOUCHDOWNS ON
FUMBLE RECOVERIES

Bentley, Ray, Cin. 1
Brandon, David, Cle. 1
Brooks, Michael, Den. 1
Childress, Ray, Hou. 1
Davenport, Charles, Pit. 1
Fuller, William, Hou. 1
Goad, Tim, N.E. 1
Harper, Dwayne, Sea. 1
Johnson, Mike, Cle. 1
Lodish, Mike, Buf. 1
Meads, Johnny, Hou. 1
Miller, Anthony, S.D. 1
Mincy, Charles, K.C. 1

NFC - TOUCHDOWNS ON
FUMBLE RECOVERIES

Goff, Robert, N.O. 2
Ball, Jerry, Det. 1
Bennett, Tony, G.B. 1
Copeland, Danny, Was. 1
Jenkins, Carlos, Min. 1
Jones, Roger, T.B. 1
Maryland, Russell, Dal. 1
Mills, Sam, N.O. 1
Parker, Anthony, Min. 1
Reynolds, Ricky, T.B. 1
Sherrard, Mike, S.F. 1
Tuggle, Jessie, Atl. 1
White, Reggie, Phi. 1

AFC FUMBLES - INDIVIDUAL

	Fum	Own Rec	Opp Rec	Yards	Tot Rec
Agnew, Ray, N.E.	0	0	1	0	1
Allen, Marcus, Rai.	1	0	0	0	0
Ambrose, Ashley, Ind.	2	0	0	0	0
Anders, Kimble, K.C.	1	0	0	0	0
Armstrong, Bruce, N.E.	0	1	0	0	1
Arthur, Mike, Cin.	4	0	0	-33	0
Atwater, Steve, Den.	0	0	2	1	2
Baldwin, Randy, Cle.	1	0	0	0	0
Ball, Eric, Cin.	1	0	2	-6	2
Banks, Chip, Ind.	0	0	1	0	1
Barnett, Tim, K.C.	1	0	0	0	0
Baty, Greg, Mia.	0	0	1	0	1
Baumann, Charlie, N.E.	0	0	1	0	1
Baxter, Brad, NY-J.	3	1	0	0	1
Baylor, John, Ind.	0	0	2	0	2
Beebe, Don, Buf.	1	0	0	0	0

	Fum	Own Rec	Opp Rec	Yards	Tot Rec
Bell, Nick, Rai.	2	1	0	0	1
Belser, Jason, Ind.	1	1	1	0	2
Bennett, Antoine, Cin.	0	0	1	0	1
Bennett, Cornelius, Buf.	0	0	3	0	3
Bentley, Ray, Cin.	0	0	1	75	1
Bernstine, Rod, S.D.	2	0	0	0	0
Bickett, Duane, Ind.	0	0	2	0	2
Bieniemy, Eric, S.D.	4	1	0	0	1
Birden, J.J., K.C.	3	1	0	0	1
Blackmon, Robert, Sea.	0	0	1	9	1
Blades, Brian, Sea.	1	0	0	0	0
Blake, Jeff, NY-J	1	0	0	0	0
Brandon, David, Cle.	0	0	3	32	3
Brister, Bubby, Pit.	2	2	0	-2	2
Brooks, Michael, Den.	0	0	2	55	2
Brooks, Bill, Ind.	0	1	0	0	1
Brown, A.B., NY-J	1	1	0	0	1
Brown, Gary, Hou.	0	1	0	0	1
Brown, J.B., Mia.	0	0	1	0	1
Brown, Roger, N.E.	0	0	1	0	1
Brown, Tim, Rai.	6	1	0	0	1
Brown, Vincent, N.E.	0	0	2	25	2
Bryant, Jeff, Sea.	0	0	1	0	1
Burkett, Chris, NY-J	1	0	0	0	0
Burnett, Rob, Cle.	0	0	2	0	2
Butts, Marion, S.D.	4	0	1	0	1
Byrd, Gill, S.D.	0	0	2	0	2
Cadrez, Glenn, NY-J	0	0	1	0	1
Cain, Joseph, Sea.	0	0	1	0	1
Call, Kevin, Ind.	0	1	0	0	1
Carlson, Jeff, N.E.	2	1	0	-4	1
Carlson, Cody, Hou.	8	3	0	-9	3
Carpenter, Rob, NY-J	3	0	0	0	0
Carter, Dale, K.C.	7	2	0	0	2
Cash, Keith, K.C.	0	1	0	0	1
Cash, Kerry, Ind.	0	2	0	0	2
Chaffey, Pat, NY-J	0	1	0	0	1
Childress, Ray, Hou.	0	0	2	8	2
Chilton, Gene, N.E.	1	2	0	0	2
Clayton, Mark, Mia.	1	1	0	0	1
Clifton, Kyle, NY-J	0	0	4	0	4
Coates, Ben, N.E.	1	0	0	0	0
Collins, Shawn, Cle.	0	1	0	0	1
Collins, Todd, N.E.	0	0	2	0	2
Cook, Marv, N.E.	3	1	0	-26	1
Cooper, Adrian, Pit.	1	0	0	0	0
Coryatt, Quentin, Ind.	0	0	1	0	1
Cox, Bryan, Mia.	0	0	1	0	1
Croel, Mike, Den.	0	0	1	0	1
Culver, Rodney, Ind.	2	1	0	0	1
Darby, Matt, Buf.	0	1	0	0	1
Davenport, Charles, Pit.	0	0	1	34	1
Davidson, Jeff, Den.	0	1	0	0	1
Davis, Kenneth, Buf.	5	2	0	0	2
Dawson, Doug, Hou.	0	1	0	0	1
Dellenbach, Jeff, Mia.	0	1	0	0	1
Dickerson, Eric, Rai.	1	0	0	0	0
Donaldson, Ray, Ind.	1	0	0	-17	0

	Fum	Own Rec	Opp Rec	Yards	Tot Rec
Dronett, Shane, Den.	0	0	2	-5	2
Duffy, Roger, NY-J	0	1	0	0	1
Dumas, Mike, Hou.	0	0	1	0	1
Duncan, Curtis, Hou.	0	1	0	0	1
Duper, Mark, Mia.	2	0	0	0	0
Edwards, Al, Buf.	1	0	0	0	0
Ellison, Riki, Rai.	0	0	2	0	2
Elway, John, Den.	12	1	0	0	1
Esiason, Boomer, Cin.	12	6	0	-9	6
Evans, Donald, Pit.	0	0	2	0	2
Evans, Vince, Rai.	1	0	0	0	0
Farrell, Sean, Sea.	0	1	0	0	1
Fenner, Derrick, Cin.	1	1	0	0	1
Figaro, Cedric, Cle.	0	1	0	0	1
Flannery, John, Hou.	0	2	0	0	2
Foster, Barry, Pit.	9	2	0	-20	2
Francis, James, Cin.	0	0	2	3	2
Fuller, William, Hou.	0	0	1	10	1
Gagliano, Bob, S.D.	1	1	0	0	1
Gannon, Chris, N.E.	1	0	0	-12	0
Gardner, Carwell, Buf.	0	2	0	0	2
Gash, Sam, N.E.	1	1	1	0	2
Gelbaugh, Stan, Sea.	9	2	0	-11	2
George, Jeff, Ind.	6	1	0	-2	1
Givins, Earnest, Hou.	3	1	0	0	1
Glover, Andrew, Rai.	1	1	0	0	1
Goad, Tim, N.E.	0	0	1	19	1
Goeas, Leo, S.D.	0	1	0	0	1
Gordon, Alex, Cin.	0	0	1	0	1
Gossett, Jeff, Rai.	1	0	0	0	0
Gray, Jerry, Hou.	0	0	2	4	2
Green, Harold, Cin.	1	1	0	0	1
Griffin, Leonard, K.C.	0	0	1	0	1
Griggs, David, Mia.	0	0	3	-5	3
Grunhard, Tim, K.C.	0	2	0	0	2
Hansen, Brian, Cle.	1	1	0	0	1
Harden, Bobby, Mia.	0	0	1	0	1
Harmon, Ronnie, S.D.	4	2	0	0	2
Harper, Dwayne, Sea.	1	1	1	52	2
Harvey, Richard, Buf.	0	0	1	0	1
Haselrig, Carlton, Pit.	0	1	0	4	1
Hasty, James, NY-J	0	0	2	0	2
Hector, Johnny, NY-J	1	1	0	0	1
Hicks, Cliff, Buf.	2	0	0	0	0
Higgs, Mark, Mia.	5	0	0	0	0
Hilliard, Randy, Cle.	0	0	1	0	1
Hitchcock, Bill, Sea.	0	2	0	0	2
Hoard, Leroy, Cle.	3	1	0	0	1
Hobley, Liffort, Mia.	0	0	1	0	1
Hodson, Tom, N.E.	2	1	0	0	1
Hoge, Merril, Pit.	3	0	0	0	0
Hollas, Donald, Cin.	6	5	0	-5	5
Hollier, Dwight, Mia.	0	1	2	0	3
Horton, Ethan, Rai.	1	2	0	0	2
Howard, David, N.E.	0	0	1	0	1
Hull, Kent, Buf.	0	2	0	0	2
Humphrey, Bobby, Mia.	2	1	0	0	1
Humphries, Stan, S.D.	9	3	0	0	3

	Fum	Own Rec	Opp Rec	Yards	Tot Rec
Hunter, Patrick, Sea.	0	0	1	2	1
Jackson, Keith, Mia.	2	0	0	0	0
Jeffires, Haywood, Hou.	1	0	0	0	0
Johnson, Anthony, Ind.	6	2	2	0	4
Johnson, David, Pit.	0	0	2	0	2
Johnson, Mike, Cle.	0	0	5	0	5
Johnson, Reggie, Den.	0	1	0	0	1
Johnson, Tracy, Sea.	0	0	1	10	1
Johnson, Vance, Den.	1	0	0	0	0
Jones, Aaron, Pit.	0	0	1	0	1
Jones, Henry, Buf.	0	0	2	0	2
Jones, James, Cle.	0	0	1	0	1
Jones, James, Sea.	0	0	1	0	1
Jones, Rod, Cin.	0	0	1	0	1
Jones, Victor, Den.	0	2	0	0	2
Jorden, Tim, Pit.	0	1	0	0	1
Kartz, Keith, Den.	0	1	0	0	1
Kelly, Jim, Buf.	8	0	0	-18	0
Kennedy, Cortez, Sea.	1	0	1	19	1
Kidd, John, S.D.	1	1	0	-9	1
Kirk, Randy, Cin.	0	1	1	7	2
Klingler, David, Cin.	3	0	0	0	0
Kosar, Bernie, Cle.	1	0	0	0	0
Krieg, Dave, K.C.	10	6	0	-15	6
Krumrie, Tim, Cin.	0	0	1	0	1
Lake, Carnell, Pit.	0	0	1	12	1
Lambert, Dion, N.E.	0	0	1	0	1
Land, Dan, Rai.	1	0	0	0	0
Lang, Le-Lo, Den.	0	0	1	0	1
Lee, Ronnie, Sea.	0	1	0	0	1
Lee, Shawn, S.D.	0	0	1	0	1
Lewis, Darryll, Hou.	0	0	1	0	1
Lewis, Greg, Den.	2	0	0	0	0
Lewis, Mo, NY-J	0	0	4	22	4
Lewis, Nate, S.D.	1	2	0	0	2
Lloyd, Greg, Pit.	1	0	4	0	4
Lockhart, Eugene, N.E.	0	0	1	0	1
Lockwood, Scott, N.E.	1	0	1	0	1
Lodish, Mike, Buf.	0	0	1	18	1
Lott, Ronnie, Rai.	0	0	1	0	1
Love, Duval, Pit.	0	1	0	7	1
Lutz, Dave, K.C.	0	1	0	0	1
Mack, Kevin, Cle.	1	0	0	0	0
Maddox, Tommy, Den.	4	2	0	0	2
Marino, Dan, Mia.	5	2	0	-12	2
Marinovich, Todd, Rai.	4	2	0	-5	2
Marshall, Arthur, Den.	3	1	0	0	1
Martin, Tony, Mia.	2	1	0	0	1
Marts, Lonnie, K.C.	0	0	1	2	1
Mathis, Terance, NY-J	2	1	0	0	1
Mayes, Rueben, Sea.	1	0	0	0	0
McCarthy, Shawn, N.E.	1	1	0	0	1
McCoy, Tony, Ind.	0	0	1	0	1
McDaniel, Terry, Rai.	0	0	1	40	1
McDonald, Ricardo, Cin.	0	0	1	4	1
McGee, Tim, Cin.	0	2	0	0	2
McGwire, Dan, Sea.	1	0	0	-1	0
McKeller, Keith, Buf.	1	0	0	0	0

	Fum	Own Rec	Opp Rec	Yards	Tot Rec
McMillan, Erik, NY-J	1	1	1	0	2
McNair, Todd, K.C.	1	1	0	0	1
McNeil, Freeman, NY-J	1	1	0	0	1
Meads, Johnny, Hou.	0	0	1	15	1
Metcalf, Eric, Cle.	6	2	0	0	2
Millen, Hugh, N.E.	8	0	0	-6	0
Miller, Eddie, Ind.	0	0	1	0	1
Miller, Anthony, S.D.	0	1	0	0	1
Miller, Scott, Mia.	2	1	0	0	1
Mills, Ernie, Pit.	2	0	0	0	0
Mills, Jeff, Den.	0	0	2	0	2
Mims, Chris, S.D.	0	0	1	0	1
Mincy, Charles, K.C.	0	0	1	30	1
Minnifield, Frank, Cle.	0	0	1	0	1
Mitchell, Scott, Mia.	1	0	0	-1	0
Mitz, Alonzo, Cin.	0	0	2	0	2
Mohr, Chris, Buf.	0	0	1	0	1
Montgomery, Alton, Den.	1	0	0	66	2
Montgomery, Glenn, Hou.	0	0	2	0	2
Montgomery, Greg, Hou.	1	1	0	-15	1
Moon, Warren, Hou.	7	0	0	-6	0
Moore, Shawn, Den.	3	0	0	0	0
Moore, Stevon, Cle.	0	0	3	115	3
Nagle, Browning, NY-J	12	3	0	-14	3
Nickerson, Hardy, Pit.	0	0	2	44	2
Odomes, Nate, Buf.	0	0	1	12	1
O'Donnell, Neil, Pit.	6	3	1	-20	4
Okoye, Christian, K.C.	2	0	0	0	0
Oliver, Louis, Mia.	0	0	1	0	1
O'Neal, Leslie, S.D.	0	0	1	0	1
Paige, Tony, Mia.	1	0	0	0	0
Parker, Glenn, Buf.	0	1	0	0	1
Parmalee, Bernie, Mia.	3	0	0	0	0
Perry, Darren, Pit.	0	0	1	0	1
Phillips, Joe, K.C.	0	0	1	0	1
Pickel, Bill, NY-J	0	0	1	0	1
Pickens, Carl, Cin.	3	2	0	0	2
Plummer, Gary, S.D.	0	1	1	0	2
Prior, Mike, Ind.	0	0	1	0	1
Radecic, Scott, Ind.	0	0	1	0	1
Rakoczy, Gregg, N.E.	1	0	0	-13	0
Reasons, Gary, Cin.	0	0	1	0	1
Redding, Reggie, N.E.	0	1	0	0	1
Reed, Andre, Buf.	4	0	0	0	0
Reich, Frank, Buf.	3	2	0	-4	2
Richard, Stanley, S.D.	0	0	1	0	1
Ritcher, Jim, Buf.	0	1	0	0	1
Rivers, Reggie, Den.	2	1	0	0	1
Robbins, Randy, N.E.	0	0	1	0	1
Robinson, Eugene, Sea.	0	0	1	0	1
Robinson, Frank, Den.	0	1	0	0	1
Rogers, Tracy, K.C.	0	0	1	0	1
Rolling, Henry, S.D.	0	0	1	0	1
Ross, Kevin, K.C.	0	0	2	0	2
Russell, Leonard, N.E.	3	0	0	0	0
Saleaumua, Dan, K.C.	0	0	1	0	1
Sargent, Kevin, Cin.	0	2	0	0	2
Schroeder, Jay, Rai.	5	0	0	0	0

	Fum	Own Rec	Opp Rec	Yards	Tot Rec
Schulz, Kurt, Buf.	0	1	1	0	2
Seau, Junior, S.D.	0	0	1	10	1
Sharpe, Shannon, Den.	1	0	0	0	0
Shelton, Richard, Pit.	0	0	2	0	2
Sims, Tom, K.C.	0	0	1	0	1
Siragusa, Tony, Ind.	0	0	1	0	1
Slaughter, Webster, Hou.	3	2	0	0	2
Smith, Al, Hou.	1	0	0	0	0
Smith, Dennis, Den.	0	0	2	0	2
Smith, Doug, Hou.	0	0	1	0	1
Smith, Neil, K.C.	0	0	2	·0	2
Stanley, Walter, N.E.	5	2	0	0	2
Stegall, Milt, Cin.	1	0	0	0	0
Stephens, John, N.E.	0	1	0	0	1
Stouffer, Kelly, Sea.	12	4	0	-8	4
Stubbs, Danny, Cin.	0	0	1	0	1
Tasker, Steve, Buf.	0	0	1	0	1
Taylor, Terry, Cle.	0	0	1	7	1
Thomas, Blair, NY-J	2	0	0	0	0
Thomas, Derrick, K.C.	0	0	3	0	3
Thomas, Doug, Sea.	1	0	0	0	0
Thomas, Robb, Sea.	1	0	0	0	0
Thomas, Thurman, Buf.	6	1	0	0	1
Thompson, Leroy, Pit.	2	0	0	0	0
Thornton, George, S.D.	0	0	1	0	1
Tillman, Lawyer, Cle.	1	0	0	0	0
Tillman, Spencer, Hou.	2	0	0	0	0
Tofflemire, Joe, Sea.	1	0	0	0	0
Tomczak, Mike, Cle.	5	0	0	-7	0
Townsend, Greg, Rai.	0	0	1	0	1
Treggs, Brian, Sea.	0	1	0	0	1
Trudeau, Jack, Ind.	3	2	0	-12	2
Tupa, Tom, Ind.	1	1	0	-1	1
Turner, Eric, Cle.	0	0	2	0	2
Turner, Marcus, NY-J	0	0	1	0	1
Turner, Kevin, N.E.	2	1	1	0	2
Turner, T.J., Mia.	0	0	2	0	2
Tuten, Rick, Sea.	2	2	0	-9	2
Uhlenhake, Jeff, Mia.	1	2	0	-4	2
Vaughn, Jon, N.E.	6	0	0	-3	0
Verdin, Clarence, Ind.	2	0	0	0	0
Vincent, Troy, Mia.	2	2	0	0	2
Vinson, Fernandus, Cin.	0	0	1	22	1
Walker, Kenny, Den.	0	0	2	0	2
Walker, Sammy, Pit.	0	0	1	0	1
Walker, Tony, Ind.	0	0	1	0	1
Wallace, Aaron, Rai.	0	0	2	0	2
Walter, Joe, Cin.	0	1	0	0	1
Warren, Chris, Sea.	2	2	0	0	2
Washington, Brian, NY-J	0	0	2	0	2
White, Dwayne, NY-J	0	1	0	-1	1
White, Lorenzo, Hou.	2	2	0	0	2
Widell, Doug, Den.	0	2	0	0	2
Wilburn, Barry, Cle.	0	0	1	5	1
Wilkerson, Bruce, Rai.	0	1	0	0	1
Williams, Darryl, Cin.	0	0	1	0	1
Williams, David, Hou.	0	1	0	0	1
Williams, Harvey, K.C.	1	0	0	0	0

	Fum	Own Rec	Opp Rec	Yards	Tot Rec
Williams, Jarvis, Mia.	1	0	1	5	1
Williams, Jerrol, Pit.	0	0	2	18	2
Williams, John L., Sea.	4	1	0	0	1
Williams, Larry, N.E.	0	1	0	0	1
Williams, Mike, Mia.	1	1	0	0	1
Withycombe, Mike, Cin.	0	1	0	0	1
Woodson, Rod, Pit.	2	0	1	9	1
Word, Barry, K.C.	2	2	1	0	3
Wright, Alexander, Rai.	1	0	0	0	0
Wright, Jeff, Buf.	0	0	1	0	1
Wyman, David, Sea.	0	0	1	6	1
Young, Lonnie, NY-J.	0	0	2	9	2
Zolak, Scott, N.E.	5	3	0	-21	3

Yards includes aborted plays, own recoveries, and opponents' recoveries.

NFC FUMBLES - INDIVIDUAL

	Fum	Own Rec	Opp Rec	Yards	Tot Rec
Adams, Scott, Min.	1	0	0	0	0
Aikman, Troy, Dal.	4	1	0	0	1
Allen, Eric, Phi.	0	0	2	0	2
Allen, Terry, Min.	9	2	0	0	2
Anderson, Neal, Chi.	6	0	0	0	0
Anderson, Gary, T.B.	3	1	0	0	1
Anderson, Willie, Rams	1	0	0	0	0
Armstrong, Trace, Chi.	0	0	1	0	1
Atkins, Gene, N.O.	0	0	1	9	1
Auzenne, Troy, Chi.	0	1	0	0	1
Bailey, Johnny, Pho.	2	2	0	0	2
Ball, Jerry, Det.	0	0	3	21	3
Barnett, Fred, Phi.	1	0	0	0	0
Barnhardt, Tommy, N.O.	2	0	0	-16	0
Beach, Sanjay, G.B.	1	0	1	0	1
Bennett, Edgar, G.B.	2	0	0	0	0
Bennett, Tony, G.B.	0	0	3	18	3
Billups, Lewis, G.B.	0	0	1	0	1
Bingham, Guy, Was.	0	0	1	0	1
Bono, Steve, S.F.	2	1	0	-3	1
Booty, John, Phi.	0	0	1	0	1
Bostic, Jeff, Was.	1	0	0	-2	0
Bouwens, Shawn, Det.	0	1	0	0	1
Bowles, Todd, Was.	0	1	0	0	1
Brady, Ed, T.B.	0	0	1	0	1
Brandes, John, NY-G	1	0	0	0	0
Brantley, John, Was.	0	0	1	0	1
Brenner, Hoby, N.O.	0	1	0	0	1
Brock, Matt, G.B.	0	0	2	34	2
Brooks, James, T.B.	1	0	0	0	0
Brostek, Bern, Rams	0	1	0	0	1
Broussard, Steve, Atl.	3	1	0	-2	1
Brown, Larry, Dal.	0	0	1	0	1
Brown, Robert, G.B.	0	0	1	0	1
Buckley, Terrell, G.B.	7	3	1	0	4

	Fum	Own Rec	Opp Rec	Yards	Tot Rec
Bunch, Jarrod, NY-G	3	1	0	0	1
Butler, LeRoy, G.B.	0	0	1	17	1
Byars, Keith, Phi.	1	1	0	0	1
Byner, Earnest, Was.	1	0	0	0	0
Campbell, Jeff, Det.	1	0	0	0	0
Campbell, Jesse, NY-G	0	0	1	0	1
Campen, James, G.B.	0	1	0	0	1
Carrier, Mark, T.B.	1	0	0	0	0
Carrier, Mark, Chi.	0	0	2	0	2
Carroll, Wesley, N.O.	1	0	0	0	0
Carter, Anthony, Min.	1	0	0	0	0
Carter, Cris, Min.	1	0	0	0	0
Case, Scott, Atl.	0	0	2	0	2
Casillas, Tony, Dal.	0	0	1	3	1
Cecil, Chuck, G.B.	1	0	0	0	0
Centers, Larry, Pho.	1	0	0	0	0
Chadwick, Jeff, Rams	1	0	0	0	0
Chandler, Chris, Pho.	9	2	0	-11	2
Clark, Gary, Was.	1	0	0	0	0
Cobb, Reggie, T.B.	3	1	0	0	1
Coleman, Monte, Was.	1	0	0	0	0
Collins, Andre, Was.	0	0	1	40	1
Colon, Harry, Det.	0	0	2	0	2
Cooper, Richard, N.O.	0	1	0	0	1
Copeland, Danny, Was.	0	0	3	15	3
Cox, Ron, Chi.	0	0	1	0	1
Craig, Roger, Min.	2	0	0	0	0
Crockett, Ray, Det.	0	0	1	15	1
Cross, Howard, NY-G	2	1	0	0	1
Cunningham, Randall, Phi.	13	3	0	0	3
Davis, Eric, S.F.	0	0	2	0	2
Dawsey, Lawrence, T.B.	1	1	0	0	1
DeBerg, Steve, T.B.	2	0	0	-7	0
DeLong, Keith, S.F.	0	0	1	-6	1
Delpino, Robert, Rams	2	2	0	0	2
Del Rio, Jack, Min.	0	0	2	0	2
Dent, Richard, Chi.	0	0	1	0	1
Doleman, Chris, Min.	0	0	3	0	3
Dombrowski, Jim, N.O.	0	1	0	0	1
Dotson, Santana, T.B.	0	0	2	42	2
Dowdell, Marcus, N.O.	4	3	0	0	3
Duckens, Mark, T.B.	0	0	1	0	1
Dukes, Jaime, Atl.	0	2	0	0	2
Dunbar, Vaughn, N.O.	3	0	0	0	0
Epps, Tory, Atl.	0	0	1	0	1
Ervins, Ricky, Was.	1	1	0	0	1
Everett, Jim, Rams	5	0	0	-9	0
Everett, Thomas, Dal.	0	0	2	15	2
Favre, Brett, G.B.	12	3	0	-12	3
Fontenot, Jerry, Chi.	1	0	0	-2	0
Fortin, Roman, Atl.	0	1	0	0	1
Fralic, Bill, Atl.	0	2	0	0	2
Fulhage, Scott, Atl.	0	1	0	0	1
Furrer, Will, Chi.	1	0	0	0	0
Gann, Mike, Atl.	0	0	2	0	2
Gannon, Rich, Min.	5	0	0	0	0
Gant, Kenneth, Dal.	0	0	1	0	1
Gardocki, Chris, Chi.	0	0	1	0	1

	Fum	Own Rec	Opp Rec	Yards	Tot Rec
Gary, Cleveland, Rams	9	1	0	0	1
Gayle, Shaun, Chi	0	0	3	0	3
Gesek, John, Dal	1	0	0	0	0
Gilbert, Sean, Rams	0	0	1	0	1
Glover, Kevin, Det	0	1	0	0	1
Goff, Robert, N.O.	0	0	3	47	3
Golic, Mike, Phi	0	0	1	0	1
Graham, Kent, NY-G	1	1	0	0	1
Grant, Alan, S.F.	1	0	0	0	0
Green, Tim, Atl	0	0	1	0	1
Green, Willie, Det	1	0	0	0	0
Greene, Kevin, Rams	0	0	4	2	4
Griffin, Don, S.F.	1	0	0	0	0
Gruber, Paul, T.B.	0	1	0	0	1
Hall, Dana, S.F.	0	0	1	0	1
Hamilton, Keith, NY-G	0	0	1	4	1
Hampton, Rodney, NY-G	1	2	0	0	2
Harbaugh, Jim, Chi.	6	3	0	0	3
Harmon, Andy, Phi.	0	0	1	0	1
Harper, Alvin, Dal.	1	0	0	0	0
Harris, Jackie, G.B.	1	0	0	0	0
Harris, Tim, S.F.	0	0	1	0	1
Harvey, Ken, Pho.	0	0	2	0	2
Hawkins, Courtney, T.B.	2	1	0	0	1
Hebert, Bobby, N.O.	3	1	0	0	1
Heller, Ron, Phi.	0	2	0	0	2
Henderson, Keith, S.F.-Min.	4	1	0	0	1
Heyward, Craig, N.O.	1	1	0	0	1
Hill, Drew, Atl.	1	0	0	0	0
Hill, Eric, Pho.	1	0	1	-2	1
Hill, Randal, Pho.	2	0	0	0	0
Hilliard, Dalton, N.O.	6	1	0	0	1
Holland, Johnny, G.B.	2	1	2	0	3
Holmes, Clayton, Dal.	0	1	0	0	1
Hoover, Houston, Atl.	0	1	0	0	1
Hostetler, Jeff, NY-G.	6	0	0	-3	0
Howard, Desmond, Was.	1	0	0	0	0
Howard, Erik, NY-G.	0	0	3	7	3
Hyche, Steve, Pho.	0	0	1	0	1
Ingram, Mark, NY-G	0	1	0	0	1
Irvin, Michael, Dal.	1	1	0	0	1
Israel, Steve, Rams	0	0	1	0	1
Jackson, Greg, NY-G	0	0	1	0	1
Jackson, Johnnie, S.F.	0	0	1	0	1
Jackson, Rickey, N.O.	0	0	3	15	3
Jamison, George, Det.	0	0	1	0	1
Jenkins, Carlos, Min.	0	0	1	22	1
Jenkins, Mel, Det.	0	0	1	0	1
Jennings, Stanford, T.B.	1	0	0	0	0
Johnson, Johnny, Pho.	2	0	0	0	0
Johnson, Sidney, Was.	1	0	0	0	0
Johnson, Pepper, NY-G	1	0	2	0	2
Johnson, Tim, Was.	0	0	1	0	1
Johnston, Daryl, Dal.	0	1	0	0	1
Jones, Tony, Atl.	0	1	0	1	1
Jones, Brent, S.F.	1	0	0	0	0
Jones, Jock, Pho.	0	0	1	0	1
Jones, Keith, Atl.	2	0	0	0	0

	Fum	Own Rec	Opp Rec	Yards	Tot Rec
Jones, Robert, Dal.	0	0	1	0	1
Jones, Roger, T.B.	0	0	2	26	2
Jordan, Buford, N.O.	1	0	1	0	1
Joyner, Seth, Phi.	0	0	1	0	1
Kelm, Larry, Rams	0	0	2	0	2
Kennard, Derek, N.O.	0	1	0	0	1
Koonce, George, G.B.	0	0	1	0	1
Kramer, Erik, Det.	4	1	0	-1	1
Lang, David, Rams	5	2	0	0	2
LeBel, Harper, Atl.	1	0	0	-37	0
Lee, Amp, S.F.	1	2	1	0	3
Lee, Carl, Min.	0	1	1	0	2
Lett, Leon, Dal.	0	0	1	0	1
Lewis, Darren, Chi.	4	1	0	0	1
Lewis, Ron, S.F.	2	0	0	0	0
Lipps, Louis, N.O.	1	0	0	0	0
Lumpkin, Sean, N.O.	0	1	0	0	1
Lynch, Lorenzo, Pho.	0	0	1	0	1
Majkowski, Don, G.B.	4	3	0	0	3
Marshall, Leonard, NY-G	0	0	2	0	2
Marshall, Wilber, Was.	0	1	2	35	3
Martin, Eric, N.O.	1	1	0	0	1
Martin, Kelvin, Dal.	2	0	0	0	0
Martin, Wayne, N.O.	0	0	2	0	2
Maryland, Russell, Dal.	0	0	2	26	2
Maxie, Brett, N.O.	0	0	1	0	1
Mayhew, Martin, Was.	0	0	1	0	1
McCaffrey, Ed, NY-G	2	0	0	0	0
McCants, Keith, T.B.	0	0	1	0	1
McDonald, Tim, Pho.	0	0	3	2	3
McDowell, Anthony, T.B.	1	0	0	0	0
McGriggs, Lamar, NY-G	0	0	1	0	1
McGruder, Michael, S.F.	0	0	1	7	1
McIntyre, Guy, S.F.	0	1	0	0	1
McJulien, Paul, G.B.	0	1	0	0	1
McMichael, Steve, Chi.	0	0	2	2	2
Meggett, Dave, NY-G	5	3	0	0	3
Merriweather, Mike, Min.	0	0	2	3	2
Miano, Rich, Phi.	0	0	2	0	2
Milinichik, Joe, Rams	0	1	0	0	1
Millard, Keith, Sea.-G.B.	0	0	2	0	2
Miller, Chris, Atl.	6	1	0	-1	1
Miller, Les, N.O.	0	0	1	0	1
Mills, Sam, N.O.	0	0	3	76	3
Mitchell, Brian, Was.	4	2	0	0	2
Mitchell, Brian, Atl.	0	0	1	0	1
Mitchell, Roland, G.B.	0	0	1	0	1
Monk, Art, Was.	1	0	0	0	0
Moran, Rich, G.B.	0	1	0	0	1
Muster, Brad, Chi.	2	0	0	0	0
Nelson, Darrin, Min.	2	2	0	0	2
Newberry, Tom, Rams	0	1	0	0	1
Newman, Anthony, Rams	0	0	3	0	3
Newman, Pat, N.O.	2	0	0	0	0
Newton, Nate, Dal.	0	1	0	0	1
Noble, Brian, G.B.	0	0	2	0	2
Noga, Al, Min.	0	0	1	3	1
Norton, Ken, Dal.	0	0	2	0	2

	Fum	Own Rec	Opp Rec	Yards	Tot Rec
Novoselsky, Brent, Min.	0	0	2	0	2
Nunn, Freddie Joe, Pho.	0	0	1	0	1
Oates, Bart, NY-G	2	0	0	-29	0
Orr, Terry, Was.	1	2	0	0	2
Owens, Dan, Det.	0	0	1	0	1
Pagel, Mike, Rams	1	1	0	-1	1
Parker, Anthony, Min.	2	1	1	58	2
Paup, Bryce, G.B.	0	0	2	0	2
Peete, Rodney, Det.	6	2	0	-7	2
Pegram, Erric, Atl.	0	3	0	1	3
Perriman, Brett, Det.	1	0	0	0	0
Perry, William, Chi.	0	0	1	0	1
Pete, Lawrence, Det.	0	0	1	0	1
Phifer, Roman, Rams	0	0	2	0	2
Price, Jim, Rams	2	2	0	0	2
Pritchard, Mike, Atl.	3	0	0	0	0
Proehl, Ricky, Pho.	5	0	0	0	0
Randle, John, Min.	0	0	1	0	1
Rathman, Tom, S.F.	1	0	0	0	0
Ray, Terry, Atl.	0	0	1	0	1
Reeves, Walter, Pho.	0	2	0	0	2
Reid, Michael, Atl.	0	0	1	0	1
Reynolds, Ricky, T.B.	0	0	2	11	2
Rice, Jerry, S.F.	2	0	0	0	0
Richards, Curvin, Dal.	3	0	0	0	0
Riesenberg, Doug, NY-G	0	2	0	0	2
Rison, Andre, Atl.	2	0	0	0	0
Rivera, Ron, Chi.	0	1	1	0	2
Robinson, Gerald, Rams	0	0	1	0	1
Rodriguez, Ruben, NY-G	0	1	0	0	1
Romanowski, Bill, S.F.	0	0	1	0	1
Rosenbach, Timm, Pho.	4	0	0	0	0
Rypien, Mark, Was.	4	2	0	0	2
Salisbury, Sean, Min.	4	3	0	-5	3
Sanders, Barry, Det.	6	2	0	0	2
Sanders, Deion, Atl.	3	1	1	0	2
Schreiber, Adam, Min.	0	1	0	0	1
Sharpe, Sterling, G.B.	2	1	0	0	1
Sherman, Heath, Phi.	3	1	1	0	2
Sherrard, Mike, S.F.	1	1	1	39	2
Simmons, Clyde, Phi.	0	0	1	0	1
Small, Jessie, Pho.	0	0	1	0	1
Smeenge, Joel, N.O.	0	0	1	0	1
Smith, Emmitt, Dal.	4	1	0	0	1
Smith, Joey, NY-G	1	0	0	0	0
Smith, Lance, Pho.	0	1	0	0	1
Smith, Tony, Atl.	4	1	0	0	1
Smith, Vinson, Dal.	0	0	2	0	2
Spencer, Jimmy, N.O.	0	0	1	0	1
Spielman, Chris, Det.	0	0	1	0	1
Stepnoski, Mark, Dal.	0	1	0	0	1
Stewart, Michael, Rams	0	0	1	0	1
Stokes, Fred, Was.	0	0	1	0	1
Swilling, Pat, N.O.	0	0	1	0	1
Sydner, Jeff, Phi.	1	0	0	0	0
Sydney, Harry, G.B.	2	2	0	0	2
Tate, David, Chi.	0	0	1	0	1
Taylor, Lawrence, NY-G	0	0	1	2	1

	Fum	Own Rec	Opp Rec	Yards	Tot Rec
Testaverde, Vinny, T.B.	4	4	0	-8	4
Thomas, Broderick, T.B.	0	0	3	-1	3
Thomas, Johnny, Was.	1	1	0	0	1
Thomas, William, Phi.	0	0	2	2	2
Thompson, Anthony, Rams	1	1	0	0	1
Thompson, Darrell, G.B.	2	0	0	0	0
Tice, Mike, Min.	0	1	0	4	1
Tippins, Kenny, Atl.	0	0	1	0	1
Tolliver, Billy Joe, Atl.	5	0	0	0	0
Tuggle, Jessie, Atl.	0	0	1	69	1
Turner, Floyd, N.O.	2	0	0	0	0
Turner, Odessa, S.F.	1	0	0	0	0
Turner, Vernon, Rams	3	0	0	0	0
Van Horne, Keith, Chi.	0	1	0	0	1
Waddle, Tom, Chi.	1	2	0	0	2
Walker, Herschel, Phi.	6	2	0	0	2
Wallace, Steve, S.F.	0	1	0	0	1
Walter, Michael, S.F.	0	0	2	0	2
Ware, Andre, Det.	6	2	0	-20	2
Warren, Frank, N.O.	0	0	1	0	1
Washington, Charles, Atl.	0	1	0	0	1
Washington, James, Dal.	0	0	1	0	1
Watters, Ricky, S.F.	2	1	0	0	1
West, Ronnie, Min.	1	0	0	0	0
White, Reggie, Phi.	0	0	1	37	1
White, William, Det.	1	0	0	0	0
Wilks, Jimmy, N.O.	0	0	1	4	1
Williams, Aeneas, Pho.	0	0	1	39	1
Williams, Jimmy, T.B.	0	0	1	0	1
Williams, Jamie, S.F.	1	0	0	0	0
Wilmsmeyer, Klaus, S.F.	1	1	0	0	1
Winters, Frank, G.B.	1	0	0	0	0
Wojciechowski, John, Chi.	0	0	1	0	1
Woolford, Donnell, Chi.	2	1	0	0	1
Workman, Vince, G.B.	4	2	0	0	2
Young, Steve, S.F.	9	3	0	-13	3
Zorich, Chris, Chi.	0	0	1	42	1

Yards includes aborted plays, own recoveries, and opponents' recoveries.

AMERICAN FOOTBALL CONFERENCE - FUMBLES

	Fum	Own Rec	Fum OB
Cleveland	19	6	1
Indianapolis	24	12	1
L.A. Raiders	25	8	2
San Diego	26	13	1
Pittsburgh	28	10	0
N.Y. Jets	28	12	1
Kansas City	28	16	3
Houston	28	15	1
Denver	29	13	2
Buffalo	31	13	1
Miami	31	13	1
Cincinnati	32	22	0
Seattle	37	17	2
New England	43	17	0
AFC Total	409	187	16
AFC Average	29.2	13.4	1.1

NATIONAL FOOTBALL CONFERENCE - FUMBLES

	Fum	Own Rec	Fum OB
Dallas	16	7	0
Washington	18	10	1
Tampa Bay	19	9	1
Chicago	23	10	3
Philadelphia	25	9	1
N.Y. Giants	25	12	0
Phoenix	26	7	1
Detroit	26	9	2
New Orleans	27	12	2
San Francisco	29	12	4
Minnesota	29	11	1
L.A. Rams	30	12	1
Atlanta	30	16	0
Green Bay	41	18	2
NFC Total	364	154	19
NFC Average	26.0	11.0	1.4
NFL Total	773	341	35
NFL Average	27.6	12.2	1.3

Fum OB= Fumbled out of bounds, includes fumbled through the end zone. Yards includes aborted plays, own recoveries, and oppponents' recoveries.

Fumbled through the end zone, ball awarded to opponents: Denver (possession awarded to Seattle).

TD	Opp Rec	TD	Fum Yards	Tot Rec
0	20	3	152	26
0	15	0	-32	27
0	7	0	35	15
1	11	0	19	24
0	21	1	86	31
0	18	0	16	30
0	15	2	17	31
0	11	3	7	26
0	16	1	117	29
0	12	1	8	25
0	14	0	-17	27
0	17	2	58	39
0	11	1	69	28
0	15	2	-41	32
1	203	16	494	390
0.1	14.5	1.1	35.3	27.9

TD	Opp Rec	TD	Fum Yards	Tot Rec
0	14	1	44	21
0	11	1	114	21
0	13	3	63	22
0	16	1	42	26
0	13	1	39	22
0	12	0	-19	24
0	12	0	28	19
0	11	1	8	20
0	20	3	135	32
0	12	1	36	24
0	14	2	85	25
0	15	0	-8	27
0	12	1	31	28
0	19	1	57	37
0	194	16	655	348
0.0	13.9	1.1	46.8	24.9
1	397	32	1149	738
0.0	14.2	1.1	41.0	26.4

NFL TEAM BY TEAM

1992 AFC, NFC, AND NFL SUMMARY

	AFC Offense Total	AFC Offense Average	AFC Defense Total	AFC Defense Average
First Downs	3762	268.7	3853	275.2
Rushing	1351	96.5	1406	100.4
Passing	2125	151.8	2157	154.1
Penalty	286	20.4	290	20.7
Rushes	6128	437.7	6383	455.9
Net Yds. Gained	24027	1716.2	24876	1776.9
Avg. Gain	——	3.9	——	3.9
Avg. Yds. per Game	——	107.3	——	111.1
Passes Attempted	6723	480.2	6613	472.4
Completed	3745	267.5	3739	267.1
% Completed	——	55.7	——	56.5
Total Yds. Gained	44841	3202.9	45208	3229.1
Times Sacked	604	43.1	597	42.6
Yds. Lost	4387	313.4	4203	300.2
Net Yds. Gained	40454	2889.6	41005	2928.9
Avg. Yds. per Game	——	180.6	——	183.1
Net Yds. per Pass Play	——	5.52	——	5.69
Yds. Gained per Comp.	——	11.97	——	12.09
Combined Net Yds. Gained	64481	4605.8	65881	4705.8
% Total Yds. Rushing	——	37.3	——	37.8
% Total Yds. Passing	——	62.7	——	62.2
Avg. Yds. per Game	——	287.9	——	294.1
Ball Control Plays	13455	961.1	13593	970.9
Avg. Yds. per Play	——	4.8	——	4.8
Third Down Efficiency	——	35.0	——	36.6
Interceptions	285	20.4	263	18.8
Yds. Returned	4397	314.1	4312	308.0
Returned for TD	24	1.7	25	1.8
Punts	1084	77.4	1061	75.8
Yds. Punted	46028	3287.7	45111	3222.2
Avg. Yds. per Punt	——	42.5	——	42.5
Punt Returns	495	35.4	513	36.6
Yds. Returned	4507	321.9	4404	314.6
Avg. Yds. per Return	——	9.1	——	8.6
Returned for TD	7	0.5	6	0.4
Kickoff Returns	678	48.4	653	46.6
Yds. Returned	12787	913.4	12347	881.9
Avg. Yds. per Return	——	18.9	——	18.9
Returned for TD	1	0.1	3	0.2

STATISTICAL SUMMARY

NFC Offense Total	NFC Offense Average	NFC Defense Total	NFC Defense Average	NFL Total	NFL Average
3985	284.6	3894	278.1	7747	276.7
1446	103.3	1391	99.4	2797	99.9
2259	161.4	2227	159.1	4384	156.6
280	20.0	276	19.7	566	20.2
6163	440.2	5908	422.0	12291	439.0
25482	1820.1	24633	1759.5	49509	1768.2
—	4.1	—	4.2	—	4.0
—	113.8	—	110.0	—	110.5
6685	477.5	6795	485.4	13408	478.9
3960	282.9	3966	283.3	7705	275.2
—	59.2	—	58.4	—	57.5
47170	3369.3	46803	3343.1	92011	3286.1
536	38.3	543	38.8	1140	40.7
3560	254.3	3744	267.4	7947	283.8
43610	3115.0	43059	3075.6	84064	3002.3
—	194.7	—	192.2	—	187.6
—	6.04	—	5.87	—	5.78
—	11.91	—	11.80	—	11.94
69092	4935.1	67692	4835.1	133573	4770.5
—	36.9	—	36.4	—	37.1
—	63.1	—	63.6	—	62.9
—	308.4	—	302.2	—	298.2
13384	956.0	13246	946.1	26839	958.5
—	5.2	—	5.1	—	5.0
—	39.5	—	37.9	—	37.2
234	16.7	256	18.3	519	18.5
3600	257.1	3685	263.2	7997	285.6
23	1.6	22	1.6	47	1.7
973	69.5	996	71.1	2057	73.5
40516	2894.0	41433	2959.5	86544	3090.9
—	41.6	—	41.6	—	42.1
479	34.2	461	32.9	974	34.8
4402	314.4	4505	321.8	8909	318.2
—	9.2	—	9.8	—	9.1
10	0.7	11	0.8	17	0.6
715	51.1	740	52.9	1393	49.8
14272	1019.4	14712	1050.9	27059	966.4
—	20.0	—	19.9	—	19.4
5	0.4	3	0.2	6	0.2

1992 AFC, NFC, AND NFL SUMMARY (CONT.)

	AFC Offense Total	AFC Offense Average	AFC Defense Total	AFC Defense Average
Fumbles	409	29.2	403	28.8
Lost	206	14.7	203	14.5
Out of Bounds	16	1.1	19	1.4
Own Rec. for TD	1	0.1	1	0.1
Opp. Rec.	203	14.5	206	14.7
Opp. Rec. for TD	16	1.1	17	1.2
Penalties	1443	103.1	1402	100.1
Yds. Penalized	11604	828.9	11193	799.5
Total Points Scored	3893	278.1	4111	293.6
Total TDs	433	30.9	459	32.8
TDs Rushing	144	10.3	156	11.1
TDs Passing	237	16.9	251	17.9
TDs on Ret. and Rec.	52	3.7	52	3.7
Extra Points	420	30.0	449	32.1
Safeties	7	0.5	7	0.5
Field Goals Made	287	20.5	298	21.3
Field Goals Attempted	393	28.1	410	29.3
% Successful	——	73.0	——	72.7

1992 AMERICAN FOOTBALL CONFERENCE OFFENSE

	Buff.	Cin.	Clev.	Den.	Hou.	Ind.
First Downs	350	248	242	234	339	267
Rushing	133	112	85	84	101	70
Passing	192	114	141	135	217	174
Penalty	25	22	16	15	21	23
Rushes	549	454	451	403	353	379
Net Yds. Gained	2436	1976	1607	1500	1626	1102
Avg. Gain	4.4	4.4	3.6	3.7	4.6	2.9
Avg. Yds. per Game	152.3	123.5	100.4	93.8	101.6	68.9
Passes Attempted	509	435	398	473	573	546
Completed	293	227	238	258	373	305
% Completed	57.6	52.2	59.8	54.5	65.1	55.9
Total Yds. Gained	3678	2284	3102	3312	4231	3584
Times Sacked	29	45	34	52	32	44
Yds. Lost	221	341	217	382	202	318
Net Yds. Gained	3457	1943	2885	2930	4029	3266
Avg. Yds. per Game	216.1	121.4	180.3	183.1	251.8	204.1
Net Yds. per Pass Play	6.43	4.05	6.68	5.58	6.66	5.54
Yds. Gained per Comp.	12.55	10.06	13.03	12.84	11.34	11.73
Combined Net Yds. Gained	5893	3919	4492	4430	5655	4368
% Total Yds. Rushing	41.3	50.4	35.8	33.9	28.8	25.2
% Total Yds. Passing	58.7	49.6	64.2	66.1	71.2	74.8
Avg. Yds. per Game	368.3	244.9	280.8	276.9	353.4	273.0
Ball Control Plays	1087	934	883	928	958	969
Avg. Yds. per Play	5.4	4.2	5.1	4.8	5.9	4.5
Avg. Time of Poss.	28:10	27:05	30:13	28:14	31:09	28:1

NFC Offense Total	NFC Offense Average	NFC Defense Total	NFC Defense Average	NFL Total	NFL Average
364	26.0	370	26.4	773	27.6
191	13.6	194	13.9	397	14.2
19	1.4	16	1.1	35	1.3
0	0.0	0	0.0	1	0.0
194	13.9	191	13.6	397	14.2
16	1.1	15	1.1	32	1.1
1238	88.4	1279	91.4	2681	95.8
10009	714.9	10420	744.3	21613	771.9
4498	321.3	4280	305.7	8391	299.7
525	37.5	499	35.6	958	34.2
189	13.5	177	12.6	333	11.9
279	19.9	265	18.9	516	18.4
57	4.1	57	4.1	109	3.9
516	36.9	487	34.8	936	33.4
5	0.4	5	0.4	12	0.4
274	19.6	263	18.8	561	20.0
380	27.1	363	25.9	773	27.6
——	72.1	——	72.5	——	72.6

K.C.	Raid.	Mia.	N.E.	N.Y.J.	Pitt.	S.D.	Sea.
246	259	316	215	252	284	302	208
87	99	101	71	94	119	118	77
134	139	194	130	137	143	161	114
25	21	21	14	21	22	23	17
446	434	407	419	424	518	489	402
1532	1794	1525	1550	1752	2156	1875	1596
3.4	4.1	3.7	3.7	4.1	4.2	3.8	4.0
95.8	112.1	95.3	96.9	109.5	134.8	117.2	99.8
413	471	563	444	495	431	496	476
230	233	332	244	251	249	282	230
55.7	49.5	59.0	55.0	50.7	57.8	56.9	48.3
3115	2950	4148	2492	2962	3046	3614	2323
48	48	28	65	39	40	33	67
323	360	173	458	283	296	268	545
2792	2590	3975	2034	2679	2750	3346	1778
174.5	161.9	248.4	127.1	167.4	171.9	209.1	111.1
6.06	4.99	6.73	4.00	5.02	5.84	6.33	3.27
13.54	12.66	12.49	10.21	11.80	12.23	12.82	10.10
4324	4384	5500	3584	4431	4906	5221	3374
35.4	40.9	27.7	43.2	39.5	43.9	35.9	47.3
64.6	59.1	72.3	56.8	60.5	56.1	64.1	52.7
270.3	274.0	343.8	224.0	276.9	306.6	326.3	210.9
907	953	998	928	958	989	1018	945
4.8	4.6	5.5	3.9	4.6	5.0	5.1	3.6
29:37	29:06	30:30	28:30	30:24	32:05	32:03	29:01

1992 AMERICAN FOOTBALL CONFERENCE OFFENSE (CONT.)

	Buff.	Cin.	Clev.	Den.	Hou.	Ind.
Third Down Efficiency	39.6	32.2	34.2	32.2	42.4	35.7
Had Intercepted	21	17	16	29	23	26
Yds. Opp Returned	423	127	213	567	367	461
Ret. by Opp. for TD	2	0	1	3	0	4
Punts	60	76	75	85	55	83
Yds. Punted	2531	3196	3083	3705	2487	3716
Avg. Yds. per Punt	42.2	42.1	41.1	43.6	45.2	44.8
Punt Returns	43	24	44	34	33	25
Yds. Returned	464	285	429	353	194	275
Avg. Yds. per Return	10.8	11.9	9.8	10.4	5.9	11.0
Returned for TD	0	1	1	0	0	2
Kickoff Returns	41	59	43	51	46	51
Yds. Returned	761	1058	880	1028	885	1001
Avg. Yds. per Return	18.6	17.9	20.5	20.2	19.2	19.6
Returned for TD	0	0	0	0	0	0
Fumbles	31	32	19	29	28	24
Lost	17	10	12	14	12	11
Out of Bounds	1	0	1	2	1	1
Own Rec. for TD	0	0	0	0	0	0
Opp. Rec. by	12	17	20	16	11	15
Opp. Rec. for TD	1	2	3	1	3	0
Penalties	103	98	104	98	111	122
Yds. Penalized	775	755	765	768	824	958
Total Points Scored	381	274	272	262	352	216
Total TDs	44	31	30	29	41	24
TDs Rushing	18	11	7	11	10	8
TDs Passing	23	16	18	16	27	13
TDs on Ret. and Rec.	3	4	5	2	4	3
Extra Points	43	31	29	28	41	24
Safeties	1	0	0	0	1	0
Field Goals Made	24	19	21	20	21	16
Field Goals Attempted	30	28	29	25	27	29
% Successful	80.0	67.9	72.4	80.0	77.8	55.2

1992 AMERICAN FOOTBALL CONFERENCE DEFENSE

	Buff.	Cin.	Clev.	Den.	Hou.	Ind.
First Downs	278	319	281	283	254	314
Rushing	77	126	86	105	93	129
Passing	185	168	170	156	139	164
Penalty	16	25	25	22	22	21
Rushes	427	490	429	489	412	493
Net Yds. Gained	1395	2007	1605	1963	1634	2174
Avg. Gain	3.3	4.1	3.7	4.0	4.0	4.4
Avg. Yds. per Game	87.2	125.4	100.3	122.7	102.1	135.9

K.C.	Raid.	Mia.	N.E.	N.Y.J.	Pitt.	S.D.	Sea.
34.3	38.5	38.8	32.3	31.4	34.6	39.4	26.6
12	23	17	19	24	14	21	23
162	345	446	232	347	235	241	231
0	2	4	0	2	1	1	4
86	77	61	103	73	74	68	108
3633	3255	2424	4227	2993	3119	2899	4760
42.2	42.3	39.7	41.0	41.0	42.1	42.6	44.1
39	41	31	37	30	32	44	38
402	402	191	274	232	364	359	283
10.3	9.8	6.2	7.4	7.7	11.4	8.2	7.4
2	0	0	0	0	1	0	0
39	43	44	64	54	48	45	50
722	744	838	1376	950	847	812	885
18.5	17.3	19.0	21.5	17.6	17.6	18.0	17.7
0	0	0	1	0	0	0	0
28	25	31	43	28	28	26	37
9	15	17	26	15	18	12	18
3	2	1	0	1	0	1	2
0	0	0	0	0	0	1	0
15	7	14	15	18	21	11	11
2	0	0	2	0	1	0	1
82	113	86	111	107	106	91	111
675	832	656	1051	873	941	813	918
348	249	340	205	220	299	335	140
40	29	36	25	23	31	36	14
14	7	9	6	8	13	18	4
15	20	24	13	12	15	16	9
11	2	3	6	3	3	2	1
39	28	34	22	23	29	35	14
0	1	0	0	1	0	3	0
23	15	30	11	19	28	26	14
25	26	37	17	30	36	32	22
92.0	57.7	81.1	64.7	63.3	77.8	81.3	63.6

K.C.	Raid.	Mia.	N.E.	N.Y.J.	Pitt.	S.D.	Sea.
256	264	273	292	276	266	250	247
97	104	92	112	110	99	80	96
145	135	168	149	146	146	157	129
14	25	13	31	20	21	13	22
441	478	428	521	460	435	365	513
1787	1683	1600	1951	1919	1841	1395	1922
4.1	3.5	3.7	3.7	4.2	4.2	3.8	3.7
111.7	105.2	100.0	121.9	119.9	115.1	87.2	120.1

1992 AMERICAN FOOTBALL CONFERENCE DEFENSE (CONT.)

	Buff.	Cin.	Clev.	Den.	Hou.	Ind.
Passes Attempted	520	489	486	462	445	470
Completed	305	288	291	268	248	260
% Completed	58.7	58.9	59.9	58.0	55.7	55.3
Total Yds. Gained	3560	3620	3467	3437	2898	3236
Times Sacked	44	45	48	50	50	39
Yds. Lost	351	294	315	317	321	336
Net Yds. Gained	3209	3326	3152	3120	2577	2900
Avg. Yds. per Game	200.6	207.9	197.0	195.0	161.1	181.3
Net Yds. per Pass Play	5.69	6.23	5.90	6.09	5.21	5.70
Yds. Gained per Comp.	11.67	12.57	11.91	12.82	11.69	12.45
Combined Net Yds. Gained	4604	5333	4757	5083	4211	5074
% Total Yds. Rushing	30.3	37.6	33.7	38.6	38.8	42.8
% Total Yds. Passing	69.7	62.4	66.3	61.4	61.2	57.2
Avg. Yds. per Game	287.8	333.3	297.3	317.7	263.2	317.1
Ball Control Plays	991	1024	963	1001	907	1004
Avg. Yds. per Play	4.6	5.2	4.9	5.1	4.6	5.1
Avg. Time of Poss.	31:50	32:55	29:47	31:46	28:51	31:43
Third Down Efficiency	38.5	45.8	37.1	36.5	35.1	35.5
Intercepted by	23	16	13	15	20	20
Yds. Returned By	325	205	222	210	181	302
Returned for TD	2	1	1	1	1	1
Punts	79	57	74	78	68	71
Yds. Punted	3465	2384	3293	3380	2939	3021
Avg. Yds. per Punt	43.9	41.8	44.5	43.3	43.2	42.5
Punt Returns	22	32	27	39	31	45
Yds. Returned	185	284	234	382	255	313
Avg. Yds. per Return	8.4	8.9	8.7	9.8	8.2	7.0
Returned for TD	0	1	0	0	0	0
Kickoff Returns	60	46	51	13	63	36
Yds. Returned	1215	1079	907	254	989	630
Avg. Yds. per Return	20.3	23.5	17.8	19.5	15.7	17.5
Returned for TD	1	2	0	0	0	0
Fumbles	29	36	33	33	24	28
Lost	12	17	20	16	11	15
Out of Bounds	2	2	1	1	0	1
Own Rec. for TD	0	0	0	0	0	0
Opp. Rec. by	17	10	12	14	12	11
Opp. Rec. for TD	1	2	0	1	2	0
Penalties	118	95	93	96	114	101
Yds. Penalized	933	797	764	715	886	836
Total Points Scored	283	364	275	329	258	302
Total TDs	31	44	29	35	28	34
TDs Rushing	8	15	5	10	6	16
TDs Passing	19	24	23	21	20	14
TDs on Ret. and Rec.	4	5	1	4	2	4
Extra Points	31	44	29	35	27	33
Safeties	0	1	0	0	0	1
Field Goals Made	22	18	24	28	21	21
Field Goals Attempted	30	30	29	38	26	28
% Successful	73.3	60.0	82.8	73.7	80.8	75.0

K.C.	Raid.	Mia.	N.E.	N.Y.J.	Pitt.	S.D.	Sea.
458	450	512	459	465	478	491	428
253	243	294	258	257	252	271	251
55.2	54.0	57.4	56.2	55.3	52.7	55.2	58.6
2928	3153	3266	3211	3201	3065	3188	2978
50	46	36	20	36	36	51	46
391	320	283	114	240	248	356	317
2537	2833	2983	3097	2961	2817	2832	2661
158.6	177.1	186.4	193.6	185.1	176.1	177.0	166.3
4.99	5.71	5.44	6.47	5.91	5.48	5.23	5.61
11.57	12.98	11.11	12.45	12.46	12.16	11.76	11.86
4324	4516	4583	5048	4880	4658	4227	4583
41.3	37.3	34.9	38.6	39.3	39.5	33.0	41.9
58.7	62.7	65.1	61.4	60.7	60.5	67.0	58.1
270.3	282.3	286.4	315.5	305.0	291.1	264.2	286.4
949	974	976	1000	961	949	907	987
4.6	4.6	4.7	5.0	5.1	4.9	4.7	4.6
30:23	30:54	29:30	31:30	29:36	27:55	27:57	30:59
35.6	32.9	40.6	36.0	35.8	33.3	36.5	32.6
24	12	18	14	21	22	25	20
403	339	458	285	269	384	405	324
6	1	3	3	3	1	1	0
80	85	74	75	70	74	80	96
3445	3615	2971	3045	2866	3107	3565	4015
43.1	42.5	40.1	40.6	40.9	42.0	44.6	41.8
40	40	33	59	26	39	24	56
328	385	382	499	189	308	244	416
8.2	9.6	11.6	8.5	7.3	7.9	10.2	7.4
1	0	1	1	0	0	1	1
64	35	65	45	33	52	54	36
1203	690	1380	749	552	1052	962	685
18.8	19.7	21.2	16.6	16.7	20.2	17.8	19.0
0	0	0	0	0	0	0	0
34	21	25	30	33	34	18	25
15	7	14	15	18	21	11	11
2	0	0	1	1	5	0	3
0	1	0	0	0	0	0	0
9	15	17	26	15	18	12	18
1	1	2	2	1	2	0	2
124	98	89	90	82	104	98	100
959	755	679	673	808	814	798	776
282	281	281	363	315	225	241	312
34	32	32	40	35	24	29	32
12	17	9	15	13	6	10	14
19	11	16	22	19	15	17	11
3	4	7	3	3	3	2	7
33	32	30	40	34	24	28	29
0	0	1	1	1	0	0	2
15	19	19	27	23	19	13	29
21	30	26	41	31	28	16	36
71.4	63.3	73.1	65.9	74.2	67.9	81.3	80.6

1992 NATIONAL FOOTBALL CONFERENCE OFFENSE

	Atl.	Chi.	Dall.	Det.	G.B.
First Downs	273	282	324	241	291
Rushing	67	101	119	83	101
Passing	194	157	183	133	171
Penalty	12	24	22	25	19
Rushes	322	427	500	378	420
Net Yds. Gained	1270	1871	2121	1644	1555
Avg. Gain	3.9	4.4	4.2	4.3	3.7
Avg. Yds. per Game	79.4	116.9	132.6	102.8	97.2
Passes Attempted	548	479	491	406	527
Completed	336	266	314	231	340
% Completed	61.3	55.5	64.0	56.9	64.5
Total Yds. Gained	3892	3334	3597	3150	3498
Times Sacked	40	45	23	59	43
Yds. Lost	259	264	112	354	268
Net Yds. Gained	3633	3070	3485	2796	3230
Avg. Yds. per Game	227.1	191.9	217.8	174.8	201.9
Net Yds. per Pass Play	6.18	5.86	6.78	6.01	5.67
Yds. Gained per Comp.	11.58	12.53	11.46	13.64	10.29
Combined Net Yds. Gained	4903	4941	5606	4440	4785
% Total Yds. Rushing	25.9	37.9	37.8	37.0	32.5
% Total Yds. Passing	74.1	62.1	62.2	63.0	67.5
Avg. Yds. per Game	306.4	308.8	350.4	277.5	299.1
Ball Control Plays	910	951	1014	843	990
Avg. Yds. per Play	5.4	5.2	5.5	5.3	4.8
Avg. Time of Poss.	28:36	29:15	33:57	27:36	32:30
Third Down Efficiency	38.4	36.4	41.8	34.3	42.5
Had Intercepted	15	24	15	21	15
Yds. Opp Returned	246	612	300	294	198
Ret. by Opp. for TD	3	6	0	1	1
Punts	70	79	61	66	68
Yds. Punted	2855	3393	2620	2846	2608
Avg. Yds. per Punt	40.8	42.9	43.0	43.1	38.4
Punt Returns	29	23	44	21	35
Yds. Returned	196	176	550	190	315
Avg. Yds. per Return	6.8	7.7	12.5	9.0	9.0
Returned for TD	0	0	2	1	1
Kickoff Returns	64	56	37	59	54
Yds. Returned	1532	1143	699	1193	1017
Avg. Yds. per Return	23.9	20.4	18.9	20.2	18.8
Returned for TD	2	1	0	1	0
Fumbles	30	23	16	26	41
Lost	14	10	9	15	21
Out of Bounds	0	3	0	2	2
Own Rec. for TD	0	0	0	0	0
Opp. Rec. by	12	16	14	11	19
Opp. Rec. for TD	1	1	1	1	1

Rams	Minn.	N.O.	N.Y.G.	Phil.	Phoe.	S.F.	T.B.	Wash.
278	288	267	271	292	277	344	281	276
83	115	92	120	138	88	135	100	104
174	157	155	119	138	161	192	165	160
21	16	20	32	16	28	17	16	12
393	497	454	458	516	395	482	438	483
1659	2030	1628	2077	2388	1491	2315	1706	1727
4.2	4.1	3.6	4.5	4.6	3.8	4.8	3.9	3.6
103.7	126.9	101.8	129.8	149.3	93.2	144.7	106.6	107.9
495	458	426	433	429	517	480	511	485
289	258	251	232	255	298	319	299	272
58.4	56.3	58.9	53.6	59.4	57.6	66.5	58.5	56.1
3422	3162	3297	2628	3054	3344	4054	3399	3339
26	40	15	45	64	36	32	45	23
204	293	119	283	462	258	174	334	176
3218	2869	3178	2345	2592	3086	3880	3065	3163
201.1	179.3	198.6	146.6	162.0	192.9	242.5	191.6	197.7
6.18	5.76	7.21	4.91	5.26	5.58	7.58	5.51	6.23
11.84	12.26	13.14	11.33	11.98	11.22	12.71	11.37	12.28
4877	4899	4806	4422	4980	4577	6195	4771	4890
34.0	41.4	33.9	47.0	48.0	32.6	37.4	35.8	35.3
66.0	58.6	66.1	53.0	52.0	67.4	62.6	64.2	64.7
304.8	306.2	300.4	276.4	311.3	286.1	387.2	298.2	305.6
914	995	895	936	1009	948	994	994	991
5.3	4.9	5.4	4.7	4.9	4.8	6.2	4.8	4.9
28:31	29:18	31:10	29:22	31:47	31:01	32:19	29:15	31:04
37.1	44.3	38.1	34.5	38.5	38.7	46.5	37.1	43.4
20	15	16	10	13	24	9	20	17
305	164	280	190	77	279	126	211	318
1	1	2	2	0	1	2	1	2
76	73	67	85	82	58	49	74	65
3122	3243	2947	3451	3459	2484	1918	3015	2555
41.1	44.4	44.0	40.6	42.2	42.8	39.1	40.7	39.3
39	33	45	27	47	33	40	26	37
345	336	231	240	555	364	389	160	355
8.8	10.2	5.1	8.9	11.8	11.0	9.7	6.2	9.6
2	0	0	0	1	0	1	0	2
63	45	42	56	48	51	42	50	48
1054	874	815	1098	987	1127	879	881	973
16.7	19.4	19.4	19.6	20.6	22.1	20.9	17.6	20.3
0	0	0	1	0	0	0	0	0
30	29	27	25	25	26	29	19	18
17	17	13	13	15	18	13	9	7
1	1	2	0	1	1	4	1	1
0	0	0	0	0	0	0	0	0
15	14	20	12	13	12	12	13	11
0	2	3	0	1	0	1	3	1

1992 NATIONAL FOOTBALL CONFERENCE OFFENSE (CONT.)

	Atl.	Chi.	Dall.	Det.	G.B.
Penalties	78	93	91	122	88
Yds. Penalized	656	776	650	903	749
Total Points Scored	327	295	409	273	276
Total TDs	39	34	48	30	30
TDs Rushing	3	15	20	9	7
TDs Passing	33	17	23	16	20
TDs on Ret. and Rec.	3	2	5	5	3
Extra Points	39	34	47	30	30
Safeties	0	0	1	0	0
Field Goals Made	18	19	24	21	22
Field Goals Attempted	22	26	35	26	29
% Successful	81.8	73.1	68.6	80.8	75.9

1992 NATIONAL FOOTBALL CONFERENCE DEFENSE

	Atl.	Chi.	Dall.	Det.	G.B.
First Downs	304	274	241	308	277
Rushing	109	109	68	119	89
Passing	172	144	147	168	170
Penalty	23	21	26	21	18
Rushes	464	468	345	460	406
Net Yds. Gained	2294	1948	1244	1841	1821
Avg. Gain	4.9	4.2	3.6	4.0	4.5
Avg. Yds. per Game	143.4	121.8	77.8	115.1	113.8
Passes Attempted	439	442	484	487	483
Completed	277	261	263	296	277
% Completed	63.1	59.0	54.3	60.8	57.3
Total Yds. Gained	3496	3290	3034	3402	3496
Times Sacked	31	43	44	29	34
Yds. Lost	241	286	347	185	219
Net Yds. Gained	3255	3004	2687	3217	3277
Avg. Yds. per Game	203.4	187.8	167.9	201.1	204.8
Net Yds. per Pass Play	6.93	6.19	5.09	6.23	6.34
Yds. Gained per Comp.	12.62	12.61	11.54	11.49	12.62
Combined Net Yds. Gained	5549	4952	3931	5058	5098
% Total Yds. Rushing	41.3	39.3	31.6	36.4	35.7
% Total Yds. Passing	58.7	60.7	68.4	63.6	64.3
Avg. Yds. per Game	346.8	309.5	245.7	316.1	318.6
Ball Control Plays	934	953	873	976	923
Avg. Yds. per Play	5.9	5.2	4.5	5.2	5.5
Avg. Time of Poss.	31:24	30:45	26:03	32:24	27:30
Third Down Efficiency	42.9	35.6	27.2	42.0	37.6
Intercepted By	11	14	17	21	15
Yds. Returned By	135	188	158	255	222
Returned for TD	0	0	1	0	1

Rams	Minn.	N.O.	N.Y.G.	Phil.	Phoe.	S.F.	T.B.	Wash.
79	99	60	87	101	85	80	91	84
592	809	567	647	807	722	636	754	741
313	374	330	306	354	243	431	267	300
38	45	35	36	44	29	54	33	30
12	19	10	20	19	11	22	12	10
23	18	19	14	20	15	29	17	15
3	8	6	2	5	3	3	4	5
38	45	33	36	40	28	53	33	30
1	1	0	0	1	1	0	0	0
15	19	29	18	16	13	18	12	30
20	25	34	23	25	26	27	22	40
75.0	76.0	85.3	78.3	64.0	50.0	66.7	54.5	75.0

Rams	Minn.	N.O.	N.Y.G.	Phil.	Phoe.	S.F.	T.B.	Wash.
319	293	246	287	242	281	277	296	249
130	113	86	115	73	101	90	100	89
175	154	146	155	146	163	174	175	138
14	26	14	17	23	17	13	21	22
467	438	381	458	387	436	351	441	406
2230	1733	1605	2012	1481	1635	1418	1675	1696
4.8	4.0	4.2	4.4	3.8	3.8	4.0	3.8	4.2
139.4	108.3	100.3	125.8	92.6	102.2	88.6	104.7	106.0
507	508	511	440	517	452	551	508	466
305	320	287	270	263	276	320	293	258
60.2	63.0	56.2	61.4	50.9	61.1	58.1	57.7	55.4
3481	3124	2846	3228	3316	3687	3642	3740	3021
31	51	57	25	55	27	41	36	39
188	342	376	197	385	196	273	230	279
3293	2782	2470	3031	2931	3491	3369	3510	2742
205.8	173.9	154.4	189.4	183.2	218.2	210.6	219.4	171.4
6.12	4.98	4.35	6.52	5.12	7.29	5.69	6.45	5.43
11.41	9.76	9.92	11.96	12.61	13.36	11.38	12.76	11.71
5523	4515	4075	5043	4412	5126	4787	5185	4438
40.4	38.4	39.4	39.9	33.6	31.9	29.6	32.3	38.2
59.6	61.6	60.6	60.1	66.4	68.1	70.4	67.7	61.8
345.2	282.2	254.7	315.2	275.8	320.4	299.2	324.1	277.4
1005	997	949	923	959	915	943	985	911
5.5	4.5	4.3	5.5	4.6	5.6	5.1	5.3	4.9
31:29	30:42	28:50	30:38	28:13	28:59	27:41	30:45	28:56
44.6	38.2	34.0	42.2	33.3	36.2	37.7	43.4	35.6
18	28	18	14	24	16	17	20	23
283	502	254	192	307	298	172	234	485
1	6	3	1	2	3	1	1	2

1992 NATIONAL FOOTBALL CONFERENCE DEFENSE (CONT.)

	Atl.	Chi.	Dall.	Det.	G.B.
Punts	61	70	87	55	68
Yds. Punted	2534	2840	3660	2263	2941
Avg. Yds. per Punt	41.5	40.6	42.1	41.1	43.3
Punt Returns	44	38	34	30	26
Yds. Returned	482	351	397	356	230
Avg. Yds. per Return	11.0	9.2	11.7	11.9	8.8
Returned for TD	4	1	0	0	1
Kickoff Returns	55	50	60	45	57
Yds. Returned	1059	1027	1217	948	901
Avg. Yds. per Return	19.3	20.5	20.3	21.1	15.8
Returned for TD	0	0	0	0	0
Fumbles	24	34	25	25	32
Lost	12	16	14	11	19
Out of Bounds	1	1	1	1	0
Own Rec. for TD	0	0	0	0	0
Opp. Rec. by	14	10	9	15	21
Opp. Rec. for TD	0	2	2	3	1
Penalties	92	90	94	111	98
Yds. Penalized	761	780	727	871	830
Total Points Scored	414	361	243	332	296
Total TDs	51	43	29	38	32
TDs Rushing	20	14	11	14	12
TDs Passing	24	20	16	20	16
TDs on Ret. and Rec.	7	9	2	4	4
Extra Points	51	43	27	38	32
Safeties	0	0	0	0	0
Field Goals Made	19	20	14	22	24
Field Goals Attempted	31	25	17	35	27
% Successful	61.3	80.0	82.4	62.9	88.9

Rams	Minn.	N.O.	N.Y.G.	Phil.	Phoe.	S.F.	T.B.	Wash.
66	76	89	64	85	62	76	64	73
2776	3182	3666	2477	3531	2656	3134	2645	3128
42.1	41.9	41.2	38.7	41.5	42.8	41.2	41.3	42.8
48	34	31	46	36	22	23	22	27
522	339	218	548	295	141	177	117	332
10.9	10.0	7.0	11.9	8.2	6.4	7.7	5.3	12.3
1	1	0	2	0	0	0	0	1
55	50	40	64	53	42	66	49	54
1128	925	923	1207	1027	767	1273	1236	1074
20.5	18.5	23.1	18.9	19.4	18.3	19.3	25.2	19.9
0	0	0	0	1	0	0	1	1
26	23	37	27	27	25	23	19	23
15	14	20	12	13	12	12	13	11
1	2	0	2	2	1	2	1	1
0	0	0	0	0	0	0	0	0
17	17	13	13	15	18	13	9	7
1	1	1	0	1	2	0	1	0
102	98	77	93	86	100	79	74	85
778	768	729	744	683	826	651	563	709
383	249	202	367	245	332	236	365	255
43	27	24	46	26	40	27	43	30
22	11	8	17	4	13	5	15	11
18	12	13	22	20	24	20	25	15
3	4	3	7	2	3	2	3	4
41	27	22	44	26	38	26	43	29
0	0	0	1	0	0	0	2	2
28	20	12	15	21	18	16	20	14
34	25	17	21	32	28	20	30	21
82.4	80.0	70.6	71.4	65.6	64.3	80.0	66.7	66.7

CLUB LEADERS

	Offense	Defense
First Downs	Buff. 350	Dall. 241
Rushing	Phil. 138	Dall. 68
Passing	Hou. 217	Sea. 129
Penalty	N.Y.G. 32	Mia.,S.D., & S.F. 13
Rushes	Buff. 549	Dall. 345
Net Yds. Gained	Buff. 2436	Dall. 1244
Avg. Gain	S.F. 4.8	Buff. 3.3
Passes Attempted	Hou. 573	Sea. 428
Completed	Hou. 373	Raid. 243
% Completed	S.F. 66.5	Phil. 50.9
Total Yds. Gained	Hou. 4231	N.O. 2846
Times Sacked	N.O. 15	N.O. 57
Yds. Lost	Dall. 112	K.C. 391
Net Yds. Gained	Hou. 4029	N.O. 2470
Net Yds. per Pass Play	S.F. 7.58	N.O. 4.35
Yds. Gained per Comp.	Det. 13.64	Minn. 9.76
Combined Net Yds. Gained	S.F. 6195	Dall. 3931
% Total Yds. Rushing	Cin. 50.4	S.F. 29.6
% Total Yds. Passing	Hou. 74.8	Ind. 57.2
Ball Control Plays	Buff. 1087	Dall. 873
Avg. Yds. per Play	S.F. 6.23	N.O. 4.29
Avg. Time of Poss.	Dall. 33:57	—
Third Down Efficiency	S.F. 46.5	Dall. 27.2
Interceptions	—	Minn. 28
Yds. Returned	—	Minn. 502
Returned for TD	—	K.C. & Minn. 6
Punts	Sea. 108	—
Yds. Punted	Sea. 4760	—
Avg. Yds. per Punt	Hou. 45.2	—
Punt Returns	Phil. 47	Buff., Pho., & T.B. 22
Yds. Returned	Phil. 555	T.B. 117
Avg. Yds. per Return	Dall. 12.5	T.B. 5.3
Returned for TD	Five with 2	—
Kickoff Returns	Atl. & N.E. 64	Den. 13
Yds. Returned	Atl. 1532	Den. 254
Avg. Yds. per Return	Atl. 23.9	Hou. 15.7
Returned for TD	Atl. 2	—
Total Points Scored	S.F. 431	N.O. 202
Total TDs	S.F. 54	N.O. & Pitt. 24
TDs Rushing	S.F. 22	Phil. 4
TDs Passing	S.F. 29	Raid. & Sea. 11
TDs on Ret. and Rec.	K.C. 11	Clev. 1
Extra Points	S.F. 53	N.O. 22
Safeties	S.D. 3	—
Field Goals Made	Mia. & Wash. 30	N.O. 12
Field Goals Attempted	Wash. 40	S.D. 16
% Successful	K.C. 92.0	Cin. 60.0

Cortez Kennedy: NFL Defensive Player of the Year.

CLUB RANKINGS BY YARDS

	OFFENSE			DEFENSE		
	Total	Rush	Pass	Total	Rush	Pass
Atlanta	10	27	4	28	28	22
Buffalo	2	*1	6	12	2T	20
Chicago	8	10	14	17	21	15
Cincinnati	26	8	27	26	24	25
Cleveland	18	19	17	14	7T	19
Dallas	4	5	5	*1	*1	5
Denver	21	25	16	22	23	18
Detroit	19	16	19	20	17T	21
Green Bay	15	21	9	23	16	23
Houston	3	18	*1	3	9	3
Indianapolis	24	28	8	21	26	11
Kansas City	25	23	20	5	15	2
L.A. Rams	13	15	10	27	27	24
L.A. Raiders	23	11	24	9	12	10
Miami	5	24	2	10T	6	14
Minnesota	11	7	18	8	14	7
New England	27	22	26	19	22	17
New Orleans	14	17	11	2	7T	*1
N.Y. Giants	22	6	25	18	25	16
N.Y. Jets	20	12	22	16	19	13
Philadelphia	7	2	23	6	5	12
Phoenix	17	26	13	24	10	27
Pittsburgh	9	4	21	13	17T	8
San Diego	6	9	7	4	2T	9
San Francisco	*1	3	3	15	4	26
Seattle	28	20	28	10T	20	4
Tampa Bay	16	14	15	25	11	28
Washington	12	13	12	7	13	6

T = Tied for position
* = League Leader

1992 AFC TAKEAWAYS/GIVEAWAYS

	— TAKEAWAYS —			— GIVEAWAYS —			NET
	Int	Fum	Total	Int	Fum	Total	DIFF.
Kansas City	24	15	39	12	9	21	18
Pittsburgh	22	21	43	14	18	32	11
Cincinnati	16	17	33	17	10	27	6
Cleveland	13	20	33	16	12	28	5
San Diego	25	11	36	21	12	33	3
N.Y. Jets	21	18	39	24	15	39	0
Miami	18	14	32	17	17	34	-2
Indianapolis	20	15	35	26	11	37	-2
Buffalo	23	12	35	21	17	38	-3
Houston	20	11	31	23	12	35	-4
Seattle	20	12	32	23	18	41	-9
Denver	15	16	31	29	15	44	-13
New England	14	15	29	19	26	45	-16
L.A. Raiders	12	7	19	23	15	38	-19

1992 NFC TAKEAWAYS/GIVEAWAYS

	— TAKEAWAYS —			— GIVEAWAYS —			NET
	Int	Fum	Total	Int	Fum	Total	DIFF.
Minnesota	28	14	42	15	17	32	10
Washington	23	11	34	17	7	24	10
New Orleans	18	20	38	16	13	29	9
Philadelphia	24	13	37	13	15	28	9
San Francisco	17	12	29	9	13	22	7
Dallas	17	14	31	15	9	24	7
Tampa Bay	20	13	33	20	9	29	4
N.Y. Giants	14	12	26	10	13	23	3
Green Bay	15	19	34	15	21	36	-2
L.A. Rams	18	15	33	20	17	37	-4
Detroit	21	11	32	21	15	6	-4
Chicago	14	16	30	24	10	34	-4
Atlanta	11	12	23	15	14	29	-6
Phoenix	16	12	28	24	18	42	-14

NFL STANDINGS
1921-1992

1921

	W	L	T	Pct.
Chicago Staleys	10	1	1	.909
Buffalo All-Americans	9	1	2	.900
Akron, Ohio, Pros	7	2	1	.778
Green Bay Packers	6	2	2	.750
Canton, Ohio, Bulldogs	4	3	3	.571
Dayton Triangles	4	3	1	.571
Rock Island Independents	5	4	1	.556
Chicago Cardinals	2	3	2	.400
Cleveland Indians	2	6	0	.250
Rochester Jeffersons	2	6	0	.250
Detroit Heralds	1	7	1	.125
Columbus Panhandles	0	6	0	.000
Cincinnati Celts	0	8	0	.000

1922

	W	L	T	Pct.
Canton, Ohio, Bulldogs	10	0	2	1.000
Chicago Bears	9	3	0	.750
Chicago Cardinals	8	3	0	.727
Toledo Maroons	5	2	2	.714
Rock Island Independents	4	2	1	.667
Dayton Triangles	4	3	1	.571
Green Bay Packers	4	3	3	.571
Racine, Wis., Legion	5	4	1	.556
Akron, Ohio, Pros	3	4	2	.429
Buffalo All-Americans	3	4	1	.429
Milwaukee Badgers	2	4	3	.333
Marion, O., Oorang Indians	2	6	0	.250
Minneapolis Marines	1	3	0	.250
Evansville Crimson Giants	0	2	0	.000
Louisville Brecks	0	3	0	.000
Rochester Jeffersons	0	3	1	.000
Hammond, Ind., Pros	0	4	1	.000
Columbus Panhandles	0	7	0	.000

1923

	W	L	T	Pct.
Canton, Ohio, Bulldogs	11	0	1	1.000
Chicago Bears	9	2	1	.818
Green Bay Packers	7	2	1	.778
Milwaukee Badgers	7	2	3	.778
Cleveland Indians	3	1	3	.750
Chicago Cardinals	8	4	0	.667
Duluth Kelleys	4	3	0	.571
Buffalo All-Americans	5	4	3	.556
Columbus Tigers	5	4	1	.556
Racine, Wis., Legion	4	4	2	.500
Toledo Maroons	2	3	2	.400
Rock Island Independents	2	3	3	.400

	W	L	T	Pct.
Minneapolis Marines	2	5	2	.286
St. Louis All-Stars	1	4	2	.200
Hammond, Ind., Pros	1	5	1	.167
Dayton Triangles	1	6	1	.143
Akron, Ohio, Indians	1	6	0	.143
Marion, O., Oorang Indians	1	10	0	.091
Rochester Jeffersons	0	2	0	.000
Louisville Brecks	0	3	0	.000

1924

	W	L	T	Pct.
Cleveland Bulldogs	7	1	1	.875
Chicago Bears	6	1	4	.857
Frankford Yellowjackets	11	2	1	.846
Duluth Kelleys	5	1	0	.833
Rock Island Independents	6	2	2	.750
Green Bay Packers	8	4	0	.667
Buffalo Bisons	6	4	0	.600
Racine, Wis., Legion	4	3	3	.571
Chicago Cardinals	5	4	1	.556
Columbus Tigers	4	4	0	.500
Hammond, Ind., Pros	2	2	1	.500
Milwaukee Badgers	5	8	0	.385
Dayton Triangles	2	7	0	.222
Kansas City Cowboys	2	7	0	.222
Akron, Ohio, Indians	1	6	0	.143
Kenosha, Wis., Maroons	0	5	1	.000
Minneapolis Marines	0	6	0	.000
Rochester Jeffersons	0	7	0	.000

1925

	W	L	T	Pct.
Chicago Cardinals	11	2	1	.846
Pottsville, Pa., Maroons	10	2	0	.833
Detroit Panthers	8	2	2	.800
New York Giants	8	4	0	.667
Akron, Ohio, Indians	4	2	2	.667
Frankford Yellowjackets	13	7	0	.650
Chicago Bears	9	5	3	.643
Rock Island Independents	5	3	3	.625
Green Bay Packers	8	5	0	.615
Providence Steamroller	6	5	1	.545
Canton, Ohio, Bulldogs	4	4	0	.500
Cleveland Bulldogs	5	8	1	.385
Kansas City Cowboys	2	5	1	.286
Hammond, Ind., Pros	1	3	0	.250
Buffalo Bisons	1	6	2	.143
Duluth Kelleys	0	3	0	.000
Rochester Jeffersons	0	6	1	.000
Milwaukee Badgers	0	6	0	.000
Dayton Triangles	0	7	1	.000
Columbus Tigers	0	9	0	.000

1926

	W	L	T	Pct.
Frankford Yellowjackets	14	1	1	.933
Chicago Bears	12	1	3	.923
Pottsville, Pa., Maroons	10	2	1	.833
Kansas City Cowboys	8	3	1	.727
Green Bay Packers	7	3	3	.700
Los Angeles Buccaneers	6	3	1	.667
New York Giants	8	4	1	.667
Duluth Eskimos	6	5	2	.545
Buffalo Rangers	4	4	2	.500
Chicago Cardinals	5	6	1	.455
Providence Steamroller	5	7	0	.417
Detroit Panthers	4	6	2	.400
Hartford Blues	3	7	0	.300
Brooklyn Lions	3	8	0	.273
Milwaukee Badgers	2	7	0	.222
Akron, Ohio, Indians	1	4	3	.200
Dayton Triangles	1	4	1	.200
Racine, Wis., Legion	1	4	0	.200
Columbus Tigers	1	6	0	.143
Canton, Ohio, Bulldogs	1	9	3	.100
Hammond, Ind., Pros	0	4	0	.000
Louisville Colonels	0	4	0	.000

1927

	W	L	T	Pct.
New York Giants	11	1	1	.917
Green Bay Packers	7	2	1	.778
Chicago Bears	9	3	2	.750
Cleveland Bulldogs	8	4	1	.667
Providence Steamroller	8	5	1	.615
New York Yankees	7	8	1	.467
Frankford Yellowjackets	6	9	3	.400
Pottsville, Pa., Maroons	5	8	0	.385
Chicago Cardinals	3	7	1	.300
Dayton Triangles	1	6	1	.143
Duluth Eskimos	1	8	0	.111
Buffalo Bisons	0	5	0	.000

1928

	W	L	T	Pct.
Providence Steamroller	8	1	2	.889
Frankford Yellowjackets	11	3	2	.786
Detroit Wolverines	7	2	1	.778
Green Bay Packers	6	4	3	.600
Chicago Bears	7	5	1	.583
New York Giants	4	7	2	.364
New York Yankees	4	8	1	.333
Pottsville, Pa., Maroons	2	8	0	.200
Chicago Cardinals	1	5	0	.167
Dayton Triangles	0	7	0	.000

1929

	W	L	T	Pct.
Green Bay Packers	12	0	1	1.000
New York Giants	13	1	1	.929
Frankford Yellowjackets	9	4	5	.692
Chicago Cardinals	6	6	1	.500
Boston Bulldogs	4	4	0	.500
Orange, N.J., Tornadoes	3	4	4	.429
Stapleton Stapes	3	4	3	.429
Providence Steamroller	4	6	2	.400
Chicago Bears	4	9	2	.308
Buffalo Bisons	1	7	1	.125
Minneapolis Red Jackets	1	9	0	.100
Dayton Triangles	0	6	0	.000

1930

	W	L	T	Pct.
Green Bay Packers	10	3	1	.769
New York Giants	13	4	0	.765
Chicago Bears	9	4	1	.692
Brooklyn Dodgers	7	4	1	.636
Providence Steamroller	6	4	1	.600
Stapleton Stapes	5	5	2	.500
Chicago Cardinals	5	6	2	.455
Portsmouth, O., Spartans	5	6	3	.455
Frankford Yellowjackets	4	14	1	.222
Minneapolis Red Jackets	1	7	1	.125
Newark Tornadoes	1	10	1	.091

1931

	W	L	T	Pct.
Green Bay Packers	12	2	0	.857
Portsmouth, O., Spartans	11	3	0	.786
Chicago Bears	8	5	0	.615
Chicago Cardinals	5	4	0	.556
New York Giants	7	6	1	.538
Providence Steamroller	4	4	3	.500
Stapleton Stapes	4	6	1	.400
Cleveland Indians	2	8	0	.200
Brooklyn Dodgers	2	12	0	.143
Frankford Yellowjackets	1	6	1	.143

1932

	W	L	T	Pct.
Chicago Bears	7	1	6	.875
Green Bay Packers	10	3	1	.769
Portsmouth, O., Spartans	6	2	4	.750
Boston Braves	4	4	2	.500
New York Giants	4	6	2	.400
Brooklyn Dodgers	3	9	0	.250
Chicago Cardinals	2	6	2	.250
Stapleton Stapes	2	7	3	.222

1933

EASTERN DIVISION

	W	L	T	Pct.	Pts.	OP
N.Y. Giants	11	3	0	.786	244	101
Brooklyn	5	4	1	.556	93	54
Boston	5	5	2	.500	103	97
Philadelphia	3	5	1	.375	77	158
Pittsburgh	3	6	2	.333	67	208

WESTERN DIVISION

	W	L	T	Pct.	Pts.	OP
Chi. Bears	10	2	1	.833	133	82
Portsmouth	6	5	0	.545	128	87
Green Bay	5	7	1	.417	170	107
Cincinnati	3	6	1	.333	38	110
Chi. Cardinals	1	9	1	.100	52	101

NFL Championship: Chicago Bears 23, N.Y. Giants 21

1934

EASTERN DIVISION	W	L	T	Pct.	Pts.	OP		WESTERN DIVISION	W	L	T	Pct.	Pts.	OP
N.Y. Giants	8	5	0	.615	147	107		Chi. Bears	13	0	0	1.000	286	86
Boston	6	6	0	.500	107	94		Detroit	10	3	0	.769	238	59
Brooklyn	4	7	0	.364	61	153		Green Bay	7	6	0	.538	156	112
Philadelphia	4	7	0	.364	127	85		Chi. Cardinals	5	6	0	.455	80	84
Pittsburgh	2	10	0	.167	51	206		St. Louis	1	2	0	.333	27	61
								Cincinnati	0	8	0	.000	10	243

NFL Championship: N.Y. Giants 30, Chicago Bears 13

1935

EASTERN DIVISION	W	L	T	Pct.	Pts.	OP		WESTERN DIVISION	W	L	T	Pct.	Pts.	OP
N.Y. Giants	9	3	0	.750	180	96		Detroit	7	3	2	.700	191	111
Brooklyn	5	6	1	.455	90	141		Green Bay	8	4	0	.667	181	96
Pittsburgh	4	8	0	.333	100	209		Chi. Bears	6	4	2	.600	192	106
Boston	2	8	1	.200	65	123		Chi. Cardinals	6	4	2	.600	99	97
Philadelphia	2	9	0	.182	60	179								

NFL Championship: Detroit 26, N.Y. Giants 7
One game between Boston and Philadelphia was canceled.

1936

EASTERN DIVISION	W	L	T	Pct.	Pts.	OP		WESTERN DIVISION	W	L	T	Pct.	Pts.	OP
Boston	7	5	0	.583	149	110		Green Bay	10	1	1	.909	248	118
Pittsburgh	6	6	0	.500	98	187		Chi. Bears	9	3	0	.750	222	94
N.Y. Giants	5	6	1	.455	115	163		Detroit	8	4	0	.667	235	102
Brooklyn	3	8	1	.273	92	161		Chi. Cardinals	3	8	1	.273	74	143
Philadelphia	1	11	0	.083	51	206								

NFL Championship: Green Bay 21, Boston 6

1937

EASTERN DIVISION	W	L	T	Pct.	Pts.	OP		WESTERN DIVISION	W	L	T	Pct.	Pts.	OP
Washington	8	3	0	.727	195	120		Chi. Bears	9	1	1	.900	201	100
N.Y. Giants	6	3	2	.667	128	109		Green Bay	7	4	0	.636	220	122
Pittsburgh	4	7	0	.364	122	145		Detroit	7	4	0	.636	180	105
Brooklyn	3	7	1	.300	82	174		Chi. Cardinals	5	5	1	.500	135	165
Philadelphia	2	8	1	.200	86	177		Cleveland	1	10	0	.091	75	207

NFL Championship: Washington 28, Chicago Bears 21

1938

EASTERN DIVISION	W	L	T	Pct.	Pts.	OP		WESTERN DIVISION	W	L	T	Pct.	Pts.	OP
N.Y Giants	8	2	1	.800	194	79		Green Bay	8	3	0	.727	223	118
Washington	6	3	2	.667	148	154		Detroit	7	4	0	.636	119	108
Brooklyn	4	4	3	.500	131	161		Chi. Bears	6	5	0	.545	194	148
Philadelphia	5	6	0	.455	154	164		Cleveland	4	7	0	.364	131	215
Pittsburgh	2	9	0	.182	79	169		Chi. Cardinals	2	9	0	.182	111	168

NFL Championship: N.Y. Giants 23, Green Bay 17

1939

EASTERN DIVISION	W	L	T	Pct.	Pts.	OP		WESTERN DIVISION	W	L	T	Pct.	Pts.	OP
N.Y. Giants	9	1	1	.900	168	85		Green Bay	9	2	0	.818	233	153
Washington	8	2	1	.800	242	94		Chi. Bears	8	3	0	.727	298	157
Brooklyn	4	6	1	.400	108	219		Detroit	6	5	0	.545	145	150
Philadelphia	1	9	1	.100	105	200		Cleveland	5	5	1	.500	195	164
Pittsburgh	1	9	1	.100	114	216		Chi. Cardinals	1	10	0	.091	84	254

NFL Championship: Green Bay 27, N.Y. Giants 0

1940

EASTERN DIVISION	W	L	T	Pct.	Pts.	OP
Washington	9	2	0	.818	245	142
Brooklyn	8	3	0	.727	186	120
N.Y. Giants	6	4	1	.600	131	133
Pittsburgh	2	7	2	.222	60	178
Philadelphia	1	10	0	.091	111	211

WESTERN DIVISION	W	L	T	Pct.	Pts.	OP
Chi. Bears	8	3	0	.727	238	152
Green Bay	6	4	1	.600	238	155
Detroit	5	5	1	.500	138	153
Cleveland	4	6	1	.400	171	191
Chi. Cardinals	2	7	2	.222	139	222

NFL Championship: Chicago Bears 73, Washington 0

1941

EASTERN DIVISION	W	L	T	Pct.	Pts.	OP
N.Y. Giants	8	3	0	.727	238	114
Brooklyn	7	4	0	.636	158	127
Washington	6	5	0	.545	176	174
Philadelphia	2	8	1	.200	119	218
Pittsburgh	1	9	1	.100	103	276

WESTERN DIVISION	W	L	T	Pct.	Pts.	OP
Chi. Bears	10	1	0	.909	396	147
Green Bay	10	1	0	.909	258	120
Detroit	4	6	1	.400	121	195
Chi. Cardinals	3	7	1	.300	127	197
Cleveland	2	9	0	.182	116	244

Western Division playoff: Chicago Bears 33, Green Bay 14
NFL Championship: Chicago Bears 37, N.Y. Giants 9

1942

EASTERN DIVISION	W	L	T	Pct.	Pts.	OP
Washington	10	1	0	.909	227	102
Pittsburgh	7	4	0	.636	167	119
N.Y. Giants	5	5	1	.500	155	139
Brooklyn	3	8	0	.273	100	168
Philadelphia	2	9	0	.182	134	239

WESTERN DIVISION	W	L	T	Pct.	Pts.	OP
Chi. Bears	11	0	0	1.000	376	84
Green Bay	8	2	1	.800	300	215
Cleveland	5	6	0	.455	150	207
Chi. Cardinals	3	8	0	.273	98	209
Detroit	0	11	0	.000	38	263

NFL Championship: Washington 14, Chicago Bears 6

1943

EASTERN DIVISION	W	L	T	Pct.	Pts.	OP
Washington	6	3	1	.667	229	137
N.Y. Giants	6	3	1	.667	197	170
Phil-Pitt	5	4	1	.556	225	230
Brooklyn	2	8	0	.200	65	234

WESTERN DIVISION	W	L	T	Pct.	Pts.	OP
Chi. Bears	8	1	1	.889	303	157
Green Bay	7	2	1	.778	264	172
Detroit	3	6	1	.333	178	218
Chi. Cardinals	0	10	0	.000	95	238

Eastern Division playoff: Washington 28, N.Y. Giants 0
NFL Championship: Chicago Bears 41, Washington 21

1944

EASTERN DIVISION	W	L	T	Pct.	Pts.	OP
N.Y. Giants	8	1	1	.889	206	75
Philadelphia	7	1	2	.875	267	131
Washington	6	3	1	.667	169	180
Boston	2	8	0	.200	82	233
Brooklyn	0	10	0	.000	69	166

WESTERN DIVISION	W	L	T	Pct.	Pts.	OP
Green Bay	8	2	0	.800	238	141
Chi. Bears	6	3	1	.667	258	172
Detroit	6	3	1	.667	216	151
Cleveland	4	6	0	.400	188	224
Card-Pitt	0	10	0	.000	108	328

NFL Championship: Green Bay 14, N.Y. Giants 7

1945

EASTERN DIVISION	W	L	T	Pct.	Pts.	OP
Washington	8	2	0	.800	209	121
Philadelphia	7	3	0	.700	272	133
N.Y. Giants	3	6	1	.333	179	198
Boston	3	6	1	.333	123	211
Pittsburgh	2	8	0	.200	79	220

WESTERN DIVISION	W	L	T	Pct.	Pts.	OP
Cleveland	9	1	0	.900	244	136
Detroit	7	3	0	.700	195	194
Green Bay	6	4	0	.600	258	173
Chi. Bears	3	7	0	.300	192	235
Chi. Cardinals	1	9	0	.100	98	228

NFL Championship: Cleveland 15, Washington 14

1946

EASTERN DIVISION	W	L	T	Pct.	Pts.	OP	WESTERN DIVISION	W	L	T	Pct.	Pts.	OP
N.Y. Giants	7	3	1	.700	236	162	Chi. Bears	8	2	1	.800	289	193
Philadelphia	6	5	0	.545	231	220	Los Angeles	6	4	1	.600	277	257
Washington	5	5	0	.500	171	191	Green Bay	6	5	0	.545	148	158
Pittsburgh	5	5	1	.500	136	117	Chi. Cardinals	6	5	0	.545	260	198
Boston	2	8	1	.200	189	273	Detroit	1	10	0	.091	142	310

NFL Championship: Chicago Bears 24, N.Y. Giants 14

1947

EASTERN DIVISION	W	L	T	Pct.	Pts.	OP	WESTERN DIVISION	W	L	T	Pct.	Pts.	OP
Philadelphia	8	4	0	.667	308	242	Chi. Cardinals	9	3	0	.750	306	231
Pittsburgh	8	4	0	.667	240	259	Chi. Bears	8	4	0	.667	363	241
Boston	4	7	1	.364	168	256	Green Bay	6	5	1	.545	274	210
Washington	4	8	0	.333	295	367	Los Angeles	6	6	0	.500	259	214
N.Y. Giants	2	8	2	.200	190	309	Detroit	3	9	0	.250	231	305

Eastern Division playoff: Philadelphia 21, Pittsburgh 0
NFL Championship: Chicago Cardinals 28, Philadelphia 21

1948

EASTERN DIVISION	W	L	T	Pct.	Pts.	OP	WESTERN DIVISION	W	L	T	Pct.	Pts.	OP
Philadelphia	9	2	1	.818	376	156	Chi. Cardinals	11	1	0	.917	395	226
Washington	7	5	0	.583	291	287	Chi. Bears	10	2	0	.833	375	151
N.Y. Giants	4	8	0	.333	297	388	Los Angeles	6	5	1	.545	327	269
Pittsburgh	4	8	0	.333	200	243	Green Bay	3	9	0	.250	154	290
Boston	3	9	0	.250	174	372	Detroit	2	10	0	.167	200	407

NFL Championship: Philadelphia 7, Chicago Cardinals 0

1949

EASTERN DIVISION	W	L	T	Pct.	Pts.	OP	WESTERN DIVISION	W	L	T	Pct.	Pts.	OP
Philadelphia	11	1	0	.917	364	134	Los Angeles	8	2	2	.800	360	239
Pittsburgh	6	5	1	.545	224	214	Chi. Bears	9	3	0	.750	332	218
N.Y. Giants	6	6	0	.500	287	298	Chi. Cardinals	6	5	1	.545	360	301
Washington	4	7	1	.364	268	339	Detroit	4	8	0	.333	237	259
N.Y. Bulldogs	1	10	1	.091	153	368	Green Bay	2	10	0	.167	114	329

NFL Championship: Philadelphia 14, Los Angeles 0

1950

AMERICAN CONFERENCE	W	L	T	Pct.	Pts.	OP	NATIONAL CONFERENCE	W	L	T	Pct.	Pts.	OP
Cleveland	10	2	0	.833	310	144	Los Angeles	9	3	0	.750	466	309
N.Y. Giants	10	2	0	.833	268	150	Chi. Bears	9	3	0	.750	279	207
Philadelphia	6	6	0	.500	254	141	N.Y. Yanks	7	5	0	.583	366	367
Pittsburgh	6	6	0	.500	180	195	Detroit	6	6	0	.500	321	285
Chi. Cardinals	5	7	0	.417	233	287	Green Bay	3	9	0	.250	244	406
Washington	3	9	0	.250	232	326	San Francisco	3	9	0	.250	213	300
							Baltimore	1	11	0	.083	213	462

American Conference playoff: Cleveland 8, N.Y. Giants 3
National Conference playoff: Los Angeles 24, Chicago Bears 14
NFL Championship: Cleveland 30, Los Angeles 28

1951

AMERICAN CONFERENCE	W	L	T	Pct.	Pts.	OP	NATIONAL CONFERENCE	W	L	T	Pct.	Pts.	OP
Cleveland	11	1	0	.917	331	152	Los Angeles	8	4	0	.667	392	261
N.Y. Giants	9	2	1	.818	254	161	Detroit	7	4	1	.636	336	259
Washington	5	7	0	.417	183	296	San Francisco	7	4	1	.636	255	205
Pittsburgh	4	7	1	.364	183	235	Chi. Bears	7	5	0	.583	286	282
Philadelphia	4	8	0	.333	234	264	Green Bay	3	9	0	.250	254	375
Chi. Cardinals	3	9	0	.250	210	287	N.Y. Yanks	1	9	2	.100	241	382

NFL Championship: Los Angeles 24, Cleveland 17

1952

AMERICAN CONFERENCE	W	L	T	Pct.	Pts.	OP
Cleveland	8	4	0	.667	310	213
N.Y. Giants	7	5	0	.583	234	231
Philadelphia	7	5	0	.583	252	271
Pittsburgh	5	7	0	.417	300	273
Chi. Cardinals	4	8	0	.333	172	221
Washington	4	8	0	.333	240	287

NATIONAL CONFERENCE	W	L	T	Pct.	Pts.	OP
Detroit	9	3	0	.750	344	192
Los Angeles	9	3	0	.750	349	234
San Francisco	7	5	0	.583	285	221
Green Bay	6	6	0	.500	295	312
Chi. Bears	5	7	0	.417	245	326
Dallas	1	11	0	.083	182	427

National Conference playoff: Detroit 31, Los Angeles 21
NFL Championship: Detroit 17, Cleveland 7

1953

EASTERN CONFERENCE	W	L	T	Pct.	Pts.	OP
Cleveland	11	1	0	.917	348	162
Philadelphia	7	4	1	.636	352	215
Washington	6	5	1	.545	208	215
Pittsburgh	6	6	0	.500	211	263
N.Y. Giants	3	9	0	.250	179	277
Chi. Cardinals	1	10	1	.091	190	337

WESTERN CONFERENCE	W	L	T	Pct.	Pts.	OP
Detroit	10	2	0	.833	271	205
San Francisco	9	3	0	.750	372	237
Los Angeles	8	3	1	.727	366	236
Chi. Bears	3	8	1	.273	218	262
Baltimore	3	9	0	.250	182	350
Green Bay	2	9	1	.182	200	338

NFL Championship: Detroit 17, Cleveland 16

1954

EASTERN CONFERENCE	W	L	T	Pct.	Pts.	OP
Cleveland	9	3	0	.750	336	162
Philadelphia	7	4	1	.636	284	230
N.Y. Giants	7	5	0	.583	293	184
Pittsburgh	5	7	0	.417	219	263
Washington	3	9	0	.250	207	432
Chi. Cardinals	2	10	0	.167	183	347

WESTERN CONFERENCE	W	L	T	Pct.	Pts.	OP
Detroit	9	2	1	.818	337	189
Chi. Bears	8	4	0	.667	301	279
San Francisco	7	4	1	.636	313	251
Los Angeles	6	5	1	.545	314	285
Green Bay	4	8	0	.333	234	251
Baltimore	3	9	0	.250	131	279

NFL Championship: Cleveland 56, Detroit 10

1955

EASTERN CONFERENCE	W	L	T	Pct.	Pts.	OP
Cleveland	9	2	1	.818	349	218
Washington	8	4	0	.667	246	222
N.Y. Giants	6	5	1	.545	267	223
Chi. Cardinals	4	7	1	.364	224	252
Philadelphia	4	7	1	.364	248	231
Pittsburgh	4	8	0	.333	195	285

WESTERN CONFERENCE	W	L	T	Pct.	Pts.	OP
Los Angeles	8	3	1	.727	260	231
Chi. Bears	8	4	0	.667	294	251
Green Bay	6	6	0	.500	258	276
Baltimore	5	6	1	.455	214	239
San Francisco	4	8	0	.333	216	298
Detroit	3	9	0	.250	230	275

NFL Championship: Cleveland 38, Los Angeles 14

1956

EASTERN CONFERENCE	W	L	T	Pct.	Pts.	OP
N.Y. Giants	8	3	1	.727	264	197
Chi. Cardinals	7	5	0	.583	240	182
Washington	6	6	0	.500	183	225
Cleveland	5	7	0	.417	167	177
Pittsburgh	5	7	0	.417	217	250
Philadelphia	3	8	1	.273	143	215

WESTERN CONFERENCE	W	L	T	Pct.	Pts.	OP
Chi. Bears	9	2	1	.818	363	246
Detroit	9	3	0	.750	300	188
San Francisco	5	6	1	.455	233	284
Baltimore	5	7	0	.417	270	322
Green Bay	4	8	0	.333	264	342
Los Angeles	4	8	0	.333	291	307

NFL Championship: N.Y. Giants 47, Chicago Bears 7

1957

EASTERN CONFERENCE

	W	L	T	Pct.	Pts.	OP
Cleveland	9	2	1	.818	269	172
N.Y. Giants	7	5	0	.583	254	211
Pittsburgh	6	6	0	.500	161	178
Washington	5	6	1	.455	251	230
Philadelphia	4	8	0	.333	173	230
Chi. Cardinals	3	9	0	.250	200	299

WESTERN CONFERENCE

	W	L	T	Pct.	Pts.	OP
Detroit	8	4	0	.667	251	231
San Francisco	8	4	0	.667	260	264
Baltimore	7	5	0	.583	303	235
Los Angeles	6	6	0	.500	307	278
Chi. Bears	5	7	0	.417	203	211
Green Bay	3	9	0	.250	218	311

Western Conference playoff: Detroit 31, San Francisco 27

NFL Championship: Detroit 59, Cleveland 14

1958

EASTERN CONFERENCE

	W	L	T	Pct.	Pts.	OP
N.Y. Giants	9	3	0	.750	246	183
Cleveland	9	3	0	.750	302	217
Pittsburgh	7	4	1	.636	261	230
Washington	4	7	1	.364	214	268
Chi. Cardinals	2	9	1	.182	261	356
Philadelphia	2	9	1	.182	235	306

WESTERN CONFERENCE

	W	L	T	Pct.	Pts.	OP
Baltimore	9	3	0	.750	381	203
Chi. Bears	8	4	0	.667	298	230
Los Angeles	8	4	0	.667	344	278
San Francisco	6	6	0	.500	257	324
Detroit	4	7	1	.364	261	276
Green Bay	1	10	1	.091	193	382

Eastern Conference playoff: N.Y. Giants 10, Cleveland 0

NFL Championship: Baltimore 23, N.Y. Giants 17, sudden-death overtime

1959

EASTERN CONFERENCE

	W	L	T	Pct.	Pts.	OP
N.Y. Giants	10	2	0	.833	284	170
Cleveland	7	5	0	.583	270	214
Philadelphia	7	5	0	.583	268	278
Pittsburgh	6	5	1	.545	257	216
Washington	3	9	0	.250	185	350
Chi. Cardinals	2	10	0	.167	234	324

WESTERN CONFERENCE

	W	L	T	Pct.	Pts.	OP
Baltimore	9	3	0	.750	374	251
Chi. Bears	8	4	0	.667	252	196
Green Bay	7	5	0	.583	248	246
San Francisco	7	5	0	.583	255	237
Detroit	3	8	1	.273	203	275
Los Angeles	2	10	0	.167	242	315

NFL Championship: Baltimore 31, N.Y. Giants 16

1960 AFL

EASTERN DIVISION

	W	L	T	Pct.	Pts.	OP
Houston	10	4	0	.714	379	285
N.Y. Titans	7	7	0	.500	382	399
Buffalo	5	8	1	.385	296	303
Boston	5	9	0	.357	286	349

WESTERN DIVISION

	W	L	T	Pct.	Pts.	OP
L.A. Chargers	10	4	0	.714	373	336
Dall. Texans	8	6	0	.571	362	253
Oakland	6	8	0	.429	319	388
Denver	4	9	1	.308	309	393

AFL Championship: Houston 24, L.A. Chargers 16

1960 NFL

EASTERN CONFERENCE

	W	L	T	Pct.	Pts.	OP
Philadelphia	10	2	0	.833	321	246
Cleveland	8	3	1	.727	362	217
N.Y. Giants	6	4	2	.600	271	261
St. Louis	6	5	1	.545	288	230
Pittsburgh	5	6	1	.455	240	275
Washington	1	9	2	.100	178	309

WESTERN CONFERENCE

	W	L	T	Pct.	Pts.	OP
Green Bay	8	4	0	.667	332	209
Detroit	7	5	0	.583	239	212
San Francisco	7	5	0	.583	208	205
Baltimore	6	6	0	.500	288	234
Chicago	5	6	1	.455	194	299
L.A. Rams	4	7	1	.364	265	297
Dall. Cowboys	0	11	1	.000	177	369

NFL Championship: Philadelphia 17, Green Bay 13

1961 AFL

EASTERN DIVISION	W	L	T	Pct.	Pts.	OP	WESTERN DIVISION	W	L	T	Pct.	Pts.	OP
Houston	10	3	1	.769	513	242	San Diego	12	2	0	.857	396	219
Boston	9	4	1	.692	413	313	Dall. Texans	6	8	0	.429	334	343
N.Y. Titans	7	7	0	.500	301	390	Denver	3	11	0	.214	251	432
Buffalo	6	8	0	.429	294	342	Oakland	2	12	0	.143	237	458

AFL Championship: Houston 10, San Diego 3

1961 NFL

EASTERN CONFERENCE	W	L	T	Pct.	Pts.	OP	WESTERN CONFERENCE	W	L	T	Pct.	Pts.	OP
N.Y. Giants	10	3	1	.769	368	220	Green Bay	11	3	0	.786	391	223
Philadelphia	10	4	0	.714	361	297	Detroit	8	5	1	.615	270	258
Cleveland	8	5	1	.615	319	270	Baltimore	8	6	0	.571	302	307
St. Louis	7	7	0	.500	279	267	Chicago	8	6	0	.571	326	302
Pittsburgh	6	8	0	.429	295	287	San Francisco	7	6	1	.538	346	272
Dall. Cowboys	4	9	1	.308	236	380	Los Angeles	4	10	0	.286	263	333
Washington	1	12	1	.077	174	392	Minnesota	3	11	0	.214	285	407

NFL Championship: Green Bay 37, N.Y. Giants 0

1962 AFL

EASTERN DIVISION	W	L	T	Pct.	Pts.	OP	WESTERN DIVISION	W	L	T	Pct.	Pts.	OP
Houston	11	3	0	.786	387	270	Dall. Texans	11	3	0	.786	389	233
Boston	9	4	1	.692	346	295	Denver	7	7	0	.500	353	334
Buffalo	7	6	1	.538	309	272	San Diego	4	10	0	.286	314	392
N.Y. Titans	5	9	0	.357	278	423	Oakland	1	13	0	.071	213	370

AFL Championship: Dallas Texans 20, Houston 17, sudden-death overtime

1962 NFL

EASTERN CONFERENCE	W	L	T	Pct.	Pts.	OP	WESTERN CONFERENCE	W	L	T	Pct.	Pts.	OP
N.Y. Giants	12	2	0	.857	398	283	Green Bay	13	1	0	.929	415	148
Pittsburgh	9	5	0	.643	312	363	Detroit	11	3	0	.786	315	177
Cleveland	7	6	1	.538	291	257	Chicago	9	5	0	.643	321	287
Washington	5	7	2	.417	305	376	Baltimore	7	7	0	.500	293	288
Dall. Cowboys	5	8	1	.385	398	402	San Francisco	6	8	0	.429	282	331
St. Louis	4	9	1	.308	287	361	Minnesota	2	11	1	.154	254	410
Philadelphia	3	10	1	.231	282	356	Los Angeles	1	12	1	.077	220	334

NFL Championship: Green Bay 16, N.Y. Giants 7

1963 AFL

EASTERN DIVISION	W	L	T	Pct.	Pts.	OP	WESTERN DIVISION	W	L	T	Pct.	Pts.	OP
Boston	7	6	1	.538	317	257	San Diego	11	3	0	.786	399	255
Buffalo	7	6	1	.538	304	291	Oakland	10	4	0	.714	363	282
Houston	6	8	0	.429	302	372	Kansas City	5	7	2	.417	347	263
N.Y. Jets	5	8	1	.385	249	399	Denver	2	11	1	.154	301	473

Eastern Division playoff: Boston 26, Buffalo 8
AFL Championship: San Diego 51, Boston 10

1963 NFL

EASTERN CONFERENCE	W	L	T	Pct.	Pts.	OP	WESTERN CONFERENCE	W	L	T	Pct.	Pts.	OP
N.Y. Giants	11	3	0	.786	448	280	Chicago	11	1	2	.917	301	144
Cleveland	10	4	0	.714	343	262	Green Bay	11	2	1	.846	369	206
St. Louis	9	5	0	.643	341	283	Baltimore	8	6	0	.571	316	285
Pittsburgh	7	4	3	.636	321	295	Detroit	5	8	1	.385	326	265
Dallas	4	10	0	.286	305	378	Minnesota	5	8	1	.385	309	390
Washington	3	11	0	.214	279	398	Los Angeles	5	9	0	.357	210	350
Philadelphia	2	10	2	.167	242	381	San Francisco	2	12	0	.143	198	391

NFL Championship: Chicago 14, N.Y. Giants 10

1964 AFL

EASTERN DIVISION	W	L	T	Pct.	Pts.	OP	WESTERN DIVISION	W	L	T	Pct.	Pts.	OP
Buffalo	12	2	0	.857	400	242	San Diego	8	5	1	.615	341	300
Boston	10	3	1	.769	365	297	Kansas City	7	7	0	.500	366	306
N.Y. Jets	5	8	1	.385	278	315	Oakland	5	7	2	.417	303	350
Houston	4	10	0	.286	310	355	Denver	2	11	1	.154	240	438

AFL Championship: Buffalo 20, San Diego 7

1964 NFL

EASTERN CONFERENCE	W	L	T	Pct.	Pts.	OP	WESTERN CONFERENCE	W	L	T	Pct.	Pts.	OP
Cleveland	10	3	1	.769	415	293	Baltimore	12	2	0	.857	428	225
St. Louis	9	3	2	.750	357	331	Green Bay	8	5	1	.615	342	245
Philadelphia	6	8	0	.429	312	313	Minnesota	8	5	1	.615	355	296
Washington	6	8	0	.429	307	305	Detroit	7	5	2	.583	280	260
Dallas	5	8	1	.385	250	289	Los Angeles	5	7	2	.417	283	339
Pittsburgh	5	9	0	.357	253	315	Chicago	5	9	0	.357	260	379
N.Y. Giants	2	10	2	.167	241	399	San Francisco	4	10	0	.286	236	330

NFL Championship: Cleveland 27, Baltimore 0

1965 AFL

EASTERN DIVISION	W	L	T	Pct.	Pts.	OP	WESTERN DIVISION	W	L	T	Pct.	Pts.	OP
Buffalo	10	3	1	.769	313	226	San Diego	9	2	3	.818	340	227
N.Y. Jets	5	8	1	.385	285	303	Oakland	8	5	1	.615	298	239
Boston	4	8	2	.333	244	302	Kansas City	7	5	2	.583	322	285
Houston	4	10	0	.286	298	429	Denver	4	10	0	.286	303	392

AFL Championship: Buffalo 23, San Diego 0

1965 NFL

EASTERN CONFERENCE	W	L	T	Pct.	Pts.	OP	WESTERN CONFERENCE	W	L	T	Pct.	Pts.	OP
Cleveland	11	3	0	.786	363	325	Green Bay	10	3	1	.769	316	224
Dallas	7	7	0	.500	325	280	Baltimore	10	3	1	.769	389	284
N.Y. Giants	7	7	0	.500	270	338	Chicago	9	5	0	.643	409	275
Washington	6	8	0	.429	257	301	San Francisco	7	6	1	.538	421	402
Philadelphia	5	9	0	.357	363	359	Minnesota	7	7	0	.500	383	403
St. Louis	5	9	0	.357	296	309	Detroit	6	7	1	.462	257	295
Pittsburgh	2	12	0	.143	202	397	Los Angeles	4	10	0	.286	269	328

Western Conference playoff: Green Bay 13, Baltimore 10, sudden-death overtime

NFL Championship: Green Bay 23, Cleveland 12

1966 AFL

EASTERN DIVISION	W	L	T	Pct.	Pts.	OP	WESTERN DIVISION	W	L	T	Pct.	Pts.	OP
Buffalo	9	4	1	.692	358	255	Kansas City	11	2	1	.846	448	276
Boston	8	4	2	.667	315	283	Oakland	8	5	1	.615	315	288
N.Y. Jets	6	6	2	.500	322	312	San Diego	7	6	1	.538	335	284
Houston	3	11	0	.214	335	396	Denver	4	10	0	.286	196	381
Miami	3	11	0	.214	213	362							

AFL Championship: Kansas City 31, Buffalo 7

1966 NFL

EASTERN CONFERENCE	W	L	T	Pct.	Pts.	OP	WESTERN CONFERENCE	W	L	T	Pct.	Pts.	OP
Dallas	10	3	1	.769	445	239	Green Bay	12	2	0	.857	335	163
Cleveland	9	5	0	.643	403	259	Baltimore	9	5	0	.643	314	226
Philadelphia	9	5	0	.643	326	340	Los Angeles	8	6	0	.571	289	212
St. Louis	8	5	1	.615	264	265	San Francisco	6	6	2	.500	320	325
Washington	7	7	0	.500	351	355	Chicago	5	7	2	.417	234	272
Pittsburgh	5	8	1	.385	316	347	Detroit	4	9	1	.308	206	317
Atlanta	3	11	0	.214	204	437	Minnesota	4	9	1	.308	292	304
N.Y. Giants	1	12	1	.077	263	501							

NFL Championship: Green Bay 34, Dallas 27

Super Bowl I: Green Bay (NFL) 35, Kansas City (AFL) 10

1967 AFL

EASTERN DIVISION	W	L	T	Pct.	Pts.	OP	WESTERN DIVISION	W	L	T	Pct.	Pts.	OP
Houston	9	4	1	.692	258	199	Oakland	13	1	0	.929	468	238
N.Y. Jets	8	5	1	.615	371	329	Kansas City	9	5	0	.643	408	254
Buffalo	4	10	0	.286	237	285	San Diego	8	5	1	.615	360	352
Miami	4	10	0	.286	219	407	Denver	3	11	0	.214	256	409
Boston	3	10	1	.231	280	389							

AFL Championship: Oakland 40, Houston 7

1967 NFL

EASTERN CONFERENCE

Capitol Division	W	L	T	Pct.	Pts.	OP	Coastal Division	W	L	T	Pct.	Pts.	OP
Dallas	9	5	0	.643	342	268	Los Angeles	11	1	2	.917	398	196
Philadelphia	6	7	1	.462	351	409	Baltimore	11	1	2	.917	394	198
Washington	5	6	3	.455	347	353	San Francisco	7	7	0	.500	273	337
New Orleans	3	11	0	.214	233	379	Atlanta	1	12	1	.077	175	422

WESTERN CONFERENCE

Century Division	W	L	T	Pct.	Pts.	OP	Central Division	W	L	T	Pct.	Pts.	OP
Cleveland	9	5	0	.643	334	297	Green Bay	9	4	1	.692	332	209
N.Y. Giants	7	7	0	.500	369	379	Chicago	7	6	1	.538	239	218
St. Louis	6	7	1	.462	333	356	Detroit	5	7	2	.417	260	259
Pittsburgh	4	9	1	.308	281	320	Minnesota	3	8	3	.273	233	294

Conference Championships: Dallas 52, Cleveland 14; Green Bay 28, Los Angeles 7
NFL Championship: Green Bay 21, Dallas 17
Super Bowl II: Green Bay (NFL) 33, Oakland (AFL) 14

1968 AFL

EASTERN DIVISION	W	L	T	Pct.	Pts.	OP	WESTERN DIVISION	W	L	T	Pct.	Pts.	OP
N.Y. Jets	11	3	0	.786	419	280	Oakland	12	2	0	.857	453	233
Houston	7	7	0	.500	303	248	Kansas City	12	2	0	.857	371	170
Miami	5	8	1	.385	276	355	San Diego	9	5	0	.643	382	310
Boston	4	10	0	.286	229	406	Denver	5	9	0	.357	255	404
Buffalo	1	12	1	.077	199	367	Cincinnati	3	11	0	.214	215	329

Western Division playoff: Oakland 41, Kansas City 6
AFL Championship: N.Y. Jets 27, Oakland 23

1968 NFL

EASTERN CONFERENCE

Capitol Division	W	L	T	Pct.	Pts.	OP	Coastal Division	W	L	T	Pct.	Pts.	OP
Dallas	12	2	0	.857	431	186	Baltimore	13	1	0	.929	402	144
N.Y. Giants	7	7	0	.500	294	325	Los Angeles	10	3	1	.769	312	200
Washington	5	9	0	.357	249	358	San Francisco	7	6	1	.538	303	310
Philadelphia	2	12	0	.143	202	351	Atlanta	2	12	0	.143	170	389

WESTERN CONFERENCE

Century Division	W	L	T	Pct.	Pts.	OP	Central Division	W	L	T	Pct.	Pts.	OP
Cleveland	10	4	0	.714	394	273	Minnesota	8	6	0	.571	282	242
St. Louis	9	4	1	.692	325	289	Chicago	7	7	0	.500	250	333
New Orleans	4	9	1	.308	246	327	Green Bay	6	7	1	.462	281	227
Pittsburgh	2	11	1	.154	244	397	Detroit	4	8	2	.333	207	241

Conference Championships: Cleveland 31, Dallas 20; Baltimore 24, Minnesota 14
NFL Championship: Baltimore 34, Cleveland 0
Super Bowl III: N.Y. Jets (AFL) 16, Baltimore (NFL) 7

1969 AFL

EASTERN DIVISION	W	L	T	Pct.	Pts.	OP
N.Y. Jets	10	4	0	.714	353	269
Houston	6	6	2	.500	278	279
Boston	4	10	0	.286	266	316
Buffalo	4	10	0	.286	230	359
Miami	3	10	1	.231	233	332

WESTERN DIVISION	W	L	T	Pct.	Pts.	OP
Oakland	12	1	1	.923	377	242
Kansas City	11	3	0	.786	359	177
San Diego	8	6	0	.571	288	276
Denver	5	8	1	.385	297	344
Cincinnati	4	9	1	.308	280	367

Divisional playoffs: Kansas City 13, N.Y. Jets 6; Oakland 56, Houston 7
AFL Championship: Kansas City 17, Oakland 7

1969 NFL

EASTERN CONFERENCE

Capitol Division

	W	L	T	Pct.	Pts.	OP
Dallas	11	2	1	.846	369	223
Washington	7	5	2	.583	307	319
New Orleans	5	9	0	.357	311	393
Philadelphia	4	9	1	.308	279	377

Century Division

	W	L	T	Pct.	Pts.	OP
Cleveland	10	3	1	.769	351	300
N.Y. Giants	6	8	0	.429	264	298
St. Louis	4	9	1	.308	314	389
Pittsburgh	1	13	0	.071	218	404

WESTERN CONFERENCE

Coastal Division

	W	L	T	Pct.	Pts.	OP
Los Angeles	11	3	0	.786	320	243
Baltimore	8	5	1	.615	279	268
Atlanta	6	8	0	.429	276	268
San Francisco	4	8	2	.333	277	319

Central Division

	W	L	T	Pct.	Pts.	OP
Minnesota	12	2	0	.857	379	133
Detroit	9	4	1	.692	259	188
Green Bay	8	6	0	.571	269	221
Chicago	1	13	0	.071	210	339

Conference Championships: Cleveland 38, Dallas 14; Minnesota 23, Los Angeles 20
NFL Championship: Minnesota 27, Cleveland 7
Super Bowl IV: Kansas City (AFL) 23, Minnesota (NFL) 7

1970

AMERICAN CONFERENCE

Eastern Division

	W	L	T	Pct.	Pts.	OP
Baltimore	11	2	1	.846	321	234
Miami*	10	4	0	.714	297	228
N.Y. Jets	4	10	0	.286	255	286
Buffalo	3	10	1	.231	204	337
Boston	2	12	0	.143	149	361

Central Division

	W	L	T	Pct.	Pts.	OP
Cincinnati	8	6	0	.571	312	255
Cleveland	7	7	0	.500	286	265
Pittsburgh	5	9	0	.357	210	272
Houston	3	10	1	.231	217	352

Western Division

	W	L	T	Pct.	Pts.	OP
Oakland	8	4	2	.667	300	293
Kansas City	7	5	2	.583	272	244
San Diego	5	6	3	.455	282	278
Denver	5	8	1	.385	253	264

NATIONAL CONFERENCE

Eastern Division

	W	L	T	Pct.	Pts.	OP
Dallas	10	4	0	.714	299	221
N.Y. Giants	9	5	0	.643	301	270
St. Louis	8	5	1	.615	325	228
Washington	6	8	0	.429	297	314
Philadelphia	3	10	1	.231	241	332

Central Division

	W	L	T	Pct.	Pts.	OP
Minnesota	12	2	0	.857	335	143
Detroit*	10	4	0	.714	347	202
Chicago	6	8	0	.429	256	261
Green Bay	6	8	0	.429	196	293

Western Division

	W	L	T	Pct.	Pts.	OP
San Francisco	10	3	1	.769	352	267
Los Angeles	9	4	1	.692	325	202
Atlanta	4	8	2	.333	206	261
New Orleans	2	11	1	.154	172	347

*Wild Card qualifier for playoffs
Divisional playoffs: Baltimore 17, Cincinnati 0; Oakland 21, Miami 14
AFC Championship: Baltimore 27, Oakland 17
Divisional playoffs: Dallas 5, Detroit 0; San Francisco 17, Minnesota 14
NFC Championship: Dallas 17, San Francisco 10
Super Bowl V: Baltimore (AFC) 16, Dallas (NFC) 13

1971

AMERICAN CONFERENCE

Eastern Division

	W	L	T	Pct.	Pts.	OP
Miami	10	3	1	.769	315	174
Baltimore*	10	4	0	.714	313	140
New England	6	8	0	.429	238	325
N.Y. Jets	6	8	0	.429	212	299
Buffalo	1	13	0	.071	184	394

Central Division

	W	L	T	Pct.	Pts.	OP
Cleveland	9	5	0	.643	285	273
Pittsburgh	6	8	0	.429	246	292
Houston	4	9	1	.308	251	330
Cincinnati	4	10	0	.286	284	265

Western Division

	W	L	T	Pct.	Pts.	OP
Kansas City	10	3	1	.769	302	208
Oakland	8	4	2	.667	344	278
San Diego	6	8	0	.429	311	341
Denver	4	9	1	.308	203	275

NATIONAL CONFERENCE

Eastern Division

	W	L	T	Pct.	Pts.	OP
Dallas	11	3	0	.786	406	222
Washington*	9	4	1	.692	276	190
Philadelphia	6	7	1	.462	221	302
St. Louis	4	9	1	.308	231	279
N.Y. Giants	4	10	0	.286	228	362

Central Division

	W	L	T	Pct.	Pts.	OP
Minnesota	11	3	0	.786	245	139
Detroit	7	6	1	.538	341	286
Chicago	6	8	0	.429	185	276
Green Bay	4	8	2	.333	274	298

Western Division

	W	L	T	Pct.	Pts.	OP
San Francisco	9	5	0	.643	300	216
Los Angeles	8	5	1	.615	313	260
Atlanta	7	6	1	.538	274	277
New Orleans	4	8	2	.333	266	347

*Wild Card qualifier for playoffs

Divisional playoffs: Miami 27, Kansas City 24, sudden-death overtime; Baltimore 20, Cleveland 3

AFC Championship: Miami 21, Baltimore 0

Divisional playoffs: Dallas 20, Minnesota 12; San Francisco 24, Washington 20

NFC Championship: Dallas 14, San Francisco 3

Super Bowl VI: Dallas (NFC) 24, Miami (AFC) 3

1972

AMERICAN CONFERENCE

Eastern Division

	W	L	T	Pct.	Pts.	OP
Miami	14	0	0	1.000	385	171
N.Y. Jets	7	7	0	.500	367	324
Baltimore	5	9	0	.357	235	252
Buffalo	4	9	1	.321	257	377
New England	3	11	0	.214	192	446

Central Division

	W	L	T	Pct.	Pts.	OP
Pittsburgh	11	3	0	.786	343	175
Cleveland*	10	4	0	.714	268	249
Cincinnati	8	6	0	.571	299	229
Houston	1	13	0	.071	164	380

Western Division

	W	L	T	Pct.	Pts.	OP
Oakland	10	3	1	.750	365	248
Kansas City	8	6	0	.571	287	254
Denver	5	9	0	.357	325	350
San Diego	4	9	1	.321	264	344

NATIONAL CONFERENCE

Eastern Division

	W	L	T	Pct.	Pts.	OP
Washington	11	3	0	.786	336	218
Dallas*	10	4	0	.714	319	240
N.Y. Giants	8	6	0	.571	331	247
St. Louis	4	9	1	.321	193	303
Philadelphia	2	11	1	.179	145	352

Central Division

	W	L	T	Pct.	Pts.	OP
Green Bay	10	4	0	.714	304	226
Detroit	8	5	1	.607	339	290
Minnesota	7	7	0	.500	301	252
Chicago	4	9	1	.321	225	275

Western Division

	W	L	T	Pct.	Pts.	OP
San Francisco	8	5	1	.607	353	249
Atlanta	7	7	0	.500	269	274
Los Angeles	6	7	1	.464	291	286
New Orleans	2	11	1	.179	215	361

*Wild Card qualifier for playoffs

Divisional playoffs: Pittsburgh 13, Oakland 7; Miami 20, Cleveland 14

AFC Championship: Miami 21, Pittsburgh 17

Divisional playoffs: Dallas 30, San Francisco 28; Washington 16, Green Bay 3

NFC Championship: Washington 26, Dallas 3

Super Bowl VII: Miami (AFC) 14, Washington (NFC) 7

1973

AMERICAN CONFERENCE

Eastern Division

	W	L	T	Pct.	Pts.	OP
Miami	12	2	0	.857	343	150
Buffalo	9	5	0	.643	259	230
New England	5	9	0	.357	258	300
Baltimore	4	10	0	.286	226	341
N.Y. Jets	4	10	0	.286	240	306

Central Division

	W	L	T	Pct.	Pts.	OP
Cincinnati	10	4	0	.714	286	231
Pittsburgh*	10	4	0	.714	347	210
Cleveland	7	5	2	.571	234	255
Houston	1	13	0	.071	199	447

Western Division

	W	L	T	Pct.	Pts.	OP
Oakland	9	4	1	.679	292	175
Denver	7	5	2	.571	354	296
Kansas City	7	5	2	.571	231	192
San Diego	2	11	1	.179	188	386

NATIONAL CONFERENCE

Eastern Division

	W	L	T	Pct.	Pts.	OP
Dallas	10	4	0	.714	382	203
Washington*	10	4	0	.714	325	198
Philadelphia	5	8	1	.393	310	393
St. Louis	4	9	1	.321	286	365
N.Y. Giants	2	11	1	.179	226	362

Central Division

	W	L	T	Pct.	Pts.	OP
Minnesota	12	2	0	.857	296	168
Detroit	6	7	1	.464	271	247
Green Bay	5	7	2	.429	202	259
Chicago	3	11	0	.214	195	334

Western Division

	W	L	T	Pct.	Pts.	OP
Los Angeles	12	2	0	.857	388	178
Atlanta	9	5	0	.643	318	224
New Orleans	5	9	0	.357	163	312
San Francisco	5	9	0	.357	262	319

*Wild Card qualifier for playoffs
Divisional playoffs: Oakland 33, Pittsburgh 14; Miami 34, Cincinnati 16
AFC Championship: Miami 27, Oakland 10
Divisional playoffs: Minnesota 27, Washington 20; Dallas 27, Los Angeles 16
NFC Championship: Minnesota 27, Dallas 10
Super Bowl VIII: Miami (AFC) 24, Minnesota (NFC) 7

1974

AMERICAN CONFERENCE

Eastern Division

	W	L	T	Pct.	Pts.	OP
Miami	11	3	0	.786	327	216
Buffalo*	9	5	0	.643	264	244
New England	7	7	0	.500	348	289
N.Y. Jets	7	7	0	.500	279	300
Baltimore	2	12	0	.143	190	329

Central Division

	W	L	T	Pct.	Pts.	OP
Pittsburgh	10	3	1	.750	305	189
Cincinnati	7	7	0	.500	283	259
Houston	7	7	0	.500	236	282
Cleveland	4	10	0	.286	251	344

Western Division

	W	L	T	Pct.	Pts.	OP
Oakland	12	2	0	.857	355	228
Denver	7	6	1	.536	302	294
Kansas City	5	9	0	.357	233	293
San Diego	5	9	0	.357	212	285

NATIONAL CONFERENCE

Eastern Division

	W	L	T	Pct.	Pts.	OP
St. Louis	10	4	0	.714	285	218
Washington*	10	4	0	.714	320	196
Dallas	8	6	0	.571	297	235
Philadelphia	7	7	0	.500	242	217
N.Y. Giants	2	12	0	.143	195	299

Central Division

	W	L	T	Pct.	Pts.	OP
Minnesota	10	4	0	.714	310	195
Detroit	7	7	0	.500	256	270
Green Bay	6	8	0	.429	210	206
Chicago	4	10	0	.286	152	279

Western Division

	W	L	T	Pct.	Pts.	OP
Los Angeles	10	4	0	.714	263	181
San Francisco	6	8	0	.429	226	236
New Orleans	5	9	0	.357	166	263
Atlanta	3	11	0	.214	111	271

*Wild Card qualifier for playoffs
Divisional playoffs: Oakland 28, Miami 26; Pittsburgh 32, Buffalo 14
AFC Championship: Pittsburgh 24, Oakland 13
Divisional playoffs: Minnesota 30, St. Louis 14; Los Angeles 19, Washington 10
NFC Championship: Minnesota 14, Los Angeles 10
Super Bowl IX: Pittsburgh (AFC) 16, Minnesota (NFC) 6

1975

AMERICAN CONFERENCE

Eastern Division

	W	L	T	Pct.	Pts.	OP
Baltimore	10	4	0	.714	395	269
Miami	10	4	0	.714	357	222
Buffalo	8	6	0	.571	420	355
New England	3	11	0	.214	258	358
N.Y. Jets	3	11	0	.214	258	433

Central Division

	W	L	T	Pct.	Pts.	OP
Pittsburgh	12	2	0	.857	373	162
Cincinnati*	11	3	0	.786	340	246
Houston	10	4	0	.714	293	226
Cleveland	3	11	0	.214	218	372

Western Division

	W	L	T	Pct.	Pts.	OP
Oakland	11	3	0	.786	375	255
Denver	6	8	0	.429	254	307
Kansas City	5	9	0	.357	282	341
San Diego	2	12	0	.143	189	345

NATIONAL CONFERENCE

Eastern Division

	W	L	T	Pct.	Pts.	OP
St. Louis	11	3	0	.786	356	276
Dallas*	10	4	0	.714	350	268
Washington	8	6	0	.571	325	276
N.Y. Giants	5	9	0	.357	216	306
Philadelphia	4	10	0	.286	225	302

Central Division

	W	L	T	Pct.	Pts.	OP
Minnesota	12	2	0	.857	377	180
Detroit	7	7	0	.500	245	262
Chicago	4	10	0	.286	191	379
Green Bay	4	10	0	.286	226	285

Western Division

	W	L	T	Pct.	Pts.	OP
Los Angeles	12	2	0	.857	312	135
San Francisco	5	9	0	.357	255	286
Atlanta	4	10	0	.286	240	289
New Orleans	2	12	0	.143	165	360

*Wild Card qualifier for playoffs

Divisional playoffs: Pittsburgh 28, Baltimore 10; Oakland 31, Cincinnati 28
AFC Championship: Pittsburgh 16, Oakland 10
Divisional playoffs: Los Angeles 35, St. Louis 23; Dallas 17, Minnesota 14
NFC Championship: Dallas 37, Los Angeles 7
Super Bowl X: Pittsburgh (AFC) 21, Dallas (NFC) 17

1976

AMERICAN CONFERENCE

Eastern Division

	W	L	T	Pct.	Pts.	OP
Baltimore	11	3	0	.786	417	246
New England*	11	3	0	.786	376	236
Miami	6	8	0	.429	263	264
N.Y. Jets	3	11	0	.214	169	383
Buffalo	2	12	0	.143	245	363

Central Division

	W	L	T	Pct.	Pts.	OP
Pittsburgh	10	4	0	.714	342	138
Cincinnati	10	4	0	.714	335	210
Cleveland	9	5	0	.643	267	287
Houston	5	9	0	.357	222	273

Western Division

	W	L	T	Pct.	Pts.	OP
Oakland	13	1	0	.929	350	237
Denver	9	5	0	.643	315	206
San Diego	6	8	0	.429	248	285
Kansas City	5	9	0	.357	290	376
Tampa Bay	0	14	0	.000	125	412

NATIONAL CONFERENCE

Eastern Division

	W	L	T	Pct.	Pts.	OP
Dallas	11	3	0	.786	296	194
Washington*	10	4	0	.714	291	217
St. Louis	10	4	0	.714	309	267
Philadelphia	4	10	0	.286	165	286
N.Y. Giants	3	11	0	.214	170	250

Central Division

	W	L	T	Pct.	Pts.	OP
Minnesota	11	2	1	.821	305	176
Chicago	7	7	0	.500	253	216
Detroit	6	8	0	.429	262	220
Green Bay	5	9	0	.357	218	299

Western Division

	W	L	T	Pct.	Pts.	OP
Los Angeles	10	3	1	.750	351	190
San Francisco	8	6	0	.571	270	190
Atlanta	4	10	0	.286	172	312
New Orleans	4	10	0	.286	253	346
Seattle	2	12	0	.143	229	429

*Wild Card qualifier for playoffs

Divisional playoffs: Oakland 24, New England 21; Pittsburgh 40, Baltimore 14
AFC Championship: Oakland 24, Pittsburgh 7
Divisional playoffs: Minnesota 35, Washington 20; Los Angeles 14, Dallas 12
NFC Championship: Minnesota 24, Los Angeles 13
Super Bowl XI: Oakland (AFC) 32, Minnesota (NFC) 14

1977

AMERICAN CONFERENCE

Eastern Division

	W	L	T	Pct.	Pts.	OP
Baltimore	10	4	0	.714	295	221
Miami	10	4	0	.714	313	197
New England	9	5	0	.643	278	217
N.Y. Jets	3	11	0	.214	191	300
Buffalo	3	11	0	.214	160	313

Central Division

	W	L	T	Pct.	Pts.	OP
Pittsburgh	9	5	0	.643	283	243
Houston	8	6	0	.571	299	230
Cincinnati	8	6	0	.571	238	235
Cleveland	6	8	0	.429	269	267

Western Division

	W	L	T	Pct.	Pts.	OP
Denver	12	2	0	.857	274	148
Oakland*	11	3	0	.786	351	230
San Diego	7	7	0	.500	222	205
Seattle	5	9	0	.357	282	373
Kansas City	2	12	0	.143	225	349

NATIONAL CONFERENCE

Eastern Division

	W	L	T	Pct.	Pts.	OP
Dallas	12	2	0	.857	345	212
Washington	9	5	0	.643	196	189
St. Louis	7	7	0	.500	272	287
Philadelphia	5	9	0	.357	220	207
N.Y. Giants	5	9	0	.357	181	265

Central Division

	W	L	T	Pct.	Pts.	OP
Minnesota	9	5	0	.643	231	227
Chicago*	9	5	0	.643	255	253
Detroit	6	8	0	.429	183	252
Green Bay	4	10	0	.286	134	219
Tampa Bay	2	12	0	.143	103	223

Western Division

	W	L	T	Pct.	Pts.	OP
Los Angeles	10	4	0	.714	302	146
Atlanta	7	7	0	.500	179	129
San Francisco	5	9	0	.357	220	260
New Orleans	3	11	0	.214	232	336

*Wild Card qualifier for playoffs

Divisional playoffs: Denver 34, Pittsburgh 21; Oakland 37, Baltimore 31, sudden-death overtime

AFC Championship: Denver 20, Oakland 17

Divisional playoffs: Dallas 37, Chicago 7; Minnesota 14, Los Angeles 7

NFC Championship: Dallas 23, Minnesota 6

Super Bowl XII: Dallas (NFC) 27, Denver (AFC) 10

1978

AMERICAN CONFERENCE

Eastern Division

	W	L	T	Pct.	Pts.	OP
New England	11	5	0	.688	358	286
Miami*	11	5	0	.688	372	254
N.Y. Jets	8	8	0	.500	359	364
Buffalo	5	11	0	.313	302	354
Baltimore	5	11	0	.313	239	421

Central Division

	W	L	T	Pct.	Pts.	OP
Pittsburgh	14	2	0	.875	356	195
Houston*	10	6	0	.625	283	298
Cleveland	8	8	0	.500	334	356
Cincinnati	4	12	0	.250	252	284

Western Division

	W	L	T	Pct.	Pts.	OP
Denver	10	6	0	.625	282	198
Oakland	9	7	0	.563	311	283
Seattle	9	7	0	.563	345	358
San Diego	9	7	0	.563	355	309
Kansas City	4	12	0	.250	243	327

NATIONAL CONFERENCE

Eastern Division

	W	L	T	Pct.	Pts.	OP
Dallas	12	4	0	.750	384	208
Philadelphia*	9	7	0	.563	270	250
Washington	8	8	0	.500	273	283
St. Louis	6	10	0	.375	248	296
N.Y. Giants	6	10	0	.375	264	298

Central Division

	W	L	T	Pct.	Pts.	OP
Minnesota	8	7	1	.531	294	306
Green Bay	8	7	1	.531	249	269
Detroit	7	9	0	.438	290	300
Chicago	7	9	0	.438	253	274
Tampa Bay	5	11	0	.313	241	259

Western Division

	W	L	T	Pct.	Pts.	OP
Los Angeles	12	4	0	.750	316	245
Atlanta*	9	7	0	.563	240	290
New Orleans	7	9	0	.438	281	298
San Francisco	2	14	0	.125	219	350

*Wild Card qualifier for playoffs

First-round playoff: Houston 17, Miami 9

Divisional playoffs: Houston 31, New England 14; Pittsburgh 33, Denver 10

AFC Championship: Pittsburgh 34, Houston 5

First-round playoff: Atlanta 14, Philadelphia 13

Divisional playoffs: Dallas 27, Atlanta 20; Los Angeles 34, Minnesota 10

NFC Championship: Dallas 28, Los Angeles 0

Super Bowl XIII: Pittsburgh (AFC) 35, Dallas (NFC) 31

1979

AMERICAN CONFERENCE
Eastern Division

	W	L	T	Pct.	Pts.	OP
Miami	10	6	0	.625	341	257
New England	9	7	0	.563	411	326
N.Y. Jets	8	8	0	.500	337	383
Buffalo	7	9	0	.438	268	279
Baltimore	5	11	0	.313	271	351

Central Division

	W	L	T	Pct.	Pts.	OP
Pittsburgh	12	4	0	.750	416	262
Houston*	11	5	0	.688	362	331
Cleveland	9	7	0	.563	359	352
Cincinnati	4	12	0	.250	337	421

Western Division

	W	L	T	Pct.	Pts.	OP
San Diego	12	4	0	.750	411	246
Denver*	10	6	0	.625	289	262
Seattle	9	7	0	.563	378	372
Oakland	9	7	0	.563	365	337
Kansas City	7	9	0	.438	238	262

NATIONAL CONFERENCE
Eastern Division

	W	L	T	Pct.	Pts.	OP
Dallas	11	5	0	.688	371	313
Philadelphia*	11	5	0	.688	339	282
Washington	10	6	0	.625	348	295
N.Y. Giants	6	10	0	.375	237	323
St. Louis	5	11	0	.313	307	358

Central Division

	W	L	T	Pct.	Pts.	OP
Tampa Bay	10	6	0	.625	273	237
Chicago*	10	6	0	.625	306	249
Minnesota	7	9	0	.438	259	337
Green Bay	5	11	0	.313	246	316
Detroit	2	14	0	.125	219	365

Western Division

	W	L	T	Pct.	Pts.	OP
Los Angeles	9	7	0	.563	323	309
New Orleans	8	8	0	.500	370	360
Atlanta	6	10	0	.375	300	388
San Francisco	2	14	0	.125	308	416

*Wild Card qualifier for playoffs
First-round playoff: Houston 13, Denver 7
Divisional playoffs: Houston 17, San Diego 14; Pittsburgh 34, Miami 14
AFC Championship: Pittsburgh 27, Houston 13
First-round playoff: Philadelphia 27, Chicago 17
Divisional playoffs: Tampa Bay 24, Philadelphia 17; Los Angeles 21, Dallas 19
NFC Championship: Los Angeles 9, Tampa Bay 0
Super Bowl XIV: Pittsburgh (AFC) 31, Los Angeles (NFC) 19

1980

AMERICAN CONFERENCE
Eastern Division

	W	L	T	Pct.	Pts.	OP
Buffalo	11	5	0	.688	320	260
New England	10	6	0	.625	441	325
Miami	8	8	0	.500	266	305
Baltimore	7	9	0	.438	355	387
N.Y. Jets	4	12	0	.250	302	395

Central Division

	W	L	T	Pct.	Pts.	OP
Cleveland	11	5	0	.688	357	310
Houston*	11	5	0	.688	295	251
Pittsburgh	9	7	0	.563	352	313
Cincinnati	6	10	0	.375	244	312

Western Division

	W	L	T	Pct.	Pts.	OP
San Diego	11	5	0	.688	418	327
Oakland*	11	5	0	.688	364	306
Kansas City	8	8	0	.500	319	336
Denver	8	8	0	.500	310	323
Seattle	4	12	0	.250	291	408

NATIONAL CONFERENCE
Eastern Division

	W	L	T	Pct.	Pts.	OP
Philadelphia	12	4	0	.750	384	222
Dallas*	12	4	0	.750	454	311
Washington	6	10	0	.375	261	293
St. Louis	5	11	0	.313	299	350
N.Y. Giants	4	12	0	.250	249	425

Central Division

	W	L	T	Pct.	Pts.	OP
Minnesota	9	7	0	.563	317	308
Detroit	9	7	0	.563	334	272
Chicago	7	9	0	.437	304	264
Tampa Bay	5	10	1	.343	271	341
Green Bay	5	10	1	.343	231	371

Western Division

	W	L	T	Pct.	Pts.	OP
Atlanta	12	4	0	.750	405	272
Los Angeles*	11	5	0	.688	424	289
San Francisco	6	10	0	.375	320	415
New Orleans	1	15	0	.063	291	487

*Wild Card qualifier for playoffs
First-round playoff: Oakland 27, Houston 7
Divisional playoffs: San Diego 20, Buffalo 14; Oakland 14, Cleveland 12
AFC Championship: Oakland 34, San Diego 27
First-round playoff: Dallas 34, Los Angeles 13
Divisional playoffs: Philadelphia 31, Minnesota 16; Dallas 30, Atlanta 27
NFC Championship: Philadelphia 20, Dallas 7
Super Bowl XV: Oakland (AFC) 27, Philadelphia (NFC) 10

1981

AMERICAN CONFERENCE
Eastern Division

	W	L	T	Pct.	Pts.	OP
Miami	11	4	1	.719	345	275
N.Y. Jets*	10	5	1	.656	355	287
Buffalo*	10	6	0	.625	311	276
Baltimore	2	14	0	.125	259	533
New England	2	14	0	.125	322	370

Central Division

	W	L	T	Pct.	Pts.	OP
Cincinnati	12	4	0	.750	421	304
Pittsburgh	8	8	0	.500	356	297
Houston	7	9	0	.438	281	355
Cleveland	5	11	0	.313	276	375

Western Division

	W	L	T	Pct.	Pts.	OP
San Diego	10	6	0	.625	478	390
Denver	10	6	0	.625	321	289
Kansas City	9	7	0	.563	343	290
Oakland	7	9	0	.438	273	343
Seattle	6	10	0	.375	322	388

NATIONAL CONFERENCE
Eastern Division

	W	L	T	Pct.	Pts.	OP
Dallas	12	4	0	.750	367	277
Philadelphia*	10	6	0	.625	368	221
N.Y. Giants*	9	7	0	.563	295	257
Washington	8	8	0	.500	347	349
St. Louis	7	9	0	.438	315	408

Central Division

	W	L	T	Pct.	Pts.	OP
Tampa Bay	9	7	0	.563	315	268
Detroit	8	8	0	.500	397	322
Green Bay	8	8	0	.500	324	361
Minnesota	7	9	0	.438	325	369
Chicago	6	10	0	.375	253	324

Western Division

	W	L	T	Pct.	Pts.	OP
San Francisco	13	3	0	.813	357	250
Atlanta	7	9	0	.438	426	355
Los Angeles	6	10	0	.375	303	351
New Orleans	4	12	0	.250	207	378

*Wild card qualifier for playoffs
First-round playoff: Buffalo 31, N.Y. Jets 27
Divisional playoffs: San Diego 41, Miami 38 (OT); Cincinnati 28, Buffalo 21
AFC Championship: Cincinnati 27, San Diego 7
First-round playoff: N.Y. Giants 27, Philadelphia 21
Divisional playoffs: Dallas 38, Tampa Bay 0; San Francisco 38, N.Y. Giants 24
NFC Championship: San Francisco 28, Dallas 27
Super Bowl XVI: San Francisco (NFC) 26, Cincinnati (AFC) 21

*1982

AMERICAN CONFERENCE

	W	L	T	Pct.	Pts.	OP
L.A. Raiders	8	1	0	.889	260	200
Miami	7	2	0	.778	198	131
Cincinnati	7	2	0	.778	232	177
Pittsburgh	6	3	0	.667	204	146
San Diego	6	3	0	.667	288	221
N.Y. Jets	6	3	0	.667	245	166
New England	5	4	0	.556	143	157
Cleveland	4	5	0	.444	140	182
Buffalo	4	5	0	.444	150	154
Seattle	4	5	0	.444	127	147
Kansas City	3	6	0	.333	176	184
Denver	2	7	0	.222	148	226
Houston	1	8	0	.111	136	245
Baltimore	0	8	1	.063	113	236

NATIONAL CONFERENCE

	W	L	T	Pct.	Pts.	OP
Washington	8	1	0	.889	190	128
Dallas	6	3	0	.667	226	145
Green Bay	5	3	1	.611	226	169
Minnesota	5	4	0	.556	187	198
Atlanta	5	4	0	.556	183	199
St. Louis	5	4	0	.556	135	170
Tampa Bay	5	4	0	.556	158	178
Detroit	4	5	0	.444	181	176
New Orleans	4	5	0	.444	129	160
N.Y. Giants	4	5	0	.444	164	160
San Francisco	3	6	0	.333	209	206
Chicago	3	6	0	.333	141	174
Philadelphia	3	6	0	.333	191	195
L.A. Rams	2	7	0	.222	200	250

*Top eight teams in each Conference qualified for playoffs under format necessitated by strike-shortened season

First-round playoffs: Miami 28, New England 13; L.A. Raiders 27, Cleveland 10; N.Y. Jets 44, Cincinnati 17; San Diego 31, Pittsburgh 28
Second-round playoffs: N.Y. Jets 17, L.A. Raiders 14; Miami 34, San Diego 13
AFC Championship: Miami 14, N.Y. Jets 0
First-round playoffs: Green Bay 41, St. Louis 16; Washington 31, Detroit 7; Minnesota 30, Atlanta 24; Dallas 30, Tampa Bay 17
Second-round playoffs: Washington 21, Minnesota 7; Dallas 37, Green Bay 26
NFC Championship: Washington 31, Dallas 17
Super Bowl XVII: Washington 27, Miami 17

1983

AMERICAN CONFERENCE

Eastern Division

	W	L	T	Pct.	Pts.	OP
Miami	12	4	0	.750	389	250
New England	8	8	0	.500	274	289
Buffalo	8	8	0	.500	283	351
Baltimore	7	9	0	.438	264	354
N.Y. Jets	7	9	0	.438	313	331

Central Division

	W	L	T	Pct.	Pts.	OP
Pittsburgh	10	6	0	.625	355	303
Cleveland	9	7	0	.562	356	342
Cincinnati	7	9	0	.438	346	302
Houston	2	14	0	.125	288	460

Western Division

	W	L	T	Pct.	Pts.	OP
L.A. Raiders	12	4	0	.750	442	338
Seattle*	9	7	0	.562	403	397
Denver*	9	7	0	.562	302	327
San Diego	6	10	0	.375	358	462
Kansas City	6	10	0	.375	386	367

NATIONAL CONFERENCE

Eastern Division

	W	L	T	Pct.	Pts.	OP
Washington	14	2	0	.875	541	332
Dallas*	12	4	0	.750	479	360
St. Louis	8	7	1	.531	374	428
Philadelphia	5	11	0	.313	233	322
N.Y. Giants	3	12	1	.219	267	347

Central Division

	W	L	T	Pct.	Pts.	OP
Detroit	9	7	0	.562	347	286
Green Bay	8	8	0	.500	429	439
Chicago	8	8	0	.500	311	301
Minnesota	8	8	0	.500	316	348
Tampa Bay	2	14	0	.125	241	380

Western Division

	W	L	T	Pct.	Pts.	OP
San Francisco	10	6	0	.625	432	293
L.A. Rams*	9	7	0	.562	361	344
New Orleans	8	8	0	.500	319	337
Atlanta	7	9	0	.438	370	389

*Wild card qualifier for playoffs

First-round playoff: Seattle 31, Denver 7
Divisional playoffs: Seattle 27, Miami 20; L.A. Raiders 38, Pittsburgh 10
AFC Championship: L.A. Raiders 30, Seattle 14
First-round playoff: L.A. Rams 24, Dallas 17
Divisional playoffs: San Francisco 24, Detroit 23; Washington 51, L.A. Rams 7
NFC Championship: Washington 24, San Francisco 21
Super Bowl XVIII: L.A. Raiders 38, Washington 9

1984

NATIONAL CONFERENCE

Eastern Division

	W	L	T	Pct.	Pts.	OP
Washington	11	5	0	.688	426	310
N.Y. Giants*	9	7	0	.563	299	301
St. Louis	9	7	0	.563	423	345
Dallas	9	7	0	.563	308	308
Philadelphia	6	9	1	.406	278	320

Central Division

	W	L	T	Pct.	Pts.	OP
Chicago	10	6	0	.625	325	248
Green Bay	8	8	0	.500	390	309
Tampa Bay	6	10	0	.375	335	380
Detroit	4	11	1	.281	283	408
Minnesota	3	13	0	.188	276	484

Western Division

	W	L	T	Pct.	Pts.	OP
San Francisco	15	1	0	.939	475	227
L.A. Rams*	10	6	0	.625	346	316
New Orleans	7	9	0	.438	298	361
Atlanta	4	12	0	.250	281	382

AMERICAN CONFERENCE

Eastern Division

	W	L	T	Pct.	Pts.	OP
Miami	14	2	0	.875	513	298
New England	9	7	0	.563	362	352
N.Y. Jets	7	9	0	.438	332	364
Indianapolis	4	12	0	.250	239	414
Buffalo	2	14	0	.125	250	454

Central Division

	W	L	T	Pct.	Pts.	OP
Pittsburgh	9	7	0	.563	387	310
Cincinnati	8	8	0	.500	339	339
Cleveland	5	11	0	.313	250	297
Houston	3	13	0	.188	240	437

Western Division

	W	L	T	Pct.	Pts.	OP
Denver	13	3	0	.813	353	241
Seattle*	12	4	0	.750	418	282
L.A. Raiders*	11	5	0	.688	368	278
Kansas City	8	8	0	.500	314	324
San Diego	7	9	0	.438	394	413

*Wild card qualifier for playoffs

Wild Card Game: N.Y. Giants 16, L.A. Rams 13
NFC Divisional playoffs: San Francisco 21, N.Y. Giants 10; Chicago 23, Washington 19
NFC Championship: San Francisco 23, Chicago 0
Wild Card Game: Seattle 13, L.A. Raiders 7
AFC Divisional playoffs: Miami 31, Seattle 10; Pittsburgh 24, Denver 17
AFC Championship: Miami 45, Pittsburgh 28
Super Bowl XIX: San Francisco 38, Miami 16

1985

AMERICAN CONFERENCE

Eastern Division

	W	L	T	Pct.	Pts.	OP
Miami	12	4	0	.750	428	320
N.Y. Jets	11	5	0	.688	393	264
New England	11	5	0	.688	362	290
Indianapolis	5	11	0	.313	320	386
Buffalo	2	14	0	.125	200	381

CENTRAL DIVISION

	W	L	T	Pct.	Pts.	OP
Cleveland	8	8	0	.500	287	294
Cincinnati	7	9	0	.438	441	437
Pittsburgh	7	9	0	.438	379	355
Houston	5	11	0	.313	284	412

WESTERN DIVISION

	W	L	T	Pct.	Pts.	OP
L.A. Raiders	12	4	0	.750	354	308
Denver	11	5	0	.688	380	329
Seattle	8	8	0	.500	349	303
San Diego	8	8	0	.500	467	435
Kansas City	6	10	0	.375	327	360

NATIONAL CONFERENCE

Eastern Division

	W	L	T	Pct.	Pts.	OP
Dallas	10	6	0	.625	357	333
N.Y. Giants	10	6	0	.625	399	283
Washington	10	6	0	.625	298	313
Philadelphia	7	9	0	.438	286	310
St. Louis	5	11	0	.313	279	415

CENTRAL DIVISION

	W	L	T	Pct.	Pts.	OP
Chicago	15	1	0	.938	456	198
Green Bay	8	8	0	.500	337	355
Minnesota	7	9	0	.438	346	359
Detroit	7	9	0	.438	307	366
Tampa Bay	2	14	0	.125	294	448

WESTERN DIVISION

	W	L	T	Pct.	Pts.	OP
L.A. Rams	11	5	0	.688	340	287
San Francisco	10	6	0	.625	411	263
New Orleans	5	11	0	.313	294	401
Atlanta	4	12	0	.250	282	452

Wild Card Game: New England 26, N.Y. Jets 14
AFC Divisional playoffs: Miami 24, Cleveland 21; New England 27, L.A. Raiders 20
AFC Championship: New England 31, Miami 14
Wild Card Game: N.Y. Giants 17, San Francisco 3
NFC Divisional playoffs: L.A. Rams 20, Dallas 0; Chicago 21, N.Y. Giants 0
NFC Championship: Chicago 24, L.A. Rams 0
Super Bowl XX: Chicago 46, New England 10

1986

AMERICAN CONFERENCE

Eastern Division

	W	L	T	Pct.	Pts.	OP
N.Y. Giants	14	2	0	.875	371	236
Washington	12	4	0	.750	368	296
Dallas	7	9	0	.438	346	337
Philadelphia	5	10	1	.344	256	312
St. Louis	4	11	1	.281	218	351

Central Division

	W	L	T	Pct.	Pts.	OP
Chicago	14	2	0	.875	352	187
Minnesota	9	7	0	.563	398	273
Detroit	5	11	0	.313	277	326
Green Bay	4	12	0	.250	254	418
Tampa Bay	2	14	0	.125	239	473

Western Division

	W	L	T	Pct.	Pts.	OP
San Francisco	10	5	1	.656	374	247
L.A. Rams	10	6	0	.625	309	267
Atlanta	7	8	1	.469	280	280
New Orleans	7	9	0	.438	288	287

NATIONAL CONFERENCE

Eastern Division

	W	L	T	Pct.	Pts.	OP
New England	11	5	0	.688	412	307
N.Y. Jets	10	6	0	.625	364	386
Miami	8	8	0	.500	430	405
Buffalo	4	12	0	.250	287	348
Indianapolis	3	13	0	.188	229	400

Central Division

	W	L	T	Pct.	Pts.	OP
Cleveland	12	4	0	.750	391	310
Cincinnati	10	6	0	.625	409	394
Pittsburgh	6	10	0	.375	307	336
Houston	5	11	0	.313	274	329

Western Division

	W	L	T	Pct.	Pts.	OP
Denver	11	5	0	.688	378	327
Kansas City	10	6	0	.625	358	326
Seattle	10	6	0	.625	366	293
L.A. Raiders	8	8	0	.500	323	346
San Diego	4	12	0	.250	335	396

NFC Wild Card Game: Washington 19, L.A. Rams 7
NFC Divisional playoffs: Washington 27, Chicago 13; N.Y. Giants 49, San Francisco 3
NFC Championship: N.Y. Giants 17, Washington 0
AFC Wild Card Game: N.Y. Jets 35, Kansas City 15
AFC Divisional playoffs: Cleveland 23, N.Y. Jets 20 (2 OT); Denver 22, New England 17
AFC Championship: Denver 23, Cleveland 20 (OT)
Super Bowl XXI: N.Y. Giants 39, Denver 20

1987

NATIONAL CONFERENCE

Eastern Division

	W	L	T	Pct.	Pts.	OP
Washington	11	4	0	.733	379	285
St. Louis	7	8	0	.467	362	368
Dallas	7	8	0	.467	340	348
Philadelphia	7	8	0	.467	337	380
N.Y. Giants	6	9	0	.400	280	312

Central Division

	W	L	T	Pct.	Pts.	OP
Chicago	11	4	0	.733	356	282
Minnesota	8	7	0	.533	336	335
Green Bay	5	9	1	.367	255	300
Tampa Bay	4	11	0	.267	286	360
Detroit	4	11	0	.267	269	384

Western Division

	W	L	T	Pct.	Pts.	OP
San Francisco	13	2	0	.867	459	253
New Orleans	12	3	0	.800	422	283
L.A. Rams	6	9	0	.400	317	361
Atlanta	3	12	0	.200	205	436

AMERICAN CONFERENCE

Eastern Division

	W	L	T	Pct.	Pts.	OP
Indianapolis	9	6	0	.600	300	238
New England	8	7	0	.533	320	293
Miami	8	7	0	.533	362	335
Buffalo	7	8	0	.467	270	305
N.Y. Jets	6	9	0	.400	334	360

Central Division

	W	L	T	Pct.	Pts.	OP
Cleveland	10	5	0	.667	390	239
Houston	9	6	0	.600	345	349
Pittsburgh	8	7	0	.533	285	299
Cincinnati	4	11	0	.267	285	370

Western Division

	W	L	T	Pct.	Pts.	OP
Denver	10	4	1	.700	379	288
Seattle	9	6	0	.600	371	314
San Diego	8	7	0	.533	253	317
L.A. Raiders	5	10	0	.333	301	289
Kansas City	4	11	0	.267	273	388

NFC Wild Card Game: Minnesota 44, New Orleans 10
NFC Divisional playoffs: Minnesota 36, San Francisco 24; Wash. 21, Chicago 17
NFC Championship: Washington 17, Minnesota 10
AFC Wild Card Game: Houston 23, Seattle 20 (OT)
AFC Divisional playoffs: Cleveland 38, Indianapolis 21; Denver 34, Houston 10
AFC Championship: Denver 38, Cleveland 33
Super Bowl XXII: Washington 42, Denver 10

1988

AMERICAN CONFERENCE

Eastern Division

	W	L	T	Pct.	Pts.	OP
Buffalo	12	4	0	.750	329	237
Indianapolis	9	7	0	.563	354	315
New England	9	7	0	.563	250	284
N.Y. Jets	8	7	1	.531	372	354
Miami	6	10	0	.375	319	380

Central Division

	W	L	T	Pct.	Pts.	OP
Cincinnati	12	4	0	.750	448	329
Cleveland	10	6	0	.625	304	288
Houston	10	6	0	.625	424	365
Pittsburgh	5	11	0	.313	336	421

Western Division

	W	L	T	Pct.	Pts.	OP
Seattle	9	7	0	.563	339	329
Denver	8	8	0	.500	327	352
L.A. Raiders	7	9	0	.438	325	369
San Diego	6	10	0	.375	231	332
Kansas City	4	11	1	.281	254	320

NATIONAL CONFERENCE

Eastern Division

	W	L	T	Pct.	Pts.	OP
Philadelphia	10	6	0	.625	379	319
N.Y. Giants	10	6	0	.625	359	304
Washington	7	9	0	.438	345	387
Phoenix	7	9	0	.438	344	398
Dallas	3	13	0	.188	265	381

Central Division

	W	L	T	Pct.	Pts.	OP
Chicago	12	4	0	.750	312	215
Minnesota	11	5	0	.688	406	233
Tampa Bay	5	11	0	.313	261	350
Detroit	4	12	0	.250	220	313
Green Bay	4	12	0	.250	240	315

Western Division

	W	L	T	Pct.	Pts.	OP
San Francisco	10	6	0	.625	369	294
L.A. Rams	10	6	0	.625	407	293
New Orleans	10	6	0	.625	312	283
Atlanta	5	11	0	.313	244	315

AFC Wild Card Game: Houston 24, Cleveland 23
AFC Divisional playoffs: Cincinnati 21, Seattle 13; Buffalo 17, Houston 10
AFC Championship: Cincinnati 21, Buffalo 10
NFC Wild Card Game: Minnesota 28, L.A. Rams 17
NFC Divisional playoffs: Chicago 20, Philadelphia 12; San Francisco 34, Minnesota 9
NFC Championship: San Francisco 28, Chicago 3
Super Bowl XXIII: San Francisco 20, Cincinnati 16

1989

AMERICAN CONFERENCE

Eastern Division

	W	L	T	Pct.	Pts.	OP
Buffalo	9	7	0	.563	409	317
Indianapolis	8	8	0	.500	298	301
Miami	8	8	0	.500	331	379
New England	5	11	0	.313	297	391
N.Y. Jets	4	12	0	.250	253	411

Central Division

	W	L	T	Pct.	Pts.	OP
Cleveland	9	6	1	.594	334	254
Houston	9	7	0	.563	365	412
Pittsburgh	9	7	0	.563	265	326
Cincinnati	8	8	0	.500	404	285

Western Division

	W	L	T	Pct.	Pts.	OP
Denver	11	5	0	.688	362	226
Kansas City	8	7	1	.531	318	286
L.A. Raiders	8	8	0	.500	315	297
Seattle	7	9	0	.438	241	327
San Diego	6	10	0	.375	266	290

NATIONAL CONFERENCE

Eastern Division

	W	L	T	Pct.	Pts.	OP
N.Y. Giants	12	4	0	.750	348	252
Philadelphia	11	5	0	.688	342	274
Washington	10	6	0	.625	386	308
Phoenix	5	11	0	.313	258	377
Dallas	1	15	0	.063	204	393

Central Division

	W	L	T	Pct.	Pts.	OP
Minnesota	10	6	0	.625	351	275
Green Bay	10	6	0	.625	362	356
Detroit	7	9	0	.438	312	364
Chicago	6	10	0	.375	358	377
Tampa Bay	5	11	0	.313	320	419

Western Division

	W	L	T	Pct.	Pts.	OP
San Francisco	14	2	0	.875	442	253
L.A. Rams	11	5	0	.688	426	344
New Orleans	9	7	0	.563	386	301
Atlanta	3	13	0	.188	279	437

AFC Wild Card Game: Pittsburgh 26, Houston 23 (OT)
AFC Divisional playoffs: Cleveland 34, Buffalo 30; Denver 24, Pittsburgh 23
AFC Championship: Denver 37, Cleveland 21
NFC Wild Card Game: L.A. Rams 21, Philadelphia 7
NFC Divisional playoffs: L.A. Rams 19, N.Y. Giants 13 (OT); San Francisco 41, Minnesota 13
NFC Championship: San Francisco 30, L.A. Rams 3
Super Bowl XXIV: San Francisco 55, Denver 10

1990

AMERICAN CONFERENCE

Eastern Division

	W	L	T	Pct.	Pts.	OP
Buffalo	13	3	0	.813	428	263
Miami	12	4	0	.750	336	242
Indianapolis	7	9	0	.438	281	353
N.Y. Jets	6	10	0	.375	295	345
New England	1	15	0	.063	181	446

Central Division

	W	L	T	Pct.	Pts.	OP
Cincinnati	9	7	0	.563	360	352
Houston	9	7	0	.563	405	307
Pittsburgh	9	7	0	.563	292	240
Cleveland	3	13	0	.188	228	462

Western Division

	W	L	T	Pct.	Pts.	OP
L.A. Raiders	12	4	0	.750	337	268
Kansas City	11	5	0	.688	369	257
Seattle	9	7	0	.563	306	286
San Diego	6	10	0	.375	315	281
Denver	5	11	0	.313	331	374

NATIONAL CONFERENCE

Eastern Division

	W	L	T	Pct.	Pts.	OP
N.Y. Giants	13	3	0	.813	335	211
Philadelphia	10	6	0	.625	396	299
Washington	10	6	0	.625	381	301
Dallas	7	9	0	.438	244	308
Phoenix	5	11	0	.313	268	396

Central Division

	W	L	T	Pct.	Pts.	OP
Chicago	11	5	0	.688	348	280
Tampa Bay	6	10	0	.375	264	367
Detroit	6	10	0	.375	373	413
Green Bay	6	10	0	.375	271	347
Minnesota	6	10	0	.375	351	326

Western Division

	W	L	T	Pct.	Pts.	OP
San Francisco	14	2	0	.875	353	239
New Orleans	8	8	0	.500	274	275
L.A. Rams	5	11	0	.313	345	412
Atlanta	5	11	0	.313	348	365

AFC First round: Miami 17, Kansas City 16; Cincinnati 41, Houston 14
AFC Divisional playoffs: Buffalo 44, Miami 34; L.A. Raiders 20, Cincinnati 10
AFC Championship: Buffalo 51, L.A. Raiders 3
NFC First round: Washington 20, Philadelphia 6; Chicago 16, New Orleans 6
NFC Divisional playoffs: San Francisco 28, Washington 10; N.Y. Giants 31, Chicago 3
NFC Championship: N.Y. Giants 15, San Francisco 13
Super Bowl XXV: N.Y. Giants 20, Buffalo 19

1991

AMERICAN CONFERENCE						NATIONAL CONFERENCE					
Eastern Division						**Eastern Division**					
	W	L	T	Pct.	Pts.	OP		W	L	T	Pct.	Pts.	OP
Buffalo	13	3	0	.813	458	318	Washington	14	2	0	.875	485	224
N.Y. Jets	8	8	0	.500	314	293	Dallas	11	5	0	.688	342	310
Miami	8	8	0	.500	343	349	Philadelphia	10	6	0	.625	285	244
New England	6	10	0	.375	211	305	N.Y. Giants	8	8	0	.500	281	297
Indianapolis	1	15	0	0.63	143	381	Phoenix	4	12	0	.250	196	344
Central Division							**Central Division**					
Houston	11	5	0	.688	386	251	Detroit	12	4	0	.750	339	295
Pittsburgh	7	9	0	.438	292	344	Chicago	11	5	0	.688	299	269
Cleveland	6	10	0	.375	293	298	Minnesota	8	8	0	.500	301	306
Cincinnati	3	13	0	.188	263	435	Green Bay	4	12	0	.250	273	313
							Tampa Bay	3	13	0	.188	199	365
Western Division							**Western Division**					
Denver	12	4	0	.750	304	235	New Orleans	11	5	0	.688	341	211
Kansas City	10	6	0	.625	322	252	Atlanta	10	6	0	.625	361	338
L.A. Raiders	9	7	0	.563	298	297	San Francisco	10	6	0	.625	393	239
Seattle	7	9	0	.438	276	261	L.A. Rams	3	13	0	.188	199	365
San Diego	4	12	0	.250	274	342							

AFC First round: Kansas City 10, L.A. Raiders 6; Houston 17, N.Y. Jets 10
AFC Divisional playoffs: Denver, 26, Houston 24; Buffalo 37, Kansas City 14
AFC Championship: Buffalo 10, Denver 7
NFC First round: Atlanta 27, New Orleans 20; Dallas 17, Chicago 13
NFC Divisional playoffs: Washington 24, Atlanta 7; Detroit 38, Dallas 6
NFC Championship: Washington 41, Detroit 10
Super Bowl XXVI: Washington 37, Buffalo 24

1992

AMERICAN CONFERENCE						NATIONAL CONFERENCE					
Eastern Division						**Eastern Division**					
	W	L	T	Pct.	Pts.	OP		W	L	T	Pct.	Pts.	OP
Miami	11	5	0	.688	340	281	Dallas	13	3	0	.813	409	243
Buffalo	11	5	0	.688	381	283	Philadelphia	11	5	0	.688	354	245
Indianapolis	9	7	0	.563	216	302	Washington	9	7	0	.563	300	255
N.Y. Jets	4	12	0	.250	220	315	N.Y. Giants	6	10	0	.375	306	367
New England	2	14	0	.125	205	363	Phoenix	4	12	0	.250	243	332
Central Division							**Central Division**					
Pittsburgh	11	5	0	.688	299	225	Minnesota	11	5	0	.688	374	249
Houston	10	6	0	.625	352	258	Green Bay	9	7	0	.563	276	296
Cleveland	7	9	0	.438	272	275	Tampa Bay	5	11	0	.313	267	365
Cincinnati	5	11	0	.313	274	364	Chicago	5	11	0	.313	295	361
							Detroit	5	11	0	.313	273	332
Western Division							**Western Division**					
San Diego	11	5	0	.688	335	241	San Francisco	14	2	0	.875	431	236
Kansas City	10	6	0	.625	348	282	New Orleans	12	4	0	.750	330	202
Denver	8	8	0	.500	262	329	Atlanta	6	10	0	.375	327	414
L.A. Raiders	7	9	0	.438	249	281	L.A. Rams	6	10	0	.375	313	383
Seattle	2	14	0	.125	140	312							

AFC Wild-Card playoffs: San Diego 17, Kansas City 0; Buffalo 41, Houston 38 (OT)
AFC Divisional playoffs: Buffalo 24, Pittsburgh 3); Miami 31, San Diego 0
AFC Championship: Buffalo 29, Miami 10
NFC Wild-Card playoffs: Washington 24, Minnesota 7; Philadelphia 36, New Orleans 20
NFC Divisional playoffs: San Francisco 20, Washington 13; Dallas 34, Philadelphia 10
NFC Championship: Dallas 30, San Francisco 20
Super Bowl XXVII: Dallas 52, Buffalo 17

1993 NFL DRAFT

(Underclassmen are designated by # in front of the name)

Player	Order No.	Pos.	College	Club	Round
Ahanotu, Chidi	145	DT	California	Tampa Bay	6
Alcorn, Daron	224	K	Akron	Tampa Bay	8
Alexander, Harold	67	P	Appalachian State	Atlanta	3
# Anderson, Richie	144	RB	Penn State	New York Jets	6
Anderson, Steve	215	WR	Grambling	Phoenix	8
Armstead, Jessie	207	LB	Miami	New York Giants	8
Arvie, Herman	124	T	Grambling	Cleveland	5
Bailey, Victor	50	WR	Missouri	Philadelphia	2
Baker, Myron	100	LB	Louisiana Tech	Chicago	4
Baker, Shannon	205	WR	Florida State	Atlanta	8
Barrow, Micheal	47	LB	Miami	Houston	2
# Bates, Patrick	12	DB	Texas A&M	Los Angeles Raiders	1
Baxter, Fred	115	TE	Auburn	New York Jets	5
Belin, Chuck	127	G	Wisconsin	Los Angeles Rams	5
# Bettis, Jerome	10	RB	Notre Dame	Los Angeles Rams	1
Biekert, Greg	181	LB	Colorado	Los Angeles Raiders	7
Bishop, Blaine	214	DB	Ball State	Houston	8
Bishop, Greg	93	T	Pacific	New York Giants	4
Blackshear, Jeff	197	G	N.E. Louisiana	Seattle	8
# Bledsoe, Drew	1	QB	Washington State	New England	1
Bonner, Melvin	154	WR	Baylor	Denver	6
Boykin, Deral	149	DB	Louisville	Los Angeles Rams	6
Bradford, Ronnie	105	DB	Colorado	Miami	4
Bradley, Chuck	158	T	Kentucky	Houston	6
Branch, Darrick	220	WR	Hawaii	Tampa Bay	8
Brisby, Vincent	56	WR	N.E. Louisiana	New England	2
Brooks, Reggie	45	RB	Notre Dame	Washington	2
Brown, Chad	199	DE	Mississippi	Phoenix	8
Brown, Chad	44	LB	Colorado	Pittsburgh	2
Brown, Corwin	110	DB	Michigan	New England	4
# Brown, Derek	109	RB	Nebraska	New Orleans	4
Brown, Gilbert	79	DT	Kansas	Minnesota	3
Brown, Troy	198	KR	Marshall	New England	8
Brunell, Mark	118	QB	Washington	Green Bay	5
Buchanan, Ray	65	DB	Louisville	Indianapolis	3
Buckley, Marcus	66	LB	Texas A&M	New York Giants	3
Buffaloe, Jeff	206	P	Memphis State	Los Angeles Rams	8
Bunn, Ed	80	P	Texas-El Paso	Washington	3
Bush, Lewis	99	LB	Washington State	San Diego	4
Caldwell, Mike	83	LB	Middle Tennessee	Cleveland	3
# Carter, Tom	17	DB	Notre Dame	Washington	1
Castle, Eric	161	DB	Oregon	San Diego	6
Cocozzo, Joe	64	G	Michigan	San Diego	3
Coleman, Ben	32	T	Wake Forest	Phoenix	2
Compton, Mike	68	C	West Virginia	Detroit	3
# Conway, Curtis	7	WR	Southern California	Chicago	1
Copeland, Horace	104	WR	Miami	Tampa Bay	4
Copeland, John	5	DE	Alabama	Cincinnati	1
# Copeland, Russell	111	WR	Memphis State	Buffalo	4
Curry, Eric	6	DE	Alabama	Tampa Bay	1

Florida State's Marvin Jones joined Jets as No. 4.

Bears' caught USC's Curtis Conway as No. 7.

Notre Dame's Jerome Bettis (10th pick) will ram for Rams.

Player	Order No.	Pos.	College	Club	Round
Dalman, Chris	166	G	Stanford	San Francisco	6
Davis, Scott	150	G	Iowa	New York Giants	6
Davis, Tyree	176	WR	Central Arkansas	Tampa Bay	7
# Dawkins, Sean	16	WR	California	Indianapolis	1
Devlin, Mike	136	C	Iowa	Buffalo	5
Dixon, Ronnie	165	NT	Cincinnati	New Orleans	6
Dotson, Earl	81	T	Texas A&I	Green Bay	3
Drayton, Troy	39	TE	Penn State	Los Angeles Rams	2
Du Bose, Demetrius	34	LB	Notre Dame	Tampa Bay	2
Duckett, Forey	117	DB	Nevada-Reno	Cincinnati	5
Dunson, Walter	134	WR	Middle Tennessee	San Diego	5
Dye, Ernest	18	T	South Carolina	Phoenix	1

Player	Order No.	Pos.	College	Club	Round
Edwards, Antonio	204	DE	Valdosta State	Seattle	8
Elam, Jason	70	P-K	Hawaii	Denver	3
Etheredge, Carlos	157	TE	Miami	Indianapolis	6
Evans, Doug	141	DB	Louisiana Tech	Green Bay	6
Everitt, Steve	14	C	Michigan	Cleveland	1
Fichtel, Brad	179	C	Eastern Illinois	Los Angeles Rams	7
Fields, Jaime	103	LB	Washington	Kansas City	4
Figures, Deon	23	DB	Colorado	Pittsburgh	1
Fontenot, Albert	112	DE	Baylor	Chicago	4
Footman, Dan	42	DE	Florida State	Cleveland	2
Frazier, Derrick	75	DB	Texas A&M	Philadelphia	3
Freeman, Reggie	53	LB	Florida State	New Orleans	2
Gedney, Chris	61	TE	Syracuse	Chicago	3
George, Ron	121	LB	Stanford	Atlanta	5
Gerak, John	57	G	Penn State	Minnesota	3
Givens, Reggie	213	DB	Penn State	Dallas	8
Gordon, Darrien	22	DB	Stanford	San Diego	1
Gordon, Dwayne	218	LB	New Hampshire	Miami	8
Gray, Carlton	30	DB	UCLA	Seattle	2
Gray, Chris	132	G	Auburn	Miami	5
Gray, Derwin	92	DB	Brigham Young	Indianapolis	4
Grbac, Elvis	219	QB	Michigan	San Francisco	8
Green, Trent	222	QB	Indiana	San Diego	8
Griffith, Richard	138	TE	Arizona	New England	5
Gunn, Lance	175	DB	Texas	Cincinnati	7
Hallock, Ty	174	LB	Michigan State	Detroit	7
Hamilton, Rick	71	LB	Central Florida	Washington	3
Hannah, Travis	102	WR	Southern California	Houston	4
Hardy, Adrian	48	DB	N.W. Louisiana	San Francisco	2
# Harper, Roger	38	DB	Ohio State	Atlanta	2
Harris, Rudy	91	RB	Clemson	Tampa Bay	4
Harris, Willie	195	WR	Mississippi State	Buffalo	7
# Hastings, Andre	76	WR	Georgia	Pittsburgh	3
Hatch, Lawrence	142	DB	Florida	New England	6
# Hearst, Garrison	3	RB	Georgia	Phoenix	1
# Henderson, Othello	193	DB	UCLA	New Orleans	7
Henry, Kevin	108	DE	Mississippi State	Pittsburgh	4
Hentrich, Craig	200	K	Notre Dame	New York Jets	8
Hill, Travis	180	LB	Nebraska	Cleveland	7
# Hobert, Billy Joe	58	QB	Washington	Los Angeles Raiders	3
Hoffman, Dave	146	LB	Washington	Chicago	6
Hollinquest, Lamont	212	LB	Southern California	Washington	8
Holmes, Lester	19	T	Jackson State	Philadelphia	1
Hopkins, Brad	13	T	Illinois	Houston	1
Hughes, Danan	186	WR	Iowa	Kansas City	7
Hughes, Tyrone	137	DB	Nebraska	New Orleans	5
Huntington, Greg	128	C	Penn State	Washington	5
Hutchins, Paul	152	T	Western Michigan	Green Bay	6
Ismail, Qadry	52	WR	Syracuse	Minnesota	2
Jeffries, Greg	147	DB	Virginia	Detroit	6
Johnson, Keshon	173	DB	Arizona	Chicago	7
Johnson, Kevin	86	NT	Texas Southern	New England	4
Johnson, Ray Lee	95	DE	Arkansas	San Diego	4
# Jones, Marvin	4	LB	Florida State	New York Jets	1
Jones, Rondell	69	DB	North Carolina	Denver	3

California's Sean Dawkins went to Colts as No. 16.

Player	Order No.	Pos.	College	Club	Round
Keith, Craig	189	TE	Lenoir-Rhyne	Pittsburgh	7
Kelly, Todd	27	DE	Tennessee	San Francisco	1
Kennedy, Lincoln	9	T	Washington	Atlanta	1
Kimbrough, Antonius	182	WR	Jackson State	Denver	7

Player	Order No.	Pos.	College	Club	Round
Kirby, Terry	78	RB	Virginia	Miami	3
Kirksey, Jon	221	NT	Cal State-Sacramento	New Orleans	8
Knapp, Lindsay	130	G	Notre Dame	Kansas City	5
Kuberski, Robert	183	DE	Navy	Green Bay	7
LaChapelle, Sean	122	WR	UCLA	Los Angeles Rams	5
Lacina, Corbin	167	T	Augustana, S.D.	Buffalo	6
Lassic, Derrick	94	RB	Alabama	Dallas	4
Lewis, Lance	184	RB	Nebraska	Indianapolis	7
Lindsay, Everett	133	T	Mississippi	Minnesota	5
London, Antonio	62	LB	Alabama	Detroit	3
Luneberg, Chris	223	T	West Chester, PA.	Buffalo	8
Lynch, John	82	DB	Stanford	Tampa Bay	3
Lyons, Mitch	151	TE	Michigan State	Atlanta	6
Marion, Brock	196	DB	Nevada-Reno	Dallas	7
McCrary, Michael	170	DE	Wake Forest	Seattle	7
McDonald, Devon	107	LB	Notre Dame	Indianapolis	4
McDuffie, O.J.	25	WR	Penn State	Miami	1
McGee, Tony	37	TE	Michigan	Cincinnati	2
McKenzie, Rich	153	LB	Penn State	Cleveland	6
McNeil, Ryan	33	DB	Miami	Detroit	2
# Means, Natrone	41	RB	North Carolina	San Diego	2
Merritt, David	191	LB	North Carolina State	Miami	7
Mickey, Joey	190	TE	Oklahoma	Philadelphia	7
Middleton, Mike	84	DB	Indiana	Dallas	3
Milburn, Glyn	43	RB	Stanford	Denver	2
Millen, Alec	171	T	Georgia	New York Jets	7
Miller, Doug	188	LB	South Dakota State	San Diego	7
Mills, John Henry	131	TE	Wake Forest	Houston	5
Miniefield, Kevin	201	DB	Arizona State	Detroit	8
Minter, Barry	168	LB	Tulsa	Dallas	6
Mirer, Rick	2	QB	Notre Dame	Seattle	1
Moore, Ronald	87	RB	Pittsburgh, Kan.	Phoenix	4
Morrison, Darryl	155	DB	Arizona	Washington	6
Murrell, Adrian	120	RB	West Virginia	New York Jets	5
Neal, Lorenzo	89	RB	Fresno State	New Orleans	4
O'Neal, Robert	164	DB	Clemson	Miami	6
Oden, Derrick	163	LB	Alabama	Philadelphia	6
Palelei, Lonnie	135	G	Nevada-Las Vegas	Pittsburgh	5
# Palmer, Sterling	101	DE	Florida State	Washington	4
Parrella, John	55	DT	Nebraska	Buffalo	2
Parten, Ty	63	DT	Arizona	Cincinnati	3
Pelfrey, Doug	202	K	Kentucky	Cincinnati	8
Perry, Todd	97	G	Kentucky	Chicago	4
Peterson, Todd	177	K	Georgia	New York Giants	7
Potts, Roosevelt	49	RB	N.E. Louisiana	Indianapolis	2
# Reid, Mike	77	DB	North Carolina State	Philadelphia	3
# Renfro, Leonard	24	DT	Colorado	Philadelphia	1
Roaf, Willie	8	T	Louisiana Tech	New Orleans	1
Robinson, Greg	208	RB	N.E. Louisiana	Los Angeles Raiders	8
Robinson, Jeff	98	DE	Idaho	Denver	4
Robinson, Patrick	187	WR	Tennessee State	Houston	7
Rucci, Todd	51	T	Penn State	New England	2
Rudolph, Coleman	36	DE	Georgia Tech	New York Jets	2
Savage, Sebastian	139	DB	North Carolina State	Buffalo	5

Colorado's Leonard Renfro was tabbed No. 24 by Eagles.

Notre Dame's Tom Carter got call as No. 17 by Redskins.

Steelers made Colorado's Deon Figures 23rd selection.

Player	Order No.	Pos.	College	Club	Round
Scott, Tom	148	T	East Carolina	Cincinnati	6
Shedd, Kenny	129	WR	Northern Iowa	New York Jets	5
Sheppard, Ashley	106	LB	Clemson	Minnesota	4
Shields, Will	74	G	Nebraska	Kansas City	3
Simmons, Marcello	90	DB	Southern Methodist	Cincinnati	4
Simmons, Wayne	15	LB	Clemson	Green Bay	1
Simpson, Carl	35	DT	Florida State	Chicago	2
Sisson, Scott	113	K	Georgia Tech	New England	5
Skene, Doug	217	T	Michigan	Philadelphia	8
Slade, Chris	31	DE	Virginia	New England	2
Smith, Artie	116	DT	Louisiana Tech	San Francisco	5
Smith, Darrin	54	LB	Miami	Dallas	2
Smith, Irv	20	TE	Notre Dame	New Orleans	1
# Smith, Robert	21	RB	Ohio State	Minnesota	1

49ers chose Kansas' Dana Stubblefield with 26th pick.

Player	Order No.	Pos.	College	Club	Round
Smith, Thomas	28	DB	North Carolina	Buffalo	1
Stablein, Brian	210	WR	Ohio State	Denver	8
Stone, Ron	96	T	Boston College	Dallas	4
Strahan, Michael	40	DE	Texas Southern	New York Giants	2
Stubblefield, Dana	26	DT	Kansas	San Francisco	1
Tanuvasa, Maa	209	DT	Hawaii	Los Angeles Rams	8
Teague, George	29	DB	Alabama	Green Bay	1
Thigpen, Tommy	123	LB	North Carolina	New York Giants	5
Thomas, Dave	203	DB	Tennessee	Dallas	8
Thomas, Lamar	60	WR	Miami	Tampa Bay	3
Thomas, Marquise	211	LB	Mississippi	Indianapolis	8
Torretta, Gino	192	QB	Miami	Minnesota	7
Tovar, Steve	59	LB	Ohio State	Cincinnati	3
Trapp, James	72	DB	Clemson	Los Angeles Raiders	3
# Truitt, Olanda	125	WR	Mississippi State	Los Angeles Raiders	5
Turner, Darius	159	RB	Washington	Kansas City	6
Van Pelt, Alex	216	QB	Pittsburgh	Pittsburgh	8
Walker, Darnell	178	DB	Oklahoma	Atlanta	7
Wallerstedt, Brett	143	LB	Arizona State	Phoenix	6

No. 1 Heisman, No. 192 (Vikings) for Miami's Gina Torretta.

Player	Order No.	Pos.	College	Club	Round
Ware, David	88	T	Virginia	New York Jets	4
Warren, Terrence	114	WR	Hampton	Seattle	5
Watson, Tim	156	DB	Howard	Green Bay	6
Wells, Dean	85	LB	Kentucky	Seattle	4
White, Russell	73	RB	California	Los Angeles Rams	3
White, Will	172	DB	Florida	Phoenix	7
Williams, Clarence	169	TE	Washington State	Denver	7
Williams, Dan	11	DE	Toledo	Denver	1
# Williams, Kevin	46	WR	Miami	Dallas	2
Williams, Kevin	126	RB	UCLA	Denver	5
Williams, Willie	162	DB	Western Carolina	Pittsburgh	6
# Willis, James	119	LB	Auburn	Green Bay	5
Wilson, Troy	194	LB	Pittsburg (Kan.)	San Francisco	7
Woodard, Marc	140	LB	Mississippi State	Pittsburgh	5
# Wycheck, Frank	160	TE	Maryland	Washington	6
Zgonina, Jeff	185	DT	Purdue	Pittsburgh	7

1993 NFL SCHEDULE

*NIGHT GAME

SUNDAY, SEPT. 5
Atlanta at Detroit
Cincinnati at Cleveland
Denver at New York Jets
Kansas City at Tampa Bay
Los Angeles Rams vs. Green Bay at Milw.
Miami at Indianapolis
Minnesota at Los Angeles Raiders
New England at Buffalo
New York Giants at Chicago
Phoenix at Philadelphia
San Francisco at Pittsburgh
Seattle at San Diego
*Houston at New Orleans

MONDAY, SEPT. 6
*Dallas at Washington

SUNDAY, SEPT. 12
Buffalo at Dallas
Chicago at Minnesota
Detroit at New England
Indianapolis at Cincinnati
Kansas City at Houston
New Orleans at Atlanta
New York Jets at Miami
Philadelphia at Green Bay
Phoenix at Washington
Pittsburgh at Los Angeles Rams
San Diego at Denver
Tampa Bay at New York Giants
*Los Angeles Raiders at Seattle

MONDAY, SEPT. 13
*San Francisco at Cleveland

SUNDAY, SEPT. 19
Atlanta at San Francisco
Cincinnati at Pittsburgh
Cleveland at Los Angeles Raiders

Detroit at New Orleans
Houston at San Diego
Los Angeles Rams at New York Giants
Seattle at New England
Washington at Philadelphia
*Dallas at Phoenix

MONDAY, SEPT. 20
*Denver at Kansas City

SUNDAY, SEPT. 26
Cleveland at Indianapolis
Green Bay at Minnesota
Los Angeles Rams at Houston
Miami at Buffalo
Phoenix at Detroit
San Francisco at New Orleans
Seattle at Cincinnati
Tampa Bay at Chicago
*New England at New York Jets

MONDAY, SEPT. 27
*Pittsburgh at Atlanta

SUNDAY, OCT. 3
Atlanta at Chicago
Detroit at Tampa Bay
Green Bay at Dallas
Indianapolis at Denver
Los Angeles Raiders at Kansas City
Minnesota at San Francisco
New Orleans at Los Angeles Rams
Philadelphia at New York Jets
San Diego at Seattle
*New York Giants at Buffalo

MONDAY, OCT. 4
*Washington at Miami

SUNDAY, OCT. 10
Chicago at Philadelphia

Sanford Dotson went from fifth-rounder to prize rookie.

Cincinnati at Kansas City
Dallas at Indianapolis
Miami at Cleveland
New England at Phoenix
New York Giants at Washington
New York Jets at Los Angeles Raiders
San Diego at Pittsburgh
Tampa Bay at Minnesota
*Denver at Green Bay

MONDAY, OCT. 11
*Houston at Buffalo

THURSDAY, OCT. 14
*Los Angeles Rams at Atlanta

SUNDAY, OCT. 17
Cleveland at Cincinnati
Houston at New England
Kansas City at San Diego
New Orleans at Pittsburgh
Philadelphia at New York Giants
San Francisco at Dallas
Seattle at Detroit
Washington at Phoenix

MONDAY, OCT. 18
*Los Angeles Raiders at Denver

SUNDAY, OCT. 24
Atlanta at New Orleans

Buffalo at New York Jets
Cincinnati at Houston
Detroit at Los Angeles Rams
Green Bay at Tampa Bay
New England at Seattle
Phoenix at San Francisco
Pittsburgh at Cleveland
*Indianapolis at Miami

MONDAY, OCT. 25
*Minnesota at Chicago

SUNDAY, OCT. 31
Chicago at Green Bay
Dallas at Philadelphia
Kansas City at Miami
Los Angeles Rams at San Francisco
New England at Indianapolis
New Orleans at Phoenix
New York Jets at New York Giants
San Diego at Los Angeles Raiders
Seattle at Denver
Tampa Bay at Atlanta
*Detroit at Minnesota

MONDAY, NOV. 1
*Washington at Buffalo

SUNDAY, NOV. 7
Buffalo at New England
Denver at Cleveland
Los Angeles Raiders at Chicago
Miami at New York Jets
New York Giants at Dallas
Philadelphia at Phoenix
Pittsburgh at Cincinnati
San Diego at Minnesota
Seattle at Houston
Tampa Bay at Detroit
*Indianapolis at Washington

MONDAY, NOV. 8
*Green Bay at Kansas City

SUNDAY, NOV. 14
Atlanta at Los Angeles Rams
Cleveland at Seattle
Green Bay at New Orleans
Houston at Cincinnati
Kansas City at Los Angeles Raiders
Miami at Philadelphia

Minnesota at Denver
New York Jets at Indianapolis
Phoenix at Dallas
San Francisco at Tampa Bay
Washington at New York Giants
*Chicago at San Diego

MONDAY, NOV. 15
*Buffalo at Pittsburgh

SUNDAY, NOV. 21
Chicago at Kansas City
Cincinnati at New York Jets
Dallas at Atlanta
Detroit vs. Green Bay at Milw.
Houston at Cleveland
Indianapolis at Buffalo
Los Angeles Raiders at San Diego
New England at Miami
New York Giants at Philadelphia
Pittsburgh at Denver
Washington at Los Angeles Rams
*Minnesota at Tampa Bay

MONDAY, NOV. 22
*New Orleans at San Francisco

THURSDAY, NOV. 25
Chicago at Detroit
Miami at Dallas

SUNDAY, NOV. 28
Buffalo at Kansas City
Cleveland at Atlanta
Denver at Seattle
Los Angeles Raiders at Cincinnati
New Orleans at Minnesota
New York Jets at New England
Philadelphia at Washington
Phoenix at New York Giants
San Francisco at Los Angeles Rams
Tampa Bay at Green Bay
*Pittsburgh at Houston

MONDAY, NOV. 29
*San Diego at Indianapolis

SUNDAY, DEC. 5
Atlanta at Houston
Denver at San Diego
Green Bay at Chicago

Indianapolis at New York Jets
Kansas City at Seattle
Los Angeles Raiders at Buffalo
Los Angeles Rams at Phoenix
Minnesota at Detroit
New England at Pittsburgh
New Orleans at Cleveland
New York Giants at Miami
Washington at Tampa Bay
*Cincinnati at San Francisco

MONDAY, DEC. 6
*Philadelphia at Dallas

SATURDAY, DEC. 11
New York Jets at Washington
San Francisco at Atlanta

SUNDAY, DEC. 12
Buffalo at Philadelphia
Chicago at Tampa Bay
Cincinnati at New England
Cleveland at Houston
Dallas at Minnesota
Detroit at Phoenix
Indianapolis at New York Giants
Kansas City at Denver
Los Angeles Rams at New Orleans
Seattle at Los Angeles Raiders
*Green Bay at San Diego

MONDAY, DEC. 13
*Pittsburgh at Miami

SATURDAY, DEC. 18
Dallas at New York Jets
Denver at Chicago

SUNDAY, DEC. 19
Atlanta at Washington
Buffalo at Miami
Houston at Pittsburgh
Los Angeles Rams at Cincinnati
Minnesota vs. Green Bay at Milw.
New England at Cleveland
Phoenix at Seattle

San Diego at Kansas City
San Francisco at Detroit
Tampa Bay at Los Angeles Raiders
*Philadelphia at Indianapolis

MONDAY, DEC. 20
*New York Giants at New Orleans

SATURDAY, DEC. 25
Houston at San Francisco

SUNDAY, DEC. 26
Atlanta at Cincinnati
Cleveland at Los Angeles Rams
Detroit at Chicago
Indianapolis at New England
Los Angeles Raiders at Green Bay
New Orleans at Philadelphia
New York Giants at Phoenix
New York Jets at Buffalo
Pittsburgh at Seattle
Tampa Bay at Denver
Washington at Dallas
*Kansas City at Minnesota

MONDAY, DEC. 27
*Miami at San Diego

FRIDAY, DEC. 31
Minnesota at Washington

SUNDAY, JAN. 2
Buffalo at Indianapolis
Chicago at Los Angeles Rams
Cincinnati at New Orleans
Cleveland at Pittsburgh
Dallas at New York Giants
Denver at Los Angeles Raiders
Green Bay at Detroit
Miami at New England
Phoenix at Atlanta
San Diego at Tampa Bay
Seattle at Kansas City
*New York Jets at Houston

MONDAY, JAN. 3
*Philadelphia at San Francisco

Nationally Televised Games

REGULAR SEASON

Sunday, Sept. 5—Minnesota at Los Angeles Raiders (day, CBS)
Houston at New Orleans (night, TNT)
Monday, Sept. 6—Dallas at Washington (night, ABC)
Sunday, Sept. 12—Buffalo at Dallas (day, NBC)
Los Angeles Raiders at Seattle (night, TNT)
Monday, Sept. 13—San Francisco at Cleveland (night, ABC)
Sunday, Sept. 19—Houston at San Diego (day, NBC)
Dallas at Phoenix (night, TNT)
Monday, Sept. 20—Denver at Kansas City (night, ABC)
Sunday, Sept. 26—San Francisco at New Orleans (day, CBS)
New England at New York Jets (night, TNT)
Monday, Sept. 27—Pittsburgh at Atlanta (night, ABC)
Sunday, Oct. 3—Minnesota at San Francisco (day, CBS)
New York Giants at Buffalo (night, TNT)
Monday, Oct. 4—Washington at Miami (night, ABC)
Sunday, Oct. 10—New York Jets at Los Angeles Raiders (day, NBC)
Denver at Green Bay (night, TNT)
Monday, Oct. 11—Houston at Buffalo (night, ABC)
Thursday, Oct. 14—Los Angeles Rams at Atlanta (night, TNT)
Sunday, Oct. 17—San Francisco at Dallas (day, CBS)
Monday, Oct. 18—Los Angeles Raiders at Denver (night, ABC)
Sunday, Oct. 24—Buffalo at New York Jets (day, NBC)
Indianapolis at Miami (night, TNT)
Monday, Oct. 25—Minnesota at Chicago (night, ABC)
Sunday, Oct. 31—Los Angeles Rams at San Francisco (day, CBS)
Detroit at Minnesota (night, TNT)
Monday, Nov. 1—Washington at Buffalo (night, ABC)
Sunday, Nov. 7—Los Angeles Raiders at Chicago (day, NBC)
Indianapolis at Washington (night, ESPN)
Monday, Nov. 8—Green Bay at Kansas City (night, ABC)
Sunday, Nov. 14—Minnesota at Denver (day, CBS)
Chicago at San Diego (night, ESPN)
Monday, Nov. 15—Buffalo at Pittsburgh (night, ABC)
Sunday, Nov. 21—Pittsburgh at Denver (day, NBC)
Minnesota at Tampa Bay (night, ESPN)
Monday, Nov. 22—New Orleans at San Francisco (night, ABC)
Thursday, Nov. 25—Chicago at Detroit (day, CBS)
Miami at Dallas (day, NBC)
Sunday, Nov. 28—San Francisco at Los Angeles Raiders (day, CBS)
Pittsburgh at Houston (night, ESPN)

It's up to David Klingler to boom without the Boomer.

Monday, Nov. 29—San Diego at Indianapolis (night, ABC)
Sunday, Dec. 5—Denver at San Diego (day, NBC)
     Cincinnati at San Francisco (night, ESPN)
Monday, Dec. 6—Philadelphia at Dallas (night, ABC)
Saturday, Dec. 11—New York Jets at Washington (day, NBC)
     San Francisco at Atlanta (day, CBS)
Sunday Dec. 12—Kansas City at Denver (day, NBC)
     Green Bay at San Diego (night, ESPN)
Monday, Dec. 13—Pittsburgh at Miami (night, ABC)
Saturday, Dec. 18—Dallas at New York Jets (day, CBS)
     Denver at Chicago (day, NBC)
Sunday, Dec. 19—San Francisco at Detroit (day, CBS)
     Philadelphia at Indianapolis (night, ESPN)
Monday, Dec. 20—New York Giants at New Orleans (night, ABC)
Saturday, Dec. 25—Houston at San Francisco (day, NBC)
Sunday, Dec. 26—Washington at Dallas (day, CBS)
     Kansas City at Minnesota (night, ESPN)
Monday, Dec. 27—Miami at San Diego (night, ABC)
Friday, Dec. 31—Minnesota at Washington (day, CBS)
Sunday, Jan. 2—Denver at Los Angeles Raiders (day, NBC)
     New York Jets at Houston (night, ESPN)
Monday, Jan. 3—Philadelphia at San Francisco (night, ABC)

POSTSEASON

Saturday, Jan. 8—AFC and NFC Wild-Card Playoffs (ABC)
Sunday, Jan. 9—AFC and NFC Wild-Card Playoffs (NBC and CBS)
Saturday, Jan. 15—AFC and NFC Divisional Playoffs (NBC amd CBS)
Sunday, Jan. 16—AFC and NFC Divisional Playoffs (NBC and CBS)
Sunday, Jan. 23—AFC and NFC Conference Championships (NBC amd CBS)
Sunday, Jan. 30—Super Bowl XXVIII at Georgia Dome, Atlanta (NBC)
Sunday, Feb. 6—AFC-NFC Pro Bowl at Honolulu (ESPN)

LIONS VETERAN ROSTER *continued from page 72*

No.	Name	Pos.	Ht.	Wt.	NFL Exp.	College
71	Tharpe, Larry	T	6-4	299	2	Tennessee State
34	Tillison, Ed	RB	6-0	225	2	NW Missouri State
8	Turner, Vernon	WR	5-8	185	3	Carson-Newman
69	Vercheval, Pierre	C-G	6-1	275	1	Western Ontario
11	Ware, Andre	QB	6-2	205	4	Houston
61	White, Mark	G	6-5	298	1	Florida
35	White, William	S	5-10	191	6	Ohio State
70	Wilson, Bernard	DT	6-2	295	1	Tennessee State

PACKERS VETERAN ROSTER *continued from page 84*

No.	Name	Pos.	Ht.	Wt.	NFL Exp.	College
41	Shavers, Tyrone	WR	6-3	205	1	Lamar
—	Showell, Malcolm	DE	6-6	270	1	Delaware State
68	Sims, Joe	T-G	6-3	294	3	Nebraska
—	Slay, Steve	G-T	6-7	295	1	Wyoming
32	Stephens, John	RB	6-1	215	6	NW Louisiana
39	Thompson, Darrell	RB	6-0	222	4	Minnesota
9	Wagner, Bryan	P	6-2	200	7	Cal-Northridge
86	West, Ed	TE	6-1	244	10	Auburn
92	White, Reggie	DE	6-5	285	9	Tennessee
29	Wilson, Marcus	RB	6-1	210	2	Virginia
20	Wilson, Robert	FB	6-0	245	2	Texas A&M
52	Winters, Frank	C-G	6-3	290	7	Western Illinois

VIKINGS VETERAN ROSTER *continued from page 104*

No.	Name	Pos.	Ht.	Wt.	NFL Exp.	College
97	Thomas, Henry	DT	6-2	268	7	LSU
87	Tice, Mike	TE	6-7	253	12	Maryland
95	Tuaolo, Esera	DT	6-2	275	3	Oregon State
8	Watkins, Slip	WR	5-9	173	1	LSU
32	Welborne, Tripp	S	6-0	205	1	Michigan
35	West, Ronnie	WR	6-1	215	1	Pittsburg State
24	Wilson, David	S	5-10	192	1	California
65	Zimmerman, Gary	T	6-6	286	8	Oregon

BUCCANEERS VETERAN ROSTER *continued from page 166*

No.	Name	Pos.	Ht.	Wt.	NFL Exp.	College
13	Vlasic, Mark	QB	6-3	205	5	Iowa
77	Wheeler, Mark	DL	6-2	280	2	Texas A&M
54	Williams, Jimmy	LB	6-3	220	12	Nebraska
84	Wilson, Charles	WR	5-10	180	3	Memphis State
19	Wilson, Walter	WR	5-10	180	2	East Carolina
46	Workman, Vince	RB	5-10	205	5	Ohio State

49ERS VETERAN ROSTER *continued from page 156*

continued from page 156

No.	Name	Pos.	Ht.	Wt.	NFL Exp.	College
61	Sapolu, Jesse	C	6-4	278	11	Hawaii
83	Seay, Mark	WR	6-0	175	1	Cal State-Long Beach
25	Singleton, Nate	WR	5-11	190	1	Grambling
65	Stewart, Andrew	DE	6-6	275	2	Cincinnati
5	Sullivan, Kent	P	6-0	206	1	California Lutheran
64	Tamm, Ralph	G-C	6-4	280	6	West Chester
47	Taylor, Brian	S	5-10	195	3	Oregon State
82	Taylor, John	WR	6-1	185	8	Delaware State
72	Thomas, Mark	DE	6-5	273	2	North Carolina State
32	Thomas, Rodney	CB	5-11	185	6	Brigham Young
86	Turner, Odessa	WR	6-3	215	7	NW Louisiana
93	Veris, Garin	DE	6-4	255	9	Stanford
27	Walker, Adam	RB	6-1	210	2	Pittsburgh
74	Wallace, Steve	T	6-5	278	8	Auburn
89	Walls, Wesley	TE	6-5	254	5	Mississippi
99	Walter, Mike	LB	6-3	246	11	Oregon
97	Washington, Ted	NT-DE	6-4	295	3	Louisville
32	Watters, Ricky	RB	6-1	212	3	Notre Dame
66	Wilkins, David	LB	6-4	240	2	Eastern Kentucky
81	Williams, Jamie	TE	6-4	245	11	Nebraska
10	Wilmsmeyer, Klaus	P	6-1	210	2	Louisville
24	Young, Charlie	RB	6-1	205	1	Stanford
8	Young, Steve	QB	6-2	200	9	Brigham Young

BROWNS VETERAN ROSTER *continued from page 211*

continued from page 211

No.	Name	Pos.	Ht.	Wt.	NFL Exp.	College
77	Trumbull, Rick	T	6-6	300	2	Missouri
29	Turner, Eric	S	6-1	207	3	UCLA
44	Vardell, Tommy	FB	6-2	238	2	Stanford
28	Walls, Everson	DB	6-1	195	13	Grambling
95	Williams, George	DT	6-2	297	2	Notre Dame
26	Wolfley, Ron	RB	6-0	230	10	West Virginia
60	Zeno, Lance	C	6-4	279	2	UCLA

DOLPHINS VETERAN ROSTER *continued from page 275*

continued from page 275

No.	Name	Pos.	Ht.	Wt.	NFL Exp.	College
71	Robbins, Kevin	T	6-6	300	2	Michigan State
4	Roby, Reggie	P	6-2	243	11	Iowa
68	Rose, Blaine	G	6-5	285	1	Maryland
77	Rowell, Tony	C	6-4	290	1	Florida
58	Sander, Mark	LB	6-2	232	2	Louisville
22	Saxon, James	FB	5-11	237	6	San Jose State
69	Sims, Keith	G	6-3	310	4	Iowa State
31	Smith, Cedric	FB	5-10	222	3	Florida
28	Smith, Frankie	CB	5-9	177	1	Baylor
10	Stoyanovich, Pete	K	5-11	181	5	Indiana
11	Taylor, Troy	QB	6-4	200	3	California
95	Turner, T.J.	DE	6-4	280	8	Houston
63	Uhlenhake, Jeff	C	6-3	284	5	Ohio State
—	Veasey, Craig	DT	6-2	300	4	Houston
23	Vincent, Troy	CB	6-0	191	2	Wisconsin
78	Webb, Richmond	T	6-6	298	4	Texas A&M
79	Webster, Larry	DT	6-5	285	2	Maryland
60	Weidner, Bert	G-C	6-2	290	4	Kent State
94	Whitaker, Danta	TE	6-4	248	4	Miss. Valley State
61	Williams, Gene	G	6-3	308	3	Iowa State
26	Williams, Jarvis	S	5-11	200	6	Florida
87	Williams, Mike	WR	5-11	183	2	Northeastern

CHIEFS VETERAN ROSTER *continued from page 254*

No.	Name	Pos.	Ht.	Wt.	NFL Exp.	College
79	Szott, Dave	G	6-4	290	4	Penn State
27	Taylor, Jay	CB	5-10	170	5	San Jose State
32	Terry, Doug	S	5-11	192	2	Kansas
58	Thomas, Derrick	OLB	6-3	242	5	Alabama
60	Thome, Chris	C	6-5	280	3	Minnesota
46	Thompson, Bennie	S	6-0	214	4	Grambling
45	Thompson, Ernie	RB	5-11	230	1	Indiana
73	Valerio, Joe	T-C	6-5	293	3	Pennsylvania
72	Villa, Danny	T-G	6-5	300	7	Arizona State
41	Whitmore, David	S	6-0	217	4	Stephen F. Austin
44	Williams, Harvey	RB	6-2	222	3	Louisiana State
23	Word, Barry	RB	6-2	245	5	Virginia
15	Young, Michael	WR	6-1	183	9	UCLA
91	Young, Todd	TE	6-5	259	2	Penn State

Brett Favre inspires visions of a QB named Starr.